The False Faces of the Iroquois

THE CIVILIZATION OF THE AMERICAN INDIAN SERIES

Dr. S. Fritz Forkel
د. سليمان فريتس فوركل
ד״ר שלמה פריץ פורקל
Skén:nen Rón:nis

The False Faces of the Iroquois

William N. Fenton

University of Oklahoma Press
Norman and London

Published in cooperation with the Museum of the American Indian—Heye Foundation

Dedication

To my father and grandfather, who collected the masks that sent me to the field, and to my many Iroquois friends, who answered my questions, interpreted their languages, took me into their homes, and admitted me to their ceremonies over the years. Most of these persons have now "gone the long trail," but to any who survive, when this book is published, my genuine appreciation for their patience and interest and for helping me learn their customs. Nia:wenh! (Thanks).

By William N. Fenton

Songs from the Iroquois Longhouse (Washington, D.C., 1942)
(Ed.) *Symposium on Local Diversity in Iroquois Culture* (Washington, D.C., 1951)
The Iroquois Eagle Dance: An Offshoot of the Calumet Dance (Washington, D.C., 1953)
(Co-editor) *Symposium on Cherokee and Iroquois Culture* (Washington, D.C., 1961)
American Indian and White Relations to 1830 (Chapel Hill, N.C., 1967)
(Ed. and trans., with E. L. Moore) *Customs of the American Indians, Compared with the Customs of Primitive Times, by Father Joseph-Francois Lafitau* (2 vols., Toronto, 1974–76)
The False Faces of the Iroquois (Norman, 1987)

Published with the assistance of the J. Paul Getty Trust and the National Endowment for the Humanities, a federal agency which supports the study of such fields as history, philosophy, literature, and languages.

Library of Congress Cataloging-in-Publication Data
Fenton, William Nelson, 1908–
The false faces of the Iroquois.
(The Civilization of the American Indian
series; 178)
Bibliography: p. 507
Includes index.
1. Iroquois Indians—Masks. 2. Iroquois Indians—
Religion and mythology. 3. Iroquois Indians—Rites
and ceremonies. 4. Masks—America. I. Title.
II. Series: Civilization of the American Indian
series; v. 178.
E99.I7F45 1987   391'43'08997   86-19360
ISBN 0-8061-2039-8 (alk. paper)

The paper in this book meets the guidelines for permanence and durability of the Committee on Production Guidelines for Book Longevity of the Council on Library Resources, Inc. ∞

Copyright © 1987 by the University of Oklahoma Press, Norman, Publishing Division of the University. All rights reserved. Manufactured in the U.S.A. First edition, 1987; second printing, 1990.

Contents

Preface / xiii

Acknowledgments / xvii

Orthography / xx

Abbreviations / xxi

1. Introduction / 3
Longhouse Communities / 3
Museum Collections / 5
The Need for a Definitive Treatment / 12
Problems and Methods / 14
History of Masked Shamanism in Iroquoia / 22
Structural Considerations / 23

PART ONE

2. Mask Types / 27
The Wooden Masks, or False Faces / 27
A Classification Based on Specimens / 30
Revised Classification / 48
The Husk Faces, or "Bushy Heads" / 54
Miniatures / 60
The Bigheads / 63
The So-called Tuscarora Faces / 63

3. Historical Setting / 65
Approach / 65
Faces in Other Media / 66
Archaeology / 66
Narratives of Early Travelers / 72

4. Time Perspective / 75
Ethnological and Linguistic Evidence / 75
The Huron Hypothesis / 75
Iroquoia: Seventeenth Century / 76
The Eighteenth Century / 78
Comments on the Literature / 82
Cultural Change in Modern Times / 85
Ethnological Literature Since Morgan / 86

PART TWO

5. The Society of Faces, or the False Face Company / 95
The Origin of the False Faces and Their Kinds / 95

6. The Window on Tradition / 129
Classes of Wooden Medicine Masks / 129
Masking of Three Orders of Medicine Societies / 138
Membership / 140
The False Face Sickness / 143

7. Of Dreams, Collectors, Scared Children, and Bundles / 159
Vicarious Forms of Participation / 159

PART THREE

8. Ritual Equipment: The Props to the Ceremony / 191
Paraphernalia / 191
Traditional Ritual of Carving the Face on a Tree / 206
Carvers and Their Art / 209

9. Carving Styles / 237
The Newtown Tradition / 237
The Grand River Style / 249
Other Carvers / 255

PART FOUR

10. The Rituals of the Society / 267
Spring and Autumn Purification of the Houses: the So-called Traveling Rite / 267

11. The Rites at Coldspring, Tonawanda, and Six Nations / 301
Local Diversity / 301

12. Family Feasts / 340
Private Rites / 340

13. "Indian New Year" / 363
Appearance of the Maskers at Midwinter / 363

PART FIVE

14. The Society of Husk Faces, or Bushy Heads / 383
Origins / 384
Powers of Curing / 400
Membership: The Society and Its Officers / 403

15. Props to the Ceremony / 405
Ritual Equipment / 405

16. The Great Husk Face Drama / 418
Appearances and Rituals of the Husk Faces / 418

PART SIX

17. Prominence and Climax / 447
Prominence of Masking and Related Concepts in Iroquois Life / 447
Masks as Material Manifestations of Dreams / 450
Attitudes: The Paradox of Fear and Humor / 451
Production and Collection of Masks / 452
Repatriation / 456

PART SEVEN

18. Comparisons and Implications for Ethnology / 461
Delaware-Munsee / 462
Seneca-Cayuga of Oklahoma / 469
Shawnee / 469
Chippewa / 471
Oneida of Wisconsin / 471
Wabanaki / 472
Eskimo / 472
The Southeast / 473
Cherokee / 475

19. Alternate Interpretations of Eastern Masking / 478
Three Levels / 478
Krusche's Revision / 480
Fogelson's Ideas on Common Folk Beliefs / 487

PART EIGHT

20. Postlude: The Startling Parallel of Carnival in Europe / 495
Preconceptions / 495
Masking the World over / 500

21. Conclusions / 501

Bibliography / 509

Index / 517

Illustrations

PLATES

1.1. Longhouses at Onondaga Valley and Coldspring / 4
1.2. Longhouses at Tonawanda and Six Nations Reserve / 5
1.3. Upper Cayuga Longhouse / 6
1.4. First masks collected by L. H. Morgan / 8
1.5. Masks collected by L. H. Morgan, ca. 1860 / 9
2.1. Mask of the Wind God / 32
2.2. Black wry-mouth and red crooked-mouth mask / 33
2.3. Grand River style / 34
2.4. Straight-lipped doorkeeper masks / 35
2.5. Spoon-lipped doorkeeper masks / 36
2.6. Hanging-mouth masks / 37
2.7. Protruding-tongue masks / 38
2.8. Wry-faced and smiling masks / 40
2.9. Early masks with pointed heads and sharp chins / 42
2.10. Whistling masks / 44
2.11. Divided mask / 46
2.12. Longnose masks / 47
2.13. Animal masks / 48
2.14. Pig masks / 49
2.15. Blind mask / 50
2.16. Husk Faces or "Bushy Heads" / 56
2.17. Twined Husk Faces / 57
2.18. Husk Faces / 57
2.19. Old men / 58
2.20. "Corn Goddess" / 59
2.21. Miniature masks / 61
2.22. Miniature masks / 62
2.23. Niagara Falls style / 64
5.1. Man-being / 109
5.2. Red mask of Levi Snow / 122
6.1. "Their Great Protector" / 130
6.2. Grand River masks representing Hadui / 132
6.3. Faces Only of the Forests / 133
6.4. Powerful masks / 134
6.5. Newtown Seneca doorkeeper masks / 136
6.6. "Doctor" mask / 137
7.1. False Face Dancer / 160
7.2. Mask and rattle of Chauncey Johnny John / 170
7.3. Masks of Henry Redeye and George Buck / 173
8.1. Turtle rattle of Jonas Snow / 192
8.2. Turtle rattles / 198
8.3. Replica of snapping-turtle rattle / 199
8.4. Making a folded bark rattle / 202
8.5. Completing a bark rattle / 205
8.6. Carving face on tree / 207

8.7. Face carved on tree / 208
8.8. Mask carved on log / 210
8.9. Six Nations carvers / 213
8.10. The carving process / 216
8.11. Taking the carving block / 217
8.12. Outlining the face / 219
8.13. Outlining feature of face / 221
8.14. Hewing face / 222
8.15. Using drawshave bench / 223
8.16. Reducing gross features / 225
8.17. Shaving and hollowing / 226
8.18. Hollowing with crooked knife / 228
8.19. Trimming chin and cutting lips / 230
8.20. Reaming mouth and rounding lips / 230
8.21. Finishing inside and scooping eye sockets / 231
8.22. Burning holes in eyes and along rim / 232
8.23. Incising teeth / 232
8.24. Final step in carving / 233
8.25. Finished unpainted model / 234
9.1. Newtown Cattaraugus Seneca style / 236
9.2. Carving doorkeeper mask in Newtown style / 239
9.3. Spoon mouth and derivatives / 245
9.4. Early Seneca black bifunnelate mask / 246
9.5. Onondaga mask from Grand River / 247
9.6. Seneca masks by Amos Snow / 248
9.7. Tom Harris replicates Grand River style / 252
9.8. Scribing the mouth opening / 253
9.9. Smoothing inside / 254
9.10. Mask B by Tom Harris / 254
9.11. Mask A by Tom Harris / 254
9.12. Avery Jimmerson and masks / 258
9.13. Mask carvers on Tonawanda WPA Arts Project / 260
9.14. Harrison Ground / 262
9.15. "Old Broken Nose" / 263
9.16. Masks by Jake Henry / 264
10.1. Maskers / 270
10.2. Doorkeeper during song / 293
11.1. Purging houses of sickness / 300
11.2. Invocation / 302
11.3. Conductor and party pass spring house / 303
11.4. Husk Face runner enters house / 304
11.5. Maskers emerge / 305
11.6. Masked clown / 305
11.7. Matron and maskers; Husk Face and conductor / 306
11.8. Dancing on way / 307

11.9. Matrons prepare feast / 308
11.10. Alice White and Red House band of maskers / 309
11.11. Bands converge on longhouse / 311
11.12. Medicine for False Faces / 327
11.13. Maskers visit springs and tobacco patches / 330
11.14. Six Nations masks / 333
11.15. Six Nations masks / 334
11.16. Matron offering tobacco to maskers / 339
12.1. Blowing Ashes Rite / 342
12.2. Private rite / 344
12.3. Cure and payment / 345
12.4. Private rite / 346
12.5. Preliminaries / 346
12.6. Maskers await signal to enter / 347
12.7. Inside / 347
12.8. Masker carries patient; feast / 348
12.9. "Buffalo" mask / 362
13.1. False Face Beggars / 368
13.2. Tonawanda Beggars / 368
13.3. Maskers circuit of houses and return / 373
13.4. Hula dancer / 374
13.5. New Coldspring longhouse / 376
15.1. Replicas of Husk Face and False Face dancers / 406
15.2. Ella T. Jimmerson / 407
15.3. Wooden-face "Bushy Head" / 407
15.4. Coiled and braided Husk Faces / 408
15.5. Twined and braided and coiled Husk Faces / 409
15.6. Grand River baroque style / 410
15.7. Braided and coiled Husk Face in European museum / 411
16.1. Husk Face tug-of-war / 423
16.2. Naked False Face dancer / 424
16.3. Husk Faces arrive at longhouse / 426
17.1. "Hidden" mask of Lucy Gordon / 449
18.1. House-post face and Eastern Ojibwa mask / 466

FIGURES

1.1. Reservations and settlements in modern Iroquoia / 4
2.1. Classification of wooden masks by mouth shape / 51
5.1. The maskers' world / 113
8.1. Crafting snapping-turtle rattle / 194
8.2. Crafting hickory-bark rattle / 201
8.3. Manufacturing Gus Yellow's mask / 214
8.4. Carving mask / 218
8.5. Directions of carving / 229
8.6. Details of mouth and eyes / 234
10.1. Music score, False Face Marching Song / 274
10.2. At Coldspring Longhouse / 276
10.3. Great Tree at center of earth / 000
10.4. Music score, False Face songs / 291
10.5. Music score, Doorkeeper Dance / 296
11.1. Tobacco invocation / 310
11.2. Purification Ceremony at Coldspring Longhouse / 310
11.3. Roster of Traveling Rite / 332
12.1. Floor plan of False Face ceremony / 353
15.1. Twining corn husk / 413
16.1. Course of Husk Face runners / 427

COLOR PLATES/following page 266

Mask attributed to the Cornplanter
First mask collected by L. H. Morgan
Seneca of Tonowanda (front and back)
Black doorkeeper mask
Spoon-lipped doorkeeper mask
Seneca seaman
Black modified spoon-mouth doorkeeper mask (front and back)
Newtown Seneca doorkeeper mask
Black hanging-mouth mask
Protruding-tongue mask
Seneca beggar mask
Whistling mask
Divided mask
"Old Broken Nose"
Niagara Falls style
Niagara variant
Delaware mask
Braided Husk Face
Twined Husk Face
Braided and coiled Husk Face (front and back)
Finely braided and coiled Husk Face

Preface

The present work fulfills a lifelong interest in a subject that goes back to my boyhood of summers on my grandfather's farm in southwestern New York State. The Fenton farm lay halfway between the Cattaraugus and Allegany reservations of the Seneca Nation of Indians, who from time out of mind had paused on their way hunting to camp on the hemlock ridge at the back of the farm. Sometime after the Civil War, Amos Snow and my grandfather W. T. Fenton became friends, hunted together, and paused in their journeys to exchange weather signs and other pleasantries. Before the turn of the century Amos entrusted to his friend for safekeeping two wooden masks, or False Faces, that he had carved and used in rites not clearly understood to the Fenton family. These were kept in a round wooden cheese box "up attic" in a room devoted to the Indian collection, which consisted mainly of archaeological specimens known as "Indian relics" that my grandfather and his neighbors had picked up during spring plowing, usually after a rain, on lots of Leon and Conewango townships in Cattaraugus County. Summers, people came from near and far to view the collection, and, when I was there, I followed upstairs and sat in a corner listening to the talk. Some of the visitors were "experts" like Arthur Parker, himself a Seneca, and his friend and colleague M. R. Harrington. And once Warren K. Moorehead, of Andover Academy, came by on his way to the Ohio mounds. On these rare occasions the talk verged on lectures that were more enlightening. Still the masks remained a mystery.

In the 1920s with the advent of a family automobile, we ventured as far as Allegany Reservation over dirt roads to find Jonas Snow, son of Amos, by then deceased. Jonas proved to be an unlimited source of huckleberries, guided my artist father to spectacular views along the Allegheny River for sketching, and soon turned up additional False Faces for our growing collection. We met such carvers as Clarence White and Chauncey Johnny John, who was known to age masks in the manure pile, and other personages. We were invited to attend the Green Corn Dance in late August, when I heard my first Seneca songs and witnessed the spectacular dancing of Johnny Armstrong.

Over the winters when work was slack on the Erie Railroad section, Jonas Snow continued to send masks to my father, John Wm. Fenton, in Westport, Connecticut. By 1930, there were some seventeen masks in the Fenton Collection, including some fine Husk Faces, which father put on view at the Salmagundi Club in New York to amuse his artist friends. Meanwhile, I had gone off to college, aiming for a career in business administration. The Crash of 1929 made that seem irrelevant.

Early in the Great Depression I discovered anthropology. In a course on the American Indian at Dartmouth, I recalled earlier reservation rambles and wrote a senior essay on the Iroquois. Because Clark Wissler, whom I knew, was teaching two days a week at the Institute of Human Relations, I was lucky to be accepted in the Yale Graduate School with the first group of anthropology students the year that Edward Sapir came from Chicago to found a new department. Graduate work renewed my interest in the family collection, particularly the Iroquois masks, which were now housed in my father's Westport studio. Sapir, recalling the Iroquois research program that he had mounted as chief of the Anthropological Survey of Canada from 1910 to 1925, encouraged my early commitment to Iroquois studies, assigned pertinent topics for presentation in his seminars on social organization and religion, which provided the opportunity to survey the literature and identify salient problems for research. This background then launched me on my first fieldwork that was financed with funds from the Institute of Human Relations.

It was in the summer of 1933 that I went to Allegany Reservation of the Seneca Nation and pitched my tent at Jonas Snow's on "Snow Street," in Coldspring. Then and there, I began my novitiate in the mysteries of the maskers. My Hawk Clan hosts urged me to come back for the "Indian New Year," the Midwinter Festival of 1934, when they honored me with an "Indian name," a personal name recently vacated by my host Jonas Snow. A return trip always validates serious intent on the part of the investigator. A second summer found me as guest of Henry, Sherman, and Clara Redeye who proved to be hosts as well as invaluable sources of information on the ceremonies at Coldspring Longhouse, of which Henry was the main speaker.

I had by then passed the preliminary orals for the doctorate at Yale and had exhausted available fellowships. An appointment as a Community Worker in the U.S. Indian Service during the Collier administration facilitated two and one-half years of continuous residence at Tonawanda, a Seneca settlement, while writing a dissertation. Still another of the medicine societies, the Iroquois Eagle Dance, and its relation to the widespread Calumet Dance of the seventeenth and eighteenth centuries seemed a more manageable topic than the False Faces, which required visitation to museum collections here and abroad and further fieldwork in other Iroquois communities. Nevertheless, while at Tonawanda I published my first exploratory paper on the Seneca Society of Faces (1937). It brought to life the Fenton Collection and called upon older masks in the museums of Buffalo and Rochester. It was also largely stimulated by the intense carving activity then going on in the Indian Arts Project, which was sponsored with WPA funds on the reservation by the then Rochester Museum of Arts and Sciences. The article prompted responses from diverse correspondents in anthropology, the arts, psychiatry, movies, and museums.

Two years later, after I was called to fill the post of J. N. B. Hewitt (1859–1937) at the Bureau of American Ethnology in the Smithsonian tower, this research appointment enabled me to extend fieldwork on the False Faces from the Seneca to the Six Nations on Grand River in Canada, to survey systematically mask collections in museums of northeastern North America, and to contribute a summary article, "Masked Medicine Societies of the Iroquois," to the *Smithsonian Report for 1940* (1941).

Iroquois fieldwork in the 1930s and 1940s differed radically from that of today. It was an advantage to be the first trained anthropologist at Allegany, and at Six Nations Reserve I was the heir to Hewitt and Alexander Goldenweiser (1880–1940) for the Anthropological Survey of Canada, 1910–14. In my day, the old people complained that the younger generation would not listen, that they were not learning Iroquoian languages, and that they failed to participate in the ceremonies at the longhouse. I listened. Indeed, the rites of the medicine societies, the stated festivals of the calendar year, and the social dances are still current, albeit in attenuated form, and masks are still being carved for the ceremonies and to sell to tourists and dealers. But with the rise of self-conscious nativism in recent years, the mask complex has intensified, and non-Indians are now excluded from the ceremonies that are not as accessible to outside observers as in former years. For this reason alone, it seemed important to write up my notes and observations on masks and masked ceremonies that span nearly a half century. Although I have published four papers on the subject (1937, 1941a, 1956, and 1972), these contributions did not satisfy the need for monographic treatment of the subject, nor did they exhaust the materials in my files.

The purpose of the present book, then, is to fulfill the need for a monograph on the False Faces and the Husk Faces in all of their aspects. Its structure derives from Iroquois culture itself, it adheres to the pattern of the ceremonies at every level, and if readers find the organization a little strange, they will sense, if they stick with it, how the Iroquois themselves regard the subject, how they share in its tradition, how they participate in "the doings," and how their activities relate to neighboring cultures in North America and to masking in general. Each major part of the book is a subject unto itself, and it may be read in order of the reader's interests.

The Society of Faces is one of the climax features of Iroquois culture. The masks are the external manifestation of cultural beliefs and represent a long tradition of relationships between humans and supernaturals. The monograph moves from the objects to the tradition and its fulfillment in ceremony. Two major concepts dominate the author's approach: Linton's concept of the "activity" that summons material and immaterial cultural resources involved in achieving a goal (ritual cleansing of the community and persons) and Sapir's stress on individual participation in culture comprising events experienced and observed vis-à-vis unconscious patterning of behavior that structures ideal fulfillment. Third, culture has temporal and spatial aspects that are revealed by employing significant aspects of Iroquois masking to probe its roots and their extension in the Eastern Woodlands. The monograph speaks to a general theory of masking, a worldwide phenomenon.

The spelling of English versions of Iroquoian names may baffle readers. Allegany Reservation of the Seneca Nation of Indians lies along the great oxbow of the Allegheny River in southwestern New York. Its derivation is of Delaware origin, a language of the Algonquian family; to the Seneca it is ʔohi:yoʔ, "a beautiful river," of which the French La Belle Rivière on seventeenth-century maps is an exact translation. Cattaraugus Reservation of the Seneca Nation borders a creek of that name that flows into Lake Erie, north and west of the divide between the Mississippi and St. Lawrence watersheds. It is an Iroquoian term derived from kaʔtä:kęskę:ǫʔ, "smelly clay" or "mud" that lined its banks and was formerly used to plaster chimneys of log houses.

The Seneca took on English names that were sometimes direct translations of personal Indian names, such as Steeprock, Burning, Snow, and Hotbread. Names like Crouse and Jemison descend from white captives. The legion of heirs and descendants of Mary Jemison, "the White Woman of the Genesee," spell their surname variously as Jemison, Jimerson, Jimmerson, and Jamieson, the latter under the influence of neighboring Scots who settled Upper Canada early in the nineteenth century. Jonas Snow, of Coldspring on Allegany Reservation, was "Jones" Snow to his neighbors; likewise Albert Jonas was Albert "Jones."

The Rochester Municipal Museum changed its name to the Rochester Museum of Arts and Sciences, and then to the Rochester Museum and Science Center some years ago after *Sputnik,* although it is commonly known as the Rochester museum, as in this book.

A word about my sources, most of whom have since gone the long trail. At Allegany, Jonas Snow, Chauncey Johnny John, Howard Jimmerson, John Jimmerson (father of Avery, later a virtuoso carver), Henry and Sherman Redeye—carvers, mask owners, ritualists, narrators all—and Clara Redeye (my interpreter), Sadie Butler, and Fannie Stevens, matrons of the Society of Faces, were my principal sources. At Tonawanda, Jesse Cornplanter, Harrison Ground, Kidd Smith, and Elon Webster were carvers; but ritualists Elijah David, Chief Lyman Johnson, Sachem Chief Henan Scrogg, and Chief Edward Black briefed me on the ceremonies; and the Reverend Peter Doctor who had grown up in the longhouse religion and loved to talk about it and Cephas Hill, foreman of the arts project and my age-mate, manifested a genuine intellectual interest in ethnology. It was in Elsina Cornplanter's kitchen where I worked with her husband and recorded singers such as Robert Shanks and others.

Jesse Cornplanter took me to his home at Cattaraugus where I came to know Kelley Lay, T. Jimerson (a Christian) but no carver as skilled or well versed as James Crow with whom I worked briefly.

At Six Nations, on Grand River in Canada, Simeon Gibson was my primary source on the rituals of the False Faces until his death in 1943 (Fenton 1944), after which his nephew Howard Sky (1900–71) assumed his role (Fenton 1972). George and Billy Buck were consistently helpful. Early on, I discussed carving problems with Jake Hess and Jake Henry before recording the technique of Tom Harris.

All of these wonderful people were my sources to a limited or full extent.

Acknowledgments

To name everyone who assisted me in accomplishing the research for this book would comprise a catalog of native Iroquois, museum directors, curators of collections, and private collectors of Iroquoiana in North America. Those persons to whom I owe the greatest debt are either mentioned in the text or acknowledged below: For access, information, and statistics on holdings, the following ethnologists and museologists are my principal creditors—Charles E. Gillette, New York State Museum; William C. Sturtevant, U.S. National Museum of Natural History, Smithsonian Institution; Charles F. Hayes, III, Rochester Museum and Science Center; Betty Robins, registrar, Buffalo Museum of Science; Rudy Busto, Peabody Museum of American Archaeology and Ethnology, Harvard; Michael K. Foster, National Museum of Man, Ottawa; Stanley Freed, American Museum of Natural History; Clark Wissler and the late Bella Weitzner, American Museum of Natural History; James G. E. Smith, Marlene Martin, and Nancy Henry, Museum of the American Indian-Heye Foundation; Anthony F. C. Wallace, Claudia Medoff, and Caroline Dosker, University Museum, University of Pennsylvania; and Edward S. Rogers, Royal Ontario Museum, Toronto.

Roland W. Force, Director of the Museum of the American Indian, saw to it that my manuscript was xeroxed in sufficient copies for readers, arranged for the reproduction from my negatives as needed for plates, and personally assisted me in their selection. Fellow trustees of the Museum of the American Indian read and criticized the manuscript at various stages: John C. Ewers, Fred Eggan, Edmund Carpenter, and William C. Sturtevant. Raymond D. Fogelson, noted Cherokee scholar at the University of Chicago, widened my horizon to encompass the Southeast and invoked current ethnological theory to enable me to perceive structural and symbolic relationships between his data and mine.

Annemarie Shimony, of Wellesley College, translated Krusche's dissertation on masking for a wider audience; and Martin W. Walsh, University of Michigan, student of the theatre, invoked parallels between his studies of Carnival in Europe and the *Relations* of seventeenth-century Jesuit missionaries in North America.

The illustrations were derived from many sources. Photographs otherwise not credited are my own. Early in my research, Clark Wissler, then Chairman of the Department of Anthropology at the American Museum of Natural History and Professor of Anthropology in the Institute of Human Relations at Yale University, supplied me with photographs of Iroquois masks in the American Museum, some of which I published in previous papers. I am similarly indebted to Arthur C. Parker, then Director of the Rochester Museum, and later to Charles F. Hayes, III, for copies of Parker's negatives. Peter T. Furst, my colleague at Albany, generously made available, for use in this book, color photographs of illustrations in *North American Indian Art* (1982). Other prints were furnished by the National Museum of Copenhagen; Museum für Völkerkunde, Frankfurt/AmMain;

and the National Museum of Man, Ottawa. The late Richard B. Congdon of Salamanca, NY, assisted me in the field and donated his negatives. After I removed to Albany, "Tip" Roseberry of the *Albany Times Union* accompanied me to the Indian New Year celebrations of 1955, shared his observations, and contributed his negatives. Five years later, the late Edmund Wilson and I attended the "doings," he became my mentor, and encouraged me to produce a classic.

At Tonawanda in the 1930s, I encouraged Ernest Smith, afterward a noted Seneca illustrator, to paint a series of canvasses and watercolors to accompany ethnological reports I was then writing. From this early period, before the many works accomplished for the Rochester Museum WPA Indian Arts Project, came the canvas of the maskers now at the Seneca Iroquois National Museum, Salamanca, NY. I am particularly grateful to Gwynneth Gillette, illustrator for the New York State Museum and Science Service, for executing the line drawings and maps for the text figures.

Support of fieldwork on masks and masking came from several sources over the years. At times, it was not appropriated for this specific purpose. It began with grants for fieldwork from the Institute of Human Relations while the writer was a graduate student in Yale University. The Smithsonian Institution was the principal source during my tenure at the Bureau of American Ethnology, 1939–51. A 1945 grant from the Viking Fund (later the Wenner-Gren Foundation for Anthropological Research) to aid the study of the Condolence Council at Six Nations Reserve enabled me to observe the autumn Traveling Rite at Onondaga Longhouse. After coming to Albany in 1954 to direct the work of the New York State Museum and Science Service, ready access to state cars facilitated brief visits to the New York reservations when masked ceremonies marked the Indian New Year. Quite often, these forays were to escort some distinguished visitor to New York State or academics from afar. The late Edmund Wilson afforded one such opportunity that grew into a lasting friendship. Finally, the writing of this book progressed during several summers in my Keene Valley study on the east branch of the Ausable River where one watches mountains and casts a fly to wary trout. Once begun, the writing consumed a fall and winter while waiting the outcome of a petition for an NEH Independent Study and Research Fellowship (no. 21664-82) to write a different book. The masks intruded on the fellowship itself. While engaged in the Documentary History of the Iroquois Project (another NEH-supported effort) at the Newberry Library, I examined the folios of Grider drawings of Iroquois masks, done at the turn of the century, which include Converse specimens that burned in the New York State Capitol fire of 1911. Of such are the twists and turns in humanistic research.

During the preliminary stages and before seeking a publisher, Dr. Force and I met with Paul H. Oehser, for many years editor at the Smithsonian, and afterward at the National Geographic Society. Over lunch at the Cosmos Club, Paul shared with us his wisdom from a lifetime of publishing scientific monographs.

From the beginning, Olive, "that white girl from Salamanca," and my wife for a half century, cooked for Indians, fitted her life around my studies, helped me with the rules of grammar, and made no profession of being an anthropologist.

To John Drayton, editor-in-chief of the University of Oklahoma Press, and his staff, my thanks for taking on the project and seeing it through the press. Robert Chadwick, editor and anthropologist, who undertook the copyediting and prepared the manuscript for the printer, came to know the stylistic peculiarities of a writer who perhaps has come to "think like an Iroquois." To Bob Chadwick, I am particularly grateful.

My colleague "Wally" Chafe, the Dr. Johnson of the Seneca language, converted my phonetic transcription of Henry Redeye's tobacco invocation to standard Seneca phonemic writing and reviewed my note on orthography.

To all of these persons and institutions, let me address a few words in the manner of the old Iroquois speakers when closing a ceremony, "Now let them all think that they have been properly thanked."

Slingerlands, New York William N. Fenton

Orthography

Both Seneca and Onondaga are Iroquoian languages and as such they share many features, but each has its phonetic peculiarities. The following note on Iroquoian orthography adheres to the model for Seneca orthography in Chafe's *Handbook of the Seneca Language* (1963) with accommodations to Fenton's phonetic transcriptions of Seneca that preceded it. Recently, Chafe has modified his system for native teachers of the language at Allegany and Cattaraugus reservations.

The *k* and *g* as well as the *t* and *d* sounds differ as to voicing. Chafe used the voiceless *k* and *t* to represent the respective phonemes. Seneca teachers prefer to use the voiced *g* and *d*, as well as the voiceless *k* and *t*. In each case, a single phoneme is involved.

In transcribing Onondaga, Hewitt and Goldenweiser used different symbols for the glottal stop, and to indicate the nasal vowels. These differences are compared with my own system and set forth in the table below under F, H, and G, respectively. We agree on stress marking, designated *x* in the table.

Four symbols are required:	F	H	G
1. Acute accent (') = stress	x	x	x
2. Top part of question mark (ʔ) = glottal stop	ʔ	'	ε
3. Greek epsilon (ε) = nasal vowel, with iota subscript	ε̨	e^n	e^n
4. Turned *c* (ɔ) = nasal *o*	ǫ	o^n	o^n

Seneca phonemes require only sixteen letters—*vowels*: a, ä, e, ɛ [ε̨], i, o, and ɔ [ǫ]; *consonants*: h, j, k, n, s, t, w, y, and ʔ [ʔ].

Vowel length is indicated by the colon : or raised period ·. Letters *a, ä, e, i,* and *o* roughly approximate written German long vowels: a = English "father"; ä = English "man"; e = French "été"; i = French "fini"; and o = English "note."

The vowels *a, ä, e,* and *o* sound slightly different when they are short and are followed by *i, j, k, s,* or *t*.

Then a = u in English *hut*, as in ja:tak, "seven"; ä = e in English *met*, as in so:wäk, "duck"; e = i in English *hit*, as the first e in sneké:äh, "take a drink!"; and o = u in English *put*, the second o in ʔo:nekanos, "water."

Nasalized vowels are ɛ (ε̨) = en in French *bien;* and ɔ (ǫ) = on in French *bon*. The Seneca o and ǫ sound like u or ų in Onondaga.

Abbreviations

Alleg.	Allegany Reservation, Seneca Nation.
AMNH	American Museum of Natural History, New York
BAE	Bureau of American Ethnology, Smithsonian Institution.
BAE-AR	Bureau of American Ethnology, Annual Report
C	Cayuga
Catt.	Cattaraugus Reservation, Seneca Nation
CIS	Cranbrook Institute of Science, Bloomfield Hills, Michigan.
DAM	Denver Art Museum
D.C.	de capo, repeated from the beginning, "from the head," in musical scores.
DMNH	Denver Museum of Natural History
F.F.	False Face
Ft. J.	Fort Johnson, Amsterdam, N.Y.
JR	Thwaites, Reuben G., ed. The Jesuit Relations and Allied Documents . . . (Cleveland, 1896–1901). 73 vols.
JRAI	Journal, Royal Anthropological Institute of Great Britain and Ireland, London.
M	Mohawk
MAI-HF	Museum of the American Indian-Heye Foundation
MPM	Milwaukee Public Museum
MME.F/M	Municipal Museum of Ethnology, Frankfurt am Main
NMC	Nationalmuseet (National Museum), Copenhagen
NMM	National Museum of Man, Ottawa, Canada.
NYCD	New York Colonial Documents. See O'Callaghan, E. B., ed.
NYSL	New York State Library, Albany
NYSM	New York State Museum, Albany
Oa.	Onondaga
Oe.	Oneida
OHA	Onondaga Historical Association, Syracuse
PMAAE	Peabody Museum of American Archaeology and Ethnology, Harvard University.
PMH	Peabody Museum, Harvard
PMS	Peabody Museum, Salem, Mass.
PMY	Peabody Museum, Yale
RMSC	Rochester Museum and Science Center
ROM	Royal Ontario Museum, Toronto
ROMA	Royal Ontario Museum of Archaeology, Toronto
SEMS	State Ethnographical Museum, Stockholm
S	Seneca
SNR	Six Nations Reserve, Canada
Tona.	Tonawanda Reservation, Basom, N.Y.
USNM	United States National Museum, Smithsonian Institution, Washington, D.C.

The False Faces of the Iroquois

1. Introduction

The Iroquois Indians of upstate New York and southern Ontario today are descended from the most illustrious native people of northeastern North America. They are among our oldest reservation Indians. Two features of their ancient culture have captured the popular imagination: their justly famous Confederacy of the Five Nations and their wooden and cornhusk masks that one sees prominently displayed in ethnographic museums of the world and that enjoy a pride of ownership among private collectors here and abroad. These so-called False Faces and Husk Faces are the subject of the present book.

A word about the confederacy and its fate in later times. In protohistoric times, the then-village chiefs of the Mohawk, Oneida, Onondaga, Cayuga, and Seneca nations accepted the Great Law of Peace, confederated, and later became Six Nations when joined by the Tuscarora early in the eighteenth century. After the American Revolution, their ancient domain, the country south of the Great Lakes, which the French named Iroquoia, and is now upstate New York, shrank to scattered islands in a sea of surrounding whites. For a century and a half, their settlements have been within marketing distance of trading and industrial centers such as Syracuse, Rochester, Buffalo, and Niagara Falls in the United States, and Montreal, Hamilton, and Brantford in Canada. Iroquois people find employment in these centers, and, in New York State, Indian children attend integrated schools adjacent to the reservations. Yet it is well known to anthropologists that traditional Iroquois culture has not disappeared and is currently undergoing a revival. The Iroquois now have their own cultural centers, libraries, and museums (Figure 1-1).

Longhouse Communities

Adjacent to the cities already mentioned, the conservative Iroquois communities are situated near the centers where Handsome Lake, the Seneca prophet, preached the "good message" of his new religion during the last decade of the eighteenth century and the first fifteen years of the nineteenth century as well as on the reserves to which his disciples emigrated. In recent years, the "code" has reached other settlements of "Praying Indians" who were converted to Catholicism in the late seventeenth century. The faithful Ongweʔǫ:we, literally "Real People," who today adhere to the *ongweʔonweka:ʔ,* "longhouse way," forty years ago lived clustered about a dance house or ceremonial structure, which is commonly referred to as the longhouse, or council house. Today, with automobiles, they may live in suburbia or even in the cities. The longhouse is where people traditionally gather for social, political, and religious purposes. The longhouse fires still burn on the Onondaga Reservation near Syracuse (Plate 1-1; Figure 1-1), not far from the site where the founders of the Iroquois confederacy kindled their council fire in protohistoric times and on the three reserva-

Plate 1-1. Longhouses. A: Onondaga Valley near Syracuse. B: Coldspring on Allegheny River, Seneca Nation.

Figure 1-1. Reservations and settlements of modern Iroquoia.

B

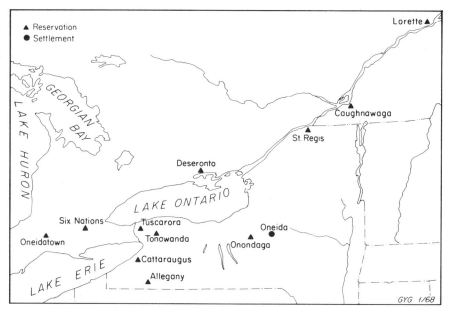

A

tions of the Seneca, east and southwest of Buffalo. The "Pagan Seneca," so-called by the Protestant missionaries at "Buffaloe Creek," maintain their fires at Tonawanda toward Batavia, at Newtown on the Cattaraugus Reservation near Gowanda, and at Coldspring (now Steamburg) on the Allegheny River below Salamanca. Allegany and Cattaraugus reservations comprise the modern Seneca Nation of Indians. Descendants of the other Iroquois—largely Cayuga and Mohawk and the Bearfoot band of Onondaga—removed after 1784 west of Niagara into Canada and settled on the banks of the Grand River, including what lands as are now known as the Six Nations Reserve near Brantford, Ontario. Today there are four congregations of Handsome Lake adherents on the reserve. The longhouse of the Upper Cayuga is at Sour Springs (Plate 1-3). Onondaga Longhouse, a center of traditional politics, stands by MacKenzie Creek opposite Middleport (Plate 1-2). Nearby, the so-called Seneca Longhouse has a congregation of mixed Onondaga, Cayuga, and Seneca descent; it reflects a schism in the Onondaga Longhouse congregation a century ago. Down below at Peter Atkins's Corners, one reaches the longhouse of the Lower Cayuga band, the most conservative group. Farther west, near London, Ontario, Oneida on the Thames comprises a small group of conservative descendants of the Oneida that did not emigrate to Green Bay, Wisconsin, and that struggles to keep up the ceremonies. Early on, their forebears in New York State were missionized by New England divines and largely became Christians. Some attenuated longhouse activity has been reported among the Wisconsin Oneida (Basehart, Lounsbury, Ritzenthaler, and Campisi). Longhouse factions have arisen recently in the predominantly Catholic communities on the St. Lawrence, both at Caughnawaga, outside Montreal, and at St. Regis, near Massena, NY. In 1939, the Akwesasneh Longhouse was a relatively recent development in the latter community, and the adherents were learning longhouse ways from Alex Clute, a Handsome Lake preacher from Tonawanda who had come from Onondaga. The number of longhouse adherents among both the Oneida and Laurentian Mohawk communities has increased in recent years. Despite this recent diffusion of the Handsome Lake religion, the longhouse adherents comprise less than a third of the Iroquois population today. As might be expected, the rituals of the masked societies are best preserved in the more conservative centers of the Seneca, among the Onondaga proper, and among the mixed Onondaga and Cayuga centers on the Six Nations Reserve in Canada. There is strong presumptive evidence that the Seneca are the focus of Iroquois masking and that the cult radiated from Buffalo Creek late in the eighteenth century.

Plate 1-2. Longhouses. A: Tonawanda, the main fire of the Handsome Lake religion, Basom, N.Y. B: Onondaga Longhouse and cookhouse at Six Nations Reserve, Canada.

Museum Collections

Important collections of Iroquois masks are to be found in the museums of eastern North America. As for European collections, Copenhagen, Stockholm, Stuttgart, Frankfurt am Main, Zurich, Nieder-Walluf, and Leningrad harbor significant specimens that come to mind. In New York City, the Museum of the American Indian-Heye Foundation, which has upward of 280 specimens, takes precedence in any world ranking of Iroquois mask collections. Together with the American Museum of Natural History, which has 55 partly field-collected pieces, New York City has more masks than Albany and Rochester. The New York State Museum at Albany holds the type specimen (Morgan 1852, 98) and has over 100 other masks. The Rochester Museum and Science Center had 27 old

Plate 1-3. Upper Cayuga Longhouse at Sour Springs, Six Nations Reserve.

masks before the WPA Indian Arts Project at Tonawanda and Cattaraugus reservations during the Great Depression provided that institution with the finest extant collection of contemporary Iroquois ethnological art, including 243 finely carved False Faces, 65 miniatures, and 41 Husk Faces—a grand total of nearly 400 Iroquois masks. Ritzenthaler (1969) published the more important examples of the 43 wooden masks at the Milwaukee Public Museum, which were collected by T. R. Roddy at Six Nations Reserve in 1906 and by S. A. Barrett a decade later among the Seneca. The Field Museum of Natural History in Chicago has some 40 specimens that are important because they were collected around the turn of the century at Grand River, Ontario, by Simms and among the New York Onondaga and the Seneca of Cattaraugus by Frederick Starr, of the University of Chicago, who was a native of Auburn, NY (Fenton 1980). A smaller but equally interesting group of masks is at The University Museum, Philadelphia, which were in part purchased in 1901 by Stewart Culin on behalf of the John Wanamaker Expedition at the Pan-American Exposition in Buffalo. This collection received an appropriate blessing by Chief Alex General (Deskaheh) in 1956 when a group of traditional Iroquois from Six Nations Reserve put on the masks and demonstrated their use for visiting scholars attending the International Congress of Anthropology and Ethnology.

In 1940, I studied and photographed 24 False Faces and several Husk Faces at the Royal Ontario Museum, Toronto, which largely represent the collecting activities of David Boyle at Six Nations on Grand River in addition to the gift of the Chiefswood Collection from Evelyn H. C. Johnson, daughter of an illustrious Mohawk chief (Hale 1885). Some fine later examples from the same place are in the Milford Chandler Collection at the Cranbrook Institute, near Detroit, which Speck published (1945a). Also from Grand River, the considerable study collection at the National Museum of Man, Ottawa, represents the fieldwork of F. W. Waugh and A. A. Goldenweiser circa 1912 and the collecting activities of C. M. Barbeau on various Iroquois reserves.

The collection at the Peabody Museum of American Archaeology and Ethnology, Harvard University, should not be overlooked. It contains fine Seneca False Faces procured at Cattaraugus in 1899 by the Reverend J. W. Sanborn for Professor Putnam. And the U.S. National Museum of Natural History of the Smithsonian Institution, Washington, received through Andrew John, Sr., representative of the Seneca Nation in Washington, the False Face attributed to John Obail, or Cornplanter, who was a celebrated Seneca war leader during and after the American Revolution (Color Plate 1). Besides, they have the masks collected by Hewitt at Six Nations in 1916 that I found infested with moths in the "old brownstone tower" during my tenure at the Bureau of American Ethnology. They also have the models carved for me by Chauncey Johnny John at Coldspring and Tom Harris at Grand River.

Two museums in Denver, the Museum of Natural History and the Denver Art Museum's Indian collection begun by Eric Douglas, each contains a dozen or more pieces.

UNDOCUMENTED BEFORE 1940

Notable as these collections are, they are largely undocumented, save as to collector, place, and year, and catalog cards convey little understanding of their function in Iroquois ceremonial life. Not until the studies of Parker (1909), Speck (1945, 1949, 1950), and my own fieldwork in the 1930s (1937, 1941) did we gain some knowledge of the role of masks in Iroquois culture.

Plate 1-4. *The first Iroquois masks collected by an ethnologist, L. H. Morgan, ca. 1850. The type specimen from an Onondaga of Grand River. New York State Museum, Albany, Cat. No. 36909.*

ETHNOLOGICAL IMPORTANCE

Wooden and cornhusk masks from the Iroquois that are often prominently displayed in museums have considerable ethnological importance as well as popular appeal. Lewis H. Morgan, of Rochester, was the first ethnologist to collect and document an Iroquois mask, and the literature on the False Faces begins with the *Fifth Annual Report of the Regents of the University,* which carries a line drawing of a mask that he acquired among the Onondaga of Six Nations Reserve for the New York State Cabinet of Antiquities. This, then, is the type specimen for all Iroquois masks (NYSM Cat. No. 36909; Fenton 1941a, Plate 6/2; here Plate 1-4). Morgan's brief report, which H. M. Lloyd included in the 1901 edition of the *League* (Morgan 1901, 1:157–60, 204–205), states tersely some beliefs regarding the False Faces as spirits, mentions the organization of the society, notes the society's attempt to prevent the spread of cholera to the Tonawanda Reservation in 1849, describes their curing activities, and relates the depredations committed by small thieving boys disguised as False Faces during the Midwinter Festival.

A decade later, Morgan furnished Count W. Raasloff, sometime Danish Ambassador to Washington, with a list of articles and prices that he subsequently collected at Tonawanda Reservation in January of 1860 for the Royal Museum of Copenhagen. These specimens, now part of the ethnographical collections of the Nationalmuseet, where I studied and photographed them in the summer of 1962, include two False Faces, one of which Morgan priced at two dollars, adding that it was "worn by members of a secret society called the False Faces."

Both masks were made in the traditional way, having holes burned in the rim for the attachment of the hair and headband. The first is a black mask with grey eyes and lacking metal reflectors; two tobacco bags are still attached; it measures seven inches by nine inches, and five holes were burned in the narrow rim (Plate 1-5). The back of the mask reveals considerable use (National Museet Cat. No. Hc369.) This mask parallels the one Morgan collected for the New York State Cabinet of Antiquities (Plate 1-4), but for which it would stand as the dated type specimen. Already, the style of carving at Tonawanda is relatively simple as compared with Grand River. The second specimen (same catalog number) is painted red; it is a smiling mask revealing tin teeth, and it has a prominent chin. It measures five-and-one-half by ten inches, and there are seven holes for the attachment of the hair. It predates a whole genre of masks collected later by Mrs. Converse.

Although J. V. H. Clark made some preliminary observations of False Face activities in the Onondaga Midwinter Festival of 1841 (Clark 1849,

---

1. Morgan Papers, University of Rochester Library, Box 24, No. 119; Box 23, No. 105. Courtesy of Professor Elisabeth Tooker.

Plate 1-5. Collected at Tonawanda (Seneca) by L. H. Morgan for Count Raasloff in January, 1860. Nationalmuseet, Copenhagen, Cat. No. Hc 369. Photo courtesy Nationalmuseet, Copenhagen.

1:57), it was DeCost Smith of Skaneateles, afterward a prominent illustrator in New York, who provided us with the first reliable source materials on the False Faces and their antics that he observed and sketched at Onondaga in January, 1888 (Smith 1888, 1889). Smith recognized the False Faces as art objects and "made a good collection" (Beauchamp 1905, 187), one of which he gave to Beauchamp. The others he later shared with the American Museum of Natural History and the Museum of the American Indian. Three specimens went to the Museum für Völkerkunde of

Berlin (Smith 1943, 354). Smith told me in 1936, when I visited him in retirement at Amenia, NY, that he had alerted the Reverend William M. Beauchamp to the function of the False Faces and to the problem of their antiquity among the Iroquois after Smith discovered one in an Indian's attic. Both men contributed a series of articles to the first two volumes of the *Journal of American Folklore,* and Smith executed a series of animated illustrations of the masks entering Onondaga Longhouse, which he afterward deposited with his mask collection in several museums. The Onondaga Historical Association ultimately received the masks that he presented to Beauchamp; the American Museum of Natural History has both the masks and the drawings that he published; and after his death his remaining collections were divided between the American Museum of Natural History and the Museum of the American Indian.

A historical particularist, Beauchamp concluded that the False Faces at Onondaga represented a recent importation from the Seneca, and his comments on them in several publications nowhere attain the coherence of Morgan or DeCost Smith (Beauchamp 1888, 197; 1905, 184–92). About the same time, David Boyle, of Toronto, was stimulated to make similar observations of the False Face ceremonies among the Iroquois of Grand River, where he collected wooden masks now in the Royal Ontario Museum (Boyle 1898, 157–64; 1900, 27–29; Killan 1983, 183–184, 203).

COLLECTORS AND THE LITERATURE

Several extensive and important study collections, which unfortunately are falsely documented, resulted from the activities of Harriet Maxwell Converse, a poet and journalist, of New York City, and friend of Indian causes who, during the years 1881 to 1903, enthusiastically amassed Iroquois materials, particularly from the Cattaraugus Seneca. Her success was accompanied by adoption into the Seneca Snipe Clan (Parker 1908, 19), and subsequently the Onondaga installed her as an honorary chief of the Six Nations (Fenton 1971; Parker 1908, 17–29). The New York State Museum has some 100 Converse masks; others were consumed in the fire of 1911; and still other Converse collections are found in the Peabody Museum of American Archaeology and Ethnology, the American Museum of Natural History, and in the Museum of the American Indian. However, it was Converse's brief published utterances on masks (1899 and 1908) and the accession records that sometimes accompany her collections that early on made me wonder about how she did her fieldwork and who were her sources. Characteristically, one finds poetic titles for particular masks suggesting fanciful roles, such as "war and scalp, clan, maternity, bird, pipe-smoker's, sun-rise, dead chief," and so forth, that no field worker among the Iroquois since her day has been able to substantiate. Even her literary executor, Arthur Parker, who had access to her notes, worked with some of the same informants, edited her literary remains, and wrote the first systematic account of Seneca medicine societies, found only four classes of masks based on function (Parker 1909, 179). We may conclude, therefore, that Mrs. Converse wrote into the record more than she was told, certainly more than she observed, and the learned world is the unwitting victim of willing informants who politely assented to leading questions. However it happened, the damage was done, and the titles *clan* and *maternity* masks continue to crop up in museum labels and in publications. (This discrepancy between museum misinformation and the knowledge and usages of living Iroquois originally sent me to the field.)

As late as 1941, Joseph Keppler, New York cartoonist and friend of George G. Heye, founder of the Museum of the American Indian, perpetuated the Converse misnomers when describing his personal collection that he donated to the museum. Keppler was adopted into the Seneca Snipe Clan at Newtown in 1898, and it is said that he succeeded to Mrs. Converse's "horns of office" at her death (Heye, in Keppler 1941, 7). Certainly, the men of Keppler's generation, including Heye, enjoyed the confidence of the Seneca, they had unique opportunities to observe, and we wish they had been more matter of fact.

Exceptional Collectors

Two exceptions among museum-trained anthropologists stand out. M. R. Harrington (1909), late of the Southwest Museum, made collections for a number of museums, including the American Museum of Natural History, the Museum of the American Indian, and the National Museum of Ethnology in Stockholm. In the summer of 1907 he visited the Iroquois reserves in Ontario and turned over to the American Museum of Natural History gratifyingly full accession records with his specimens. Years later, Simeon Gibson, my interpreter, recalled the pleasure of having served Harrington as driver and front man. Harrington's notes suggest only a few generalized mask types that agree with the findings of Morgan, Parker, and the writer. In 1962 at Stockholm, I found a Harrington collection of False Faces from Cattaraugus with the usual documentation.

The other exception was Alanson Skinner. Skinner collected for several museums, notably the American Museum of Natural History, the Milwaukee Public Museum, and the Museum of the American Indian. Although he made his principal contribution to the ethnology of the prairie tribes before his untimely death at age thirty-nine (Harrington 1925), Skinner attended the Midwinter Festival at Allegany that year, observed and described the False Faces in action, and collected two wooden masks for the Museum of the American Indian whose staff he had joined. He properly speaks of certain "hidden masks" that rarely appear in public ceremonies, but I believe he was mistaken about so-called "clan masks" (Skinner 1925, 201, 202–203). He poignantly described a young man hastening to carve a mask under the pressure of a dream that had to be fulfilled (Skinner 1925, 202–203). Dorothy Skinner, his widow, continued fieldwork among the Seneca until just before I arrived at Coldspring in 1933.

Making a collection for a museum was the accepted way of financing ethnological fieldwork before 1930. The Bureau of American Ethnology and the National Museum of Canada alone supported fieldwork for its own sake. Frank G. Speck, of the University of Pennsylvania, for many years counted on partial support of his field expeditions from Labrador to the Carolinas in this way. In 1931, he had followed the Delaware and Munsee to the Six Nations Reserve, which led naturally to a systematic study, *The Midwinter Rites of the Upper Cayuga Long House* (1949), which was especially about the False Face Society. The masks that Speck collected are the ones that he observed in use or that amplify statements of his informants. Although Speck's book appeared a decade after my first two papers on masks, he had served as my mentor before I went to the field, and he had provided me with a model for studying the ceremonies.

Of late the subject has attracted the attention of an art historian, Zena Pearlstone-Mathews (Mathews 1978), whose dissertation finds a negative correlation between Iroquois False Faces and faces on prehistoric Seneca and Huron clay pipes, an avenue of research that Parker first proposed. Perhaps the present work will illuminate broader issues raised by other studies (Krusche 1975; Ritzenthaler 1969; Zerries 1954, 1961).

The Need for a Definitive Treatment

In 1940, I noted that extensive extant collections of Iroquois masks are commonly undocumented or labeled so as to conform to dubious sources that contradict the concepts that the Iroquois themselves hold regarding the masks and the ways that they use them in the ceremonies (Fenton 1941a, 400). Instead of finding detailed catalog entries—as to collector, date, place, tribe, source, use, and the like—establishing the provenience of the museum specimen, I encountered a lore that had come down through successive curators as to the supposed function of the masks in Iroquois culture. As one might expect, functions that were ascribed to the masks on the basis of their appearance and the classification that had grown up in the museums differed markedly from the ideas that I met among the Iroquois who still carved and used masks. Clearly, at some time two streams of culture had diverged, and my gut feeling was that the Iroquois had less reason to speculate and were probably more trustworthy custodians of their own tradition.

That such confusion then existed in the face of a rather extensive literature on the False Faces only served to emphasize the need for an adequate monograph. So I set out to gather the materials to describe and classify the masks in terms of the myths in which they figure, and I observed the rituals in which they participate, took texts of the prayers and invocations, recorded the songs, and employed pictures of the masks in museums to prompt informants to talk about them, to classify them, and to stimulate carvers. I was aware that one might derive a typological classification from the masks themselves after the manner of archaeologists, and this I subsequently attempted. But I wondered whether such a classification, although it might make a system out of the material, would bear any relation to how the Iroquois themselves grouped the mask beings of which the masks are portraits.

There were several questions on which I needed information. How do individuals join the Society of Faces? How is the society organized internally? How do the False Faces relate to the other Iroquois medicine societies? Getting answers to these questions required keeping a detailed account of the rituals, repeating observations, and following up with queries. And then I hoped to stimulate participants to keep records of their own activity within the society.

Operating with Linton's concept of the "activity" (Linton 1936, 397), I sought out and described the manufacture and use of all ceremonial equipment associated with the False Faces, including the wooden and husk masks themselves. Certain items no longer in use were in museums, but informants responded to pictures, and one or two items were restored to use. Chapter 8 covers ritual equipment.

IROQUOIS MASKING IN ETHNOGRAPHIC PERSPECTIVE

In the 1940s, some estimate was needed of the importance of masked shamanism in Iroquois life and of its position in the ethnographic perspective of the Northeast. Iroquoianists then thought of the Iroquois as essentially a southeastern people intrusive in the Northeast, but a revolution in prehistory, sparked by Griffin and MacNeish, advanced the in-situ hypothesis, which is now widely accepted and explains how Iroquois culture evolved from earlier prehistoric cultures in their homeland. Elements of northern shamanism and the concept of "master of the game animals" found in Delaware and Iroquois tales relate to the hunting cultures of the northern forests. And the Iroquois themselves may be the focus of masking in the Eastern Woodlands, possessing the complex in its climax form. Or is this but the cultural moraine of some ancient, more widely distributed complex, as Krusche (1975) has suggested?

The present work addresses these and related problems. It brings up to date what we know of the subject, presenting for the first time materials that were only glossed in earlier papers. In the late 1930s, while serving as a Community Worker to the Tonawanda Seneca, I approached these problems in a general paper (1937). It reached a wide audience of readers outside of ethnology and promptly went out of print. The same response greeted a more systematic treatment of the problems generated by the first article (1941a). Masks evidently hold an especial fascination for a wide range of people in the creative arts, whereas shamanism has implications for medicine and professions concerned with the human psyche (Kroeber and Holt, 1920; Eliade 1972; Fenton 1972b, 1979; Macgowan and Rosse 1923; Pasztory 1975; Wilson 1960; Wissler 1928).

Problems and Methods

CLASSIFICATION

The problems that continue to confront us are those of mental stereotypes and overt behavior, of mental constructs and cultural forms. Are there formal types of masks, and how do the Iroquois classify them? Does a systematic classification based on formal features have any cultural validity? To what extent do the mask types recognized by the Iroquois reflect cultural stereotypes found in their mythology? Conversely, are the formal characteristics specified in myths for mask spirits and the shapes that they assume in dreams and visions simply projections into the spirit world of the grotesque wooden masks worn by human beings? Goldenweiser (1922, 231–32) first asked this question.

LOCAL STYLES

As my studies progressed, both in the field and with museum collections, it became evident that there are local styles of carving (Fenton 1956, 352). This led me to consider how the individual learns to carve, how his personal style develops, and to what extent he is captive of a local tradition. I interviewed carvers and watched them at work. Sometimes they were carving freely, and at other times they were executing a commission for some person who had a particular dream calling for a specific kind of mask. How was it that masks carved at Allegany or Cattaraugus (Seneca) came out one way and those at Six Nations another way? Despite the tyranny of tradition, new kinds of masks are created. There is no better illustration of the impact of culture on the individual artist and his impact on culture. After me, Hendry (1964, 377, 394) explored this problem at Onondaga.

As Hendry points out, the really great carvers are also users. They are members of the Society of Faces and performers in its rituals. No words adequately convey the dramatic behavior of these actors; there is no substitute for seeing the False Faces in action. The mildest persons become transformed in these roles. Native theory goes out the window in ritual practice. Even if the Iroquois were to make a formal distinction between mask types based on the content of myths, it should be noted that the members of the society do not consistently use the same mask always to portray the same being, and the same mask does not perform a consistent function in the ceremony. But with it, the individual owner performs several roles of increasing importance during his lifetime. This disregard of native theory in ritual practice makes a shambles of overnice formal distinctions. As we shall see, the False Faces are like people: They express different moods and characteristics.

METHOD

The approach in this study has been circular. I first attempted to find out the meaning of masks in a family collection, and I hoped to observe their use in ceremonies. Undocumented museum collections presented the same problem. On my first field trip in 1933 to the Seneca at Allegany Reservation, the source of our collection, I carried photographs of masks that had been collected among them. My host, Jonas Snow, was a carver. Both he and his neighbors expressed great interest in seeing pictures of their handiwork, and they identified particular masks with the individuals who had carved them or used them in the ceremonies. I recorded their comments along with Seneca terms for various mask types. I repeated this procedure with other carvers whenever opportunity afforded.

The method that I employed in the field was not standardized or controlled; rather, it was open-ended—I made it a rule never to stop an informant who volunteered tangential information but recorded his comments. Nor did I insist that he adhere to a protocol. This loose procedure elicited, often enough, explanatory myths, and it evoked relations of human adventures with the False Faces, which I took down. Unless offered, I directly asked all informants for the origin myths, and particularly to relate their personal histories as members of the Society of Faces. These case histories disclose information on the kinds of illnesses cured by the False Faces, entrance to the society through dreams and visions, accounts of hysteria on seeing the masks, the hazards of ridicule, dangers of neglect, and the compulsion for renewal of ceremonial obligations. These accounts of participation in cures produced some lengthy descriptions of the rituals.

The masks may be art forms and the myths, tales, and human adventures oral literature, but the performance of the maskers is high drama.

Observations

I first witnessed a performance of the False Face rites in August of 1933, when the matrons of the Hawk Clan at Allegany, into which clan I was soon adopted, offered to celebrate a private rite in my honor as the best way of satisfying my questions. After that, I observed the ceremony many times at Allegany, both private and public rites, and again at Tonawanda during the two and one-half years I was resident there for the U.S. Indian Service, when I also witnessed the climax performance at Onondaga, near Syracuse, NY, during a midwinter festival. After joining the Bureau of American Ethnology in 1939, I commenced fieldwork on the Six Nations Reserve, where a private rite was put on for me while recording the music for the Library of Congress, and I was once present for the public autumn Traveling Rite at the Onondaga Longhouse near Middleport.

Informant interviews prepare one for observing, but observation provides a further background for questioning because the outside observer notes both significant and accidental detail, and not until one's informant describes the same performance does the ethnologist begin to perceive the pattern that governs the conduct of the ritual and gain some notion of what the ceremony actually means to participants. It is all too easy for the observer to make a complete but spurious record of behavior and fail to grasp what is culturally meaningful. An unedited motion picture of the ceremonies would have the same spurious weakness.

PHOTOGRAPHIC ETHNOLOGY

From my first fieldwork at Allegany I used a black-and-white camera and kept a running log of the negatives. Often enough, this catalog was my only record of certain activities. The quarter-plate camera has certain advantages for publication, requiring little enlargement and affording two cuts to the plate. Only later did I resort to 35-mm cameras when color became available. Then the catalog began to flag. From street scenes, the ball ground, people, and social events, it was a gradual progression to the ceremonies. I was soon permitted to photograph the False Face ceremonies, usually at a private house during the Midwinter Festival, first at Tonawanda, and after 1940 at Coldspring. But here again it proved more successful to enlist someone who knew the ritual and have him compose a series of what he considered the essential phases of a curing ritual. Chauncey Johnny John at Allegany is responsible for the series that has now been published the world over (Brasser 1967; Fenton 1941a, Plates 19–21; Ritzenthaler 1969; Sturtevant and Trigger 1978, 461). Simeon Gibson arranged such sessions at Six Nations; Cephas Hill at Tonawanda. The still camera freezes characteristic posture and gesture, and it also catches the contemporary scene. Illustration, like imaginative writing, creates the scene, which may be an attempt at historical reconstruction.

By 1941 it was possible to photograph actual ceremonies such as the spring purge of the settlement by the False Faces. Photographic ethnology may serve to document a ceremonial event and illustrate its structure better than words. It is unlikely that this kind of fieldwork could be replicated today.

In studies of material culture, photography is an essential supplement to observation. With the camera I recorded the technique of mask making at Tonawanda, at Coldspring, and on Grand River. The camera catches positions of work and ways of handling tools. This I found the best way to learn about artistic styles, what freedom the individual carver might enjoy in devising new forms, how he learned his craft, and to what degree he conformed to local canons of art. The carving of the masks was formerly ritualized, and it is still hedged in by the fragments of a broken-down ceremonial procedure. During this century, however, the ritual of carving the mask on a tree is only a cultural memory.

The same technique was used in recording the manufacture of snapping-turtle shell rattles. One such type specimen by Jonas Snow was collected for the Yale Peabody Museum (Fenton 1937, 236; Cat. no. 25289). Conklin and Sturtevant (1953) afterward made a thorough study of Seneca "singing tools."

A Native Painter

Ernest Smith, of Tonawanda, was a young painter in the 1930s, with little formal training, but he had grown up in the traditional culture. I commissioned Smith to make some illustrations of the False Face ceremonies, as he imagined they were performed a century earlier, and to feel free to consult with my older informants. Indeed, they were all then employed on the WPA Indian Arts Project for the Rochester Museum of Arts and Sciences, for whom in the course of the next five years Smith was to do several hundred canvases and watercolor illustrations (Plate 12-1). In later years, Smith sold his drawings and paintings widely, and those now held by private collectors command high prices. Smith's illustrations of traditional Seneca life stand in the same relationship to my photographs as informant descriptions do to the ethnologist's observations. They represent ideal patterns—native theory in contrast with actual practice.

MUSEUM STUDIES

In seven seasons of fieldwork up to 1940, I failed to confirm the poetic titles that Converse assigned to masks in the several collections that she made for museums. Therefore, its seemed advisable to study her extensive collections in Albany and in New York City. As controls, I visited Rochester, Buffalo, and Toronto. I went equipped with typewriter, two quarter-plate cameras, copystand, and lamps. The technique employed was to record information on a selected series of criteria on slips that developed in the field and increased or narrowed as the study progressed. These were color, form of chin, shape of mouth, nose, presence or absence of supplementary wrinkles and supraorbital ridges, spines on the nose bridge extending to the forehead, shape and method of attaching metal eyes,[2] and presence of tobacco bags. And, turning to the back of the mask, I noted the number of holes for head and hair attachment,[3] evidence of use, carving-tool marks, species of wood, and other noteworthy features. Having recorded these data and the museum catalog numbers, I then photographed each specimen front and back and afterward cataloged the negatives serially to agree with the data sheets and the museum catalog. But for the substitution of 35-mm cameras and the want of a typewriter, this procedure became my standard technique for studying museum specimens in five trips to Europe while hunting for older American collections. A summary of the collections seen and examined in this way is given in Table 1.

By 1940, I had seen and examined about 200 masks, besides photographs furnished by museums that I could not visit. Since then, I have seen and studied 100 more, including 25 in European museums. William C. Sturtevant has given the subject serious attention, both in the field and in the museum, although his results are not available. The one serious student who exceeded my sample and confirmed most of my results, Zena Pearlstone-Mathews, examined 335 wooden masks—264 full-face and 71 miniatures—largely from the Seneca and compared them to archaeological predecessors both in Iroquoia and in Huronia (Mathews 1978, 88, 127), disposing of an important historical problem.

Museum-Fieldwork Reciprocity
The relationship of these museum studies to continuing fieldwork on the Society of Faces was reciprocal, if not circular. As soon as my photographs were developed and printed, they were mounted on sheets with accompanying data on five-by-eight-inch slips pasted below. I used these photographs and data both for stimulating informants to share their knowledge and later for classifying the masks. I never succeeded in devising a controlled technique for testing the attitudes and recording remarks of living sources about the pictures. Tape recorders were not yet available. All of my Iroquois collaborators regarded the pictures of masks with great interest, and sometimes with considerable amusement, often hailing passing neighbors to come share in their experience. Interest seemed to vary with the evident age and horrific appearance of a mask and its implied power, which might evoke a statement of awe—"it ought not to be in a

2. In 1687, Father Beschefer mentioned kettles as the source of brass eye reflectors (Thwaites 1896–1901 [hereafter *Jesuit relations* (*JR*)] 63:289). Some old masks, however, have no eye plates. Why? Is crimping older than tacking eye sconces in place? I would suspect so because tacks or metal triangles like glazier's points had to be procured or made. Most museum specimens have tin eye reflectors that were cut out of tin cans, and these constitute another criterion of age.
3. As I shall discuss later under mask carving, older masks have from five to seven holes in the rims for attaching hair and head ties; later the hair and ties were tacked on like a baseball catcher's mask.

museum unfed and uncared for"—or sometimes the mask proved an excellent caricature of some local personality, which relieved the tension in shared amusement. Indeed, the Iroquois manifest ambivalence—they are both amused and awed by these pathetically humorous portraits of supernatural beings whom they see dramatized in the ceremonies of the False Face Society and who appear to them in dreams. The same ambivalence occurs during ritual celebrations. Although I never obtained from all informants consistent data on each mask or was satisfied how they fit into a native classification, often enough the informant would recognize the picture as a mask that he had carved, had owned, or that he had seen in a ceremony. All of these volunteered incidents proved grist for my mill.

The pictures proved of value later in segregating formal mask types and determining art styles by localities (Fenton 1956; Mathews 1978). Early on, I thought I could analyze the masks into salient features and plot their distribution: mouth shape, bent nose, spines on forehead, presence or absence of supplementary wrinkles. I came to recognize local styles, often by the makers; tribal art styles would remain fuzzy and elusive. Informants were not always verbal in answering such questions, possibly because, as Sturtevant pointed out in reading my manuscript, much art and material culture are surely very conscious but are difficult to verbalize. I am rather inclined to think that much of formal art and a great part of the skills involved in material culture are transmitted on the level of unconscious behavior patterns.

FOLKLORE AND TEXTS

There is no want of verbal lore on the False Faces, however, and this ranges from formal prayers, set myths, human encounters, and personal documents of misfortune and cures to the hazards of not renewing one's ceremonial obligations. As a student of Franz Boas's famous pupils— Edward Sapir, Clark Wissler, and Leslie Spier—I was urged, even though it was then unfashionable, to record texts in the Iroquoian languages of myths, prayers, and even accounts of individual participation in the culture. I took texts, first in Seneca, then in Onondaga, employing the phonetic transcription in use before the discovery of phonemics. This practice grew to proficiency and remained useful even after the advent of electronic sound recorders, first on discs and then on wire and tape. It also preceded Chafe's work on Seneca grammar and his dictionary (Chafe 1963, 1967), which triggered the recent explosion in Iroquoian linguistics. In the long run, the recording devices are a wonderful crutch, preserving the original voices in song and prayer, but the records still have to be transcribed and analyzed. There is no substitute for the native language in the study of ceremonies: Often enough the prayer texts contain archaic words that are the keys to unlock concepts that are no longer verbalized by con-

Table 1-1. *Museums Visited and Mask Collections Seen and Studied*

Date	Museum	Wooden	Husk	Miniature wood	Miniature husk	On tree	Other	Total	Studied	Photographs
1935	Buffalo Historical Society	55						55	9	×
1935	Buffalo Museum of Science	27	9					36	×	×
1936	Onondaga Historical Association	30						30	2	×
1934	Peabody Museum, Yale		1					1	×	×
1935	Fenton Collection (now MAI)	[11]	[2]				Cloth [1]	[14]	[14]	×
1940	New York State Museum	113	11	4	2	1		132	85	×
1940	Montgomery County Historical Society, Amsterdam, NY	6						6	×	×
1940	Royal Ontario Museum	37	7					44	24	×
1940	Rochester Museum & Science Center									
	(older)	27	12	5	1	2		47	16	×
	(Seneca Arts)	243	41	65				349		
1940	Museum of the American Indian-Heye Foundation	215	47	18	2	2		284	35	×
1940	American Museum of Natural History	31	15	5		1		52		×
1940	U.S. National Museum	31	10	3		1		46	10	×
1945	Cranbrook Institute of Science	8	8				1 cloth	17	1	×
1947	Milwaukee Public Museum	43	2	3		1		49		×
1956	University Museum, Philadelphia	21						21	6	
1959	Peabody Museum, Harvard	6	7					13		

Table 1-1. *Continued*

Date	Museum	Wooden	Husk	Miniature wood	Miniature husk	On tree	Other	Total	Studied	Photographs
1962	Field Museum of Natural History	40	4	2	1			47		×
1962	National Museum of Man, Ottawa	75	41	29	2	3		150	20	×
1962	Rijksmuseum voor Volkenkunde, Leiden	1						1	×	×
1962	Nationalmuseet, Copenhagen	2	2					4	4	×
1962	State Ethnographical Museum, Stockholm	4	2	1				5	5	×
1962	Municipal Museum of Ethnology, Frankfurt am Main	3	2					5	5	×
1962	Speyer Collection, Nieder Walluf	1						1		
1962	Linden Museum, Stuttgart	3						3	3	×
1962	Ethnological Collection, University of Zurich	1	1					2	2	×
1962	Hotz Collection, Zurich	3						3	3	×
1962	Museum of Ethnography, Geneva	1						1	1	×
1963	Arizona State Museum, Tucson	1						1	1	×
1964	Institute of Ethnography, Leningrad	4	4					8	1	
1973	Denver Museum of Natural History	69	23 (2 wood)	1	1	1	2 long nose	97	×	
	Denver Art Museum [large collection: seen but not studied]									
Totals		1,101	249	136	7	12	4	1,509	+ 2 turtle shell = 1,511	

temporary members of society. Apart from any interest in linguistic research, I early discovered that the recorded texts would lead me to the ethnological materials I was seeking. Thus, from the tobacco invocation to the False Faces one derives the term for the "sponsor" of a medicine society ceremony. One can find this same term in a similar form in the writings of seventeenth-century Jesuit missionaries among the Huron, and from this we infer that the present role of sponsor has an historical depth of 300 years and that the term and role are probably pre-Columbian. Although there are hazards in deriving Iroquois customs from the Huron, the two cultures were similar, and the common trait helps to explain why the business of feast making, which amounts to a compulsion, permeates all of Iroquois ceremonialism (Cf. Sapir 1916, 51ff.).

History of Masked Shamanism in Iroquoia

Both the direct historic approach of ethnohistory and the comparative method can be employed to place Iroquois masked shamanism in ethnographic perspective. I first suggested this approach nearly forty years ago, when I wrote:

> If we can show that the complex has a historical depth reaching back to the first white contacts with the Iroquois, it would be relevant to investigate whether the Iroquois possess the complex in a greater degree of detail than their Algonquian neighbors. If we could determine the center whence the masking spread throughout the northeast, some light might shine on the problem of whether Iroquois masking is a diagnostic trait pointing to their alleged southern origin, or whether it is related to northern shamanism and the use of masks across the Arctic litoral, or whether the complex was original with the Iroquois themselves from whom it spread to the neighboring Delaware. [Fenton 1941a, 405]

Just then evidence to support a southeastern migration hypothesis was not forthcoming, and the in situ theory for the development of the Iroquois was barely perceptible on the horizon, although it would soon displace the first alternative. Evidence for a northern affiliation of the masking complex was not much better, if as good. The sensible alternative was to concentrate on the third, the Iroquois focus, for which there are manageable data. In 1956, I returned to the first alternative, but the whole problem of the derivation of the masking complex must be revised in the light of two recent studies (Krusche 1975; Mathews 1978), which I shall discuss later.

Structural Considerations

HIERARCHY OF MEDICINE SOCIETIES

Of the dozen medicine societies that have survived into modern times (Parker 1909), "undisputed preeminence among [them] was held by the False-faces" (Goldenweiser 1922, 72). This statement is certainly true in the popular imagination of both the Iroquois and collectors of masks, although more recent studies of the Little Water Society and of its affiliated societies—Hadí:ʔdo:s (the Medicine Company), its celebration group, and of the Eagle Dance—afford a more balanced view of the maskers' position (Fenton 1953, 1979; Shimony 1961). Goldenweiser himself, in an earlier statement (1912, 472–73), accorded first rank to the Medicine Company as most sacred and influential and grouped the False Faces with several shamanistic societies having animal tutelaries in second place. The False Faces, nevertheless, with their spectacular public appearances in spring and autumn to purge the settlement and as beggars and throwers of hot ashes at the height of the Midwinter Festival remain the best known.

ORDERS OF MEMBERSHIP

As with the other medicine societies, orders of membership in the Society of Faces derive from specific cures, particular dreams, and participation. As we shall see, the False Faces specialize in the "red diseases" (nosebleed, etc.), paralysis, and dental and muscular disorders. One may dream of a mask, of a ritual, or it may be prescribed. There is some belief in inheritance of unfulfilled obligations from one's forebears. And there are cases of hysterical possession when the maskers appear. These matters will be treated later.

FORM AND CONTENT OF RITUALS

As I shall explain presently, three orders of medicine societies employ masks, namely the Society of Faces (wooden masks), the Husk Faces, or "Bushy Heads," and the Society of Mystic Animals, or the Medicine Company (Hadí:ʔdo:s). Each of these orders has its own specialized ritual equipment, which has to be prepared for the purpose, and each order has its own rituals. In the case of the False Faces, the most prominent aspect of preparing the ritual paraphernalia is the traditional ritual of carving the mask. In general terms, the several rituals of the False Faces and of the Husk Faces conform to a pattern or sequence that governs all Iroquois medicine feasts. I first pointed this out in 1936 and then in later works. The pattern consists of an invitation by messenger, an announcement of intent at the meeting, a tobacco invocation to the spirit forces requesting their cooperation, the specific ritual, and a terminal feast. There is usually an acknowledgment of thanks to those who participated, specific roles being mentioned.

IMPORTANCE IN IROQUOIS LIFE

Although the number of longhouse adherents is less than one-third of the reservation population today, no Iroquois descendant would be prepared to deny the importance of the False Faces in his or her cultural heritage. With the makers and users of masks there can be no question, but some others who belong to various Christian sects and regularly attend church also attend the doings at the longhouse during the height of the Midwinter Festival. Others are dealers in Indian crafts and readers of books, and all Iroquois are great museum goers. There are cases of Christian and non-longhouse Iroquois who have called in the False Faces, although the frequency of such visitations is probably less today. So we are confronted with a wide range of attitudes toward the maskers and the masks themselves. I vividly recall one Christian Delaware on the Six Nations Reserve who proudly showed to me as a treasured heirloom a mask that had been confiscated by a missionary from the Delaware Big House on the reserve in the last century. I have known Iroquois who possessed and treasured such masks from as far from home as Los Angeles. Indeed, the rage for ethnological art is not confined to persons other than Native Americans.

So let us turn to the masks themselves.

PART ONE

2. Mask Types

The Wooden Masks, or False Faces

A few museum visitors, if they are traditional Iroquois, may appreciate that the weird human likenesses that mock them from the display cases are actually memorials to generations of nightmares. They were carved in response to particular dreams. They are portraits carved in wood of several types of mythical beings whom the old Iroquois say only a little while ago inhabited the rocky regions at the rim of the earth or wandered about in the forests. The Seneca term for "mask" (*gagǫ́hsaʔ*) is *face,* but the Onondaga commonly refer to the progenitor as Hadúʔiʔ, or Hodó:wiʔ, "Hunchback." Among the Mohawk, the term is simply "face" (*gagú:wara*). Everywhere in Reservation English the masks are called "False Faces," and they are so designated in the literature.

THEIR TRUE MEANING

The tradition is that Iroquois hunters, when traveling in the forest, frequently met strange, quasi-human beings who darted from tree to tree and who often appeared to be disembodied heads with long, snapping hair. These forest creatures agreed not to molest human beings, saying that they merely wanted Indian tobacco (*Nicotiniana rustica* L.), and they asked that mush be made from the white corn meal that hunters and warriors carried. More powerful than the forest faces, however, is the being of the wry mouth and broken nose, whom the Seneca call Shagodyowéhgo:wa:h, "Our Great Defender," but who is Haduʔiʔgó:nah, "The Great Humpbacked One," to the Onondaga. He has appeared to few humans because he promised the Creator to abide in inaccessible places on the rim of the earth. This latter being is prominent in mythology and familiar from his counterparts—the maskers that represent him in the ceremonies.

The Faces of the Forest have also claimed to possess the power to control sickness. They have instructed dreamers to carve likenesses in the form of masks, promising that whenever anyone makes ready the feast, invokes their help while burning tobacco, and sings the curing songs, supernatural power to cure disease will be conferred on human beings who wear the masks. They further specified that dancers should carry turtle rattles and a peeled hickory staff and speak a weird, unintelligible language composed entirely of nasals: *hǫ hǫ hǫ hǫ!* Furthermore, the power is given to maskers to scoop up ashes with glowing embers in their bare hands without suffering burns when they administer hot ashes on the sick person by blowing.

Though conforming to generalized styles, the masks are also as varied as the individual visions that inspired them. The visions, too, conform to consistent patterns. Sick persons often dream of a particular kind of mask, and the range of variation reflects artistic license of individual carvers who sculpt the masks from single blocks of living basswood, or some seasoned substitute.

NATIVE CLASSIFICATION POORLY UNDERSTOOD

Iroquois sources became perplexed when asked to classify the great range of False Faces into types. A classification based on morphological features alone, a game in which archaeologists have frequently indulged, and at the time seemed like an interesting experiment employing photographs of masks in museum collections, failed to satisfy the native Iroquois view of masks. The one feature that they most often mentioned was the shape of the mouth, but other considerations entered into their view, as we shall see later.

Spirits and People

Henry Redeye, the preacher of the Handsome Lake religion at Coldspring Longhouse, declared that there are as many types of False Faces as there are people. Some masks are portraits of youths; others are of old men having long white hair and wrinkled faces. There are angry individuals with broken noses and mouths skewed to one side as if they were victims of paralytic strokes. Such masks are likely to sweat and cause their owner illness if he neglects to supplicate them with tobacco offerings. Others have distended, open lips as if they were blowing ashes. A few masks with standing hair and raised eyebrows are whistling and merely want tobacco, whereas others protrude red tongues in pain, or laugh, revealing irregular rows of wooden or bone teeth. Their similarities, one to another, represent the patterns that the local culture has prescribed in dreams and the styles developed by resident carvers.

Tradition in Visions

Tradition has dictated the forms that the faces assume in visions, and the craftsmen (only men are carvers!) emphasize these features in carving. Indeed, these are the very features that the Seneca mention when describing the original forest folk. It is sufficient for the carver to single out particular features of the face for artistic expression. How he achieves this is up to him, given the limitations of the medium in which he works, the tools available to him, and his personal skill. The face portrays the being, and the wearer must dramatize the other attributes of the supernatural he represents: his erect or slouching gait, his awful mien, and the nonsensical, nasal speech that the actor accompanies by shaking a rattle or rubbing it on some surface. To the Iroquois, the total effect is both terrifying and extremely humorous. Having watched these performances repeatedly over the years, I can say that the distance between a collection of masks in a museum and the False Face society in action is of the order of a transport into another world.

Iroquois conceptions of the supernaturals whom these dramatizations impersonate have unquestionably been influenced by projecting tradition in dreams, both in the form of masks present in the community and the behavior of the actors who perform in the ceremonies. It was Goldenweiser who first perceived that

> various grotesque spirits must be regarded as derived either from dreams or visions or to be the outgrowth of the free play of the imagination. Not infrequently, artificial objects or artistic conventions must have had an influence on the formal character of the spirits. Thus, it is highly probable that the False-face spirits of the Iroquois are the projections into the spiritual world of the grotesque wooden masks worn by the members of the False-face Society. [Goldenweiser 1922, 231–32]

Use and Type

From an Iroquois standpoint, any consideration of mask types is contingent on the uses to which they are put. They are not rigidly definable on the basis of form alone because, to a large extent, use determines type. Role supersedes form, native practice disregards native theory, and the overnice taxonomic distinctions based on form alone fail to find confirmation in Iroquois culture. A carver may indeed be guided by the mythological incident when Haduʔiʔ broke his nose on the advancing mountain, and the carver may intend his mask to represent that being, but a subsequent owner may ignore the incident in using the mask. Conversely, a mask that was never intended to represent more than a common face of the forest may in time be called upon to perform the curing role of the great world-rim dweller in the doorkeeper ritual. Thus, all old masks tend to become ultimately "doctor" masks. On occasion, even some of these more potent doctor masks get into the hands of small boys who impersonate the beggars of the forest during the Midwinter Festival. Therefore, only with certain limits and allowing for such exceptions would my Iroquois mentors even attempt to assign a series of masks to specific functions and categories.

Dramatic Behavior of Maskers

As already indicated, the dramatic behavior of the men who don the masks counts far more in the roles in which the masks appear than the form of the mask itself. The roles are assigned. Individual talent in acting and dancing determines the effectiveness of the ceremony. Certain individuals in the several Iroquois communities are known to be good performers in the role of doorkeeper. Conductors of a ceremony remember great performances and notice new actors. Sometimes such an actor possesses a fine old mask that is suited to the role, and in time both he and his mask come to be cast in that role. But, as he grows older, that man may be selected as conductor by the sponsor of the ceremony, and he readily finds a younger man to wear his old mask. However, the elders in the community easily distinguish the mask and its owner and identify the second wearer as new in the role.

In general terms, Iroquois False Faces have the following features: They have deep-set eyes that are rendered bright by tin or brass sconces; noses are large and frequently bent. The arched brows are deeply wrinkled and are sometimes divided longitudinally by a crease or comb of spines—a motif that Jesse Cornplanter called "turtle-tail" because of its resemblance to the processes on a snapping turtle's tail. The mouth is the most variable feature and spans a range of contortions depending on mood, function, and local style. Both mouth corners may be upturned in a smile or a grimace showing teeth. Or the mouth is distended ovally for blowing ashes, sometimes with protruding tongue, or it is puckered as if whistling, or puckered with conventionalized tongue and spoonlike lips, as if the cheeks were sucked in. The mouth may assume the shape of bifunnelate, flared lips for blowing ashes or a square mouth blower revealing teeth. Still others have large, straight, distended lips that may be twisted up at one corner or down at the other corner, accompanied by a bent nose. Finally, both corners may be turned down in an expression of extreme anguish. Thick, distended lips protrude beneath the nose, and a series of modifying wrinkles augments the distorted expression. Cheekbones are sometimes suggested, and a prominent chin, a feature on masks from Grand River, and sometimes from Allegany Reservation, serves as a convenient grip for the wearer to adjust the mask to his face. The face is usually framed by a long wig that is commonly cut from black horse tails, which fall on either side from a part in the middle of the forehead. (This was a hairstyle affected by young American women in the 1960s and 1970s, which always suggested to me, when I looked out over an undergraduate lecture section, a meeting of the Society of Faces.) A startling effect is produced by reversing the natural grain of the hair on some beggar masks. On still older masks, and quite possibly more anciently, cornhusk braids, shredded bast of basswood, or buffalo mane served as hair.

A Classification Based on Specimens

My approach to classifying masks takes into consideration formal types based on variations in the masks themselves and local styles of carving. A particular formal feature, such as the bent nose or the twisted mouth, is likely to be shared by two or more local groups, but what distinguishes the masks of a particular local group, say the Seneca of Newtown, from the masks by artisans of another community, the Onondaga of Nedrow near Syracuse or the carvers of Six Nations, on Grand River in Canada, is the manner in which the individual carver expresses the local artistic tradition in the general conformation of the whole face.

Early on I discovered, with the help of my Iroquois collaborators, that the mouth is the mask's most variable feature. This enabled me to range photographs in a series of categories illustrating progressive changes in mouth shape from upturned corners to downturned corners. This seemed a promising and reasonable basis for distinguishing formal types. The tendency of the Iroquois themselves to designate the mouth as a criterion for naming the masks gives this arrangement significance. The masks do not have personal names except as they are given the names of the tutelary spirits. The names are rather descriptive referents to various facial expressions.

Interviews with various informants, in which they arranged the photographs typologically, yielded twelve mask types.[1] The last four of the twelve types, which I published early in the study (Fenton 1941, 408–12), represented other types of wooden masking, to which I have now added another category under a separate heading—the so-called "Tuscarora" faces.

Beginning at the middle of the series, the twelve types are the following:

1. The crooked-mouth mask, which is so named because "his mouth is twisted" (*hahsagai:de?*). One corner of the mouth is pulled down or up.[2] Such masks occur among the Seneca, among the Onondaga, and at Six Nations where carvers make them intentionally horrific to frighten away disease, with bent nose and twisted mouth and supplementary wrinkles. The latter is virutally a Grand River style, today exemplified in the work of Jake Thomas. At first, I thought this type was the commonest among all the Iroquois (1941, 408), but I was mistaken (Plates 2-1–2-3).

2. The mask with straight lips, "his mouth is straight" (*hodesadógęhdǫ*). Straight distended lips like a duckbill run the width of the mouth across the whole face. With its variants, this one and the two that follow are sometimes ornamented with a vertical crest of spines or "teeth," or "knots" extending up the forehead from the nose bridge (Plate 2-4A, B).

---

1. It all came together one summer afternoon when Chauncey Johnny John, one of the great carvers at Coldspring, drove over with me to the Cattaraugus Reservation, where he had grown up, to visit James Crow, of Newtown, the acknowledged premier carver of that community. Together we examined my photographs of museum specimens. I produced the pictures and let my informants arrange them while I noted their comments. They naturally began with types most familiar to them in their own localities. Later, I repeated the process with other informants in other localities: with Jesse Cornplanter, of Tonawanda (with whom I also went to see James Crow, for Jesse, too, had been reared at Newtown); with Simeon Gibson (Onondaga-Cayuga), of Grand River; and with Sherman Redeye, back at Coldspring.

2. In reading the manuscript, Raymond Fogelson raised an interesting question for future research: "Is there any consistency here in which side of the mouth is pulled up or down, and if this tendency exists among known masks, is it ultimately related to Bell's palsy or some other paralysis, which may offer suggestions on brain lateralization?" One might go through photographs of crooked-mouth masks in collections with this question in mind.

Plate 2-1. Crooked-mouth masks: classic portraits of Hadui (Plates 2-1 to 2-3). Mask of the Wind God, a red mask collected by J. N. B. Hewitt at Grand River, Canada, 1916. U.S. National Museum, Washington, D.C., Cat. No. 381410.

Plate 2-2. A–B: A black wry-mouth mask in the Grand River style. New York State Museum, Albany, Cat. No. 37019. Two views. C: A massive red crooked-mouth mask from Grand River. Chiefswood Collection, Royal Ontario Museum, Toronto, Cat. No. HD 12635.

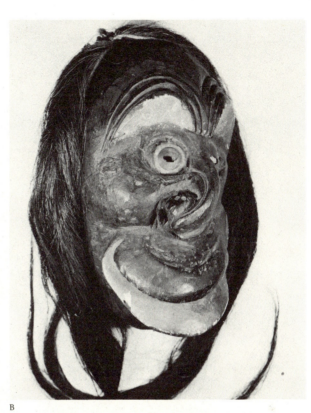

Plate 2-3. A modern version in the Grand River style by Chief Jacob Thomas (Cayuga), the reigning carver at Six Nations Reserve, ca. 1956. Collection of David Bartholomew, Hudson, N.Y.

Plate 2-4. Straight-lipped doorkeeper masks. A: Black mask with distended lips, collected by J. W. Fenton from Jonas Snow, 1924. Probably carved by Clarence White ca. 1915. Fenton Collection from Allegany, Museum of the American Indian–Heye Foundation, Cat. No. 20/2841. B: Black doorkeeper mask with red flared lips. Seneca. New York State Museum, Albany, Cat. No. 37023.

A

B

3. Spoon-lipped, or spoon-mouthed, mask, having "double spoons made on it" (*odógwaʔshodoʔ*). Conventionalized flared or puckered lips as in blowing may be accompanied by a rudimentary tongue that projects beneath the pursed mouth aperture (Plate 2-5A–D). Spoon-lipped masks are common at Newtown on Seneca Cattaraugus Reservation, where they have been in use since the earliest memory of my informants—the last quarter of the nineteenth century—and they consider the straight-lipped and the spoon-mouthed mask types, which they pair in the doorkeeper ritual, to be the classic Seneca representations of the great world-rim dweller. Among the Seneca of Coldspring, on Allegany Reservation, spoon lips become funnel-shaped.

4. Hanging-mouth mask, so-called because "the corners of his mouth are hanging" (*hosę́:ʔdǫ*), not unlike the muse of tragedy. An old type among the Seneca, it is present in collections made at the old Buffaloe Creek Reservation, from Onondaga Valley, and Tonawanda. One such specimen is reported to have been taken beyond the Niagara frontier into Canada in the late eighteenth century (Plate 2-6A–D). Another such specimen, collected in Oklahoma, was probably taken there from Grand River, Ontario. An inconstant feature of this type is a crest of spines on the forehead.

5. "Protruding-tongue" (*dodänǫhgáwęh*) masks are supposed to portray pain. DeCost Smith collected such at Onondaga, and Lewis H. Morgan and David Boyle found them among the Onondaga of Grand River. Uncommon among the Seneca, this type may be considered Onondaga (Plates 1-4, 2-7A–D).

6. Smiling mask (*hayóndihaʔ*), "he is smiling." As one informant remarked, "Maybe he saw a pretty girl, and he is smiling." Surely not all masks are wry-faced. The type occurs frequently as beggar masks among the Seneca of Coldspring on Allegheny, but among the Onondaga of Grand River smiling masks are likely to be quite heavy, having thick, leering lips, heavy chins, and puffy cheeks (Plates 2-8A–D). Some of these masks were unquestionably involved in curing. Early Seneca beggar masks frequently have pointy heads and sharp chins, and sometimes ears, as if intended to be caricatures of men and women (Plate 2-9A–E).

7. Whistling masks, designated "he is whistling" (*hanǫ́:gagah*). This one is also called the "blowing spirit mask," or the Whistling God (Djinnagáhi-häh [Hewitt]). The type has a puckered mouth, which is frequently enhanced by supplementary wrinkles. Several examples from the Seneca appear quite old and have tobacco bags attached suggesting rewards for cures; still other such specimens are regarded merely as beggar or dancing masks. Further examples come from the Onondaga of Six Nations Reserve in Canada (Plate 2-10A–D).

8. The divided mask "his body is split in halves" (*dęhodyaʔtgai:ewęh*).³

---

3. See the myths that Hewitt had from Chiefs John and Joshua Buck, Chapter 5.

Plate 2-5. Spoon-lipped doorkeeper masks. Seneca of Cattaraugus. A: Black (formerly red) with brass eyes. Collected by A. C. Parker in 1909. NYSM, Cat. No. 37042. B: Old red mask, with pierced ears and silver eyes. Note spines on forehead and nose and mouth pursed as if blowing. Buffalo Historical Society, Buffalo, N.Y. C: Red-brown mask with grayish hair in the classic Newton Seneca style. Collected by T. R. Teft, of Collins, N.Y., 1923. Rochester Museum and Science Center, Cat. No. AE 7.1.0/404. D: Mask in the smooth Newtown style, Cattaraugus Reservation. Joseph Keppler Collection, MAI-HF, Cat. No. 9133.

A

B

C

D

Such a mask collected by Hewitt at Six Nations was said by Chiefs John and Joshua Buck to represent a god whose body is half-human and half-supernatural; hence his face is divided between deep red and pure black, symbolizing east and west. He is free to wander at large, even among the people. Only a few informants at the Tonawanda Seneca Reservation had heard of this being; rather he seems to be a Cayuga–Onondaga spirit localized on Grand River, where there are a few masks representing him; but he is not well known even there (Plate 2-11). Possibly the divided-face concept derived from the Delaware-Munsee settled among the Upper Cayuga at Sour Springs.

9. "Longnose" (*hagónde:s*), or thin-nose, mask. Such masks always amuse the Iroquois because they suggest Longnose (Hagónde:s), a trickster, with whom they were threatened as naughty children. Longnose masks were anciently made of buckskin but later of cloth at Coldspring (Plate 2-12A–C). Probably few such masks in collections were meant to represent this trickster.[4] A few similar masks at Onondaga, DeCost Smith

4. The Iroquois and their northern Algonquian neighbors use buckskin masks to impersonate a cannibal clown who is said sometimes to kidnap naughty children. The Seneca call this clown Hagónde:s, "Longnose," because of his elongated proboscis. He is the Iroquois bogeyman:

> They say he chases bad children when the old people are sleeping. He mimics them, crying out as he runs after them. But the old folks do not wake up, since he has bewitched them so that they will remain sleeping. This goes on all night until the child gives up and agrees to behave, or else Hagonde:s makes away with the child, carrying it off in a huge pack basket.

A male kinsman would suddenly appear from the bush shouldering a pack

Plate 2-6. Hanging-mouth masks. A: An old reddish mask with cross-hatched nose, said to have been "taken to Canada before the Revolutionary War." Collected at Grand River by H. M. Converse, ca. 1895. NYSM, Cat. No. 37057. B: A nineteenth-century Onondaga mask. Note massive carving and brass eyes. Collected by DeCost Smith or Wm. M. Beauchamp ca. 1880. Onondaga Historical Association, Syracuse, Cat. No. 486. C: A typical Tonawanda Seneca mask. Collected by A. C. Parker from Sachem Chief Chauncey Abrams. RM&SC, Cat. No. AE2871. D: Black doorkeeper mask by Clarence White of Coldspring, Allegany Seneca, ca. 1920. Collected by J. W. Fenton, ca. 1925. Fenton Collection, MAIHF, Cat. No. 20/2840.

A

B

C

D

Plate 2-7. Protruding-tongue masks. A: Massively carved mask from Onondaga Reservation, N.Y. Collected by DeCost Smith ca. 1888. MAI-HF, Cat. No. 20/1245. B: Mask carved by John Styres at Grand River ca. 1829. Collected by David Boyle, 1899. ROM, Cat. No. 17020. Note the heavy carving, bent nose, bifunnelate lips, and lolling tongue.

A

B

basket in which Longnose was supposed to carry off children. The fright usually sufficed to send the errant child screaming to the arms of his or her mother or grandmother.

Clara Redeye, my Seneca interpreter at Allegany, recalled a bad dream during childhood which was confirmed by her mother, Emma Turkey, matron of the Hawk Clan into which I was adopted. I heard similar accounts from other Seneca sources and at Six Nations, on Grand River. The clan mother commented, "It is not right to whip little children," a profound conviction regarding child rearing among all the Iroquois. She added that formerly stubborn children who would not go to bed were sometimes sent out of the house at dusk to meet Longnose impersonated by a relative wearing a cloth mask (Plate 2-11A–C). The child would immediately run into the house. She further stated that it is not considered right to use the great wooden masks of the Society of Faces for scaring little children. The great Faces are deemed sacred and should not be ridiculed, lest the beings they represent might, through the mask, "poison" the child, or "spoil his face." Such an act would bring bad luck to the impersonator.

C: The mask that Howard Jimmerson brought from Grand River to Coldspring. It was carved by Jerry Aarons in the Grand River style and purchased by Howard of Robert Smoke, a Seneca at Six Nations. The legend around the tin eyes reads: "How would you like to be the ice man?" Fenton Collection, MAI-HF Cat. No. 20/2844. D: Stone mask with lolling tongue. From near the Mission Station of Freedenslintfer, Wyalusing, Pa. Collected by A. B. Skinner. MAI-HF, Cat. No. 5/2501.

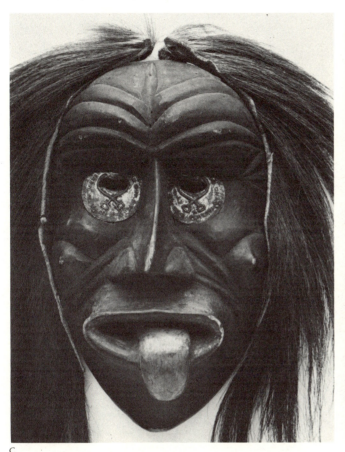

was told, were inspired by a certain puckish wooden figure that stood during the 1890s on the sidewalk before a Syracuse tobacconist's shop.

10. The horned mask (donǵgao:t). This so-called "buffalo"-type mask, according to Jesse Cornplanter, was devised as recently as 1900 by Austin Jacobs, of Newtown, on Cattaraugus Reservation. Since that time, masks of this character have acquired power and usurped the roles formerly reserved for the so-called "doctor" masks (Plate 2-13A). Some of these horned masks were possibly intended as caricatures of the missionaries' version of the devil or of blacks that came to settle near the Seneca at Buffalo Creek.

11. The animal masks. Masks representing animal spirits are not as common among the Iroquois as are anthropomorphic likenesses. I know of only one such mask representing Dew Eagle (Shadaʔgéa:ʔ), tutelary of the Eagle Society (Fenton 1953), or possibly Giant Raven (Gáhgago:wa:). The mask suggests the origin legend of the Little Water Society in which

Plate 2-8. Wry-faced and smiling masks. A: Jonas Snow's masterpiece, ca. 1920. Seneca of Coldspring. Regarded as a beggar mask. Fenton Collection, MAI-HF, Cat. No. 20/2839.

B: Massive smiling mask. Provenience unknown. Buffalo Museum of Science Photo, courtesy Buffalo Museum of Science. C: A heavy mask with thick smiling lips from Grand River. Collected by E. Pauline Johnson from George Buck, an Onondaga. MAI-HF, Cat. No. 1/1535. D: An Oneida mask from near St. Thomas, Ontario. Collected by M. R. Harrington, ca. 1907. It is evidently old and has seen much use: it was scraped, repainted, and rubbed with oil. It was originally red, then black, later white. MAI-HF, Cat. No. 2/7962.

B

C

D

Plate 2-9. Some early masks have pointed heads and sharp chins, sometimes ears, as if caricatures of old men and women. A: Black, smiling mask with square eye apertures. Converse Collection, NYSM, Cat. No. 37026. B: Black Seneca beggar mask. Cronon Collection 1884, Municipal Museum of Ethnology, Frankfurt am Main, Cat. No. N8399. Photo courtesy Museum für Völkerkunde, Frankfurt am Main. C: Black smiling mask, which Chauncey Johnny John made for his wife's brother, Howard Jimmerson, ca. 1900. Veteran of numerous cures. Fenton Collection, MAI-HF, Cat. No. 20/2843. D: Red mask with ears, ear bobs, and braided black hair—a caricature possibly of an old woman. The tobacco bags at the forehead attest to medicinal use. Converse Collection, NYSM. Cat. No. 37035. E: Black mask with red, smiling mouth, cleft chin, and ears. Attributed without documentation to the great Cornplanter,

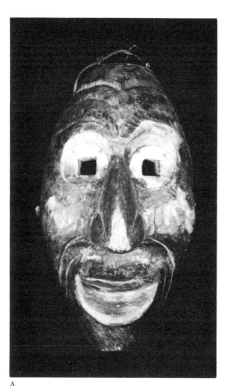

A

B

late eighteenth century. Photographed at Montgomery County Historical Society, Ft. Johnson, N.Y., 1940.

C

D

E

Plate 2-10. Whistling masks are likenesses of forest spirits who merely want tobacco. A: An old red flat-faced whistler, veteran of many cures. Recalled as very old in the Coldspring settlement, as first a beggar, later a "doctor." Fenton Collection ca. 1920, MAI-HF, Cat. No. 20/2838. B: A red-faced whistler from Tonawanda (?). Note the pock-marked forehead and long hair. John M. Clark Collection, NYSM, Cat. No. 36867. C: A black mask from Grand River; likeness of the Whistling God. Chiefswood Collection, ROM, Cat. No. HD12634. D: Red whistler mask with black painted moustache and eyebrows. NYSM, Cat. No. 36914.

A

B

Mask Types

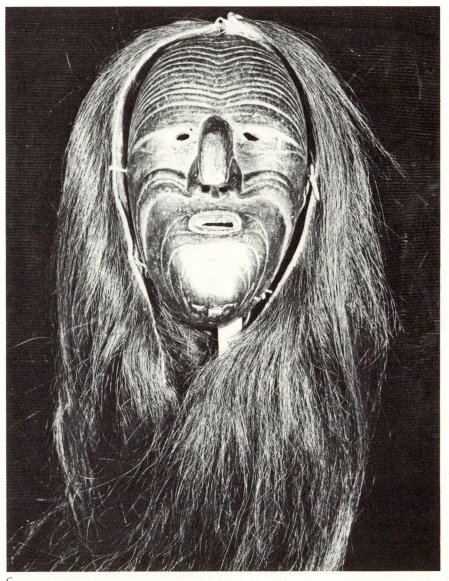
C

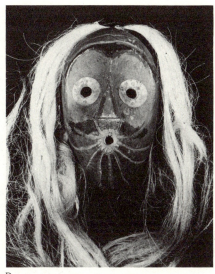
D

Plate 2-11. Divided mask. Probably carved by Jake Hess Cayuga at Six Nations Reserve, ca. 1925. ROM, Cat. No. 27032.

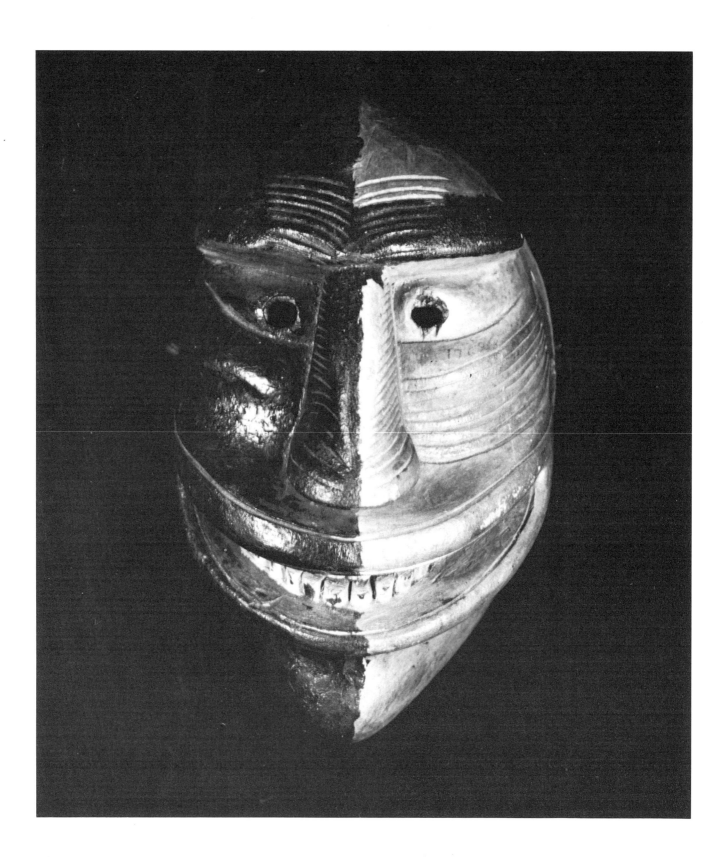

Plate 2-12. Longnose masks frighten children and amuse adults. A: A cloth mask of Longnose made to frighten a naughty child by Clara Redeye, Seneca, Allegany Reservation. Collected by the author in 1934 and donated to the U.S. National Museum, 1940. B: A puckish mask by Eli Schenandoah, Onondaga Reservation, N.Y. Collected by M. R. Harrington. MAI-HF, Cat. No. 1/6672. C: A mask improvised from a pinetree trunk and branch. Modern Seneca, Cattaraugus Reservation. MAI-HF, Cat. No. 20/1879.

A

B

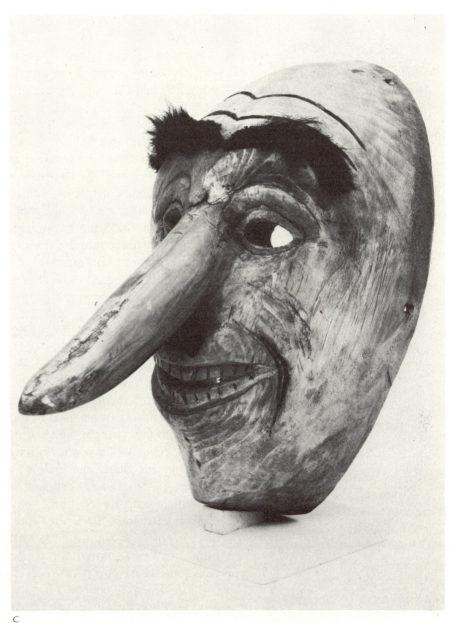

C

Plate 2-13. Animal masks are uncommon among the Iroquois. A: Horned masks: the so-called buffalo masks of the Seneca. Note the ears and earrings present on some masks. NYSM, Cat. No. 37608. B: The bird mask with bloody scalp in its beak probably represents either Dew Eagle or Raven in the Little Water Society origin myth. Buffalo Historical Society.

the great bird fetches the bloody scalp of the good hunter from the Cherokee lodge (Plate 2-13B).

Pig masks (Plate 2-14A–C) are fairly common from the Seneca of Allegany and Cattaraugus and among the Cayuga of Grand River (Plate 2-14C). We know that the pig supplanted the bear as the principal medicine society feast food, and possibly pig masks derived from masks representing the bear, although there is no evidence that such masks were ever worn in the Bear Society ritual (Plate 2-14D). James Crow, of Newtown, formerly had a pig mask that was featured as doorkeeper in a ceremony fulfilling a dream that involved the Delaware Skin-beating Dance. In one of his early drawings, Jesse Cornplanter illustrated the traveling rite entering Newtown Longhouse in which the wearer of a pig mask and having a long tail is crawling on all fours to one side of the throng of maskers. The male conductor at the longhouse door carries the striped emblem pole topped with the insignia of his office (New York State Library, Cat. No. 12845-24; reproduced in Trigger 1978, 462). At Coldspring, during the 1930s and 1940s, the pig appeared as a beggar mask at the Midwinter Festival and in the traveling rite.

12. The "blind mask" (*dágǫgwegǫ gagóhsaʔ*). Masks of this type present something of an enigma. They lack eyeholes or have the eyeholes covered, and we know little about them because they became obsolete ca. 1900 and were already out of use when Arthur C. Parker worked at Cattaraugus. Of the models that he had made for the New York State Museum, he wrote, "These masks are never used in the rites of the False Face Company, and differ from them in that they have no metal eyes" (Parker 1909, 173–74). Some specimens, however, do have metal eye covers. They formerly appeared in one rite of the I:ʔdo:s Society, as Parker says, but Jesse Cornplanter, son of Edward Cornplanter, Parker's chief informant, told me that his father remembered blind masks in use during his youth, when a masked shaman in the I:ʔdo:s ritual demonstrated his powers by finding hidden objects, juggling hot stones, and knocking over a standing doll from an inverted corn mortar. Although a blind I:ʔdo:s Society mask having metal eye covers (Plate 2-15) and a blind masquette (MAI-HF Cat. No. 2/4337) were collected from the Seneca of Grand River early in this century, I was unable to learn anything of their use a generation later.

Revised Classification

In 1956, at the invitation of Harold Conklin, I returned to the questions of classification and typology, which I originally had proposed in 1940 (Fenton 1941a, 95–100) and which were based on museum studies undertaken during the most intensive period of my fieldwork. Speck had accepted my classification and typology, which encouraged me, and he extended it by suggesting five variant Husk Face types for the Canadian

Plate 2-14. Pig masks are relatively common, both as Seneca beggar masks, and in the Hadi:doʔs ceremony. A: Pig beggar mask. Buffalo Historical Society, Cat. No. 249. B: Pig mask from Grand River. MAI-HF, Cat. No. 13/9404. C: Pig mask suggesting a bear. Collected at Grand River by F. W. Waugh, *1918. National Museum of Man, Ottawa, Cat. No. III.I. 1080. Three real teeth are mounted on either side of the snout. D: Bear mask. New and unused. Buffalo Historical Society, Cat. No. T-38.*

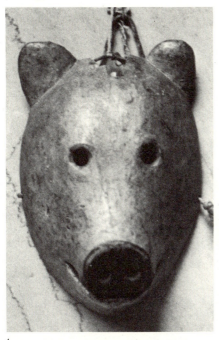
A

B

C

Cayuga (Speck 1942, 1945b, 1949, 1950). Up until now, the classification that I proposed in my lecture at the New York Academy of Sciences (Fenton 1956) has not been seriously questioned. Hendry (1964, 369–71) reviewed the issues; Ritzenthaler (1969, 23–25) adhered to it; and Zena Pearlstone-Mathews (Mathews 1978, 60–128) reexamined it with a larger sample and overwhelmingly confirmed it.[5]

Reexamination of my 1940 classification resulted in a regrouping of my original twelve-fold classification, as illustrated in the chart drawn by Gwyneth Gillette and reprinted from the 1956 paper (Figure 2-1). By rearranging the continuous series of eleven mouth categories so as to place together those shapes most nearly alike, and adding three categories— oval distended, bifunnelate blower, and modified distended, variation spoon mouth, which were variations in the original classification—one

D

5. In preparing the New York Academy of Sciences lecture in 1956, I reviewed three archive boxes of notes, photographs, and a fourth of publications on the False Faces that I had systematized for the book that I have just now written. At the time I was directing the work of the New York State Museum and Science Service, and I asked then-State Archaeologist William A. Ritchie and Curator of Archaeology Charles E. Gillette to take the photographs, which I had classified in folders, and to review my results. With a minimum of consultation, the three of us independently reviewed and confirmed the twelve types of wooden masks that I had found in 1940. Although we disagreed on the placement of certain specimens, the types held with slight alteration.

Plate 2-15. Blind mask from Seneca of Six Nations on Grand River, Canada. MAI-HF, Cat. No. 6/1105.

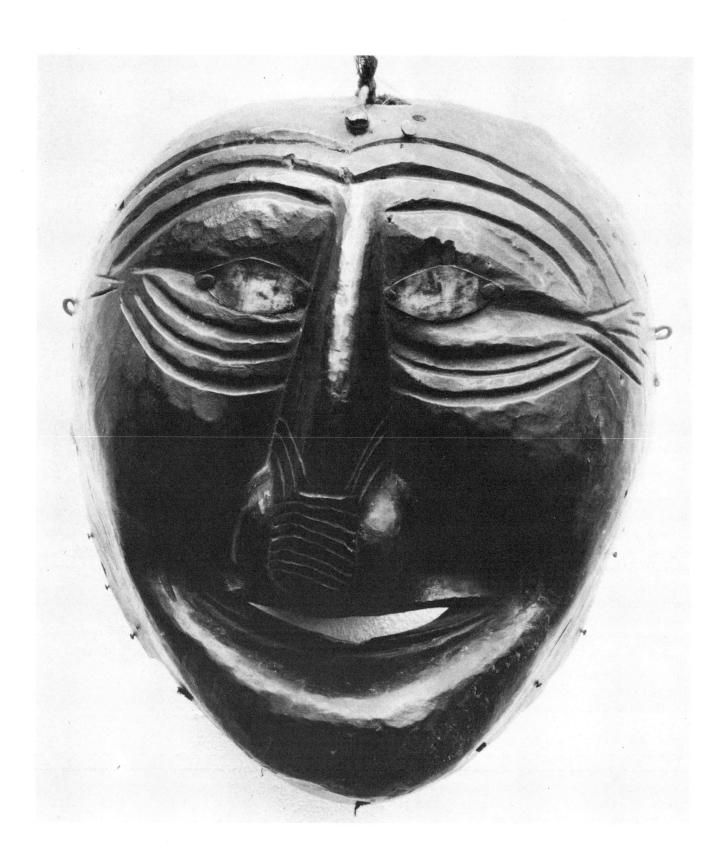

Figure 2-1. Classification of wooden masks by mouth shape. After Fenton 1956, 249.

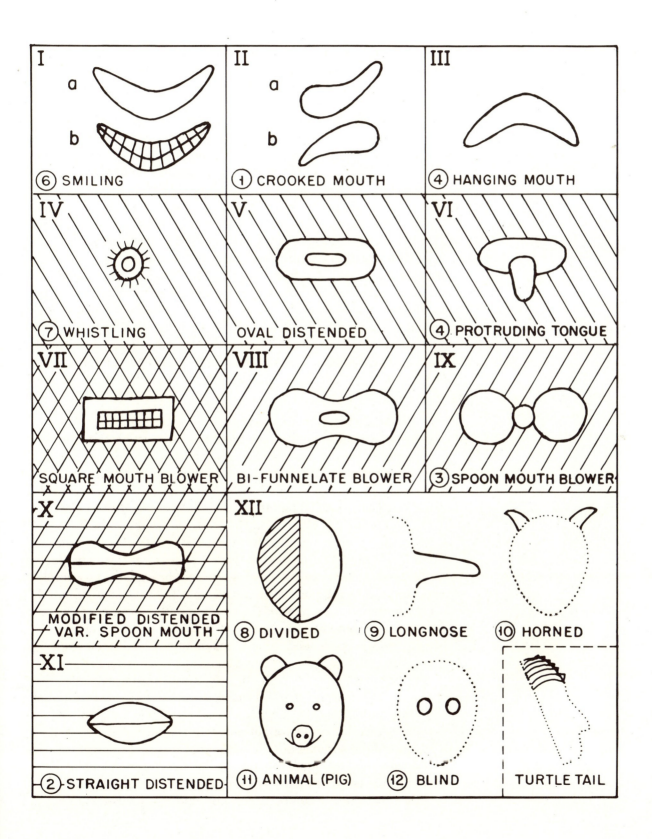

can see relationships that are marked with left and right diagonals, cross-hatching, and horizontal lines. The diagram illustrates how the eleven mouth variations are reducible to seven types. The twelfth category lumps the novelties.

If the series had been larger and composed of over 500 masks, and if, in such a series, as many as 100 fell into one class, it should be possible to validate the types statistically. One such attempt to put my smaller series on a computer yielded only some significant clusters on local styles.

A later study of Iroquois mask morphology, which investigated the question of a possible relation of Seneca False Face masks to faces on pottery pipes and other archaeological specimens from western New York and Ontario, involved a sample of 335 masks (Mathews 1978, 88, 127). Starting with my 1956 classification (1956, 60), Mathews, an art historian turned anthropologist, critically examined the masks in her sample in terms of my categories and findings. There was considerable overlap between the masks in her sample and those in mine because we both studied several of the same collections, and she had complete access to my notes and files of photographs. Our findings differ to some degree, particularly where I made flat judgments on local styles that her data do not support; but in the main we agree. Her findings are best summarized in her own words:

> This study began by organizing masks according to mouth types. Fenton has long recognized the mouth as the most obvious and apparent feature of masks and it is by mouth configuration that the Iroquois organized the faces. Since one primary function of the False Face Society is to cure by blowing ashes upon the patient it is not surprising that the mouths of the masks are their most elaborate and noticeable feature. . . . It is only the mouths which are essential in curing. Perhaps all the mouths on False Faces would signify blowing if curing was the sole function of the Society. But the False Face Society and its masks cannot be explained so simply.
>
> In the foregoing analysis of data Fenton's (1956) system of mouth classification was employed. His eleven mouth types were reduced to seven by combining his "spoon mouth," "bi-funnelate blower," and "modified distended variable spoon mouth" in a single category, and reducing his "straight distended," "oval distended," and "square mouth blower" to another. With this modification, *this study overwhelmingly confirms Fenton's mouth categories*. Out of a total of 335 masks (264 full-size and seventy-one miniatures) only twenty-eight did not fit comfortably into his categories. . . .
>
> Most of the observations about mouth types by Fenton are also verified here. Protruding tongues . . . are not common among the Seneca; the hanging mouth is an old type and sometimes is accompanied by a crest of spines; spoon lips (and bi-funnelate mouths)

are most common at Cattaraugus and often have a rudimentary tongue; and distended mouths are often accompanied by a crest of spines. [Mathews 1978, 126–27; italics added]

But Mathews found three instances where her results diverge slightly from my findings: "(1) distorted mouths are not as common as Fenton has implied; (2) only a slight correspondence between spoon/bi-funnelate mouths and forehead spines is indicated; and (3) there is less facial wrinkling on Grand River masks than Fenton's observations suggest." She added that I was not just looking at Seneca masks from Grand River (1978, 127–28).

Going beyond my observations, Mathews found "(1) Five stylistic clusters of smiling-mouth masks" from the two reservations of the Seneca Nation. "Four are from Cattaraugus: 'clowns,' faces with rectangular ears, faces with a broad flat nose and a cluster based on a similar face shape." From Allegany, she found a cluster with chin dimples. She also found (2) two such clusters for distended-mouth masks, both from Cattaraugus:

One has the crispness of execution of Cattaraugus bi-funnelate mouths, the other has oval lips with a protruding bottom lip.
(3) Two variations were distinguished for whistling mouth masks, crease and funnel. (4) . . . distended mouths are primarily Cattaraugus forms. The individual styles of Amos Snow [originally of Cattaraugus], Jonas Snow and Clarence White [of Allegany] have been verified.

And a style attributable to James Crow, of Cattaraugus, has been isolated (Fenton 1956, 353; Mathews 1978, 128).

STURTEVANT'S CRITIQUE

Sturtevant, who kindly read the manuscript of this book, has posed some critical strictures. He maintains that not only are the native classifications poorly understood but "all attempts to discover *the* single classification based only on form have failed. Evidently there are many classifications that are based only in part on form."

Sturtevant finds problems with the classification by form; he admits that they are not readily solvable but suggests mentioning them. As I discovered, "the mouth typology itself is not simple," and the crosshatching in my diagram of 1956 indicates overlaps. I was unaware that the overlaps were "based on several attributes given unequal weighting." He notes that Class 12 intersects with other mouth types in unstated ways, and, except for the animal subtype, it includes other attributes than the mouth. To be certain, it is a catchall. He goes on to list other attributes that could serve for classification, which have unequal weight and in my view are not as controlling as the mouths. Hair type and color are accidental. Thickness or weight relates to carving style. I have treated colors in other contexts. The chin type, treatment of cheeks, eye shape, and surface finish are important stylistic features. I have stressed features at the back of masks: thinness of rim, number of holes bored for the attachment of hair and harness, indication of use, and so forth. Sturtevant holds that these features "are not randomly associated correlations representing local and individual and temporal styles." I disagree. He does not find "convincing that the mouth types are most salient for the Iroquois" but adds that "other characteristics are recognized too." It is to be hoped that he or another student will undertake an art-historical study that will take into account these other attributes. Inherent in such a study are problems relating to archaeology and art history and the logic of classification that I am not prepared to discuss in this volume.

The Husk Faces, or "Bushy Heads"

HUNTERS AND FARMERS FROM ANOTHER WORLD

Closely associated in the ceremonies with the wooden False Faces are the Husk Faces, or "Bushy Heads," who represent a people from the other side of the world where the seasons are reversed. They are another class of earthbound spirits or supernatural beings who formed a pact with human beings and taught them the arts of hunting and agriculture. Indeed, their dramatic appearance to climax the Midwinter Festival symbolizes the gift of maize–beans–squash horticulture to the Iroquois by another people living nearer the source of its diffusion in eastern North America.

The techniques of braiding and twining cornhusks in the manufacture of mats, shoes, and dishes and, later, bottles with stoppers for salt have been present since Contact times (Megapolensis 1909, 173) and may be even more ancient. I shall refer to the two techniques in making Husk Faces as "braided" and "twined." The so-called braided masks are actually coiled. Historically, the use of braided and coiled Husk Faces is probably no older than the sewing of braided cornhusks into coils, like a braided rug, for seats and foot mats. The two are related in the Iroquois mind. Both the Husk Faces, including beings that they represent, and the fringed mats bear the same name: *gajíhsaʔ,* meaning "bushy," "fuzzy," or "awry." Indeed, husk masks bear some resemblance to doormats, the major difference being that such a mask, having eyes and mouth, comprises a triangle of three coils, and the pile is sheared on the inside. But Husk Faces and mats share a ragged fringe of hair. My Seneca hosts used to chide me that a person awaking with his hair standing awry, like the pile of a foot mat, looked like *gajíhsaʔ*—"a bushy head." This bit of participant observation to the contrary, Chafe maintains—and he may be correct—that the term *kajíhsaʔ* is unanalyzable (Chafe 1967, #851, p. 62).[6]

Husk Face masks are age-graded and sexed, as are the beings whom they represent in the rites. They are both men and women, old people and young people. There are "grandfather" and "grandmother" Husk Faces, although there are few if any wooden masks of women, despite the misnomer of the "maternity mask"; if there are any such, those old Seneca masks with ears are the most likely candidates (Keppler 1941, Plate VI; here Plate 2-13A). The attributes of age and sex in Husk Faces derive from the technique achieved in the medium of cornhusks, notably cosmetics.

TECHNIQUES

The several types of Husk Faces depend heavily on technique and reflect local styles.

Braiding

Most common, in both collections and available photographs, by about ten to one are the braided and coiled faces. Long strips of cornhusk braid are sewn into three coils to form the eyes and mouth, and the nose, which is often a sheathed corncob, and the fringe is then added. Protruding ends are then sheared off inside to protect the wearer's face, but rarely are they lined with cloth. Little knobs of covered husk appended to the fringe (hair), nose (snot), and eyes (tears) designate females (Plate 2-16). Rougher-looking specimens are deemed to be old men or "grandfathers," a generic term for husk and wooden masks alike (Plate 2-17). The smoother masks are of youths (Plate 2-18A). Among the Seneca at Allegany and Cattaraugus, Husk Face mouths are small and round. This is partly a function of the medium and the coiling technique. But at Grand River, Husk Faces are more coarsely braided, and mouths purse to resemble a funnel spout, or they take on the shapes of mouths on the wooden faces. Grand River husk masks more completely cover the entire heads of the wearers (Plate 2-19A). The fine weave and smooth surface of Seneca husk masks contrast with the baroque character of their cousins from Grand River, characteristics that are consistent with the carving techniques or styles of the two localities (Plate 2-18B).

Twining

Twined husk faces were made by old Seneca women at Allegany and Cattaraugus until just before the period of my fieldwork. Ella T. Jimerson

---

6. *K* and *g* and *t* and *d* in Seneca are intermediate sounds, comprising single phonemes. Chafe's "Handbook" (1963) and his *Seneca Morphology and Dictionary* (1967) employ the voiceless forms. I hear the forms as voiced.

Plate 2-16. The Husk Faces, or "Bushy Heads." A: An old lady with tears and runny nose. Cayuga, Grand River. Collected by F. G. Speck, ca. 1935. MAI-HF, Cat. No. 18/6097. B: Grandmother and grandfather. Cattaraugus Seneca. ROM, Cat. No. HD8125, HD8126.

B

A

Plate 2-17. Above: Twined Husk Faces of Chauncey Lee, Allegany Reservation of the Seneca Nation, 1933. A: A rugged grandfather (left). B: A grandmother painted with round red spots for ceremonial (right).

Plate 2-18. Below: Husk Faces are age-graded and reflect local styles. A: Large, smooth twined Husk Face from Coldspring Longhouse, Allegany Reservation. Collected by J. W. Fenton from Orphie Redeye, 1919. It represents a young woman. MAI-HF, Cat. No. 20/2835. B: Grand River baroque. Cayuga. Collected by F. G. Speck. MAI-HF, Cat. No. 18/6096.

2-17A

2-17B

2-18A

2-18B

Plate 2-19. The rougher-looking specimens are of old men. At Grand River they run to pursed mouths and accented eyebrows. A: "Grandfather" and "Grandmother." Laidlaw Collection, ROM, Cat. Nos. 43347, 21468. B: Wooden Gajihsa, or "Bushy Head." Collected by M. R. Harrington from Albert Silversmith, Onondaga of Six Nations on Grand River, 1907. The lines on the chin represent tattooing or face painting, sometimes incised on wooden masks. NYSM, Cat. No. 37018.

B

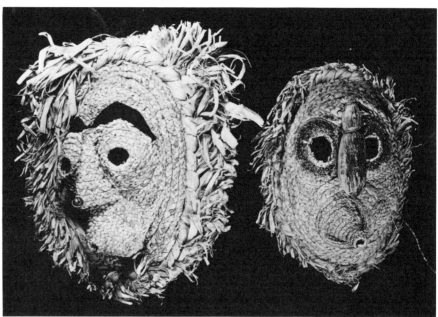

A

(Redeye), of Coldspring, knew the technique and reconstructed it for me. Twining commences at the nose with a nucleus of four interlocking husk elements that are again divided to make eight warps, which are later extended and subdivided by twisting on new elements. Then a pair of wefts is twisted around each standing warp as it is passed until one reaches the rim of the mask.

Not all of the details were available to me. There were several such masks at Coldspring in the 1930s, and I had pictures of museum specimens. The poorly crafted ones with stubble on the cheeks were termed "grandfathers," and the smooth-faced "bushy heads" with a round red spot painted on each cheek were said to be of young people bound for religious festivals at the longhouse (Plates 2-16 and 2-18A).

Wood Fringed with Husk

A third variety known as "Wooden Bushy Head" (Owę́ʔga Gajíhsaʔ) occurs in collections from Grand River (Plate 2-19B). This is a wooden face in natural finish, or painted in light tones, with red ceremonial markings consisting of a round red spot on each cheek and a series of vertical lines or marking in red beneath the lower lip. The mouth is pursed as in blowing. The face is smooth and in no way distorted. The cornhusk fringe of hair puts it in the camp of the Husk Faces, and it is credited with being more powerful than its all-husk companions (Harrington 1909, 89).

Also from the Grand River, there is a Husk Face of a "Corn Goddess," which has a large cloth sunflower at the brow and a smaller cloth flower

Plate 2-20. The "Corn Goddess," with associated sunflowers. Collected by J. N. B. Hewitt at Six Nations, 1916. USNM, Cat. No. 381402.

depended from the chin. Hewitt illustrated this mask in his report of fieldwork on the Six Nations Reserve in 1916, when he collected a series of masks and musical instruments for the United States National Museum (Hewitt 1916, 124, 128, Figure 123; USNM Cat. No. 381402). The accompanying Onondaga texts, which Hewitt had from John Buck, document the involvement of the Husk Faces in agriculture and their role as messengers for the False Faces (Plate 2-20).

SPECK'S CLASSIFICATION

Speck's informants at the Upper Cayuga Longhouse at Six Nations recognized five distinct types of Husk Faces: (1) eyedropper; (2) cornflower (Plate 2-20); (3) bisexual face; (4) one called "disappearing," having a miniature husk mask attached; and (5) "old man" (Speck 1945b, 70). The last is chief of the mask company, and his "hoary age is symbolized by puffy cheeks, nose, and lips, and wrinkles." A specimen collected in 1932 is illustrated from the Cranbrook Collection (No. 1259) (Speck 1945, 70).

The mask collected by Hewitt equates with Speck's later category of "smiling blossom" (*awahayǫ́de*), which he identifies as the Burr Marigold (Speck 1949, 98), replacing his second category. Its use is restricted to private rites.

Speck's monograph on the ceremonies makes no reference to his earlier classification but specifies five variations (Speck 1949, 98). He says that all are braided and sewed. He notes that the technique allows use of the bristly ends to surround the face, to form eyebrows, and sometimes to form chin whiskers. All are popeyed and "have pointed, pursed mouths with small openings." He specifies and illustrates masks (1) with braided nose; (2) with single-piece stuffed nose; (3) with puffy cheeks; (4) with "medicine drops" (Seneca: "tears"), "small packets of powdered herbs, attached to eyes, nose, lips"; and (5) the "helmet" type, which encloses the entire head and is exceptional.

Husk Faces in collections frequently have small bags of tobacco attached at the forehead, which, as on wooden masks, are tokens of curing rites performed.

Speck came to realize that our attempts to classify masks from museum specimens bear small resemblance to the native Iroquois classification, in which the differences in form are inevitably vague (1949, 100), showing a schematic arrangement of mask types and functions that admits of four possible types (1949, 101).

The confusion lies among morphology, function, and native names. The fact that the Iroquois themselves are not clear about these matters makes it that much more difficult for the ethnologist. The Husk Faces are what they do, as will become apparent from the origin myths and the rituals.

Miniatures

For all the varieties of wooden and cornhusk masks, there may be miniatures, or masquettes. These assume the characteristic types and art styles of the localities where they are made (Plate 2-21, 2-22).

Among the Seneca, miniature False Faces, being close replicas of the large wooden masks and representing the same spirits, are kept to protect the health of the owners. They may be hung in the house in some inconspicuous place, and like the large False Faces, protect the household from high winds. The Seneca say that a masquette attached to the hair at the forehead of a large wooden mask represents the child of the larger one. It usually has the same color and features. This is as close as my data come to the "maternity" concept and may be the origin of the confusion started by Converse and continued by Keppler (Plate 2-22C).

BOYS AND CARVING

At Allegany, Seneca sources add that small boys sometimes learn to carve by first making small masks. The Seneca believe that such preoccupation with the False Faces can make one ill, and then one must receive the rites of the society and become a member. But, in the main, small masks are kept as talismans, or personal charms, to commemorate a dream that led to a cure. They are sometimes hung on larger masks and "ride along" in the ceremonies (Plate 2-21A–D). An unmasked Seneca matron leads the traveling rites at Cattaraugus, when her staff of office consists of a pole on which are hung a miniature False Face, a Husk Face, diminuitive snapping-turtle rattle, and a tiny tobacco basket (Plate 2-22A–C).

DREAM OBJECTS

The Iroquois are naturally quite reticent about dream objects because the dream is the expressed wish of the soul. Consequently, it is difficult to learn precisely what the miniature masks represent. Cayuga sources explained to Speck (1945, 71) that miniatures serve as surrogates for the larger masks worn in the curing ceremonies, and they may be invoked for aid when the larger masks are not present. Speck also learned (1950, 17) that, when one dreams or has a fleeting vision of a Husk Face, one should attach a miniature cornhusk mask to the larger mask that one is obliged to make in response.

Miniature Husk Faces and False Faces are made and presented to the dreamer by the person who guesses the dream during the Midwinter Festival. This rite is no longer viable among the Seneca, but it flourishes at Onondaga, N.Y. (Blau 1966, 568), and I received an account of it at Onon-

Plate 2-21. Miniature masks are kept as personal guardians. A: Top left, blind masquette from Grand River. MAI-HF, Cat. No. 2/4337. B: Spoon-mouth masquette from Cattaraugus Seneca. MAI-HF, Cat. No. 2/9809. C: Seneca miniature bushy head (front). D: Note the tobacco bag (back). MAI-HF, Cat. No. 7/9888. Joaquin Arraga photos.

A

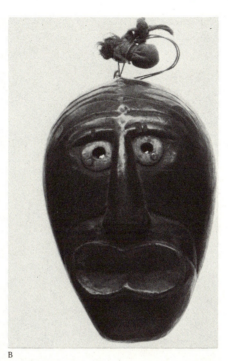

B

C

D

Plate 2-22. Miniatures, private and public. A: Husk Faces, male and female. Nobs or "tears" designate females. Cattaraugus Seneca. MAI-HF, Cat. Nos. 1656, 6/365. B: False Face and Husk Face for leader's pole. Left, red doorkeeper mask with straight lips and white hair, tobacco bag at scalp. Right, braided and coiled Husk Face with single tobacco bag attached top rear. Collected by A. C. Parker, 1923. RMSC, Cat. No. AE 7,1.0/363. C: False Face with masquette riding on the hair. NYSM, Cat. No. 37060.

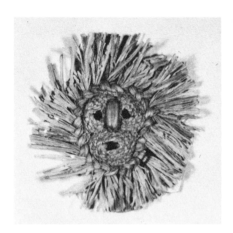

A

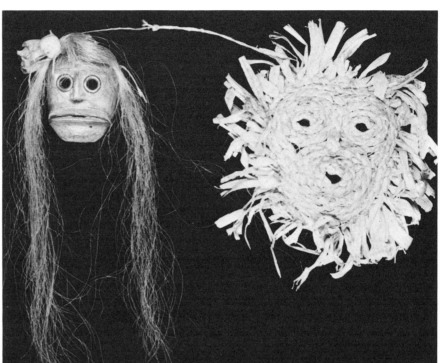

B

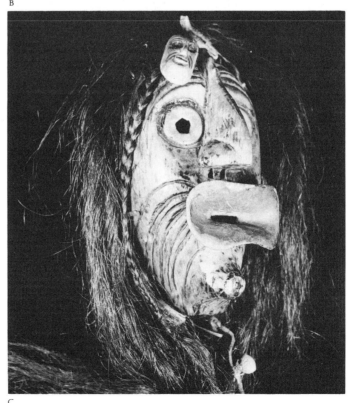

C

daga Longhouse on Grand River (Fenton 1842b, 15). Speck reported it from Upper Cayuga Longhouse (Speck 1950, 18).

As a response to a dream, as a token presented by the dream guesser, as an object kept to remember a cure, the whole question of talismans, or dream objects, in Iroquois culture remains obscure because of the personal reticence of owners and the rapid obsolescence of the associated customs in recent years. Dream guessing during the Midwinter Festival had been abandoned before my fieldwork commenced among the Seneca in the 1930s. I was faced with a problem of historical reconstruction, of examining the past in the light of the present.

The Bigheads

Not to be confused with the wooden False Faces or the Husk Faces, who form two linked but also distinct medicine societies, are the Bigheads, known familiarly as "Our Uncles," who announce the Seneca New Year, the Feast of Dreams, or the Midwinter Festival. The two men from opposite moieties who impersonate the uncles are not really masked; they are dressed by two women, also from opposite moieties, in buffalo robes—today old blankets that they bind on with ropes of braided cornhusks from which the ears have been pulled as consumed. The two uncles wear cornhusk anklets with a tailpiece and a wisp of husk at the head, and they carry corn pounders striped with ceremonial red paint with which they stir the ashes in the houses that they visit on a circuit of the village three times on the morning of the new year. This first stirring of the ashes, which heralds the Feast of Dreams, recalls similar passages through the hearth fires of Huronia. Their costumes symbolize the union of the trophies of the hunt and the fruits of the harvest, men and women's subsistence activities respectively, in winter and summer.

The So-called Tuscarora Faces

William Sturtevant first called my attention to these exotic masks that feature exaggerated supraorbitals, prominent cheeks, pronounced distortion of nose and mouth, teeth, and a spade-shaped projecting chin. Sturtevant discovered these caricatures of familiar Iroquois False Faces in a tourist museum at Niagara Falls, NY, and named them the "Niagara Falls Style" in 1953. Specimens that I have examined in collections here and abroad are mostly shallow at the back, show little if any use, and have three-hole attachment for buckskin head ties. They have been attributed to the nearby Tuscarora Reservation and to Caughnawaga. Tuscarora has no False Face society. These masks appear to be the work of a single artist and were most probably carved for the tourist trade. They must have attracted the

Plate 2-23. The Niagara Falls Style: The so-called Tuscarora face. The type specimen. Cronon collection, Municipal Museum of Ethnology, Frankfurt am Main, Cat. No. 8398. 6¾ × 11 × 2¾ inches deep. Photo courtesy MME F/M.

fancy of individual Iroquois, however, because there are two examples that were field-collected, one in the Keppler Collection (MAI-HF Cat. No. 16/2029), said to be from Cattaraugus, and a second in the National Museum of Man in Ottawa (Cat. No. III-I-418), which Alexander Goldenweiser collected at Grand River Reserve in 1911. (The latter mask is hollowed out for use). I have seen and photographed other examples in the Hotz Collection, Zurich, attributed to the Tuscarora, and the Arizona State Museum, Tucson. The U.S. National Museum received seven examples of this genre with the undocumented Evans Collection, and seven others were loaned from the Lenman Collection, five of which were part of the Edward M. Nelson Collection of Houston in 1966, all of which were photographed (Sturtevant, personal communication, September, 1979).

The type specimen of this genre (Municipal Museum of Ethnology, Frankfurt am Main, Cat. No. 8398) is greatly prized by German ethnologists as one of the finer examples of Iroquois art, but two other masks in their collection better represent the False Face Society. The former mask, the type specimen, was illustrated in a publication honoring the fiftieth anniversary of the Frobenius Institut (Zerries 1948, 29) and again in a work on exotic masks (Kutscher 1953, 61) (here Plate 2-23).

3. Historical Setting

Approach

My inclination as an ethnohistorian is to exhaust the direct historic approach to the recent past, to the period of historical records, and to prehistory before turning to comparisons of masking in adjacent ethnographic provinces. The direction of such research is what I have previously termed "upstreaming," but the presentation of the record will follow chronology. Comparisons, except as they immediately touch the Iroquois, are deferred to later in this book. In both instances one proceeds from the known to the unknown. I learned long ago that in fieldwork or in documentary research the investigator finds out pretty much what he or she knows or what the state of ethnological theory at the moment prepares one to discover. Therefore, it may be helpful to state what one should be looking for in the sources. Just as the archaeologist needs some frame of reference for interpreting the bits and pieces of cultural refuse, likewise the ethnohistorian must inevitably employ the ethnologists' descriptions of cultural activities in the recent past for evaluating the passing remarks of early historical writers on masking customs that they were not prepared to understand or obliged to describe amply. Therefore, at the expense of anticipating my description of the activities of the False Faces, let me be explicit as to what we should be looking for.

The first thing to look for is evidence of the False Faces themselves: wooden masks with metal eye plates, or the eye plates alone; rattles of the snapping turtle (*Chelydra serpentina*), or fragments of the carapace and plastron. Second, one may search for descriptions of the maskers themselves and of their gear, some of which, notably staves and bark rattles, cannot be expected to survive. Third, references to curing activities of medicine societies that employ or display masks of wood or plant fibres may occur in the literature. The False Faces disguised as hunchbacks have a peculiar crawling gait and a unique nonsensical speech; they defy frost and cold and appear seminaked in winter; they handle hot fire; and they blow hot ashes on patients. The False Faces preserve in fossil form these traits that are associated with northern shamanism, and we may expect to find them mentioned in descriptions of the activities of unmasked shamans at an earlier time. Fourth, the so-called "Traveling Rite" of the False Faces, while purging the settlement in spring and fall, passes through the houses on the way to the longhouse where the main feast occurs. This going from house to house, also at midwinter, relates to the progresses of other medicine societies during the Midwinter Festival for which we should expect to find earlier descriptions, as indeed we shall. Finally, there may be earlier examples of the mask and rattle as a bundle kept by its owner in prescribed ways.

Faces in Other Media

The Iroquois preoccupation with dreams and the self would lead us to expect to find faces in other forms. Masquettes, we know, are kept as charms, as talismans, and may be called upon to substitute for the larger forms. Faces may be expected to occur in other media—in pottery, pictographs, stone, and bone. Quite obviously, I am anticipating what may be discovered by stating what one may expect to find. The dialogue between present and past is reciprocal: One illuminates the other, as Father Lafitau perceived 250 years ago (Fenton and Moore 1974, 1:xlviii, 2ff.).

Archaeology

Unmistakable evidence of the existence of the False Faces in prehistoric times is difficult to come by, and such evidence as there is occurs in media other than wood and calls for considerable explanation. Early in this century, archaeologists who had observed the False Faces in action, notably Harrington, Parker, and Skinner, were prepared to find such evidence, and they immediately intuited that human faces with hands to mouth on pottery pipes that they found in sites in western New York were representations of the False Faces blowing ashes (Harrington 1922, 234; Mathews 1978, 145; Parker 1922, 146; Wintemberg 1931, 78; 1936, 75).

Certainly, the appearance of some of the human and animal faces modeled on the bowls of earthenware pipes, usually made to face the smoker, suggest that they were intended to represent wooden masks, but they are open to other interpretations (Mathews 1978, 129ff.). The closest resemblance between these pottery faces and Iroquois masking is to the miniature False Faces, or masquettes.

In the only thoroughgoing published study of the relationship of human face representations on archaeological specimens and Iroquois masks in museum collections, Zena Pearlstone-Mathews found little if any stylistic relationship between these archaeological human faces and wooden False Face masks of recent ethnological provenience. In her view, the only evidence that the Seneca used masks before the period of the Huron wars (1648–49) rests on two objects, the second of which is lost to science. The first is an antler figurine from the Cameron site, dated 1575 to 1600, which portrays a person adjusting a mask to his face by the chin (Mathews 1978, 138; Rochester Museum and Science Center, Rock Foundation Collection, Cameron 5066/41). The second bit of evidence consists of a terse statement in the field notebook of the late Harry Schoff, an industrious amateur digger in cemeteries of the Seneca Nation, that he found, in a grave at the Dutch Hollow site (1600–25), a "fragment of a wooden mask preserved by a sheet brass eye and parts of the carapace of a snapping turtle." There are no known photographs of the specimens, and the material was dispersed at auction after Schoff's demise. That this may indeed have been a False Face is the fact that masks are sometimes buried with their owners (Fenton 1937, 230), although an important mask is normally given to a friend or relative of the deceased at the Ten Days Feast. Up to now in this inquiry, evidence that the Seneca may have had masks before 1650 is at best shaky.

Hamell's Views

A somewhat broader view of this question and certainly some helpful insights come from the yet-unpublished researches of another scholar, George R. Hamell, formerly associate curator of anthropology at the Rochester Museum and Science Center, and now with the New York State Museum, Albany.[1] In a study of wooden smoking pipes, he found that brass and copper inlay on wood flourished during the last half of the seventeenth century. It is in this period, after the Huron wars, that the earliest archaeological and documentary evidence of full-sized wooden masks, or False Faces, occurs among the Seneca. The evidence consists of inlaid brass (copper) eyes and teeth. Just such a specimen was found and taken by Indians allied with the Denonville Expedition in 1687, of which there are two eyewitness accounts, which I will document presently. What may be interpreted as cut sheet brass (copper) inlays for teeth (two examples) and three specimens of eyes for such masks have been inventoried in the archaeological collections of the Rochester museum from Seneca sites, which range in date from A.D. 1645 to 1687.

The Snapping-Turtle Rattle Enigma

The alleged want of evidence that the ubiquitous snapping-turtle shell rattle—the most important item in the False Face masker's gear and the main prop of Great Feather Dance singers—was present before the mid-nineteenth century (Morgan 1851, 279) and its almost complete absence from archaeological sites is most baffling. In fact, the familiar snapping-turtle rattle was in use among the Caughnawaga Iroquois as early as 1710 as one of the two prevailing types of rattles, the other being the gourd rattle (Lafitau 1724, in Fenton and Moore 1974, 153ff.). That it had been around for a while is implied by its expected use in the land of the dead

---

1. In a series of research memoranda (Hamell, personal communications, August 16, 17, 22, 1979), Hamell has shared with me his ideas about Iroquois masks and human face representations, which he developed while working with the extensive Iroquois collections of the Rochester Museum and Science Center, and he has given me carte blanche to "do with them what you like."

(Fenton and Moore 1974, 258).[2] Nevertheless, in his report on the excavation of an early historic Seneca site, Ritchie (1954, 63–64) stated flatly that "until then [Morgan 1851] no archaeological evidence of the prehistoric or historic use of such rattles has been found in central and western New York State."

Historic evidence of shamans using snapping-turtle rattles among the Huron is not wanting. Franciscan Gabriel Sagard who made the long journey to Huronia in 1623 illustrated one such rattle in the frontispiece to his published journal (1632). Lafitau, in the next century, had this plate redrawn as Plate VIII of his *Moeurs des sauvages* . . . (1724) (Fenton and Moore 1974, 1:153). In Plate VIII, Figure 6, Lafitau illustrated the rattle itself as the "tortoise or sistrum of the Iroquois, Huron, and northern Indians." Sturtevant, having made a special study of the sources of Lafitau's illustrations, ascribed this one to Champlain, Sagard's contemporary. The several illustrations show the wooden handle projecting at the turtle's tail and terminating in a proximal knob, instead of being inserted at the neck with the head and neck stretched over the wooden rod and stitched as in modern Iroquois turtle rattles, in which the legs and tail are removed and the apertures closed. Possibly Champlain or Lafitau's illustrator misconstrued instructions or sought to bring the illustration into conformity with the other rattles on the same plate. We shall never know.

To back this up, in later decades of the seventeenth century, we have the observations of the Jesuit missionaries to Huronia and Iroquoia, previously cited. One poignant query by Father Lalement in 1639 (JR 17:157) links the turtle rattle to the cosmology: "There is a mysterious something, I know not what, in this semblance of a Tortoise, to which these people attribute their origin. We shall know in time what there is to it." In all the many versions of the Iroquoian cosmology, the earth rests on the back of a giant snapping turtle swimming in the primal sea (Fenton 1962).

Perhaps it is too much to expect to find snapping-turtle rattles, whole or in part, in burials and refuse heaps, inasmuch as solid evidence of full-sized False Faces in seventeenth and eighteenth-century sites, particularly from burials, is wanting. This anomaly is difficult to explain in the light of Iroquoian cosmology. Sophisticated archaeologists certainly know what to look for: edges of the carapace worn from beating out songs on wooden surfaces; a decayed snapping turtle would have lost its wooden handle, its lashing, and the sewn-up apertures where feet and vertebrae were re-

2. Its use in Huronia as early as 1639 is described by Jesuit missionaries (JR 15:179; 16:197; 17:157, 213; 20:23). Father Lalement described it in some detail (JR 17:157), and Fathers Dablon and Chaumonot witnessed its use in the Feather Dance at Onondaga in 1655 (JR 42:149). A possible reason for the want of archaeological evidence is the report that the faith had made such progress among the Mohawk by 1669 that shamans were throwing their "tortoise drums" into the fire (JR 53:237). It would appear that the turtle-shell rattle was the signature of shamans both in Huronia and in Iroquoia at an early date.

moved. Although archaeologists do not report finding snapping-turtle rattles, the snapping turtle is represented in the refuse bones from sites ranging from the Late Archaic State (ca. 2500 B.C.) down to the late prehistoric period. It is assumed that the ancestors of the Iroquois ate these turtles, which, if true, violates a later taboo against eating snapping turtles lest "one be a long time dying." Eight other species of turtles are also reported (Hamell, personal communication, August 22, 1979).

Box Turtle Rattles
Instead of what one might expect, the archaeologists present us with a case of the almost exclusive use of the box turtle (*Terrapene carolina*) for rattles on sites dating from 2500 B.C. until the third decade of the eighteenth century. The lone exception is a rattle made from the shell of the wood turtle (*Clemmys insculpta*) (Ritchie 1969, 107, 118, Plate 41, No. 1).[3]

Regardless of the findings by archaeologists, or lack of them, it is clear from the ethnohistorical sources that both Huron and Iroquois shamans knew and used turtle-shell rattles.

Masquettes
The case for the antiquity of the miniature, or the False Face masquette, is much stronger and derives strength from the wide range of media in which faces are portrayed in Iroquois art. Representations of the human face are known archaeologically from the Late Middle or Early Late Woodland stages (Hamell, personal communication, August 16, 1979). But they do not become common until the late prehistoric period (fifteenth century), and they become increasingly common during the next two centuries. These art forms comprise apparent miniature masks, effigies on the

---

3. The Carolina terrapin is said to be extinct in central and western New York, although in recent years it has extended its range. I have seen it in Cattaraugus County. This species is much sought after by Seneca women, who highly prize the few box-turtle rattles that they still possess for use in the *tonwi:sas* rite at the Green Corn Dance and the Midwinter Festival, when they celebrate their association with the Three Sisters—corn, beans, and squash—the traditional cultivated crops.

The box-turtle rattle belongs to the cultures of the Southeast. Such rattles are always perforated and are worn in clusters on the calves of Cherokee and Muskogean women dancers. Sturtevant (1961, 200–201), in his comment on Kurath's discussion of Iroquois music, dance, and environment (1961, 174ff.), concluded that box-turtle rattles were used by the Iroquois long before they adopted the *thonwi:sas* rite from the Cherokee and that this rattle form need not have been introduced from the Southeast. Its use and distribution offer a check to the suggestion (Ritchie 1954, 63–64) that sometime in the late seventeenth century the Seneca (and other Iroquois) shifted to the use of the snapping turtle for rattles as box turtles became scarce or extinct. Sturtevant suggests "other rattle forms."

bowls of smoking pipes, usually facing the smoker, and decorations beneath the cornered rims, or so-called "castellations," on Iroquois pots. Besides clay, the media include antler, stone, bone, shell, and wood. Miniature pictographic carvings of human faces persist into the nineteenth century on canes employed to recall the rituals for mourning a dead chief and for installing his successor in the Condolence Council (Fenton 1950, 35, Figures 2, 3, Plates 7, 8). These images find their antithesis in the concept of "Death, The Faceless" that stalks the trails and strikes unexpectedly and in the custom of not putting faces on cornhusk dolls lest they be used in witchcraft. The rule seems to be—no face, no person. In contrast, "to hold some person's face up to the crowd" is the metaphorical expression used in the Condolence Council, when, at the climax of the ceremony, the matron stands her candidate before the assembly to have him charged with the duties of the title in which he is installed and for which she is trustee.

Face Motif
Although Pearlstone-Mathews (1978) concluded that there is little stylistic relationship between the human faces found on archaeological specimens from the fifteenth to the eighteenth centuries and wooden False Face masks known to ethnology and she ascribed the so-called blowing faces on pottery pipes to other forms of shamanism than the False Faces, nevertheless, archaeologists see these forms as related to Iroquois masking (Hamell, personal communication, August 16, 1979; Ritchie 1965, 299; Tuck 1971, 213; 1978, 330). Indeed, these forms begin to appear with some frequency in the Chance Horizon (ca. A.D. 1450) (Tuck 1978, 323), a period when the Iroquois began to concentrate in large towns, form political alliances leading to the league, and celebrate the rites of medicine societies such as the False Faces (Tuck 1971, 213). Such activities became possible under the new conditions, but we have no solid evidence of what was really going on.

Hamell, having given considerable thought to these questions, accepts Pearlstone-Mathews's finding regarding the lack of stylistic relationship between prehistoric human effigy forms and recent Iroquois False Faces, both of which she studied in detail. But he disagrees with the conclusion implicit in her arguments that as a consequence "the archeological human face representations have no relationship to Iroquoian masking" (Hamell, personal communication, August 16, 1979). Limiting his argument to archaeological masquettes—in the forms and materials mentioned previously—Hamell observes that these forms were "complete unto themselves," they were attached to other artifacts, or they were worn as pendants. From the Rochester Museum and Science Center collections, he has presented nine examples of stylized human faces that appear to be miniature masks, illustrate a gradual evolution from naturalistic to grotesque, and contain features found in later Iroquois mask types. If, indeed, the progression is form naturalistic to grotesque, it is the same process that I have noted in the later development of Iroquois masks, which become more stylized and grotesque in later times. Possibly this was a continuous development from archaeological masquettes through ethnological False Faces. One specimen (R1302/72.34) from Onondaga territory appears to portray a False Face carved on a tree! A second is the Cameron Figurine, which Mathews accepts, of a person adjusting a mask to his face. A third, a wooden masquette, was originally painted red and has copper and brass staining in the eye sockets (Cameron-Wray 85/159); it conforms to my hanging-mouth type.

The archaeological evidence, in Hamell's view, supports either of two alternative explanations: (1) The specimens in question are miniatures of a class of False Faces no longer being carved and perhaps not recognized by modern Iroquois; or (2) they are miniature versions of the False Faces and the beings they represent and comprise one end of an evolutionary sequence of style that began in prehistory with naturalistic representations and evolved into the grotesque masks of the ethnological present. The latter alternative seems the more plausible.

EVOLUTION OF STYLE

Previously, I ascribed the evolution of style in Iroquois masks from plain likenesses to progressively ornate and grotesque caricatures of spirits and disease states to the influence of better tools (Fenton 1941a, 416). Metal carving tools became available to the Iroquois through the trade soon after Europeans reached these shores. Early in the sixteenth century, the French were on the St. Lawrence, and in the next century the Dutch were on the Hudson and the Swedes on the Delaware. There were even earlier visitors to Chesapeake Bay, which receives the Susquehanna drainage that reaches within fifteen miles of the main Iroquois settlements. The new cultural gifts that came with the trade were a mixed blessing because contact with Europeans brought new diseases to which the natives had no immunity. Hamell argues that the new diseases may have been more important than access to metal tools in changing carving styles of both wooden pipes and masks. He points out (and rightly) that metal carving tools are not requisite for an artistic renaissance, as witness the art of the Adena and Hopewell cultures. One might add the Key Marco wooden sculptures from Florida.

Rather, Hamell has a different idea. He suggests that when traditional curing rites failed to cope with epidemics of European diseases that swept through Iroquois towns every few years, greatly reducing the population, the resulting traumata brought a reevaluation of the spirit forces that govern the medicine societies. As we shall see, the False Faces are both agents and curers of diseases that are conceived as "windborne." As these diseases became more virulent and disfiguring, notably small pox, Hamell argues, the Iroquois changed their perception of the supernaturals: They saw them as increasingly grotesque in appearance. He views this changing perception of the relationship of people to supernaturals as one aspect of a broader pattern of psychological dislocations following European contact. The trauma is mirrored in the art of the carvers in the shift in style from naturalistic to grotesque forms.

In favor of this explanation is Hamell's observation that archaeological masquettes have their closest parallels with the older masquettes in Iroquois ethnographic collections: Both tend to be smooth and plainly carved. Masquettes of this type have a wider distribution from archaeological sites in the Susquehanna and Delaware drainages (Fenstermaker: 1959, 152, Figure 24D; Kinsey 1977, 96; Kraft, personal communication, 1954). In my view, style is not a function of size because there are miniature masks in later ethnographic collections that reproduce elaborate features of full-scale wooden masks. Moreover, an additional note to which I shall return: Archaeological masquettes from the Iroquois area resemble Delaware ethnological masks and the carvings on center house posts of the ceremonial chamber, which are supposed to resemble the Creator.

From the speculative interpretations of objects from prehistory we turn to the fragmentary records of direct history for which few if any objects survive in museum collections.

Narratives of Early Travelers

From the earliest contact of Europeans with Iroquoian-speaking peoples, nearly 450 years ago, explorers and missionaries mention or describe some form of ritual behavior, although masks are not always specified, that is associated later with ceremonies involving masks. In September of 1535, the headmen at Stadacona (now Quebec) devised a ruse to prevent Cartier from going up to Hochelaga (Montreal). They dressed three "devils" in black-and-white dog skins, "with horns as long as one's arm and their faces coloured black as coal," and shoved them off in a canoe to confront Cartier's ships. Their speaker feigned to bring a message from the gods at Hochelaga of impending winter freeze up in which Cartier's crew would perish (Biggar 1924, 136–39). This reminds one of the later weather predictions of the maskers at the Midwinter Festival.[4]

As one reads the classic Huron literature of the next century and recalls repeated observations of Iroquois masked shamanism 300 years later, it would seem that the ritualized behavior of the actors in current cere-

---

4. This account suggests skin masks, and, given the distribution of skin masks, Fogelson suggests that these possibly might be considered ancestral to wooden faces.

monies is older than the form of the masks themselves and has kept alive old tricks of the Huron *oki,* or medicine man, who was not always masked. The *oki* handled hot coals and juggled hot rocks and blew ashes on his patients; the first and last feats are perpetuated by the False Faces, and the juggling of hot stones is a boast of ʔi:ʔdo:s singers. The *oki* was actually the familiar spirit of Huron shamans, with whom he communicated in a trance state, a divine frenzy that is the essence of true shamanism, and he prescribed one of twelve rituals; this function is perpetuated today by the clairvoyant in Iroquois communities, and, as Tooker (1964, 106n.) points out, there are twelve Iroquois medicine societies today, a tempting parallel.

The Huron *oki* not only handled hot coals and blew ashes on his patients, but in his hysterical frenzy relieved the compulsive possession of neurotic women who "walked on all fours like beasts" until the masked company was summoned to displace their possession by blowing upon them to the din of their turtle rattles (Champlain [1616] 1929, 3:153–55). Champlain adds that they "parade the length of the village while the feast is being prepared for the masquers, who return very tired, having taken enough exercise to empty the kettle of its Migan" (Champlain 1929, 3:153). Later on, he mentions the public appearance of beggar maskers, both men and women, visiting each other's villages much as they now go from house to house at midwinter (Champlain 1929, 3:166). The okis were still in business seven years later when Champlain invited Father Gabriel Sagard to spend an exciting winter in Huronia. Sagard, who sometimes parroted Champlain, witnessed an unmistakable example of the doorkeeper's role in the modern False Face ceremony. The actor in this role wore a bearskin garb such as the Delaware and Onondaga maskers used in later times, but Sagard does not mention a wooden mask (Sagard 1939, 117). He wrote:

> I have seen them dressed . . . in masquerades or mummeries, a bear-skin covering the whole body, the ears erect on top of their head, their face covered up except for the eyes; and these persons were only acting as door-keepers or jesters and took no part in the dance except at intervals, because they were there for a different purpose.

Moreover, Sagard goes on to describe in a medicine dance for a sick woman typical False Face behavior that I have observed at Grand River: On the repetition of a particular song the doctors carry her, and at the next song she is made to walk a little and then to dance, while they encourage her to recover. As is true now, there was a terminal feast for guests (Sagard 1939, 118). Although these early descriptions of medicine society curing rites do not fit the modern ceremonies precisely, one can recognize elements in them out of which the modern rituals have evolved.

The most vivid descriptions of the rituals of Huron medicine societies are contained in the "Relations" of Father Brébeuf during the midwinter festivals of 1636 and 1637. He suggests the antics of the False Faces and of their Husk Face doorkeepers when he writes:

> You would have seem some with a sack on the head, pierced only for the eyes; others were stuffed with straw around the middle, to imitate a pregnant woman. Several were naked as the hand. (*Jesuit Relations* [*JR*] 10:203).

Intimation of pregnancy is a trait of the Husk Faces when they visit the Seneca longhouses at midwinter, whereas modern beggar maskers go naked to the waist and feign not to feel the cold. Brébeuf tells us that on the following December at the great Huron village of Ossosané, members of a curing society "donned their masks and danced, to drive away disease" (*JR* 13:175). It was during this winter that a blind clairvoyant named Tsondacöuané came into prominence among the Huron. Not only is his name preserved to us but also a case history of his revelations and orders to perform curing ceremonies. When, in 1936, I read the relation to my Seneca mentors at Tonawanda, they immediately equated the name Tsondacoüané with their own term for the individual who sponsors a medicine feast: *godę́syoni*, "she sponsors the ritual"; *sadę́syoni,*, "you sponsor." (The Huron form may be the third-person singular masculine.) In one such dance that he ordered to drive away pestilence and for the recovery of a patient, the relation reads:

> All the dancers were disguised as hunchbacks, with wooden masks which were altogether ridiculous, and each had a stick in his hand. An excellent medicine, forsooth! At the end of the dance, at the command of the sorcerer *Tsondacoüané* all these masks were hung at the end of poles, and placed over every cabin, with the straw men at the doors, to frighten the malady [and the spirits who brought it]. [*JR* 13:263]

Then as now, individual householders burned tobacco in the hearth and asked the mask spirits for protection of the resident family. One urged the masks to keep a good watch over his door. On the third day, men beat upon pieces of bark in all the cabins, making a great din, and then both the wooden masks and the straw men that had been hung over the houses were appealed to with tobacco offerings (*JR* 13:261–67; see also Tooker 1964, 108–9). On another occasion, fearing that pestilence might spread, the inhabitants of a neighboring town decked out with wooden masks and straw figures all the houses in the environs within forty-eight hours of the sorcerer's edict (*JR* 13:231).

In Huronia, as later in Iroquoia, particular medicine societies had officers, and persons who had the society perform its dance for them afterward became members of that society, an obligation that descended to their children (*JR* 17:139, 197; Tooker 1964, 109). Particular dreams also foretold the need to join a particular society.

4. Time Perspective

Ethnological and Linguistic Evidence

Whether these same beliefs and practices described in the previous chapter were current among the Five Nations Iroquois south of Lake Ontario during the first half of the seventeenth century confronts scholars with an enigma inasmuch as the first observers to go among the Iroquois at midcentury fail to mention masked ceremonies. Surely the Jesuits who had been in Huronia before the destruction and dispersal of the Huron by the Iroquois in 1648 and 1649 should remember the maskers or had read of them in the relations. The Iroquois themselves could not have been ignorant of the beliefs and practices of their neighbors to the north; indeed, Iroquois warriors were prisoners in Huron towns for protracted periods and then escaped. And Huron warriors had similarly lived in Iroquois communities. One lesson that ethnology teaches is that where peoples live in contact they learn and take on each other's customs. The Iroquois are no exception to this rule: They are avid learners of new songs an dances, and their repertoire of ceremonial songs and social dances reflects this process over centuries.

The Huron Hypothesis

In earlier papers (Fenton 1937, 218–20; 1941a, 412–16), I followed the lead of Beauchamp (1905, 184–85), who first suggested that masks may have been brought to the Iroquois by Huron captives late in the seventeenth century, even though Parker (1909, 181) disagreed. At issue is the question of whether the failure of seventeenth-century observers to mention masks before 1650 means that the Iroquois had no masks, or whether observers jaded with accounts of Huron masking failed to mention the custom among the Iroquois because it was no new thing (Tooker 1964, 108, n. 1). The resolution depends on how one interprets the sources.

MOHAWK "FACE" MOTIF

Although the face motif appears on seventeenth-century northeastern war clubs (National Museum of Denmark; Birket-Smith 1920, Plate 2), and if these are indeed Mohawk war clubs, there is no reference to the Mohawk having had a Society of Faces at an early date. Beauchamp (1905, 185) asserts that Bruyas's *Radices verborum iroquaeorum* (ca. 1680; 1863) records no Mohawk word meaning "mask," or referring to its use. But if such existed, it would have the same root as "face," -*kǫhs*-, as in the other northern Iroquoian languages.[1]

---

1. Indeed, Beauchamp may be mistaken, for Bruyas (p. 50) records *gagonsa*, "visage" (face). He also gives *gagonhara*, *le milieu ou le gros os du nez*, "the mid or large

How early the Mohawk knew masks is not clear, but Lafitau (1724, 1:368; 1974, 1:234–35), in describing the Feast of Dreams (Midwinter Festival), which he witnessed at Caughnawaga during the second decade of the eighteenth century, mentions masks made of tree bark, or from a sack pierced for the eyes and mouth, and says that "they comb their hair and dress in an extremely bizarre manner. In this costume they run like madmen from house to house, breaking, destroying, and overthrowing everything, without anyone's finding this a procedure to be criticized" (Lafitau 1974, 1:235). Moreover, he describes a typical Iroquois witchhunt, involving a famous hermit named Shonnonkouiretsi, "The Very Long-haired One," whose powers suggest the False Faces who also have long hair and represent great shamans (Lafitau 1724, 1:390–93; 1974, 1:247–48). And he also speaks of "the ash-throwing dance of our Indians," which again suggests False Face behavior (1724, 1:526; 1974, 1:322). Lafitau had access to the notes of Father Bruyas, and he comes closest to describing a masked medicine society among the Mohawk of his day.

Iroquoia: Seventeenth Century

The descriptions of the Onondaga Feast of Dreams, or Midwinter Festival, at midseventeenth century are not specific enough to be certain that the Onondaga then used masks or had a Society of Faces. Jesuit Fathers Dablon and Chaumonot witnessed the dream feast in February, 1656, but failed to mention masks as such. Instead, they describe their host's brother "dressing himself somewhat like a Satyr, and decking his person from top to toe with husks of Indian corn" (*JR* 42:156, 161). As companions, he had two women disguised "as veritable Megeras,—their hair flying, . . . faces coal-black, their persons cloathed with a couple of Wolfskins, and each armed with a handspike or large stake."

---

bone of the nose," after which Hewitt wrote in my copy: *agonwara*. Michelson (1973, 149), under the entry *-kuhs-*, "face" (*okuhsa*, p. 73), adds a derisive form, *-kuhwara* (*kaku:wara*, p. 73). Could this latter mean "bare face," afer *Agon, estre nud, vuide,* "to be nude (bare), or empty" (Bruyas 1863, 22)? Michelson, in "Upstreaming Bruyas" (1974, 43), noted: "48 *Gagenrion*, rouler (to roll), and *Atragenrion*, se rouler dans le cendres (to roll in the ashes)," which he ascribes to False Faces at midwinter. The trouble with all of this is, as Sturtevant pointed out to me in reading the manuscript of this book, that Bruyas defines these terms as referring only to faces and does not mention "masks" as such. Contemporary Mohawks of Akwesasneh (St. Regis) know the term *okonhsa?*, "face," and for "mask," *iontkonwaroroktha?*, which suggests that it is a descriptive term composed recently (Mithun, 1977, 28, 50), and that the False Faces are something recently introduced. A generic form (*kakonwara*) is known at Six Nations Reserve, where the Upper Mohawk have long been in contact with Cayuga and Onondaga among whom the Society of Faces is long extant.

Their procession through the village, the two mad women preceding him and knocking, with their stakes, whatever came under their hands, is open to two interpretations. One recalls the Bigheads and their women dressers announcing the Feast of Dreams, and the second interpretation suggests the Husk Faces of later times. The Satyr, finding his own house stripped, later went begging through the village to recover his losses (*JR* 42:167). Earlier, a shaman is described as striking a turtle shell rattle against a mat for a group of women dancers to banish disease, which could be either the Feather Dance or a False Face dance (*JR* 42:149). Other False Face traits of later times are going naked in winter, handling, stirring, scattering, and blowing ashes, throwing water, casting excrement, and breaking kettles and other household goods (*JR* 42: 157). But our observers were limited to what they saw, and we are grateful for what they relate.

Dablon and Chaumonot imply that some of these dream-fulfilment rites were the performances of companies, or society dances (*JR* 42:165). And twenty years later, Lamberville, in Dablon's relation of 1676–77 (*JR* 60: 191), tells of a girl patient who had had nine feasts performed to fulfill such a dream. These included what appears to be an ancestor of the modern Medicine Company, in which shamans boast and demonstrate their powers, and a performance of the Bear Dance Society. One reads of casting spells, possession, and throwing ashes. The sixth feast involved both casting and removing spells; guests were covered with feathers from head to foot, and all were masked. At a later stage, eight masked men emerged from the house followed by eight others carrying pouches filled with charms; they formed two opposing ranks and danced to gourd rattles, casting feather charms at one another, and some falling to the ground to writhe and roll (*JR* 60:191). This act of "shooting spells" is reminiscent of the Midé of the Ojibwa and is characteristic of one degree of the Iroquois Medicine Company.

For another decade, the Jesuit writers seem unsure of whether the Iroquois had masks and rites such as they had seen in Huronia. But Father Beschefer, who accompanied De Nonville's Expedition against the Seneca towns, wrote in October, 1687, to Villermont describing the booty looted from Seneca towns and cemeteries:

> I was mistaken when I told you that the Iroquois wore no masks. They make some very hideous ones with pieces of wood, which they carve according to their fancy. When our people burned the villages of the Tsonnontouans, a young man made every effort in his power to get one that a outaouae [Ottawa] had found in a cabin, but the latter would not part with it. It was a foot and a half long, and wide in proportion; 2 pieces of a kettle, very neatly fitted to it, and pierced with a small hole in the center, represented the eyes. (*JR* 63:289).

If the mask had fallen into French hands, it most probably would have been shipped to France to adorn some cabinet of curiosities, along with the "24 bark dishes of various sizes," "2 wooden spoons," and other ethnographic objects that Father Beschefer was shipping to his correspondent. Had it survived, this would have been our earliest dated type specimen from the Seneca.

It is true that the Seneca had one Huron town after 1648, and there were Huron captives distributed among the other league towns including Onondaga, which lends credence to Beauchamp's hypothesis that the Huron may have introduced the False Face Society among the Seneca, whence it spread to the other towns of Iroquoia. But the resolution of this proposition cannot be determined by the ethnohistorical data and will rest with archaeology and art history. Evidence is building that it was there before the midseventeenth century.

The Eighteenth Century

Certainly, the False Faces were well established at Onondaga a century later. John Bartram, the Philadelphia naturalist, who accompanied Conrad Weiser, the Pennsylvania interpreter, and Lewis Evans, mapmaker, to Onondaga in 1743, left us an unmistakable description of a False Face beggar who kept them awake of a July night.

> At night, soon after we were laid down to sleep, and our fire almost burnt out, we were entertained by a comical fellow, disguised in as odd a dress as *Indian* folly could invent; he had on a clumsy vizard of wood, colour'd black, with a nose 4 or 5 inches long, a grining mouth set awry, furnished with long teeth, round the eyes circles of bright brass, surrounded by a larger circle of white paint, from his forehead hung long tresses of buffaloes hair, and from the catch part of his head ropes made of the plated husks of *Indian* corn; I cannot recollect the whole of his dress, but that it was equally uncouth: he carried in one hand a large staff, in the other a calabash with small stones in it, for a rattle, and this he rubbed up and down his staff; he would sometimes hold up his head and make a hideous noise like the braying of an ass; he came in at the further end, and made this noise at first, whether it was because he could not surprise us too suddenly I can't say. [Bartram 1751, 43]

When Bartram asked Weiser, who like him lay next to the alley, what the noise was, Shickallamy, their Indian guide, thinking Bartram somewhat scared, "called out: 'lye still *John.*' I never heard him speak so much plain *English* before." Their guide's familiarity with the act indicates that the Oneida, too, knew the play. He goes on:

> The jack-pudding presently came up to us, and an *Indian* boy came with him and kindled our fire, that we might see his glittering eyes and antick postures as he hobbled round the fire, sometimes he would turn the Buffaloes hair on one side that we might take the better view of his ill-favoured phyz, when he had tired himself, which was sometime after he had well tired us, the boy that attended him struck 2 or 3 smart blows on the floor, at which the hobgoblin seemed surprised and on repeating them he jumped fairly out of doors and disappeared. I suppose this was to divert us and get some tobacco for himself, for as he danced about he would hold out his hand to any he came by to receive this gratification which as often as any one gave him he would return an awkward compliment. By this I found it no new diversion to any but my self. In my whim I saw a vizard of this kind hang by the side of one of their cabins to another town. [Bartram 1751, 44]

Neither Evans nor Weiser, whose mission was political, bothered to mention this incident. Shikellamy, though he bore a Delaware name, was an Oneida chief whom the League Council at Onondaga had placed on the Upper Susquehanna River to watch over dependent bands who had accepted the principles of the Great Peace. At Shamokin, near the forks, he well might have observed the masked being or spirit whom the Delaware thought to be master of the game. The Reverend David Zeisberger, a Moravian missionary of the period, wrote of the mask spirit in these words:

> The only idol which the Indians have, and which may properly be called an idol, is their Wsinkhoalican, that is image. It is an image cut in wood, representing a human head, in miniature, which they always carry about them either on a string around their neck or in a bag. They often bring offerings to it. In their houses of sacrifice they have a head of this idol as large as life put upon a pole in the middle of the room. (Zeisberger n.d., 141, quoted in Speck 1931, 41).

The reference here is to both miniature faces used as talismans and to stationary faces carved on posts of the Big House. But the Delaware mask spirit also had an ambulatory aspect in the guise of a shaman dressed in bearskins who wore a wooden mask, employed a turtle shell rattle, and carried a staff like the Iroquois False Faces. The relevance of Delaware masking to Iroquois masked medicine societies is that the two peoples were in contact: They were both drifting westward during the eighteenth century, and they would meet in adjacent towns on the Upper Allegheny River. Then later, they would merge in Ohio where the Iroquoian Mingo would comprise a motley assemblage of displaced League Iroquois and other Iroquoian remnants living side by side with Algonquian-speaking Delaware, Shawnee, and others. Under these circumstances, their cultures were bound to merge and feed back to the Seneca and others of the Five Nation Iroquois.

While the Delaware were yet at Shamokin, the Reverend David Brainerd witnessed a performance of the masker in 1745 and described his dress and behavior:

> His *pontifical garb* . . . was a coat of *bear skins,* dressed with the hair on, and hanging down to his toes; a pair of bear skin stockings; and a great *wooden* face painted, the one half black, the other half tawny, about the colour of an Indian's skin, with an extravagant mouth, cut very much awry; the face fastened to a bear skin cap, which was drawn over his head. He advanced towards me with the instrument in his hand, which he used for music in his idolatrous worship; which was a dry *tortoise shell* with some corn in it, and the neck of it drawn on to a piece of wood, which made a very convenient handle. As he came forward, he beat his tune with the rattle, and danced with all his might, but did not suffer any part of his body, not so much as his fingers, to be seen. No one could imagine from his appearance or actions, that he could have been a human creature, if they had not had some intimation otherwise. When he came near me, I could not but shrink away from him, although it was then noon day, and I knew who it was; his appearance and gestures were so prodigiously frightful. [Brainerd, quoted in Edwards 1822, 237–38]

This is the first mention of the divided mask in the literature, a type that appears later on the Six Nations Reserve in Canada and may reflect Delaware influence. Otherwise, the behavior is typical of Iroquois False Faces, and Brainerd's reaction was in no way different from Indians and later anthropologists who have had such experiences.

Somewhat later on the Muskingum in Ohio, the Reverend John Heckewelder, having followed the Delaware westward, encountered a masked "doctor" dressed as a bear walking on its hind legs enroute to treat a bewitched person. But there is no mention of a wooden face. Heckewelder and his informant engage in a philosophical discussion of the "doctor" role in their two cultures (1819 [1881], 233–36).

Nicholas Cresswell, an English traveler and trader, had a similar encounter in Ohio when he "saw an Indian Conjuror dressed in a coat of Bearskin with a Visor made of wood, frightful enough to scare the Devil" (Cresswell [1775] 1924, 109).

It was inevitable that white captives taken during the frontier wars would meet and mention the False Faces. Mary Jemison, who started her captivity among Delaware in Ohio but lived most of her life on the Genesse River among the Seneca, tells how the officials for the Midwinter Festival don bearskin leggings, and on the fourth day

> make false faces of husks, in which they run about, making a frightful but ludicrous appearance. In this dress (still wearing the bear-skin) they run to the council-house, smearing themselves with dirt and bedaub everyone who refuses to contribute something toward filling the baskets of incense [tobacco], which they continue to carry, soliciting alms. During all this time they collect the evil spirit, or drive it off entirely, for the present, and also concentrate within themselves all the sins of their tribe, however numerous or heinous. [Seaver 1932, 166]

Although Mary Jemison fails to mention wooden masks, one may infer that Thomas Peart did see wooden False Faces near Kanasadega (modern Geneva) and west of Seneca Lake in 1778. He presumed that they were trying to frighten him. He was taken by a young Indian about two miles into the bush "where several Indians were collected, dressed in horrid masks, in order, as he supposed, to make sport of his fears" (Gilbert Narrative, in Walton 1904, 124).

The Sullivan–Clinton campaign of 1779, which destroyed the crops and graineries of the Iroquois and burned most of their towns, inevitably committed much ethnographic art to their bonfires. Von Schaick's detachment, in its drive against Onondaga, is said to have burned a house full of masks, according to an unverified note of a conversation with DeCost Smith in 1935. Officers of Sullivan's main army, however, report having collected some masks at Chemung in August, and some of these ended up in Du Simitiere's Museum.[2] The museum catalog reads:

> November 1779: A vizor or mask of wood representing a ghastly human face, the colour of an Indian with a mouth painted red, the eyes of yellow copper with a round hole in the middle to peep through [,] the forehead covered with a piece of bear skin by way of a cap. found with several more to the number of about 40, in an Indian town called Chemung which was burnt by the cont'l army under Gen. Sullivan in his expedition last summer into the country of the Six Nations. These visors are commonly called Manitoe-faces and Serve for the Indian conjurors or Pawaws. . . . There is also a long horse [hose?] that belonged to it with a coat of bear Skins, but this was destroyed by the Soldiery. All these masks were different from each others.

Whoever wrote this catalog entry possibly had access to Brainerd and had far more detailed information on the numbers collected than is found in journals of the soldier collectors, who, perhaps, found time for reflection on their return.

2. Cook 1887, 139, 229; Du Simitiere's Memoranda 1774–83, MS notebook in the Library of Congress, Manuscript Division.

The entry of November, 1779, after listing several other items, concludes: "All of the above with the visor were given by Dr. Wilson of the continental hospital at the recommendation of Gen. Mifflin and Dr. J. Potts." I judge that these medical men received the loot from hospitalized soldiers. Two years later, the museum acquired "an Indian face carved in red stone," presumably of catlinite, "about two inches high and broad in proportion," having "behind the ears two Small holes thro' which leather were passed, and it was suspended to the neck of an Indian chief, called the King of Kanada Sego [Geneva, NY]," who was killed at the battle of New Town. This miniature was a gift of General Sullivan. Not to be outdone, Governor Clinton, of New York, donated three items, including "a meneeto-face or mask of an Indian conjuror, with a border of bear skin round the forehead and a tuft of feathers in the center."[3]

Comments on the Literature

Two comments on the ethnohistorical literature so far discussed seem in order. Most European observers, and especially the missionaries, who encountered the maskers or saw faces carved on house posts, were imbued with the Judeo-Christian preoccupation with "graven images" and regarded them as evidences of idolatry. They were all fearful. Only John Bar-

3. None of these masks or masquettes are extant today in the museums of Philadelphia. Peale's Museum, which flourished from 1784 until the midnineteenth century, apparently incorporated some of the specimens from Du Simitiere's American Museum, which expired just then. Peale's Museum contained a number of Indian items, but a "description of the objects displayed" in his museum while it was in the state house fails to list any masks from the Iroquois (Peale Papers, Historical Society of Pennsylvania, No. 481). It is conceivable that Peale acquired several of the "idols" mentioned in Du Simitiere's catalog. Peale's Museum featured an "Indian Room," and among its contents, listed in the catalog of the sheriff's sale in 1848, were "1 case, Female dresses and figures of Idols, etc." (Sellers 1980, 317). Whether any of these "idols" were indeed Iroquois masks is open to question. P. T. Barnum acquired the collection; parts of it burned in a fire, and parts of it ended in Boston, where the ethnological specimens were ultimately transferred to the Peabody Museum of Archaeology and Ethnology, at Harvard. Among its older Iroquois masks are possible candidates, unless otherwise ascribed to other sources on good authority. None of the Iroquois masks at the University Museum, in Philadelphia, dates before 1901, but eight of these were collected by Stewart Culin at the Pan-American Exposition, Buffalo. Although these are fine old nineteenth-century Iroquois masks and among the best examples extant, they cannot be attributed to Peale, Du Simitiere, or Sullivan's soldiers. I am indebted to Anthony F. C. Wallace, Claudia Medoff, and Carline Dosker, of the University Museum, for this search (Wallace to Fenton, personal communication, June 23, 1980). On Du Simitiere and Peale's museums, see also Hallowell 1976, 130–31.

tram, the naturalist, described what he saw in the manner of an ethnographer. Such are the limitations of the sources. Second, the sources do establish that the Delaware had portable masks; the masker carried a turtle rattle and was dressed in a bearskin suit; and the Delaware carved faces on the posts of the Big House, the ceremonial chamber. Moreover, Delaware faces were sometimes divided vertically between red and black sections. In general, the faces were smooth, but there is some mention of distorted mouths.

FACES CARVED ON POSTS

Heretofore, the preoccupation of scholars with the variety of Iroquois masks and the viability of Iroquois masked medicine societies have blinded us to the fact that the Iroquois also carved faces on posts around which they danced. These were posts erected at the gates of villages, on gable ends of houses, as well as on trees. We owe this notice to the researches of Krusche (1975, 166ff.), which contradict the flat statement of Speck (1950, 18) that the Iroquois, unlike the Delaware and other southeastern peoples, did not carve stationary face images. I find no evidence, however, that the Iroquois sculptured images on the house posts of the longhouses in the manner of the Delaware Big House.

The case that Krusche (1975, 166ff.) makes in answer to his own question—"Did the northern Iroquois have similar sculptures?"—is not altogether convincing. The sources that he cites are not quite clear whether they are talking about faces, pictures, or carvings. These vague terms are ascribed to the seventeenth-century Mohawk and Oneida. Charlevoix's journal, written early in the eighteenth century, is somewhat more specific and ascribes the burning of the Iroquois towns during the previous century by the French as the reason for the decline in architecture and ornamentation. He writes:

> Formerly the Iroquois built their cabins in a better manner than the other nations, and even than themselves do at this day; these were adorned with figures in relievo, but of very course workmanship; and as almost all their towns have since been burned in different expeditions, they have not taken the trouble to rebuild them with their former magnificence. [Charlevoix 1761, 2:127–28]

Were these reliefs of humans or animals?

The Dutch journal of 1635, now attributed to Van den Bogaert, the surgeon of Fort Orange, specifies that as they marched through the gate of Oneida Castle, atop the gate there were three big wooden images, carved like men (Jameson 1909, 148).

The next evidence comes a century and a half later from the village of Chemung, probably Seneca, where some forty masks were collected by personnel of Sullivan's army. Major Norris wrote: "In what we supposed to be a Chapple was found indeed an Idol, which might well enough be worshipped without breach of the 2d Commandment" (Beauchamp 1905, 173, quoting Norris in Cook 1887, 229).

The famous wooden statue of a man or deity, which stood in Cornplanter's village on the Upper Allegheny River in 1791, around which the Seneca inhabitants danced at stated festivals marking the new moon, and its fate during the Quaker–Handsome Lake reformations is well documented.[4] This literature yields some important facts about the statue. It must have been carved on a pine log at least thirty feet in length, for the figure of the man is described as about nine feet on a twelve-foot pedestal, and it was erected in the center of the village near the council house, which meant digging a hole deep enough to support it in an upright position. It was painted to represent an Indian of peace, which Wallace (1970, 192) alone has equated with Teharonhiawagon, "The Holder of the Heavens," or the Creator. This painted figure wore breechclout and leggings and a sash over one shoulder. It stood near the riverbank at Cornplanter's upper village of Genesinguhta for a generation until Henry Abeel, son of Cornplanter, in his enthusiasm for the new religion toppled the figure and rolled it into the river. Col. Daniel Brodhead's report of 1779 of the Allegheny campaign speaks of "a painted image or war post, clothed in dogskin, . . . at the upper Seneca Towns" (Conover 1887, 308). Such painted war posts were not uncommon in Seneca towns, as witness the place-name Painted Post, a thriving community today near Corning, New York.

Despite the distribution in Seneca towns of painted war posts and posts for hanging white dogs at the Midwinter Festival, other than the carved statue in Cornplanter's upper town and possibly a carved house post in Chemung, dance posts or house posts having human faces carved on them were not typical of the Iroquois in the late eighteenth century. The two examples noted in the literature are in towns closest to towns occupied by the Delaware. One cannot argue from a single good example that a whole cult of worshipping idols carved on posts disappeared after the arrival of the Quaker missionaries on the Upper Allegheny and the rise of the Handsome Lake religion. To be certain, Henry Abeel's act of vandalism disposed of the idol, but the worship dances that went on around it continued. Handsome Lake restructured the ceremonies, preserving the Feather Dance, Drum Dance, Personal Chant, and the Bowl Game as four sacred rites, but he preached against the medicine societies

---

4. The primary sources are the Quaker journals of Halliday Jackson, John Phillips, Joshua Sharpless, and Henry Simmons; and that of Col. Thomas Proctor [1792] (1832, 154). The Quaker journals have been edited and published in part by Deardorff and Snyderman (1956); Jackson (1830); Snyderman (1957); and A. F. C. Wallace (1952). Secondary sources on the wooden statue are Beauchamp (1905, 144); Deardorff (1951, 85); Krusche (1975, 167–68); and Wallace (1970, 53, 192, 229, 249, 257, 297).

and their feasts that had become drunken brawls. The societies and their rites went underground to emerge within a decade. They survived in communities beyond the reach of the prophet's voice, and their celebration soon became an integral part of the new religion. Indeed, keeping up one's obligations to the medicine societies is the hallmark of participation in the longhouse religion.

If the False Faces paused in their rounds of the upper Cornplanter town to rub their rattles on the stump and derive power from the carved wooden statue, the literature is silent. But such activity may be assumed from the affinity of masks to trees: the giant elm standing at the center of the earth where the mythical masker pauses at noon to rub his rattle and replenish his strength; the former rite of carving masks on living basswood trees; burning tobacco and asking the tree to impart its medicinal power to the mask; and the rubbing of rattles on house posts, door posts, and wooden surfaces of buildings. Nonetheless, in my opinion, the Iroquois never had the carved-human-face-on-house-post concept to the degree reported from the Delaware and Shawnee (Krusche 1975, 169).

Cultural Change in Modern Times

At the opening of the nineteenth century, the Seneca were occupying their present reservations: Allegany, Cattaraugus, and Tonawanda, besides Genesee and Buffalo Creek. Yet there is no good account of the Seneca Society of Faces until that of Morgan at the midcentury. Seneca folklore, collected soon after that by Curtin and Hewitt (1918, 537), is peopled by flying heads, the spirit of whirlwind, and the "Great Defender" (Shagodyowéhgo:wah), the principal mask spirit. All of these folk characters were subjects for masks. Specimens of these masks, sometimes attributed to "Buffaloe Creek" Reservation, mutely witness an undocumented activity. Moreover, the mask that Morgan collected at Six Nations Reserve on Grand River, where refugees from Onondaga, Cayuga, and Seneca enclaves joined with Brant's Mohawk after 1784, exhibits a well-developed art style and has become the type specimen for all Iroquois masks (NYSM Cat. No. 36909; Morgan 1852, 98; 1901, 2:157–58).

The Seneca in the westward drift into Ohio during the previous century carried with them the Midwinter Festival (and presumably the rest of the annual round of ceremonies). Midwinter of February, 1830, was marked by the White Dog Sacrifice and climaxed by the appearance of a False Face intruder who rushed to the fire, scattered ashes, and frightened the children. Samuel Crowell, who witnessed these events at Sandusky, fills the void in the literature with this account:

> Just as this dance ended, an Indian boy ran to me, and with fear strongly depicted on his countenance, caught me by the arm, and drew me to the door, pointing with his other hand towards some-

thing he wished me to observe. I looked in that direction, and saw the appearance of an Indian running at full speed to the council house; in an instant he was in the house, and literally in the fire, which he took in his hands, and threw coals of fire and hot ashes in various directions, through the house, and apparently all over himself! At his entrance, the young Indians, much alarmed, had all fled to the further end of the house, where they remained crowded, in great dread of this personification of the evil spirit! After diverting himself with the fire a few moments, at the expense of the young ones, to their no small joy he disappeared. This was an Indian disguised with a hideous false face, having horns on his head, and his hands and feet protected from the effects of the fire. And though not a professed fire king, he certainly performed his part to admiration. [Crowell 1877, 331–32]

Several comments from my own observation of such acts may be pertinent. The masker coming at full speed in the manner of the Husk Faces interrupted the dances. The withdrawal of the children (boys) in genuine or feigned fright is typical. Humans avoid hot ashes and the power of the mask spirit. The lesson is not to get involved unless one is obligated or desires a cure. The masker's hands and feet were apparently bare, yet he was not burned. The horns on the mask led this nineteenth-century observer to equate his appearance with the Devil. In doing so, he dates masks with horns, such as appear later at Cattaraugus, which I formerly thought were modern.

There are a few brief notices of the False Faces among the Seneca before Morgan's time. David Cusick, the Tuscarora historian of the Six Nations, writing about 1825, mentions that "they have a certain time of worship: the false faces first commence the dances; they visit the houses to drive away sickness, etc." (Beauchamp 1892, 30; 1905, 185). Their role in the Onondaga Midwinter Festival of 1849 is described in J. V. H. Clark's local history (Clark 1849, 1:57ff.), which observations are supplanted by DeCost Smith (1888, 1889), and afterward by Beauchamp.

Ethnological Literature Since Morgan

After Morgan's time, the ethnological literature on the False Faces commences, but there are few solid contributions until the turn of the present century, when Parker (1909) published his famous paper on the medicine societies of the Seneca. This was at a time when Lowie, Wissler, and others were researching age-grade societies on the Plains. After that, the literature expanded markedly in quality and quantity, particularly in the work of Speck, Shimony, and the writer (see Table 4-1 for a summary of this literature in tabular form).

Table 4-1. *Ethnological Literature*

					Secondary	
Author	Period	Publication	Collection	Primary	Theoretical	General
Morgan	1849–51	1852, 98; 1901, 1:157; BAE-AR 3:144	NYSM	Tonawanda Six Nations	×	×
Smith, DeC.	1888	1888; 1889; 1943, 342–85	OHA AMNH MAI-HF	Onondaga		
Converse	1890s	1899; 1908, 74–78; 1930	NYSM AMNH MAI-HF PMAAE Ft. J.	Cattaraugus		× face on tree
Beauchamp	1880–1920	1905, 187; 1905, 184–92	NYSM (Converse)	Onondaga	Post 1656	
Boyle	1897–98	1898, 157–58; 1900, 27–29	ROMA	Mohawk & Onondaga at SNR		
Keppler	1898–1920	1941	MAI-HF	Cattaraugus Allegany Tonawanda SNR		×
Harrington	1903	1909	AMNH MAI-HF	Cattaraugus Allegany Tonawanda SNR		× carving
Parker	1903–11	1906; 1908; 1909, 179–84; 1910b; 1923, 8, 342, 347, 399, 400–1, 435	NYSM	Cattaraugus Tonawanda	×	× FF pudding Tree motif War bundle origin (294) face on tree halts Naked Bear with tobacco
Hewitt	1880–1930	1916, 8, 122; 1918 AR-BAE, 32:357–65, 436–81;	USNM	Cattaraugus SNR		texts: Oa., C., S., M.

Table 4-1. *Ethnological Literature*

Author	Period	Publication	Collection	Primary	Secondary Theoretical	General
		1921 AR-BAE 21:197, 201;		Myth		
		1928 AR-BAE, 43		Myth		
Waugh	1910–18	1913, 478, 480; 1916, 103	NMM	FF pudding		×
Goldenweiser	1911–12	1912, 13; 1913, 465	"	Six Nations Reserve	× × phratry societies	×
Barbeau	1910–11	1912, 10; 1913, 4	"	Wyandot, Ok		
Kroeber & Holt		1920, JRAI			×	×
Wissler		1928				×
MacGowan		1923				×
Fenton	1933–45	1936, 9–10, et seq.; 1937; 1940(1a); 1941a; 1942; 1956; 1972	MAIHF	Seneca S. & SNR music	societies × × classification	× × ×
Cornplanter	1895–1905 1935–37	1903; 1938; 1978, 458, 461, 462	NYSL	drawings drawings Catt., Tona.		tales
Speck	1930–45	1942;				Review of Fenton 1941
		1945a;	CIS			×
		1949;		Cayuga	×	×
		1950			×	
Conklin & Sturtevant	1951	1953		Seneca	×	×
Wallace	1952	1970		Seneca	×	×
Kurath	1947–50	1951; 1961; 1964		dance & music	× × ×	× ×

Table 4-1. *Continued*

Author	Period	Publication	Collection	Primary	Secondary Theoretical	General
Shimony		1961		SNR	×	
Blau	1962–64	1966		Onondaga	×	
Hendry	1950	1964		Onondaga	×	×
Ritzenthaler		1969	MPM			×
Krusche		1975			×	×
Pearlstone-Mathews		1978	AMNH DAM DMNH MAIHF MPM NMM NYSM PMH PMS RMSC ROM	Art	×	×
Isaacs & Lex		1980		Psychotherapy ×		
Sturtevant	1951–63, 1983			Seneca	×	×

The subject has continued to attract scholars of whom Blau, Hendry, and Ritzenthaler are the more important contributors. And Wallace, in his great work on the Handsome Lake revival (1970), has put the whole subject in perspective and offers the best explanation of how and why the society and the masks have survived. Their place in the structure of Seneca ceremonies is set forth in Tooker (1970). The broader culture-historical implications of Delaware and Iroquois masking for the origin of masking in the Eastern Woodlands have been undertaken with great thoroughness and common sense by Krusche (1975), who from the relative isolation of Leipsig has been limited to libraries and museums without benefit of fieldwork. Most recently, Mathews (1978) has brought a new dimension to the subject from art history.

Several scholarly trends may be seen in this literature, which parallel the development of anthropology as a discipline. The old preoccupation with origins and antiquity, which persists to a degree, has given way to solid ethnographic description. This, in turn, has enabled undertaking problems of a more theoretical nature—classification, the nature of form and function, the formation and operation of social groupings such as clans and phratries (or moieties), symbolism, and psychotherapy.

The question of the age of Iroquois masking is at once a culture-historical problem and a problem of change and stability in culture. Certain traits of Iroquois masking are very old and unquestionably go back to aboriginal times. Others are innovations over time, and some are quite new. The ethnohistorical literature is inadequate to solve this dilemma; ethnological studies may be used to interpret the past, but more and more we are turning to archaeology and art history for the roots of cultural traits and behavior that survive in the False Face Society of today. A few examples may be helpful.

The Reverend William Beauchamp (1800–1925), an Episcopal missionary to the Onondaga for forty years, from 1880 to 1920, consistently held the view that much of Onondaga culture as it confronted him was of recent development since colonial times. He continually sought historical evidence for Iroquois customs and refused to acknowledge its lack as open to explanations of ignorance, secrecy, or tradition. He summarized his view in the statement: "In Indian history there is no more uncertain element than time" (1905, 189).

Beauchamp maintained that the masks were not necessarily old, that neither DeCost Smith nor Boyle in Canada encountered masks that he considered 100 years old. The great age that Converse attributed to certain masks, particularly a few old masks that she collected for the New York State Museum (Converse, in Beauchamp 1905, 190), was based on their rude character and evidence of use. I am inclined to give more weight to such evidence than was Beauchamp, who discounted appearance and wear as being due to the skill of the carver and the care of the owner (Beauchamp 1905, 109). The back of a mask tells more than the front as to material, age, and use—the species of wood from which it was carved, the tools that were used, thinness of rim, the method of attaching the hair and head ties, whether by seven holes burned through the rim or merely three, and the hair tacked on, as in modern False Faces. Specimens of known early date, and several old masks in the New York State Museum collection that survived the fire of 1911, reveal these characteristics and support Converse's contention, although we only know when they were collected.[5]

5. The attribution of age to a mask by its collector can be misleading. Joseph Keppler collected some of the finest masks in the Museum of the American Indian, primarily at Cattaraugus, Allegany, and Tonawanda among the Seneca, but he also went to Six Nations in Canada taking Chief Lyman Johnson as his guide. The museum catalog and Keppler's publication (1941) specify where individual masks were collected, but the attributions of class, function, and probable age are unreliable. It is as if Converse were leaning over his shoulder as he wrote.

Beauchamp's third point is that one should not disregard tradition, which is of small value unless substantiated by direct history. However, one can sometimes infer from an accession date, from the structure and performance of then-contemporary rituals, and from the prominence of the masking cult in a given community how long it has been going on.

Finally, Beauchamp consistently held that wooden masks first appeared in Iroquoia during the last half of the seventeenth century. He ascribed the greatest intensity of their use to the Seneca whence the cult spread to Onondaga. He was positive that masks were not in use during the Midwinter Festival of 1656; but we know from Bartram's observation that False Faces were well understood at Onondaga a century later. Also, the Handsome Lake religion reached Onondaga in 1815, when the Seneca prophet died there, and in its aftermath the medicine societies intensified. The "new religion" became the foundation of what Beauchamp regarded as "Onondaga paganism," which he attributed mostly to the Seneca.

One last point intrigues me. Although deferential to the then-considerable reputation of Mrs. Converse both among Indians and New York State officialdom, Beauchamp remained skeptical of the uses and names that Converse imputed to the masks that she collected for museums. His Onondaga sources had never heard of them, and so he said the information might be Seneca. He confirms a point that I have made previously, but it is worth repeating because museum catalogs and the literature have become clouded by Converse's followers.

During the 135 years of their known history, Iroquois masks have retained the essential character of the type specimen that Morgan collected. At the same time, they have evolved and been elaborated, and modern features have been introduced. They have also increased enormously in value. In the 1880s, with little trouble and expense, DeCost Smith picked up a large collection at Onondaga. Aware that the Onondaga had adopted black persons, he inquired about two masks having protruding lips whose owners dated them ca. 1860, which led Beauchamp to think that masks

---

Keppler contributed to ethnological confusion and did the museum a disservice in perpetuating Converse's error concerning the so-called "Wolf Clan Mask" (MAI-HF No. 6/1104; Keppler 1941, 35–36; Plate XI), which Converse collected at Grand River in Canada in 1892 with the information that it "was taken over to Canada when the Mohawks departed from N. Y. State with Brant (Thayendanegea) during the Revolutionary war." The mask has since been attributed to Brant himself, rather than to a follower, and has been proudly displayed as part of the Brant memorabilia. Brant was a lifelong adherent to the Anglican faith and probably never owned a False Face. Converse's statement to the contrary, there is no other evidence that the Iroquois had clan masks or that they were paired by sexes. To be certain, the mask itself is a splendid specimen of the Grand River carving style, and it may well date from the late eighteenth century. It is of comparable importance with the mask collected there in 1850 by Morgan.

having broad, puckered, or pointed lips were recent (1905, 191). He also set down the following as modern features: moustaches, projections on the forehead, mouth, and nose. His own Figure 141 (1905, 191, Plate 32), which to him suggested certain Japanese masks, is a typical "whistler" (Fenton's Type 7), of which there are early examples. We are in agreement, however, that the evolution of the carver's art has been from the smoother, less elaborate, to the more grotesque. And each age has introduced into the class of beggar masks the folk heroes of its own time.

In trying to fulfill the need for a careful reconstruction of Iroquois masking as it exists (Hendry 1964, 364), we have not satisfied all of the problems in this section. There remains the question as to whether the Iroquois were innovators, copiers, or merely survivors of a masking complex once prevalent in the Eastern Woodlands, as Krusche (1975) has proposed. I shall defer this question to a later chapter, for it may be what Boas called a *scheinproblem* for which the data do not exist in sufficient amplitude to make it researchable.

PART TWO

5. The Society of Faces, or the False Face Company

The Origin of the False Faces and Their Kinds

Among the Iroquois there are two prevailing types of origin legends for the wooden False Faces. The first is a mythical epic pertaining to the creation; the second is a human adventure, and tales of this type are far more common and varied in content. Each is associated with a different class of beings.

THE EPIC STRUGGLE FOR CONTROL OF THE EARTH

Invariably informants say that "this is what we heard from the old folks." I have made my own version of what Chauncey Johnny John and Henry Redeye told me in the summers of 1933 and 1934 at Allegany (Fenton 1941a, 418–19). I then give the two versions pretty much as recorded.

> Now when our maker was finishing this earth, he went walking around inspecting it and banishing evil spirits from his premises. He divested the Stone Coats and banished them as harmful to men. He removed the stone shirts from the Little People and permitted them to remain to help hunters and cure illness. As the Creator went on his way westward, on the rim of the world, he met a huge fellow—the headman of all the Faces. The Creator asked the stranger, as he had asked the others, whence he came. The stranger replied that he came from the Rocky Mountains to the west and that he had been living on this earth since he made it. They argued as to whose earth they traversed and who created it but agreed to settle the title by contest. The Creator agreed to call the stranger "headman" should he demonstrate sufficient magic strength to summon a distant mountain toward them. The two sat down together facing the east with their backs to the west and held their breath. Now the great False Face shook his giant turtle rattle and the uproar frightened the game animals. He summoned the mountain toward them, but it moved only part way. Now it was the Creator's turn. He conjured and summoned the mountain to come toward them, and it came directly up to them. However, his rival, becoming impatient, suddenly looked around and the mountain struck his face. The impact broke his nose, and pain distorted his mouth. Now then the Creator realized that this fellow had great power. Therefore he assigned him the task of driving disease from the earth and assisting the people who were presently to travel to and fro hunting. The loser of the contest agreed that if humans would make portrait masks of him, call him "grandfather," make tobacco offerings, and set down a kettle of mush, that they too should have the power to cure disease by blowing hot ashes. The Creator assigned

him a place to dwell in the rocky hills to the west near the rim of the earth, and the mask being agreed to come in which ever direction the people might summon him.

The Version of Chauncey Johnny John (Turtle Clan, Cayuga-Seneca) I wrote this down in the summers of 1933 and 1934 at Allegany.

This is a pretty long story. Now you see you may not believe it, but this is the story as I had it from my father, Abraham Johnny John [Seneca of Cattaraugus].

Now a man who is the Great Spirit, Our Maker, goes walking around the edge of the world, and then he saw a man (Hadúʔiʔ or Gagǫ́hsaʔ) approaching him. When he met the man Our Maker asked him, "Who are you and where do you come from?"

And he answered, "I come from way down west near the Rocky Mountains! You had better go away; this is my country."

Our Maker says, "No I cannot leave for I made this world."

Gagǫ́hsaʔ says, "I am the first man and no one else is. This is my property." Now both of them think this earth belongs to them, and Gagǫ́hsaʔ adds: "I don't want anyone else besides myself living in this world."

So the Great Spirit says, "I tell you what I will do. I will bet with you. We two will have a contest. You may indeed be the boss [headman] if you can induce those Rocky Mountains out there to come toward you. Then I will call you boss [hásenowa:nenh, "exalted name"—the word for "chief"].

And this fellow agreed saying, "Alright, I can move that mountain out there and bring it toward me. You sit down here and face the east with your back to that mountain."

So the Great Spirit turned around and looked off into east while Gagǫ́hsaʔ shook his snapping-turtle rattle (haʔno:wa) and rubbed it on the shagbark hickory tree and talked to that mountain in his language [the nonsensical hǫ hǫ hǫ or yǫ ʔyǫ ʔyǫ of the False Faces].

Presently, Our Maker says, "How long are you going to be doing it?"

The conjuror answered, "It is about time now. You may turn around." And the Maker did, but old man False Face had not moved the mountain; it was solid rock.

So then Our Maker decided that it was his turn, and so he said, "You turn around this time and face the east." He did this and Our Maker continued, "You rock yonder, come over here (gá:jiʔ)." And then the mountain commenced approaching until it was as a wall behind Gagǫ́hsaʔ's head. Then the Great Spirit spoke: "ó:nenh" ["Now, already," or "right now"].

Gagǫ́hsaʔ was eager to see the mountain moving, and, turning around quickly, he struck his nose on a stone and smashed it. *And that is why his nose has ever since been crooked,* and when masks are made to represent him they have their noses bent to one side and sometimes flattened.[1]

Dá neʔho [And so it is finished].

The term for the masker, Gagǫ́hsaʔ, is the Shagodyowéhgo:wa:h of Henry Redeye and other informants. Because Gagǫ́hsaʔ means "Face," Shagodyoweh is probably the name of the mask spirit. Haduʔiʔ is another name, more commonly used among Onondaga and Cayuga.

Henry Redeye's Explanation of Shagodyowéhgo:wa:h

This is about the Creator and the four classes of beings whom he outwits and appoints to specific duties toward man.

> When Our Maker had first finished this earth he was walking around inspecting it. And as he was walking, he first met a very small man, a pygmy (jǫkáːǫʔ), or elf. This little fellow was wearing a stone dress (ajadowíshäʔ). Our Maker greeted him and asked him where he came from. This person said, "I have always been here." The maker merely looked at the pygmy for a long time wondering what that person could possibly do, just what he was good for. And then he stripped off the little fellow's stone dress. Then he told the pygmy that he was to help the people who were about to live on the earth and gave him permission to live in the neighborhood where the people were going to live. The pygmies do help the people to get well when they are sick.
>
> Our Maker went on his way and presently he met another man. This one was huge, and this one was Shagodyowéhgo:wa:h, the head of all the False Faces. When he met this one, he asked him the same question: "Where did you come from?" The great one replied similarly, "I have been living here for a long time." Our Maker looked him up and down for a long time and finally told him that he might not stay around that place because there were going to be people living there on this earth. The Maker told him to go away to the far end of the earth, off to the west, where the sun sets. The Maker

---

1. Fogelson suggests a possible hypothesis regarding facial deformation: "Is there any regularity in the museum specimens in the direction in which the nose is bent? Following literally from the myth, if Gagǫ́hsaʔ was facing East and turned in the traditional Iroquoian counterclockwise direction to be bumped by the mountain, the resultant 'out-of-joint' nose would be tilted to the right." Again, this question relates to mouth deformation, and its answer requires returning to the photographs of museum specimens. My own hunch is that the mouths and noses are deflected to the same side, and the distribution between left and right is random. Carvers may not always be mindful of the myth or its internal logic.

knew that this giant could harm the people because he was "poison" (*hotgǫʔ*) [having maleficent supernatural power or strength]. Therefore he banished him.

When asked about the classic mountain moving incident, Henry said that incident was part of another story, which he attributed to a contest between the Maker and the Thunderer. But in J. N. B. Hewitt's "Iroquoian Cosmology—Part II," the contest is between the Creator, or Skyholder, and Haduʔiʔ (Fenton 1962, 294; Hewitt 1928, 533–37).

Creator versus Hiʔnǫʔ (Thunderer)
In Henry Redeye's version,

> The Maker went along and presently he met another, a third man, whom he saw coming in the distance. He, too, was a large man, and like the pygmy, wore a stone coat or shirt. Likewise, Our Maker, when he was close to him, looked him up and down thoroughly before divesting him of his stone dress and throwing it away, as he had done with the stone shirt of the pygmy. He decided that this man, too, was evil and banished him far to the West, to the other end of the earth.
>
> Once more Our Maker proceeded on his way toward the sunset. He met another man, the fourth. Unlike two of the others he was not of tremendous size, but he wore a beard and it was a big one. This person was Hiʔnǫʔ, the Thunderer. The Maker asked him the same questions: Whence he came and how long he had been there. The Thunderer answered that he had been there all the time. Further, he said that he made the earth. So they both sat down together, the Maker and Hiʔnǫʔ. Far off there was a hill and when they sat down the hill was behind them. The Maker said to Hiʔnǫʔ, "If you made this earth, we will turn our backs to that hill, and when we turn around again, the hill will have moved toward us." [In other variants, the contestants are described as conjuring and commanding the mountain to move toward them.]
>
> When they turned around again, the hill had moved a little ways toward them. The Hiʔnǫʔ said, "It is your turn to try to make the hill move." So once more they turned their backs to the hill. And when they looked around, the hill was directly behind them. [The nose-smashing incident is omitted from this version.]
>
> So the Maker had a talk with this fellow saying, "Indeed you have strength (*gaʔhaxteshäʔ*). [My informants had never heard of *orenda;* they thought it probably a Mohawk word! For a fact it is cognate with *ʔoenǫʔ*, "song".] So you can be of help to the people. Just now my brother is making all kinds of fierce animals of destruction who will harm the people, should they come to the surface of the earth. And it is your work, Hiʔnǫʔ, to keep them down in the ground."

Further, the Maker told him that it was his work to help the plants when they start to grow, and the people when they plant; to help keep all sources of water—springs, brooks, etc.—fresh. Further that he should come from the west, from the sunset, and go toward sunrise whenever he traverses the earth, above it, until the end of the world.

Da neʔ ho (And so it is finished.)

Although these two Seneca versions from the same community differ in content, they contain some of the same incidents, and the plot is identical. Chauncey Johnny John's is the classical version, like that of Chief John Arthur Gibson (Hewitt 1928, 533–37). The Creator meets other mythical beings on his tour of the world rim, four in all, the magical number, in the Redeye version, including the Stone Coats and the Little People of the Dark Dance. For Chauncey the world-rim encounter was but a preface to human adventures that followed immediately and that I shall defer.[2]

The association of the Stone Coats or Stone Giants, a race of inimical cannibals dangerous to humans, occurs in versions of the origin of the False Faces that Parker (1923, 394–96, 398) collected at Cattaraugus early in the century, in which the Gé:no:skwaʔ (it literally means "It Used to Eat Skin [or Leather]") are the source of the masks. These primordial Iroquoian monsters have their counterparts among the Cherokee (Fogelson 1980). Parker himself (1909, 180–81) regarded the Stone Coats as sources of masks to be somewhat dubious, although he collected a mask representing a Stone Giant's face from a woman who claimed to be keeper of secret masks (1909, Plate VIII, Figure 2; Report of the Director of the New York State Museum, 1906).

---

2. Each of these supernaturals claims to have been there all of the time. This is characteristic Seneca behavior. In the summer of 1933, when I first arrived at Allegany Reservation to take up fieldwork, I did not find Chauncey Johnny John, whom I already knew, at home. Neighbors informed me he was away. The next day I asked him where he was the day before, why he was not at home. He replied, "I was there all the time, in the corn field tending my crops. . . . I knew you were there. Why didn't you come look in the cornfield? I was home all the while." The cornfield was located about 300 yards back of the house on the Allegheny River bottom. Later in the summer, Chauncey arrived late to a meeting at the Coldspring Longhouse where he was expected to sing. People were waiting inside. When twitted about his tardiness he replied, "I have been here quite a while sitting outside. Why did someone not invite me to come in when you were ready to commence?"

For a sketch of Chauncey's personality, see my Eagle Dance monograph (Fenton 1953, 49–53). His behavior was that of an extraordinarily talented individual operating within a cultural context and is typical of both.

Skyholder versus Hadu?i?

The classic version of the contest between Skyholder and Hadu?i? is that of Chief John Arthur Gibson in the "Iroquoian Cosmology—Part II" (Hewitt 1928, 533–37). Although Hewitt collected different versions from other informants, he never published them. Simeon Gibson and I reviewed the main incidents of his father's version during the period that we worked together from 1939 until his tragic death in 1943 (Fenton 1944). These incidents are Skyholder out inspecting the recently completed earth meets Hadu?i?, and a controversy ensues over its creation and control. They agree to settle the dispute in a contest of power that involves moving a hill that stands afar beyond a field. Hadu?i? conjures, shakes his rattle, and fails to move the hill but half way. He is then directed to turn his back while the Creator conjures and moves the hill directly up behind them. But Hadu?i? is impatient, when told, and suddenly looks around and bumps his nose, which is why masks representing him have bent noses and crooked mouths. (The protruding tongue is given in some versions as portraying pain.) In return for a grant of life, Hadu?i? goes west.

Simeon Gibson commented:

> These False Faces which we have here at Grand River are only an imitation, or likenesses of the real one (Hadu?i?). When they burn tobacco for the masks, the speakers always refer to the real one way out west on the rim of the world. You see, in their agreement. Hadu?i? pledged, "I will go back west and I will do my best to help the people." And so he did. He said, "I shall never be here [present] myself, but you will make likenesses of me and they will be around here."

Gibson knew no stories of hunters encountering False Faces.

SIX NATIONS VERSIONS

The origin myths for the Society of Faces have survived at Six Nations on Grand River in greater detail than among the Seneca of western New York. The Canadian Onondaga recitations allude to several types of masks not mentioned in the Seneca tales. Again, the False Face myths are of two general types—the epic of the Creator and a rival shaman known as Hadu?i?, besides a series of explanatory myths assigning special functions, powers, and world quarters to the several ranks of spirits represented by masks. Second, there are the traditions of the adventures by hunters who have encountered the lesser spirits in the bush. However, unlike the Seneca who are full of the experiences of their ancestors, my informants at Onondaga Longhouse in Canada knew only the myth of the Creator and Hadu?i?, whereas Goldenweiser and Waugh, working a generation earlier, collected visionary experiences like those of my Seneca sources. Moreover, the very best information, such as was no longer available from informants in 1940, was patiently recorded in phonetic texts by J. N. B. Hewitt from such extraordinary ritualists as Chief John Arthur Gibson and Chiefs John and Joshua Buck. The former, though Seneca, was speaker of the Onondaga Longhouse, and the latter two were of Onondaga and Tutelo descent. These texts I was able to arrange and retranslate in the field with Simeon Gibson.

Epic Myths Recited at Ceremonies
The long cosmological legend of the contest between the Creator and the original humpbacked shaman, Haduʔiʔ, for control of the earth was fully known to but few individuals in the 1940s, but everyone who attended the ceremonies at Onondaga Longhouse had heard it. Sometimes the account is abbreviated. A member of the congregation of that longhouse when asked how False Faces came into the world might simply reply:

> When God created the world he went on an inspection tour. He saw a False Face that looked like a human being. God asked him who he was. He said that he was False Face, and that he would forever help and cure the people if God permitted him to stay on the earth. And so his wish was granted. [George Gibson to A. A. Goldenweiser, *Field Notes,* Vol. 16]

Frequently at the two annual meetings of the society this legend was repeated so that the young people might listen and learn how the Society of Faces originated.

John Jamieson, Sr., a Cayuga who then regularly conducted the maskers in the Traveling Rite, on August 15, 1915, summarized for F. W. Waugh the address to the congregation at Onondaga Longhouse.

> The preacher at the two annual meetings of the False Face Society (that is when they go from house to house in spring and fall) tells them, among a variety of things, that God and the False Face were the first beings on earth. God looked at him and saw that he was pretty ugly-looking, so he said to him, "Can you do what I can do?" The False Face said, "I can make that mountain yonder come closer." So he told the mountain to move closer. It moved just a little way. The False Face then turned the other way. Then God told the mountain to come closer. It came right up close to them. The False Face turned around suddenly and struck his nose against the mountain, knocking his nose to one side (just as in the masks).
>
> God told this False Face to beg the other False Faces to keep quiet and not to bring disease to the people. They must be "doctors" to the people.
>
> God and the False Face made a bargain that the latter should be allowed to stay on the earth, but not with the people. He should

stay off somewhere. God realized that the False Face had power. So the False Face said that whenever the people offered tobacco and asked them to help that they would hear, wherever they might be, and would come and cure.

A soothsayer or fortune-teller—(there was only one at this time) was chosen to tell what was wrong [in cases of sickness] and what [procedure or ceremony] was needed. This one man was also endowed with knowledge of medicine.

A Matron of the Society at Six Nations Reserve
Simeon Gibson took me to Mrs. Peter Williams, one of the leading officers for the Deer Clan at Onondaga Longhouse. Mrs. Williams had frequently officiated at the ceremony of oiling the masks before they set out through the settlement, and she had faithfully attended the semiannual meetings of the society in the longhouse. This is her version given to me on August 15, 1940, with Simeon Gibson acting as interpreter.

The Creator himself was traveling about inspecting his earth after the flood. He met a man and this man asked, "Where did you come from?" The Creator replied, "I am just traveling about looking over the works that I have accomplished on the earth that I have just created." "No," the stranger said, "I made the world myself." Thereupon the Creator said, "We shall soon find out who is the maker of this earth."

"See that mountain over there? If you can cause that mountain to move up here, then you are surely the one who made this world."

They both turned about facing the other way. So now the stranger had his chance first. He tried to move that mountain toward them. He said, "Mountain over there, come towards both of us." When they turned again, the mountain had only moved half way to where they were standing.

Now the Creator said, "It is my turn to try to cause that mountain over there to move this way." "Mountain," he said, "move up towards the two of us." The mountain came right up to where they were standing. Just as it came up to them, the Creator said, "Now let us turn around." So they did. And the mountain was right at their backs.

This stranger, who was Haduʔiʔ, quickly turned around, striking his nose on the rocks. [*That is why he has a crooked nose now.*] And he twisted his mouth. [No, his tongue did not protrude.] Just then this fellow felt ashamed, and he did not know what to do. So he merely rubbed his rattle [made of a snapping turtle] on the rock.

Haduʔiʔ begged of the Master, "Will you let me live? May I continue to live on this earth?" The Creator replied, "Yes, but what relationship will you bear to these people who presently are to reside here on this earth?" "I will take them as my grandchildren (*keya-deʔshǫʔǫ*)," he said. "I have the power. I can stop the high wind storms (*ęgayenáhdaʔ*) and I can drive away disease!"

The Creator answered, "I will permit you to live on the earth, and I shall plant the great tobacco (*gayęʔgwaʔnowasgó:na*) here, and the people shall employ that for transmitting messages [making offerings] to you, whenever they require your assistance. Furthermore, there shall be a certain way. It will come through dreams that it is necessary to make a feast (*ęyųdęʔniyó:dę:ʔ*). Also we shall make imitations (*dewadenyędę́stikh*) of the way you look (*tsaʔnihayaʔdo:dę:ʔ*) [likenesses]." [The account makes it clear that the Creator, and not Haduʔiʔ, suggests that the people shall make the masks, which are, literally, likenesses. It is the reverse in the later account of John Buck.]

The people shall use these likenesses to cure the sick by blowing ashes on the sick one. There shall be two colors, namely *red* and *black*. (*This one whom the Creator met had a red-appearing face*.) And so they shall also make black ones. He (*the black one*) shall stand in second rank (*hoyaʔdawę́hdeʔ*) [*Black therefore has not as much power as the red masks.*]

The Versions of Chiefs Joshua and John Buck

During several field seasons on the Six Nations Reserve circa 1916, Hewitt collected six texts in Onondaga from Joshua Buck that purport to explain the ranking of the various supernatural patrons of the False Face and the Husk Face societies (Hewitt 1916, 128). Hewitt kept revising these texts during subsequent years of fieldwork until 1931; in the process of revision he took several additional texts from Chief John Buck, after his brother Joshua's demise in 1920 (1929, 182). Other than brief reports of fieldwork, none of this material has been published. One or two texts that remained untranslated at Hewitt's passing were rendered into English by Simeon Gibson. Meanwhile, John Buck had also died circa 1933. Gibson was particularly interested in the texts because they contain archaic Onondaga terms seldom heard in the 1940s, and for this reason he urged me to publish the original texts so that future generations of longhouse people might learn them. His translations afford ethnological data for a fine group of masks that Hewitt collected for the U.S. National Museum. This documented series provides us with a conceptual scheme for classifying other masks collected from the Grand River Reserve. The scheme is sufficiently elastic to allow for great individual variation in artistic execution of a few basic suggestions as to how the portraits of the original medicine men should be rendered in wood and cornhusk. Conversely, the conception of the supernaturals has been influenced by the appearance of the wooden masks whose physical forms are reflected in the myths.

The ordering of Hewitt's materials is difficult and uncertain. He had numbered his manuscripts in red crayon, and I have adhered to that order, but there are inserts and addenda that are difficult to place and do not always quite fit. Ultimately, he was aiming for a version of his own, the one true version, that never came off.

Onondaga Myth of the Wry-Faced Man-Being (The Split-Faced Man-Being) Dehotgǫhsgá:yęh, from Joshua Buck, 1918. (Hewitt MS No. 2350.) (The confusion of terms between *wry* and *split* is in Hewitt's title.)

The split-faced man-being dwells at the side of the midsky, the South, there along the margin of the earth.

It is stated that the man-being, the east side of whose body is red, but the west side of whose body is dark, full black, dwells chiefly in darkness. These are the persons who bear away, or drive away whatever in the way of evil might menace or befall the inhabitants of the earth. Furthermore, his staff is the whole peeled trunk of a huge hickory tree, and his girdle [belt] is made of the bark of a huge hickory tree, and his robe is the flayed skin of a monster bear. Such then is the power possessed by the split-faced man-being that when he sounds his rattle, the people of the entire earth will become aware of him.

It is said that his Chief (Master) said to him: "There thou shalt abide at the side of the middle sky [South], so that then it will be easily understood when the human inhabitants shall turn their thoughts to thee. And accordingly, it shall become the principal thing, namely the native tobacco, when human beings shall turn their thoughts to thee for help."

So then, it is said, the *red* Man-being (Twęhdai:gǫʔ) was assigned to the margin of the earth on the side of the *sunrise*.

So now the Dark, Pure *Black* Man-Being (ʔOhswęʔdo:gǫʔ) was assigned to the side of the *sunsetting* along the ends of the earth there. The Master of Life said to him: "There at that side, you [deprecative second-person singular] shall continue to dwell. That is the quarter [side] that shall be responsible (when you may be needed). Therefore, it shall be the custom whenever someone shall turn in thought to you for assistance. The Sun will have passed the midsky [noonmark] when that appeal shall become the main thing. [So at Tonawanda it is said that the black faces come after noon.] Then you shall make use of your power inasmuch as you have promised to aid human beings residing on the earth. And then, as is fitting, native tobacco shall be one of the essential things. And then you shall use all the power which your chief, the Great Humpbacked Man-being conferred on all of you [masks]."

He of the Divided Body (Dehodyaʔthgá:węh). Hewitt marked this English translation "A" 1929. It is probably from John Buck. The Onondaga text is not available to me. The mask that illustrates the text is USNM Cat. No. 381412, Hewitt (1916, Figure 122); Plate 2-11 in this volume.

The symbolism of life and death, red and black, human and supernatural, of death and resurrection, the upright, and the humpbacked comprise a series of dyads. There is also the generational gap of grandfather and grandchildren, besides the concept of the divided body and the divided mask, which occurred in face painting (Relation of 1645, *JR* 27:269). The association of Haduʔiʔ and the "Faces Only," the common False Faces, and the complementary relationship of all the wooden masks to the Husk Faces is noteworthy. Moreover, the Husk Faces are to the matrons and horticulture as Haduʔiʔ relates to luck of hunters and control of the game.

I have left Hewitt's English unchanged.

Hewitt's version of the myth of Dehodyaʔtgá·wɛh (i.e., He Whose Body Is Riven in Twain).

> It is said to be a fact that he is free, is a master of his own person, and that it is possible for him to aid mankind who dwell (on the earth). It is also declared that he, the Great Humpbacked One (personage) (i.e., Hadu'i'gō⁀năh), said, "It is the thing to do perhaps, that I should transform the body of the man which lies yonder. So, I will take up one-half of the body of the human being, the flesh body of a human being, wherein thou shalt continue to live."
>
> The Great Humpbacked Person (Hadu'i'gō⁀năh) then went thither to the place where lay the flesh body of the human being. Forthwith he divided that body in twain, that body of the dead human being. Then the Great Humpbacked Personage (Hadu'i'gō⁀năh) exclaimed, "Come hither, thou who art my brother." So now he went there, and he divided in twain the body of his brother, and taking up one of the halves of the flesh body of the dead human being he conjoined it with one half of the body of his brother, and the two halves combining became one body. "So they [meaning mankind] will continue to name thee De'hodyăʔtgāe⁀wᵉⁿh (or Deohodyă'tgāe⁀eñh) (i.e., He Whose Body Is Divided in Twain), and our grandfather, Hadu'i' (i.e., the Humpbacked). So then thou shalt have one half of thy head covered with the pure white hair of a human being, and the other half of thy head shall be covered with the black hair of a Hadu'i' (i.e., of a humpbacked personage).
>
> ["]And then, also, thou shalt when addressing human beings make use of the words, 'my grandchildren'. And then, too, it will be possible for thee to be of assistance to mankind. And next it will also be possible for you and them to converse together. And in the next place, therefore, they will continue to be fortunate and successful. So do thou no injury to them. And now I permit thee to go free. There, in the forests shall be thy habitation."

So, now, verily, at this time and place he exclaimed, "I [*deprecative*] now I depart to my far away home. Never again shall one of mankind see me again. I verily am Hadu'i'goⁿnăh, the Great Humpbacked One."

So now Deʿhodyă'tgāe'ĕñh (He Whose Body Is Riven in Twain) became verily a free and independent personage.

After the lapse of some time he then saw a number of men who were hunting. Now, verily, he declared, saying, "I desired that you and I might meet one another (to become acquainted). I indeed am Deʿhodyă'tgāe'ĕñʿ (He Whose Body Is Riven in Twain). In going from place to place I accompany the Man-being who is called Ogoⁿʿ'sō'goⁿ' (i.e., He Who Is Only Face) and who is a wild nomad of the forests, and also Hadji''să' (i.e., He Who Is Attired in Corn Husks), our Chief. It would not be good for you should you unfortunately see him.

["]So then you shall have good fortune in your hunting, for I will cause it to be so.

["]So then I [*deprecative* form] will now pass on, for I am going about from place to place considering the various peoples who dwell in diverse habitations."

Now, it came to pass that he came to a place where several matrons had planted a field with corn. They were indeed surprised to behold a Man-being coming towards them in that place. He arrived near them and to allay their apprehensions said, "Verily, I have you for my grandchildren; verily, I am he whom you people name, ʿDeʿhodyă'tgāe'wĕⁿh (for Deʿhodyă'tgāe'ĕñh), i.e., He Whose Body Is Riven in Twain, who customarily wanders about from place to place, and whom people also name, Hadu''i' (i.e., He Who Is Humpbacked). I am indeed a being whose body is one half human. Then, let no one become alarmed should one inadvertently see me somewhere in my travels. I have the power to give assistance to you [pl.], so that you shall be successful and fortunate at all times.

["]I have the power also to devote care to your planted fields (that they may be productive). It is also possible for me to render aid to your warriors who travel from place to place hunting the game animals.

["]So then do you inform them when you [pl.] will have returned to the dwelling-places of your people that you and I have seen one another. That then you shall tell them saying, 'We indeed have seen Deʿhodyă'tgāe'ĕñh (He Whose Body Is Riven in Twain), the Hadu''i' (the Humpbacked Man-being)'."

The Great Hunchback. In 1918, Joshua Buck, of Onondaga-Tutelo descent, dictated the following text to Hewitt, which the author revised and edited from a new text by Simeon Gibson in 1941 (Hewitt MS No. 2347).

This myth of the Great Hunchback, including his contest with the Creator, is an origin legend and also serves as an opening address by the speaker for the Society of Faces at their public rituals in the longhouse.

The speaker opens the session for the Hondu?i? with these words concerning Hadu?i?go:na, "The Great Humpbacked One":

> That one who created this earth, namely the Sapling, while on his rounds looking over the entire earth that he had just completed, saw in that place a man [or man-being]. [This is the time the Creator, named the Sapling, asks Hadu?i? who he is. When the Creator first met him, the man's face was not twisted; his face was straight yet. (S. Gibson).] And at that time he asked him, he said, "Where do you come from?" And then he answered him, saying, "I am the owner of this earth." And then the Sapling said, "I think that I made this earth myself, which is the reason that I am traveling along." And so now the man answered, saying, "I am the owner of this earth and I am the very first being you have discovered." Then the Sapling replied, saying, "Perhaps then (try if) you are able to move toward us yonder ridge." And he added, "It will prove surely whether you can do it, that is, move that yonder mountain this way toward us." Then the Sapling said, "Let us both turn around." Then he said to that man-being, "Can you move it this way toward us?" Now the man-begin said, "Move over this way, yonder mountain." At that time they both turned about, and for certain it had moved there a little way toward them. At that point the man said, "It is your turn, it is up to you to move the mountain toward us, that ridge yonder." Then Sapling said, "Let us both turn about," and they both did turn about. It was Sapling who then said, "Move this way yonder mountain, for I am the Maker of the whole earth." And so this did happen, as they faced around again, so quickly did he [the man-being] turn around that he struck his nose on the rock which was hard against their backs, and it was then and there that he bent his nose.
>
> Just then Hadu?i? said, "Will it be possible to let me live in the parts of the earth that I habitually inhabited, inasmuch as you intend there shall be released here human beings who are about to be created? Furthermore, I shall stand in the relation of grandparent to them and call them 'my grandchildren.' Moreover, it might not do for them to see me close at hand. Therefore, I quit this place and leave for that place where the earth is ragged (to the north where no person travels)."
>
> Then Sapling spoke, "Indeed it would not be pleasant for you as the first being who did travel here on earth. It isn't that you don't know where you hail from, though perhaps [it appears] that you travel the way the wind blows." [Sapling thinks that Hadu?i? came with the wind.]

Then the being named Haduʔiʔgo:nah declared: "I have given myself over to dwell in a certain quarter where the land is rough. The reason that I do this is that it will not result in good should I be seen by human beings. So then I have resigned myself to dwell in places where men are not accustomed to frequent. Therefore I go to the *north,* and then I shall continue to dwell in the north, the place of cold, because I am not affected by it in any way." [This is the rationale for the maskers going nearly naked at midwinter.]

"So now then, for a fact, you are as brothers to one another have seated yourselves respectively in your proper places" [Here the speaker refers to the moieties in the longhouse]. Entirely *Red* One (Tgwęhdai:goʔ) chose to pass by on the *north* side. Entirely *Black* One (ʔOhswęʔdo:goʔ) chose to pass by on the side of the setting sun [west]. But the one with the *divided* face (Dęhotgǫhsga:yęːʔ), or He Whose Body Is Cleft in Twain (Dęhotdyaʔtgai:węh), is *not restricted* in his wanderings to any one place. Indeed it is possible for him to travel back and forth beside a person.

Similarly, the man-being [the one] who is entirely face [face only] (Neːʔ ogǫhsóːgoʔ) is independent [not restricted] in his goings and comings. He frequents the paths in the *depths of the forest*. (Face Only is a fast runner. Regularly he travels amongst the high winds. He travels rapidly. Therefore he has great power as well.)

The man-being with cleft body and two faces, one a wooden face and the other a husk face, back to back, takes the lead when those associated with him [in the medicine society] set out on a mission of curing (Plate 5-1). He is the one that has two faces—back and front. He also looks out from behind the shield of the sun upon all his associates as they go to make their visits. [His face would appear dark from behind the sun.] [Simeon Gibson had not seen such a mask, so it must belong to an earlier period at the Onondaga Longhouse where it has since gone out of use. But he has seen divided masks in miniature.]

So you have all seated yourselves [taken your proper places] wherever may be your respective places on the face of the earth."

Haduʔiʔ, the Humpbacked Man-Being. This incomplete Onondaga text provides the rationale for four kinds of masks plus the Husk Face messenger: entirely black on the west, pure red on the east, Face Only in the forests, divided face in the midsky (South)—deep red/pure black and wry mouth, and the Husk Face messenger, a female spirit. I have simplified Hewitt's ornate English to conform to the text.

There was a man in the Onondaga country who owned a legend of Haduʔiʔ. He was named Honǫhsihathaʔ, "He Who Habitually Passes by the House," and he had been a great man in the native land of the Onondaga people. And he had a cousin by the name of

Plate 5-1. The man-being with cleft body and two faces: one Husk the other wooden: Gajihsa and Hadui. Collected by J. N. B. Hewitt, Grand River, 1916. Courtesy USNM.

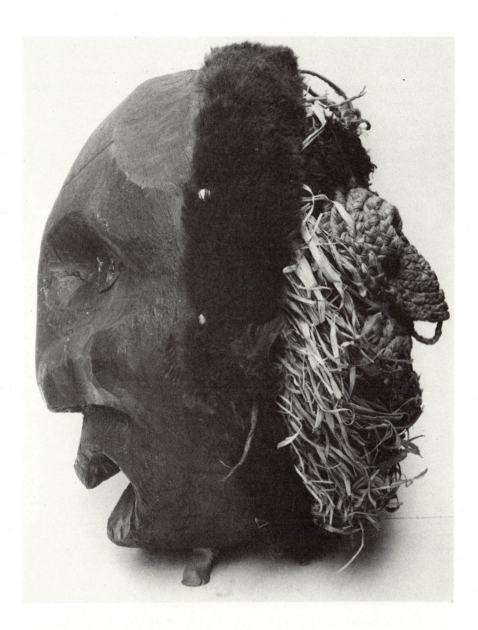

Gahiʔkdóːdǫʔ, "Standing Thorns." They were both chiefs and leaders of their people in the country of the Onondagas.

The two men fell to discussing the question as to when the Humpbacked Beings, the Hǫndúʔiʔ, might again visit the people resident there. They did this because they both believed that Humpbacked Beings were helpful to their people.

The uncertainty arose over the question as to the place of origin of the first Haduʔiʔ, when he was first seen on the face of the earth. They both recalled that it was Dehaǫhiyawáʔgih, "Holder of

Heavens" [the Master of Life] who first saw him as he traveled along inspecting the earth.

What made these two men give some thought to this question was that they realized that Haduʔiʔ possessed magic power, and his strength was such that he was invulnerable, since he was quite immune to any hostile agency.

(At that time these two chiefs understood that the humans then inhabiting the earth were subject to visions, mysterious ills, and to fearful contagions.) [This passage by Hewitt is not in the text] (They took comfort from recalling the tradition of the meeting between Sapling, the Master of Life, and Haduʔiʔ.) They recalled that at this meeting that when the Master of Life perceived that Haduʔiʔ had great power, he asked him, saying, "Where did you come from?" And Haduʔiʔ replied saying, "I have always lived here on the earth. I indeed am owner of it." Then the Master of Life rejoined, "I myself made the earth as it is, and so I believe that I am master of it. Indeed through my power human beings are about to inhabit it. So then let the two of us put our contentions to a test. Way over there stands a rock cliff. If you are as capable as you boast, can't you make it move this way to our backs?"

At that time Haduʔiʔ replied, "Just so shall it happen." Whereupon the Master of Life said, "You shall have first try." Then Haduʔiʔ said, "Yonder rock cliff, move here at our backs," and turning to Sapling said, "Let us turn our backs towards it," and they turned. Shortly, they turned back and saw that the rock cliff had indeed moved about half the distance to where they were standing.

Then Haduʔiʔ exclaimed, "You are next." [The Onondaga text, which is incomplete, stops here, but Hewitt's English translation continues.] Thereupon the Master of Life spoke, saying, "Yonder rock cliff far off, move here to our very backs." Again they both turned their backs. Whereupon the rock cliff rushed up with so much noise and commotion that Haduʔiʔ was struck with fear and whirled around suddenly, thus striking his face and shoulder violently against the rock cliff with the result that his nose became crooked and his back was humped permanently as the penalty for his defeat. *This is why his entire offspring are misshapen and ugly,* according to tradition.

Then it was that Haduʔiʔ humbly acknowledging his discomfort exclaimed, "Oh, Master of Life, let me live and I will serve you and the people whom you are about to create on this earth."

The two Onondaga leaders remembered that Haduʔiʔ at that time had made a promise to the Master of Life saying, "I can be of assistance to those human beings, if only they will make a likeness of my physique. It is feasible that the likeness of my figure and face can be taken from the living wood of growing trees. Then it shall be the way that wherever and whenever a human being shall become ill by reason of the fact that I myself was the first to traverse the face of the earth and in so doing infected it with contagions and evil influences [black magic] of my person, by means of such likenesses it shall be possible to help such a sick person. And even if there should be an epidemic among the people, these likenesses are capable of expelling it from the community. Such then is the extent of my power." The two Onondaga leaders also knew that the Master of Life said to Haduʔiʔ, "You shall live. But I think that it would not result in any good that you should linger here any longer. Therefore you should move away."

So, when the two chiefs, Honǫhsihátaʔ and his cousin Gahiʔkdó:dǫʔ, realized that some disaster was about to happen to their people, they resolved to act.

So they collected as many as possible of the masks from the diverse lodges of their people and they carried them to a cavern in a mountain to conceal them. Their country was invaded, and the Onondaga lodges were destroyed and burned.³ Then and there at that cavern in the mountain, the old men made a selection of the masks; they took two apiece for each kinship group and carried them from there to temporary homes.

Among the masks that they selected were the following: the Ohswęʔdó:gǫʔ, "The Entirely Black One"; then Tkwęhdai:gęʔ, "The Pure Red Mask"; and then Ogǫhsó:gǫʔ, "The Face Only Mask," or the Bald Hunchbacked Being of the Forests; then Dęhotgǫhsgá:ęh, The Mask Whose Face Is Divided, one side [a] deep red color, and the other side pure black; and then Hadjíhsaʔ for Yedjihsaʔ, "Husk Mask," the cornhusk mask who travels about in advance and who then touches [notifies] the persons of the heads of the houses, so that they shall know that the Hǫnduʔiʔ, the maskers or the Humpbacked Beings, are on their customary round of driving out the disease spirits.

And so it was that when the red-faced being met the Holder of Heavens (the Master of Life), it was at a suggestion of the master that the mask-being promised him, saying, "On the side of the sunrise I will stay and in the rough desert country of the earth where human beings do not usually go; there I shall continually remain. It will then be quite impossible for human beings to look upon me to behold the living shape of my body and person."

In like manner, Ohswęʔdo:gǫʔ, The Entirely Black Mask, passed over to the side of the sunsetting. He, too, was told to inhabit the

---

3. Onondaga was twice invaded and burned by European armies: in 1696 by Frontenac and again in 1779 by Van Schaick during the Sullivan–Clinton campaign of the American Revolution.

rough desert places of the earth, where human beings do not go. "There," he said, "I will continue to stay."

And Dehotgǫhsgaéęnh, that is, The Crooked-faced Mask, was sent to the midsky, to the South, by the master.

Hogǫhsó:gǫʔ, the mask that is a face only, was sent to inhabit the forests, for he is wild, that is—he is free: He goes about in the deep forests examining things as he travels. He and Owä:deʔ, that is, the Wind Mask, go around together; the latter is said to change everything.

[From this information it is possible to chart the maskers' world in a diagram; see Figure 5-1.]

A few comments on the preceding account are contained in a scrap on the False Faces in Hewitt, Ms. No. 3634.

When the people see the Husk Face messenger coming, they are aware that the Honduʔiʔ, the Humpbacked Beings, are coming there.

The moiety division of masks is equal. Each side has a full complement of masks. Each phratry of clans (at Onondaga when faced with disaster) chose one black, one crooked face, one divided mask, one white face, one bald head (round face, everything straight and plane). [The latter is the equivalent of the Seneca Common Face of the forest.]

The wind being who travels with the face alone in the forests changes every day.

How the Masks Got to Grand River. After Honǫhsihátha? secluded the masks and apportioned them, "that is what they brought here," Hewitt's informant added, "It started there from Onondaga where the Onondaga people lived in ancient times. They migrated [here] from there, and they brought that [the masks] with them whenever they removed from there."

When they arrived [at the Grand River], they conjoined their lands here [with those of the other Five Nations remnants]. They had with them what masks Honǫhsihátha? had saved for them. Now and again as necessary they made use of the Faces which they had brought from Onondaga to Grand River, namely the Honduʔiʔ (Humpbacked Beings). "Clear Sky," Oęhiyogé:węh, was the other name of Honǫhsihátha?, and he was the leader and director of the Five Nations of the Iroquois League.

Hewitt ended his notes on the maskers' world view (Ms. No. 3634) with the comment:

When the Crooked Face (Dęhotgǫhsgá:ęh) stands at the center of the midsky, the left side of his body appears black and the right side is red. [This has to do with his position relative to the path of

Figure 5-1. The maskers' world.

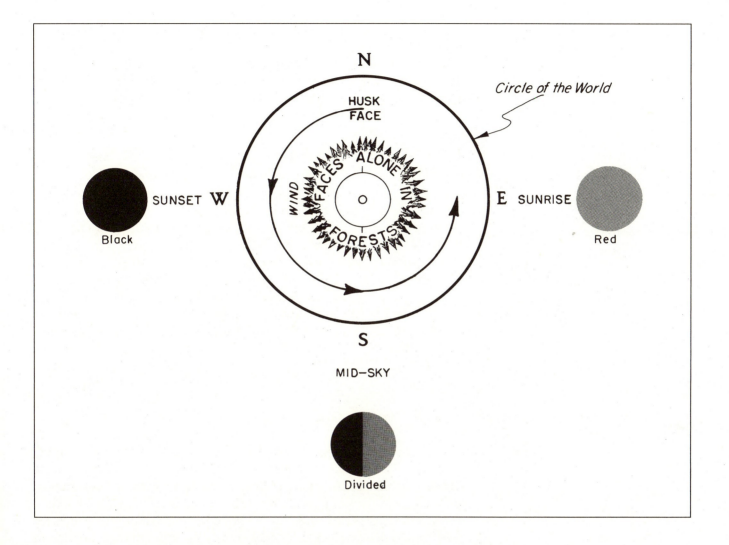

the sun.] When he makes his turtle-shell rattle sound, the hunchbacked beings of the whole earth will become aware of it.

Another note (Ms. No. 3522) speaks of his contract with the Creator in return for life

> to provide for human welfare by curing the sick, dying and wounded, provided that occasional feasts be held in his behalf. His mouth extended diagonally across his face from one cheekbone to the lower part of his jaw on the opposite side of his face. There is a secret society [at Grand River] whose members must wear wooden masks having the like diagonal mouth carved on them.

This concept is transferred to the firmament in the belief that "the three stars comprising the belt of the constellation *Orion* are translated

Hatú?i?," and the image is that of "death with the agony of dying persons depicted on his face."

The Seneca world view of the masker is somewhat different. They say that the great False Face follows the daily path of the sun and at noon stops to rub his rattle on the giant elm or pine that stands in the center of the earth. Arthur Parker had a drawing made of this concept, which appears in several of his papers (1909, 183; 1913, 154; 1923, 431–44). He writes:

> The Seneca world-tree . . . , whose branches pierce the sky and whose roots run down into the underground waters of the underworld . . . is mentioned in various . . . rites . . . the Great Face, chief of all the False Faces, is said to be the invisible giant that guards the world tree. He rubs his turtle shell rattle upon it to obtain its power and this he imparts to all the visible faces worn by the Company. In visible token of this belief the members of the Company rub their turtle rattles on pine tree trunks, beliving that they become filled with both the earth and sky-power . . . the turtle shell rattle . . . is perhaps a recognition of the connection between the turtle and the world-tree that grows upon the primal turtle's back. [1923, 435]

HUMAN ADVENTURES

The adventure of the good hunter and the False Faces is the common theme of most Seneca narrations of the beginnings of the Society of Faces. The cosmic encounter, just described, serves as a preface to some human encounter with beings in the forest. This is the common plot for several medicine society origin tales. Among the tales that Parker collected at the turn of the century (1923, 347), in one the False Face saves the hero from the monster Naked Bear, and in return the hero pays the False Face tobacco. In another (1923, 399–400), the hunter has a vision in which he dreams and awakes at the foot of a basswood tree that unfolds to reveal the Face. Genonskwa? (Stone Coat) speaks to him from behind the tree, instructing him to carve. Gathering up the many faces he has carved, the hunter returns to his village, now an old man, and relates his adventure. This association of the Stone Coats with the False Faces is typical of early Seneca versions. In a third tale, a homeless boy, the typical Iroquois folk hero, the rejected orphan of No-Father, has a vision of the great False Face in which he is instructed to lead a war party west of the Mississippi. The False Face spoke four times, the magic number, but people only laugh at the revelation. In the engagement, False Face stands in the bow of the first canoe, catches arrows on a great shield, while the hero shoots the enemy (1923, 342–43).

The role of False Face in suppressing cannibal spirits permeates early Seneca tales. In one of these contests, False Face reduces a forest to dead trees by hammering on the bark, and then works on an evil elder brother until he disappears (Curtin and Hewitt 1918, 119, 271; Parker 1923, 29, 176, 264, 345).

Henry Redeye: How the False Faces Came to the People
In Henry Redeye's account of how the False Faces came to the people, a tale of the common forest False Faces, Hodigǫhsósgaʔa,

> There were two Seneca hunters who in the fall went into the woods hunting. They built a hemlock-brush shanty or lean-to. Outside of the shelter they built a fireplace for cooking. Every time the two hunters went out in the morning and returned from hunting, as was their custom, they discovered that their fireplace was destroyed, and the ashes were strewn over the ground as if someone had been playing in them, and there were the marks of some great, dirty hand where someone had grasped a house post for support as he leaned over and pawed in the fire. This continued for a few days. Then the hunters decided to find out who had done this.
>
> One morning they hid in the brush nearby to watch for the intruder. In a few hours they saw a peculiar man, the like of whom they had never seen before, approaching. His face was *red,* and he had long hair which was parted in the middle and fell down on each side. His eyes were shiny as if something encircled them. Thus they saw him from a distance. [Clara Redeye, my interpreter, commented: "He was carrying a rattle made from the mud turtle, but the story does not say so."] Crouching, he would look at their shelter, and then again stand erect. And then he would drop again to his knees and crawl a little way on one hip. Shortly, he would stop again, stand and look suspiciously in the direction of the lean-to.
>
> Having made sure the shanty was empty, he went straight up to the fireplace and scattered the ashes.
>
> Meanwhile, the hunters lying in ambush decided to return to their shanty and find out who the stranger might be. When they reached their camp they intended to shoot the intruder, if he were still there. They were carrying muskets. [Henry Redeye remarked that the story says they were carrying muskets, and so, he added, "this was not so very long ago." In the Chauncey Johnny John version, which follows, the hunter carried a bow and arrow.] As they approached, the stranger ran back into the brush. The hunters were not able to move to shoot him; they stood frozen, paralyzed, so great was his power.
>
> Undismayed, the two hunters repaired their fireplace and went to sleep. During the night one of the hunters dreamed about this

False Face whom they had seen. In the dream, the visitant told the hunter that he was hungry and that he wanted some of the hunters' mush, which hunters were accustomed to prepare of roasted white corn that is afterward pounded in a mortar, parched, and cooked into a gruel. They carried the parched meal dry with them into the woods. Both hunters and warriors always carried this meal ready prepared in a small bundle at the waist when they followed the chase or the warpath.

The next day the hunter made the mush as directed in the dream. When he had finished it, he put some Indian tobacco in the fire, as he was also directed. While he was so engaged, two False Faces arrived—their previous guest and a companion who looked just like the other one. They carried turtle rattles. In the dream the False Face had taught the hunter a third thing: Hodigǫhsóskaʔah, "The Faces Only," their song for curing and how to sing it. And so borrowing the rattle from one of the False Faces, he sang this song and they danced standing erect. When they had finished dancing [and this is always the first dance of the False Face ritual], he gave each of them some mush, whereupon they vanished.

The following night the hunter had a second dream in which the two False Faces asked the two hunters always to remember them, and by way of commemoration to "put up a dance" for them every year. They also told this hunter that this species of False Faces, the Hodigǫhsóskaʔah, "Nothing but Faces," or the Common Faces, were everywhere in the forest, that they were always among the trees, and that if the hunters did as he instructed them, they would have good luck in the future.

[It is apparent that one hunter has the dream, and one False Face consistently is his familiar in the dream. Just as one hunter has a companion, so has the False Face.]

The two hunters returned to their homes and told their village what had happened to them. This was in the fall [since Indians always went hunting in the fall]. Now the chief of that village asked the hunters what had really happened. And so they told him what they had seen and related what one of them dreamed. They told him they had seen a False Face, and the dreamer recited his vision, relating how he had put up a dance [made a feast for them], making the mush and putting tobacco in the fire.

It was now that this hunter [the one who it seems is always having the dream] had another dream. The same two False Faces again appeared to him. This time they wanted faces made of wood in representation of them. [The story does not say what particular kind of likenesses.] Further, they desired the whole village to give a dance for them. [This is the one that is held for them in the longhouse every spring and fall.] They instructed him how to conduct the ceremony.

Then the two hunters made the False Faces because they knew how the forest spirits looked. They made several such masks. When they had finished preparing these False Faces, the chief said, "We shall now have a meeting." This was in the beginning. [And women are not mentioned as running the ceremony. Nor is there any mention of moiety alignments.]

The two hunters did all the work: They made the mush, they taught the men how to dance, and at the ceremony they put the Indian tobacco in the fire. They alone knew how to do it and what to say.

This first meeting was held on behalf of the whole village, and that is how it originated and that is why people have to continually put up dances for the False Faces up to the present.

Da neʔhoh ("That is it, so it happened, so it is spoken").

Howard Jimmerson: A Downriver Hunt. Also in the Coldspring Longhouse community on the Allegany Reservation of the Seneca Nation, Howard Jimmerson, of the Wolf Clan, then 76, related essentially the same tale of a family's adventure with the False Faces while on the fall hunt. For him it was only one or two generations away.

My mother who is long since dead told me that the old folks used to go down the Allegheny River every fall. They hunted in the hills on either side of the river, and some years they stayed there in the hunting camps until March near Pittsburgh. Some years they would come home in midwinter for the Feast of Dreams, and sometimes they would not return until spring planting. Some families stayed downriver for a year or more.

One time a man went downriver with his family to hunt for meat, and they took up residence in an old house. A white man accompanied them. They hunted during the day. When this white man returned home at night from his hunting, he discovered the fireplace ashes strewn all over the dirt floor. The fireplace was in the middle of the room on the bare earth. Imprinted on one of the house posts near the fire was the mark of a great hand which had been whitened with ashes. The handprint indicated where some giant of a person had grabbed the post to support himself as he scattered the ashes.

A few days later the white man saw a great False Face person. His face was red and greasy from constant perspiration. His long hair fell to his knees from either side of his head. He rubbed his great turtle rattle on the walls and house posts, while saying hǫʔ hǫʔǫʔǫʔǫʔ. The white man got scared and went home.

The Indian returned from his hunting. He was not afraid because he had Indian tobacco. "He cannot do anything to me," he said, "He is merely playing in the fireplace."

The Indian family stayed on for two months in this hunting camp. The False Face came frequently to play in the ashes during the day while they were off hunting. The Indian family finally decided that their visitor wanted mush and tobacco. So he put [burned] some tobacco in the fire so that his family might not have trouble with the False Face, and they left a kettle of mush when they went hunting.

This was the first time.

Later Encounters. But of even more recent date, Howard Jimmerson's step-father saw one across the Allegheny River at High Bank when he was young. "He was spearing fish near the Big Bend west of Wolf Run. The one that he saw was a tall fellow and he shook his rattle as he walked."

The prevailing opinion among the Seneca is that the False Faces are supposed to be hunting for tobacco when they thrust their hands into the fire and scatter the ashes. The corresponding belief is that if one "puts tobacco" in the fire, which amounts to burning it on the live embers, the False Faces will scent it and derive benefit, or find it there in the fireplace. The hunter in Howard's story knew that the False Face wanted tobacco and mush, and which other narrators describe them as demanding. The culture had already provided a ready method for handling this situation.

The Hunter and the False Faces

Chauncey Johnny John, who had married and lived many years with Howard Jimmerson's sister Betsy, began his narrative, "The Hunter and the False Faces," immediately following the myth of the Creator and the mountain-moving incident as a preface, already related.

And now soon another man went hunting. He carried roasted corn meal and remained in the woods all fall. He also had Indian tobacco [*Nicotiana rustica* L.] which he carried pulverized in a doe-skin bag.

Early one morning he took his bow and arrows, knife, and tomahawk to go hunting. He was walking about, traversing the forests, when, presently, he saw someone who proved to be an old man sitting on a log staring at him. He shot an arrow at him, and the old man fell over backwards behind the log. As the hunter approached, the man got up and standing erect, said, "You come take your arrow." And the hunter pulled it from the old man's wound. Apparently, it had not hurt him.

This man said, "I do not want anything from you, nor have I come here to harm you. The headman of the False Faces sent me here to tell you because we know you have tobacco and meal which we like. Presently we will come here, and I am giving you two days' notice to make bark dishes, 100 of them, before we arrive. You are to cook that meal and make mush. Make enough so that everyone of us can have some in our bark dishes. (There are to be 100 of them.) Also you must have tobacco ready."

The hunter replied, "Very well, I will make the dishes within two days, cook enough mush for all of them, and I will have tobacco ready."

When they had reached an agreement, this man went away.

In two days time the hunter was ready. By then he had made 100 dishes of elm bark, he had cooked the mush, and he had tobacco ready.

Soon another man appeared to ask the hunter, "Are you ready?"

"Yes."

"We shall come then," and he returned for his company of one hundred. And they prepared themselves.

[Projected into the folktale is the contemporary usage. Men of the False Face Society don their masks outside of dwellings before entering, and it is the duty of the matron in charge to see that their host is prepared and has met all of the requirements: mush and tobacco. Then she goes and summons them.]

Soon he saw many men approaching wearing masks (Gagǫ́hsaʔ, "Face"); and this hunter built a small fire. He watched them while they seated themselves in a circle about his fire. [Again, the maskers enter a house crawling and sit about the stove as the headman sprinkles tobacco in the fire pit. Since the old fireplaces were on the center line of bark longhouses directly beneath the smoke holes in the ridge, the old-time meetings did not differ essentially from the mythical forest meeting, except for being beneath a roof.] Some of the visitors were grown men; others were youths. They were of all sizes and appearances just like people.

And then this old man, who was head of the Gagǫ́hsaʔ, asked, "Where is your tobacco?" And the hunter turned about and reached for his tobacco bag, which he handed to the Gagǫ́hsaʔ.

This fellow then said, "You man listen to me. Hear what I shall say. Then you will know how we do it [customarily perform]."

The hunter said, "Alright, I will listen."

Whereupon the old man, the False Face, stepped to the fire with the tobacco and sprinkled it on the flames a pinch at a time as he talked. This is *hayęʔtgǫntwas,* "throwing the tobacco." When he finished, he turned to the hunter saying: "Did you listen? Can you do it?"

"Yes."

"Well then come here to the fire and take the tobacco and repeat what I have just said." And the hunter did this.

"Come here to the fire once more," and he did. "We now give you some medicine." Every one of the False Faces put his hands into the red hot ashes, and taking great handfuls, rubbed them together. Their leader continued, "We will make a dance for you. You must listen to my song, which we call Hodigǫhsóskaʔah, 'the Faces Only'."

[The contract concept enters into nearly all Seneca medicine society rites. In return for tobacco, which man has and the spirits desire, they agree to remove sickness that they also have the power of inflicting. The maskers scoop up handsful of hot ashes and rub their hands together to distribute the heat evenly and so as not to burn them. This is a learned technique.]

And so the headman sang these three songs:

1. *Shagodyowéhgo:wa: hadyaʔdotaʔ*
   Great False Face   cure him
2. [Nonsense words, see song texts later.]
3. *o:nęh neʔho*
   Now there (Now that is it).

And then when he had finished singing, the headman asked this hunter, "Can you sing them?"

The hunter said, "Yes."

"Well then, that is good enough. Where is your mush?" The man went and got his kettle [Chauncey thinks it was an earthen pot], and he distributed bark dishes, one to each of the 100 False Faces. Then he filled them with mush. Their headman continued, "When you get back to your people, tell someone what you have seen." [One is supposed to relate all dreams and visions (Parker 1913, 26). Confession and dream guessing dominated the old midwinter ceremonies. And today the officers on their rounds of the houses announcing the ceremony urge people to reveal particular dreams.]

When the hunter reached his village, as was the custom, he related his vision to the headman of the town where he lived. Immediately the headman sent runners summoning the people to the meeting place, the council house. Now the headman of the False Faces had also given the hunter a miniature mask so that he might remember how they looked and that he might copy it on a larger scale. He was obliged to keep it during his lifetime.

Everyone came to the council house because they wanted to see the man whom they had heard had had a strange adventure. They were anxious to hear his story and to inspect the tiny False Face which they had heard had been given to him to keep during his lifetime. The hunter stood and told the story of all that he had seen and experienced. It was now the middle of winter, and he had been hunting all fall. Everyone saw and inspected the tiny mask, which he directed them to return home and carve in larger sized masks, using this small one as a pattern. This was just as the headman of the False Faces had directed.

All the men went home and carved masks of cucumber, butternut, black walnut, and a few of hard maple, and some of basswood. A few carvers made False Faces immediately, but others watched them and copied. Gradually the knowledge spread.

Now this is how the people came to have a False Face Company, even up to now.

Encounters with Flying Heads

Bodyless heads that flit from tree to tree sometimes disclose themselves to hunters and are grouped with the Common Faces of the Forest. Several of my Seneca informants had tales about these flying heads. Jonas Snow, my host at Coldspring in the first summer of my fieldwork, related this adventure of a hunter:

The first time, a man went hunting and met the False Face in the forest. Before he saw him he heard him moaning. He did not know what it was. The sound came from up a tree where he looked. At first he could not find the source because it kept hiding on the opposite side of trees, darting from tree to tree through the forest. It was only a head with long hair streaming out behind. Its face was red and it talked [in its peculiar nasal way]. It was Hodigǫhsóskaʔah, "The Faces Alone."

Presently the man's nose commenced to bleed. When he reached home he put tobacco in the fire for the False Face he had seen and soon his nose stopped bleeding. He thought that Gagǫ́hsaʔ caused it to bleed.

Now it seems that this False Face, while talking, had told the hunter that he desired tobacco and mush. "That is all I eat," it said. "Maybe you will have good luck when you fulfill that every time. I cure, whenever you are sick, toothache, eyes, etc. You only need put tobacco and call me and I will always come and help you."

A Tonawanda Seneca Tradition. Two years later at Tonawanda, Chief Barber Black related a similar hunting adventure.

There used to be big woods all over [western New York]. In the fall the Indians would go there to hunt the wild animals such as the deer and the bear. A man went hunting deer in the fall. He approached the big woods and saw a strange face, a Gagǫ́hsaʔ, peering at him from behind a big tree, looking first from one side and then peeking curiously from the other side like a child playing peek-a-boo. (The False Face was standing behind a big tree peering alternately at the man from both sides.) The man approached and the False Face spoke to him, saying: "I will help you during your lifetime." He said that he craved the old-fashioned tobacco. "You

Plate 5-2. *The powerful red mask of Levi Snow, Coldspring, Allegany Reservation, 1933.*

put it on the fire and speak, asking my help. And you make white corn-meal mush (*ʔoji:skwaʔ*). Use this now whenever someone is sick."

False Face Encounters a Stone Giant

Helia Jones, a young man of the Hawk Clan at Allegany, whose mother was Jonas Snow's sister, and parallel cousin of Clara Redeye, related a legend of how the headman of the False Faces bested a Stone Coat, and how one hunter escaped from the False Faces. The association of the False Faces with the Sone Coats is never clear, but one gets the impression from these tales that the False Faces are slightly superior beings and on the side of man.

> Shagodyowéhgo:wa:h is the headman of the False Faces. One day he was out sunning himself on a rock and while asleep was disturbed by a Stone Coat (*Gęːnǫːskwaʔ*) [customarily eats skin or leather]. These are big fellows that eat stray hunters.
>
> The headman of the False Faces was annoyed to be rudely awakened while warming himself on a rock. The Stone Coat asked him who he thought was the stronger and threatened to eat him.
>
> The False Face headman replied, "I have a hatchet, and if I cannot break a stone with it, you may eat me. But if I succeed in breaking the rock, I will use it on you as well."
>
> The Stone Giant agreed, saying, "I will watch you."
>
> So the old man of the False Faces picked up a stone some eight inches in diameter and used the rock on which he had been sleeping as an anvil. He said, "In one blow I will split it, or you may eat me." He struck at the stone with his mighty strength and crushed it.
>
> Now the Stone Giant witnessing his rival's success ran as fast as he could. Meanwhile Shagodyowéhgo:wa:h lay down and went back to sleep.

It was Helia's opinion that masks representing Shagodyowéhgo:wa:h are "poison" or *ʔotgǫʔ* (evil power). He specifically named two masks then in the community, a black mask belonging to Amos Johnny John and a red mask belonging to Levi Snow (Plate 5-2). "It can be of any shape, so long as it is poison, and then it is Shagodyowéhgo:wa:ʔ. They will be 'poison' when they are old."

A Hunter Escapes from the False Faces

The preceding myth was by way of preface to the following tale. Helia Jones remembers that Mandy Gordon of the Wolf Clan, "whom we called Wändi, was an old lady who came to live with us. She used to tell me stories."

A hunter went in the forest and he heard False Faces all around him in every direction. He attempted to follow the voices. Finally he saw a man by a pine tree, rubbing his rattle on the tree. He had long hair which reached to his ankles. Soon others appeared whose long hair dragged on the ground.

The hunter took out his tobacco, which he carried, and he kindled a little fire. He spread some tobacco on the fire and asked them not to bother him and to let him pass unmolested. While he was casting tobacco, they all disappeared and let him pass through.

A Hunter Meets a Black False Face

From my host, Jonas Snow of the Seneca Hawk Clan, in the summer of 1933, I heard a second tale, "The Black False Face."

Another man was walking in the woods, and he saw a huge black gagǫ́hsaʔ, a jẹ:stáʔẹ:ʔ gagǫ́hsaʔ. He was walking along and he was carrying a whole pine tree in his right hand for a walking stick. [The giant pine as a walking stick of Shagodyowéhgo:wa:h is specified in the text of the tobacco-burning invocation of Henry Redeye which follows later.] As he walked, his steps jarred the earth [a belief confirmed by Sadie Butler of the Wolf Clan, matron of the society]. He went along and presently stopped to rest at a particular tree, and then returned to rest at the same tree, a giant elm (gaǫgä́hgo:wa:ʔ), which stands at the center of the earth. The hunter watched this strange giant go by several times, and for a long time the being was unaware that he was being watched. He did not see the man. He was carrying a bark rattle (gasnǫ gastawẹʔsäʔ), *for the turtle rattle is late and the Gagǫhsaʔ first used the bark rattle.*

The hunter had no idea what this stranger was doing. He thought that he was a strange animal, as if he were a new species come to live in the timber. Only later did he find out what he is.

This big fellow talked a strange, unintelligible language: *hǫʔǫʔǫʔ ǫʔǫʔ* (I heard it about five years ago [1928] when they were laying an extra track along the Erie railroad. It was raining. There must still be some of them alive.)

Every time Gagǫhsaʔ rested he rubbed his rattle on the tree, where the bark was all gone thin where his rattle had polished it smooth. He circled the tree, rubbing his rattle up and down all over it, emitting his mournful complaint: *hǫʔǫʔǫʔǫʔǫʔ*.

At last this hunter and Gagǫhsaʔ fell to talking, and Gagǫhsaʔ told the hunter what he wanted. First, he wanted tobacco, and secondly, corn soup (the other one in the forest wanted mush. Both kinds talk the same language.) He said, "I can cure any kind of disease, no matter what it may be. I kill all disease. It does not matter whether the people know what kind it is. You merely call me with tobacco and I will come and help you."

Long afterward this same hunter made up the name Diyę?si?da-dí?as, "It Bumps Its Feet," for this kind of False Face. This kind has its own song which the hunter learned. They are supposed to wear *black* faces [masks].

Albert Jones (Snipe Clan) who was married to Jonas Snow's sister of the Hawk Clan confirmed that the great one carries a giant pine tree with the limbs lopped off from the ground to the top as a cane, and that he travels all over the world in a short time, but because he is "poison" (*?otgǫ?*) no one sees him. Masks representing Shagodyowéhgo:wa:h are black.

How the Seneca Learned What the False Face Likes to Eat
Clara Redeye, whose mother was Emma Turkey of the Hawk Clan and sister of Jonas Snow, served as my interpreter in early fieldwork at Allegany Reservation, but she had a fund of stories in her own right that she had heard from her grandmother, her father's mother, Lucy Gordon. The following False Face tale was collected in the summer of 1938 by my student Ann Schafer. (For Lucy Gordon's mask see Skinner 1925, 201, and Plate 17-1, p. 449 below.)

Real people lived here long ago who had faces like this. They lived underground in caves and tunnels, but they don't live there anymore. The Great Spirit drove them away. He considered them not fit to live among humans. They were not supposed to mingle with humans, but they really did no harm. Long ago when people were braver than now, they would go out into the rough places where they would see these creatures. They would appear in the daytime.

There were two Indians who went hunting. They planned to stay for some days. (There is a certain thing that they prepare and take along for meals. If you eat it you won't get hungry for a while. This food was made of white corn roasted in a roasting pan in the fire. Then it is ground in a mortar and made into flour. Before people had sugar they added maple sugar. All hunters long ago used to take that with them. A bit of it will stop hunger. When they reached camp they would cook it by adding water to make a gruel, but when traveling, they would eat it raw.) Each of those hunters took along some of that flour. They would have to walk for days before they got ready to camp. Then they would stay there in the woods until they would get enough game to take home. They fixed up a camp and built a fireplace outside where they cooked their meals. When they finished their camp and straightened the fireplace, then they cooked something to eat. They had kindled a fire in the fireplace.

On the third day since they were in camp, when they returned in the evening from hunting, they found that someone had raided their fireplace, scattering the ashes and their gear. At first they blamed a bear or a wolf, or some animal. Well, this went on for two days. It was always the same way when they returned, ashes scattered everywhere.

The next morning they decided to find out who came to their fireplace. They pretended to go hunting. But they stayed near camp. They hid in the bushes from where they could see the fireplace. Pretty soon they saw someone come from the forest, and they did not know what it was. It had a face like that [mask]. They had never seen anything like it before. Their first impulse was to run, but they stayed. They watched it come up to their camp for two mornings. One of the two said, "Let us stay for a couple more days to see if it would harm us."

The night before they were to leave, this same man had a dream that he was talking with what they had seen. That creature told him that he wanted some of their corn flour. He said that if they would give it to him, he would help them to have good luck. When they reached home they were to tell their people about him and the others [of his kind]. He was not the only one. Whenever they wanted to talk to him, they should throw Indian tobacco in the fire. Then, while they talked, he would hear them, and that that was the proper way.

And that is the way the ceremony for the False Faces began. He also taught this hunter what song they were to sing.

This hunter remembered all that he was told—what to do and what to say when he talked with the Indian tobacco. The visitor said that he had great power to help the sick. He added that the reason he could not appear himself to the people was because they [the False Faces] were too powerful. People would get nosebleed. So he instructed the hunter to make these masks to represent them, that the masks would be just as effective as they themselves. They were always to have mush of that powdered corn when they performed the ceremony and thought of him. That was what he liked. Further, when anyone became sick, people would have the power to cure if they appealed to him.

The two hunters returned home and remembered everything that this False Face had told them, which they related to the chiefs of their village. When the chiefs of a village hear anything like that they always call a council and talk over what they have heard. And the chiefs thought it would be of great help to them if they followed this advice. So that is how the False Face Society started.

And they still keep it up in the same way. One has to make that mush of roasted corn.

AN ONONDAGA HAPPENING

The False Face Society has maintained its preeminence at Onondaga Valley, near Syracuse, from the midnineteenth century (Beauchamp 1892, 1905; DeCost Smith 1888, 1889) to the present day (Blau 1966, 1967; Hendry 1964). Humans have encountered the masks spirits in rocky places amid the glaciated hills and valleys east of Onondaga. Beauchamp (1892, 84–85) recorded a story connected with Green Pond, west of Jamesville, known as Tue-yah-dah-so, "Hemlocks in the Water."

> This pond was the reputed ancient resort of the False Faces for their great mysteries. An Onondaga one night heard many voices there, and crept quietly to the edge of the high rocks [that bound the pond on three sides]. Looking down from the brink of the precipice, he saw the False Faces coming up out of the water, heavily loaded with fish. They were merrily shouting, "*hoh! hoh-o-o-oh!*" as they came. But their leader called out, "Someone is coming! Look out!" So they entered the rock wall in single file. The hunter heard their voices in the rocks far under him, until their songs died away, and all was quiet again.

THE GOOD HUNTER, THE FALSE FACES, AND THE STONE GIANTS: GIBSON-GOLDENWEISER

In the second decade of this century Alexander Goldenweiser, working with Chief Gibson, of the Onondaga Longhouse, at Middleport, on Grand River, collected an extended English version, about thirty-six typescript pages, of the adventures of the Good Hunter among the False Faces and the Stone Giants. In his summary report for 1912, he characterized this long myth as follows:

> The prevailing type of myth is an epic account of the wanderings and achievements of a pure young man, often an orphan, who is an expert runner and hunter. Possessed by a wanderlust or a desire to find out where the dead people go he starts out alone, or accompanied by his bride, for the forest, hunts as he goes on, secures the friendship of the wild animals by sharing with them the produce of his chase, has encounters with the stone giants or pygmies, or the False Faces, obtains from them, often in exchange for some power of his own, various magical objects, incidentally witnesses the performance of the Death Feast or Dark Dance or a lacrosse game (which he subsequently introduces among his people), safely returns to his village, and henceforth becomes an influential man owing to his knowledge and powers.

> In these myths a day is always equal to a year, and animals always appear in the shape of men.
>
> In one myth [the one in question], an Indian stranded in an unknown country, wanders on through the forest. Every night he addresses the wild animals and leaves for them the larger part of the products of his chase; the animals in turn protect him; he meets the False-face, enters the False-face village; presents them with 12 wooden bowls [actually elm bark bowls], and 12 bows and arrows of his own making. In return they promise to appear to him in dreams and warn him of dangers. Later he meets the Stone-Giant, narrowly escapes death from his terrible voice, is pursued by the giant [whom he foils at a river crossing], but finally cuts him to pieces with the giant's own axe. [Stone Giants have pointed heads and fused necks and cannot swim.] From him he obtains a magic skin which gives him power over all the animals, and a stone finger, which, in falling, indicates a desired direction. The Indian returns to his village and, being warned by the False-faces, of the approaching enemy, organizes a war party, falls upon the enemy, and exterminates them [Goldenweiser 1914, 474]

The plot of the myth of the Good Hunter, in its variant versions, is essentially that of the origin of the Little Water Society and of the Eagle Dance (Fenton 1953, 80; 1979, 607).

ASSOCIATING WITH TREES

There is a strong belief that False Faces are associated with trees, particularly the basswood that imparts its medicinal qualities to masks. F. W. Waugh, a persistent fieldworker for the National Museum of Canada at Six Nations Reserve on Grand River, in 1914 heard from Peter John a story of the origin of the False Faces that was then current in the neighborhood of Onondaga Longhouse:

> A long time ago a man was out in the bush when he heard a noise such as False Faces are supposed to make. He looked around and after a while saw a False Face attached to and forming part of a tree. He then chopped the False Face off the tree and took it home. This occurred way off in the West where the False Faces are supposed to live. Afterward, he hollowed the False Face out and put it on. Others then made False Faces like this one.

Jonas Snow, a Seneca carver at Allegany, told me this same story in 1924, when, as a lad of sixteen, I accompanied my father on a collecting trip.

According to Peter John, there are only two kinds of False Faces: the red and the black. In his view, the red have more power, and a man having a red mask will put it on and dance for a sick person and scatter ashes on his head, to cure a person having a sickness caused by False Faces. But Simeon Gibson held that both kinds of masks have the same powers. And Albert Jonas, a Seneca of Allegany, maintained that the black ones are more powerful. There seems to be no consensus on color.

FURTHER BELIEFS CONCERNING FALSE FACES

Not only are False Faces derived from trees, but they can disappear into trees. And the Thunders—"Our Grandfathers Whose Voices Reverberate from Toward the Sunset"—have some power of regulating them. According to Jake Hess, a Cayuga ritualist and carver at Six Nations, "gagǫ́hsa? draws lightning when it goes into a tree to hide itself. Then the lightning will strike and smash it to pieces. Moreover it can change its face and form many times as it goes from tree to tree." (J. Hess to F. W. Waugh, Field Notebook No. 9 [1915].)

The trees with which False Faces are specifically associated cover a wide range in my field notes. Some informants mention the giant pine or elm that stands in the center of the earth, where the mask spirit stops to rub his rattle and from which he restores his strength. Others identify the basswood or the cucumber; and a Seneca ritualist said the common False Faces frequent groves of hard maples and that carving blocks were taken from these hardwood trees. I have seen a few maple masks, many of pine, cucumber, and basswood, but never of elm.

Other folk beliefs concerning the masks occur presently in connection with their care and neglect.

6. The Window on Tradition

Classes of Wooden Medicine Masks

Rationalizing from the two prevailing types of origin legends, the Iroquois conceive two main classes of False Faces. As Hewitt insisted, the masks that represent the beings in the legends are likenesses or representations, and in no way disguises. The masks that represent the great figures of mythology operate on the principle of substituting a part for the whole; they suggest the being to the beholder, and it is not necessary to depict the entire figure. First is the leader of the False Faces, the great fellow who lived on the rim of the earth, and second, his underlings, the common forest people whose faces are against the trees.

SHAGODYOWEH, OR HADUʔIʔ: THE DOORKEEPER

The Seneca and Onondaga, and their counterparts at Six Nations Reserve, conceive the "great one" somewhat differently. The Seneca call the great one *Shagodyowehgo:wa:h hadjaʔdothaʔ*, literally, "The Great Defender, or Protector/He Doctors," or "Our Protector the Doctor." He is earthbound and travels from east to west following the path of the sun. He is tall and carries a great staff, made from a giant pine or shagbark hickory tree with its branches lopped off to the top. He walks rapidly with great strides, bumping his staff and shaking the earth. In his right hand he carries a huge snapping-turtle rattle, and he stops at noon to rest and rub his rattle on the giant elm or pine that stands in the center of the earth and from which he derives great strength or power (Plate 6-1, Figure 6-1). Sources at Tonawanda said that his face is red in the morning as he comes from the east (for the sun precedes him and illuminates his face), but black in the afternoon as he looks back from the direction of the sun setting behind him. He controls high winds and has a wary eye for pestilences that are thought to be windborn and might destroy the people. One of his songs refers to this power to control wind and disease. Because of his magic power, few persons have seen him. He has two characteristic dances: In one he kicks out his feet and spars, his thumbs pointed in the air as if he were about to fall over backward. (In ritual, the masker dances opposite a woman as in a square dance routine, and the gestures have a suggestive sexual connotation.) Having made the people imitate him, in the second, he organizes them in a round dance in which they bump their feet alternately as if to shake the earth, while he or his partner watches the door to see that no one leaves or enters.

The Onondaga and their counterparts in Canada call him Haduʔiʔgo:na, "The Great Hunchbacked One," and stress this aspect of his demeanor. He claims the same rites.

Masks representing him have long hair. They are painted red or black and portray the broken nose and pain he suffered when the mountain

Plate 6-1. Shagodyowehgo:wa:h, "Their Great Protector," as portrayed by Sherman Redeye, wearing his father's mask. Allegany Reservation, 1933.

struck his face. Among the Seneca a few masks have high-bridged noses, and all have protruding lips, which are twisted with the nose or away from it, or are straight, hanging or flaring like two funnels, or flattened like spoons, for blowing ashes.

Recalling the legend of how the Onondaga masks reached Grand River and reconsidering my reconstructed chart of the maskers' world (Figure 5-1), it seems possible that the divided mask that has both a crooked face and is red on the East and black on the West sides has as its prototype the mask spirit standing at the midsky looking south. Such masks, however, represent a possibility of native theory that is seldom actualized in practice. Most masks representing this being from Grand River are either red or black (Plate 6-2).

COMMON FACES OF THE FORESTS, OR "FACES ALONE": DANCING MASKS

The second class of wooden masks are the so-called Common Faces, literally "Only Faces," who inhabit the forests (Plate 6-3A,B). Primarily bodiless heads, they are represented in myth and ritual as deformed beings, either hunchbacked or crippled below the waist. Some carry rattles, made by folding a rind of hickory bark; a few possess turtle rattles; others only have tincans filled with stones. Still others have only a stick or pole that they all carry. They crave mush and beg for tobacco. They have their own songs and a dance, during which they cure by blowing hot ashes. Masks of this category are ill-defined and include a great variety, among them the so-called beggar masks.

BEGGAR MASKS

Frequently new masks make their debut as beggars at the Midwinter Festival, or they appear first with the Common Faces in their ritual; but after they have been worn in many performances of the blowing-ashes rite, or they are borrowed and pass through the hands of several owners, they have accumulated several bags of tobacco offerings for their services, attained an antique color, and achieved sufficient prestige to graduate into the class of great doctor masks, where their sanctity is preserved by reputation. Everyone acknowledges that the older masks have more power.

MASKS OF RESTRICTED FUNCTION

Besides the first two categories and the beggar masks, which are not ordinarily used for curing, there are a number of masks of restricted func-

Plate 6-2. *Most Grand River masks representing Hadui, the world-rim dweller, are black or red. AMNH, Cat. No. 50/6480. Photo courtesy AMNH, New York.*

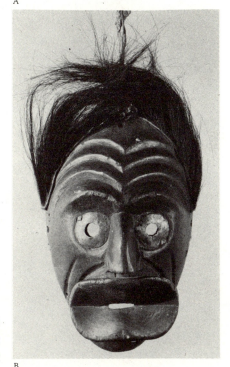

Plate 6-3. Faces Only of the Forests. A: These masks frequently feature upstanding hair. NYSM, Cat. No. 37051. B: A red beggar mask with upstanding hair. AMNH, Cat. No. 50.2/1153. Photo courtesy AMNH. (With long hair it might pass as a doorkeeper mask.)

tion about which little is known. Among these are the odd mask representing a Stone Giant (Parker 1909, Plate VIII, 2), certain "secret" masks used by the ʔI:ʔdo:s Medicine Society, particularly the so-called blind masks (those with restricted or no eyeholes) (Parker 1909, 173 and Plate 2-15). However, I have seen one or two particularly powerful masks of the False Face Company appear at Allegany during the rites of the Hadi:ʔdo:s, Parker's "Society of the Mystic Animals."

JOHN JIMMERSON'S CLASSES

John Jimmerson, of High Bank, who grew up at Cattaraugus and was the father of Avery Jimmerson, the distinguished carver of masks, specified four classes of False Faces known from his youth at Plank Road Longhouse.

> In the olden times there were four kinds of societies [four orders of masks]: (1) *Hodigohsóskaʔah* [Faces Only], the Forest Faces. A great company, sometimes a hundred, would enter the longhouse behind a leader who sings the song to the wind, moon and thunder (*ganoío:wi:ʔ*) [which is believed to quiet the wind]. (2) A few maskers of the same class enter a private house, or the longhouse, when everything [tobacco and mush] is ready for them. [These two orders constitute the Common Faces.] (3) The greatest of all are the *shagodyowéhgo:wa:h*—the great wind masks; and they are four faces of all [different] colors: one is red, one is white, another is black, and the last is blue, which is a secret mask. [The white and blue are of a class of secret masks belonging to Honǫtshinǫhkɛʔ, the so-called Charmholder's Society.[1]]
>
> He [Shagodyowéhgo:wa:h] is the same all over [everywhere]. He is a tall fellow. His cane is of a great pine tree with the limbs lopped off to the top. As he traverses the earth, he stops to rest in the center of the world where stands a giant pine on which he rubs his rattle. These faces are generally *red*. He has a big distended mouth.

I asked John specifically about the face with bifunnelate lips, which he said "is any kind." It could belong to several orders. He volunteered that the "funny-looking masks are beggars" and added that "the whistling one is also a beggar and merely wants tobacco. Still others cure."

He later described a medicine society ritual at Cattaraugus that involved his four colored faces, already mentioned, in which each was asso-

---

1. John then owned a white face that he said was secret and belonged to this order. He added, "It is the grandfather of all the False Faces." A decade later John's son Avery, having inherited the mask, stated that his father "used it if a woman had a hard time when a baby came." (Avery Jimmerson, personal communication to C. E. Congdon, 1942.) This is the only recent suggestion, unconfirmed, of the

Plate 6-4. Especially powerful masks may be held "secret" or secluded. A: John Jimmerson's white mask, with multiple bundles, alleged to have been used in childbirth. Courtesy C. E. Congdon. B: The medicine mask of William Lee, which graduated through the ranks to the class of "doctor."

A

B

ciated with a cardinal direction: red (south), white (west), black (east), and blue (north). Deferring the description of the rite to a later chapter, its importance here is that his orientation of the black and red masks contradicts the usual placement of red (east) and black (west).

East–West Color Symbolism at Tonawanda

On two occasions, Chief Lyman Johnson (Thäwa:nyaʔs), of the Wolf Clan and speaker of Tonawanda Longhouse, showed me his masks and explained the east–west, red-black symbolism. He said that an old black mask with a broken nose was Shagodyowéhgo:wa:h, the great doctor or wind mask. The other two were merely common faces of the forest. Dáhon, as we called him, said that the old people told him that if one summoned the False Faces in the morning, the red ones would appear; toward evening or at night, the black ones would appear. This is especially true if the person is sponsoring the Doorkeeper Dance. Chief Johnson explained the color symbolism of the divided mask to me the following year.

> The Great False Face promised the Creator: "I am sitting both on the east and on the west. If someone calls me in the morning, I will come down from the east; if someone calls me in the afternoon, I will come down from the west." When he comes from the east his face is red (because he is looking toward the sun which he follows); and when he comes from the west, his face is black (because the sun is behind him). He follows the path of the sun.

Chief Johnson had never seen a divided mask that is half red and half black at Tonawanda. This maks is usually longitudinally separated into a red half on the left and black on the right, or vice versa. But he had seen it in Canada, among the Onondaga at Syracuse, and at Newtown among the Cattaraugus Seneca. He had once accompanied Joseph Keppler (Gayentwaʔkeh) on a collecting trip to Canada.

Jesse Cornplanter's Two Classic Doorkeepers

The one person to whom I owe much of my understanding of the False

---

"maternity" concept, which midwives whom I consulted consistently denied. Note the apparent confusion between this group of secret masks and the leaders of the False Faces proper, the so-called Shagodyowéhgo:wa:h. Henry Redeye confirmed the notion that a whole group of masks at Allegany was affiliated with the Charm Holder's Society. He named John Jimmerson's white mask; William Lee's mask, then owned by his son (Plate 6-4A, B); and a mask of Hannah Abrams, known as Yändi, that had belonged to her late husband. John called his last group or class (No. 4) *deyɛhsiʔtatíus*, which is the name of the round dance in which the maskers organize the public into joining, in which they alternately bump their feet. It is the so-called Doorkeeper's Dance. These are the doorkeeper masks, so called from their office and rite.

Faces was Jesse Cornplanter, of Tonawanda, a native of Newtown on Cattaraugus whose ways he preferred. Both in conversations and in his book (1938, 210), he recalled, specified, and illustrated the spoon mouth with spines over the nose, which he called "turtle's tail," as the proper doorkeeper, or medicine mask. Its Newtown counterpart was a similar mask having straight, distended lips. He illustrated these two mask types time and again in his letters and carved beautiful examples during the 1930s (Plate 2-4B; 6-5A, B). Unlike James Crow and Kelley Lay who carved many such masks at Newtown, now in museum collections, Jesse omitted the "turtle tail" motif in the example illustrated (Plate 6-5A, C; and Plate 2-4B).

Allegany Seneca sources were less specific as to what type of mask should perform the role of doorkeeper. Some ritualists specified black masks, but others said color was unimportant. But they asserted that the two men in this role must be of opposite moieties. Still others said that color was specified in the dream, or perhaps the patient dreamed of both colors, but clearly the culture has not resolved this issue (Plate 6-6).

Ambiguity over Restricted Function
Nor is it clear which masks have a restricted function. Chauncey Johnny John, of Allegany, asserted that no special mask serves in ʔi:ʔdo:s; it need be only an old False Face. "Sometime they use mine" (Plate 7-2C). As for the blind masks in the New York State Museum (Parker 1909, 173), Chauncey treated them as a joke. He pretended that he had never heard of them, although he grew up at Cattaraugus at the time. Either he was censoring, or he was ignorant, and I suspect the latter. He did recall, however, that, in his youth at Cattaraugus, they had a special mask at Plank Road Longhouse settlement that was used in ʔi:ʔdo:s. It belonged to old Sam Jimmerson, father of John, already quoted, and it was a white one. Whenever Sam Jimmerson sponsored a feast for ʔi:ʔdo:s (the Medicine Company), "he would take it out of the box and let someone use it" to impersonate the False Face. Chauncey said it resembled one in the U.S. National Museum (Catalog # 221,152) of which I showed Chauncey a picture. "It was painted white and it had white hair. The lips were painted red. But when I came to live at Coldspring [Allegany] I found they used any mask for ʔi:ʔdo:s." He added that the Jimmerson mask was definitely not of the spoonmouth type. Chauncey's observation confirms my own record of an ʔi:ʔdo:s ceremony that I witnessed at Coldspring Longhouse in September of 1939. On that occasion Jonas Snow impersonated the masked visitor.

Jesse Cornplanter was the one person who should have had some knowledge of blind masks because Edward Cornplanter, his father, was Parker's informant. Three months after my discussion with Chauncey in June of 1940, I asked Jesse about the appearance of a blind mask in the ʔi:ʔdo:s ceremony. Jesse asserted that he had never witnessed a blind mask in this ceremony. His father, however, related how certain songs in his

Plate 6-5. Classic Newtown Seneca doorkeeper masks. A: Spoon-mouth mask by Jesse Cornplanter, Tonawanda, 1936. RMSC Collection. B: Doorkeeper mask with straight distended lips. The second of paired doorkeepers by Jesse Cornplanter, 1935–36. RMSC Collection. C: Spoon or flare-mouth mask from Newtown, Cattaraugus Reservation, by James Crow or Kelly Lay. Note the "turtle tail" motif in the ridge of spines above the nose in B and C. MAI-HF, Cat. No. 16/4795.

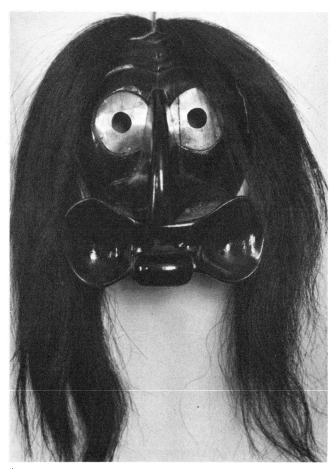

A

B

C

version of the rite refer to "limestone," which marks the place in the ceremony where a shaman entered wearing a blind mask.

Now, ʔi:ʔdo:s is the "play ritual" of the Medicine Company, in which shamans would juggle hot stones, and one wearing a blind mask would brush over a corn husk doll (which is referred to in particular songs as gayaʔdaʔ) that stood on the bottom of an inverted corn mortar. These feats demonstrated the power of the shaman to see through a mask that lacked eyeholes.

MINIATURES

Miniature False Faces constitute a class apart only by virtue of their diminutive size. Treated earlier in the formal classification, I shall add here some specifics garnered in the Coldspring Longhouse community. By 1933 the Small False Face (nigagǫsáʔah) had ceased to be a dream object. Emma Turkey, matron of the Hawk Clan, had an old one that was made

Plate 6-6. *An old black "doctor" mask with rudimentary bifunnelate mouth, attributed to the Seneca of the Genesee Valley. Keppler Collection, MAI-HF, Cat. No. 9148.*

by some Canadian Iroquois at Six Nations Reserve. It was considered a household protector. I was told that miniatures were sometimes hung on the large masks so that they would carry them along in their Traveling Rite.

Small boys frequently commence carving by making miniatures. I watched Bemis Snow making a small one when I was resident with the family of Jonas Snow, a renowned carver. It was by way of practice prefatory to making larger ones.

The following summer, Sherman Redeye, then a grown man, spent a large part of his spare time during the two weeks of August before the Green Corn Dance carving a miniature False Face about five inches long from a chunk of basswood. His wife, Clara, anticipated sponsoring a meeting of the Common False Faces (Hodigǫhsóskaʔah) when it was finished. "Then the headman will burn tobacco and ask this miniature False Face to protect this house and the land." She added, "Sherman is anxious to keep his mother's estate that was awarded him in the Ten Days' Feast after she died from the claim of the senior children of his mother by her first husband." Sherman's father, Henry Redeye, the second husband, "went to Canada last fall to preach the Handsome Lake revelation at the Canadian longhouses." While there "a man told Henry that if he had a miniature False Face made, it would protect the house."

Because larger masks are thought to protect a house, it would seem that miniatures are used in covert ways and are thought to have more power even as surrogates than the larger masks that they represent.

The more serious aspects of miniature masks as dream objects made and presented by the dream guesser to the dreamer continue at Onondaga (Blau 1967, 568) and at Six Nations (Fenton 1942b, 16–18; Shimony 1961, 183). Persons who have had these particular dreams keep such objects during their lifetimes, renew the ceremonies on anniversaries of their presentation, and regard them as sacred. In the same communities, miniatures are made for the tourist trade and sold in Indian curio shops along with other knicknacks. Thus, there is a fine line between the sacred and the profane.

Masking of Three Orders of Medicine Societies

SEMIANNUAL HOUSE PURGING: THE TRAVELING RITE

Among the contemporary Iroquois, three distinct medicine societies employ masks. These societies perform their rituals in public or in private, usually with a prepared feast, but sometimes without. At Six Nations, this is called "dry pole," when no kettle is hung for the maskers (Shimony 1961, 283).

The Society of (Wooden) Faces

The False Face Company, they who wear the wooden masks, comprises both orders of medicine masks—the Common Faces and the Shagodyoweh, or Hadu?i?—who have three distinct rituals. Most spectacular and perhaps best known are their public appearances. In spring and autumn, the entire company goes from house to house and then to the longhouse exorcising diseases from the settlement, concluding with the performance of all their rites and a feast involving the entire community. Then, at the Midwinter Festival, smaller bands appear at the longhouse to enable persons to fulfill particular dreams or renew them. If one is present when either of these appearances occurs, it is impossible to remain ignorant of their existence, and in this sense the False Faces are not a secret society. Among the Seneca, the public appearance of the beggars and thieves during several nights of the midwinter ceremonies are merely a motley group of boys (and girls at Tonawanda) who sometimes "take sick" afterward and thereby gain admittance to the society.

The Common Faces

The second ritual belongs to the Common Faces who enter a house, dance, and blow ashes on a patient. This is sometimes called the "Blowing Ashes Rite" (Plate 12-1).

The Doorkeeper's Dance

The third rite is when the Common Faces combine with, and are followed by, the two maskers representing the great world-rim dweller whose ritual is the Doorkeeper's Dance. This, as we shall see, has two parts. Sponsors or patients may belong and celebrate any combination of these rites. The Society of Faces, therefore, is the body of people who have been cured by the masked company of the wooden faces of whatever rank. Husk Face messengers are optional in the two previous rites.

THE HUSK FACES, OR "BUSHY HEADS"

The separate society of Husk Faces has its own invocation, its own songs, and a special curing dance. The Husk Faces appear publicly at least twice during the Seneca Midwinter Festival. Membership is gained by dream or cure, though nonmenbers join in their public dances at the end of the line. Both among the Seneca and in Canada, Husk Faces act as heralds for the False Faces, watch the door, and police the rites. Among the Canadian Iroquois the Husk Faces seem more specialized.

HADI:ʔDO:S: THE MEDICINE COMPANY, OR THE SOCIETY OF MYSTIC ANIMALS

The third society that employs masks is the Medicine Company (Hadi:-ʔdo:s, Seneca, or Hanáhi:ʔdo:s, Onondaga), which Parker called the Society of Mystic Animals. I have already alluded to the magic feats of the shaman wearing a blind mask, the juggling of hot stones, and other boasts of power. Its celebrations involve a round dance (*ganónyahgwę̨ʔ*), and its more elaborate phase, a great round dance (*ganonyahgwę̨ʔgo:wa:*).

Membership

LIMITED PARTICIPATION

The Society of Faces, or the False Face Society, is a restricted medicine society in that participation in its rites is limited to its members, but it is in no way a secret society. Its membership is known to most persons in the community, and the maskers, having impersonated the supernaturals in the rites, reenter the lodge of the patient and share in the feast afterward. Only in the Traveling Rite do the maskers enter a house and leave still masked and do not return unmasked for the feast, which is set down for them at the longhouse, where they enter, leave, and then return unmasked.

My views on the question of secrecy differ from those of earlier writers on the subject, notably Morgan (1901, 1:159), Parker (1909, 179), as implied by the title of his article, and most recently, Hendry (1964, 365). Parker is the one to be respected in this matter, but it is important to know that he was deeply involved in Masonic mysteries. This is evident in a later treatment of the subject (Parker 1923, 400–401), in which two things emerge: the element of secrecy and the derivation of power from the Genonsgwaʔ, or Stone Giants. "The society was to be a most secret one and only for a qualified number. Its mettings were to be held only when the moon was away." We read further that "the Company was to have no outward sign and members were to recognize one another only by having sat together in a ceremony." Parker's source was Edward Cornplanter, father of Jesse, but in all of my conversations with the son nothing of this emerged. Perhaps I was among the Seneca in a more relaxed period. Today, secrecy and sacredness are watchwords of the militants who spurn ethnologists and insist that museums remove all masks from exhibit and return them.

OTHER VIEWS ON "SECRECY"

The Reverend William Beauchamp of Onondaga (1892, 84) at first thought the False Faces formed a secret society but later changed his mind after reading David Boyle's report of fieldwork at the Grand River Reserve (Boyle 1898, 157ff.). Boyle was ambivalent as to whether the False Faces were indeed a secret society. He quotes Morgan's report to the regents (1852) and says he undertook his inquiry at the suggestion of Gen. John S. Clark of Auburn, NY. Informants denied the existence of any such society until "one intelligent Indian assured me that he knew everyone who took part," that no attempt was made at secrecy, and the dancers might be viewed at any time, both before and after masking. Boyle acknowledged that such openness might be recent (Boyle 1898, 158). On further inquiry, he did find out that there was a second "secret" order of False Faces, of which most Indians on the reserve were ignorant. He speaks of new members being approved by existing members, rather than entering via a dream or cure, and he cites a formal charge to the neophyte by the "Chief False Face" and a pledge to adhere to the ancient customs, followed by the announcement of his name in the longhouse, and there was a provision for censoring errant members. Boyle concluded: "To a very large extent the secrecy that formerly characterized the False Faces no longer exists" (p. 159). They held regular meetings from which nonmembers were excluded, so in that sense it was a restricted, rather than secret, society. Two matrons acted as mediums of communication between the society and outsiders, just as Morgan stated, but these women mainly cook the feast. In 1898, Abraham Buck (Onondaga) served as "Chief of the False Faces" (Plate XV, near p. 81 of Boyle 1898).

OFFICERS

The officers of the False Face Society are known by the following terms in Onondaga and in Seneca. The Onondaga terms were given by Simeon Gibson in 1940; the Seneca terms come from several sources.

1. Male leader of the Company on semiannual rounds
   (a) (Onondaga) *honduʔiʔ họwagowa:neh,* "headman, or commander of *haduʔiʔ*"
   (b) (Seneca) *hodigọhsaʔshọʔọ honọsteistọ,* "False Face conductor"
2. Women cooks, one from each moiety, appointed for life to cook for the society at the longhouse
   (a) (Onondaga) *deyọhéhgwih o:nasdeisdi,* "our food they manage"
   (b) (Seneca) *deknisenowa.neh shagodyoweh,* "the two head women of the False Faces"
3. Women who oil the masks (distinct from the preceding)
   (a) (Onondaga) *howadiʔhnai:s gagọ́hsaʔ,* "they oil the masks"

(b) (Seneca) This office not found among Seneca, but women who dress the maskers: hawenǫhsya:ni

Membership is open to both men and women, but women never wear the wooden masks. Seneca girls do put on Husk Faces to represent male visitors, and boys dress as female spirits, when the entire company visits the longhouse at midwinter.

As in other Iroquois medicine societies, entrance to the Society of Faces follows a particular dream, when a clairvoyant prescribes one of its rituals to cure a sickness, or by particpation. A patient automatically joins all of the societies that assist in his or her recovery, and he or she must afterward sponsor any combination of rituals that has assisted his or her recovery. Thus, the Society of Faces includes all persons who have been cured by the False Face Company. Membership in the several orders of the society, or participation in the rituals of the masked company, depend on the personal history of the individual. The masked company is composed of men who wear masks of the orders that cured them, but both men and women sponsor the rituals and belong to the orders that have accepted them for membership in the society by making them sick in the first instance. It is the spirits and not the maskers, except by transference, who cause and relieve the False Face sickness. Afterward, members are obliged to "put up a feast" every year for the orders that have helped them. Among the Seneca, the patient or sponsor calls in the headwoman of the opposite moiety and asks her to conduct the ceremony.

Membership rarely ceases, but that occurs when one dreams that one has been released. Then the person knows that he or she is no longer a member. So it has been since Morgan first described it (1852; 1901, 1:158).

Matrons

Among the Cattaraugus Seneca, the woman leader assumes a more active role than at Allegany. She actually leads the band of maskers as they go from house to house, and she carries, as emblem of her office, a staff from which hang, at the top, a miniature False Face and Husk Face. Sturtevant (1983) has recently written from the viewpoint of his fieldwork at Cattaraugus.

The Seneca, to my knowledge, have no chief male officer of the False Faces. On a given occasion, some knowledgeable man is appointed to lead the band of maskers and speak for them, make the tobacco invocations, and perhaps sing for them. This role tends to devolve on the same person, or persons, as occasion demands. Ability to perform is the main criterion. At Allegany, however, there are two matrons of the society, one from each moiety, who determine the date of the ceremony, prepare and direct the feast, appoint conductors, speakers and singers, keep the bag of community-owned Husk Faces, dress the maskers, and direct their annual appearance at the Midwinter Festival. We shall encounter these officers again and learn more of their duties in the descriptions of actual ceremonies.

Conductor, Singers, Invoker

Other than the matrons, there are no other formal statuses in the Society of Faces. The conductor of the ritual, the singers, and the invoker who burns tobacco and addresses the spirits of the maskers are roles performed by persons, normally men, who are selected by the matrons because they know the songs and prayers. There is a tendency for the same individuals to fulfill these roles on repeated occasions because their knowledge is recognized in the community, and they are called upon repeatedly. But others can and do perform these roles, although they may not be so much in evidence until the first choices are unavailable. Such knowledge was more widely shared a generation or two ago than at present. Today the matrons have fewer choices. I have always been amazed how in a crisis someone surfaces and the ceremonies go on.

Women Who Oil the Masks

In the 1940s, I found the False Face Society among the adherents to the Onondaga Longhouse on Grand River apparently as active as it was thirty years earlier when observed by Alexander Goldenweiser. They still celebrate their ceremony twice a year, in spring and late autumn (Goldenweiser's notes read "summer"), and they participate in the Midwinter Festival. As in Goldenweiser's time, there are women members, one of whom is appointed to annoint the masks with sunflower oil (*uwä?ų sa ?ó?hna?*) before the maskers start out of the longhouse to visit the houses of the settlement. Since my observations, Speck (1949) and Shimony (1961) have confirmed that the society is alive and well in the Upper and Lower Cayuga longhouses at Six Nations Reserve.

The False Face Sickness

SYMPTOMS

Symptoms of the False Face sickness are ailments of the head, shoulders, and joints. Masks are believed to cause and cure swelling of the face, toothache, inflammation of the eyes, nose bleeding, sore chin, earache, and facial paralysis. At Tonawanda, appearance of red spots on the patient's face are deemed False Face symptoms and call for the red Faces to dance in the morning before sunrise. Black spots require the use of black masks at night. Imaginary hair lying on the patient's face, indicated by attempts to brush it aside, is interpreted as a False Face symptom. When the patient complains to the old people, they consult a clairvoyant who prescribes a False Face ceremony. To ridicule the masks or any of their ceremonies is to invite sickness or misfortune, as later cases will demonstrate.

Participation by nonmembers in the doings of the society and by young boys who aspire to carving or join the maskers in their rounds may lead to sickness, curing, and lifelong membership. One learns at Grand River that the men who wear the wooden faces represent the so-called False Face or Humpbacked people who are spirits (*da:gwa*) capable of sending sickness, pestilence, and famine. It is said that they used to live on a big mountain near Onondaga Castle in New York but that they became scattered during the American Revolution, at the time some of the Onondaga removed toward Grand River. Now they are thought to live somewhere in the west where there are no people. "No one ever sees them now," Goldenweiser was told in 1912. His informant (possibly Peter John) said he never saw one of the spirits, nor had he ever met anyone who had seen them, but some people he had met knew other people who had seen them. So the belief lingers that the spirits exist and that they can and do cause illnesses. The source continued that a boy who becomes preoccupied with carving miniature False Faces often becomes ill and joins the society at the suggestion of his parents. He is cured and becomes a member of the society. Therefore, in later life when he puts on his mask and joins the company of maskers during their semiannual rounds of the houses, he does so in the belief that he has the power to cure any of the symptoms mentioned previously. It is unimportant that his contemporaries in the society have not encountered supernatural medicine men wandering in the forests because the origin myths, as narrated by the old people at the big ceremony twice a year, remind the laity of their heritage and of their obligations. (Simeon Gibson, on reviewing Goldenweiser's field notes on August 15, 1940.)

One of Goldenweiser's sources held that one way to join the society was to wear a mask when the False Faces go about, to get sick, be cured, and then become a member. This informant believed that the motivation to join was deliberate. In his *Summary Report of 1912,* Goldenweiser cited the caseof a then-skilled carver who as a young boy used to amuse himself by carving small False Faces. "His parents objected to the practice and put a stop to it. About two months later the boy fell sick. Then his parents advised him to join the False Faces. He was cured and became a member of the society" (1913, 472). This is the same case mentioned previously.

CASES

Goldenweiser did record a partial vision. He writes:

> Some three years ago [1909] an Oneida man of powerful frame and great strength, suddenly became ill. He could not locate the source

of his trouble but felt his strength waning from day to day. His weight was rapidly decreasing. While . . . thus afflicted, it so happened that he was traveling alone in the woods. Suddenly he heard a strange whistle which he readily identified as the voice of the False-face. Being of a skeptical disposition, he did not pay much heed to the incident, and reached home. Meanwhile his illness grew worse, and twice the False-face appeared to him in a dream, and spoke to him. Then he resolved to call in the False-faces. They performed their rites, and presently he felt relieved. Of course he joined the society. [Goldenweiser 1913, 472. Recorded in Oneida text; later translated by S. Gibson for the author]

The sickness can occur without an accompanying dream. Then it is up to the parents to consult a clairvoyant. Clairvoyants are certain old people who are well versed in the traditional lore. These prophets interpret dreams, practice divinations, and in a subtle way contribute to the maintenance of the old ways (Goldenweiser 1913, 473; Shimony 1961). On accepting the advice, the patient appeals to the appropriate medicine society, which he thereby joins and is afterward obligated to maintain its ceremony lest the spirits take revenge and he become again afflicted.

Goldenweiser's field notes supplemented by Simeon Gibson's translation of the Oneida text, amplify Goldenweiser's published statement of the case.

How Oneida Chief John Danford joined the False Face Society. The following bit of life history was dictated in Oneida and recorded in phonetic text in the manner that Boas trained his students. Chief Danford was then (1912) the oldest living man at Oneidatown (near London, Ontario), and he used to come and board with the family of Chief John A. Gibson while working for Goldenweiser. Simeon Gibson, then a boy at home, recalls the circumstances and was, therefore, the ideal person to interpret the text for me. Simeon recalled that Danford's tongue, conditioned as it was to speaking Oneida, could only render his employer's name "Goldenwisla," which became somewhat of a joke in the Gibson family. This case history represents almost our total knowlege of the False Face society among the Oneida in Canada. This aspect of traditional Oneida culture seems to have been derived and renewed by the Iroquois of Six Nations Reserve. Experiences of individuals among the Oneida like Chief Danford who were raised in the Christian faith, according to Simeon Gibson, were all that served to keep the Oneidatown Longhouse alive; indeed it almost died out in 1906 when Chief John Gibson was called there to requicken it.

Before I was a member of their organization whose guardian (lundluʔswayendʌ) has its face covered (atguʔsulʌ) (of the society whose guardian wears a mask), whenever they performed a feast they asked me as a favor to help them fulfill their ceremony. But I did not own membership [belong] at that time and for a long time afterward.

Long ago it happened that when on occasion I was walking at night in the bush, I heard behind me the sound of a rattle (ʔusdawɛ́sla) making a very loud noise. Also they were wearing masks and cried yµ yµ ʔµʔµʔµʔµh, and as I walked on for a ways, one made a noise with the rattle. Then I saw a fire beside the path. Just as I reached there I took out my pouch, and then I crushed the leaves. Then I cast the tobacco on the fire, saying, "Grandparent, the smoke arises." I asked him to please not molest me, and then I walked by very quietly. And then the noise ceased.

Not once did this recur for a long time. After many years' time I heard it again. At once I recalled what had happened the previous time. Immediately then I reached under my roof (dugadaʔsgwahɛlĩ) [either a camp or house roof], and again that time procured real tobacco which I cast on the fire, saying: "You all partake of the tobacco, you who wear masks (swatgµʔsulų́). Please don't let it happen to me again in the future days and nights to come. That is the length of the message."

For some time I had noticed that I felt queerly on my body, and I had no feelings of pain. I was growing weaker as I moved around. Moreover I then noticed that I was failing in flesh. [Later he became quite ill. One wonders whether these are classic anxiety neurosis symptoms?]

And then after a very long time it happened again. This time right where I was sleeping. Now he came there, the one of the mask (neʔ atgµsulų́), saying, "We want you to give us the kind of food we eat. Furthermore, offer tobacco for us. Now you know who I am." That is the way that the one who appeared in my dream said it should be.

[There follows an interpolation of what the old people said afterward.]

The old people warned me, saying, "Until you put up a feast, only then will you feel well disposed. And also you will recover when you become a member of the society (ladiyóhgwayɛʔ) of the False Face wearers (atgµso:lµ) as they are called." And then they told me, "They were the cause of your failing health."

Accordingly, when I awoke, and afterwards I noticed that immediately I was feeling better.

So then their officers made a feast for me. I gave these officers corn that had been parched and pounded into flour, made into mush of hominy corn, with lard thrown in. Then they invited the society of the mask wearers. They asked me for Indian tobacco, which I gave to them in the amount that the women officials had requested.

And then at nightfall the ceremony commenced. And then someone of my cousin side (*ugyalaʔgíshę*) [the opposite moiety] cast tobacco in the fire and prayed to the masked ones. And he also told them that everything they liked the most was ready for them: That there was a kettle set down full of mush. And he asked them to release me. And addressing me he said, "Now again you will be well and up and traveling in the days to come." This is the length of the prayer.

Now they called the masked ones there close to the fire. Then I sat down there [the patient sits by the fire], and then they commenced to blow ashes on me. And when they finished on me they stood me up, and then I was made to go around there where the masked ones were dancing.

And then the women [as if matrons of the society] made everyone stand up and dance. [Plainly this is the round dance called *deyolasiʔdadíhas,* "they put one foot in front," which will be discussed later at greater length.]

When he finished singing the song of the masks, their own song, it was then that the masked ones shared up their food. [This is the familiar Iroquois distribution in equal shares.]

Then at that time the speaker on my cousin side [of the opposite moiety] spoke: "Now it is fulfilled. We only hope that the ceremony will help him who invited us. Therefore [addressing the society] you shall all think that he has released us. So let us depart, keeping this in our minds, that we shall go now in under our own roofs (*dyųgwadaʔsgwaxlúnyų*) (to our homes).

[This ends the ceremony.]

Now after the time of that feast I noticed the beginning of a change (for the better) in my life. Now from that time, I say, I feel much better until the present. I believe that (this ceremony) is what helped me to be in as good health as I am now experiencing. That is what I truly believe.

These are all the words.

Other cases of neglected dreams and visionary experiences among the semi-Christianized Oneida of the Thames, which Chief Danford related to Goldenweiser, follow the discussion of hysterical possession on seeing the maskers in action.

HYSTERIA

Most Iroquoianists have heard of cases when persons became possessed and simulated False Face behavior when the maskers appeared and performed in the longhouse. Others perhaps resisted the commands of the maskers to join the round dance. No Iroquoianist, to my knowledge, has actually witnessed such an instance of catatonic behavior. These personality crises are not confined to either sex, although cases of women, reported from earliest times, may be more common. One is reminded of the descriptions of Huron shamans of the early seventeenth century handling live coals, pretending to swallow them, and throwing red-hot ashes in the eyes of onlookers (Champlain 1922–36, 3:151–52). Indeed, Champlain expressed amazement that patients did not die of the noise and confusion, let alone the violent treatment. He wrote: "There are also women who go into these rages," but they were less violent than the men and did less harm. Possessed, "they walk on fours like wild beasts," and he witnessed one instance when a shaman blew on her to bring the pronograde woman out of hysteria, in the manner of False Face doctors. Huron shamans also employed the familiar turtle-shell rattle. One order of maskers reminded Champlain of the Mardi Gras in France, when they paraded the length of the village while the feast was being prepared and the kettle set down for them (Champlain, Biggar, ed., 1922–36, 3:154–55). Although it may be tenuous to extrapolate from Huron to early Iroquois culture, the two people shared similar patterns including shamanistic behavior and quite possibly the same medicine societies. Dutch visitors to Oneida in January, 1635, were invited to attend a shamanistic rite more reminiscent of honaʔhi:do:s, the modern Medicine Company, than the False Faces, but participants handled and ate fire, and a turtle rattle was used (Jameson 1909, 152; Van den Bogaert Journal, MS. in the Henry E. Huntington Library).

It was Peter W. Doctor, a Seneca lay preacher at Tonawanda, who, during my residence in that community for the U.S. Indian Service in 1935 to 1938, called my attention to the phenomenon of hysterical possession that he thought was confined to certain nervous women who became possessed of the False Faces whenever the masked men appeared. On hearing the rumpus of whining and shaking rattles, which marks the approach of the maskers, a certain woman, whose case he cited, would fall into spasms, imitate their cry, and crawl toward the fire, and, unless she was restrained, plunge her hands into the glowing embers and scatter the fire, as if she herself were a False Face searching the hearth for tobacco. Someone always grabbed her and restrained her while someone else burned tobacco, imploring the masked men to cure her. The ritual usually restored her normal composure.

There were other women who became possessed of the tutelaries of the Bear and Buffalo societies. Peter Doctor used to think that these women became possessed to draw attention to themselves, or to show off. He added that some of these women were also clairvoyants.

Case 1. The Neophyte Masker and Mary Shongo. Peter Doctor, who related this case, remembered the former longhouse on Sand Hill near the southern end of Tonawanda Reservation. He was then a boy and in regular attendance at longhouse ceremonies. He recalled an incident that occurred on one Indian New Year (Midwinter Festival) that is best told in his own words:

> It was midday and quiet in the settlement when I, although I did not belong to the False Face Company, decided to put on a False Face, carry a rattle, and make the rounds of the houses in the settlement. (The regular ceremonial circuit to be visited included five houses—Isaac Hill's, Willie Peters's grandmother's, Mrs. Isaac Doxdater's, John Fish's, and Mary Shongo's—before returning to the longhouse. The longhouse stood east of the road, south of the present abandoned schoolhouse.)
>
> I had made the round without event, begging a little tobacco here, and food there. As I neared Mary Shongo's house, I heard voices conversing inside. Coming around the house, I rubbed the huge turtle rattle that I was carrying on the house wall, and I gave the cry of the False Face. As I came around to the door, I heard a crash within, and the reply of someone imitating a False Face. It was Mary crying like a False Face and crawling toward the fire pit. They held her as she attempted to plunge her bare hands into the coals. I went in. They wanted me to blow ashes on her. They put her on a chair. [My notes do not say that someone burned tobacco and made an invocation.] I blew hot ashes on her head, shoulders, and arms; and I felt of all her joints, pumping her arms and legs to take the stiffness out of them. I got hold of her breast too and shook that a little. [Here Peter laughed.] They sang two songs. I danced. They gave me lots of Indian tobacco.
>
> They never recognized me, but I cured her, even though I was not a full-fledged believer nor a bona fide member of the False Faces. My experimental journey about the settlement was sheer adventure.

Within Peter's observation, this form of hysteria seems to have been confined to women. Its particular form depended on the spirit that possessed them. "When a lady becomes possessed (waʔagodzaʔdo:wiʔ [Seneca], the hysteria signifies that the being [tutelary] has accepted her." Peter remembered a whole group of women at Tonawanda who formerly manifested hysteria whenever the False Faces appeared. "I always supposed that they wanted to show off." He mentioned a living woman who regularly went into hysteria and acted like a False Face.

If Peter Doctor was right in his sexist interpretation of hysteria, in that all of his cases were women, this type of possession is doubly interesting because the beings whom the False Faces represent are always dramatized by men. Although he did not recall having heard of men becoming possessed, he recognized the term hodzaʔdo:wiʔ, "he is possessed." But there are numerous male possession cases, as we shall see momentarily.

Case 2. An Onondaga Woman Possessed of a Bear. Peter Doctor visited Onondaga Longhouse at Syracuse years ago.

> I remember a woman there who was *godzaʔdowiʔ*, or hysterical from a bear. It was during the Midwinter Festival, because I remember that the Onondaga dream heralds, the "Bigheads," dress in old blankets, instead of buffalo robes, and they run down the road at top speed carrying hoes instead of pestles. Instead of a route laid out by the faith keepers, they visit every home. The greater part of the Onondaga festival is devoted to guessing riddles. There are two houses, the longhouse and a smaller house [the Mud House] west of it. A moiety occupies each, and they visit back and forth, guessing each other's dreams. They spend the rest of the winter on Saturday nights putting up feasts to fulfill dream obligations.
>
> It was during this spate of dream guessing that a woman, named Mary Lyon, over in one corner commenced having "bear trouble." Although she was a small woman of scarcely 100 pounds, she manifested great strength. She grunted and snorted air between her closed teeth. While two men held her, someone procured a jar of blackberries and gave her a tablespoonful. But she suddenly clamped down on the proffered tin spoon of berry juice, denting the bowl so badly that it appeared to have been suddenly folded by some great force.

Case 3. Possession by Buffalo. About 1880, when Peter Doctor was living near Sand Hill Longhouse, Sarah Jimmerson's older sister Nancy had hysteria caused from possession by the buffalo (*degiyáʔgo*). The seizure occurred during the Midwinter Festival; the Seneca call the festival *hodinäyaʔse:ʔ,* "they are deranged," referring to the accumulation of ceremonial obligations they have to fulfill. [This accords with the seventeenth-century descriptions of the feast as described by Sagard and the Jesuits among the Huron, and later at Onondaga.]

> During that particular Midwinter Festival, of perhaps 1880, I was loafing around the Sand Hill Longhouse with a group of boys. It was in the afternoon and nothing was happening. About four o'clock someone came in looking for dancers. He said that someone was possessed. We all volunteered—all of us youngsters. None of us belonged to the particular medicine society, but, being curious we went along with the messenger.
>
> Arriving at the house of Blodgett Sundown, we found everything ready. They had prepared a kettle of mush with grease, such as they set down for the False Faces. This woman, the patient, lived with Blodgett, and he was holding her. She was intermittently convulsing and bellowing, letting out a great roar from within her. Every once in a while she would bellow like a mad bull.

They had an announcer [speaker], and the other ritual manager [conductor] had come after us. Someone burned tobacco and made the invocation. They had a singer and we danced, butting into each other as if we were Buffalos. Coming around the singer, where he sat astride a bench in the middle of the house, one of the boys made a gesture toward the patient as if he were going to butt her. She burst away from Blodgett and joined the dance, butting into all of us as we went by.

We cured her and got a lunch of mush out of it.

These fits of hysteria, or tremens, seem to occur during the Midwinter Festival [Peter thought] from cases of overwrought nerves.

It seems that the patient, Nancy Hill, had previously belonged to the Buffalo Dance Society, and we have no way of knowing whether she became hysterical before, during, or after the preparation of the feast for her. There is some evidence that these seizures represent a kind of expected role behavior. At Coldspring in the 1930s, I recall seeing one older male traditionalist join in the dance that he had sponsored and simulate Buffalo behavior, but younger people at Coldspring remarked that his enthusiasm for the roles of the old culture exceeded propriety.

I have included the two cases of bear and buffalo possession with cases of False Face possession because they are different manifestations of a single phenomenon. In common, they represent a heritage of derangement that descends from the Feast of Fools as the seventeenth-century Jesuits called the Dream Feast, of which the Midwinter Festival is heir.

In commenting on his cases, Peter Doctor remarked that Mary Shongo (Case 1) belonged to the False Face Company, and her reaction to his utterance of the False Face cry and the rasping of the rattle on the wall was a manifestation of surprise. She was a sensitive person who told fortunes. She worked through dreams. Peter conveyed to me that these persons were essentially neurotics. He himself was one of the few extraverted Iroquois that I have known. His willingness to assume roles that might be dangerous is typical. He remarked that his band of buffalo dancers were not members of the society; they had no real right to participate, and yet their dancing effected the desired cure. There was no doubt in Peter's mind that the messenger, speaker, singer, and others present at Nancy's feast belonged to the Buffalo Society. A particular dream, or a special manifestation of hysterical possession, calls for a medicine society to perform its unique ceremony and release the patient from his or her obligation or affliction. Indeed, this is the common purpose of the Midwinter Festival.

Case 4. A Tonawanda Matron in the 1930s. Ernest Smith, the well-known Seneca artist who commenced painting for me in 1935, identified a certain woman of the Turtle Clan who regularly became possessed of the False Faces. "I don't know whether she put that on or not, but she was always doing it." Ernest recalled a quite recent episode but gave no particulars.

He thought possession was not sexbound, and gave the following terms: "she is possessed": *waʔagodjaʔdo:wi:ʔ*; "he is possessed": *wao djaʔdo:wi:ʔ*; *ǫga djaʔdo:wi:ʔ*: "it is possessed."

There is a parallel with the term for the marching rite of the False Faces and their song to quiet the wind. It is called *honóiowi:ʔ* (Tonawanda Seneca Field Notes, April 3, 1937).

Case 5. An Onondaga Boy Who Volunteered. DeCost Smith (1889, 279) reports the case of a boy at Onondaga who entered the society without benefit of a feast. On entering the longhouse for the first time wearing a False Face, the lad was seized by a frenzy to dash into the fireplace and burrow into the coals in search of tobacco. He was observed scattering coals with bare hands and was enveloped by flames. He was promised tobacco to come out of the fire, which he did. He was reported not burned. In a way, this incident mirrors a more or less formal mock struggle between the masked leader of the False Faces on entering the longhouse and the headman (conductor). When the masker attempts to dive into the fire in search of tobacco that has been burned there, the headman quiets him with the promise of tobacco.

Case 6. The Man Who Ridiculed the Masks. A ritual holder at the Coldspring Longhouse (Seneca) related a case of what happened to a man who ridiculed the masks.

> A half-breed from Red House [toward Salamanca] came to the New Year dance and made fun of the faces. "Nothing to it; just the wood." He talked out loud in the longhouse. "They do not mean anything," he said. Then, a while after the New Year's Dance, he got what he was looking for. These False Faces pulled his mouth to one side clear up to his ear. He could not talk. When he tried to talk, he sounded like *gagǫ́hsaʔ* [mask]. He called the society over there, and four men from here went over to help him. They gave him six blows of hot ashes a piece, and that crooked mouth was all gone. And, if we didn't treat him, he would be dead by this time because these faces are "poison" (*ʔotgǫʔ*) and are derived from live, hard maple trees. That is why we think it is not right for anyone to make fun of the masks.

> And so this man, he says: "I will not do *that* again." And so they treat this man every year now, and he says he is going to keep it up all his life. And this man is living today, and he believes in the False Faces.

Case 7. A Man at Six Nations Who Ridiculed the Masks. Simeon Gibson, an Onondaga-Cayuga, and until his death, my interpreter and colleague (Fenton 1944), recalled three instances of possession arising from ridicule, singing the songs out of context, and neglect by a Christian Mohawk.

> A man who formerly was living here libeled the False Faces when

they were going around the houses. He called them evil names and insulted them. Soon afterwards he got sick, and his mouth and face twisted to one side. Nothing else they tried would help him until they had a feast for him. They invited in the False Faces. He got better afterward. He is now deceased.

This case conforms to the preceding.

Case 8. One Who Dared Sing the Songs Whenever They Occurred to Him. This case by Simeon Gibson took a different twist.

My mother told of her brother, the late Chief Abraham Charles (Cayuga), how as a young man he went about singing *haduʔiʔgéhaʔ*—the song belonging to the medicine man. The old people warned him not to do this, but he did not heed them. Time came and he took sick. At that time they used to have open fireplaces in the log houses. The fire was going briskly, when he was suddenly taken, and he jumped into the fire. And he made that noise. His mouth and nose were crooked [distorted], and he kept trying to get after the ashes. The people at home ran and held him back. The old folks hurriedly looked for tobacco, which they burned, promising the Haduʔiʔ that they would hold the False Face feast. As soon as the message ascended in the smoke of the tobacco, he quieted down.

A few days later the men came with their False Faces and put the ashes on him. And he got over his ailment immediately.

Case 9. A Christian Mohawk, North of Ohsweken. Simeon Gibson had this account from the victim's brother.

William was sick for a while. He did not recover. Finally he got worse. When he became delirious they had doctors [white physicians] for him but to no avail. They could not hold him down. He was *strong,* and he made *sounds like a Haduʔiʔ crying for tobacco.* And he was *blowing.*

At last someone remembered that there were fortune-tellers among the longhouse people. His people inquired for one of these clairvoyants and consulted him. The fortune-teller instructed them that he must have a feast for the False Faces. The family did not know how to prepare it since they were Christians and unfamiliar with longhouse ways. So they hired some longhouse people to prepare the feast, and when it was ready the False Face Company arrived. They had merely to blow ashes on him, and after the feast he recovered without taking any other medicine.

Simeon commented on this case:

A man when sick may get delirious. The old people can recognize the symptoms, and immediately when they discover that this [False Faces] is the cause, they burn tobacco. The speaker of the invocation promises that the family will make a feast as soon as the patient recovers. And generally he improves immediately.

Case 10. A Tonawanda Seneca Who Imitated a False Face to Scare Friends. F. W. Waugh recorded this story in 1912.

> False Faces are seen along lonely roads and especially up in trees. One young man disbelieved these stories. He thought he would frighten a friend by climbing up into a tree and imitating the False Face. While in the tree he heard a noise above him, and looking up he saw a False Face. He jumped from the tree and ran for his life. He never disbelieved stories after this.

Whether this incident was followed by possession and a cure is not stated.

Case 11. A Seneca at Newtown, Cattaraugus, Who Resisted a Doorkeeper's Command to Dance. Jesse J. Cornplanter who grew up at Newtown Longhouse on the Cattaraugus Seneca reservation recalled an incident that happened in the first decade of this century. A man became possessed for resisting the command of the masked doorkeeper to join the round dance.

> When the masked ritual conductor nudged him with his rattle, he obstinately refused to join the round dance. They struggled, and the man, overcome with fear, fell into a spasm and cried like a False Face. Afterward the man did not remember his behavior.

Case 12. Another Trickster Done In. From David Key of Onondaga Longhouse on Grand River, Waugh heard a case of a man who set out to trick his friends and lost his mind.

> There was a road along the river where just about sundown people used to see a False Face sitting on the limb of an oak tree. [The narrator added] False Faces have bodies and legs and big eyes.
>
> Three young fellows didn't believe it. The worst of the three thought he would play a trick on the others. He waited until sundown and then climbed up to about the second limb and put on the False Face. [This greatly amused Simeon Gibson with whom I reviewed this case.] He heard the other fellows coming. They stopped a little piece off, and one said, "My God, there's two big fellows now!" The two turned and went back.
>
> The prankster wondered what they meant by "two of them." He looked up just then and saw a second False Face just above him. He dropped down, calling on the others to wait, and ran home as fast as he could. When he got home he jumped for the door and fell down inside. That was the last he remembered. He lost his mind. When he got better, he told the old people about the trick.
>
> Whoever sees a False Face will have nosebleed very badly [This calls for a cure.]

In the story the False Face was always seen in a particular tree, an oak. "Some man went and cut down the tree and burned it, and people did not see it anymore."

Case 13. A White Observer Who Made Game of the Masks. As in Case 6, this time a white man ridicules the masks and becomes possessed. Peter John recalled for Waugh in 1913 that

> a white man present at a False Face dance was making game of the False Faces. He took very sick—"got crazy"—and danced all around like the False Faces. He called in one of the company and was told [that to recover] he must procure a pig's head and some white corn for bread (although for him wheat flour would do). The company came together, [one] sprinkled Indian tobacco on the fire, and the leader made a speech asking the False Faces not to hurt this man [from now on] because he was giving them a feast to make it right.

Case 14. Phoebe Halfwhite Possessed During the Visitation of the Maskers at Midwinter. Not unlike Peter Doctor's experience with Mary Shongo (Case No. 1), Phoebe Halfwhite of Coldspring was frightened into hysteria by the False Faces making their rounds of the houses at dawn during the Midwinter Festival. Henry Redeye and Charles Logan (father of my interpreter, Clara Redeye) were the two maskers. Phoebe Halfwhite's house stood just east of the Presbyterian church on the riverbank. The two lads were approaching the house when Robert Halfwhite came out and started down the hill toward the spring carrying a lantern and a pail for water. The two lads stood and shook their rattles but did not make the False Face cry. The man returned to the house without fetching water. He told his wife what he had seen.

> "I have just heard ghosts talking," he told her. She told him to lock the door, but before he could slide the bolt, the two maskers threw themselves against the door and entered. They threw themselves on the floor and crawled in. Phoebe jumped up and ran behind the stove and commenced to rub her hands on the stovepipe and cry like a False Face. Her mouth was drawn to one side (*yehsagái:deʔ*). Her husband then told the two lads that they would have to cure her. They blew ashes on her, this apparently cured her, and they departed.

It is bad enough to neglect or ridicule the False Faces, but it is worse to insult them. A Coldspring Seneca told me a story of a man at Newtown on Cattaraugus Reservation who remarked about defecating in a mask. "Long Horns," a noted medicine man, is said to have burned tobacco and cast a spell on the man who became sick. Then they had to have a ceremony to cure him.

Nosebleed from Failure to Put on a Feast

Accounts of cures involving nosebleed, facial paralysis, and similar ailments of head and shoulders are fairly abundant in the life histories of Iroquois sources.

George Gibson, one of Goldenweiser's informants at Six Nations, circa 1912, recalled that some fifteen years previously he called upon a woman who was bleeding heavily from both nostrils. He got some tobacco, prayed to the False Faces, and while he was praying the blood began to come in drops, and soon stopped. Later Gibson called in three other men (including John Jamieson, a noted False Face leader), and a feast was given them. The patient was then well and became a member of the society.

It was evidently a prevalent belief at Six Nations that to see a red False Face in the bush would cause nosebleed. The vision or apparition of a black False Face was believed to cause headache. Waugh's informant, Sam John, who had such an experience, recommended drinking a decoction of Red Osier Dogwood in the first instance.

A Persistent Belief. In reviewing these cases with Simeon Gibson in 1940, I learned that *nosebleed may follow failure to put up a feast.*

> There was a case this summer of a woman [in Simeon's neighborhood] who took sick for failure to put up a feast. The woman had a severe nosebleed that lasted all during one day. They did everything they could think of to stop it and failed. But toward night they happened to think of this society. She really belonged to it, having joined it a long time ago. So they decided to burn tobacco, which they did. They promised that they would make a feast, that they would make mush also, and that they would hold the ceremony as soon as they could. The minute that they burned tobacco and promised everything that is required, that bleeding stopped.
>
> Just a few days afterward they managed to have a feast for the company. She has not been bothered since.
>
> It is funny that these church people get sick this way. Although a church member, she had to have that (ceremony) nevertheless.

Such cures are well-nigh endless. The obligation to renew human debts to the supernaturals goes on from generation to generation. In a sense, one inherits from previous generations membership in the medicine societies and to overlook or neglect this association is dangerous. Indeed this compulsion to fulfill one's ceremonial debts is what keeps the traditional culture going. In a 1912 field interview with F. W. Waugh, Seth Newhouse, the chronicler of the Iroquois confederacy, held that because his father was in the False Faces, so all of his family were in it by inheritance. They must make a feast once a year. He cited a man who neglected this obligation and had his mouth drawn to one side.

Participation. When asked how they joined the False Faces, Iroquois informants will often relate their personal case histories or describe some cure in which they participated. Chief Lyman Johnson, speaker of Tonawanda Longhouse in the 1930s and 1940s, told me:

> I was sick for a long time when I was a little boy. It was then that I joined Gagǫ́hsaʔ, False Face. He is good for any kind of sickness. One just says to him, "Help me." And he will cure.
>
> A woman tells me that she is sick. She lies there and it seems to her as if hair is lying on her face. She reaches to brush it aside, and nothing is there. Repeatedly she reaches to brush the hair off her face. But she never sees it.
>
> She complains to her old people. They go to a fortune-teller, He says, "It is Gagǫ́hsaʔ [False Face]; that is False Face hair that is making her sick." She put up that [ceremony for the False Face Company], and so now she is getting better.
>
> This happened long ago.

Toothache

Next to nosebleed, toothache is a common cause for joining the False Faces. The Seneca frequently mention it in personal histories. Indeed the incidence of caries is high among Iroquois, and it is no new thing; skulls from Owasco sites and later Seneca graves of the protohistoric and prehistoric periods show a high degree of caries and tooth loss (Ritchie, personal communications, 1954, 1983; 1965, 275). This has been ascribed to the high incidence in the diet of starch from corn soup (Leechman 1934).

Inflammation of the eyes is another symptom. Again this is nothing new. Early travelers mention the smoke of longhouse fires irritating the eyes. Conjunctivitis and sometimes venereal infection occurs. I observed one such case at Tonawanda.

Clairvoyant Prescribes

The girl was born with infectious gonococcoid eyes. She was eight years old when I saw her. After six months of hospital care, she came home uncured, but her mother was told that she might outgrow the condition. They advised washing her eyes with boric acid. Evidently, her family had not cooperated. Only recently had she been accepted at school.

A Combination Prescription. Alex Clute, a native of Tonawanda Reservation, returned home to preach the Handsome Lake code at the Six Nations meeting in September of 1934. Clute was blind himself, and he had left Tonawanda some years previously to live and preach at Onondaga. Most recently he had carried the "Good Message" to Akwesasne (St. Regis), where I found him in 1939 spreading Handsome Lake's words and teaching Seneca songs and dances to the Mohawk. (This was the beginning of a cultural renaissance that is now thought to be quite ancient.) As a prophet he had been telling fortunes, divining the causes of real and supposed ailments. The girl's mother told me:

> We asked him to do for our little girl's eyes. He said, "Let her come up to me," and he placed his hands on her chest. [Although Clute was blind, one wonders about the laying on of hands: Was it borrowed from Christian doctrine?][2] Presently he said, "You should put up a False Face Dance for her and also a Dark Dance [the ritual of the Little People]. Then go out in the woods and cut a small sassafras sapling. Take the soft part in the center, the pith, and steep that in hot water. Wash out her eyes. She will get well." [The latter was an act of imitative magic because the pith of Sassafras resembles pus.]

Facial Paralysis, a Classic Syndrome

The following case recounted by an Allegany Seneca matron on January 26, 1936, to Marjorie Lismer is typical.

Mrs. C. did not believe in the value of the False Face Society. She thought it was all superstition, but now she knows better. When she was a young girl, a man from Cornplanter Reservation (just south of the Pennsylvania state line) came to visit his brother who lived next door to the narrator.

> The man had been taken sick at Cornplanter [a Christian Seneca settlement] and [white] doctors said that he could not be cured. He was badly paralyzed, and one side of his face was all twisted up like the real False Faces. His eyelids would not work either [sounds like Bell's palsy]. The one side of his face was all hard like wood. Although this man did not believe in the False Faces, one person put on a mask and visited him. After that he felt better. So he decided to go and visit his brother who was a longhouse member and see if he could be cured. The evening after his arrival at his brother's place he was visited by the False Faces. He was cured and his face returned to normal. [The narrator remembers seeing the patient both before and after his cure.]

---

2. The Cherokee laid on hands warmed by fire, which suggests that the practice was pre-Christian (Fogelson, personal communication).

7. Of Dreams, Collectors, Scared Children, and Bundles

Vicarious Forms of Participation

DREAMS: THE WINDOW ON THE SOUL

From the seventeenth century onward, missionaries deplored Iroquois preoccupation with dreams, both the belief that they revealed the wishes of the soul and the acts of fulfillment. This literature provided one anthropologist with rich fare for analysis (Wallace 1958). The interpretation of particular dreams, the ritual of dream guessing, and the rites of acting out their consequences became the main supports of the Midwinter Festival and together the strongest positive force for maintaining the traditional culture. One dare not disregard such revelations even though they compel one to fulfill a number of rites until one hits on the particular spirit force that only can be released by the celebration of its ceremony, with the obligation of renewing that ceremony annually so long as one lives. Although other anthropologists have sensed this, it was Wallace who first advanced Iroquois dream fulfillment as a psychoanalytic theory, and Shimony (1961) who demonstrated it as the principal force in Iroquois conservatism.

It is in this context that the following cases of False Face dreams take on meaning.

Case 1: A Sick Boy
Jonas Snow, of the Hawk Clan, my host at Allegany in 1933, and himself a carver of note, told me in our first interview that "if a boy is sick and dreams of *gagóhsaʔ*, he tells his parents. They notify the False Faces, and they come the following night and dance two dances: the rite of the Common Faces and the Doorkeeper Dance. Before the dance, someone prays and burns tobacco." Jonas thought it inadvisable for boys to use False Faces; "it will spoil their face," he added. Later on, his own youngest son, Bemis, began to carve a miniature mask, with the usual result: He had to join the society.

Such instances are documented over and over again in the field notes of earlier ethnologists. Although boys often start by carving miniature Faces (*nigǫhsáʔa*), Avery Jimmerson, one of the great Seneca carvers of recent years who was but a lad during my first summer at Allegany, was already making drawings of maskers and started out making full-scale masks during the 1930s (see Plate 7-1, an early drawing by Avery Jemison, done in 1933).

Case 2. A Nonbeliever
Sadie Butler of the Wolf Clan and Fannie Stevens of the Heron Clan were the two headwomen of the False Faces for their respective moieties at Coldspring Longhouse during the 1930s. As a girl, Sadie did not believe in the power of the False Faces. But she got sick and was cured by them. Her head was so sore that she could not even comb her hair. Her eyes

Plate 7.1. Drawing of a False Face Dancer by Avery J. Jemison, age sixteen. High Bank, Allegany Reservation, 1933. Photo by Joaquin Arriaga, MAI-HF. Author's collection.

were sore, and she saw False Faces everywhere when she closed her eyes. They were around her bed. Previously, she had attended the ceremonies of the society at the longhouse because she liked the way the food was prepared and she liked to watch the dances. Later, through the efforts of her family, Sadie was elected headwoman for her side. The office is for life, and it tends to descend in the clan. Her opposite number, Fanny Stevens, was even newer to the office. Two other headwomen opposite her had died previously during Sadie's tenure. People appeal to the headwomen when the rites of the society are called for to cure someone. Other than organizing the ceremony and staging the fall and spring Traveling, or house-to-house cleansing, Rite, the headwomen never put on masks, and they do not themselves own masks. However, they do keep the sack of Husk Faces that are used when this supernatural race of horticulturists appears at the Midwinter Festival, and they dress the participants. They also oversee the cooking and preparation of the medicine at the longhouse during the spring and fall ceremonies, and they pass the medicine to the congregation. They themselves are the first to take the medicine and the first to receive the ashes from the maskers. Besides the two headwomen, there are other women members of the False Faces who supply intermediate roles on demand and report to the head ladies. These deputies may be the first to hear of dreams that require the services of the society.

Case 3. A White Trader and Unbeliever

John Holt for years kept the store at Quaker Bridge. It was said of him by Seneca women who obviously liked him that "I wouldn't trust any man, not even John Holt!" John understood Seneca and spoke a little. He used to kid his Seneca customers about their customs. He made fun of the False Faces. And like Sadie Butler, "he saw False Faces all over the place." He was cured by the company. So it was said in Coldspring.

Case 4. A Collector of Masks "Poisoned"

Soon after I arrived at Coldspring to live with the family of Jonas Snow on "Snow Street," there was a rumor going the rounds very similar to the story about John Holt. It seems that Amos Johnny John, son of Chauncey, was showing my father John Wm. Fenton, artist and collector of masks, how the gagóhsaʔ were used. This event is supposed to have happened during the 1920s. It is said that Amos entered the house wearing a mask and carrying a rattle. My father is reported to have commenced "jumping up and down, 'poisoned' (hodjáʔda:wiʔ) by the mask, but Amos was able to cure him." Jonas Snow is reported to be the author of this story. Although a classic case of "possession," like those cases already described, it is similar in outline to the story about John Holt.

The story may also have been intended to warn me of the dangers involved in such inquiries, but it also reflects a certain amount of tension between the Snow and Johnny John families, which came out when I commenced to work with Chauncey.

Miniature Masks as Personal Dream Guardians

Although reported from Onondaga (Blau 1966, 1967), the feature of divining dreams by guessing contests at the Midwinter Festival is no longer observed in the three Seneca longhouse communities in New York—Coldspring on Allegany, Newtown on Cattaraugus, and Tonawanda. The inquiring ethnologist soon learns that Six Nations on Grand River in Canada is the place and Onondaga Longhouse in particular. Goldenweiser collected a number of cases of persons joining the False Face Society through dreams and being presented with a miniature mask as a memento and personal guardian. In 1940, I reviewed these cases with Simeon Gibson, and his analysis and explanation follows.[1]

Case 1. A Woman with Swollen Face. A Mohawk woman named "Drags a Canoe" (Gųwahá:wiʔ), otherwise Lydia Sugar, had a swollen face. She dreamed of two men wearing False Faces who entered her door saying, "We come to cure you." They blew at her through their hands and departed. Next morning she was better. Then later they came with other maskers and a leader; they burned Indian tobacco, rubbed her with ashes, and ate mush. She has been well ever since and invites them to her house periodically. This cure occurred before the turn of the century.

She added that there are no real False Faces around here now. They have gone somewhere.

Case 2. A Cayuga Matron and a Man Bearing Talismans. Gawęʔnanu:wę, a Cayuga matron of the Bear Clan and wife of George Gibson, Goldenweiser's interpreter, some years previous to the interview dreamed that Chief David Skye, a prominent figure at Six Nations, came in carrying a large False Face in one hand, and in the other a hockey stick. He said, "I brought these to protect you and to cure you." Her face had been swollen on one side, and for three days and nights relatives had tried to relieve her, but in vain. Exhausted, she and her attendants had fallen asleep. When she awoke, David Skye was visited.

The dream occurred just before the Midwinter Festival; the chiefs were informed, and they ordered the appropriate dream objects made. One version says that Chief Skye's son was ordered to make her a little False Face and a little hockey stick. The other version says that Chief Skye himself made them.

They returned with the leader of the False Faces, presumeably old John

---

1. Sturtevant maintains that there is no necessary connection between having a dream and joining the False Faces, nor does this depend on midwinter dream guessing. At Cattaraugus in the 1950s, he collected cases of dreams, their diagnosis, and joining the False Faces. At Cattaraugus, there has been no dream guessing in recent years. The same is true at Coldspring.

Jamieson, Sr., who always led the society. The False Face curing ceremony was gone through while Chief David Skye stood by wearing a large mask. Then Mrs. Gibson recovered and became a member of the society. Afterward, she put up an annual feast for the False Faces, inviting the men to play hockey when David Skye was present with his mask. She thoroughly believed that these miniature dream objects warded off sickness.

Case 3. How Participation Got George Gibson in Trouble. Gibson had joined the society about thirty years before the interview. An elderly woman named Silversmith was sick, and, outside the leader, old John Jamieson, no members of the False Face Society could be found. George consented to put on a mask and play the part. Later he got sick. He asked his mother for help. She went to a fortune-teller, who explained the situation. Subsequently the society was invited to eat mush. Old John Jamieson burned a little tobacco and addressed the False Faces and asked the maskers present to put ashes on George's head. Then other members of the society came in, ate the mush, and left. Thus George became a member and invites the False Face Society to his house once a year to eat mush. On these occasions the leader of the False Face Society always burns tobacco and speaks to the False Faces in the following manner.

Prayer to the False Faces by George Gibson
This prayer was taken by Goldenweiser and corrected by Simeon Gibson and the author on August 13, 1940. The text is in Seneca.

> o:nɛ ɛswadahɔsi′yo:sdaʔ swa:duʔi:ʔ o:nɛ weswa:′yɔ
> Now you do all listen   you   now you came here
>   maskers

> čaʔnɔ́:wi heˆyetcinɔ́:gi neʔ etciya:de:ʔ / onɛ díʔh
> a certain they did   your   so now then
> place   summon   grandchildren
>   you

> we:ʔswayɛʔgwaʔsɔ́:wiʔ o:nɛ   hwagaiyɛʔgwái:dɛ /
> you inhale tobacco   (which) the smoke arises
> (savor)   now

> o:nɛ díh waʔetciyadɔheʔsɛ́:ʔgwɛ ɛyetciyaʔdagé:nhaʔ
> Now then she your help requested you would relieve her[2]

> etciya:de:ʔ / na:yeʔ néʔ ganadjíya:yɛʔ etcijisgɔnyé:ni
> Your   And so   a full kettle of mush cooked especially
> grandchild   set down   for you [maskers]

---

2. In Iroquoian usage, the third person singular female form is made to stand for the people. It is either "she" or "people" who requested help.

hegaʔnaɛːʔtwi ʔohgwaiʔohnaːʔ / oːnɛ dih´ swashasdɛʔsäːgwéːgi
poured into it bear oil   Now then use all your strength
                                              (power)

ɛyetciyaʔdagéːnhaʔ / oːn ɛ díh waʔoyɛgwaʔsɔ́ːwi
you to help her   Now then it did savor the tobacco

sadadíʔtshɛʔ hadegaɛhóhsaːʔdi oːnɛnoːga / oːnɛ oʔnaː
your cane   entirely stripped hickory   Now another
             of branches

waʔoyɛʔgwaʔsɔːwi neʔ swasdawɛːʔshäːʔ / neʔtho´ nigaːwénage
it tobacco received your rattle   These are all the words

oːnɛ ɛwadiːwáhdɛdia ɛyetciyáːɛːdaʔtɔʔ /
Now let the ceremony you treat her with ashes
    proceed

Free translation:

> Now all of you Hunchbacked beings listen. Now you came here to a certain place where you were summoned by your grandchildren. So now then inhale [savor] the tobacco smoke, the smoke that now arises. Now then one [or the people] requested your assistance that you would relieve her, namely your grandchild. And there is a full kettle resting on the ground of mush prepared especially for you, into which bear oil has been poured. Now therefore use all your power (strength) to help her. Now then (also) that has partaken of the tobacco, namely your cane (staff) which is a hickory entirely stripped of its branches. Now also it has partaken of tobacco, your rattle.
>
> Therefore these then are all the words.
>
> Now let the ceremony proceed in which you treat her by blowing ashes.[3]

Case 4. A Boy and Cardboard Masks. (from Goldenweiser manuscript). While still a boy, George Gibson's stepson used to make cardboard masks. Presently, his face swelled and also his head. He dreamed that he had three cardboard False Faces. Three maskers came in and wanted mush. He awoke and told his mother. The boy's stepfather notified John Jamieson, the leader of the False Face Society, who came with three men. They went through the ceremony, and the boy was well the same evening. Thus he became a member.

As we have seen elsewhere, and so at Six Nations, a nonmember who takes part in any of the activities associated with the False Faces risks illness, he or she requires a cure to release the spirit forces and as a conse-

---

3. Fogelson remarks how similar this tobacco invocation is in form to Cherokee formulas of ceremonies written in the Sequoia vocabulary.

quence becomes a member of the society. This could mean a woman cooking a feast for another woman, a boy carving faces, or a boy joining the maskers in some rite. One gets sick, and the solution is revealed in a dream. Indeed, the anthropologist who meddles in such affairs assumes the same risks, in the eyes of traditionalists.

Miniature Masks and Classes of Membership
In the light of the preceding cases noted by Goldenweiser, who preceded me by nearly thirty years at Six Nations, Simeon Gibson set out to enlighten me on the classes of membership in the society. At the pain of anticipating Chapter 8 on the rituals, I shall keep his explanation together as he stated it on August 11, 1940.

> A person is sick and it seems that no medicine can cure her. Sometimes it comes through a dream while the person is sick. The person dreams that he [or] she must have a small False Face and joins the society.
>
> Should this happen anytime in the fall, then at the time of the midwinter ceremonies, they take the dream and report it to the old people at the longhouse. The officials will hold a guessing contest until someone comes up with what this sick person wants. At the longhouse each person present will have a chance to guess what the dreamer needs. When someone guesses correctly, the conductor who introduces the dream, shouts *goh go:h* (high tone). The person who guesses correctly has to make the miniature mask (or whatever) for the sick person.
>
> The seventh day of the Midwinter Festival at Onondaga Longhouse on Six Nations is the time that the designated maker of the miniature dream object brings the masquette to the longhouse. After the Drum Dance, the speaker (one from each moiety appointed for occasion) or the man himself announces to the public that this mask belongs to a named sick person and that it shall be her guardian for the rest of her life. Then the masquette is delivered to the person by the particular medicine society.
>
> The second of the two ways of joining is to employ a clairvoyant or fortune-teller (*hadraota:ʔ,* Cayuga). Some relative or a friend makes a bundle of green tea and sleeps on it under the pillow overnight. Next morning the person [female] takes it to a fortune-teller. The fortune-teller makes tea of the little bundle. She puts it in a cup, pours the contents of the cup into a saucer, and then "reads" the tea grounds left in the cup. The clairvoyant sees perhaps a miniature face in the tea leaves, and says: "The person must join the False Face Society." Likewise, he/she tells that "someone must make a guardian for her" [or him] (*ęyųdadwęnaha:goʔ*), that "she will be protected" (*ęyagoyadanǫ́hna:k*). So they (family of sick person) take

the dream and its interpretation to the longhouse committee. The dream reporter for their moiety announces that someone has had a dream, and the guessing goes on [as described in the first instance].

All the men guess. The one who divines the dream goes home and makes the masquette. Having finished it, he returns with it to the longhouse. The speaker announces that someone is about to make a present of a guardian to a sick person (or someone who was sick and is now well). The miniature is presented to the person if present, or taken to the sick person if still confined. And then they set the date for some night when they will have the feast for the False Face Company.

At the meeting when the sick person joins the Society of Faces, there is a tobacco invocation, after which the ceremony of the False Faces begins.

Address to the False Faces When One (She) Joins the Society. The text is in Onondaga and was rendered by Simeon Gibson.

 o:nɛ näńgɛ wɛndá:di: o:nɛ nɛ: ´ higá:yɛ oyɛʔgwaʔɔ:we
 now this day now this at hand tobacco

ná:ye ɛyɔ:dwɛnɔnyáːʔdaʔ na:ye: he:iwa:neʔkha:ʔ nehneh
which they request help namely a favor so that

dɔsayɔ:dawɛ:nye: tcahɔhwɛ́:djadeʔ ɔsayɔdahgaí:dat nɛ:
she may travel here on earth she shall get relief from this about

gonowákdanekh nehto ni:yo:t waʔagoi:sɛ:dakséhaʔ na:yeʔ[4]
her sickness it seems she did dream that
       that

deyodɔwɛ:dyo´hwi[5] ne:ʔ ɛ:yodadwɛnahä:́gwaʔ ne.ʔ gagɔhsaʔ
it is necessary that she must have a namely a mask
(demanded) guardian

na:yeʔ ɛyagoyaʔdadɔhna:k neʔ ohɛ:ndɔ
which it will protect her in future

wahwɛda:deníyɔdiye: / nɛndiʔi iga:yɛʔ neʔ gagɔhsaʔ
days to come Now it is here this mas[quette]
      then

---

4. The speaker acts on behalf of the sick woman employing the tobacco as a message to ask a blessing of the grandparent, the masker.
5. "It seems that Haduʔiʔ wants her to have this miniature False Face as a guardian. The demand must be fulfilled. If she fails to fulfill, she will never get better. The verb is very specific" (Simeon Gibson).

na:ye wa?ɔ:dadwɛnahä:´gwa?⁶ / o:nɛ di:? heyahdɔdáhgwi?
this (mask) which she   Now so   she shall belong to it
requested be given to her   (from   (the society)
                                now on)

etisó:da? hadu?i?/ o:nɛ di ga:yɛ? ne? oji:sgwa?
our grandparent   Now then it   the mush
                  is ready

héswaya?dagweníyo? / o:nɛ ne?tho nigawɛ́nage?
for all of you it is   Now these are all the words.
intended

Free Translation. An English translation of the Onondaga text of the prayer for burning tobacco when a person joins the society follows:

> Now this very day, such as it is, genuine Indian tobacco, by which the family requests a favor, the favor being that she shall travel about /get well/ on the earth, that she shall get relief from her sickness.⁷ It seems that she did dream that it is necessary that she must have a guardian, namely, a mask,⁸ by means of which she shall be protected in the future days to come.
>
> Now then it is here, this mask /the miniature/, which she desired to have given to her as requested in her dream.⁹
>
> Therefore from now on she will belong /to the society/ of our grandparent, the hunchbacked /medicine man/. Now then the mush is ready for all of you for whom it is intended.¹⁰
>
> Now these are the words.

A typical miniature False Face, illustrated in one of Goldenweiser's notebooks and now in the collection of the National Museum of Man, Ottawa (Cat. No. NMM(C)III.1663), fulfills Simeon Gibson's explanation. It measures two inches long, and one inch and one-half at the widest place. It was painted red with white lead eyes. Its appearance suggests a beggar mask with smiling mouth.

---

6. "To give her what she requested in her dream. It shall be hers forever" (Simeon Gibson).
7. Simeon explained: "The speaker acts on behalf of the sick woman [person], and he uses the tobacco as a message [a means of communicating] to ask a blessing of the grandparent, the mask.
8. "It seems that Hadu?i? wants her to have this miniature False Face as a guardian. It must be fulfilled. If she does not do this, she will never get better."
9. Literally, "to have a present given as requested."
10. "So you all can share it. The men bring small lard pails, and after the ceremony, the mush is divided equally among the men who wore the masks. But the mush is intended for the real medicine man, the miniatures, the larger masks, as well as for the members of the society" (Simeon Gibson).

Dreamers Who Do Not Hold "Guardians"
Some members, of this second class, do not have small False Faces as guardians. But for them it must come through a dream that they should join the society. "I belong but have no miniature. When I was a small boy, someone went to a fortune-teller and he told that I should join. Only certain ones have to have a miniature as guardian."

Divided Masks. Simeon's eldest sister dreamed when she was sick that she must have a miniature False Face that was half red and half black, "divided down the nose. They took it to the longhouse and someone guessed."

During a half century at Six Nations, Simeon Gibson said that he never saw a large, divided mask. He stated that he knew of only two kinds—red and black. He added that his sister could use either color mask when she was sick. Divided masks certainly were not common, but they were present on the reserve during my interpreter's lifetime. As we have seen, Hewitt collected mythology on divided beings, and such masks occur in museum collections from the reserve.

CHILDREN AND THE MASKERS

Within my observation, little children are frightened when the maskers appear at the longhouse. They frequently cry and are comforted by their mothers or grandmothers. They had been warned in advance not to be afraid when the maskers entered.[11] Because the masks are believed to possess supernatural power, it is felt that they can harm children who are cautioned not to touch them where they may hang in houses or to pry into bundles. And it is strongly stated that it is wrong to employ a False Face to discipline a naughty child because the child might be seriously harmed. Discipline is left to Hagónde:s, or Longnose, a cannibal clown, whose mask and function was described in Chapter 2. Here I shall mention one or two cases as described by Emma Turkey, matron of the Hawk Clan at Allegany, who as my clan mother thought I should know something about child rearing.

In general, whipping children is deplored. But when a child is really bad, it was customary to cut twelve whips of the Red Osier Dogwood, which is known as a medicine. Each whip is used once and thrown away until the child relents, when the mother is supposed to cease whipping. It may take all twelve to subdue an obdurate youngster.

Ducking in water is another reported corrective measure. Emma pre-

---

11. One year Sturtevant took his four-year-old daughter with him to Allegany, and they were present for the traveling rite. Sibbie Snow, their hostess, warned her not to be frightened when the False Faces entered her house on their rounds, and she took care to do this before they appeared.

ferred to push a child out into the night, saying óʔowa:ʔ ęsaye:nǫʔ, "owl will get you." The frightened child is left outdoors until he or she promises to be good.

Emma's husband Myron Turkey had a mask resembling Longnose. He would put it on and emerge from behind the barn or appear at the woods' edge to scare his wife's grandchildren. He made no noise. Longnose is believed to be outside at night, as already indicated, but he is distinct from the False Faces, and he has no society. His victims owe him no obligation, except to reform, and no feast or renewal is involved.

The daughter of Clara Redeye, my interpreter, and granddaughter of Emma Turkey is now a grown woman. But one time as a little girl it is said she was bad. She insisted on remaining out of doors on a cold afternoon. "We could not make her stay in the house." It was then that Myron Turkey went behind the barn and put on the Hagónde:s mask of white cloth. He struck the building with a stick to attract attention. The little girl looked that way and saw the figure of the masked clown staring her in the face. "She came running into the house, crying gádathe:wat, 'I repent.'"

The impersonator of Longnose can be a woman.

SIGHTINGS OF LONGNOSE

It is believed that such folk characters used to inhabit the woods and that the old folks frequently saw them, "when they were around here." Henry Redeye, of the Bear Clan, a respected speaker at the Coldspring Longhouse and preacher of the Handsome Lake code, claimed to have seen one. He told me, "Hagonde:s is small, scarcely four feet tall." Djíwaʔ [Henry's nickname], Dáhdo:t, and Gáʔnǫʔ ("arrow"), three brothers, once went spear fishing with torches along the Allegheny River at Coldspring. Djiwaʔ sighted one. "He was walking near an old barn and stood out clearly in the torchlight. His nose was so long as to nearly rest on the ground." The three brothers disembarked and tried to catch him. Djiwaʔ went around one side of the barn and Dáhdo:t went the other way. Gaʔnoʔ did not see him. They lost him and were unable to find him anywhere.

THE BUNDLE: MASK, RATTLE, AND TOBACCO

Men belonging to the Society of Faces usually own a bundle containing a turtle rattle and one or more masks decorated with bags of sacred tobacco. Masks are seldom owned by women, although they may have temporary custody. When not being used, the mask is laid away, face down (not face up like a corpse) with its hair wreathed around the face and the turtle shell of the rattle nested in the hollow back of the mask. The whole mask is wrapped in the cloth head cover. Occasionally unwrapped masks are hung upstairs, but facing the wall. This rule is not always followed. It is said that a mask facing outward should be covered, lest some person see it, become frightened and possessed. False Faces require considerable care. If a mask falls, the owner burns a tobacco offering, makes an appropriate prayer, and then ties a small bundle of the sacred tobacco at the ear or forehead of the mask. Whenever the owner dreams of the Face, he should rise and repeat the ritual. Such offerings should be removed from the mask when it is sold to white people. The owner burns tobacco and tells the mask it is going away; he asks it especially not to return and harm him or the new owner. (Chauncey Johnny John dictated the prayer text to me and posed for my camera [Plate 7-2A–C].)

Any member of the society may use another member's mask. A new owner will add a package of tobacco to a mask, and if the mask he purchases already has several such bundles attached to its forehead, he adds one of his own. But a carver does not tie tobacco to a mask if he intends to sell and not use it. Masks are thought to become hungry for tobacco and mush. Owners rub the lips with mush and annoint the faces with sunflower oil, which adds a rich luster. A man without heirs may request that his mask be buried with him. Other Seneca sources held that women may own masks; they agree that they never wear them but lend them out to men for use in the curing ceremonies.

Dependencies

At Onondaga, New York, Harold Blau discovered and formulated a series of dependency relationships between mask and man, some eighteen in number, which do not essentially contradict Seneca beliefs, and which he summarized in a table of dyads between malevolent power for ill treatment and benevolent power for proper treatment (Blau 1966, 572–76):

Ill Treatment	Malevolent Power	Benevolent Power
Hung face up	*Causes noise*	*Cures ills*
Hair comes loose	*High winds*	*Enables sight*
Neglect tobacco	*Fire, trouble*	*Drives out evil*
Falls down	*Death, illness*	*Handle coals*
Neglect feeding	*Bad dreams*	*Withstand cold*
Ridicule	*Illness*	*Perform witchcraft*

Blau finds a high degree of concordance between these themes and the descriptions of Huron practices in the seventeenth century; he notes that most themes imply cooperation between man and the spirits (or the masks); and third, that sanctions are implicit in neglect or fulfillment of requirements. Further, he sees parallels between the False Face Society and human society—one being a projection of the other. He reminds us that the False Faces have a cosmology of their own in which the hunchback theme, evident in the dance behavior of Cayuga and Seneca actors, is most prominent among the Onondaga (Blau 1966, 577).

Plate 7.2. *The mask and rattle of Chauncey Johnny John, Seneca. A: Chauncey poses with mask and rattle. B: Chauncey instructs his mask with tobacco. C: The mask itself.*

Care

Masks require both constant care and frequent use. Unused masks can be a source of illness, at least a serious annoyance, as DeCost Smith (1888, 193) was told at Onondaga. There it was said that a woman's mouth had commenced to grow crooked because of a neglected mask that had not been danced for but her cure commenced when the mask was used in a dance following a proper tobacco invocation. In making one of the early collections, Smith was instructed on taking a mask away by its former owner that one must attach a small bundle of tobacco at the head tie and make a proper invocation at the fire. This act should be repeated every three months, renewing the tobacco in the bag. In this way the new owner would be free of frights and illness that the mask might cause. It is this failure to feed and sacrifice tobacco to the spirits that worries traditionalists about collections of masks in museums. There are all manner of stories about the Morgan and Converse collections in the New York State Museum and the great fire in the state capitol of 1911.

During my tenure as assistant commissioner for the State Museum and Science Service one of our maintenance helpers fell through a plate glass case during the renovation of Morgan Hall. This accident was ascribed to the False Faces. Later, I had Chief Corbett Sundown of Tonawanda make the proper invocation for the collection.

Although not an Iroquois himself, William Guy Spittal, proprietor of *Iroqrafts* at Caledonia by Six Nations Reserve, has created a steady market for Iroquois carvers and has inquired into the masking complex (Spittal

1961). Inasmuch as he sells to collectors and to museums, his remarks on the care of masks seem appropriate as representing thought at Six Nations.

> In the "old days" masks were carved from living trees, while tobacco was burned and a turtle rattle scraped along the tree. This is occasionally done today but most people don't want to talk about it. Now when a mask is made it is carved from a block of basswood, pine, ash, poplar, or maple. . . . It is then painted and given hair [of] horse tail. Anciently, shredded basswood bark or cedar bark were used. . . . At the False Face ceremony tobacco is burned and the Great Defender is asked to bestow power on the mask; then the mask is implored to help and protect his new owner, and to help other people, when called upon. A . . . bag of cloth or skin is tied to the forehead, inside as an offering of . . . Indian tobacco, the food of False Faces. Next the mask is rubbed with grease or melted lard—formerly sunflower seed oil and wild animal grease. It is now a blessed mask.
>
> The person for whom the mask was made is now the centre of the False Face curing rite. If the . . . new mask is used in the curing, it is given a second bag of tobacco. [Spittal 1961, 4].

It is apparently optional whether the owner leaves succeeding tobacco offerings attached to the mask, or removes them as new ones are added. It is believed that under no circumstances should an owner sell a consecrated mask. We know that such theory is neglected in practice, for museums are full of such masks. It is believed also that the owner will become ill if the owner is careless and loses some of the mask's hair. Should this happen, he should make every effort to find and restore it. A few strands might be overlooked, but an entire bunch pulled out in passing through a wire fence during the traveling rite through the community should be searched for.

When not in use, Spittal observes, the mask is usually kept in some remote part of the house or in an outbuilding, sacked with the rattle in a burlap bag in which it is transported; the same is used as a "headthrow" when the mask is put on. If, during the year, the mask is not used, the owner should grease its face, offer tobacco, and provide a feast of mush. These are considered signs of respect between the owner and his "friend" (Spittal 1961).

This close relationship between an owner and his bundle is widespread in North America and certainly is not new among the Iroquois. Although one cannot be certain that a False Face is involved, a seventeenth-century Mohawk manifested similar respect for his "idol." The author of the Dutch Journal of 1634–35 noted that on succeeding days "this chief showed me his idol; it was a head with teeth sticking out; it was dressed in red cloth" (Wilson 1896, 88). He goes on to list other fetishes for good luck.

Transfer of Ownership

Early on in fieldwork among the Seneca at Allegany, again at Tonawanda, and later at the Six Nations Reserve, I inquired into the care, ownership, borrowing, transfer, and inheritance of masks. My sources were both carvers and owners. Jonas Snow, one of the more active carvers at Allegany in 1933, assured me that he only put tobacco on a mask when he intended it for use. From tobacco grown in his garden and dried over the stove, he pulverized a pinch, wrapped it in a tiny sack, and tied to the top of the mask. He then burned tobacco in a fire offering the incense to the Great False Face. Properly, each member of the society has such a bag of tobacco on his mask, but it should be removed before selling the mask. Masks are personally owned but are readily shared with members of the False Face Company. In this sense, they are common property for use. Leaving a medicine bag on a mask and selling it might lead it its harming a new owner, particularly white people.

During the Midwinter Festival of 1934 at Coldspring Longhouse, I slept upstairs in the house of Henry Redeye. Although speaker of the longhouse and properly informed, Henry kept his False Face hanging on the wall at the head of the stairs next to his son's mask, face out and uncovered. I recall awaking on a winter's night to see the moonlight from the snow reflected by the brass sconces around its eyes. Henry knew that some people covered masks, but he felt that his mask protected the house from high winds.

This remarkable red mask was carved by Lewis Twoguns of Coldspring in 1889 (Plate 7-3A). Although not then a member of the society, Henry commissioned the mask, but he did not witness it being carved. It was afterward that Henry dreamed that the mask appeared to him and asked for tobacco, promising to be his guardian in every respect. In this vision, Henry acquired both rituals—Common Faces and the Doorkeeper's Dance—at the same time. Owning the mask caused him to dream, put up a feast, and thereby join the society. To judge by the number of bags of tobacco attached to it, this mask had received considerable use in the community. Henry remarked, "Whenever I go out to cure people, after the ceremony they give me tobacco. I bring it home and tie a little on the mask."

Another notable mask in the Coldspring community was owned by Chauncey Johnny John who carved it himself, instructed me in its care and use, and then reproduced it for the record. (This original mask was most recently in the Congdon Collection in Salamanca, Plate 7-2C.) The case history of this mask represents the interface of museum studies and fieldwork during 1940. Arthur C. Parker, then-director of the Rochester museum and my predecessor in False Face studies, had told me that masks used to be rubbed with oil and that they were scraped; that Ginseng berries were rubbed on the eyes to give second sight. Informants at

Plate 7-3. A: The mask of Henry Redeye, Seneca, Allegany Reservation. B: The five masks of George Buck, Lower Cayuga Longhouse, Six Nations Reserve. C: George Buck displays his collection, 1940.

Coldspring knew about oiling but had never heard of the latter two practices (personal communication, May, 1940).

At the turn of the century, David Boyle was collecting masks on the Six Nations Reserve for what is now the Royal Ontario Museum. He left a vivid account of how an owner parted with a mask and the ritual procedure. The owner stirred the fire, approached the fire wearing the mask from an adjoining room, uttering the False Face cry. He then hung the mask by the head ties over a chair back, invoked the spirits with tobacco, and tied a packet of tobacco to the forehead. He then stroked its long hair affectionately and spoke vis-à-vis to the mask, telling it that it was going away, mentioned their long-time association and participation in cures, urged it to go on doing good for its new-named owner, and promised that the new owner would from time to time burn tobacco for it. The new owner was instructed to rub its face with oil once or twice a year. (Boyle 1900, 28–29.)

This account seemed entirely familiar to Chauncey Johnny John who said he would do the same thing. He commented on rubbing masks with sunflower oil.

> Last fall when the False Face Company went by the houses, then I rubbed sunflower oil on my mask before he went to the longhouse. I did not wear it myself but loaned it to another person. But before he went out of the house, I put a little oil on his face. However, this spring when the company went by I did not do it. Every mask owner is supposed to treat his mask this way. But I do not know what others do.

He was adamant that the Coldspring people never scrape masks. "I just leave it when I get done with it." They are not oiled after use. He added, "We keep them covered in a sack made for this purpose." While he was talking, I could see his mask and two masks of his grandson hanging face out in the adjoining bedroom. Once more, native practice contradicts native theory.

The Mask of Chauncey Johnny John (Seneca)

The case history of this mask is important to the present study because Chauncey was to subsequently reproduce it in various stages to illustrate carving techniques and because it furnished me clues of what to look for in examining older masks in museum collections. It also conveys the feeling of a man for an object of his own creation.

Chauncey made his own mask for his own use without first having had a dream. "I just thought I would try to make one for myself. The first time, it was no good. This one represents the second time I made it."

> I was then living at Cattaraugus Reservation, and I was about thirteen years old. [This would date the mask ca. 1893, for in

June, 1940, Chauncey was in his sixties.] Later I made another just like it, a copy of this one for a Tonawanda boy named Lee Snyder (Djidoʔdoʔ), long since dead, who came here to Coldspring and asked me to make one for him. Afterward he went and sold it to a museum in Buffalo where I saw it.

Close behind our house at Cattaraugus there were woods. I went into the woods and found a cucumber tree (*Magnolia acuminata*). I had brought tobacco with me, and I told the tree what I was going to make. I did not build a fire but just sprinkled tobacco around the tree where it stands. It makes no difference which side of the tree one takes, just so the grain is straight. That tree grew back again where I took out the chunk.

This is what I said when taking a chunk from a living tree to carve a mask [Seneca text]:

neʔ nängę́ ʔishe:t ęgadyäʔdak niwáʔa:ʔ
right here you stand I will a small piece
                                take

ęgęsiono:niʔ ęyǫgwayaʔdanó:nǫ:k agyǫ́:gwe
I am going it will protect us we people
to make
   onǫhgwaʔshεʔ ęyǫgwadǫʔssęǫ:k /
   medicine we shall be using/

o:nęh oyęʔgwaʔǫ:we: ǫgǫʔnigǫjsionya:t
now tobacco real I reward you with

aję:nóniʔgeh ogyä:ʔdak skε:nǫʔ ęsenǫʔdanyǫ:k nängęʔishé:t
take good I shall use well you will be this you stand
care of me   disposed

hęnisasäno:ʔdę: neʔ neʔ agwa:dǫ geóndane:khe:h
what we name namely we say

From you who stand right here I am going to use a little piece [with which] I am going to make (something) that will protect us people, namely as medicine that we shall be using. Now the genuine tobacco with which I have rewarded you [is given] in good faith so that you shall be well disposed (not feel badly when I take away the timber) from you who stand here, namely that which we call the particular tree (cucumber).

That is all.

Medicinal Power from the Living Tree

It is strange in view of Parker's published accounts and pictures that Chauncey seemed unfamiliar with the method and ritual of carving the face on a living basswood tree. James Crow, a noted carver and ritualist then living at Newtown on Cattaraugus, whom Chauncey and I visited, said: "Yes, because the tree is living. Therefore they make the face on the living tree to give the mask greater strength. Then they cut the face off the living tree and bring it home to finish it."

Chauncey, however, stated that he simply chopped half-way through the standing tree, below and above, to get a chunk long and thick enough to make a face and then brought home the living block to carve. To emphasize that he did not carve the face on the living tree, he made a joke about a totem pole with faces on it that a neighbor in Coldspring had carved and erected in the manner of the Northwest Coast peoples.

Besides the ax, the essential steel tools for mask-making are a jackknife and a gouge-adze called a "howel" used by coopers in barrel making. Other tools come into use during the observed carving sessions.

Burning in Woodworking

Before the introduction of steel tools, which had an inevitable effect on carving techniques, the old Iroquois method of woodworking was burning. Indeed burning was practiced throughout the Eastern Woodlands.

> My father (Abraham Johnny John who came from Buffalo Creek) used to tell how they made the faces long ago. They used to burn them out. They made a little fire and watched it, scraping with a stone where it burned around. Father had two or three such stones sharpened at one end which he called a "skinning knife used in olden times." Chauncey supposed that the method was similar to making a corn mortar, which he still made in this way. One chops as far as he can, then lights a fire with chips, and watches that it does not run away and spoil the desired shape.

On older masks, the holes burned through the rim with a red hot awl or wire serve for hair attachment. In modern times, the horse hair is tacked on. Chauncey learned this distinction from his father.

With Chauncey's help and comment, I took measurements and recorded specifications of his red doorkeeper mask (Plate 7-2C), both front and back views, to establish diagnostic clues for describing and dating undocumented specimens that I was to encounter both in the field and in museums.

Front. On the forehead, a ridge of four spines (*onóskeʔ; onóskeot*) extends vertically from the nose to the hairline. This feature is prominent on doorkeeper masks from Cattaraugus but not all have it. At first Chauncey did not seem to know the term *turtle tail* for this motif but then said that his term meant the same thing. He added that Common Faces are not made this way.

Mouth. The flared mouth reveals ten teeth, which are not present in all doorkeeper masks. The outline of the flared lips is rectangular, rather than bifunnelate. Chauncey denied knowing Seneca terms for various mouth types.

Backside. The rim is perforated for seven-hole attachment of the hair and head ties: one hole at the brow, two at the forehead level, two at the ears, and two at the chin. The top and ear perforations serve to hold leather thongs fixing the mask to the wearer's head. The remaining pairs of holes are for securing the hair by loops of thong.

Tobacco Bag. Chauncey claimed that the tobacco bag attached at the upper left was the original.

Finish. The rim edges are thin as in other finely finished masks. The inside was finished smoothly and showed much use. Although the wood resembles maple, which Chauncey said was too heavy for comfort, his was carved of cucumber, which is lighter.

Chin. This mask lacks a definite chin in common with many Seneca masks; instead, the wearer adjusts it to his face by grasping the lips.

Paint. The mask is painted red and is well patinated from use. "I painted it red because I like that color." Evidence of ashes at the mouth recalled many curings. He regularly "fed it" with sunflower oil.

Horses were introduced to Iroquoia late in the seventeenth century. All known False Faces having horsetail hair must date well after that. Before horses came to the Senecas, Chauncey thought that they used bearskin or deer tails for hair on masks. His father had one with bearskin hair, such as Heckewelder (1881, 235–36) describes for the Delaware. He had no knowledge of Basswood hair.

The Dedication of the Completed Mask. Chauncey outlined the steps as follows:

> When I make a mask and paint it, and put some tin around the eyes, I put him by the fire [Plate 7-2B], throw tobacco in the fire, and tell him to do the best that he can to help the people where he is going to stay. Then I call the Indian name of the person who will take him away. Every new mask must be told what he is supposed to do.
>
> After that I put a little tobacco on the brow of the mask, and he goes away to the other person's house, or stays home with me, as the case may be.
>
> See this bag of tobacco [attached to the upper left hole loop]; it is the original one that I put on the mask when I made it.

When I mentioned having seen several such bags of tobacco attached to other masks, particularly that of Henry Redeye, Chauncey remarked that he had no idea why Henry Redeye should have so many bags attached to his mask. This comment may tell more about interpersonal relations than about the care of masks.

Invocation to the Completed Mask. Chauncey hangs the mask facing him on a chair back set near the fire (Plate 7-2B). He holds a cup of tobacco that he commits to embers, while saying:

ęsadiwátonda:t doʔgaʔah niyowɛnǫ:ge:
you listen   a few   words

ęsaʔnigǫįdo:gęh héneya:wę oęndǫ:gwa neʔ nängę́: hǫ:gwe
you will know it will   in future   this very person [name
               happen   of person]

neʔ hęsha:ʔ neʔ dędjadiya:k heh nyawɛníshäge:
who will take   to stay with him as long as he lives.
you along

You listen to the few words by which you shall know how it will be in the future, for this very person (who is named) will take you along to live with him for as long as he shall live.

Then the packet of tobacco is tied to the forehead, whether the mask goes away or stays with him, as attested by the original packet attached to the mask from the time he finished it.

Mask Ownership at Six Nations
Simeon Gibson introduced me to the masking complex at Six Nations Reserve. As a lad, he had assisted M. R. Harrington in collecting, and he had interpreted for A. A. Goldenweiser. He was himself a member of the society. There is no bundle or bag of False Faces at Six Nations that belongs to the whole False Face Society. Individuals, however, may own as many as three to a half-dozen masks that they keep on hand to loan to persons not having any. The then-leader of the company had but one, but Simeon's friend Robert Skye had, besides the one he wore, two or three extra masks to loan to persons to wear at a feast or to go around in the spring and fall traveling rite. "On the latter occasions they always try to make as big a turnout as possible, and those not having masks know where to borrow them."

Borrowing. Extra masks may be loaned or sold, in the opinion of persons I interviewed in 1940. But a mask that comes to a person through a dream and is made for him especially as a guardian, either the miniature or the large mask, must be kept during the owner's lifetime, or unless he dreams otherwise. These particular masks are one's protection.

Borrowing masks between members of the society at Six Nations was an accepted practice. A member who did not own a mask simply borrowed from another. Simeon regularly borrowed from his friend Robert Skye, a member of the opposite moiety. "He would burn tobacco and tell the mask that I was just going to use it for a few days, whereupon I would return it." When a borrower fails to return a mask, the owner may burn tobacco a second time and instruct his mask "to bother that person wherever he may be. It will come out in a dream" that the borrower must return it to its rightful owner. The delinquent borrower will also get sick.

A person may dream of a particular mask that is then borrowed. After Gaylor Smoke's death, Simeon inherited his mask.

> There was one time after that when a certain Cayuga lady on a neighboring road took sick and dreamt that she must have this face that Gaylor formerly owned. That was the only thing that would cure her. So they went all the way up to my place to borrow it. I let them have it. I burned a little tobacco. They used it on that lady and brought it back. Afterward she got better—real well again.

Although he had inherited a mask, my interpreter knew of no case of burying a mask with its owner. He explained how it came to him and how he disposed of it.

> I formerly had a False Face. It must have been an old one because the hair had all fallen off. The hair should be renewed every twenty-five years anyway. One must offer tobacco when the hair is renewed. They always put gray hair on an old mask.

When Gaylor Smoke (Onondaga), Simeon's first wife's mother's brother, died, they gave his mask to Simeon at the Ten Days' Feast. Simeon had helped him while he was sick. Although not one of those appointed to help during the funeral ceremonies, it was awarded to him nevertheless. Simeon kept the mask for ten years, until the hair all came off. He then sold it to the museum in Brantford. "It was a black one. It must have been an old one. They never told me where it came from." It is the custom when a man dies that they distribute everything that he owns among his relatives and friends. The responsibility for how things are distributed and to whom rests with the matron of the particular maternal family. Her say is law. "However, they must give a mask to a member of the False Face Society." Until then Simeon had generally borrowed a mask.

Ownership and Care at Six Nations. George Buck of Lower Cayuga Longhouse proudly displayed for the Smithsonian camera five masks from his collection, while he held a sixth, a beggar mask from Newtown on Cattaraugus Reservation of the Seneca Nation (Plate 7-3B, C). Of the five, four are clearly in the Grand River style, and the fifth appears to be a Seneca mask of the straight-lipped doorkeeper variety from Newtown. Indeed, it was associated with the Seneca Longhouse at Six Nations. From left to right: one and two are the work of John Snow, an Onondaga who died after 1900; both have the vertical ridge of spines above the nose; both are crooked mouthed; both have fine wrinkles over the face, forehead, and nose; but one has the nose to the left, and the second to the right; both are black with black hair; the first has cornered brass eyes, and the second round brass eyes; both have three or more tobacco bags at the forehead. The third is a smiling black Mongoloid or broad-faced mask, with prominent chin and straight nose, and small, closely set eyes. This was George Buck's personal mask, and he claimed it to be the oldest. It also had long black hair and the usual tobacco offerings. The fourth, a smiling wry mouth, with nose bent slightly left, broad faced like the third, and chestnut hair, was painted red. George said this mask led the procession in the traveling rite. The fifth, already commented on, was also red; the spines above the forehead, straight nose, and straight lips are reminiscent of one of two types of doorkeeper masks carved at Newtown. Several of these masks were employed later in a private feast for Simeon Gibson.

In the informant statements on the care of masks at Six Nations, I failed to confirm Arthur Parker's statement that masks were scraped. Gibson said that an owner could scrape and repaint a mask. Oiling the masks is believed to freshen their power; "individual owners do not do this but bring them to the community feast in the spring at the longhouse when all masks are oiled at the same time. The oil is food for the mask and renews its power." The owner's duty is to tie some tobacco into a packet and attach it to the top of the mask whenever it is used to cure a person. This explains multiple packets attached to old masks. A mask in the New York State Museum (Cat. No. 37044) has a tobacco bag hanging at the nose; I found no explanation for this.

Chief John Arthur Gibson, learned as he was in myth and ritual, never told his son about the care of masks. "We never had any while he was living." (He died in 1912.) Whenever Chief Gibson celebrated the feast for the *hana?hi?do:s* (Medicine Company), which requires a mask, it was brought by one of the members. Simeon offered these admonitions:

> Keep the mask upstairs out of reach, especially of children. Oh yes, children are afraid of masks. Hang it on the wall. [He did not seem to think that it must be covered.] Sometimes we put them in a sack so dirt does not get on them, and to keep moths away from the hair.[12]
>
> A falling mask—from its hook in the house—means that someone is going to call on the society to cure.
>
> When a mask sweats, that is a sign that someone is sick, and will call on the maskers in a few days.
>
> Sometimes the rattle will sound indicating that surely someone will call on them for help.
>
> Generally, it is proper to keep the mask in a bag, out of sight of nonmembers, lest they, or the children of the house, see it and become sick.

---

12. Fogelson reminds me that the idea of keeping a mask covered may help to retain its power. He points to the widespread idea in North America of keeping not only medicine bundles but medicine itself covered or wrapped so as to retain its potency. No Iroquois has ever suggested this as an explanation, to the author's knowledge.

Maternity Masks. The so-called "maternity mask," a term that occurs on museum labels (NYSM Cat. Nos. 3760, 37021) and in the literature (e.g., Keppler 1941, 29, Plate V) is evidently a misnomer. Some older masks having ears and earrings appear to be portraits of old women, and there are larger masks to which a miniature is attached to the hair, as if "riding along." Everywhere I inquired systematically about childbirth and whether masks were ever used to facilitate difficult deliveries, and universally the answer from old midwives was "no!" These experienced practitioners were horrified at the thought. However, just as I was satisfied that I had laid this ghost to rest, Avery Jimerson told C. E. Congdon that his father's white mask was called out in such emergencies.

As we have seen, members of the Society of Faces at Six Nations keep miniature masks as personal guardians, having acquired them through a particular dream or by order of a clairvoyant. These talismans are ordinarily kept at home and are not worn publicly on the larger masks. "The masquette belongs to but one person; while anyone might borrow or use the larger mask, providing the borrower is a member of the society."

Invocations for Making and Owning a Mask. To draw all of his previous remarks together, Simeon Gibson systematically dictated and explained six sets of invocations involved in making and owning a mask, as follows:

1. Making the mask
   a. Taking the wood from the tree
   b. When the mask is ready to use
2. Rehairing a mask
3. Promising to hold a feast
4. Loaning the mask
   a. Failure to return
5. Transferring ownership: telling the mask it is going away
6. When a mask falls

Making the Mask. John Snow, a Seneca, already deceased in 1940, lived near Seneca Longhouse, on the north side of the Vth Line Road, just over MacKenzie Creek. He used to make masks around the turn of the century, during Simeon's boyhood (recall that George Buck had two examples of his carving; George Buck identified John Snow as Onondaga). Simeon Gibson did not witness the act, but John Snow told him that he always burned tobacco at the basswood tree where he took the block for carving. Apparently he commenced carving the face on the standing tree and then hollowed out the back before bringing the block home, where he refined the features of the face. Having finished carving the mask, he burned tobacco informing the spirits that the new one was joining the society. He specified in Onondaga the following tools for carving:

1. Curved blade knife   diyudahshá:kdųʔ
2. Curved adze for hollowing out the back   ʔumgaɛ:ʔdahgwá:ʔthaʔ

3. Straight-bladed knife with fine point: *odása:gwáisu̧*
   various sizes
4. Drawknife for trimming edges   *washai:s*

Recent masks are more elaborate than the older ones, which are rather plain. Simeon made this observation after seeing photographs of masks in the New York State Museum. He felt that in recent years carvers had made an effort to make the masks appear "rougher" to scare away disease. This entails more carving and is facilitated by available steel tools.

TAKING THE WOOD FROM THE TREE. The tobacco offering at the tree is addressed to Haduʔiʔgo:na ("the Great Humpedback Being"), telling him that the carver is about to make one (mask) that will be in the society. John Snow spoke Seneca but also Cayuga or Onondaga, as befitted the occasion. The text is in Onondaga.

> o:nɛ waʔgayɛʔgwaidɛʔ ne:ʔ oyɛʔgwaʔɔ́:we nayé:ʔ
> Now the smoke arises   tobacco   which
> (from)   sacred
>
> ɛgadowɛnónyaʔdaʔ
> I will transmit a message
>
> nayé:ʔ dewagadɔhwédyo:nik ɛgeshä:niyaʔ ʔaʔse: gagɔhsaʔ
> as to what I desire (want)   I shall make a new Mask
>
> ʔagwidi:ʔstɛ:ʔ ne saʔnigɔhäwéhaʔ ʔi:s ne;ʔ saduʔiʔgo:na
> don't be   in your mind   you   the great medicine
> contrary   person
> opposed

Then he tells the basswood tree that he is going to cut it:

> nayeʔ di nängé ohóhsäʔ gähe:ˊdaʔ naye:ʔ ɛʔkhgɔhsɔnyáʔtaʔ
> This then this basswood tree from which I shall make a mask

Here he is telling Haduʔiʔgó:na, "The Great Humpbacked One," that he is going to cut the basswood tree so as to carve a mask. He will cut down the whole tree and split it, for it will die anyway. It would blow over.

This is Iroquois pragmatism in the face of native theory.

Now the smoke arises from the sacred tobacco by which I will transmit a message, namely that I desire to make a new mask; so don't be opposed to it in your mind,[13] you the Great Humpbacked

---

13. "The tobacco carries the message to Haduʔiʔ, whom he asks not to interfere with him. Otherwise he might get sick for failure to offer tobacco" (Simeon Gibson).

One. And so it is from this very basswood tree that I shall make the mask.

In this way, he also informs the basswood tree that he is going to cut it. He is also informing Haduʔiʔgo:na that the tree is cut to make a mask. He will end by felling the whole tree and splitting it. "It will die anyway or blow over."

WHEN THE NEW MASK IS READY FOR USE. The masks reside in various houses around the reserve, and this one is about to join the fellowship of the others. Just now the maker owns the mask, just finished, until someone comes along and buys it, when the maker will burn tobacco again, whatever its destination. He should say:

o:nɛ waʔagayɛʔgwaidɛʔ oyɛʔgwaʔo:we wagadowɛnonyaʔthaʔ
Now the smoke arises   sacred tobacco   I send my message

ʔi:s wesayɛʔgwaʔsɔ:wi neʔ saduʔiʔgo:na na:yeʔ o:nɛ
you to inhale the tobacco   thou great one   which   now

wage:yɛnɛndáʔnhaʔ/ o:nɛ dǐh ɛgayaʔdaʔnhaʔ neʔ tcaʔnɔ:we:
I have finished it   Now then it will join   where ever

hɛnídɛ:ʔ ɔkiso:daʔ / da sadɛniyéhtadih neʔ gaʔsasdɛ́ʔsha:ʔ
reside our   So you convey   the power [to this mask].
grandparents

Now the smoke arises from the sacred tobacco by which I transmit my message. Inhale the smoke, you the Great Hunchbacked One, for this one which now I have finished. Now then it will join our grandfathers wherever they are settled. So you should convey power [to this new mask].

REHAIRING A MASK. Deer hide was used before the coming of horses to provide tails for mask hair. Shredded bark of basswood, which strips readily between June and August, appears on recent masks in the Royal Ontario Museum in Toronto and is still used occasionally on the reserve. One cuts the basswood tree at the bottom and pulls off the bast in long shreds by hand. Nowadays whenever a horse dies, the mask makers come and cut off the tail and mane. This is then stretched until dry. Then the tail and mane are cut into thin strips, long enough to go around the rim of the mask. The hair strips are tied with strong cord in loops through holes in the edge of the mask. The best cord for the purpose is twisted groundhog (woodchuck) skin. "For this kill a groundhog and pull out the hair while it is still hot." Then the skin is stretched, and when dry a thin line can be stripped by going around the margins of the hide with a jackknife, the width is then gauged with the thumb. "They claim that that will last longer than the hair on the mask."

The five-hole attachment—at the chin, eyes, and one at top—is considered the proper way to attach hair to a mask. "They claim that one is not supposed to use tacks on a mask; woodchuck skin ties is the proper way." A big loop is left at the forehead (crown) to hang the tobacco offerings.

To the same opening sentence, add:

o:nę nängę wendá:deʔ o:nęo:yaʔ
Now this very day   now another

ʔá:seʔ ęskonǫkhwéʔedęʔ
new   I shall put new hair on you

ɛkhgájiaʔdi:h neʔ sanǫkhkwehäga:yǫ Dá neʔtho
I shall   it your old hair.   That is all.
remove

Now today there is another thing. I am about to put new hair on you (the mask); I shall first remove your old hair.

PROMISING TO HOLD A FEAST FOR A SICK PERSON. When signs of sickness appear that are associated with masks, which are detailed after the text, use the same opening sentence, and add the following words:

oyęʔgwaʔsǫ́:wi sadúʔiʔ naye:ʔ nängę́ deyaguiwadiyéndani
                                        sickness possessed her

gonǫhwákhdanik gonujánohwaks naye:ʔ ʔayę:ʔä naye:ʔ
she is sick   she has   which it seems that
                toothache

deyodohwę:jóhwi neʔ ʔaseyagę́hä:kh neʔthodih neyawę́haʔ
it is necessary   for you to   therefore it shall be
                   blow ashes
                   on her

ęyǫdęʔniyu:dęʔ gagwe:gi ęyagodeʔsáʔikh tcaʔnowahodęʔ
she shall fulfill all   she will have   with what kind
(hold feast)   ready

saiwhanowę́hgwi neʔtho dih nigawę́nage:
you do prefer   these are all the words

Now the smoke arises from the sacred tobacco by which I would transmit a message. Inhale (partake) the tobacco, Haduʔiʔ, and it is because sickness has possessed her, for she is ill with toothache [or whatever specific complaint], which it seems that it requires that you blow ashes on her. Therefore (accordingly) this shall be fulfilled, for she will have everything ready that you require for your feast. And so these are all the words.

KINDS OF FALSE FACE SICKNESS. These are thought to be caused by the mask or require its ministration: toothache (*ganodjianúhwakhs*) (Onondaga); swelling of face (*gotgǫhsɛʔgwɛʔ*); earache (*gohuᵐhdanǫ́hwakhs*); nosebleed (*deyeniukha:s*); possession, jumping in fire for hot ashes: "she has mask sickness" (*gotgǫhsoyɛ:nik*); Twisted mouth, or nose (*deyagotsadá:seʔ*), (*deyagodeniyuhsadá:seʔ*); mask sickness (*ɛ:yagotgǫhso:yɛʔ*) (Onondaga), (*ɛyagotgǫ́hsonyɛʔ*) (Cayuga), (*yatgotguwaró:nyɛʔ*) (Mohawk).

LOANING THE MASK. One burns tobacco and notifies the mask that it will leave the place for a while. To the opening sentence add:

ʔi:s neʔ ʔakhgǫ́hsaʔ ɛgoyaʔthto:yɛʔ
to you my mask I shall instruct you

na:yeʔ ɛsahdɛ́:diyaʻ doga:ʔ niwendage na:yeʔ neʔ waheyɛniháʔdɛʔ
that you shall go for a few days in that I am loaning you
away to him

na:yeʔ neʔ ɛgyá:tsi x
(to) that friend
is my

[Now the smoke arises from the sacred tobacco by which I transmit my message] to you my mask, for I am going to instruct you that you shall be going away for a few days because I am loaning you to my male friend.

FAILURE TO RETURN. The original owner can burn tobacco and instruct his mask to "come through a dream" (appear in a vision to the borrower), saying that he [the mask] wants to come home. It is believed that someone in the family of the delinquent borrower might get sick. "Or the owner can instruct the mask to make someone sick, and indicate through a dream that he wants to return home."

To the usual opening sentence, add:

ʔi:s weʔsayɛʔgwaʔsǫ́:wi neʔ ʔakhgǫ́hsaʔ
you inhale tobacco it my mask

se:yadidáʔsi:ɛʔ gaisɛʔdagú:wa neʔ dǫda:híɛʔdä:ʔne
you will in (his) dream to bring home
appear

diyɛ:ʔgwa hi:yaːʔ sǫgwanowahoʔdɛʔ ɛyagotgǫhso:yɛʔ tcaʔ
if not someone one will get in that
mask sickness

ʔe:ʔwadjiya:yɛʔ DaneʔthonigaːwɛnagexDaneʔtho ni:ga:wɛnage x
in that family So these are all the words.

[Now the smoke arises from the sacred tobacco by which I transmit my message.] You, my mask, inhale the tobacco, so that you will appear in her dream to be brought home. If this is not done somebody in that maternal family will surely get mask sickness. So these are all the words.

TRANSFERRING OWNERSHIP. The maker owns the mask until he transfers it to the person for whom it is made. He will then tell the mask its duties and name the Iroquois personal name of the new owner. If the mask is going to a museum, *diyekdǫʔthaʔ,* "a place where people pass in and out to look," where he says "lots of people will be coming in to see you," he then charges the mask: "You shall go back with him to the museum, and don't create any disturbance there, for you shall remain there forever from now on."

Simeon recalled that M. R. Harrington, the ethnologist, when collecting for the American Museum of Natural History and the Museum of the American Indian among others, was careful to make an invocation to the departing masks at Six Nations. "And he promised to repeat it again in New York. My father helped him. They told the masks they were going away never to return here." Simeon manifest considerable respect for *Djisgogo,* "Robbin," Harrington's Iroquois name.

To the usual opening sentence, add:

ná:yeʔ o:nę waʔgadęhní:yǫ: o:nę ęsahdéndiyah
which now I have sold you   now you shall go away
is

na:yeʔ dí:h nängę hę́:gwe na:yeʔ ętcís:ne   na:yeʔ tcaʔnǫ:we
along with this   man   and   you go   wherever
                                          with him

tonǫhsa:yę ne'tho hęʔsidę́:ndak   naye:ʔ dih dęsè:yęʔniyá:dǫk
he resides there   you shall reside there   and you shall protect
                                                                them

neʔ ʔtgahwajiyä:yęʔ tcaʔno:we hęjisníyǫ
that maternal   wherever you both reach there x
family

[Now the smoke arises from the sacred tobacco which carries my message] that now I have sold you. Now you shall leave here with this man, and you shall go with him to wherever he lives. And there you shall protect the members of that maternal family wherever you both shall arrive.

WHEN A MASK FALLS. One promises to hold a feast when a mask falls from the wall where it is hanging. Such a happening is "a sure sign that somebody is thinking of him [the mask] and will call upon him to blow ashes on her." Such a person might be sick and dreaming of that particular mask. The keeper or owner of the mask makes the offering.

nängę̑ sadúʔiʔ naːyeʔ dih gę̑hjikhgishę̑ʔ
this   what   then perhaps

songwanowá:hodę̑ʔ ę̑yé:yoʔ ę̑yesayaʔdaʔnhaʔ neʔ ʔaseyaʔgę̑hä:kh
someone   will call she will ask you   that you will blow
                   here   a favor   ashes on her x

[Now the smoke arises from the sacred tobacco carrying my message] to you the Hunchbacked one because quite possibly someone will call here asking for your services namely that you will blow ashes on her.

At the pain of some detail we have discussed the nature of the relationship between a man and his mask, the responsibilities of care, and the transfer of ownership. Let us turn now to other props to the ritual, their use and manufacture, before reconstructing the traditional ritual of carving the mask on the tree and describing carvers and their art.

PART THREE

8. Ritual Equipment
The Props to the Ceremony

Paraphernalia

The actors of the False Face Company carry wooden staves or canes and employ three instruments: the classic Iroquois snapping-turtle rattle, a folded bark rattle, and a wooden billet for the singer. In recent years, a tincan filled with stones with stick handle thrust through the ends has replaced the traditional folded bark hickory rattle. Although Conklin and Sturtevant (1953, 264–73) have included these instruments in their discussion of "seneca singing tools," I shall record here my own observations.

TURTLE RATTLE

On late spring evenings, before summer's heat peels the turtle's shell, Iroquois craftsmen, who are often the mask carvers, watch for snapping turtles (*Chelydra serpentina*), otherwise háʔno:wa:h, about ponds and creeks. Of an evening, one may meet a man bearing a burlap sack containing a live turtle, or he carries it by the tail well out from his body; he is bound for the house of a friend whom he knows can "fix it" for a rattle.

Jonas Snow—Maker
In July of 1933, I watched Jonas Snow make two such rattles, recorded his comments, and photographed the steps in their manufacture. One of these specimens now reposes in the Yale Peabody Museum (Catalog No. 25289) (Plate 8-1A).

There are several ways of killing a turtle. One is to drive a nail through its head. Jonas's way was to induce it to bite a soft pine stick and then pry the head out of the shell, as the turtle is reluctant to let go until its neck is fully distended. Then Jonas was able to thrust the tongue of a steel file into its mouth and make an incision with a knife in the side of the neck to slit the jugular vein. He then hung it in a tree by the tail and left it to hang for several days. He remarked, "Turtles do not die until after sundown, and some people say ten days." Other Seneca rattlemakers cut off the tail and hang the turtle by the head, as I was afterward told at Tonawanda and Conklin and Sturtevant (1953) learned at Allegany. The same procedure is followed at Six Nations on Grand River.

Jonas next cut off the feet with a knife and removed the entrails (ʔoksó:wɛʔ) through the apertures left by removing the hind legs. He then removed the front feet and slit the neck up both sides and removed the vertebrae and limb bones. He then inserted a piece of pine to replace the spinal column so as to stretch the neck while it was curing. He threw away the entrails and gave the meat to the dog because turtle meat is not eaten, according to other members of his extended family. "They say you will be ten days dying!" The carapace was then hung in a tree well removed from the house where flies and worms consumed the meat from the interior.

Plate 8-1. Jonas Snow, Seneca, makes a turtle rattle. A: His 1933 model. PMY. Cat. No. 25,289. B: Cleaning the turtle. C: Detail of handle. D: Lashing the handle. E: Completing the lashing with a whip knot.

When the shell was thoroughly dried, he soaked it in the rain barrel for several days to soften the skin so that it would be readily workable. He cautioned that one must not soak the turtle too long lest the carapace shed its scales soon after the rattle has been finished. He also observed that some care must be taken in selecting the time to kill a turtle, as it may be shedding its outer plates and will continue to do so in death (Plate 8-1B).

Details of Manufacture. The following notes were made while observing the manufacture of a second specimen.

The turtle had been soaking in the rain barrel for four days, when Jonas commenced sewing up the big apertures. He remarked that it had remained in the water too long as the skin commenced peeling from the head. He customarily used eel gut for thread, as I observed in the first specimen, but he was out of it. His supply had become too brittle to work. The substitute was raw calfskin that he was cutting with a pair of barber's scissors. Thus there are two kinds of thread for this purpose: gut and rawhide. When eel fishing, Jonas saved the guts, which could be twisted between palm and thigh into a thread having great tensile strength. This he used in the first specimen.

A second type of thread can be spun out of rawhide lines. To cut lines, one sticks a knife upright in a board, notches the edges of a skin so as to grasp the tag end of the coming line. The gauge is a stick with a notch mortised in one side of an end, the width of the proposed line. He held this gauge against the knife with his right hand and drew the line with his left. The skin, being to the left of the knife blade, revolved in a clockwise direction. The line was cut around the periphery. (Chauncey Johnny John employed the same technique in making buckskin lines.)

As fast as Jonas cut the line, his son stretched it. Then the two men, facing in opposite directions, commenced twisting the line between right palm and thigh, working from opposite ends of the line. The entire line rapidly twisted into thread. When working alone, one end of the line is attached to a stationary object. The thread is then stretched and wrapped around two upright objects, such as a chair back.

The whole posterior ventral skin of the turtle is open because the tail has been removed here with the back legs. This, as well as the other apertures, has to be stitched. If the hide is still in raw condition, a handful of table salt or potassium nitrate can be put inside the shell. Edges are trimmed. Sewing commences at the posterior ventral medial line of the rear hole, at the point where the tail was. The stitch commences on the inside with a knot, and the seam proceeds in two directions successively. In this example, the left rear leg hole was sewn first, and then the right, each time from the medial line. The hide is pierced with an awl, and the holes are spaced a quarter of an inch apart on the inner row and a half-inch apart on the outer row, so as to gather the skin in sewing on an arc, for the outer row requires twice the gathering. The stitch is like that used in sewing baseballs. In the "ball stitch," the needle is inserted from the lower side. At the end of each of four seams, the thread is drawn tight and a knot tied on the outside (Figure 8-1A).

Some rattles that I have seen have their rear aperture sewed from the two ends converging to the middle. The knots are on the inside where the stitching starts, and the two ends are tied on the outside where the two seams converge at the median line. A small rattle made by Jonas Snow before 1924 is stitched continuously from side to side. Two from Lyn Dowdy in 1930 were sewed from either side to the middle. Their maker is unknown.

The apertures on either side of the neck where the front legs were skinned out are next stitched. Again, he commenced with a knot on the

Figure 8-1. Stages in the crafting of a snapping-turtle rattle. A: Sewing detail of rear leg aperture. B: Handle detail: side view and top view. C: Ventral splint. D: Dorsal splints.

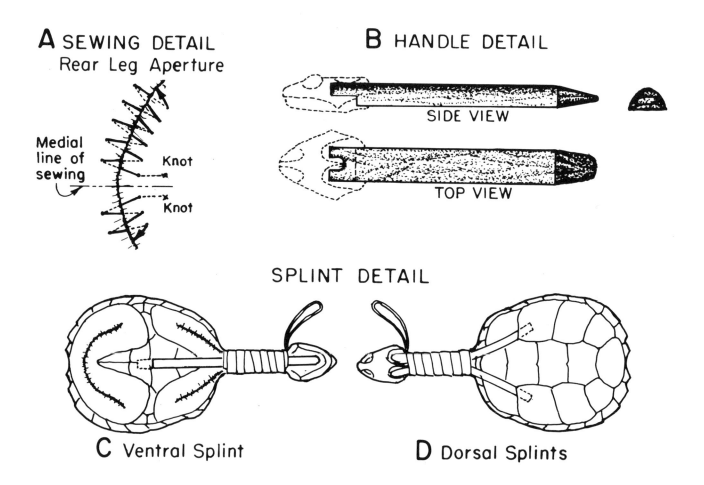

inside, at the posterior end of one of the vents and sewed it completely to the head where a knot was tied on the outside. The opposite aperture is still open. This time the holes for the stitches are spaced equally.

A handful of chokecherry pits were then poured inside the shell, and the sewing commenced again. Jonas gathered cherry pits in the summer, dried them, and stored them in a paper bag, which could be seen hanging from the rafters of his house. Having used what was needed, he tied the bag, handed it to his son, and his wife hung it up again. The cherry pits provide percussion, although other seeds, kernels of corn, and small pebbles may be substituted.

The next problem of providing a stiff handle for the rattle must be solved before completely closing the remaining neck seam. An inner handle must be inserted and fitted to distend the neck and provide a rigid grip. Dry pine is usually selected for the handle (*gatgé:saʔ*) because it is readily whittled with a jackknife. It is measured to extend from the heel of the hand to the extended thumb, which is the distance from the atlas vertebra of the turtle's neck well into the shell—some five or six inches overall. Orienting the handle with the turtle, the proximal end is mortised on the ventral side and cut away and its end is then notched to form a "V" so that the two prongs will extend into the turtle's cranium. The distal end is tapered on its dorsal and ventral surfaces so as to fit between the shell and the sternum plate. Then the whole ventral surface is planed flat (Figure 8-1B). I watched Jonas thrust the distal end into the shell through the remaining aperture (Plate 8-1C), after which he stretched the turtle's head over the proximal, notched end of the stick, which he turned until the prongs articulated with the basal end of the skull.

Other craftsmen mortise the proximal end of the handle on the dorsal side, leaving no prongs to grip the cranial foramina, but they make a ventral tongue that extends into the mandible, holding the turtle's mouth forever open. Jonas insisted that it is better to notch the stick on the ventral side, secure the prongs into the skull, and close the mouth with the ventral splint on the outside.

The remainder of the neck may now be closed. When Jonas reached the end of a seam and because his stitches originated on the inside, he looped the thread on itself and passed the needle through the bight, making a half-hitch on the outside of the seam. Then he cut the thread.

The last problem is to brace the handle sufficiently rigidly so as to withstand the lateral strain of beating the edge of the shell rattle on a bench when singing Great Feather Dance in the longhouse or the False Face dance songs. There is also the vertical strain of a dancer leaning his weight on the top of the handle as he pushes the rattle before him when crawling into a house during the False Face ritual. Three splints, two on top at either side (sometimes three), and a third along the bottom, absorb these stresses. These splints are inserted in slots cut in the shell and lashed about the neck to form the grip. They are called braces (*degádǫgo* Figure 8-1C, D). The term for the two dorsal splints is *degáieǫ*. The splints are of green hickory timber, which is split and worked down like basket handles. Jonas drew them under his jackknife, held in his right hand on his right knee until they were reduced to measure one-half inch wide by one-eighth inch thick. In cross section they are planoconvex, with one flat surface for the inside. He measured them the width of his hand with thumb extended plus two fingers, or nine inches.

He next cut three slits in the shell to receive the splint braces: one on either side of the dorsomedial line at the sutures of the first and second lateral scales, about a quarter of the distance back on the carapace (Figure 8-1D); the third slit was made about a quarter of the way down the sternum on the medial line. This was for the ventral splint (Figure 8-1C). On some rattles, this slot is directly in the center of the bone. (If there are four splints, a third is added on the dorsal side and enters the shell in the middle of the second medial scale. Henry Redeye had such a rattle fabricated by Chauncey Warrior.)

Each splint, in turn, is inserted in its proper slot and bent with the hands to correspond to the curvature of the shell. The ventral splint is straight and extends up under the mandible where it terminates in a rounded end that closes the turtle's jaw (Figure 8-1C). The dorsolateral splints are cut off at the back of the head on a line parallel with the lower jaw (Figure 8-1D). The green splints are now wound in place with a withe of inner hickory bark, and the rattle is hung until they dry in shape.

Lashing the handle or grip is the final step (Plate 8-1D). The grip is whipped with rawhide, buckskin, or hickory bark withe. The lashing commences at the shell with three turns over one end of the lash and terminates at the base of the skull, where the free end is tucked under the last two winds and drawn taught as in whipping a rope (Plate 8-1E). A loop may be formed by tying two free ends together to serve as a hanger; frequently, turtle rattles have a string loop through one of the eyeholes and the mouth.

Raw hickory-bark lashing has the advantage of drying in shape and making a permanent handle. Sometimes skin or raw hide is sewn over the splints.

In recent years, turtle shell rattles have been varnished, but anciently they were not painted in any way.

There was a ready market among Feather Dance singers and members of the False Face Society for turtle shell rattles. Jonas Snow frequently bartered rattles for wanted items; but in 1933 he charged but one dollar to "fix one." I had difficulty keeping the one I acquired for the Peabody Museum at Yale because every singer who saw it wanted it. Besides Jonas Snow, there were four other makers of these rattles at Coldspring in the 1930s—Chauncey Johnny John, Chauncey Warrior, and John and Avery Jimmerson, father and son. Each of them had made a great many, but seldom did they possess more than one or two at a time. In my observation, nearly every longhouse member at Coldspring had at least one turtle rattle. And they could be readily borrowed.

Six Nations

The method of making a giant turtle rattle (*ganyaʔdęgo:na gasdawęʔsä:ʔ* [Onondaga]) at Six Nations Reserve is essentially the same. The turtles are caught in the spring when they first come out from wintering in the muck of ponds and swamps. (Simeon Gibson had observed the turtles migrating from the swamp near his house into the Grand River in springtime.) A wire is tied around the turtle's neck, and it is hung from a tree. After two weeks it is taken down, and the neck and legs are slit; it is eviscerated, and the meat is cleaned out. (Contrary to Seneca sources, Gibson held that the meat is good medicine for smallpox and other contagious diseases such as measles or laryngitis. The meat is spread in the sun until dry and put away for the winter.) Then the eviscerated turtle is hung again until thoroughly dry. Then it is soaked so that the seams can be sewn. String of woodchuck skin is used because basswood string is not strong enough. (Gibson had watched Gaylor Smoke, the mask maker at work on turtle rattles.) The strut or splint of round wood that distends the neck is forked at the head and pointed aft, as in Jonas Snow's rattles, and is driven into the shell to secure it. Again, three splints—two on top and one underneath—are wound in place with woodchuck hide to form a grip. Before it is entirely closed, cherry pits are put inside for percussion.

Simeon recalled a giant snapping turtle rattle formerly at Onondaga Longhouse for the sole purpose of the Hadu?i?. The first masked man to enter the longhouse carried this giant rattle (Plate 8-2D).

Wooden Replicas

Wooden replicas of snapping-turtle rattles never were common, but they do exist in collections. One such example (New York State Museum, Catalog No. 36945/04-C) (Plate 8-3A, B), which was probably collected by Harriet Maxwell Converse at the turn of the century, is a faithful reproduction of a snapping-turtle rattle, complete with extended neck and head, and a tin plastron tacked on the ventral side. It was carved from some hard wood, probably maple. The only feature lacking is the wooden splints, here unnecessary to brace the handle as on genuine snapping-turtle rattles. This reproduction illustrates a tendency of the Iroquois to play around with their art by transferring a form to a different medium. In the process, a structural invention becomes an objet d'art. Such wooden turtles also had a utilitarian purpose; at Cattaraugus they were the instrument for accompanying the Great Feather Dance, and they were used by singers for the False Faces. Although I have never seen one in use, Sturtevant found it employed at Newtown Longhouse in 1950.

BARK RATTLES

Before tincans reached the reservations, maskers who lacked turtle rattles carried rattles made of folded hickory or elm bark. They are easily made. First, I will give the generalities of their use and then the details. In June when bark peels readily, a cylinder of green hickory bark is slit longitudinally and then peeled around the tree. The maker spreads the slit cylinder at the middle by inserting his thumbs and then folds it end to end, placing one curled end inside the other (Plate 8-3C). A few cherry pits, pebbles, or kernels of corn provide the necessary percussion. There is no set number as among the Cherokee who always used seven, the magic number (Fogelson, personal communication). Iroquois makers plug the open end with a corncob or stick and lashes the handle with a bark withe. A man can make a dozen such bark rattles in a summer afternoon and toss them in the loft overhead to dry.

There they repose until the next Midwinter Festival, when a band of

Plate 8-2. *Turtle rattles in museum collections. A: Collected by Morgan at Tonawanda, 1860. Nationalmuseet, Copenhagen, Cat. No. H.c.363. Photo courtesy NMC. B: Fenton Collection from Lyndsey Dowdy at Coldspring, Allegany Seneca Reservation, 1924. MAI-HF. C: Ventral view showing splint and stitching of leg holes. D: Turtle rattle with serrated splints. MVF/M, Cat. No. R236/57. Courtesy MVF/M.*

A

B

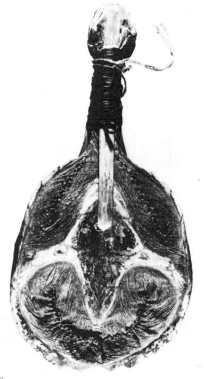

C

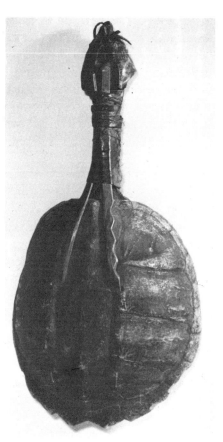

D

Plate 8-3. A, B: Wooden replica of snapping-turtle rattle (front and back). Seneca of Cattaraugus. NYSM, Cat. No. 36945. C: Folded bark rattle by Jonas Snow of Allegany. D: Folded bark rattle by Chauncey Johnny John, Seneca of Allegany.

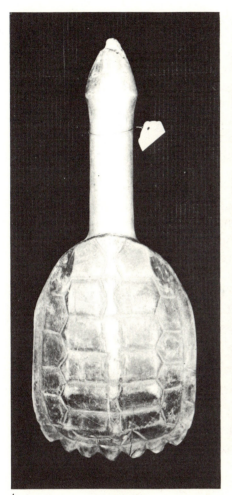

A

B

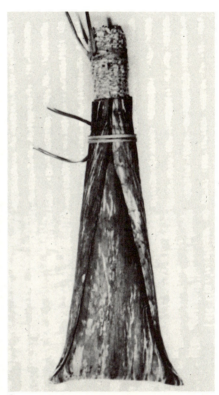

C

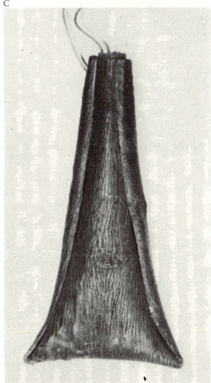

D

outlandishly attired little boys wearing beggar masks may visit that house on their rounds to solicit or pilfer food and tobacco for a feast. The rattle maker will reward them, and then, reaching overhead, distribute his bark rattles to those poor youngsters who were unable to locate turtle rattles and may be carrying sticks of kindling wood or tincans filled with pebbles. The rattle maker may have no children of his own, or he may belong to the generation of classificatory grandparents who befriend and teach youngsters the old ways. He will invariably sing for them, and they will dance individually and together for the amusement of the household before they depart.

A rattle borrowed from a dancer or a stick of firewood is good enough to beat time for the False Face dancers. The Iroquois are ingenious in making do with whatever comes to hand. There are special dance tempo beaters that range in design from wooden cudgels to the elaborate wooden replicas of snapping-turtle rattles already described. But singers do very well without them.

Although I have observed several craftsmen making bark rattles, I shall describe the work of one artisan that represents my first recording of the process when my eyes were focused on the details that became routine later. Then I shall describe a repeated observation seven years later in the same community.

Jonas Snow—Maker

One June evening after supper in 1933, my host Jonas Snow was stripping bark from green white hickory sticks about two and one-half inches in diameter that he intended to split and fashion into basket handles.

Hickory bark is readily stripped by tearing a longitudinal stripe a half-inch wide the length of the stick. The remaining bark will then peel easily and is then saved for folding into rattles, or it can be split into withes for binding splint basket rims. If it is not used immediately to make rattles, or split into strips, it will curl of itself and become useless.

While the bark is still green and wet with sap, it is simple to make rattles. The thumbs are inserted at the middle and the bark cylinder is spread with the hands; this separates the curled edges. The bark naturally buckles, and it can be folded readily between the thumbs and the first two fingers of each hand. The top end (Figure 8-2B[1]) is then folded into the bottom end (8-2B[2]); the folded bark is now half its former length, about twelve inches, and it is triangular in shape (Figure 8-2A–C).

The inner edges (Figure 8-2C[3, 4]) of the bottom half are trimmed with a knife so this end in curling will embrace the folded end (B[1]) that curls on itself. The whole handle is then wrapped with a withe of hickory bark, and it is left to dry. The rough ends are trimmed to the desired length overall, about ten inches. When the triangle of folded bark has dried, kernels of corn or cherry pits are poured into the open end, which can now be corked (Figure 8-2C[5]). The plug can be a corncob, a piece

Figure 8-2. Stages in the crafting of a hickory-bark rattle. A: The roll of bark. B: Spreading the bark cylinder with thumbs. C: Folded, tied, and plugged (with detail of loop).

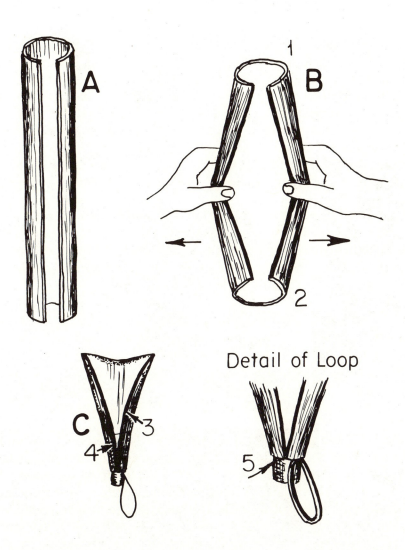

of whittled pine, or a cork. A hole is bored in one edge of the bark near the end and a loop of string inserted for a hanger. Jonas, however, drove the string in with the cork.

Chauncey Johnny John—Maker
The folded hickory bark rattle antedated the snapping-turtle rattle, in the estimation of Chauncey Johnny John, of Coldspring, whom I found ready to go into the woods to peel bark in June of 1940. He commented that "in olden times they used no turtle rattles. They just had the folded hickory bark rattles. This is the old-time rattle of the False Faces." Although informant testimony on history is notably unreliable, for we know that turtle rattles go back to the seventeenth century, the association of the bark

Plate 8-4. The steps in making a folded bark rattle, by Chauncey Johnny John, Seneca of Allegany. A: Peeling bark from a hickory tree. B: Peeling the strip around the tree. C: The roll of bark. D: Folding one end into the other.

rattle with the False Faces is firm, their manufacture is consistent with other Iroquois bark technology, and the fact that we have no early documentary records of them may be due to their perishable nature. Chauncey continued, "Now is the time to slip the bark and make these rattles." He had been thinking of going into the woods after bark. "Just slip the bark and fold, tie until dry, and plug the end with a corncob." Making a hickory bark rattle is that simple (*djogä:ga:s ʔosnǫʔ gasdawɛʔshɛʔ*).

We found several clumps of young bitternut hickory trees growing near a brook on the south side of Pierce's Run, just west of the Allegheny River. Chauncey, an experienced woodsman, selected a clump having smooth bark and trunks some four inches in diameter. He notched the bark with an ax about four feet above ground and then slit the length of the trunk down to a second cut just above ground. Then with his hands he peeled the bark around the trunk (Plate 8-4A–D). In one instance he left a strip of bark two inches wide, saying that it would not then kill the tree. In all, he took bark from three trees. Pragmatist that he was, he made no tobacco invocation. Similar rattles can be made as late as August from soft maple bark.

The accompanying drawing from my field notebook (Figure 8-2) and photographs illustrate the stages of manufacture (Plate 8-4B, C).

On reaching home, while the bark was still green, he took a section of shelled bark about three feet long and, selecting a place for the bend, tapered and trimmed from the bend about twelve inches in each direction. One end was trimmed so that it would turn inside the other. He tried several times to bend one folded end into the curve of the other end. Finally, he shortened the end that would fold inside (Plate 8-4D).

He next tied the folded bark in place with string of basswood bark, or strips of inner hickory bark. The ties were made in three places by running the string around the broader end, and knotting the string at each crossing (Plate 8-5A). Then he trimmed off the longer, outer end (Plate 8-5B).

The finished rattle measured thirteen by seven inches. It was put aside to dry.

Commenting on his creation, Chauncey advised:

> Before it is thoroughly dry, put some fine round stones inside and plug the open end with a corncob. The corncob will never come out because its sides are rough. When the rattle finally dries, take off the strings. This is the best kind of rattle for *hǫ hǫ* [the nickname of the False Faces from their cry].

Here Chauncey shook the rattle edgewise, rubbing the smooth side on the floor in the manner of the maskers.

Smooth bark hickory (*djogä:ga:s ʔosnǫʔ gáhsǫwi:yo:*), literally, "hickory bark smooth kind," is also used.

A finished Johnny John rattle was presented to the U.S. National Museum (Cat. No. 380918).

MINIATURE MASKS

Miniature masks have been discussed as personal talismans, in connection with dreams, and with respect to membership in the Society of Faces. We have seen that they sometimes ride along on the hair of other masks in the traveling rite. At Cattaraugus, the leader of the society, a matron, carried as her staff of office a striped pole on which hung a small tobacco basket, a miniature wooden face, a tiny Husk Face, a diminutive turtle rattle, and a tiny basket for tobacco. With this ritual baggage she led the masked company when they visited the houses exorcising plagues in spring and fall.

Besides this emblem pole, the carvers have seen fit to sculpt miniature masks on canes.

MASKER'S COSTUME

At one time, Iroquois maskers wore suits of bearskin, like the Delaware. Of late, any outlandish disguise, such as tattered blankets or burlap sacks and flour sacks, which also serve as headthrows, is worn over overalls or blue jeans that were the official reservation uniform long before these working garments were taken up by undergraduates and became high fashion.

CANE

The great world-rim dweller carries a giant hickory tree (*onɛno:ga ʔgó:na* [Onondaga]), the limbs lopped off to the top, as he travels the earth shaking the ground. His staff is imitated by the poles that the maskers carry in their rounds today. If one forgets to save an old cane from a previous ceremony, which by now is dry and lighter, one goes to the woods and cuts a new one, leaving on the bark but stripping the branches. These staffs are not painted or striped.

EMBLEM POLE (MATRON'S STAFF)

As already described, the decorations on the matron's staff at Cattaraugus—miniature False Face, Husk Face, snapping-turtle rattle, and tiny tobacco basket—were the charms that individual members of the society might keep as guardians. Parker (1909, 180) specified the attachments to the leader's pole but not the sex of the leader. Jesse Cornplanter frequently mentioned the emblem pole in conversation but did not describe it in his published account of the False Faces (1938, 204–6). At least one such

Plate 8-5. Steps in completing a bark rattle.
A: Ties. B: Ready to dry. C: Finished rattle
(front) USNM, Cat. No. 380918.

staff was reproduced by the Seneca arts project at Tonawanda for the Rochester museum. I do not recall seeing one in another collection.

A boyhood drawing by Jesse Cornplanter (1903), in the New York State Library, of the False Faces on their rounds at Cattaraugus shows the two leaders carrying hickory canes striped with hematite and decorated as mentioned, but the two leaders are clearly males (Tooker 1978, 462).

Traditional Ritual of Carving the Face on a Tree

It is the official tradition everywhere in Iroquoia that False Faces were carved on living basswood trees and that the procedure was highly ritualized. A recent scholar of the subject has pointed out that this ceremonial procedure lacks historical substance and suggests that our knowledge of it is a reconstruction (Hendry 1964, 379–80). Indeed, all of the extant museum specimens of faces carved on a basswood tree trunk were commissioned for exhibit purposes as illustrations of this tradition.

PARKER'S RECONSTRUCTION

There is no historical record antedating 1905, when Parker prompted his Newtown informants at Cattaraugus Reservation to pose for his camera offering tobacco and sculpting the face on a living basswood tree (Parker 1910b, 61–62, Plate 18; here Plate 8-6). The type specimen is in the New York State Museum (Cat. No. 36917; Plate 8-7). Parker's report to the then-director of the state museum carries the illustration, and the caption reads:

> False faces are carved upon living tree trunks of basswood trees by a wood carver chosen by the False Face Company. While he carves, an officer of the company chants the carving song, casting native tobacco on the ceremonial fire as he sings. When the mask is rudely formed, the tree is cut and the mask taken from the log to be finished elsewhere.

This is the only mention of the carving song in the literature. None of my sources mentioned it.

Parker extended his remarks in a later publication (1923, 401–2). Masks were carved on living trees because supposedly they would "contain a portion of the life spirit of the tree." The absorbent quality of basswood for drawing out diseases and for healing wounds is well known in Iroquois medicine. Parker adds that the tree was visited for three days: (1) On the first they gathered and offered tobacco from the roots to the branches; (2) at sunrise next day the prayer was repeated, beseeching the tree to help someone; (3) on the third day, the prayer was repeated. "If at

Plate 8-6. The ritual of carving a face on a living basswood tree. Arthur C. Parker photo for NYSM; Negative now in RMSC, RM 2088. Photo courtesy RMSC.

the first stroke of the ax the tree remains firm, it has consented." The Face was outlined on the bark and then cut into the tree six inches. The tree was thanked and the block removed (cf. Parker 1923).

In an interview with Parker in July of 1940, he recalled that in 1905 carving on a tree was said to be an old method. However, it had by then gone out of use. Parker succeeded in getting the process reconstructed. In the picture of the carvers at work that was published in the state museum director's report (Parker 1910b, 62; Plate 18), he said: "Ward B. Snow is the fat fellow looking on; Delos Kettle is offering tobacco, and the carver is a chap named Green who lived near Newtown Longhouse." Note that there is a curved adze or howel stuck in the tree trunk. At the time of his fieldwork, Parker saw a number of these adzes, which were made by a

Plate 8-7. The type specimen of a face carved on a tree. A, B: Specimen and detail. A. C. Parker, collector. NYSM, Cat. No. 36917. Photographs by N. E. Baldwin, courtesy NYSM.

A

B

local blacksmith in Collins, in use among carvers. In his day as in mine, instead of carving on living trees, carvers sought sections of well-seasoned barn beams of soft clear pine. Easily carved, they made good False Face blocks. Green wood checks. "Ward Snow used to soak the block he was working in the creek to keep it from checking." Burning holes in the rim of the mask for the attachment of the hair was still common practice among Seneca carvers in 1905. Even when augurs and drill bits were available, Parker witnessed Seneca farmers burning holes in whiffle trees with a red hot iron rod.

After Parker's publication, other museums acquired similar specimens for exhibit. George Heye procured at Cattaraugus Reservation a "live mask carved on a basswood log 46 inches long" (MAI-HF Cat. No. 18/8655; Plate 8-8). The mask face is in the typical Newtown style. It measures eight and three-fourths inches from the top of the forehead to the lowest edge of the extended lips.

Such masks carved on a living tree or believed to have been done in accordance with ritual are considered more powerful. Even masks of unknown provenience may receive this attribution. Sherman Redeye believed that this was the way his father's mask was carved and "that is why it is poison." However, Henry's mask was carved out of pine, and it was commissioned to Lewis Two Guns.

We are indebted to Parker for his pioneer attempt to recover the activity, for the ceremony is no longer observed by the Iroquois, and it is not an activity that an anthropologist can readily witness. This much is certain, however; the three essential parts of the traditional ritual of carving the mask on a tree are (1) the prayer or invocation to the tree; (2) the actual carving; and (3) the invocation to the finished mask.

In 1940, one could observe carvers at work; one could elicit comment on local styles of carving and recover ample data on the carving process.

Carvers and Their Art

We have detailed observations of at least a half-dozen carvers at work with comments on style that span the first half of this century. Starting with Goldenweiser's record of Gus Yellow's carving at Six Nations in 1912, I followed with Chauncey Johnny John's demonstration in 1940, which engendered comments by Jesse Cornplanter on the Newtown tradition. In the same year, Marjorie Lismer and I did a case history of Tom Harris at Six Nations; there are my interviews with Jonas Snow; and during two and one-half years of residence at Tonawanda during the 1930s, I made notes on carvers working on the Seneca Arts Project.[1] These details are worth

---

1. Sturtevant made detailed notes and photographed Ed Curry carving a False Face at Allegany in 1958.

Plate 8-8. Other museums sought replicas. Live mask carved on a basswood log, 46 inches long. A, B: Specimen and detail. Seneca, N.Y. MAI-HF, Cat. No. 18/8655. Courtesy MAI-HF.

A

B

preserving, and they do add up to a pattern. First, I will present the case histories.

GUS YELLOW AT SIX NATIONS RESERVE (GOLDENWEISER, 1912, 474–75) (PLATE 8-9A)

Of the little time that Goldenweiser spent on material culture, the False Faces interested him as artistic creations. Before writing up his notes, I reviewed them with Simeon Gibson who interpreted for Goldenweiser and was present during the carving sessions. F. W. Waugh, also of the Anthropological Survey of Canada, which employed Goldenweiser on contract, photographed the operation. The original manuscript and negatives are in the National Museum of Man at Ottawa. After the mandatory summary report, Goldenweiser published only a paragraph or two on this subject in his two textbooks—*Early Civilization* (1922) and *Anthropology* (1937). In his usual perceptive way, he noticed the contrast of wide variation and pattern; he was aware of the problem of style; and he foresaw later interest in color symbolism. He hoped these data might undergird a more elaborate study of False Face technique and styles from an artistic point of view.

In keeping with the practice of his contemporaries at Six Nations, Gus Yellow did not burn tobacco in the bush. According to Gibson, "He had the block ready when we got there. He simply took it off the woodpile. It is better to have dry wood anyway because green wood checks."

Gus Yellow, or Deyunaʔkwagí, as Goldenweiser rendered his Onondaga name, selected a block of poplar wood and converted it into a chunk of appropriate size with an ax. First, he took off a little wood from the undersurface with a knife (probably the drawshave [II]); and then hollowed out the inner surface (the back) with a curved adze (I). During this operation, he sat straddle of a wooden bench as in Waugh's photographs (Plate 8-9A, B), or on a drawshave horse, which enables holding the work firm and freeing both hands for the drawshave. Otherwise, he held the work with his left hand and worked with his right, the direction of strokes being toward him. An even surface was achieved by long strokes. Having finished hollowing the back with the adze, he returned to the outer surface (front) and worked with the drawshave. (Goldenweiser made drawings of the adze and two sizes of drawshave and listed the pertinent terms.[2])

The worker sits with both legs on the one side of the bank and holds the chunk between his thighs so as to free both hands for the drawknife (II).

2.   I Adze   ksaʔdụnyaʔthaʔ; or uagonyaʔthaʔ (Simeon Gibson)
        II Drawknife   washai:s; yoʔwisá:ta
        III Little knife   krinaʔdaʔkhwa, "I'll whittle with it" ʔása:ʔ (S.G.)
        IV Curved knife diudaʔshará:gda

He then holds the chunk in front of himself and adzes (I) the eye grooves by a single stroke from the eyebrows downward. Then he does this in the opposite direction. He continues in the same way to hollow out along the cheeks, leaving an elevation for the nose (geʔnyu̜su̜ʹnyaʔ, "I make a nose") (see Figure 8-3A, B). The mouth follows, with the adze (I) at the lower edge of the nose.

Holding the chunk with forehead toward himself, the carver employs the drawknife (II) to reduce the section below the nose. Then he uses it to even down the sides. He next smooths down the surface under the nose a little. Switching to the adze (I), he cuts a little deeper, making vertical lines beneath nose and eyebrows. Then measuring by eye to a point beneath the nose, he planes the mouth. Again with the adze (I), grooves are cut on both sides of the nose.

Taking up the little knife (III), the carver cuts around the eyes, beneath the nose, and the lower edge of the nose, and the sides of the nose are made deeper. In working with the little knife (ʔásaːʔ), the chunk is held with the left hand. The worker deepens grooves previously made and forms the alares (wings) of the nose. He deepens surfaces of the cheeks and sharpens the upper edges of the eyes. Then cutting away the lower edge of the nose, he forms the nostrils.

With the drawknife (II), he smoothes the surface below the nose on which the mouth will appear. He then cuts out the mouth by first making a small groove just below the nose. (The mouth is to be bifunnelate in shape). The shape of the mouth is achieved by grooving out the surrounding surfaces, beneath the lips to form the chin and indenting both sides of the lower cheeks. The cheeks that have now become excessively protuberant from cutting in the eyeholes and lips are reduced (Figure 8-3C).

Returning to the eyebrows, then making the nostrils flare on both sides, then refining the lips, the face begins to assume recognizable form (Figure 8-3D).

The shape of the chin, a prominent feature on Grand River masks, is then accented. Using the adze (I), the carver makes a groove just below the center of the lower lip. It is completed with the curved knife (III). The groove beneath the lower lip is now made very deep, thus bringing out the flared mouth and chin. The carver then completes the inside of the mouth and finishes the upper edge of the upper lip and the lower edge of

---

V Bore (awl)		khgaʔrundasdáʔkhwaʔ, "I bore with it"
VI Narrow blade knife		ngayu̜ʔdaʔa; ʔasaːʔnigayu̜ʔdaʔaʔ (S.G.), "little knife with fine pointed blade"

These terms are subject to verification. Goldenweiser's phonetics were erratic at best. His effort to learn the native terms for tools and stages of the production is laudable. I have listed these terms because he follows them through his notes and identifies each tool by Roman numeral.

Plate 8-9. Six Nations carvers at work, 1912. F. W. Waugh photos, courtesy NMM, Ottawa. A: Gus Yellow, astride bench, using curved adze. B: Gus Yellow, astride bench indoors, hollowing back of mask with curved adze. C: Chief David Key, Seneca, carving.

A B C

the nose. Cutting off the outer corners of the upper lip draws attention to the cheeks.

The cheeks are then hollowed out from the middle of the face to the upper lip and then lower on the side toward the chin. This permits deepening the surfaces above, below, and to the sides of the mouth.

Until now, the chin has ended square with the chunk. It is then cut down perpendicularly to the chunk, and the lower edge is smoothed and rounded with the drawknife (II). (To accomplish the reduction of the chin, the carver sits with both legs on the front of the bank, left curved behind the right, holding the chin upward between his knees, using his legs and arms and hands in coordination to pull off shavings.) Similarly, the edges are planed smooth with the drawknife.

Attention is next directed to the eyes with the small knife (III). Cutting the lower edge of the nose still shorter and deepening the nostrils increase the distance from nose to mouth considerably. The wings of the nose are accented by cutting the underside back so that the tip of the nose protrudes downward.

Typical of the Grand River style of carving is the treatment of eyebrows and forehead. A series of as many as five sets of parallel radiating wavelike wrinkles crease the forehead above the eyebrows (Figure 8-3-E). Similar grooves beneath the eyes and on the cheeks around the mouth enhance

Figure 8-3. Stages in the manufacture of Gus Yellow's mask. A: Making grooves for eyes and cheeks. B: Working lower part of face. C: Reducing the cheeks. D: Treatment of eyebrows, flaring nostrils, refining lips. E: Treatment of forehead—five sets of radiating wrinkles. F: Boring five holes for attachment and trimming inside to fit face.

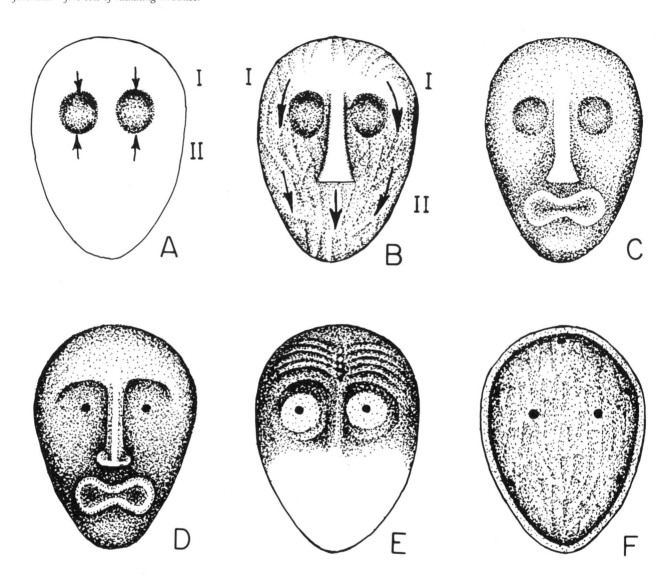

the shapes of eyes and mouth. (See the illustrations of the masks of George Buck and other masks from Grand River: Plate 7-3B, C.) Goldenweiser noted some ten steps in the carving of these grooves.

Turning to the back or inside of the mask, the block is hollowed out with the adze (I). The reason given for not doing this earlier is to afford greater resistance to the previous steps in carving the face. Otherwise, pressure might break through to the back. Holes are now perforated for eyes (III). Similar holes are made for the corners of the mouth and nostrils with the gimlet (V) (ęhá:kdaʔ). The inner surfaces are then cleaned out with a knife (III).

The knife with the small blade (VI) serves to complete all inner features: mouth, eyes, and space for wearer's nose.

Gus Yellow tried on the mask several times, taking off inner surfaces here and there to fit his face. A hook-nosed scraper (VII) (deyudaʔsá:khdų "small bent knife") is used for smoothing inner surfaces (Figure 8-3F).

Gus Yellow then made five holes (V) in the rim for the cords to attach the hair and the mask to the wearer: one at top, a pair at eye level, and a pair near the chin. (Note that he did not burn these holes with a hot wire but used a gimlet. Older masks have seven holes for attachment.)

The mask is now ready to paint. Gus Yellow specified the plants to produce black or red dye, but Goldenweiser failed to record or collect the species involved. F. W. Waugh has a list of such plant dyes in his notes. Gus also described how the dyes were produced once plants were collected by boiling down the bark until the proper color was achieved.

Goldenweiser's notes end by stating that the entire operation took Gus Yellow some five and one-half hours.

It will be interesting to compare these notes with the observations of Tom Harris carving at Grand River in 1940 (Case 4).

CHAUNCEY JOHNNY JOHN'S DEMONSTRATION AT ALLEGANY, 1940

Tools Used in Mask Making

The following tools are used in mask making:

    ax: *ado·gę'*; **askwisa'*
    tool handle: *gatge·'sa'*
    drawshave: *deyo'weno·n*—two (double) handles; handle on either side
    pencil (charcoal when so used): *yeyadǫhgwa'*—to mark with
    handsaw: *dęnyenesdiya''tʿa'*—"they cut boards with it; a board-cutting instrument" (literally); *ganestɛ'*—"board"
    small handax: *niwa''skwisa''a*

Plate 8-10. Chauncey Johnny John, Allegany Seneca, demonstrates the carving process. A: Selecting a basswood tree. B: Notching the tree.

Cutting or drawshave bench: *deyowenon gadzi′gaya'*—"two-handled (cutting) chair"

chisel: *yohgeogwa't'a'*—"a chip [*ohga′·'*]-removing tool; something with which to take a chip out"

gouge adze, or "howel": *o'so′'doshɛ'*—"round edge ax[?]"[3]

Crooked knife (with antler handle): *deyotganya′'sekdo·*—"knife (*gaga′nya'shɛ·'*) that is crooked (*deyosak′do·*)"

Chauncey's knife bears a hallmark that is no longer legible.

Selecting a Tree

Along the river road below Ononville and Jock's Point, toward Cornplanter and just above State Line Run, Chauncey looked for a tall, straight basswood tree growing on the lower river terrace. He selected such a tree growing on the bank of the first river terrace that he deemed suitable for carving a mask (NYSM Herbarium specimen No. 460). This tree was probably sixty feet high and sixteen inches wide at the butt. It was straight and free of knots for about twenty feet up to the first branch. This is important for insuring a "clear" block for carving (Plate 8-10A).

Chauncey first notched the tree halfway through with the ax. Then he cut a stalk of black cohosh (*Cimicifuga racemosa*) that was growing nearby and measured the depth of the cut. Then he measured two lengths of twelve inches up the trunk above the first notch and started a second, upper notch (Plate 8-10B; Figure 8-4A). Chauncey said it was better to take home the block and dry it than to cut the face on it because the block would check in drying out and split any mask that was carved on the standing tree.

Having finished the cuts, Chauncey cut a wedge of iron wood and sharpened the end to a point against the tree trunk. He thus produced a series of wedges for splitting away the block (Plate 8-11A, 1; Figure 8-4B).

Using one of the wedges as a spud, he peeled the bark away from the trunk to expose the block, and drove two wedges into a slit started with the ax (Plate 8-11B), driving the second wedge below the first. When this operation failed except to illustrate how it was formerly done, as a last resort he decided to fell the tree and cut out the whole section to take home for making two masks.

---

3. According to Charles E. Congdon, of Salamanca, this tool was formerly known as a "howel" and was much used by the early settlers in the manufacture of sap tubs, butter bowls, and dugout canoes. Blacksmiths formerly made these tools for the Seneca, and Chauncey obtained his howel, which he sold to a museum collector, from the blacksmith at North Collins, New York, near Cattaraugus Reservation. This one had double bits: one edge was straight and the other curved. Some had only one curved cutting edge. Before these tools were introduced, the Seneca used to burn out the back of masks as in making a corn mortar.

Plate 8-11. Taking the carving block.
A: Sharpening wedges. B: Driving wedges.

A

B

Preparing the Block

That evening Chauncey split the block and stood the two halves behind the stove to season.

Ten days later after the blocks had seasoned, he finally selected one from the back half of the tree because it had better grain. He also remarked that the round side presented a better surface for carving. He said it was not necessary to carve the mask on the sunny side of the tree. He hewed one side of the block for a working surface.

Outlining the Features

Having removed the hair from his own mask, which he was about to reproduce, he laid the mask down on the hewed flat surface and traced around it with a piece of charcoal. "Injuns don't use no pencil," he remarked; "white men only use pencil." (Later I observed him using a pencil) (Plate 8-12A, 1). He went to the chopping block and hewed around the charcoal line. Then he turned the slab end for end and hewed the side,

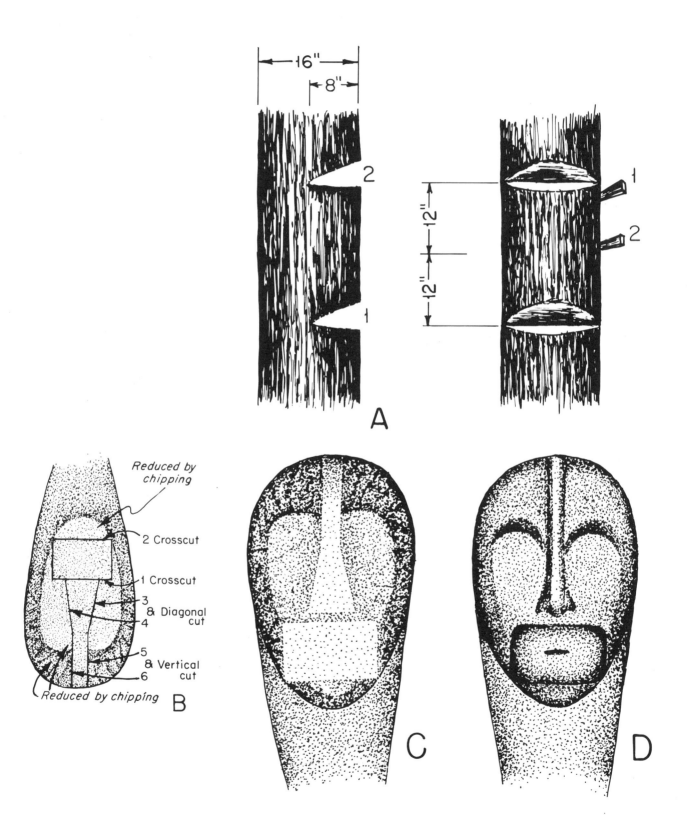

Figure 8-4. Stages in carving Chauncey Johnny John's mask. A: Notching the tree and wedging out block. B: Detail of saw cuts on face. C: Beginning mouth. D: Cheeks flattened and mouth hole begun.

Plate 8-12. Outlining the face. A: Hewing around the outline. B: Hewing both sides and top.

rounding the forehead end. He remarked, "My ax isn't sharp enough for this kind of timber."

In this way, he completely rounded the forehead end of the mask (Plate 8-12B). He now employed a tape measure to estimate the length of the forehead at the front.

Measurements

On the round side of the block, he gauged the proportions of the face with a rule and marked them off vertically. From crown to chin, his three divisions were (1) above the eyes to where the top of the nose projects; (2) below the eyes at the tip of the nose; and (3) at the chin. Having determined the midline with a rule, he drew the midline to guide in carving the two sides of the face. He next made a gauge of a splint, and having determined the width of the mouth on his own mask, doubled it, and spaced the outer limits of the mouth with reference to the median. He did likewise with the eyes. Then, in exaggerated style, he drew the features of the lips, face, and eyes, the proportions of which would be reduced in carving (Plate 8-13A).

Now he set the forehead end of the mask on the cutting block and shaped the forehead, imparting a slope to it with the ax (Plate 8-13B). Then turning the object end for end he hewed the sides to the outline on the back and to lateral lines of the face on the front. He reduced both sides until the work tapered to a point beyond the chin (Plate 8-14A).

He then announced, "Now I will rub deer tallow (*neogɛʔ o·nǫʔ*) on the forehead and let it stand two or three days so that it will not check further." The green basswood block had commenced to check, and I was assured that deer tallow is regularly used to prevent checking when carving green timber. No wonder Seneca carvers of late prefer to get seasoned barn beams as mask material (Plate 8-14B).

Now that the block had seasoned for six days since he had rubbed deer tallow into it, Chauncey took it to the cutting bench and smoothed off the back working surface with the drawshave (Plate 8-15A). Then he turned the block over and planed the face side toward the forehead.

Once more he took the original mask that he was copying and retraced the outline of the mask on the back of the block (Plate 8-15B). This time, however, he used a pencil.

Because the tail end of the block below the chin was no longer useful, he cut it off below the chin with the handsaw, chipping away the green wood from below with the ax when the saw bound (Plate 8-15C). The block was now ready to carve.

In making facial measurements, carvers employ their fingers as calipers. Chauncey originally determined the distance between his eyes by bringing the ends of his first and second fingers up to the middle of his eyeballs and transferring this unit to the mask via a rule—two and a half inches. Similarly, he measured the distance across his nose—one and a half

Plate 8-13. A: Outlining features of face with charcoal. B: Cutting away forehead.

Plate 8-14. Hewing and rubbing with tallow. A: Hewing sides to outline of face (back and front). B: Rubbing deer tallow into forehead to prevent checking.

Plate 8-15. Working on the drawshave bench.
A: Planing the block. B: Tracing the outline
from his own mask. C: Cutting off the chin.

inches. The thumb and first or second finger, a common method in Seneca mensuration, were similarly used to determine bizygomatic width and face height. These measurements that had been determined for his original mask were transferred by rule to the new mask.

In commencing the face, the first step is to saw a crosscut under the nose and above the upper lip with a handsaw. Next Chauncey marked out the lower line of the lower lip and made a second crosscut. Then, measuring equidistant from midline, he made diagonal and vertical cuts one inch on either side of the nose bridge (the wood was still very green). He made similar cuts on either side of the mouth and where the nose bridge extends up over the forehead (Figure 8-4B).

The next problem was to reduce the level of the cheeks and chin so as to leave nose and mouth areas in relief. He cut a short length of poplar log and reduced one end for a handle. Using this device as a maul or mallet, he drove the blade of a small handax into the edge of the block, chipping away the wood up to the saw cuts around the mouth (Plate 8-16A, B). (This was difficult work because the wood was still green.) During this process, he held the block on or between his knees while sitting on the cutting bench. In the same way, he split away the wood on either side of the nose bridge thus reducing the cheeks to eye level (Figure 8-4C).

With the main features of the face now in relief, he went to the chopping block and hewed the back of the mask block on both sides to the outline that he had traced on its back from the original mask. Then he hewed away the sides of the face on either side of the mouth and nose. For the first time, the block now assumed the ovoid shape of the human head.

After an hour and a quarter of work, he decided to abandon further work for that day because the wood was yet too green for carving. To prevent further checking in drying, he applied more tallow and put the work away about three o'clock.

A week later, he had flattened the cheeks and begun the mouth hole (Figure 8-4D). He resumed shaving the sides of the face (Plate 8-17A) with a jackknife, holding the work in the crook of his left arm against his chest and cutting away from himself. For opening the mouth, he used a mallet and chisel (*yohgeogwá:tha?*). (I observed that the block had checked around the chin and over the right eye.)

Hollowing the Back

Having blocked out the features of the face, he could now commence hollowing the back of the mask (Plate 8-17B). Chauncey worked both the front and back of a mask at the same time. He commented that before steel tools were introduced, the Seneca used to burn out the back of a mask in the same way as in excavating a corn mortar but that this process of alternately charring and scraping was abandoned when they could procure curved steel adzes from traders or smiths. (Although the curved adze was present in the Archaic cultures of western New York, its use was un-

Plate 8-16. Reducing the gross features.
A: Chipping around mouth with handax and maul to bring mouth and nose into relief.
B: Reducing cheeks to eye level by chipping either side of nose bridge.

Plate 8-17. A: Shaving sides of face with jackknife; mouth hole begun. B: Hollowing back of mask. His great-grandson watches.

known among modern Iroquois carvers. The modern curved steel adze, or howel, employed by coopers in making barrels is not the lineal descendant of the Archaic curved stone adze, although the techniques of using the two implements were probably similar.) Chauncey no longer possessed a curved adze (oʔsóʔdǫshɛʔ), which a blacksmith at North Collins, New York, had made for him when he was living at Cattaraugus Reservation, but he employed the handax in a similar way. Working from the chin end, he chopped a series of clefts toward the middle of the back, and then turned the work around and cut back from the forehead end (Figure 8-5A) (Plate 8-17B). Alternately working first from the chin end and then from the forehead end, he gradually enlarged the cavity (Figure 8-5B). He said, "When I get this down a little bit, then I will get my crooked knife and you can take another picture." He continued with the ax until the cut was two inches deep and the edges about an inch thick.

Then he took the crooked knife and commenced to smooth out the inside (Plate 8-18A). In working with the crooked knife, the handle is grasped near the blade firmly in the right hand, and the work is held in the crook of the left hand and arm and against the right knee and chest. The direction of the knife is necessarily toward the worker. It is desirable to have a left- and right-handed curved knife so that when the grain of wood demands a knife that is curved in the opposite direction, it is possible to work without turning the object or changing the direction of work. Chauncey did not possess a second knife (Plate 8-18B).

He decided to stop at eleven forty-five in the morning, after working an hour and a half. "I will not put it by the stove tonight. It would check again." I was told to return the following Friday.

Refining the Face
During the ensuing week, Chauncey had been working in his spare time at shaping the lips. He had reduced the surface of the lips below the level of the nose tip, by paring them with a jackknife. To separate the lower end of the nose from the edge of the upper lip, he shortened the nose with the saw. Then with lead pencil he gauged and marked the depth of the flare of the outer lips from which point they would be cut back toward the face. Then he shaved the upperlip with his jackknife (Figure 8-5C, D).

Next he smoothed the sides of the face, cutting toward himself, and shaped the chin below the mouth. Then he turned the mask around and trimmed down the other side of the chin, this time cutting away from himself (Plate 8-19A). This narrowed the cheeks and exaggerated the flare of the lips. Then, with his left hand, he held the work against his chest while he cut back under the lips to bring out the flare (Plate 8-19B). Both sides of the chin were now shaved, and he began to point the chin by cutting away from the mouth. He then planed the mask face all over with the jackknife. The angle remained sharp between eye level and the sides of the face.

Plate 8-18. A: Hollowing the back of the mask with crooked knife. B: Detail of the use of crooked knife.

Figure 8-5. Directions of carving at back of mask. A: Scoring with ax. B: Enlarging the cavity. C: Shaping the lips (full face). D: Shaping the nose (profile) and flaring mouth.

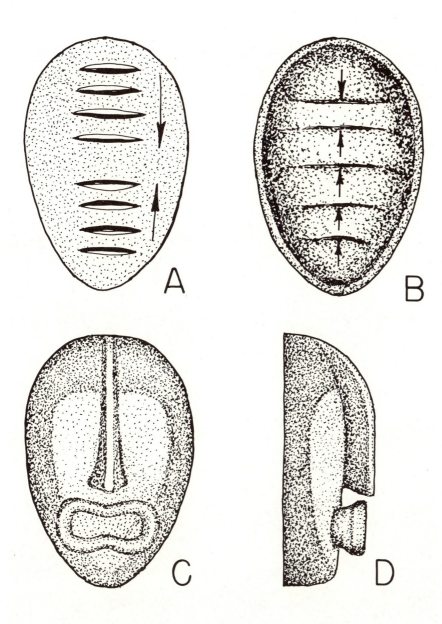

Plate 8-19. A: Trimming the chin to impart flare to lips. B: Cutting back lips to impart flare.

Plate 8-20. A and B: Reaming out the mouth. C: Rounding inner surface of lips to flare outward.

 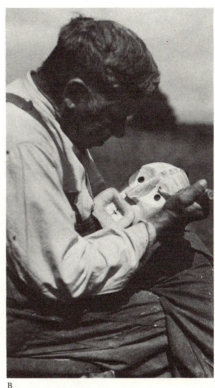

Plate 8-21. A: Finishing inside of mask with crooked knife. B: Scooping eye sockets.

To ream out the mouth, he propped the mask between his knees and held it with his left hand. To protect his thumb, he wore a thumb guard when cutting toward it and rounded off the inner surfaces of the lips to enhance the outward flare (Plate 8-20). He rotated the work as he proceeded (Figure 8-6A–C).

Carver's Comment on Mouth Types. Several points came up in conversation while Chauncey worked on the mouth regarding types of mouths on Iroquois masks, which I had recently studied in museums and which Chauncey had observed in his lifetime. I remarked on having seen a *mask with protruding tongue* in the Boyle Collection at the Royal Ontario Museum of Archaeology in Toronto (Cat. No. OPM 17020). "That's the way they make them over there [at Six Nations Reserve]," he replied. "Howard Jimerson had one [Fenton Collection; MAI-HF Cat. No. 20/2844; Plate 2-7C]; Levi Snow and John Coury also have that kind from over there [Six Nations]. They make them long over there." Recall that the Morgan mask at the state museum also has a protruding tongue (Plate 1-4).

The flaring mouth with visible teeth, of the type of mask he was then making, "is old at Cattaraugus where it came with the Senecas from Buffalo Creek Reservation. George Hemlock who came to Cattaraugus from Buffalo Creek had one that had been made by Henry Stevens of Buffalo Reservation."

Plate 8-22. A: Burning eyeholes with hot iron punch. B: Burning seven holes in rim with red hot iron for attaching hair and head straps.

Plate 8-23. A and B: Incising teeth with jackknife.

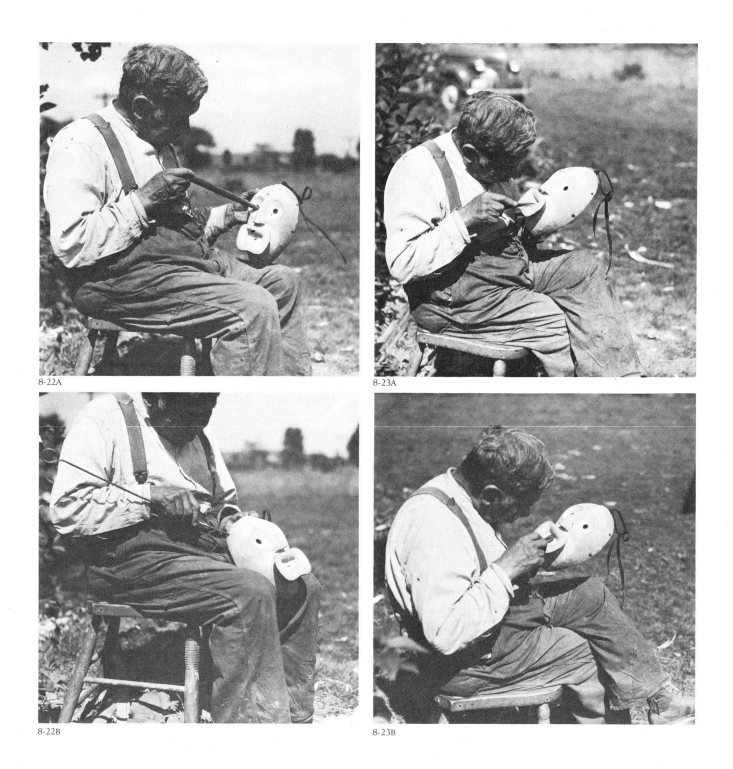

Plate 8-24. The final step in mask carving: engraving brow wrinkles and notching spines above nose bridge.

A close relative, the so-called "spoon-mouth" type, a conventualized flare mouth with incipient tongue, was also early at Cattaraugus. "My brother had one like that also made by Henry Stevens." It was borrowed, never returned, and ultimately sold to a Buffalo collector.

Forehead Detail

Turning from the mouth, he marked out the limits of the forehead in pencil; the new line was slightly below and inside the earlier one. All along, he said that he had made it heavier, so now he reduced the brow line to the new marks, and then shaved back the whole forehead. "Later I will take glass and scrape it smooth." Next he planed off places for the eyes, cutting toward himself with the jackknife on the right side, and turning the mask away from himself on the left side (Figure 8-6B). The direction of work was determined by necessity.

Finally, after two hours, before laying aside the work, he marked out the median on the nose with a rule. It was now late afternoon, and we stopped for the day. It also ended my notetaking. From here on I relied on the camera.

Burning Holes for Attachment

The remaining steps in finishing the mask are carried by the legends to the plates (Plates 8-21A, B, 8-22, 8-23, 8-24). These steps comprised finishing the inside of the mask with the crooked knife, scooping the eye sockets with the crooked knife, burning the eyeholes with the hot iron

Plate 8-25. Below: The finished but unpainted model. USNM, Cat. No. 381020. A: Semi-profile. B: Back.

Figure 8-26. Above: A and B: Details of the mouth and eyes. C: Finished mask.

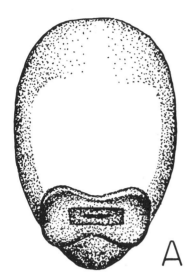
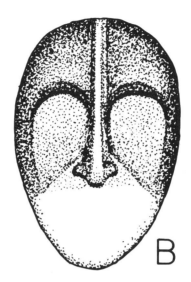
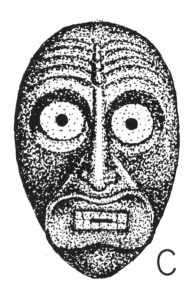

A　　　　　　　B　　　　　　　C

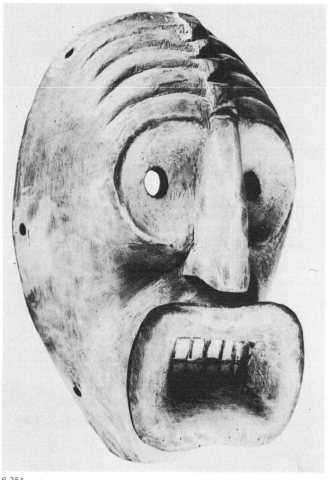
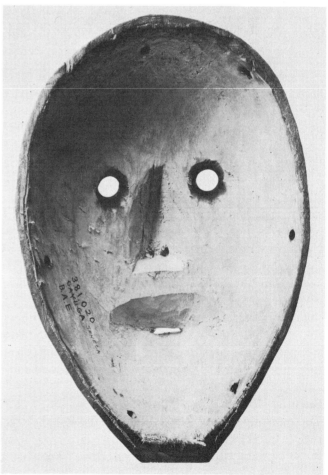

8-25A　　　　　　　　　　　　　　　　8-25B

punch, burning the seven holes in the rim for attaching hair and head straps, incising the teeth with the jackknife, engraving the brow wrinkles, and notching the spines above the nose bridge—the final step in carving.

The finished but unpainted model was deposited in the U.S. National Museum of Natural History (Cat. No. 381020). It measures six and one-half inches by ten inches with three and seven-eights of an inch prognathism (Plate 8-25A, B).

Plate 9-1. Masks in the Newtown, Cattaraugus Seneca style of the early 1900s. MAI-HF, Cat. Nos. (top row, left to right) 4126, 6/335, 9145; (bottom row) 8/7804, 8/7810, 8/7807.

9. Carving Styles

The Newtown Tradition

Newtown, on Cattaraugus Reservation of the Seneca Nation, has been a center of mask carving since the nineteenth century, and it has developed its own distinctive style. It was here that Harriet Maxwell Converse, at the close of the century, and after her Arthur C. Parker made the first large collections. Fortunately, R. A. Grider, in 1897, made full-scale watercolor drawings of nearly 100 of these masks, many of which went to the New York State Museum only to be consumed with much of the Morgan Collection in the fire of 1911 that destroyed the New York state capitol. A few of the Grider drawings are of masks from Tonawanda. I examined the grider portfolios at the Newberry Library in April of 1981. They document informant statements that the distinctive Newtown style present in the carvings of Sanonʔgai:s (James Crow) and Jesse Cornplanter had roots deep in the nineteenth century. Both the spoon-mouthed and straight-lipped doorkeeper masks were already present. In contrast with the larger, deeper wrinkled masks from Grand River, which often feature protuberant tongues, as previously noted, Newtown masks are smaller in overall dimension, chinless, smooth faced, and feature the ridge of spines and accompanying wrinkles above the nose (Cornplanter 1938, 210) (Plate 9-1).

Parker's contemporaries—M. R. Harrington, George Heye, Joseph Keppler (1941), and Alanson Skinner—made frequent collecting trips to Newtown, not to mention private collectors from Buffalo and western New York. There are probably more masks of Newtown provenience in museums than from any other single Iroquois community. Several of the Allegany carvers—Chauncey Johnny John, John Jimmerson, Jonas Snow through his father Amos Snow—were native sons and did their first carving at Cattaraugus or learned from mentors of that tradition. This is not to say that all Newtown masks are spoon lipped or have straight distended lips and have a comb of spines above the nose; they are not. There is a great variety of beggar masks that are predominantly smooth faced and often smiling, and sometimes with ears pierced for earrings (Grider 1897, 19, 20, 32, 37, 44; Keppler 1941, Plate VI, frontispiece). Indeed, the older masks are simpler and more human in appearance (Plate 2-5). The fiercer types appear to have developed in later times from protoypes already represented in the older collections.

CLASSIC DOORKEEPERS

Jesse Cornplanter was living at Tonawanda in the 1930s, but he was a native of Newtown and identified with its traditions (Fenton 1978). His father, Edward Cornplanter, Parker's main informant, was a leader in the Newtown Longhouse and preacher of the Handsome Lake code. Jess imbibed the Newtown ways with his mother's milk and corn soup. He was a boy wonder as an artist (Fenton 1980; Parker 1909, 1910a, 1913), but he turned to carving masks much later during the Tonawanda WPA Indian Arts Project (1935–38). He specialized in doorkeeper masks—either spoon mouthed or with straight, distended lips—in the Newtown tradition that were finely finished and on which he lavished time and affection (Plate 9-2A, B; see also Plate 6-5). In his letters to me and in his published book of letters (1938), he projected into the mythology what he constantly reiterated. Jesse's version of the origin myth has the mask spirit specify that the people shall offer the Creator's gift of tobacco at the basswood tree and carve his image on the tree. We are told that masks made from the basswood tree have as much power as the original mask being. The carver is supposed to make the offering at the tree before he carves the mask. If this is done properly, then it is believed that the full spirit of the woodland, that is, the mask spirit, enters into the mask (Cornplanter 1938, 215).

The Basswood Tradition
Basswood, then, has the prestige of tradition, but carvers whom I interviewed at Tonawanda and at Allegany preferred softer woods such as willow, cucumber, and pine. The following generalized statement derives from informant interviews at Allegany and Tonawanda when Cornplanter interpreted, and, despite his Newtown prejudices, he acceded to older men.

> Anciently, a man went into the forest to carve his masks. He carried native tobacco and sought a living Basswood tree. Now he kindled a small fire and committed the tobacco to the burning embers, a pinch at a time, addressing his prayer to the tree and to the beings whom the False Faces represent. Then he carved the face on the living tree and having roughed it out, he notched the tree with an ax above the forehead and below the chin and cleaved away his sculpture in a solid block. It is said that the carving never broke because one had put tobacco and asked the tree for its life. Nor did the tree die. Within 4 years, the scar healed over. He took home his block, covered it, and worked on it at his leisure. When the features of the face were finished, he hollowed out the inside, and perforated the eyes, nose and mouth. He encircled the eyes with metal, for the eyes of Shagodyowéhgo:wah are bright. Then he painted it. They say at Tonawanda: "If he had sought his tree in the morning, he painted the mask red; but if he found the tree and commenced carving after noon, the mask would be black." This color symbolism originates with the theory as to the morning and afternoon appearance of the giant, world-rim resident. During his daily journey following the path of the sun, in the morning his face would appear red, but dark in the afternoon when the sun [which always

Plate 9.2. A: Stages in carving a doorkeeper mask in the Newtown traditional style. By Jesse Cornplanter, 1940. B: An earlier spoon-mouth doorkeeper mask, probably from the Cattaraugus Seneca. Courtesy Buffalo Museum of Science, Cat. No. 11118.

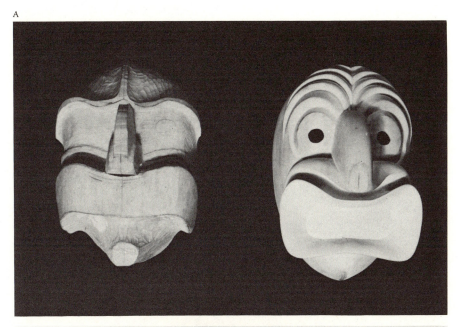

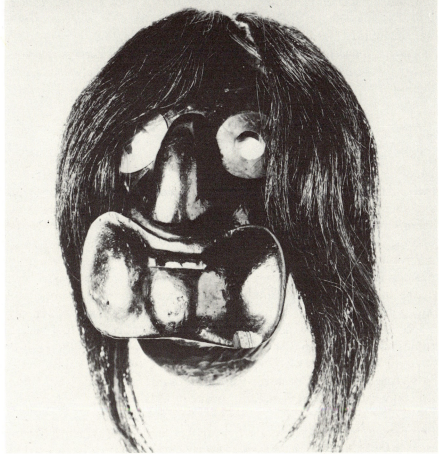

precedes] is behind him. [When the masker looks back from toward the setting sun, he appears dark in profile.] For the long hair which falls on either side to his knees, the mask maker attaches horse tails to the forehead. These are tanned with deer brains. [After Fenton 1941a, 423–24]

Out of respect for Jesse's preference for Newtown ways, he and I once made a trip there to inquire into such matters. As far as I could learn none of the then-extant carvers whom we interviewed—James Crow (Sanonʔgai:s), Kelly Lay, Jake Jack, and Roy Jimmerson—carved masks on living basswood trees. They all preferred seasoned blocks of clear timber.

Another carver, Francis Kettle, Jesse's boyhood companion, is credited with having created a distinctive "Buffalo mask," which has horns and a fierce countenance and is painted black. It enjoys a certain favor in the I:ʔdo:s rite. I learned virtually nothing about the so-called "blind masks" that Parker (1909, 173) associated with this rite.

Older masks in the Buffalo Museum of Science are notably simpler in surface treatment than masks carved afterward at Newtown by emigrees from Buffalo Creek (Plate 2-8B). Certainly, the acquisition of steel carving tools has enabled carvers to elaborate their art. This was very evident at the Tonawanda Arts Project during my residence there in the mid-1930s, when the Rochester museum made available to Seneca carvers the finest of woodworking tools. Jesse Cornplanter, as one of the beneficiaries, remarked on this himself.

TWO ESSENTIAL TYPES: MEDICINE AND BEGGARS

For Jesse, there were two classes of masks based on function. There were the so-called "beggar masks" that exhibit a bewildering variety of forms, and there were the "doorkeepers," the great doctors, which were either spoon-mouthed or had straight, distended lips. Other mouth types fall into the doorkeeper class and assume this role, but for the moment I shall not confuse the reader or contradict Jesse's views. Jesse documented his position in two ways. In the winter of 1935–36 he carved two doorkeeper masks in the Newtown tradition for the Rochester museum: one with spoon lips and painted red, reminiscent of one his father once owned, and a second with straight, distended lips, also painted red, with a ridge of spines above the nose (Plate 6-5A, B). This pair of masks differed from anything being carved by other craftsmen on the Tonawanda WPA Indian Arts Project. The first mask is reminiscent of the "great wind mask" published by Parker (1909, Plate IX, opposite p. 182), possibly from the Keppler Collection (cf. MAI Cat. No. 9133). Second, after the appearance of Keppler's *Comments on Certain Iroquois Masks* (1941), which I had reviewed for the *American Anthropologist* (Fenton 1942a) and procured for him, Jesse wrote me two important letters (personal communications, October 10, 1941, and November 11, 1941).

Although Jesse had great respect for Keppler as a father figure, nevertheless, he stated his own views.

> All I know is: *Ga-gonh-sah* or *Sa-go-dyo-weh-go-wah*. There are two types that I was told. The first and the older type is the Medicine type or Door-keepers and the other type is the beggar-mask, . . . used in Mid-winter when they go [the] rounds house-to-house. This type is never blessed with the Native Tobacco and never have that small bundle at the top string of the Face. The Door-keeper mask is never used in this sort of dancing, that is, to beg tobacco, but only when he goes out to do what a doctor does when on a call.
>
> I will tell you of an incident that has caused me to really believe in the potency of the ritual and power of the Sa-go-dyo-weh-go-wah. This happened at Young Lay's place years ago. I stooped down to pick up something under the stairs, it was semidark; all at once a drop of water fell on my neck. It sort of scared me, there under the stair-way. I looked up to see what could have caused this, and there hung Young Lay's mask. It was wet with what appeared to be perspiration all over the mask, and it was running down the side and dripping down. I went and told Young Lay about it. He just laughed and said that they would be called upon to go out and doctor somebody—that he [the mask] was just overanxious about it. . . . Inside of two hours, his sister [Sophia Jones] came and notified him to go to a certain place to dance and administer the rites of the Door-keepers' Ceremony.

MATERNITY REVISITED

Jesse went on to admit that he had heard once or twice about the maternity mask and the wind spirit mask, but he thought it was from white writers who sought to embellish their stories and make them sound more exotic. "Father never mentioned to us, nor [did] anyone else that I can recall" these erudite versions of the mask symbolism.

Jesse, a World War I veteran, returned to the subject in a long epistle written on Armistice Day, which had special meaning for him.

> It is my opinion that [the] different types of masks are the work of various mask carvers. They make a Face that might typify a certain belief, and that [mask] becomes a certain variety and is accepted as such. There are some [faces] that typify the Stone Giants, and some [individuals] claim that the whistling type are the Wind-spirit

mask. Then too, when collectors come [to the reservation], some are prone to enlarge their version as to types and purposes, mostly [out] of their own imagination. Naturally, it is accepted as truth. Take the case of Mrs. Converse: she took about the first choice [of specimens] from the Cattaraugus Reservation. She was a writer for some newspaper. She made many errors. The same applies to her collection [and publication] on Brooches. She made the same mistakes that remain today.

Jesse returned to Newtown from World War I to discover that after his father's death, a certain black spoon-mouthed doorkeeper mask had been sold to a collector nearby from whom Joseph Keppler was negotiating its purchase. In correspondence with Keppler, his foster father, in 1928 Jesse described the mask and his efforts to repossess it. "It is gloss black with spoon mouth, wrinkled forehead and Brass eye piece" (Keppler Papers, MAI, Fol. C.8.4, No. 25). Late in December, Jesse was certain that Keppler had it; he wrote:

But this one [the black mask with spoon mouth], we bought that from Albert Jones. He claims to have made it from a live tree with due ceremony. There is quite a history to the mask. . . . Upon my father's death, Eliza Phillips had it for safe keeping [and] for use during the New Year Dance. He is 'Doorkeeper.'

Jesse went on to say how various private collectors wanted it, how he borrowed money from one of them, and how he returned to Newtown after World War I to learn that the mask had been "stolen." He was certain that Keppler had it (Keppler Papers, MAI, Fol. C.8.4, No. 27). In a later letter, dated 10 January 1929 (Kepper Papers, MAI, Fol. C.8.4, No. 28), he was more positive but willing to let Keppler keep it for the original valuation of twenty-five dollars of which Jesse had already received twenty. Keppler had evidently paid Taft, a local collector, ten dollars for the mask. For an additional five dollars, Jesse promised its full history. The full documentation is in a folder of letters that I received from M. R. Harrington (Cornplanter Letters, American Philosophical Society Library).

The copy of Cornplanter's letter to Keppler in 1929 reads:

Concerning Ga-gon-sa—It was made by Albert Jones . . . for himself. . . . Dad and I coaxed him to part with it. It was the understanding that we are to always keep it in the family and never sell it. So it was kept until my dad's death. Then Mrs. Phillips had custody of it. From there it was kept to Delos Kettle's old place on the corners—then finally lost or stolen. I will give the ceremony whenever I get there.

After commenting on how a certain collector was reputed to operate in persuading masks to leave the reservation, Jess continued:

> The other two Sacred Old Masks are—one owned by Young M. Lay, [a] (Very Old Doorkeeper), and Jacob Bennett's also old [mask]— their history unknown. Whether they were carved out of life tree I am not certain.

After listing several other doorkeeper masks and their owners, stating that they were not for sale, and quoting current prices offered by collectors, he returned to the first one:

> This one you have of *ours* was the cause of one death. Viz.:— A certain Layman or Preacher from Pine Woods was at New Town years ago. Our mask was used and kept near [the] longhouse. This Indian Minister was opposed to "Ong-weh-on-weh-kah" [the Indian Way or longhouse religion], and saw this mask laying on the bed. He grabbed same and started to abuse it, saying "It was one of the craziest, despicing [?] Wooden Bowl he ever saw," and was in the act of pulling the hair off when the Woman of the house took it away from him, just in time. Well, the matter was reported to [the] headmen, and Jim Crow and someone else burned o-yen-gwa-oh-weh [Indian Tobacco] to the spirit of Ga-goh-sah for revenge or punishment to the nonbeliever.
>
> In the course of two weeks news came that a certain Preacher of Christianity was suffering a strange Malady—mocking the noise of Ga-gon-sah, and asking this certain Mask to come and help him. Runners were sent to Newtown—to Dad, Jim Crow, etc. for the Ceremony with the certain Mask. It was all refused flatly. Result— One Indian Minister just passed out after days of intense suffering. All kinds of offers were made to induce the Dance.

Some of the Cornplanter–Keppler correspondence came to me through the kindness of M. R. Harrington after the passing of both men. With these letters are several from Jesse to Jiskoko, "Robbin," Harrington's adopted Iroquois name. Harrington had been one of the more assiduous collectors of masks for museums, as Jesse commented in October of 1955, two years before his own passing.

> You fellows should be satisfied by now. You've cleaned us out on our masks. We still have some left. But they are not for sale any more. What good are they doing behind glass cases? They belong right in our reservations. Maybe in a few years there will be no more of us left to wear them. . . . I know of a few old ones over in Plank Road [Cattaraugus], but they are not for sale. Money can't buy them. . . . I made quite a few of them in my good days. I made myself one real Doctor or Guardian Mask during our WPA Project . . . in my spare time. It was a Spoon Mouthed type, or what we call "Door Keeper Type." . . . Keppler in that Booklet he wrote on Masks (1941) . . . called it "Maternity Mask." I wonder where in the world he got that

silly idea? I never heard of anybody calling them that name. Its foolish. In fact, they [Senecas] had few names of types.

This letter disposes of the "maternity" issue. It also foretells a then-growing attitude among traditional Iroquois about mask collections in museums, and it anticipates later efforts to repatriate them.

SOME PROTOTYPES

Before leaving the Newtown tradition, one should acknowledge some prototypes of Cornplanter's classic doorkeepers and their variants. We should also look at the work of contemporary Newtown carvers who during Jesse's boyhood there and after he departed were still carving. There are earlier examples of spoon-mouthed doorkeeper masks from Cattaraugus in museum collections (Plate 9-3A). Grider illustrated several. Occasionally, they feature spines over the nose bridge, but otherwise they are smooth. James Crow developed this style to an elaborate art form. The Keppler Collection at the Museum of the American Indian contains his early pieces, and the Rochester museum holds the work he did on the arts project at Cattaraugus. The work of Roy Jimmerson, a Christian Seneca of Gowanda, is equally interesting. A carpenter most of his life, he enjoyed carving and joined the arts project. The backs of his masks are unfinished and do not show use (Plate 9-3B).

The spoon-lipped and straight-distended mouth types that Jesse Cornplanter identified as the classic Newtown doorkeeper masks represent the extremes of a range of variant mouth shapes that have a wider distribution. If the spoon-mouth exaggerates the sunken cheeks of the pursed, blowing shaman, its counterpart, frequently used as a doorkeeper, is the bifunnelate blower that distends the lips in the same mouth conformation and frequently exposes the teeth. Roy Jimmerson, Kelly Lay, and James Crow carved such masks (Plate 9-3C, D). Such mouth shapes occur at Allegany, is a type specimen of this class (Plate 7-3A). Masks with straight-distended lips are frequently modified varieties of bifunnelate or spoon-Allegany, is a type specimen of this class (Plate 7-2A). Masks with straight-distended lips are frequently modified varieties of bifunnelate or spoon-mouthed masks, and although they occur in collections from Cattaraugus (Plate 9-4D), they were collected at Allegany, at Tonawanda, at Six Nations (Plate 9-4C), and Onondaga (Plate 9-5A, B). Variation is a matter of artistic license. At least two appear to be the work of the same carver. As the Iroquois say, they all are of the same spirit manifesting variant moods and expressions.

Plate 9.3. The Spoon mouth and its derivatives. A: An early example from Cattaraugus. NYSM, Cat. No. 36868. B: Roy Jimmerson's modern version, ca. 1936. RMSC. Bifunnelate mouths with teeth, Cattaraugus. C: Collected by E. R. Burmester, 1925. RMSC, Cat. No. AE 7.1.07/309. D: By Kelly Lay, Cattaraugus, 1936. Red mask. Denver Art Museum, Cat. No. NSen.14.Ex. Photo courtesy Denver Art Museum.

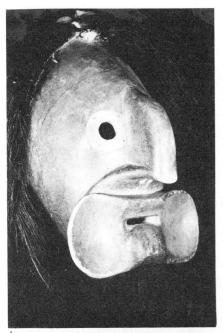

A

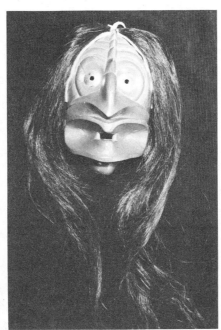

B

C

D

Plate 9.4. Very early Seneca black bifunnelate mask with teeth. NYSM, Cat. No. 37016. A: Front. Note face is flat and broad. B: Back. Reveals age and use, multiple tobacco offerings. Appears to be of maple. Upper row of teeth set in with pegs. C: Red doorkeeper from Six Nations with round brass eye sconces and small bifunnelate mouth, Chiefswood Collection, ROM, Cat. No. HD10371. D: A very old mask of the Allegany mouth type. Collected by H. M. Converse, NYSM, Cat. No. 37054.

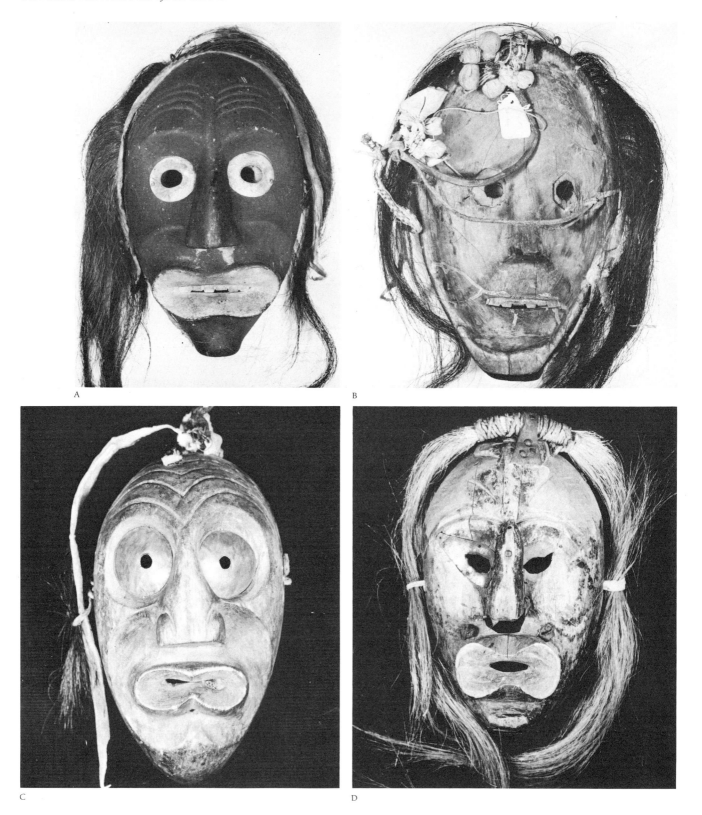

Plate 9.5. A: An Onondaga mask from Grand River, with pointed chin and straight, slightly bifunnelate mouth, crimped brass eyes, painted red with red hair. Collected by W. L. Bryant. MAI-HF, Cat. No. 10/4015. Compare this mask with that of Lucy Gordon, of Allegany, collected by Skinner but attributed to a local carver who could have carved both specimens (Cf. Plate 17-1). B: A mask of dubious ascription: not in the Newtown style, but the work of Jonas Snow. Tioga Point Museum, Athens, Pa., Cat. No. 36,223.

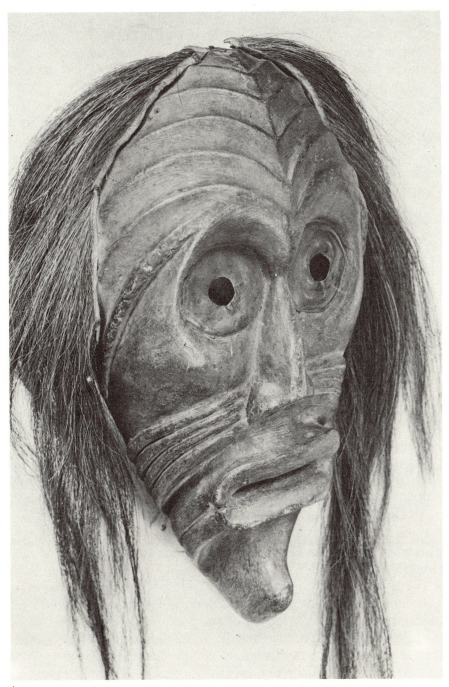

Plate 9-6. Two Seneca masks by Amos Snow, ca. 1850. A: Red doorkeeper mask with straight nose, square funnelate mouth, tin eyes, and chestnut hair. Fenton Collection, MAI-HF 20/2836. B: A classic Shagodyoweh doorkeeper with flattened nose, crooked mouth, and spines on forehead. Fenton Collection, MAI-HF, Cat. No. 20/2837.

A

B

Amos Snow's Work

Still another variant of the spoon-mouth blower has a square, bifunnelate mouth for blowing ashes (MAI-HF 20/2836; Plate 9-6A). When this mouth appears twisted down at one corner, as in the second mask of Amos Snow (MAI-HF 20/2837; Plate 9-6B), it is still assigned to the doorkeeper role by informants. Amos Snow, of Cattaraugus, carved both of these masks before the Civil War, and they were acquired for the Fenton Collection in 1897. They illustrate variation in mouth types cast in the doorkeeper role, and they are also examples of the rough-and-ready carving style at Cattaraugus and Allegany reservations of the Seneca Nation that preceded the finely finished masks of recent carvers.

A MUSEUM MISNOMER

One bit of evidence questions the overnice distinction that Jesse Cornplanter made for Newtown doorkeeper masks of his boyhood and that derives from a museum piece that has been attributed to his father. In 1950, there was a black mask with red, smiling lips and visible regular teeth in the Tioga Point Museum in Athens, Pennsylvania (Cat. No. U.S. 36.223; Plate 8-30B). The Tioga museum acquired it in 1936 from a private collector. It was then said to be fifty years old. The accession record states that it belonged to Ga-na-da-dah and was later given to his son who passed it on to So-son-da-wa. No location is specified.

The then-curator, Charles L. Lucy, came up to Red House for an Iroquois conference, met Sherman Redeye, and afterward wrote to him to learn the identity of the Seneca names. The Redeyes readily recognized Sosondo:wah, "Dark Night," as the name of Edward Cornplanter, the well-known preacher of the Handsome Lake code (Parker 1913, Plate 2) and father of Jesse. They did not assign the familiar Seneca name Kanɛʔtatɛʔ, "Hemlock Bows Lying," to any known person. This is all very plausible, but it is open to another interpretation (Lucy, personal communication, March 9, 1950).

The style of mask conforms neither to Jesse's view of the Newtown style, nor does it resemble his description of masks once owned by his father. Rather, the treatment of the chin and face resembles other masks carved by Jonas Snow, of Allegany. Ascriptions of age are often exaggerated. If we accept fifty years, or even a generation, it is right for Edward Cornplanter, but it also fits another person, whom Sherman Redeye forgot. Chauncey Johnny John, of Coldspring, also had the name Kanɛʔtatɛʔtɛǫʔ, "Hemlock Boughs Lying Down," and his son Amos, after the death of Edward Cornplanter, was also named Sosondó:wah. They were neighbors of Jonas Snow and could have been the persons involved. I regret now that I did not check out this identification while these persons were living. The mask itself suggested the lead while writing this book.

I shall treat Jonas Snow and his carving later. But before turning to him, let us follow through the carving of a mask by a Grand River craftsman. Crooked mouth masks as portraits of Haduʔiʔ appear frequently in the Grand River style.

The Grand River Style

TOM HARRIS AT SIX NATIONS ON GRAND RIVER

Of the modern carvers at Grand River, Chief Jacob Thomas is probably the greatest living artist, and his work is represented in many collections (Plate 2-3). But in 1940, Tom Harris, an Onondaga-speaking Seneca of Onondaga Longhouse, was considered the reigning exponent of the Grand River tradition. I witnessed the carving of a crooked face mask with Marjorie Lismer of Toronto, herself the daughter of Arthur Lismer, one of Canada's famous "seven" painters; she had spent a season in a field school I had run at Allegany and was then a graduate student at Columbia.

When I contracted with Tom Harris to make a mask for me, he asked what kind I wanted. He said that he could make any kind and that he usually left the decision up to the person who hired him. We agreed on a typical Onondaga crooked face, representing Haduʔi:ʔ after the mountain struck his face. My instructions were explicit to carve it in the true Six Nations Reserve style. (He said that often the person making the request brought a picture of the type of mask desired.)

We arrived on the appointed morning (August 18, 1940) about nine to find that he had already completed one mask (B) of two labeled "A & B." He had carved it the day before in about eight hours, he told us. He had a second block of basswood ready to carve another mask (A), which we were to witness. Harris preferred basswood (*ohó:sɛʔ*) (*Tilia americana* L.) for carving. (The first day that I had talked with him, he professed not to know about going into the woods and carving the mask on the standing tree.) He said that pine or poplar are also used, but he told Lismer that pine is harder to work.

While he was working, Harris told us that "every house is supposed to have a mask in it to protect the building and occupants from high winds." He added that even if the householder is not a member of the False Face Society, he can have a mask. [Simeon Gibson later confirmed this.] Such masks are hung and covered with a cloth "so children will not see him and get sick."

Although Tom did not profess knowing about carving masks on living basswood trees, he told Lismer: "A False Face should be made in the bush where no one sees it being made. If you have to leave it, it must be covered with leaves and hidden." Then he added, "A real False Face has to be cut on the west side of the tree. Haduʔi:ʔ comes from the west like the thunders, and he comes and protects us with the thunder, too. (Both are called 'grandfather'.)" Tom said that he burns tobacco "to make it [the mask] alive."

(The preceding contradictions and specific information about carving on living basswood trees are interesting because they illustrate how informant testimony may differ with a second ethnologist in separate interviews.)

One of us asked about the problem with unseasoned wood checking. "It is best to cut the wood in the spring and then it won't crack up [check]."

Tom's grandfather was John Jamieson, Sr., the reputed leader of the Faces at Onondaga Longhouse for many years. His father was not a carver. Tom watched other carvers at work and was largely self-taught. He had been making masks for about twenty years. Six Nations people paid him to make their masks.

Apropos of carving masks in concealed places, there is a belief at Six Nations that a carver may cut himself when people are watching. Tom considered it not quite right for people to watch. Once he cut himself when people were watching. For this reason and the fact that it also lacked the tobacco invocation, he said of the mask he was then carving: "It won't be a real False Face."

Harris also made miniature masks. He said that they were not used by members of the society, which contradicts other information. "It takes between five and six hours to carve one. They have to be done mainly with the jackknife."

The preceding are mainly the artist's comments before or while working. My observations of the carver at work follow:

1. The carver roughs out the block with an ax.
2. He saws a diagonal crosscut that will be the base of the nose. Then with the adze, he chops out the lower area toward the chin. (With strong, sure blows he removed large chips at a time.)
3. The carver gouges out the eye sockets with curved adze or howel: first, a little from the left eye and then a little from the right. Now, using a curved gouge or straight chisel, he removes the wood on either side of the nose bridge below the brow ridge. (He holds the chisel in the left hand and strikes it with the pole of the adze.) With the chisel, the carver continues to remove wood from the cheeks and then from the eye areas, thus forming the brow ridges (supraorbitals). Now, the carver holds the mask upside down and trims down the upper side of the brow ridges.
4. With gouge (round chisel), the carver trims down sides of the nose and the inner corners of the eyes.
5. With the saw, he makes a final, clean-cut line diagonally across the lower end of the nose. (Tom remarked that the crooked-nose type takes longer to make.)

6. With a pencil the carver makes a single line to outline the mouth.

7. With a chisel, he continues to remove chips from the cheeks to lower the level. This leaves the area outlined by the pencil lines outstanding in relief. This area will form the protruding lips and the supplementary wrinkles at the mouth corner.

8. The areas of the eyes, cheeks, and chin have been now blocked out. With the ax the carver trims around the edges or margins of the block.

9. With round chisel or gouge and hammer end of adze, the carver makes a line, undercutting the raised lip. Then with the chisel, he removes still more beneath the mouth and upward toward the cheeks.

(Harris generally works with the head of the mask down away from him, and the chisel moves away from the carver toward the forehead. The position of the tools was observed to be quite irregular, according to the convenience of the moment.)

10. Now the carver trims the forehead with the ax, removing small thin flakes. And he smooths the forehead with a spokeshave. (During this operation the carver stands at the bench. All previous work was accomplished with the mask resting on a block of wood on the ground in front of the carver who sat on a low seat, an old soda box.)

11. Trimming entails more work around the mouth with the round chisel; then under the brow ridges and the sides of the nose. Further trimming is done around the eyes with straight chisel.

12. For cutting down the sides of the mouth, the carver employs a jackknife for cutting down and removing thin shavings from the cheeks, and over the nose. This produces a smooth finish. (The carver uses a small, narrow blade, drawing the knife toward himself. He holds the knife in the right hand and applies pressure with the left, while clasping the mask between his knees. Also, when the situation suggests it, the carver employs the motion of cutting away from himself.) He smooths the surface of the mouth with the jackknife.

[The notes to this point are largely the observations of Lismer. Here the author returned to observe and photograph the operation. From this point his notes are combined with Lismer's.]

As with other carvers, work proceeds from the front to the back of the mask.

13. Having blocked out the features of the face, the carver hollows out the back with the curved adze (howel). The first cut is from the forehead down, and then the block is turned around and adzed in the opposite direction, the carver working alternately from either end. (Plate 9-7A,B. Note Mask B on the ground.) (During this operation Tom held the mask with his left hand underneath and between his knees, cutting toward himself.) This operation continues until the excavation reaches the proper depth and size.

14. Then the carver returns to the front of the mask. He outlines the mouth with the small blade of the jackknife, cutting away the edge of the

Plate 9-7. Tom Harris, Seneca of Onondaga Longhouse, Six Nations, replicates the Grand River style. A: Hollowing the back of the mask. B: Detail of carving supplementary wrinkles at mouth corner.

Carving Styles

lip. Then he outlines two supplementary wrinkles where the mouth is pulled up at the right corner. He carves these with the knife point. Then he shaves the lips with the adze and cuts back with the knife (Plate 9-7B).

15. Here the artist gives the name to the mask, which in Onondaga is called *hagǫhsaʔgą́i:heʔ*, "his face is twisted." The carver then pauses to sharpen the knife on a whetstone. A sharp point is important for the following steps.

16. The carver uses the point of the knife as a graver to outline the aperture of the mouth (Plate 9-8A, B).

17. Again working at the back, the carver puts the crooked knife into play to shave down the inside. (Harris had one knife curved to the right and a second curved to the left for conveniently reaching all surfaces (Plate 9-9A, B).

18. With the narrow blade of the jackknife as a graver, the carver makes the supraorbital wrinkles on the brow, cutting from a median line above the nose around the right ridge and returning along the same line. Then he does the same thing with the left ridge.

19. The carver cuts holes for the nose, eyes, and mouth from the front inward. He makes holes for attachment with a jackknife (not burned with a hot wire or awl). Tom made three, but when asked, knew of the seven-hole attachment, which he said was the method used before hair was tacked on, as in modern masks.

20. Tin eyes were punched in from the front and nailed at the inner and outer corners. Other carvers use copper that is crimped into sockets prepared to receive and hold the reflectors.

21. Tom painted this mask red because most False Faces are painted red. He claimed not to know any difference between red and black masks. Nor did he know how to prepare the old paints from barks and roots. He said there are very few black masks at Six Nations. (A count would show them to be about equally divided.)

The following tools were used: ax, curved adze, gouge, chisel, saw, jackknife, curved or crooked-knife—right and left—and a spokeshave.

Mask B (Plate 9-10A, B) took eight hours to make; Mask A, as observed in process, took two and one-half hours (Plate 9-11A, B). The two were collected as specimens for the U.S. National Museum of Natural History (Cat. Nos. 381369[B], 381468[A]).

The Onondaga terms for the tools of the mask making are as follows: ax (*ʔaskwiśaʔ*); draw knife (*washai:s*); straight blade knife (fine point) (*oda:sa gwai'śu*); curved knife (*diyudahshá:kduʔ*); and curved adze (*ʔumgaɛ:ʔdahgwa:ʔthaʔ*).

Plate 9-8. Scribing the mouth opening. A: With knife point as graver. B: The same continued.

Plate 9-9. Smoothing the inside with crooked knife. A: Right-handed. B: Left-handed.

Plate 9-10. Mask B by Tom Harris. USNM, Cat. No. 381369 (B). A: Front semiprofile. B: Back.

Plate 9-11. Mask A by Tom Harris (unfinished). USNM, Cat. No. 381368 (A). A: Front. B: Back.

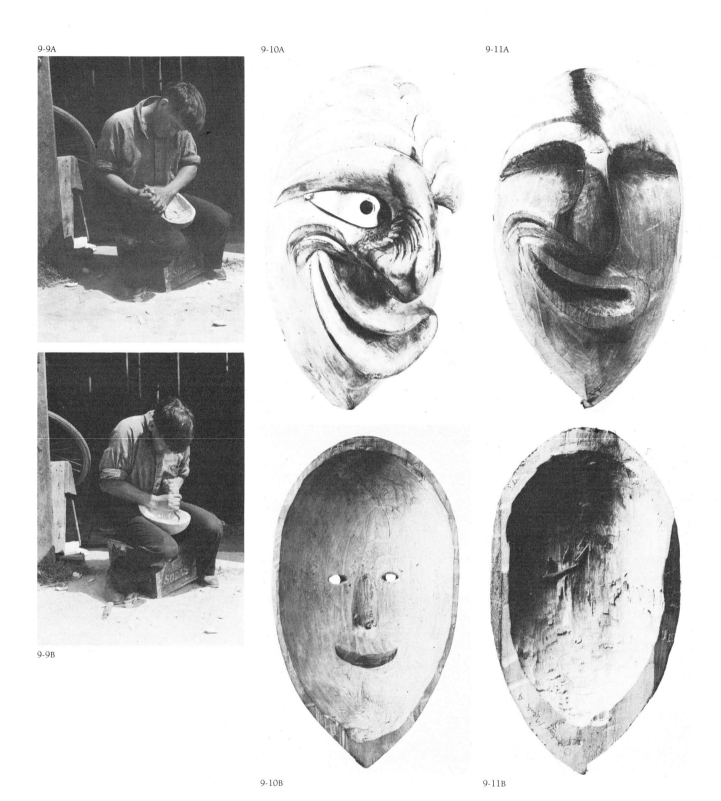

Other Carvers

JONAS SNOW

Jonas Snow, of Coldspring, Allegany Reservation, was a prolific carver of False Faces. He was not carving but working on the railroad in the summer of 1933 when I boarded with his family on Snow Street. A popular member of the Coldspring Singers, a boon companion, collector of snapping turtles and rattlesnakes, he was the recognized local genius in all branches of material culture. He could fix anything in a hurry, usually at the last minute, and he enjoyed a reputation for brilliant and feverish execution (Fenton 1953, 44). In the 1920s he had carved several masks for my father during winters when work was slack. His masks show a rough but sure hand, but a few of them are finely finished. Jonas or "Jones," as his neighbors called him, was a merry fellow, and his False Faces are invariably smiling or wry-faced. There is extant at least one masterpiece. Note that the cleft chin is a hallmark of his masks. (Fenton Collection, MAI-HF 20/2846 "wry mouth"; MAI-HF 20/2847 "beggar mask"; and MAI-HF 20/2839; Jonas Snow's masterpiece for Willie Titus circa 1920, Plate 2-8A.)

Jonas was not carving masks when I returned to interview him in June of 1940 but was fixing turtle rattles again. He told me that he went into the woods and selected one of three trees: first, cucumber (*Magnolia acuminata*); second, white pine; and third, basswood. Masks of basswood, in his experience, were liable to break from checking. He much preferred cucumber for carving. He offerred tobacco. (Fire was not mentioned.) He professed to carve the face on the living tree and bring home the block. He explained that it was easiest to carve the face on the tree, which prevented accidents of driving a chisel into one's leg when shaving the chin. Besides the chisel, his tools included a jackknife, handsaw, gouge adze, and curved knife for hollowing out the back. He said that he worked out the features of the face with knife and chisel, separated the nose from the upper lip with the handsaw, and formed the crooked mouth.

He cleaved away the block (probably with ax and wooden wedges) and brought it home to hollow out with adze and crooked knife. He assured me that the tree lives because he offered tobacco. Any season is suitable.

It takes about three hours to outline the face on the tree. (He did not specify the hours required for finishing.)

Formerly, Jonas made several masks a year, but it had been several years since he had carved any. Jonas then was in his late fifties or early sixties; he had little energy to spare after working as a section hand on the Erie Railroad, and his productive years were waning.

ALBERT JONES

A great singer and frequent speaker in the longhouse during the 1930s was Albert Jones, or familiarly "Albert, the Buck," who sired several families and for years was married to Jonas Snow's sister Alice. They lived toward Red House on Allegany, and Albert was frequently called upon to lead the band of False Faces from the upper end to Coldspring Longhouse. Though not a carver himself, his views are important. He distinguished first, the "Common Faces" Hodigǫnhsóskaʔah, which means "Bare Faces," or "Only Faces." "These are red faces, and they used to jump on to a person. These are the ones who are constantly picking out whom they are going to get to burn tobacco for them. See those weeds out there—look at them; then select the ones that are good for medicine. Just so, the mask spirits pick out certain people." Second, he mentioned certain "old faces," which are "poison" (*ʔotgǫ́ʔ*), that is, powerful. "These faces come from a live, hard maple tree."

Albert is not unique in deriving powerful masks from hard maple trees, but none of the carvers interviewed preferred to work in this medium: "They just take out a piece big enough to make a false face and let the tree stand. Before taking away the block for the mask, they used to set a small fire of pine branches or knots near the tree. They would burn tobacco and speak to this tree, telling the tree that you are going to take a piece out to help the people."

TOBACCO PRAYER TO THE MAPLE

The version of A. Jonas, A Seneca.

     oʔgáyęʔgweodęʔ oyęʔgwaʔǫ:we skwadjęnókdaʔo saiwisáʔǫ
     smoke arises   from tobacco   you our Creator you intended
                                                  (promised)

     ne:ʔ ęwǫdjä́:ʔdak gaidigwaʔǫ:we nęgáye:ɛt ne:ʔ dih nangę́
     it   for our use   wherever   (smoke)   this
                                              wanders

     wáhdaʔ
     very hard maple

     ge:i:t ęwowęʔdáhshǫ:k ne:ʔ ęyǫgwayáʔdage:haʔ neh ǫgwęǫ:we
     tree but a small piece it   will help us (people the Indians)

     ne:ʔ agwadoíšǫʔgwaʔ ęswayaʔdage:heǫ:k ne:ʔ ęswayɛ́:ʔdak
     this we plead (pray) you all (False Faces)   that you will use
                                   will help the people

heh niswaʔahaste:ʔ	nęko	ęwǫdjä:́ʔdak	oʔgęhda:yę:ʔ	ne:ʔ
all your strength	besides	you will employ	hot ashes from the hearth	which

swadjɛ:ʔdáhgwaʔ	ęswádjaʔdo:dę́ʔ	Dá neʔhoh ni gawɛnǫ:ge:
what you employ	when you treat anyone.	That is all the words.

[Free translation]
The smoke arises from the sacred tobacco which you our Creator intended for our use. Wherever the maples are situated the smoke wanders. Of this particular hard maple tree but a small piece will help the real people (Indians). This we plead (pray) that all of you (False Faces) will help them and that you will use all of your strength (power), that besides, you will employ hot ashes from the hearth, which is what you use when you treat anyone. These are all the words.

Albert went on:
Where the mask is taken, the tree heals over. The Faces fly about from one tree to another among the hard maples. They travel all over the world wherever the hard maple grows. We people do not see them, for they are "poison" (*ʔotgǫʔ*). Whoever makes fun of them might get her mouth or nose crooked. Then these Faces have to come and remove the crooked mouth by administering hot ashes: two to four blows of each masker will take that (crookedness) out. One has to burn tobacco and tell them (the Forest Spirits) to remove it.

Albert then cited several cases already described. His association of the False Face spirits with the sugar bush is interesting. Indeed, the Faces are forest spirits, so common throughout the Americas (Zerries 1954), and for the Iroquois the sugar maple is the forest tree par excellence.

AVERY JIMMERSON, OF HIGH BANK (1914–1986)

Avery Jimmerson (his adult spelling), of High Bank on the Allegheny River, became the preeminent carver of False Faces among the Seneca of Allegany Reservation. He was but a lad in 1933 when I first commenced working with John Jimmerson, the crusty old ritualist and my principal critic at Coldspring Longhouse, but Avery, his youngest son who would inherit the father's erudition, was already making drawings of False Faces (see Plate 7-1), and he had carved at least one beggar mask that was then owned by Sherman Redeye (Plate 9-12A). Avery had arranged the tin plates as eye reflectors, which are put on to make the eyes appear bright at

Plate 9-12. Avery Jimmerson, premier carver at Allegany, 1958. A: His first beggar mask, 1933, for Sherman Redeye. B: At the height of his career, 1958, with the author. C: Masks at various stages.

A

B

C

a distance, in opposing fashion, one vertical and one horizontal, so that the mask appears to be winking. Round eye sconces are more common in Seneca masks. Old Onondaga masks collected by DeCost Smith have ovoid eye plates drawn out to fine points, as do certain masks from Six Nations.

Twenty-five years later, when Avery was at the height of his career as a carver and swamped with orders for masks, I found him surrounded by a woodyard of blanks in various stages of completion (Plate 9-12B, C). I never had the chance to follow him through the carving process. One of Avery's more famous pieces was inspired from published photographs of a creation of Elon Webster, an Onondaga living at Tonawanda, during the Seneca arts project, the type specimen of which is in the Cranbrook Institute of Science.

In December, 1964, after moving into a modern house, Avery had stopped carving. The surroundings were not right, and he had no place to work (Fenton 1967, 18).

Avery had told me that he liked to work out under the trees, and, like many artists, he felt uncomfortable when other persons were watching. In summer, 1981, I revisited Allegany after a lapse of several years. Avery and Fidelia had sold their modern, suburban ranchtype house in Jimersontown and had removed once more to High Bank, not far from where I had first met him fifty years ago. "It was a question of privacy," he said, and because he was busy with construction of an addition, I did not press him about carving.

TONAWANDA SENECA CARVERS

Besides Jesse Cornplanter, of the Newtown tradition, the principal carvers of masks at Tonawanda, whom I had a unique opportunity to observe daily between the winter of 1935 and late summer of 1937, included Harrison Ground, Kidd Smith, Jimmy Jonathan, Willie Gordon, and Elon Webster. All of them were employed on the Seneca Arts Project of the Rochester museum with WPA funds. The project included the group of carvers that worked at Cattaraugus—notably James Crow and Kelley Lay—and it yielded for the collections of the Rochester museum some 243 False Faces, 65 miniature masks, and 41 Husk Faces (George Hamel, personal communication, August 10, 1979) (Plate 9-13).

Of the artisans who produced this treasure of modern Iroquois art, which has been widely exhibited but never adequately studied, I shall comment on the work of two carvers—Harrison Ground and Elon Webster.

Harrison Ground

Harrison Ground, of a leading longhouse family at Tonawanda, in 1935 was in his prime as singer, speaker, and exponent of the traditional mate-

Plate 9-13. Mask carvers on the Tonawanda WPA Arts Project, 1935. Left to right: Jimmy Jonathan, Willie Gordon, Harrison Ground, and Elon Webster. Photo courtesy RMSC.

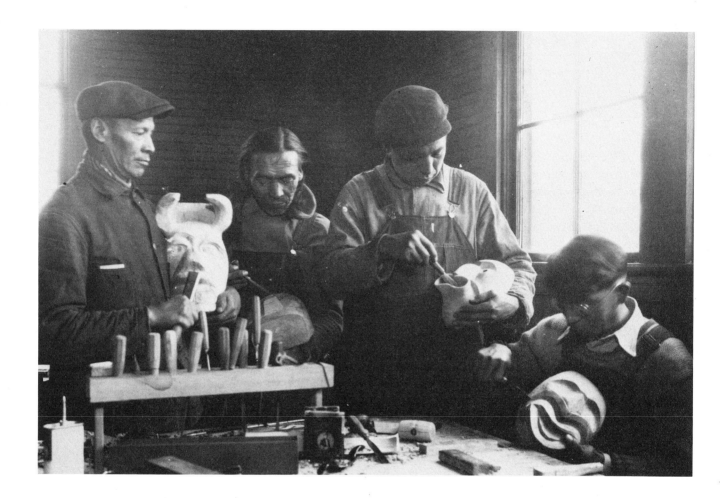

rial culture of his people. One day at the arts project I observed him making a False Face of willow wood in a traditional Seneca pattern with a bifunnelate mouth (Plate 9-13, third from left). He said that he would paint this mask red because he began it in the morning. Had he commenced carving it after noon, it would be black.

Again we meet the native theory so often recited by carvers but so frequently neglected in practice: Ordinarily, Harrison said, he would go to a basswood tree, build a fire, make the proper tobacco invocation asking the tree for its wood, and then commence to carve. When it was well blocked out, he continued, he notched the tree above and below the face, and cleaved away the whole block. He said that it never breaks if one offers tobacco. Within four years the bark will have grown over the wound.

Harrison Ground did not think it proper to sing while carving the face on the tree, but Cephas Hill, who was present, had heard that someone else had heard a man singing in the forest on the Cattaraugus Reservation.

Harrison did not intend to put tobacco offerings on this particular mask that he was carving because it was going to the Rochester museum. He added that he did not like to sell Indian things to collectors.

The fine German wood-carver's tools, which the Rochester museum supplied to the arts project carvers, greatly enhanced the range of technique. Before that, Harrison had used a chisel and a bent farrier's knife for carving masks. His own special mark fulfilled his thought that the eyebrows of a carved mask should come to a point over the nose bridge (Fenton, Tonawanda Journal, 1935, 6–7) (Plate 9-14).

Harrison Ground was probably the most productive carver of False Faces on the Tonawanda arts project, but the palm for originality goes to another wood-carver.

Elon Webster's Masterpiece

Elon Webster, an Onondaga married to a Tonawanda Seneca woman and a long-time resident of the community, originated a downtwisted mouth mask with the nose also crooked to the left, which, for its very distortion of the face, has instant artistic appeal to both Iroquois and Iroquoianists. It has been widely copied from my published photographs (Fenton 1937, 234), notably by Avery Jimmerson of Allegany. It was a joke around the arts project that Elon's creation was a portrait of Howard Pierce, a Tonawanda resident, whose face was severely distorted from a construction accident when a crane cable snapped. Robert Hatt, director of the Cranbrook Institute of Science, had written to me asking me to commission some Tonawanda carver to execute a mask for an exhibit. Elon Webster undertook the commission. The original went to Cranbrook, and Webster afterward reproduced it for the Rochester museum on the project. (Cranbrook Institute of Science, Cat. No. 3754; Speck 1945b, 68; Plate 9-15).

JAKE HENRY (CAYUGA) OF SIX NATIONS RESERVE

The work of Jake Henry speaks to two points: the local tradition and individual style. In summer, 1940, Simeon Gibson took me to visit him. He was a Cayuga living near Onondaga Longhouse on Six Nations Reserve, who was a mask maker to both the Onondaga at Middleport and the Cayuga of Lower Cayuga Longhouse. Although Jake was not then carving, he showed me three of his masks, which he hung for me to photograph (Plate 9-16A), and then posed wearing his favorite most powerful face (Plate 9-16B). From left to right, they are, first, a black mask with huge smiling mouth, a bent, lined nose, and heavily lined cheeks and supraorbital wrinkles. The tin eye sconces were tacked at the outer corners. The mask wore a mustache, but the hair had been temporarily removed. Tobacco bags were still attached to the forehad, and it had seven holes in the rim for attachment of hair and head strap. The overall appearance is that of an old man—Grandfather Haʔduʔiʔ.

Plate 9-14. Harrison Ground, Tonawanda's most productive carver, 1935.

Plate 9-15. Elon Webster's "Old Broken Nose," commissioned for Cranbrook Institute of Science, 1936, Cat. No. 3754. Photo by the author.

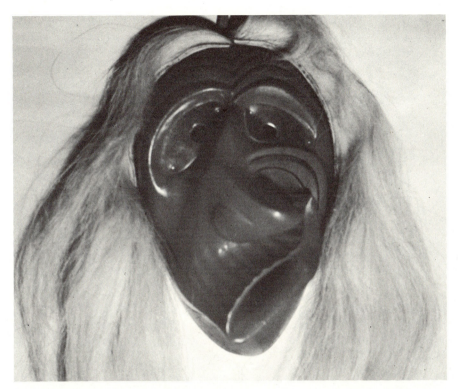

The second, in which Jake afterward posed, is a natural or "white" unpainted mask, heavily impregnated with oil; it is massively carved with prominent cheeks, smiling mouth revealing two rows of regular teeth, and pronounced chin. Four sets of supraorbital wrinkles crease the brow in matching crescents. Again, the tin eyes are nailed at the corners. Unlike the first, the chestnut hair was tacked on, and there were but three holes for attachment. Jake had carved this mask of poplar wood recently. He valued it at ten dollars.

The third is a red mask with long black hair. Again the nose is straight, and teeth project from the smiling lips. Ridged cheeks accent the mouth and nose. It has round tin eyes. There are only two sets of matching crescent brow wrinkles. Again tacked-on hair and three-hole attachment bespeak its modernity.

All three masks were heavily impregnated with sunflower oil from use in the local ceremonies. Jake claimed to have carved all three. He said that the style of the mask is left to the carver's whim. "You will find that every carver makes them differently." The massive carving and the heavily accented lines are in the Grand River style. Jake's masks seem to run to smiling mouths. The chin on the second mask is a Grand River feature. When I described a Seneca mask I had seen, he remarked, "The spoon-mouth mask is not made here!" But he added that he thought he could make it.

I think this reaffirms a point already made in discussion of the Newtown style.

Plate 9-16. Three masks by Jake Henry, Cayuga, carver to maskers of Onondaga and Lower Cayuga Longhouses on Grand River. A: Left to right: (1) a black mask, (2) smiling mask au naturel, and (3) red smiling mask with teeth. B: Jake Henry impersonates Hadui, wearing his most "powerful" mask. The corn pounder is used at family feasts.

A

B

PART FOUR

Mask attributed to the Cornplanter. 12 by 7¼ inches. U.S. National Museum, Cat. No. 221152. Courtesy Peter Furst.

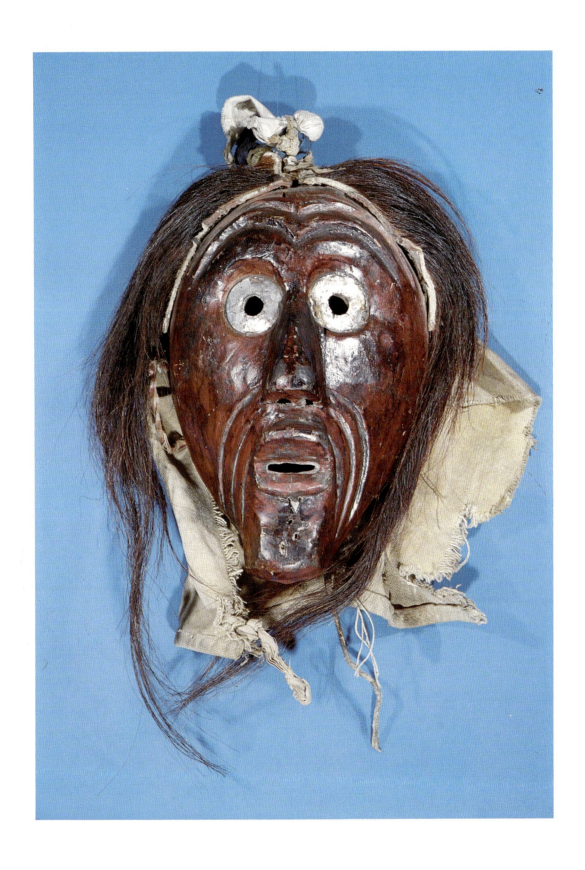

The first mask collected by an ethnologist, Lewis Henry Morgan. Onondaga of Grand River, 1850. 10½ by 6¾ inches. New York State Museum, Cat. No. 3609. Courtesy Peter Furst.

Seneca of Tonawanda. Collected by Lewis Henry Morgan, January, 1860. Nationalmuseet, Copenhagen, Cat. No. Hc369 (front and back). 7 by 10¼ inches.

Black doorkeeper mask with red flared lips. Seneca. NYSM, Cat. No. 37023. Eleven by six inches. Courtesy Peter Furst.

Spoon-lipped doorkeeper mask by Jesse Cornplanter, 1936. Commissioned for Seneca boy in the Navy at San Diego.

A homesick Seneca seaman celebrates.

Black modified spoon-mouth doorkeeper mask. Collected by M. R. Harrington at Cattaraugus, 1909. State Ethnographical Museum, Stockholm, Cat. No. 09,18.2/427/2.

Back of mask at left, showing head ties, tobacco bag, and three-hole hair attachment. 6 by 10 inches.

Classic Newtown Seneca doorkeeper. Museum of the American Indian-Heye Foundation, Cat. No. 21/1035.

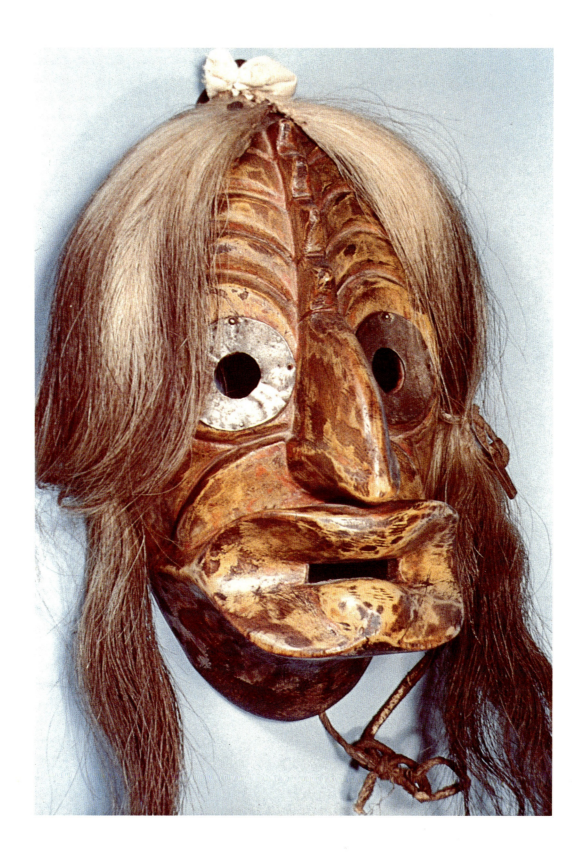

Black hanging-mouth mask with husk head throw and feather. Onondaga of N.Y. MAI-HF, Cat. No. 6/1103.

Protruding-tongue mask in the Grand River Style by Jerry Aarons. Collected by J. W. Fenton ca. 1924 from Howard Jimmerson, of Allegany. Fenton Collection, MAI-HF, Cat. No. 20/2844.

Seneca beggar mask, a remarkable likeness of an Iroquois face. Collected by M. R. Harrington. SEM/S, Cat. No. 09.18.2/427/1. 10 × 6½ inches.

Whistling mask from Tonawanda Seneca. Collected by J. M. Clark, NYSM, Cat. No. 36867. Note pock-marked forehead and long hair. 10 × 6¾ inches. Courtesy Peter Furst.

Divided mask. Collected by J. N. B. Hewitt at Six Nations on Grand River, 1916. USNM, Cat. No. 381412. 11 × 6¼ inches. Courtesy Peter Furst.

"Old Broken Nose," carved by Elon Webster, Onondaga at Tonawanda, 1936. Commissioned for Cranbrook Institute of Science, Cat. No. 3754. Courtesy Cranbrook Institute of Science.

"The Niagara Falls Style": the so-called Tuscarora Faces. The type specimen. Municipal Museum of Ethnology, Frankfurt am Main, Cat. No. 8398. 6¾ × 11 inches; shallow: 2¾ inches.

A Niagara variant. Arizona State Museum, Tucson. Cat. No. E-361.

Delaware mask of Elliott Moses. Ohsweken, Six Nations Reserve, 1956.

Braided Husk Face, male. Collected by M. R. Harrington. Seneca of Cattaraugus. SEMS, Cat. No. 09.18.6[1].

Twined Husk Face. Collected by L. H. Morgan at Tonawanda, 1860. NMC, Cat. No. H 3010.

Braided and coiled Husk Face, ca. 1900. Cronan Collection. MMEF/M, Cat. No. 10264.

Back of Husk Face at left, showing detail of coiling and braiding.

Finely braided and coiled Husk Face. Zurich University Museum, Cat. No. 3234.

10. The Rituals of the Society

The False Faces participate in three kinds of ceremonies during the year. There is first and foremost the public ceremony to purge the settlement of disease in spring and autumn. These semiannual appearances are also called the "rite of purification" of the houses, or simply the "Traveling Rite." The second series consists of private feasts of varying complexity depending on the particular dream of a sponsor. The third is the better known participation of the False Faces at the Midwinter Festival. The association of the Husk Faces with the False Faces, both as heralds, and in their separate capacity, will be touched on here and considered systematically in Chapter 14.

Spring and Autumn Purification of the Houses: The So-called Traveling Rite

In the spring and fall, when sickness lingers in the settlements, a great company of maskers goes through the houses frightening disease spirits. In Seneca, this is called *hɛnǫhnǫsoteowih*, "they drive away sickness," or *onǫhsodayǫːʔ hɛnondoːwiʔ*, "sickness they purge." At Coldspring, two parties of maskers start at opposite ends of the settlement, visit all houses and springs on the way, and converge at the longhouse. They are preceded by Husk Face runners. Along the way, members of the society take down their masks and rattles and join the procession as it passes. The masked exterminators wear old burlap sacks or tattered blankets; some go naked to the waist; they are armed with turtle shell or bark rattles that they shake to scare away the spirit of sickness; and they carry pine boughs to brush away malefic influences. They are led by an unmasked conductor who sings the song to quiet the wind when approaching the houses of members of the society, for sickness is believed to be windborne. Enroute, they scour the exterior of the houses, enter crawling, visit every room, haul people out of bed, blow ashes on the household as requested, and demand in return only tobacco, which their conductor collects in a basket or paper sack for the great invocation at the longhouse. (These are the main features, which are elaborated upon later, as we discuss the components of the ritual pattern that governs the ceremony. Then with respect to local diversity, so important to the Iroquois, observations of the ceremony at Coldspring, Newtown, Tonawanda, and Six Nations follow with comments.)

False Face ceremonies follow a ritual pattern that is shared with other medicine society rites. The components of the pattern are organization, collection of food and tobacco in the settlement with a declaration of purpose, a thanksgiving speech, a tobacco invocation, the specific program of dances and songs of the particular society, a terminal feast, and a blessing on those who have turned out and participated (Fenton 1953, 144).

For the purification of the houses, the essential parts of the ritual pattern involve preparations at the longhouse, collecting tobacco, singing the marching song to the wind, returning of thanks at the longhouse, the tobacco invocation, the rite of the Common Faces in private houses and at the longhouse, dispensing the medicine, the Doorkeeper's Dance, and the terminal feast of mush.

Invariably in the following discussion, the ceremonies at Coldspring Longhouse are paramount because Coldspring is where my fieldwork began, and I have returned there most frequently.

PREPARATIONS

Among the Coldspring Seneca, two matrons, one from each moiety of four clans, have charge of the spring and autumn ceremonies, and they serve for life. They set the date. They each co-opt a man from each respective side to conduct one of the two bands of maskers; they appoint a speaker who also makes the tobacco invocation; and they enlist singers. They prepare the medicine, supervise the cooking at the longhouse, and see to the distribution of the medicine and the feast.

All of their servants are men. The matrons appoint two masked men as water waiters (hinɛgiya?kǫ) to pass the medicine to the crowd and to act as doorkeepers. The two matrons dance opposite these two masked men, and they receive the blowing of ashes from the maskers whom they pay off with tobacco and with a share of the feast.

Sadie Butler (Wolf Clan) (Ganɛdowa:kǫ) and Fannie Stevens (Heron Clan) (Ganónhsdi:yo?) were the matrons in the 1930s and early 1940s. In 1941, Alta Abrams (Beaver) had succeeded Sadie who was then ill. Although Sadie Butler's tenure has been mentioned previously, she described her duties as follows:

> I am the one to say: "Now we will have it again," who will help and who will go out collecting the food. Everyone must contribute. Mrs. Stevens and I are of opposite sides [moieties], "cousins." I have four clans on my side—Wolf, Bear, Beaver, Turtle—and I can ask them [the men] to get water and cut wood. Everyone belongs. If someone on my side gets sick, the opposite side [moiety] does the work at the house. Fannie's side includes Heron, Hawk, Snipe, and Deer clans.

Collecting Tobacco

After the two matrons have decided when to hold the ceremony, each appoints a man from her side to conduct one group of maskers. He carries a basket or bag in which he collects Indian tobacco for that group, which is later combined and burned in the fire at the longhouse by the appointed speaker. The conductor notifies the members of the time and place of the ceremony and the appointed place to dress. Each conductor asks one man to put on a Husk Face and run ahead of the maskers to notify householders of their approach. If no one is at home, that house does not get purified.

Food and Medicine

During Mrs. Butler's tenure and my observations at Coldspring Longhouse, one group of maskers started at Quaker Bridge, and the other group came from Red House to meet at the Council House about noon. Then they adjourned for lunch at two houses close by: Alice White entertained the Red House side, and Hannah Abrams hosted the Quaker Bridge side. Mrs. Butler, herself a renowned cook, said the selection of houses was a matter of convenience where the two matrons could prepare the food for the participants as well as prepare the food to be consumed later at the Council House (longhouse). The heavy cooking was always done at the cookhouse adjacent to the longhouse. Preparation of food and medicine starts the day before the ceremony and occupies the next morning while the maskers are visiting the houses. The round of the houses is supposed to be over by noon, but it is frequently delayed by a late start (Sadie Butler, interviewed by Marjorie Lismer, July 28, 1938).

The False Faces are believed to be "medicine" capable of dispersing any kind of disease from the houses. Their semiannual visitation relies both on symbolic therapy and the dispensing of a special plant decoction. When the members of the Society of Faces put on masks, take up turtle rattles, carry pine boughs to whisk disease and misfortune out from under the beds and corners, they are impersonating Shagodyowéhgo:wah'—the biggest man of the forest people—who habitually carries an uprooted pine tree trimmed to the top as a cane. (Other sources specify a shagbark hickory with its limbs lopped to the top.) It was he who taught the people the two dances—that of the Common Faces Alone and the Alternate Feet Dance of the doorkeepers. These are described later.

The matrons prepare two kinds of False Face medicine. The sole ingredient of the first is manroot (*Ipomoea pandurata* Meyer), *ongweʔ okteäʔ*, which Seneca herbalists used to dig at Old Town and at Cornplanter, both of which sites are now flooded by Kinzua Dam.[1] It is said to grow at Onondaga. The Coldspring False Face Company, in 1933, had used the same root for years ever since Hannah Abrams's husband, then deceased, dug it down below. Only a root that is found growing in situ in a vertical

---

1. The tuber and vine of *Impomoea padurata* Meyer has an Ohio River distribution; it may have been domesticated by previous generations of Seneca herbalists, and it was available to other Iroquois communities by trade. It is said to grow at Onondaga.

Plate 10-1. A: Shagodyoweh takes over the author's Packard, 1934. B: Six Nations maskers sometimes go naked to the waist, affect animal skins, and tether the turtle rattle to the belt. Cayuga at Grand River, ca. 1908. MAI-HF, Neg. No. 2657.

"living" position is believed effective as medicine; a horizontal root is believed to be "poison" and is used in witchcraft. The second ingredient is sunflower seeds *ʔaweǫhsaʔ* (*Helianthus annuus*).

The manroot is scraped lengthwise until there is a teacupful. It usually takes three teacupfuls. The powder is steeped in the proportions of a teacupful in each of three pails of water.

Sunflower Medicine. The sunflower seeds are gathered when ripe, sacked, and stored. To make the medicine, one roasts and pounds them. Anciently they used a small mortar and pestle, but the matrons now wrap the roasted seeds in a cloth and pound them with a hammer (Jonas Snow showed me the side of a large corn mortar in which there was a small depression for this purpose). Three cups of seeds are steeped separately in three pails of water. They sometimes lack the sunflower seeds and omit them.

Corn Soup and Mush. For the fall meeting, the matrons make a big kettle of corn soup and another kettle of mush. (It was implied that corn was not always available in March.)

The amounts of medicine and food are in proportion to the size of the anticipated crowd. Often there is but a single pail of each kind of medicine.

HOUSE TO HOUSE: PURGING SICKNESS AND COLLECTING TOBACCO

The going from house to house is called *hadinonhdíʔthaʔ*. One band used to rendezvous at Quaker Bridge, dress, and start out under the appointed leader to visit houses upriver toward the longhouse at Coldspring. The other band gathered at Red House, formerly at Albert Jones's place, and he led them downstream to Coldspring. Theoretically, the two leaders should be of opposite moieties, an ideal seldom fulfilled in practice. As the morning wore on they converged at Coldspring.

Maskers are supposed to walk. Early one winter they rode in automobiles, making a wild sight as they sped up the valley road in open Fords, their hair whipping in the chill wind. They rubbed their turtle rattles on the car doors and uttered their terrifying cries whenever they swerved to pass a stranger. One Seneca masker rather fancied my 1926 Packard roadster and posed behind the wheel (Plate 10-1A).

Costumes are as outlandish as one's imagination can conceive. Maskers no longer wear bearskins, but a tattered blanket, burlap sacks, and sweat pants are de rigueur. Some go naked to the waist (Plate 10-1B). It is believed that a masker will not become sick from exposure while traveling in cold weather nor will he suffer burns from plunging his bare hands into the fire pit and rubbing embers and hot ashes to blow on patients.

The conductor does not sing as the band of maskers approaches a dwelling. Householders are alerted by the Husk Face runner. The conductor asks for tobacco as his maskers enter a house: *oyę ʔgwaʔǫ́:we ʔęjo:tgáʔ ganyoʔgo:yęʔ* ("Indian tobacco contribute if any available"). Some sources specify that the conductor sings the first verse of the song that quiets the wind.

The Seneca comment on their own failure to observe ceremonial protocol. Indian time is an hour after the appointed hour. They say the maskers should come around in the morning, and the big meeting should convene at the longhouse at noon, but more often it occurred at three o'clock. And when the maskers come after noon they do not find people in bed, unless they are ill. "The maskers go to every house, and walk through all the rooms. Whoever they find in bed they pull out and handle roughly. Long ago they found more victims for their amusement." They commit indignities on lazy people.

The maskers carry only rattles with which they rub the house all over and pine boughs with which they whisk disease spirits and sickness out from under the beds and corners inside the houses. It is believed that the False Faces ward off great plagues and prevent whirlwinds from destroying the settlement. During the cholera epidemic of 1849 in western New York, the False Faces went from house to house "down below" in the longhouse district of Tonawanda performing the rite of purification to expel the pestilence (Morgan 1901, 1:159). The Allegany folk say that high winds never hit their reservation, and they recall that the small pox epidemic came only to Red House, which is the northern fringe of the False Face beat.

Jesse Cornplanter recalled that once at Newtown, a conductor was about to gather his company of exterminators and depart for another house when he noticed that one was missing. They heard a most terrifying racket in the loft and climbed up to discover the missing masker violently shaking an old straw bed ticking from which the bedbugs were fleeing by the score. This was Jim Crow (Sanonʔgai:s), later a famous carver and medicine man, possessed of an extraordinary sense of the ridiculous, who was shaking his rattle and crying in the most orthodox manner. This example of the frivolity that may pervade an otherwise serious ritual conveys the ambivalent way that the Iroquois regard the False Faces: They are at once both terrifying and amusing.

During the progress through the houses, if someone sets down a kettle for the maskers, the conductor burns tobacco, appeals to the patron spirits, and asks the masked company to blow ashes on the patient. The only fee is native tobacco that the leader collects in a twined husk basket. However, if the maskers are not rewarded and given the least opportunity, members of the party will steal food for a feast at the longhouse. Women watch their cupboards.

THE HUSK FACE RUNNERS

There must be two Husk Faces, one for each band of the False Faces. The Husk Face go ahead and pass through houses; anciently they traversed the length of the longhouses, but now they go in the front door and out the back. This passage is to let the people know that the maskers are coming. The Husk Face runner does not speak. At any house where he is denied admittance, he signals to the company by waving his pole and they bypass that house. The Husk Faces dress in old clothes like the other maskers. They no longer go stripped.

Clara Redeye offered this amusing comment on the selection of runners.

> They used to get Jerry Jimerson, who was considered foolish, to wear a Husk Face and send him ahead to see whether the dogs at certain houses would bite the maskers. Indeed some dogs run out and bite the False Faces. If dogs ran out at Jerry, the company would know not to go there. Jerry was not afraid of anything.

Implicit in this comment is the belief that the wearer of a Husk Face is immune to physical injury.

The masked company enter houses where people admit them. They walk in; they do not crawl. After going over the premises with turtle rattles and pine bows, should any resident want to be cured, he or she must provide tobacco. They set out a chair for the patient and administer the ashes. The False Face impersonators then take off their masks and eat the mush that is set down for them on the premises, before remasking and proceeding to the next house.

Chauncey Johnny John expanded on the role of the conductor. Unmasked he precedes the company into the house carrying a bag for tobacco that he is collecting for the invocation at the longhouse. He tells the people to go to the Council House as soon as the masked company has passed. He says:

> agwatayineʔ ganǫhsosgeh waʔǫgwinǫdjeʔ deswaʔsá:yɛʔ
> we are   to the   we are going   You all hurry
> traveling   longhouse

> gagwe:gǫh neʔho hɛswe: onǫʔgwaʔshɛʔ swanegeɛ:ʔ
> everyone   there that   medicine   you all shall drink
>   way

> oyɛʔgwaʔǫ:we kho ǫgweǫdjeʔ
> Indian tobacco   we are collecting.
> also

[Free translation:] We are proceeding toward the longhouse. All of you hurry in that direction where you shall all drink medicine.

Also we are collecting tobacco.
   Everyone is bound to give him a little tobacco.

Coldspring takes its name Dyo:negano:h ("Cold Water") from a flowing spring that joins the creek of that name and enters the Allegheny River south of the then longhouse behind the former residence of Chauncey Johnny John. Chauncey had remarked when we were carving a mask that he tries to take the block from the east side of the tree because, in the purification of the houses rite, they should start out early in the morning and visit all the springs. At Cattaraugus, they stationed a masked person at each spring to purify the drinking water (Cornplanter 1938, 209).[2]

THE SO-CALLED "MARCHING SONG": GANǪEOWI:ʔ— THE "DAWN SONG" THAT QUIETS THE WIND

This is the dream song (*ganonhwai´wi:ʔ*), the Onondaga variant, related to the songs sung when stirring ashes at the Midwinter Festival for revealing and fulfilling dreams. It is addressed to the spirit forces of the mid-pantheon—thunder, sun, moon, and, in the case of the False Faces, the wind. It is sung by the unmasked conductor as he leads the company of maskers toward the scene of the feast. The song has a marvelous melodic quality, and it calms the human spirit as well as the wind. The old Iroquois believed that disease was airborne, so in their minds the song prevents the spread of sickness as well as averting storm damage. It appeals to the spirit, whom the Seneca call Shagodyowehgo:wa:h and the Onondaga Hadúʔi:ʔ, who is believed to have the power to control the wind.

In the recorded version that Jesse Cornplanter had from his father at Newtown on Cattaraugus Reservation, the first verse is sung on approaching a house and the second on entering the longhouse.[3] (Figure 10-1; transcription after Kurath 1964, 207).

   [1] gawęnode:[1] ye: gę'ęne:
      yo: wige wige
      yo: wige wige :] (repeat)

---

2. The concept of purification by running water lies deep in Iroquois culture consciousness. A stream runs beneath the earth into which weapons were symbolically cast, an act that removed the taint of death in warfare. This was the metaphor of burying the hatchet. Water for medicine is always dipped with the current, never against it. Purification by invocation of running water to wash away disease underlies the Cherokee ritual of "going to water."
3. Fenton-Huot Collection of 1936, Record 6, a and b. Indiana University Archive of Traditional Music, No. 784.24. Kurath's transcription 1964, 207 (Figure 10-1).
4. *gawɛnondeʔ*, or *gawɛnonde:*, "a voice floating," or "a long voice."

Figure 10-1. Musical score of the False Face Marching or Dawn Song. From Kurath 1964, 207.

[2. This is the second verse, used only at the longhouse on approaching and entering]

niyawęne:⁵ niyawęnehe	It might happen
ha i ge heʔe :] DC and end here	
shagodyowehgo:wa: ha	From mighty Shagodyoweh
ha i ge heʔe	
ǫgwadeʔɛ ʔshewahdǫʔ⁶	Our luck shall derive
ha i ge heʔe (repeat)	

Joshua "Billy" Buck, one of the virtuoso Iroquois performers of this century, a Tonawanda Seneca through his mother but a frequent resident at Six Nations where his father lived, recorded for me, in 1941, a variant version of the "Dream Song Which They Sing for our Grandparents (the False Faces)." This has been published in album form (Fenton 1942, text at page 25 of Program Notes.) There is but one verse.

gowęnodeʔe yo:wige hano:] [Repeat ad lib]
A voice is rising.

THE CONDUCTOR'S ANNOUNCEMENT

As the maskers crawl into the longhouse and approach the fire and eagerly search amid the embers for tobacco of previous invocations that they have smelled, the conductor addresses them briefly to indicate what is in store for them. Simeon Gibson made this announcement in Ononaga on the record:

| nigaiwagwáhaʔ | ęswadahǫsíyosdaʔ | neʔ skwaso:daʔ |
| a few words | you all shall listen | you grand parents attentively |

| o:nɛh deswa:yǫ | tcaʔnų:we niyagoyaʔdayeisthaʔ | neʔ hegagwegi |
| now you arrived | here where people gather | all of them |

| gohųgoyaʔgídiʔ | ęsheswadę:nó:tas | ęswadųhä̀hsę: | neʔtho |
| he is appointed | he shall sing for you | you will enjoy rejoice | That's it. |

[Translation] You shall all pay attention for a little while, you grandparents who have now arrived here where people customarily gather together, for a man has been appointed to sing for you so that you may rejoice. That's all.

5. *neyaw neʔ*, "it might happen."
6. *ogwadę:ʔshiʔwahdǫʔ*, "we derive our fortune" (*odęʔswaʔ*). There is a difference between song text and spoken language.

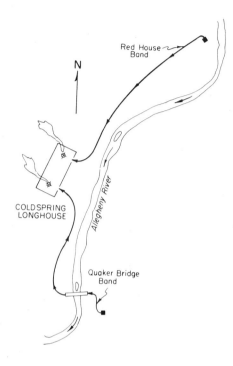

Figure 10-2. At the Coldspring Longhouse. The longhouse is cleared and, the benches are set aside until after the first dance. The singers' bench is then put back in the center for the Doorkeepers' Dance. The two companies of False Faces enter the longhouse crawling and sit around the fire listening to the invocation. The first dance is for "the Faces alone" (Hodigǫnhsóskaah). They dance all over the floor, using the same songs. Two appointed maskers pass the medicine. The Doorkeepers' Dance (Diyę:hsitatías) follows.

AT THE LONGHOUSE

Meanwhile, the community has assembled at the longhouse (Figure 10-2). An appointed speaker returns thanks to all the spirit forces from earth to the sky world. This is the familiar Ganǫ́:nyǫk, or Thanksgiving Speech (Chafe 1961, 16ff.). The tobacco invocation will soon follow, and the medicine, already described, will be served to the public by two appointed waiters. Meanwhile, suspense builds as the assembly anticipates the arrival of the maskers. At Coldspring, the Husk Face runners burst into the room from opposite ends, cross in the middle, and exit from the opposite door. This is a signal that the False Faces are coming. Outside, the two groups of maskers approach the longhouse from opposite sides. The unmasked conductor of each group carries a turtle rattle for accompanying the dance songs and a sack of tobacco collected in the houses. When the two parties of maskers reach halfway between the houses where they had lunch and the longhouse, the conductor of each band commences to sing the marching song. They enter by the north and south doors, respectively. Clamoring into the room, the False Faces crawl toward the fire, sliding on one hip, right hand resting on a turtle rattle that is slid forward at each hitch, and propelled with the pole in the left hand. The maskers gather around the stove where the speaker or priest awaits them. Each of the matrons meanwhile entrusts a pail of the medicine to one of the maskers whom she designates as "water waiter" for her moiety. Lest the maskers scatter ashes and live embers about the room, the priest who will make the invocation addresses them briefly, urging them to be patient and hear his message. Then, with the sack or tray of tobacco, levied in the houses and now combined into one, he implores the False Faces through their tutelary to protect the people against epidemics and tornadoes. Persons near enough the fire to hear the words of the prayer may learn snatches of the cosmology where myth and ritual merge. The priest reserves some of the tobacco for distribution among the maskers after they dance and make medicine.

TOBACCO INVOCATION

Tobacco invocations vary with the speaker and the occasion. The following text is the one that Henry Redeye made in the spring of 1940 at Coldspring Longhouse, when the False Faces went from house to house driving out sickness. It is essentially the same as the one he would use in the fall. He learned it by listening to Oscar Crow and Jackson Titus who used to say this prayer before him. Chauncey Johnny John, learned as he was, remarked that he would listen to Henry the next time he performed. Old people regarded this man as a particularly fine speaker.

Other versions were obtained from Elijah David of Tonawanda, from

John Jimmerson, of Coldspring, and from Simeon Gibson, at Grand River. Arthur Parker (1913: 128–29) published a Newtown version in English, and I included an English translation of Henry Redeye's prayer at a private feast held in January of 1934 in a summary paper (Fenton 1941a, 426–27).

The value of these texts is that they provide the keys to the Iroquois view of the False Faces and spell out the relation of the people to the spirits of the maskers whom the False Faces represent. These same concepts are inherent in the mythology, as we have seen.

It is first of all apparent that the False Faces who crouch around the fire are only an imitation of the real faces who dwell on the edge of the earth and the Faces that hunters see going from tree to tree in the forest. The latter are "Faces Alone," for they are seemingly without bodies or legs; it is this aspect that the men impersonate in crawling into a fireside. But the one whom the Seneca call Shagodyowehgo:wa:h and the Onondaga Hadu?i:?, who dwells on the rim of the earth, is a whole, erect, and walking giant anthropomorphic spirit. The formula also calls for specifying and gratifying items of ritual paraphernalia: the staff, which is a tall pine or hickory with the limbs lopped off to the top; the snapping-turtle rattle; the giant elm at the center of the earth where the mask spirit pauses to rub the rattle and renew his strength; the provisions for the feast—mush and corn soup. The contract fulfilled, it is then up to the maskers to arise and make medicine. This means blowing ashes on their grandchildren.

A Coldspring Prayer
I took the original text in phonetic script from Henry Redeye in June, 1940. Wallace L. Chafe, the authority on the Seneca language and my colleague, kindly edited and retranscribed the text with interlinear translation in 1982, employing the present Seneca orthography. I am publishing his version with grateful acknowledgment. The free translation is my own.

> Da: o:nęh swadáǫhdi:yos wa?étshi:nǫ:k.
> So now   you all listen   you summoned them.

> Da: ne? wai swagwe:nyǫ: ęyetshiyá?tage:ha?, ne? hoiwihsa?ǫ
> So truly you are able   you will help them   he planned it

géǫya?ge hę?dyǫ?, o:nęh o?désnyadade:gę?, ne? dzadi:wihsá?ǫh
in   he   now   you two meet   you two contracted
heaven   dwells

ęyetshiyá?dage:ha? nę:gę: neh wa:goya:tga? ǫgwe.
to help them   this   the he released them people.

> Da: o:neh dih o:neh eswaye?gwásǫ:wi? nę:gę: wa:dǫh
> So now   then now   You all will   this   it says
>   partake of the
>   tobacco

shagodyowéhgo:wa:h i:s dyodyéęhdǫh o:nęh ęswaye?gwáhso:wi?
Great False Face   you it's first   now   you all will partake of
                                                 the tobacco

we:ęh diswe?s dzǫędzadih.
far   you all   on the other side of
  are   the earth.
  there

Da: ne? gwá: neh swathǫ́dehji:węh o:nęh o?wadye?gweodę?
So   especially you all listen   now the smoke arises
                 carefully

oyę́?gwa?ǫ:weh.
the Indian tobacco.

Da: o:nęh dih ne?i:s ęswayę?gwáhso:wi? nę:gę́: gahadagǫ́shǫ?
So now   too you   you all will partake here   in the forests
                    of the tobacco

deswadawę:nye: wa:dǫh hodigǫhsósga?ah ętshiyadya?dǫdáhgǫh.
you all are   it says the faces alone you are taking their
moving about   place.

Da: o:nęh dih gagwe:gǫh o:nęh eswayę?gwahsǫ:wi? ne? dih nae
So now   too all   now   you all will partake of indeed
                              the tobacco

hodi:wayeisdǫh wa?etshiyę?gwayę́ǫs.
they have   you provided tobacco for them.
fulfilled it

Da: ne? khoh tgaye:i? swanǫ́?dzayę? ojísgwa?
So further- fittingly you all have mush
    more   set down the
                        kettle

degä:nǫ́gǫhdǫh ne? khoh neh yohga: neh gisgwi:s o:nǫ?.
it has been   also the it has the pig   fat.
sweetened   been
                               spread

Da: o:nęh ne? i:s hodi:wayeisdǫh ganǫ́?dzayę? onǫ́:hgwa?
So now   you   they have   the kettle   hulled corn soup
                 fulfilled it   has been set
                                 down

ne? ga:negaga?ǫsdáhgǫh nę:gę́: neh yǫ:ne?shä?géshǫ?
the liquid has been   this   the in the clearings
   flavored

deyodawę́nye:nǫʔ.
they used to move about.

    Da: o:nęh dih o:nęh waʔoyęʔgwáhsǫ:wiʔ nę:gę: neh
    So   now   too now   it partakes of the   this   the
                                       tobacco

swanǫhgwaʔshäʔ khoh nę:gę: sadáʔdishäʔ oʔsoäʔgo:wa:
your medicine   also this   your cane   giant pine

haʔdegaioʔsęhdǫh neʔ dzá:dahgwaʔ neʔ gę:s oʔsyäʔdak
something stripped   you use it   habitually you use it

oʔse:gęʔ gwisdęʔ dahsáʔęno:dęʔ.
you see some-   you stick it with the pole (staff, cane).
it   thing

    Da: o:nęh neʔ khoh hę́:ǫweh ni:s dehsadawę́nyaʔthaʔ
    So   now   also   where   you you move about

gado:gę: hę́:ǫweh ni:s dehsadawę́nyaʔthaʔ.
a certain where   you you move about [travel].
[place]

Da: neʔ dih neh waʔoyęʔgwáhsǫ:wiʔ khoh nę:gę: hę́:ǫweh
So   then   it partakes of the   also this   where [place]
                    tobacco

sadǫishę́hdahgwaʔ haʔdeyǫędzaęh gä:it gáǫgähgo:wa: neʔho
you use it for   in the middle   tree great elm   there
resting   of the earth

seʔnowagä:nyáʔthaʔ. Da: o:nęh dih   oyęʔgwáhsǫ:wiʔ.
you rub the turtle   So   now   then it partakes of the tobacco.
rattle

    Da: o:nęh dih háeʔgwah oyęʔgwáhsǫ:wiʔ neh saʔno:waʔ.
    So   now   then also   it partakes of   the your turtle rattle.
                                tobacco

    Da: neʔ dih waęnǫdóisyǫk nę:gę: neh skę:nǫʔ heh ni:yǫ:n
    So   then they pray   this   the good   as many as
                                      health

yagǫ:heʔ hadiksaʔshǫʔǫh heh dyo:doʔk
they are the children   it's complete
living

skę:nǫʔ aęnęnǫhdǫnyǫ́:ǫk
well they should be disposed

sagwe:nyǫ: wak?a: ęswaye:is nę: ganǫ:kdéshä? gä:tye?s
you are   short   you all   this sickness   on the wind
able   will ac-
                    complish
                    it

deyä:węnye: ne? oyę?gwa?ǫ:weh wa:diyá:?dak heh
the wind is   Indian tobacco they use it   when they
moving
  hęnǫdóisyǫhgwa?
  pray

neh do:gęs ne?hoh neya:węh ne? sę?ę wá:di:waye:is.
surely   that   it will   because they accomplished it.
               happen

  Da: o:nęh dih gaiwayędahgǫh i:s neh do:gęs ne?hoh
  So now then the responsibility you surely   that

neya:węh skę:nǫ? aęnęnǫhdǫnyó:ǫk ne? gáiǫ:nih heh ahsǫh
it will   well   they should be   because   still
happen   disposed

hęnǫ:he? hadiksa?shǫ́?ǫh hagęhjiishǫ́?ǫh.
they are the children   the old people.
living

  Da: o:nęh dih ó:ya? ne?hoh nę? i:s swayę?gwawęhde?
  So now then another that   you you all add the tobacco
              one

nę:gę: wa:dǫh ethíso:t hegä:hgwę́?skwa: diswéhdahkwa?
this it says our   from toward the you all come from there
              grand-   sunset
              parents

swa?hástesyowa:neh nę? i:s?ah.
you all have great   yourselves.
power

  Da: ne? dih o:nęh nę?i:s ęswayę?gwáhsǫ:wi? neh do:gęs
  So   then now you   you all will partake of   surely
                              the tobacco

ne?hoh neya:węh nę:gę: waęnǫdǫisyǫk heh ni:yǫ:n
that   it will   this   they pray   as many as
       happen

goya?dogǫ́hsotha?.
they survive.

Da: ne? dih neh wa?oyę?gwáhso:wi? nę:gę: ne? i:s?ah
So then it partakes of the this you
 tobacco

swadyä:?dáhgwa? eyetshiyádya?do:dę? nę:gę: oji:sta?.
you all use it you cure them these embers.

Da: ne? dih so:ga:? ę:yę:? a:gadya?do:dę? da: o:nęh dih
So then some- will want it should So now then
 one cure them

gaiwayędahgoh.
the responsibility.

Da: o:nę dih ó:ya? ne? deswayenǫwǫ?khǫ? nę:gę:
So now then another You all work these
 one together

neh wa:dǫh akhíhso:t gajíhsa? niswahsęno?dę:. da: ne?hoh
 it says our husk what your So that
 grand- faces name is.
 parents

ne? i:s jiyá?dä:dye? o?gáiwaye:i?t.
 you you two are it came to pass.
 part of it

Da: o:nęh dih eswayę?gwáhso:wi? wa:dǫh akhíhso:t.
So now then you all partake of it says our grandparents.
 tobacco

Da: ne? dih neh gaiwayéisdǫh ni:s na?ot saiwanǫ́hgǫh
So then it is you what you like
 accomplished

onę:hsǫ́hgwa?.
popcorn.

Da: o:nęh dih nę? i:s gaiwayędahgǫh deswaye:no:?
So now then you responsiblity you all will work together

ęyetshiyá?dage:ha? oyę́?gwa?o:weh nę? i:s ęswaǫgá?dak.
you all will help Indian tobacco you you all will hear with it.
them

Da: o:nęh dih naeh o?wadyęnę:da?t o:nęh dih naeh ne? dih neh
So now then Indeed it is finished now then indeed then

ęgaiwaye:i?t ęswanǫnyahsǫ:wi? khoh ne? deyę:si?dadías
it will be you all will par- and alternating feet dance
accom- take of the dance
plished

ęgáiwaye:iʔt haeʔgwah khoh nę:gę: akhíhso:t gajíhsaʔ
it will be   also   and this   our   husk faces
accom-   grand-
plished   parents

waodinǫnyahsǫ:wiʔ haeʔgwah.
they partake of   also.
the dance

  Da: nehoh dih nǫʔgawenǫgeʔheʔt o:nęh dih nä: dyadé:shat.
  So that then the entire message now   then indeed you two stir

  Dá: neʔhoh.
  So that [is it].

Translation[7]
  Now all of you listen attentively, whom you, the people, did summon.[1]
  For indeed you are able to help them [the people], just as the one who lives in the sky world ordained. Now that your two groups are joined just as you two contracted[2] to help these people whom he did release on earth.
  So now then you all shall partake of the scent of the tobacco, the one people call Shagodyowehgo:wa:h, for you are of first importance. Now you shall savor the scent of the tobacco where you abide at the far side of the earth.[3] So particularly you all are listening carefully (attentively) to the message that arises in the tobacco smoke.
  So now then you too shall all partake of the scent of tobacco, namely you who are roaming in the forests, whom people call the "Faces Alone,"[4] for whom you maskers are substituting.[5]
  So now then all of you (both real and False Faces) will partake of the tobacco, which the people have fulfilled by providing tobacco for them.[6]
  So, furthermore, fittingly you all have set down a kettle of mush which has been sweetened and topped with lard. And so now it is for you that they (people) have fulfilled it by setting down a kettle of hulled corn soup which is flavored with game that used to move about in the clearings.[7]

---

7. The numbers that follow in brackets represent the comments of the interpreter Clara Redeye, and they are numbered at the points in the translation where they occurred. These then follow the translation, bearing the same numbers. In a sense they are her footnotes on the text, which she felt needed clarification. Inevitably some of the notes are my interpretation of what she sought to convey in her comments. These again are in brackets.

So now then that too which is your "medicine" partakes of tobacco, namely your cane [staff], which is a giant pine stripped to its top, which you habitually employ should you see something (evil): you impale it (stick it with a pole).[8]

So now this also: where you habitually travel there is a certain place where you regularly go. Therefore it partakes of the tobacco, namely this special place where you rest at the middle of the earth, which is a great elm tree on which you rub your turtle rattle.[9] So now then it partakes of the tobacco.

So now then this too: your turtle rattle partakes of the tobacco.

So this then they pray: that all the children now living shall enjoy good health (for the next six months), for you are capable of diverting sickness that is drifting on the wind. It is this genuine tobacco that the people use when they pray so that surely it will eventuate because they have fulfilled all the requirements.[10]

So now then the responsibility is yours to ensure that it happens that they will feel well, namely the children and old people yet living.[11]

So now then another thing. It is the ones with whom you share tobacco whom the people call "our grandparents" who do come from toward the sunset. You have great power of your own.[12]

So then now you all shall partake of the tobacco, for surely all of those who (as many as) survive pray that this will happen.

So this then partakes of the tobacco, namely these live embers which you employ in treating someone.[13]

Accordingly, in case someone wants to have ashes blown on her, then it is up to that person to come forward.[14]

So now then another thing. You all do work together, these who are called "our grandparents," the Husk Faces, as you are named. Moreover you two came along together as is customary.[15]

So now then you all will partake of the tobacco whom people call "our grandparents." Accordingly that which you like is provided, namely popcorn.

And so now then it is your responsibility for you all to work together and help them. This tobacco is the means of your hearing.

So now then indeed the prayer is finished. Now then surely a dance shall be performed for your enjoyment.[16] You will all take part in the alternating feet dance. And besides that our grandparents, the Husk Faces, shall enjoy their dance as well.

That then is the entire message. Now for certain get up and make medicine.

That is all.

Here the invoker casts the rest of the tobacco in the fire, except for what has been reserved to pay off the maskers.

Explanatory Notes on the Prayer Clara Redeye, as interpreter, provided the following explanatory notes:

[1] The invoker addresses the False Faces gathered around him. They have been around town all morning going from house to house, and now they have gathered at the longhouse fire.

[2] The Creator and Shagodyoweh agreed that the latter should look after the people whom the maker was about to release on earth.

[3] Shagodyoweh inhabits the far edge of the earth. Sometimes the invoker says: *heyodoędzo:k,* "on the rim of the earth."

[4] The Faces Alone. They say that they see only faces, no bodies, going from tree to tree in the forest; but Shagodyoweh—they see the whole man. Therefore, humans crawl to impersonate the Faces Alone.

[5] The False Faces (maskers) at the fire are only an imitation of the real Faces. The human actors perform the role of the Common Faces, the Faces Alone, who roam everywhere in the forests. It is implied that they substitute for the great ones who wander in the rocky valleys and mountains at the edge of the earth (Parker 1913, 128).

[6] All faces, both real and false, now partake of the tobacco which the people have donated.

[7] The reference is to game animals that formerly, before going into the kettle, roamed the land. [Of late the pig has replaced them as a feast food.]

[8] Shagodyoweh, with his staff fashioned from a giant pine or shagbark hickory from which the limbs were stripped, impales snakes and other evil things encountered in his travels. [The idea of the shaman and his magic staff is shared by the Cherokee.]

[9] Shagodyoweh travels a restricted route over the earth, stopping to rest at a certain spot at the middle of the earth where stands a great elm on which he rubs his turtle rattle to renew his strength, or power.

[10] The people now have awarded tobacco to everything.

[11] [It is customary at periodic ceremonies for the people to return thanks for life and health during the past and hope for good health and long life in the future. This plea includes the children as well as the old people.]

[12] He here refers to the thunders, "our grandfathers of the rumbling voices who come from toward the sunset."

[13] He offers tobacco to the live embers which the maskers use when they cure by blowing.

[14] He addresses members of the society who need to renew their membership or require treatment. The patients come to the fire and sit on the bench provided.

[15] [The False Faces and the Husk Faces collaborate in curing the

people.] Two Husk Faces came along with the False Faces as messengers.

[16] The ritual will be performed properly, and there will be a dance for the False Faces and for the Husk Faces after they finish curing. [These rites are specified.]

A Tonawanda Variant
Elijah David, of the Hawk Clan, was leader of his moiety in the Tonawanda Longhouse ceremonies. He had worked previously with F. W. Waugh on medicines, and so I sought him out. At the time he made the invocation to the False Faces in the longhouse. His variant, which he learned from William Poudry, has interesting cosmological implications and contains the rationale for the identification of red faces with the East and black faces with the West. Jesse Cornplanter, in interpreting the text, commented on the style and added his summary of the cosmology.

Lyman Johnson, of the Wolf Clan, was the speaker for the other moiety, but I never recorded in text his extended version of the tobacco invocation to the False Faces, which I heard him give in the longhouse. We did, however, discuss its content.

Elijah's text is short, and is probably much abbreviated.

Tobacco Invocation to the False Faces. (By Elijah David, 'Twenty Kettles', moiety officer and Hawk Clan leader at Tonawanda Longhouse; Jesse Cornplanter, Snipe Clan, interpreter; edited by Wallace L. Chafe, 1982.)

oʔsayęʔgwáhsǫ:wiʔ	shagodyowéhgo:wa:	i:sę:	dewogadawenyé:ak
you partake of the tobacco	(false face prototype)	you said	I will be traveling

hetgę́:gwa:	ne yǫędzadeʔ	neʔ neh ękheyaʔdagé:heǫk	neh yǫędzageʔ
above	the earth	I will be helping them	on earth

deyogadawényé:[1]	neʔ neh dedzá:ǫgwa:	deyǫędzoʔkdáʔoh
are traveling	on both sides	the ends of the earth

·egíʔdyǫ:ędak[2]	gáędiʔgwah	nigáʔa:	niyó:waʔgeh	ęyǫ́gasha:aʔt
I will abide	whatever (however)	small	what time	they will remember me

neʔ giʔshęh	oʔgä:sʔa:né:gwa:	heyǫ́gasha:aʔt	neʔhó:gwa:
maybe	at dusk	they will remember me	whichever direction

khoh nai	ętge:hdak neʔ	giʔshęh	ne sedéhjiah	ęyǫ́gasha:aʔt
and indeed	I will come from there	maybe	in the morning	they will remember me

ne?hó:gwa: nae khoh ętge:hdak [3] hé:gwa: tgä:hgwitge?s.
whichever in- and I will come from the east.
direction deed from there that direction

    Da: ne? dih neh ękä:idak ha?deyǫ́ędzahsę:nǫ? ne?hoh
    So then the tree will in the middle of the there
                be there   earth

ęgi?nowagä:nya?dak ne? neh o̱"sóä?go:wa:. [4]
I will use it for rubbing the great pine.
the turtle rattle

    Da: ne? khoh ęwǫgyä´:?dak neh adá?dishä? neh onǫnogá:?go:wa:
    So also I will use the cane [staff] the great hickory

ne? dih gę:s ęgada?dísyo:dę? ne? khoh ęwǫgyá:?dak ne? gę:s
then habit- I will thump the and I will use habitually
    ually   cane

ęge:k neh ojískwa?.
I will eat the mush.

    Da: ne? khoh neh ęwǫkhnǫnyáhso:wi? sǫ:dí?gwah
    So also I will partake of the whoever
                         dance

ękheya?dágeha?.
I will help

    Da: ne?hoh.
    So that [is it].

Translation by Jesse Cornplanter[8]

Partake of this tobacco, Oh Great Wind Being (Shagodyoweh-go:wa:h), for it was you who said, "I will travel back and forth over the earth's surface, so that I shall be continually helping those people who roam the earth.[1] And I will sit (reside) on both sides at the ends of the earth.[2] However brief a span of time they will remember me, in whichever direction it is, whether it be evening, or should it be in the morning, I shall come straightaway; should it be in the morning, I shall come straightaway; should it be in the morning

---

8. Jesse Cornplanter interpreted Elijah David's prayer. The numbers in brackets key his comments to the text and the commentary that follows his interpretation. These were things that he evidently felt I should know, and being highly versed in Seneca and quite literate in English, his commentary required little editing on my part. Those passages that are clearly my own appear in brackets.

Figure 10-3. The great tree at the center of the earth.

that someone remembers me I shall come straightaway from toward the sunrise.[3] Then there is the tree which will stand in the center of the earth, namely a giant pine tree, and there I will use it for rubbing my turtle rattle.[4] And also I shall carry a staff (cane) made of a giant hickory tree, which I shall thump as I go along.[5] And moreover I shall expect that which I customarily eat, namely mush.

And, besides, I will participate in a dance with whomever I cure (help).

That is all.

Commentary by Jesse Cornplanter.

[1] Shagodyoweh is in the wind or air but earthbound. Whereas Hiʔnoʔ (Thunder) is in the clouds and therefore is of the midpantheon. The Creator appointed him to take care of the earth.

[2] [Shagodyoweh is conceived as traveling continually back and forth across the earth from rim to rim], and he stops to rest at the great elm tree which stands in the middle of the earth where he rubs his rattle. [The text says pine, as does Parker (1913, 128). But Henry Redeye and Jesse agree on elm.]

[It is believed that he derives his strength from this tree, which Jesse conceived as having double-spreading limbs that figure as the central unit in the double-curve motif in Seneca art. The tree stands at the middle of the earth that is symbolized by a flat curve. Overhead is the sky dome, and just beneath it are the sun and moon, which are in the midpantheon. Above is the sky world. The earth rests on the back of the turtle, which is surrounded by water on all sides. This is the central theme in Iroquois cosmology (Figure 10-3).]

[3] If one remembers and summons Shagodyoweh in the morning, he will come from the East, from toward the sunrise, because he is following the path of the sun! Should one call him in the

afternoon, he would appear from the opposite rim of the earth, from toward the sunset, the West. [Later that summer, Lyman Johnson said that if one summons False Faces before noon, the red ones appear; if afternoon, the black ones appear. This color symbolism keyed to the cardinal directions is no longer intact at Tonawanda, where it seems to be unique, but the idea of red for morning and black for afternoon strengthens the East-West pattern in the text. East is the direction of light; therefore it is red; West is the direction of darkness; therefore it is black. One might speculate as to whether this pattern supports color symbolism for moieties, especially when two masks are employed, one representing each moiety, one red one black, in the Doorkeeper's Dance.]

[4] The False Face (Shagodyoweh) wants tobacco, mush, and a chance to dance. In return he will cure.

[5] [Throughout the text Elijah uses the first person] because he is reciting the message of the False Face as it was given to someone long ago, [perhaps the hunter of the origin legend].

PUBLIC TAKES THE MEDICINE

Just after the invocation, each matron hands a pail of medicine to a previously appointed masker as he enters the longhouse; the two waiters then pass the medicine water among the public. People of both sexes imbibe the medicine as the Common Faces are performing. Meanwhile, the two Husk Face messengers guard the doors to ensure that no one leaves or enters. However, one can sometimes bribe a doorkeeper with a pinch of tobacco. There is some discrepancy in my infomation as to when the passing of the medicine occurs: Clayton White, in his 1944 account of the ceremony, puts this activity later, after the Common Faces have performed. The medicine is supposed to ward off disease and evil spirits. Each person attending drinks all that he can, for herbal philosophy holds that a patient should take all the medicine he wants—drink as much as he can. The chances are, nevertheless, that this act of preventive medicine is counterbalanced by the hazard of everyone's drinking from common dippers, thereby spreading whatever infectious disease may be going around. Passing the medicine is a Coldspring custom not shared by the other longhouses.

THE DANCES

There are dances for each class of Face—common, husk, and doorkeeper. Each has the power of curing.

The Common Faces

At the close of the invocation, as the invoker charges the maskers to perform, an appointed singer takes up a turtle rattle, straddles a bench that has been set to one side of the longhouse to clear the floor, and sings for the Common Faces. They stand up and dance, dip their hands in the embers, rub them together, utter their nasal whines, and blow ashes on the head, shoulders, elbows, and knees of patients who have come forward as required by dreams or who are obliged to renew a former cure. Sometimes the maskers are little boys wearing masks for the first time who have to be held up by their elders to reach a patient's head when blowing ashes. A clever little fellow may puff the ashes from his upturned hand. As they leave, the maskers cure each other. A matron distributes tobacco among them, and each masker returns thanks by blowing ashes on her head. They depart with their kettle of mush. The performance is the same when the maskers are called upon to blow ashes in the houses enroute to the longhouse and at private feasts.

The False Face dances have been described and choreographed by Gertrude Kurath (1964, 9, 61, 97, 99), and she has also transcribed the music of the songs and published the texts that I recorded. The six songs of Hodigǫhsóskaʔa, "The Faces Alone," or the Common Faces, which are accompanied by the shaking of the dancers' rattles and their moans and roars, are among the most archaic and rugged melodies in the Iroquois repertoire. They feature repetitious themes and exhibit a narrow compass and intervals of a second and third, preceded and followed by three chromatic calls of "*hoi*," which lead directly into the next song. (Kurath 1964, 9). By virtue of their individual choreography, the False Face dances fall in a category with Husk Face and War Dance; but the archaic music of the two kinds of maskers and their function as shamans may be regarded as the ancient form of Iroquois ritualism (Kurath 1964, 61).

With the exception of the Marching Songs, which Billie Buck, Jesse Cornplanter, and Edward Black recorded at Tonawanda, and I have already described, in 1941 Chauncey Johnny John at Allegany recorded the complete cycle of False Face and Husk Face songs for the Library of Contress (Kurath 1964, 103–4, Figures 39–41). Chauncey was considered the greatest then-living exponent of this music. The singer accompanies himself with a turtle rattle or a stick with which he beats on the bench that he straddles. At Cattaraugus and at Grand River, the singer may strike a wooden corn pestle with a stick, but at Allegany only a stick or rattle is used. Like many musicians, Chauncey preferred his own instrument and always took his own turtle rattle with him whenever and wherever he was called upon to sing.

HODIGǪHSÓSKAʔAH

    1. heʔ haʔiyę heʔe haiyę
       heʔe haʔi haiye:
       heʔę hęhe haiye: :] Repeat

2. he shagodyoweh shagodyoweh he haja?dota?	the great doctor (protector) cures (with ashes)
3. he?e dehaskayǫndye?a [9] he?ę hę dehaskayǫnddye?a :]	the (maskers) are coming in they are coming in
4. he?e honǫhsǫni?ga?a :] (repeat) he hę?ę he :] D.C.	He is of the League (Iroquois) people He belongs to the Iroquois people
5. haja?tgaha:to? agegǫhsa? [10] wi: hih :]	Turn over, my Face
6. o:nęh ne?ho haja?dota? [11] shagodyoweh o:nęh ne?ho onęh ne?ho:] ha hai hoi:	Right now then cure (doctor) False Face (name) right now Right now." "That's enough" (signature).

With the signature of the sixth song, the False Faces go out, receiving tobacco from the conductor or the matron, in reward for their services. Having removed their masks outside, the actors return inside the house for mush.[12]

The musical scores for these six songs appear in Kurath (1964, Figure 39, p. 129) (see Figure 10-4A, B).

9. This is an old word meaning "they are entering," and it refers to the False Faces who crawl into the room and make for the fireplace to tackle the ashes. *Dethodiyǫ?,* "they are back inside," is a modern form, according to Chauncey Johnny John.

10. Verse four claims the False Face spirit for the Iroquois people. Verse five calls on him to turn a flip. Here a masker may tumble. "Sometimes they lie down and roll over in fun to make people laugh."

11. Verse six is the signal for the maskers to tackle hot ashes and blow them on the patient.

12. At longhouse ceremonies, the cooks prepare two kettles of mush—one for the maskers, a second for the crowd. This feast food is known as *gagǫ́hsa? ojí:skwa?,* "False Face pudding," or simply *?ojiskwa?,* "mush." Parker (1910, 79), who first described it, wrote:

> This was a ceremonial pudding eaten at the False Face dances, at special private lodge feasts, or in the ceremonies of healing the sick. It was composed of boiled parched cornmeal mixed with maple sugar. Sunflower or bear oil was used wth it in special cases. This pudding is considered a most delicious food and believed to be a very powerful factor for pleasing the masks. No one must make a disrespectful remark while eating this pudding as the mysterious faces were thought to be able to punish the

Figure 10-4. A: Musical score of False Face songs. B: Stick figures of dancers. From Kurath 1964.

a.

b.

Dance. The dance steps and choreography are best described in Kurath's words (1964, 9). As already mentioned the conductor leads the company of maskers into the longhouse; the maskers crawl toward the fire, and await the tobacco invocation. When enjoined to perform:

> Step—jump on both feet, hop on left; then reverse, raising free leg out in angualr fashion, bending torso from side to side, and raising arms with bent elbows. Sometimes grotesque improvisation, foot twists, hip shaking. Ritual action—ashes . . . rubbed on arms, legs, and hair of patient, seated on the singer's bench. . . . Patient in a passive role.

Figure 10-4B shows False Faces (stick figures) dancing (Kurath 1964, 97, 101).

Husk Faces

As the occasion may require, Husk Faces next perform, receive popcorn, and bound out of the room. They have no speech, and their songs are most abbreviated and of narrow melodic line. (Their songs and dance steps are treated later.)

The Doorkeeper's Dance

The Doorkeeper's Dance is the English term, since Parker's day, for a salient feature of two sets of dances, which comprise the second part of the ritual that the Seneca and other Iroquois term Deyẹ:hsiʔtatías, literally "They Alternately Bump Their Feet." In the round dance, humans simulate the earth-shaking behavior of their patron Shagodyoweh. It is then that one of the maskers guards the door while his cousin clears the benches, forcing everyone in attendance to join the dancing circle. Hence its name. As the song commences, two men, who are appointed by the matrons of opposite moieties, appear wearing the medicine masks representing the great world-rim beings. Albert Jones, of Coldspring, said the masks representing Shagodyowéhgo:wa:h are black, but he admitted that black and red masks appear together in this role helping one another. "The black one has more 'poison' to it."

The two maskers dance first with the matrons, each facing the woman of the opposite moiety. A couple dances in unison, hopping on the left

---

offender by distorting their faces, and cases are cited to prove this assertion.

Parker wrote from his Seneca experience circa 1904. In modern times lard had replaced bear oil, and strips of fried pork or bacon were laid on top of the kettle. (Waugh (1916, 103) repeated Parker but added that nut meat oil is sometimes substituted for sunflower oil (F. W. Waugh, Notebook A, 51; see also Shimony 1961, 152 for more recent usages). It is much the same at Six Nations on Grand River.

Plate 10-2. The Doorkeeper looks in during each song. He allows no one to enter or leave during the ritual.

foot while bending the right knee and then kicking out the right foot. At the same time they spar with each other, alternately with left and right hand, pointing the thumb upward. The masker's turtle rattle dangles by the loop through the nose of the turtle. Then the matrons pair men and women in couples who dance imitating the maskers and matrons. As they spar at each other, a bold woman may sometimes back a bashful man from the floor. There is an element of railery and sexual aggression in this activity. One of the two masked doorkeepers looks inside once during each song, as if to ensure that it is being done properly (Plate 10-2).

The Seneca call this picking out of a lady and man *da:dinyotha?*, and the sparring *deyotyohkéotha?*, literally, "they put their thumbs up." While the wooden maskers are engaged in this pleasantry with the matrons, a Husk Face masker who enters with them watches the door. If there is a particular sponsor of this rite, the two wooden maskers dance opposite the lady who sponsors the feast and is the patient. Chauncey Johnny John who recorded the music said the same song was used throughout and that the False Faces paired the couples to dance opposite each other. There is probably a difference in the conduct of the public ceremony in spring and fall at the longhouse and its celebration at private feasts.

I shall let Kurath describe the dance and then the song texts. The songs are similar to those of the Common Faces, entirely with intervals of a third (Kurath 1964, 9).

> Step—hop-kick step on alternate feet, that is, hop on right while raising left knee and then kicking foot forward; reverse. Thumbs-up—left arm extended forward, right arm flexed close to shoulder, fingers closed into palm, both thumbs pointed vertically upward. Participants—two False Faces and two matrons of the society paired face to face, the men backing up toward the door; then in turn other coupled society members; one Husk Face watching the door. [Kurath 1964, 9–10]

The Thumbs-Up Songs.[13]—The first song is sung for the dance of the masker and the lady sponsor.

> 7. (1) ye haiyo gaiyo
>   haiyo gaiyoo
>   henǫwio haiyo:]
>   he?ę haiyo haiyo hai hai (end)
>
> 8. (2) (The same song with shorter words)
>   haiyo haiyo, etc.

---

13. Chauncey Johnny John recorded these songs for the Library of Congress. Numbers seven and eight place these two songs (a first and second with shorter words) in the entire sequence of the False Face repetoire.

During this song, the two False Faces go around the room and pick out men and women to dance together.

The Round Dance (Deyę:hsiʔdadías, "They Bump Their Feet Alternately"). "Now everyone has to dance." To Chauncey Johnny John, the singer of the Round Dance, its name means "They Put One Foot Down Ahead of the Other." A dancer lifts his foot, bumps his heel, and sets it down again ahead of the other. This alternate bumping of the heels simulates the gait of Shagodyoweh who shakes the earth as he walks. This dance is organized and policed by the two doorkeepers who return to the room and compel everyone inside to join in the Round Dance. One doorkeeper directs the dance, while his cousin of the opposite moiety watches the door to see that no one escapes participating in the ritual. Seneca Chief Henan Scrogg, of Tonawanda, who had performed this role, stated the following:

> The member who wears the mask to impersonate the doorkeeper is supposed to know the members of the society. You can pick out the members. They look scared. They look at you hard, or they pretend to be busy about some other affair of their own. You can discern them through the mask. If any are reluctant to join, you have the power to force them, a strength against which they dare not resist. The mask tells who is a member. Sometimes fights occur. If one is not able, his partner, the other doorkeeper, will help him. Members *must* dance. Those who resist become possessed.

Those who become possessed on these occasions may be temporarily cured by having ashes blown on them, but in a few days they will have to prepare hulled-corn soup for the Society of Faces. "Then we all go over and remove the 'poison' from her or him." Albert Jones, a famous singer, who imparted this information remarked: "It's a funny thing. I almost never wear masks; the matrons always put me to sing." He added that women never wear masks. "They [the old people] claim that the real ones are all males. But women are really members, although they may not wear masks like men."

But there is a way out of participation. Albert commented on his long observation as singer for the rite: "The Faces are rough when they want to get rough. They will throw disturbers out. If you don't want to dance, or are unwell, whisper to the False Face and look on; but if you are well, they will make you dance or throw you out."

KURATH'S COMMENT ON THE ROUND DANCE SONGS. On the songs of the Round Dance, which Johnny John recorded for me and Kurath transcribed, she comments (1964, 9):

> Tonality and compass [are] similar to previous songs, but with reiteration of a skipping rhythm and with discrepancy between song and rattle tempi. Husk Faces in this Round Dance—two songs with repetitive motifs and syncopated rattle beat.

Kurath's scores (1964, 130–31, Figures 40–41) (Figure 10-5) reproduce this rhythmic peculiarity. Kurath has analyzed the dance step and scored the choreography (1964, 10, 99). She writes:

> Step—male heel-bumping, that is, right foot flat forward, right heel raised and forcibly thumped on the floor; reverse; female enskanye step [women's shuffle dance] . . . . counterclockwise circling. Participants—by compulsion, all members, men line up first, women in the rear; by option, all present. During sponsor's song (16) special entrance of sponsor into the round, under guidance of a husk face. During two special songs (17 and 18) entrance of two husk faces to the round. Final dances—ash blowing on the sponsor and patient by two false faces and a husk face.

[*The Songs.*—"Now everyone has to dance."]

9. (1)   o:nęh negi   "Now we must be stir our
       oʔsǫgwayaʔdǫya:nǫ[14] he   bodies"
       shagodyowehgo:wa:h hane   "For the greatest
       hai h h yai yoho:]   Shagodyoweh"
       he he (end)

10. (2)   hodayędǫsǫyondyeʔs[15]   "He peers around
       shagodyowehgo:wa:h hane   the greatest doctor"
       hai hęʔę hai hęʔę
       hai yo ho
       hai he he
       hai hęʔę:]

[The first song in the set is frequently repeated, urging people to dance.]

11–13. (3–6) Burden syllables.
       wiyawęne :] hęʔę
       haiyoho
       a a b
       c c ;] DC

12.   wiyaw neha::]
       hai yoho hai hęʔ
       a a
       a a :] DC

14. This is the first song for the whole assembly. Here, one of the two False Face doorkeepers clears the benches so that everyone as to bestir himself or herself to join the dance.

15. Here one of the two False Faces looks about to see who, of the members present, should be dancing.

Figure 10-5. Musical score, Doorkeeper Dance. Kurath 1964.

13. wiya haʔne wiya haʔneha
　　　hai hęhę
　　　a b
　　　c d:] DC hai hai (end)

14. (Not recorded)
　　　wiyo: o hęne :]　　　　　"It is good" (fair, beautiful)
　　　a a
　　　a a hęne :] (4 times) hai hai
　　　(end)

15. (7) gaiyǫhiyadéhaʔ :]¹⁶　　　"On the sky"
　　　hai yoho
　　　hai hehe:
　　　hoi yoho¹⁷ :] hai hai (end)

16. (8) yo agedawɛnǫnę́dagǫ　　　"Yo my voice echoes on
　　　gaihiyǫhiyade¹⁸　　　　　the sky"
　　　hai hęhę
　　　wiyohęne:]　　　　　　　"It is good."

17. (9) The sponsor's dance song. The Husk Face enters, goes over to where the sponsor is seated, as in Chanters for the Dead (ʔOhgi:we:), and starts her off in the dance.
　　　esagoyaʔdonyánǫ:ʔ　　　"You her body stir (start)"
　　　shagodyowéhgowa:haneʔ¹⁹　"Oh Greatest Doctor"
　　　eyagowęnonénta:k　　　　"For she sponsored the
　　　hai yoho (etc.)　　　　　ceremony"
　　　hai hęhę :]

18. (10) Two songs follow for the Husk Face in the Round Dance. According to Chauncey Johnny John, "There is always one Husk Face in *deyę:hsiʔdadías,* and the Husk Face has to dance, too. He goes around in the dance and goes out with the two False Faces who finish by putting ashes on the sponsor." These songs are not the same as those sung for the Husk Faces at midwinter.

---

16. The form *gayǫhiyáde,* "against the sky," when sung, derives from spoken *geǫyǫhiyáde.*
17. The nonsense vocables *hai* and *hoi* are interchangeable. The latter is more characteristic of the False Faces.
18. *agedawɛnǫnę́dagǫ geǫhiyǫhiyade wiyo: hęne,* "my voice echoes against the sky, it is good [sounds well]." "Shagodyoweh is playing in the woods; his voice reverberates from the sky, and it pleases him" (Chauncey Johnny John).
19. Although the song is addressed to the spirit of the wooden masks, as if this were Shagodyoweh's role, Chauncey attributed the business to the Husk Face who is generally present during this rite.

	wiyoho ganiyǫndǫʔǫʔǫh [20]	"Pretty hanging 'knobs' [pods]"
19. (11)	gayehe honiyǫndǫʔ hai hęhę: hai hęhę: :]	"His hanging knobs of husk"
20. (12)	hai hęʔ hęʔ hę :] 3 times odaʔgę: odágwę o:nęh [21] ashes flying now	"Now the ashes are flying"
21. (13)	hai hęhę hai hęhę hę́ nyawęne nyawę he o:nęh ;] hai hęhę: hę́ nyawę́ nyawę́ ne o:nęh :]	"Thanks, thanks now" "Thanks, thanks again."

Once again the people and the Faces thank each other for renewing their mutual contract.

Albert Jones, a frequent singer of these songs, said:

> At the end of the last song it tells that a Face has to go to the stove and tackle ashes and blow on the one who put up the feast for the society. All sit down while the ashes are being put on. Each patient receives five or six blows: (1) top of the head; (2) back of the head; (3) between the shoulders; (4) tops of both shoulders; (5) elbows; (6) hands. The last one is on the small of the back but not the knees unless they are sore. Finally, the masked one blows once or twice on each matron's head. That is all. Each matron has tobacco which she gives to each masker. That ends it. They go out.

TERMINAL FEAST

The feast is hulled-corn soup. White squaw corn is shelled, leached, washed three times, boiled for hours with appropriate meat, and then ladled out of the great kettles that assistants bring in from the cookhouse

---

20. The song calls for Husk Faces for this rite that are decorated with small pods or balls like fruit, and are sometimes called "tears." Chauncey claimed these masks represent males; other informants have said that these masks represent old ladies (Plates 2-16, 2-17). We did not pursue the analogy.

21. "Now the ashes fly in all directions." Chauncey elaborated: "All three types of maskers, the two wooden False Faces who are the doorkeepers, and the Husk Face, go to the fire pit, dip their hands in the hot coals, and blow the hot ashes on the sponsor or patient. At the semiannual ceremony for the whole community, the maskers treat a number of patients and each other, and the two matrons of the society receive ashes before paying tobacco to the maskers" [The author's rendering of Chauncey's reservation English].

adjacent to the longhouse (see Fenton 1953, 137, 152, Plates 25–26). The distribution follows a common pattern in all Iroquois feasts. Persons attending bring pails. At the command of the matron or conductor, they set their pails down around the kettle of their choice, and the matron ladles soup into each vessel, a dipper at a time, in a counterclockwise direction, until all pails are full or the soup is gone. Then at her or his command, "Come pick them up," each person retrieves his or her pail or kettle and starts for home.

Frequently, while waiting on the cooks or during the distribution, the speaker holds forth on the meaning of the ceremony, taking his text from one of the origin myths, or explaining elements of the ceremony and relating it to cosmology. These recitals are listened to with rapt attention. Or he may publish the news of upcoming socials or ceremonies in the near future. Sunday night social dances are a means of raising funds for the greater feasts at the longhouse.

Finally, the speaker returns thanks to all who have participated.

Plate 11-1. Purging the houses of sickness, 1941. A: The Quaker Bridge maskers dress at dawn. B: Before donning masks, the maskers assemble with their conductor, who carries a sack of extra masks for volunteers en route.

11. The Rites at Coldspring, Tonawanda, and Six Nations

Local Diversity

OBSERVATIONS AT COLDSPRING LONGHOUSE

I was privileged to witness the ceremony of cleansing the houses on April 12, 1941, and make a photographic record of it. Richard B. Congdon, of Salamanca, assisted me with a second camera, duplicating some shots and supplementing others. Our combined efforts comprise the photographic essay that speaks for itself. The legends are drawn from notes taken at the time or written shortly afterward.

This essay is followed by accounts of two ceremonies in succeeding years that take the form of letters written in reservation English to Merle H. Deardorff, of Warren, Pennsylvania, who collaborated in this fieldwork by getting Clayton White, a faithkeeper in the longhouse, to produce these ethnological gems. They have been edited only to clarify his Seneca syntax and spelling.

The Purging of Sickness (*hęnǫhnǫhsodéowiʔ*): A Photographic Essay

First, one band of maskers assembles at Quaker Bridge to dress before traveling upriver to Coldspring. The photographs and legends that follow document the several stages of the ceremony.

1. At dawn, the maskers dress in the yard and shed at Atkins Coury's (Plate 11-1: the Husk Face runner ties his headthrow while chatting with the author (Plate 11-1A; before donning their masks the group assembles in the shed with their conductor (Plate 11-1B): left to right, Spencer Warrior (Deer Clan), Kenneth Fatty (Heron Clan), Aldrich "Ostrich" Bill (Canadian), Fred Clark (Snipe Clan), conductor and singer, and Arthur Johnny John (Beaver Clan). The conductor carries a sack of spare masks for persons who volunteer enroute.

The first ceremonial act before setting out to visit the houses is the invocation. Here, Henry Redeye (Bear Clan) burns tobacco and invokes the spirit guardians as the maskers stand by listening. Note the mask on the stove that is being blessed. Masks should be oiled before setting out (Plate 11-2A).

2. The band poses for a group picture before setting out: One masker defies the camera in jest (Plate 11-2B). Note the Husk Face runner on the left, the invoker, and the other maskers. They are, from left to right: Husk Face runner (Arthur Johnny John); invoker (Henry Redeye); pig mask (Avery Jimmerson); smiling mask of Chauncey Johnny John (Spencer Warrior); a clown in burlap, a substitute for bearskin (Aldrich "Ostrich" Bill); spoonmouth mask (Donald Black); and smiling beggar mask (Kenneth Fatty) (Plate 11-2B).

3. The conductor and his party pass a spring house (Plate 11-3A).

4. The pig masker carrying a cane that rattles brings up the rear (A. Jimmerson) (Plate 11-3B).

Plate 11-2. A: The invocation before setting out to visit the houses. Note the mask on the stove being blessed. R. B. Congdon, photo. B: The band poses before going house to house over the paths and fields to the longhouse.

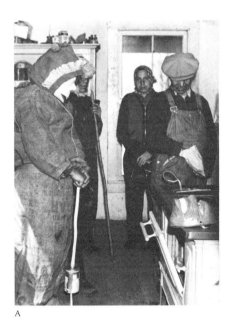

A

B

5. The Husk Face runs ahead to warn householders, and the conductor and his band follow (Plate 11-3C).

6. The conductor (Fred Clark) precedes the ragged band of maskers (Plate 11-3D).

7. The Husk Face runner enters the house of Emma Turkey (Hawk Clan matron) (Plate 11-4A).

8. The False Faces and their conductor go all through the house, while the Husk Face runner waits unmasked outside (Plate 11-4B).

9. The maskers emerge: The first to appear is the persistent clown; the others follow one by one (Plate 11-5A).

10. The conductor marshalls his band as the Husk Face waits in the distance (Plate 11-5B).

11. A clowning masker (A. Bill) takes the author into custody (Plate 11-6).

12. On the road, a matron thanks the False Faces with tobacco (Plate 11-7A), as the Husk Face and conductor wait by the road (Plate 11-7B).

13. A beggar mask dances on the doorstep after purifying the house of Chauncey Johnny John (Plate 11-8A).

14. The company rejoices with an impromptu dance on the road, while the conductor sings and the Husk Face messenger stands by. The pine boughs gathered enroute are for brushing aside disease (Plate 11-8B).

15. Meanwhile, at the longhouse kitchen, the two matrons of the society prepare the feast (Plate 11-9A). Fannie Stevens (Heron Clan) and Alta Abrams (Beaver Clan), who has succeeded Sadie Butler (Wolf Clan) as matron of her moiety, boil the corn soup and stir the mush for the feast.

Plate 11-3. A: Conductor and party pass a spring house. B: A lone pig masker carries a cane that rattles and brings up the rear. C: Husk Face runs ahead to warn householders; conductor and band follows. D: Conductor precedes the ragged company of maskers.

Plate 11-4. A: Husk Face runner enters a house. B: False Faces enter a house followed by conductor, while unmasked Husk Face waits outside. R. B. Congdon photo.

Plate 11-5. A: The maskers emerge one by one, first the persistent clown. B: The conductor marshalls his band outside.

Plate 11-6. A masked clown takes the ethnologist into custody. Aldrich ("Ostrich") Bill and the author.

Plate 11-7. A: A matron thanks the maskers with tobacco. R. B. Congdon photo. B: Husk Face and conductor wait by the road for maskers. R. B. Congdon photo.

Plate 11-8. Dancing on the way. A: A masker dances on the doorstep after purifying a house. B: Nearing Coldspring, the maskers hold an impromptu dance in the road, while the conductor sings for them and the Husk Face runner stands by.

A

B

Plate 11-9. A: The two head matrons prepare the feast at the cookhouse. B: Stirring soup and mush. R. B. Congdon photo.

Plate 11-10. A: Alice White, gaindahkwa (Wolf Clan matron), hostess to the Red House band of maskers. B: The Red House band of maskers at Alice White's. R. B. Congdon photos.

The date over the fireplace (September 23, 1932) and the initials (J. L.) tell when Jake Logan laid the chimney for the Coldspring cookhouse (Plate 11-9B).

16. At midday the Quaker Bridge band stopped for lunch at Yendi Abram's house, and the Red House band arrived for lunch at the home of Alice White (Plate 11-10A, B).

17. After lunch, the two bands approach the longhouse: The Quaker Bridge band from the south passed the cookhouse, and the Red House band from the north approached the men's door at the north end of the longhouse. Note that each party is preceded by a Husk Face and conducted by an unmasked singer who also speaks for them (Plate 11-11A, B). As they converge on the longhouse, first, the Husk Face runners race through the building from opposite ends, crossing in the middle and slamming the doors as they exit. The conductor of each band sings the Dream Song of the great masked being that is believed to quiet the wind and is the Marching Song of the False Faces. The matrons each meet one of the columns and entrust a pail of the medicine to a responsible and knowledgeable masker (Plate 11-11 A-B).

18. A Husk Face leads the Quaker Bridge band to the south or women's door of the Coldspring Longhouse. Henry Redeye (with cane and pail under his arm) sings the Marching Song. Note the masker in the center carrying the medicine pail, with a folded bark rattle in his left hand. The matron, Fannie Stevens, is just entering the women's door, and Alta Abrams (white apron) stands by; Alice White (arms akimbo) is second from the left (Plate 11-11A).

19. The Husk Face heralds, having just raced through the longhouse, usher the north band who carry pine boughs and rattles. (It would appear that the composition of the two bands was rearranged, and the moieties mixed.) Note that the pig masker with the medicine pail who started out with the Quaker Bridge band has now joined the Red House band. Albert Jones (Snipe Clan), having just sung the Marching Song for them, now instructs them, and he will perform as speaker and invoker for the main ceremony inside (Plate 11-11B).

20. The tobacco invocation at the south or women's stove has been reduced to a schematic drawing. Note that a Husk Face guards the door as the company recline around the fire listening to the words of the prayer. Meanwhile, the two medicine waiters who will later impersonate Shagodyoweh sit to one side at the left (Figure 11-1).

A second schematic drawing maps the ceremony at Coldspring Longhouse and summarizes the main features of the ritual program (Figure 11-2). Arrows indicate the entrance and passage of the two Husk Face runners from opposite ends of the longhouse, passing at midhouse, and emerging at the far door. The procession of the two bands of maskers (M M M M), led by a singer, diagrams the Marching Song. Entering by two doors, the False Faces crawl to the south fire and await the tobacco invoca-

Figure 11-1. The tobacco invocation at the south, or women's fire.

Figure 11-2. Maps and program of the 1941 Purification Ceremony at Coldspring Longhouse. A: Husk Face passage. B: False Faces enter. See Figure 10-2, p. 276, for program.

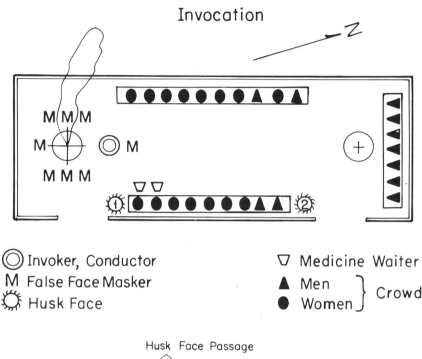

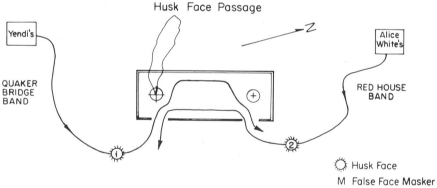

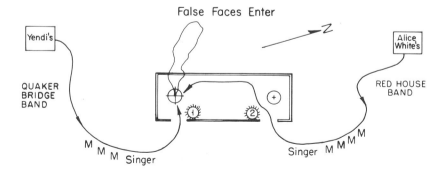

Plate 11-11. After lunch the two bands converge on the longhouse. A: A Husk Face leads the Quaker Bridge band past the cookhouse to the south door of Coldspring Longhouse. Note the masker carrying the pail of medicine.

B: The Husk Face heralds, having just raced through the longhouse, usher the Red House band of maskers to the north door.

A

B

tion. Following the prayer, the False Faces alone dance and blow ashes on patients who come forward to the bench placed by the fire; Husk Faces man the doors. During this business, the medicine is passed among the crowd from two pails. Then comes the Thumbs-up Dance on the west side of the longhouse: The maskers form two parallel facing rows, with the invoker at the end of the line facing into the room, and the two matrons opposite him at the end of the line facing the wall. When each set of paired facing dancers completes its routine, a singer straddles a bench placed in the center of the room and summons the maskers and the crowd to join in the Alternate Feet, or Doorkeeper's Dance. The two maskers who had passed the medicine assume the roles of doorkeeper and bench clearer. Again there is opportunity for administration of ashes; on this occasion Jonas Snow was patient, also Weni Abrams, and the maskers did not neglect the two matrons before departing. At the end of the dance one can observe False Faces blowing ashes on each other.

A Note on Costumes
The costuming on these occasions is various and assorted. I noted: braided cornhusk masks; maskers armed with long canes or staffs; a few had turtle rattles, or folded hickory bark rattles; one cane, as previously noted, transfixed a tincan of pebbles. There were two complete costumes of sewn burlap bags, worn by A. Bill of Canada and Avery Jimmerson, his neighbor, that were reminiscent of the bearskin suits of old. No special shoes or moccasins were evident. Maskers carried pine boughs gathered enroute to the longhouse. Other than husk and wood, there was no special differentiation of masks according to roles. Doorkeeper masks as such did not materialize.

From the longhouse, one could observe people coming on the road carrying pails for mush and soup in the wake of the maskers. Few people arrived at the longhouse in advance of the maskers.

Clayton White's Accounts of Two Spring False Face Visits
The following year the spring purification rite was held early, and neither Richard Congdon nor I was present. Fortunately, Merle Deardorff, of Warren, Pennsylvania, who had attended in 1941, covered the ceremony by arranging for Clayton White, one of the faithkeepers, to record his own observations in the form of letters, which Deardorff transcribed and shared with the Congdons and me. It is interesting to have an inside view of the ceremony written in Reservation English that mirrors Seneca syntax. I have edited these observations as little as possible to make them intelligible to other readers. Deardorff subsequently interviewed Clayton and the questions and answers about various points in the letter follow.

Coldspring
March 26, 1942

Dear M. H. Deardorff,

I am sending you Three Sheet[s] of all about the False Face Visit [to] the houses on Sunday March 15th. I like to do my Best and tell you if I [know] [about] any thing you like to [know] [He promises more in the next few days.]

Cold Spring Longhouse
Sunday March 15th, 1942

The False Face Men's visit [to] the houses today.

There are 20 False Faces in all, and two Husk Faces.

Atkins Curry, Leader on the South End, he have 16 False Face and one Husk Face.

They visit every house.

On the East they begin at the home of Delbert John, and on South End they begin at the home of Jasper Watt. The East End False Face Men stopped to rest at the home of Ruben White, and they go to Annie Abram's to have a Lunch. The South End False Face Men stopped to rest at the home of Annie Abram where they have lunch. After the Lunch they go to the Longhouse.

Albert Jones do the sing[ing] of GAR NA WE [gaṇǵeowi:ʔ] for the East End False Faces, and Atkins Curry do the sing[ing] . . . for the South End. . . . And when they get to the longhouse on [the] outside now they meet, the False Faces, and they shake hands. And the Husk Faces do the same.

Both of the Husk Faces went into the Longhouse before the False Faces come [arrived], and [it was] afterward [that they] shake hands. The East End False Face Men come back to the North End Door, and now they went in; and the South End False Face Men come in on the South End Door. . . . They both . . . crawl. They all go near the Stove on [the] South End. And now Albert Jones come to the stove.

Albert did the throwing of the Indian Tobacco in the Fire. First to say, "Now keep Quiet of you False Face[s]. And also of the Husk Face[s]. Now listen. Hear [by means of] the Indian Tobacco. Now the Smoke arises to Make [enable] you to Smell: [that is], all you False Faces and all who are running in the Big woods. And it Means [includes] both [kinds] of you, [namely] the Red False Face[s] and the Black False Face[s]. And here the Indian Tobacco Smoke rises to Make you Full understanding of what your grand Children want you to do. And now here the Indian Tobacco Smoke rise[s] [for you] to Smell [inhale] to [from] the Fire, which is used to burn the Indian Tobacco [so as] to Make it Smell, and to Make them hear . . . whatever [they] are wanted to hear.

And here is another thing: Indian Tobacco Smoke rises to Smell of [to] the Fire, and to the Ashes, for this is what you use when you . . . treat . . . the People.

And here the Indian Tobacco Smoke rises to smell of [for] [the] Turtle Rattle . . . which you always Carry on your traveling.

And here another Indian Tobacco Smoke rises to smell, of which you are a great Interesting [importance], [namely] that Big Pine Tree which stands in the Middle of the World . . . [where] you . . . scrub your Turtle Rattle, and [which is] your Meeting Place.

Now here again the Indian Tobacco Smoke rises to make [enable] you [to] Smell [inhale]—all the False Faces in this World, to give you a full understanding of what your grand Children wants you to do. That is, your grand Children want you to take away all kinds of Sickness or Bad Diseases, or any Bad Storm or Strong Wind—because you have Power to take these away from this Indian Reservation. And your grand Children are wishing [praying] for your great help to us.

And here the Indian Tobacco Smoke rises. Now you Husk Faces . . . listen when you Smell [partake] of this Indian Tobacco Smoke. That you are a great Interesting [of great importance] too. And all of you Husk Faces who are Running the World [coursing the earth], you shall smell [partake] of this Indian Tobacco Smoke. Know that this Indian Tobacco Smoke will go all over the world. And here again the Indian Tobacco smoke rises. Now you will hear that your grand children wanted you to help because we are in full belief that you have a great Power. So your grand children are wishing [pleading] for your great help in taking away all of the Bad Diseases. And also the Bad Storm, or a bad [severe] Strong Wind.

And here another Indian Tobacco Smoke rises. Now you listen, both you Red False Face and the Black False Face, and you Husk Face. Now you shall give your Treatment to your grand Children. And use your full Power. This means all of you.

And now Atkins Curry and Albert Jones sing so [that] the False Faces [may] dance. And at the same time they do their Treatment to the People, [that is], whoever wanted it. And now the Husk Faces dance, as sung by C. J. John, and it is all over.

[Thumbs-Up Dance]

And now Atkins Curry and Albert Jones sing again so the False Faces [may] dance on the East Side and the People on the West Side.

[Round Dance]

And after this now they all dance around the long bench. And now Everybody dances. And the Husk Face Stand[s] Guard at both doors so [that] no body [man] go out to Run away. Because [the rule] is Every[one] has to dance.

And During the False [Faces] [are] doing their Treatment, Two False Face Men Pass around to the People a Pail full of their Medicine to Drink on [the part of] Everybody. This Medicine is Made of Sun Flower Seed [ground and] made into some kind of a Tea.

[Here Clayton offered an explanation of kinship between the Faces and the people.] [The] False Face and the Husk Face is our Great Grand Parent. So this is why the False Faces say "Our Grand Children" to the People. [This is] because both the False Face and the Husk Face [were] first to be [let] live in this World.

Clayton added that the way to make a False Face powerful is to use Indian Tobacco when the carver takes the timber to make a mask. He specified basswood, cucumber, and pine, which is the best.

On receiving the copy of Clayton's letter, I wrote to Merle Deardorff commenting on several points and raising some questions. I identified the song sung by the leaders on approaching the longhouse. The two companies of maskers meeting and shaking hands had escaped my notice, and no other source mentions it. What most interested me, and continues to plague translators of Seneca prayer texts, is the meaning of the verb *sǫ:wiʔ*, which my interpreters rendered "partake," and for which Clayton wrote "smell." This verb appears in combination with "tobacco," *oyęʔgwáhsǫ:wiʔ*, in all prayers in which tobacco is offered or burned. Clayton neglected to mention one significant ingredient of the False Face medicine, namely manroot, which was previously specified. Also, none of the Coldspring accounts notices the Six Nations custom of annointing the masks with sunflower oil before setting out.

Within a week, Deardorff took my comments to Alice and Clayton White for clarification. Mrs. White affirmed that, of course, the False Faces actually smell the sacred tobacco smoke. She added that many people who have the power can actually lay their hands on the heaps of smouldering tobacco without burning themselves. The maskers do this and then raise a hand to the mask that it may better smell the incense. People who do not have the power try this and get burned. This happened at the purification ceremony that Clayton describes (Deardorff, personal communication, April 4, 1942). Deardorff previously wrote Clayton five specific questions about his account of the purification ceremonial, and Clayton replied on April 2. The schedule of questions and answers yielded some new information.

Clayton failed to name the ceremonial but stated that its purpose is to ward off contagious disease and dispel high wind storms in the spring and fall. Second, there is no set time, governed by stars or moons. The third question as to the disparate size of the two bands of maskers—five from the East, and 17 from the South ends—ascertained that this was a matter of available men; fewer traditionalists lived toward Red House. Fourth, on the difference between red and black False Faces, the answer was: the red False Face does not have to go around the bench in the Alternate Feet

Dance; the black False Face performs that role and gets everybody to dance. (This statement refers to clearing the benches of onlookers, not the singers' bench.) The answer to the final question as to who prepares the sunflower seed medicine confirms previous knowledge that it is the role of the two matrons who also do the cooking.

Although Clayton White continued to chronicle the ceremonies at Coldspring Longhouse during the next year, his next record of the False Faces followed two years after his first account. Merle Deardorff attended and commented on the record (Clayton C. White, Coldspring Notes, Sunday, April 9, 1944).

> The False Face bands were scheduled to start, one from each end of the Allegany Reservation, at 9:30 A.M., Sunday the 9th. The company from the South End was supposed to meet at the house of Atkins Curry, above the Quaker Bridge creamery. I was there; but Albert Jones had arrived before that to say that—because of a small number this year (so many working, sick, Saturday night, etc.)—they would not start till afternoon and then from Mrs. Abrams' house closeby the Longhouse on that end. Atkins said they used to start at 7:00 A.M. and go to every house; but things are different now.

Indeed, the record shows a considerable decline in participation. A number of Coldspring lads were away fighting in World War II.

The 1944 Performance. Two years later Clayton White filed a second communiqué on Sunday, April 9, 1944.

> 9:50 A.M., E.S.W.T.—Chief Levi Snow, [headman of his moiety], came to the Longhouse and began to cut pole wood, to get ready to make a fire at the big fire place, in the Cookhouse to cook for the False Face Men [who] are coming to the Longhouse sometime this afternoon.
>
> 1:15 P.M.: The False Face Medicine Men got in at Coldspring Longhouse. Just one End [band] came. Only the East End [Red House], and the leader was Albert Jones. The band from the South End did not come.
>
> When the False Face Medicine Men come to the Longhouse, their Leader sings GAR-NAN-WEE [*gangeowi:ʔ*]. The False Face Medicine Men came from Hanna Abrams' house where they have been resting a little while waiting for the South End False Face Medicine Men to come, but their leader heard that the South End band are not coming. So the East End False Face Medicine Men just went to the Longhouse. Of these there are five little boys and two men, and one Husk Face Man who came to the Longhouse. And when they get in they all go to near to the stove at the South end of the Longhouse. Their leader got C. J. John to do the Indian Tobacco throwing in the

Fire. And the matron Fannie Stevens came over to C. J. John. She gave him instructions as to what to say and what is [the purpose] . . . that the False Face Medicine Men [have] in visiting the houses. And so after all she told him, so the C. J. John goes to the stove and now he begins: But first he says: "Now, please all of you be quiet and now all be listening."

[INVOCATION]

Now he says, "Now here goes the Smoke of the Indian Tobacco. Now receive you the Tobacco, you Shagodyowehgowa, the Great False Face. Now it is that you have come to where your grandchildren are gathering this afternoon. And now here goes of the Indian Tobacco Smoke to make [it possible] for you all to smell—all of the False Faces living, and all of you who are running all over the World. And it takes just a little while to reach the other side of the World, from wherever your grandchildren are calling you, or else that your grandchildren are in Danger. And you the False Face Men all have great and powerful sight, [so that] you False Face Men are seeing all over the World. And in the same way you all have great and powerful Hearing, [so that] you hear good anytime that your grandchildren are calling you for help, from any where in the World. And now this afternoon your grandchildren are gathering right here at our Indian gathering place, and that your grandchildren call for your help. [This is] because that Night ago the Dream came to your grandchildren that you have notice that a Dangerous Disease is coming to attack your grandchildren. So you are given a warning that you are wanted [needed] to do your duty [of] protecting all the grandchildren. [This is] because our Creator gave you a great and powerful sight and powerful hearing. And so be a great Power to protect all of your grandchildren in this world. And now this day is now the time that has come. Now your grandchildren try to do what you . . . want done. Because our Creator [caused] a Dream to [occur] to the People; [it was] to give some warning and . . . also to tell [us] what to do. And this is why you are here now. [Or this is why you are hearing of it now.] And now your grandchildren want you False Face Men to [use] all of your great Power to stop that Dangerous Disease [so that it does] not come on the Indian Reservation and not attack all of your grandchildren. [This is] because this day that your grandchildren do the best they can to satisfy you, namely all of you False Face Men and in the same way the Husk Face Men. There is but only one thing that they don't have that you like, the Corn Soup. [This is] because the White Corn we cannot find. Nobody has it. So we only have Mush and very sweet with sugar and the Frying Pork, with a Big

Slice as Big as your foot. [Here the maskers roll in ecstasy and try to put their feet in their mouths.] And so your grandchildren think that you False Faces shall be satisfied enough because you know very well that there is no Corn Soup.

"And now for the Husk Face men. Now you listen to a few words. That your grandchildren are [assembled] in here at our Indian gathering place this very afternoon. And that your Corn Husk Face tribes shall all hear of what your grandchildren want you to help them. And that you are hearing just the same as the False Face Members do, and your grandchildren think that they have every thing ready of what you [hold in great esteem]. First, the Indian Tobacco and the Pop Corn, and [understand] that we have it all ready.

"And now another thing. Your Grandchildren want you to help them. This means both you False Faces and you Husk Faces. That is that your grandchildren want you to protect all you can those of your grandchildren who are in very dangerous fighting zones at this time. And we know that you False Faces and you Husk Faces that you all know of the whereabouts of our Boys. So this is why we are asking you to help them to all come home, all of them, all of the Boys who belong to this Longhouse.[1] And this is about all that I can say to tell you." (End of the Indian tobacco throwing in the Fire.)

Common Faces. The ritual now followed its usual pattern.

And now the C. J. John went back and sat on the Bench, and now he [sang] about 5 or 6 times The False Face Members' Dance. And after this Albert Jones stand to speak just to tell the People: that it is now open for a little while if anybody wanted to have a False Face or the Husk Face to blow the Hot Ashes to them. Then almost every one of them came near to the Stove.

[THUMBS-UP DANCE]

And after this, again Albert Jones spoke to tell the People that they the False Face Men shall be lined up on one side of the Room, and all of the People shall be lined up on the other side so as to dance. And everyone came and Albert Jones sang about 5 times and it was over.

[ALTERNATE FEET DANCE]

The False Face Men put back the long bench to the middle of the floor. So the Albert Jones came and got Amos J. John to help him to sing, and the False Face Men got C. J. John and Levi Snow to be leaders of the dance. And now everybody go to dance, and one of

---

1. At least three Coldspring Longhouse boys were killed during the American offensive in France.

the False Face Members passes around a pail of the False Face Medicine to Everybody to drink.² And Albert and Amos sing about 10 times and all is over the Dance.

[BLOWING ASHES ON THE MATRON]

And now the False Face Men go to the stove, and now the Fannie Stevens [the matron] came foward so that the False Face Men [could] blow the Hot Ashes to her. And then she gave each one [of the maskers] the Indian Tobacco for their Pay. And the Husk Face does the same. And now they went out and [it] is over.

[THANKS AND THE FEAST]

And now C. J. John stands up to speak. "Now please listen in this gathering. That we have all done now what our Grandfather wants us to do. And now it is up to them now to deliver of their help to us. And now for the Head Women of the False Faces and the Husk Faces, they are very great thankful to all of you who do this kind of work, because this kind [of ceremony] is of great benefit to our Indian people, and we are hoping that all of you shall be willing if anybody wants help. And now this will be enough about this. It is all over, just [as soon] after the Mush is to be distributed to everybody. So this is all that I can say."

End at 2:30 P.M.

Comment on the Coldspring Observations

The relationship and differences between informant testimony, the ethnologist's own observations, and the recorded observations of a native deserve comment. When asked to describe the sequence of a ceremony, informants will invariably outline the ideal pattern that is supposed to be followed, and they can describe with reasonable accuracy ritual events that the ethnologist may have witnessed and that the informant did not attend. Informants know what is significant behavior and what is appropriate to the occasion. The ethnologist's observations run rather to spurious detail and frequently contain notes or memories of accidental behavior that is not significant to the informant. Some balance between the two kinds of information is required. Clayton White's two sets of observations contain elements of both. In writing, I was puzzled by my notes as to just when the passing of medicine occurs. My 1942 observations put it after the Thumbs-up Dance and before the Alternate Foot Dance. Later I shifted it ahead to commence right after the Tobacco Invocation. One or two informants said this was the case. This is why Clayton White's two accounts are so important. A lifetime attendant at these rites, he unconsciously knew what was supposed to happen, and yet his attention to detail is almost compulsive. His 1942 account puts the passing of the medicine dur-

---

2. Other accounts put the serving of the medicine earlier, just after the Common Faces perform.

ing the Alternate Feet Dance. It is the same in 1944. Moreover, it is interesting to compare his Indian English version of the tobacco invocations with the texts that I had from Henry Redeye and others. That the False Face spirits are believed to inhale and savor the smoke of the burning tobacco offering is implied by his use of the English word *smell*. Deardorff confirmed this by direct inquiry.

The ceremonies were declining at Coldspring Longhouse during the war years when the young men were overseas. They revived for a time after they returned and then tapered off during the 1950s until 1965 when the longhouse was abandoned with fitting ceremony and the fire moved to Steamburg because of the construction of the Kinzua Dam (Abrams 1967, 23). Clayton White's second report already notices the failure of the east end band of maskers to show up, and it also illustrates the readiness of the Seneca to adapt to new circumstances. Since the removal to the new longhouse, I am told, the rounds of the False Faces to the houses have been abandoned altogether because housewives objected to having their new doors marred by turtle rattles and mud tracked in on their hardwood floors. Other changes will be presented in connection with the Midwinter Festival. Another factor affecting all of the ceremonies is that all of the great speakers are gone and have taken their words with them into their graves.

OBSERVATIONS AT TONAWANDA, WITH NEWTOWN OVERTONES

In 1935, I was stationed at Tonawanda for the U.S. Indian Field Service, which gave me an unparalled opportunity to observe the "doings" at the longhouse. Several of the leaders felt that I should understand what I was seeing and went out of their way to explain ceremonials to me. Among them, Elijah David, Chief Lyman Johnson, and Chief Henan Scrogg, himself a Handsome Lake preacher, were my principal sources. Jesse Cornplanter interpreted for informants who were not completely bilingual, and because he was most familiar with the ceremonies at Newtown Longhouse on Cattaraugus where he was reared, his remarks and footnotes to other sources have that ring.

On Easter Sunday, April 20, 1935, the headman of the False Faces, Harrison Ground (Turtle Clan), was appointed to organize two bands of False Faces to purge the houses of sickness. Chief Scrogg failed to say who did the appointing but presumably it was the two matrons, one from each moiety, whom he mentions later, who are the heirs of Morgan's "Mistress of the Band" (1901, 1:158). The status of headman, as we shall see, is typical of the Onondaga at Grand River.

At each house that they purge, the maskers are supposed to collect tobacco for an invocation at the longhouse. Their unmasked leader sings

Ganǫeowi:ʔ, the Dawn Song, when approaching and entering houses where members of the society live. The maskers rub their rattles on the building, go upstairs, and shake out of bed any who are sick, and peer into every nook and cranny and crevice where the spirit of sickness may be hiding. They look under the beds, shake their rattles, and utter their querulous complaint—*hǫʔǫʔǫʔǫʔ*.

Here Jesse recalled the incident of the strayed masker at Newtown driving bedbugs out of an old bed ticking that has been cited.

The Origin of the Custom of the False Faces Driving Sickness from the Houses

The following origin legend is unique in the literature, and has the virtue of having been volunteered. Chief Scrogg asked me:

> Do you know how this custom first started? I mean this ritual of going from house to house in the spring driving out sickness. I heard the old folks talking once about it and how it first got started.
>
> Frequently there were several families living in a single house. This time there were four families living in one house and they had children who also lived with them. Some people became ill and soon all of the occupants of the house went down sick. One night as they were all lying on the platforms under the place where the roof slants, they all peered up through the smoke hole. They thought that they heard someone on the roof. They looked. They discerned someone coming down through the smoke hole. (The end doors were closed at night.)
>
> He was the one who caused the sickness, *onǫ́hsodayǫʔ*, indeed the Spirit of Sickness Sǫdowéhgo:wa:h, the great faceless—the harbinger of death. They covered up their faces that they might not see him. He went about over their prostrate forms and tried to pull back the covers and peer into their faces. They resisted. While he was looking, just then they heard a great noise outside, the noise of the Great False Face shaking his rattle, and *hǫʔǫʔǫʔǫʔ*, his terrifying cry outside the door.[3]
>
> The Spirit of Sickness became frightened, and ran about inside the house trying to find a way out, for the door was blocked by the Great False Face.[4] A False Face chased him and he finally escaped through the smoke hole where he had entered.
>
> The False Faces scared away the sickness and all of the people got well.

3. This recalls the approach of the maskers and how they sound to persons within the house.
4. Here is the origin of the doorkeeper role and of doorkeeper masks and their ritual during which no one is allowed to enter or leave. They peer in during the ritual. It is then that sickness goes up the flue.

And that is how it started, the custom of going from house to house. It is in the spring when people usually are sick and the season when we lost most of our people by death. Grippe, epidemics, and spring fever occur then. People feel lazy and logy. The old people used to take emetics then to cleanse themselves of a winter's accumulation. It is believed that this man, the Spirit of Sickness, goes about the houses in the spring. Wherever he lingers, sickness occurs. Thus we go about the houses wearing masks in imitation of the shagodyowehs, to scare him away.

Plagues
Chief Scrogg continued his explanation.

Toward the close of the first World War, when the "Flu" came to Syracuse, and afflicted the Onondagas, they claim that they saw this man. It is said that a policeman discovered him on the streets of Syracuse and arrested him as a vagrant. He refused nourishment in jail and escaped. People saw him going about Onondaga village and noticed that he traveled a few inches above the ground. They jailed him once more, and again he escaped. He told them that it was no use trying to keep him in jail.

Jesse Cornplanter commented:

The False Faces, our grandfathers, are the last resort in times of plague when no earthly medicine—herbs, grasses, and barks—will cure the sickness. Then the people, their grandchildren, may call upon the False Faces to aid them. Someone who holds a sacred medicine mask may dream of a coming plague or windstorm. Delos Kettle at Newtown once had such a mask with three bundles of sacred tobacco attached. The mask spoke to him in a dream, saying: "I am coming to help you, for a wind will come of such magnitude and strength as to level the houses and bare the earth of all its vegetation." Delos called a meeting of the Society. They went from house to house driving away the sickness and they gathered tobacco. The people assembled at Newtown Longhouse, as instructed. An invocation was made imploring the False Faces to divert the oncoming high winds from the settlement. They drank a medicine brewed of parched Sunflower seeds."

Manroot is not added to the brew at Tonawanda and Newtown. Scrogg added that the old Tonawanda people employed only the seeds of white sunflowers that still grow in his garden.

The concern with plagues has a long history among the Iroquois, although the first record of mustering the False Faces to ward off disease dates from the mid-nineteenth century. During the cholera epidemic that swept New York State in 1849, the False Face company, properly costumed, went from house to house in the longhouse district "down below" at Tonawanda, performing the customary purification rite (Morgan 1901, 1:159). Indeed, by then this custom was well established and must have descended from even more traumatic times when smallpox and other pestilences wiped out large portions of Iroquois towns during the preceding two centuries. One wonders, therefore, how these pandemics may have contributed to the public health functions of the masked company. Regretably we lack the data to demonstrate this hypothesis.

I had witnessed the ceremony at Tonawanda but naturally made no notes during its progress. The session with Chief Scrogg and Cornplanter followed soon afterward, and I wrote up my notes the next day. Their explanations seemed more important than the details that I could immediately recall of my own observations, which took the form of questions.

Components: The Leader's Dawn or Marching Song

Jesse Cornplanter, who frequently performed in this role and later recorded the songs, sang over the text of the Dawn or Marching Song for Scrogg's comments (song texts and transcriptions by Kurath 1964, 207).

In going about the houses, the headman sings only when approaching houses occupied by members of the Society. Then they will know what to expect. The headman sings again while entering the longhouse, but the two songs are distinct.

[I]
go: wę no di:	(gawęnǫdeʔ, "long voice")
yo wi ge yowige wige:, etc.	

[II]
ne ya węne: węnehe	(niyaw ne:, "it might happen")
ha i ge: heʔ i:	
shagodyowehgo:wa:ʔa:	(Great False Face)
hai i ge:......	
agadę́sewahdǫ	(-ataeʔswaʔ, "luck")
	I a charm derive

ha i ge: heʔ i:

"It might occur that I shall derive my luck from the Great False Face." It also means, "Maybe I will derive my strength (power) to cure from the Great False Face."

Scrogg noted that the new Seneca speech is different from the archaic language of song and prayer. The text sounded to him as if it might be derived from *niyawęne: agadę́sewahdǫ*, "it might happen I derive luck from," which means that the people would derive luck (power to cure) from the great False Face. And this interpretation accords with the origin legend in the Iroquoian cosmology (Fenton 1962, 294; Hewitt 1928).

At Tonawanda they speak of the False Faces in the plural as *hadigohsaʔshǫ́ʔǫ;* in the singular as *gagǫhsaʔ*. They are aware that the mask spirit is called *hadúːhiʔ* by the Cayuga and Onondaga in Canada.

Curing Songs. Besides the song *ganyeowiːʔ*, which their leader sings on entering houses and is their song to the wind, they have, as at Coldspring, two curing songs and two sets of rites.

CURING WITH ASHES. Immediately following the tobacco invocation comes Hodigǫhsóskaʔah, "Their Faces Alone," or "Only the Faces." This is when they dance by themselves and blow ashes on the patient.

THE SECOND CURING SONG. The second ritual, Deyę:hsiʔdadías, "they place one foot ahead of the other" (literally, "Alternate Their Feet") is the general term applied to the latter part of the ceremony, which consists of several parts. It includes the dance of couples, the Thumbs-up Dance, wherein the two maskers oppose the two headwomen who are of complementary moieties, followed by a similar pairing of all members of the society into couples of men and women. Finally, there is the Round Dance (Ganónyahgwenh), from which the ritual derives the name "Doorkeepers' Dance." Here two maskers in the role of doorkeepers compel every member present to join in the Round Dance in which they alternate their feet and bump their heels with each forward step.

It was here that Chief Scrogg described the remarkable power that wearing a mask to impersonate the doorkeeper confers on the masker to discern who are the members and force them into the line.

SIX NATIONS

Information on the False Face Society and its rites at the Six Nations Reserve on Grand River, Canada, is based on the writings of L. H. Morgan, David Boyle (1898, 157), Goldenweiser's field notes, Speck (1949), my own fieldwork with Simeon Gibson and personal observation of a Traveling Rite at Onondaga Longhouse, and Shimony (1961, 148–53), whose observations are the most extensive. One striking difference between the society in Canada and among the Seneca of western New York is that the False Face societies at the several longhouses on Grand River are headed by men instead of women (Shimony 1961, 148), and this male dominance has obtained throughout the present century. Goldenweiser, in 1912, learned from George Gibson, Simeon's father's brother, that anciently the longhouse officers appointed a man to lead the False Face Society in its annual spring and fall rounds of the community. For years at Onondaga Longhouse, old John Jamieson, Sr., an Onondaga of the Deer Clan, was the officer for his and Simeon's moiety. George Davis, of the same clan, succeeded him during the period that Simeon was active in the society. In 1940, when I commenced these inquiries, George Davis was living but crippled and could no longer endure the long walk. As Simeon said, "It must be a smart [agile] man." By then a younger man, Thomas Miller, an Onondaga of the Turtle Clan of the opposite moiety, was acting leader. Bill Sherry performed that role in Shimony's time (1961, 153), some fifteen years later.

The women do have a role, however. They provide corn flour for the mush, they cook, and they oil masks. At the last night of medicine society dances during the Midwinter Festival, the False Face company is promised a kettle of mush; but this present is not delivered for another two months afterward when the society makes its spring round of the settlement driving out disease.

In fulfillment of that promise, the families who are going to the longhouse for the spring False Face rite must bring flour for the mush. Each family parches white corn, and when it is half burnt, they crack it in the corn pounder. Then it is sifted and pounded again until it is reduced to flour. About sundown, the families go to the longhouse taking about a half pail of flour for the mush.

At the longhouse two women are in charge of the kitchen, as at Coldspring.

> They are officers appointed by the people to take care of the cooking for the False Faces. They are supposed to be from each moiety, they are appointed for life, and they serve as long as they are able to carry out the duties. Then new ones are appointed. These women come around within the longhouse collecting flour from the people who have brought it, when they think that all the donors have arrived. Then they take the flour to the kitchen and make the mush. The two matrons usually have the lard ready and sugar to sweeten it, but by rights they should use maple sugar. In the olden times each family would bring a brick of maple sugar. Also persons are expected to bring a small portion of sacred tobacco, which the matrons also collect for the invocation. There are times when they have lots of mush flour on hand, so they make two big kettles of mush. They give one pot to the hadúʔiʔ who eat it after their performance, and the other pot is divided among the people to take home.

It is apparent that the unmasked leader also collects tobacco at the houses visited by the traveling maskers; he may use part of it for small invocations at houses where the maskers are requested to cure someone, but the accumulation of collections and rewards goes for the big invocation at the longhouse.

The Rite of Oiling the Masks
Simeon Gibson volunteered an account of the ceremony:

> Did you ever hear how the matrons oil the False Faces in the spring? In the spring, about the first week of May, on a date set by

the longhouse officers, all the men who are members bring their own masks to an appointed fireplace. [For many years the place was at Simeon Gibson's fire.] Usually when they set the date the officers appoint two or three of the eldest women to go there with the ingredients of the oil. [To a bowl full of sunflower seed hot water is added and then it is boiled to try out the oil. It is let boil until the oil is rendered.] When the men arrive they set their masks down around the fireplace.

When they think that everyone has arrived they have the oldest man of the society burn tobacco. The elder offers a prayer to the masks before they are oiled and before they start out to purge the settlement.

Prayer to the Masks Before Oiling and Setting Out on Their Mission
Simeon Gibson prayed in Onondaga (Plate 11-12 A, B):

o:nɛ nɛgɛ wɛnda:de o:nɛ ɛyagwanadíde'da' o:nɛ di'ih
now this day   now we shall the village now then
                                 go over[5]

nɛ: i:ga:yɛ' oyɛ'gwa'ɔ:we ɛyagwadowɛnónya'da[6]'nɛ'
it is here native tobacco we a favor are asking it

oyɛ'gwa'ɔ́:we ne' wa'agwaihwané:gɛ[7] ne' sadu'igó:na
native tobacco it is our request   you the great hunch back
              (we did ask)   medicine man

ne' hu:da'skwa:yu' ne' gasha'sdéshä:' tca' ganɔhsayé:du[8]
to give us   the power   each houses scattered

hɛyagwa:yu deyagwadawɛnye:[9] tca' hena:gé: ne' sheyadesɔ́'ah
we do enter as we travel   this settlement of your grand-
                                                children

na:ye wa'agwaiwa'ne:gɛ' ne' skɛ:nɔ tháyenage:k[10] tca'
which we requested of you in health they shall live each

gonɔhsayɛ:dɔ' he:hwadjiyɛgéhɛ:' hayagoda'gaidényɔ:k[11] ne'
in their   all maternal   they shall have good the health
several homes families

5. "We are going to go about the whole village or neighborhood."
6. "We are asking for something [a favor] for the whole public."
7. "We have requested," or "our request." Note the difference in style from Seneca invocations that say: "Now then partake [savor] the smoke of the sacred tobacco which is rising, etc."
8. "Houses here and there," or "scattered homesteads."
9. Hence the name Traveling Rite.
10. "They shall live in health."
11. "They shall be healthy."

Plate 11-12. Medicine for the False Faces. A: Native tobacco (Nicotiana rustica) growing at Six Nations Reserve on Grand River. C. M. Barbeau photo, 1949. NMM, Neg. No. J2992. B: Sunflowers for oil. C. M. Barbeau photo, 1949. NMM, Neg. No. J3040.

A   B

    ohɛ́:ndų? wahwɛdadeniyúndiye o:nɛ dih wa?gɔdiyɛnɛdá?nha:?
    future   days to come   now then the women have done

    wa?gɔdinohgá:k ne? gagɔhsa?sú?ah tca? nɔdagɔdiyeɛ́:ne
    they women   the masks   as they customarily have done
    have oiled them

    ne? ohná?gɛ dawɛdadéniyɔdie:
    in the past   days

      o:nɛ dih   ne?tho nigawɛ́nage
      Now then these are all the words.
      [or] dan:ne?tu
         so there

[Translation]
Now today, we are just now about to go over the settlement. Now accordingly here is the native tobacco by means of which we are asking a favor. With the tobacco we are requesting you the Great Hunchback [Medicine Man] to confer upon us the power as we enter each of the scattered houses during our travel about this settlement of your grandchildren. And we are requesting you that they each live in health in in their several homes (scattered houses), namely that all the maternal families shall be healthy in the days to come.

Now the women have completed oiling the masks just as they have done in former days.
Now then these are all of the words.
So there.

The Women's Role in Oiling the Faces
Then the old ladies who belong to the society oil the faces of the masks, having previously prepared the ingredients. Mrs. Peter Williams (Onondaga), who had acted in this role, indicated that the name of the ceremony, Watowẹnǫgwísdaʔ, literally, "They Are Honoring Them," reflects the reverance of the people for the masks. Its purpose is to show the masks the people's appreciation for what the masks are about to do in visiting the houses. So it is done before they start out. The matrons who oil the masks, according to Mrs. Williams, are the longhouse leaders of their respective moieties. They also supervise the cooking. For the autumn feast of the Traveling Rite, they mix pumpkin in with the mush. It is cut up fine, peeled, and added to the corn flour.

Then the women folks, any old ladies who belong to the society, begin to oil the faces of the masks. They have previously prepared the oil. [There is no moiety differentiation of roles at Onondaga on Grand River or complementary behavior in curing, as among the Seneca. However, Gibson thought it a good idea.] After the women have finished oiling then each man can pick up his mask. Then they retire outside the house to dress before re-entering. The maskers chose one man to lead them. He sings one song of ganǫháo:wi: [Cayuga], and they march in behind him. As the maskers enter the door the leader marches around the room and the maskers crawl in behind him, shaking their rattles and crying yµʔµʔµ:. . . . As he makes the circuit of the room the maskers fall in behind him. When he gets back to the door again, he sings a second kind of song, which is called haduʔi:géha: [Cayuga] and haduʔigéhaʔ [Onondaga], 'mask kind.' [-géha: refers to a class, or kind, or genre of dance songs. What follows takes place at each of the houses visited in the traveling rite.]

Now they all stand erect on their feet and dance. Now if there is a person resident there who belongs to the society they will put the ashes on her head. The patient will sit by the fire and the ashes are blown on. She will also have mush ready. The ashes are blown on the patient's head, hands, and joints. If the patient is a man, one of the maskers will pick him up and carry him pickaback around in the dance. They do not do that with women—just let her dance.

When the leader offers tobacco he divides it and sets aside part of it for the masked performers who receive this payment just before they blow ashes.

As they go about the houses the mush pot is sometimes set outside for them. Then they will take off their masks and eat. At other times it is given to them as they depart from the house. Sometimes householders give them cookies with the mush.

Husk Face Runner
As among the Seneca, a Husk Face runner precedes the traveling maskers; he runs through the houses, and says nothing.

In visiting the houses the *gadjíhsaʔ* goes ahead and bursts through the door. He visits all the rooms of the house. He says nothing. Then he departs for the next house when he sees that the main body is following.

The group of traveling maskers comes in behind their leader who sings. They visit all the rooms of the house. They creep through all the rooms. They even go upstairs. The noise they make with their rattle and their cry is supposed to drive disease out of the house. They don't bother people who sit quietly in a corner.

[Simeon Gibson continues his narrative:] In going from house to house we sometimes come upon a sick person who belongs to the False Face Society. She usually wants us to put ashes on her head. The head of the house reports the fact to the leader of the masked company before they enter. He in turn informs his band so that they are prepared to cure with ashes after they go in. The leader burns tobacco in a special offering.

Tobacco Prayer for a Particular Person
The leader speaks for the sick person

oːnę	wendaːdeʔ	waʔgayę̨ʔgwaideʔ	oyę̨ʔgwaʔuːwe	ʔiːs
Now	today	the smoke arises	from real tobacco/	

swayaʔdagweníyuʔ	wehswayɛʔgwaʔsǫ́ːwiʔ	gwasoːdaʔ	swadúʔi
you are the proprietors (the intended)	you shall inhale	our grandparents	you hunchbacks

naːyeʔ	waʔetciwahnéːgęʔ	nęgę́	ganowakdéːsäː	deyagoiwadiyędáni
and this	she asks you	this	sickness	that she is suffering

naːyeʔ	neʔ	gawéʔih	ęyetciyaʔdagéːnhaʔ	ęyatciyaʔgę́häːk
which		she decided	for you to help her	you shall doctor her with ashes

ųːsayǫdaʔgáidaːt	dǫsayędawɛnyeːʔ	tcaʔ uhwę́ːdjadeʔ	godeʔsaʔi	diːh
that she shall get well	she shall again travel about	here on earth	She has prepared	then

Plate 11-13. The maskers visit springs and tobacco patches. A: Hadui visits a tobacco patch at Six Nations. C. M. Barbeau photo. NMM, Neg. No. J2989, 1949. B: His compatriot. C. M. Barbeau photo, NMM, Neg. No. J2990. Both masks are in the Grand River style.

godinaʔdja:yɛʔneʔ odjí:sgwaʔ
she a kettle   of mush
set down

na:yeʔ neʔtu nigawénage:
And   these are the words

[Translation]
Now today the smoke arises from the native tobacco which is intended for you exclusively so that you shall inhale the tobacco fumes, our grandparents, you hunchbacks. And this she asks you with respect to this sickness that she is suffering, which she has decided for you to help her by doctoring her with ashes so that she shall get well again and so that she shall again travel about here on the earth. Accordingly she has prepared and set down a kettle of mush. And these are all the words.

Now the leader will call the men [maskers] in, but as he starts to sing only a few of the maskers will enter. The senior men of the company are chosen who know how to put on the ashes. The younger men who perhaps have not done that before remain outside until the ceremony is over.

After this dance of curing, then the leader calls in the whole company. When the whole procedure is completed, then the maskers take the mush pot outside and everyone shares it. Sometimes the patient serves cookies with the mush.

This happens about every other house on the rounds. The maskers finally arrive at the longhouse about dark. But we don't get hungry because we eat mush here and there.

Traveling

The masked band expands in numbers as it goes along and sometimes divides and apportions the districts to separate groups. They visit springs and tobacco patches (Plate 11-13). Simeon recalled:

Very often when we reached Longboat's Corners we would meet a crowd of members who were arriving late and had not come in time to have their masks oiled. The leader carries tobacco collected at the houses already visited, and so he would give each of the recruits a pinch as he joined the brigade. If there were then too many maskers in the party, the leader would divide them into two parties and appoint another man to lead the second party. Our party would go down the river road from Longboat's Corners toward the Grand River and half way to Owen's Corners, and then cut across the fields. (We did not go below that point, or to Beaver's Corners because that is the territory of Lower Cayuga Longhouse, and their members cleanse that neighborhood.) We came out again on the road on Concession V near Seneca Longhouse, halfway between Peter Atkins' Corners and Silversmith's Corners, and from there we would go to Onondaga Longhouse. (The Seneca Longhouse maskers visit some of the same houses.) If the other party was not there we would wait for them.

The other party would go south along Stone Ridge Road past Onondaga Longhouse, past Silversmith's Corners, to Stone Ridge Corners. There they called at David Thomas's. Then they would visit W. Williams on Concession IV above Stone Ridge Corners, and thence into the bush and north visiting a number of houses to emerge on the Vth road half way to St. John's Corners. From there they would return to Silversmith's Corners to wait for us. Then both parties would combine again and go to the Onondaga Longhouse (Figure 11-3).

At the Longhouse
Here occurs the long awaited climax to the Traveling Rite. People await the arrival of the False Faces (Plates 11-14, 11-15). The cooks having collected flour would be making a great pot of mush. Each person brings a small bundle of tobacco for the invocation. People know the False Faces are coming when the Husk Face runners burst into the room, circle, and go out. (Onondaga Longhouse has but one door midway on the east wall.) When the leader arrives with the party of maskers outside the longhouse, the maskers wait outside while he goes in alone. At first he does not sing. He goes counterclockwise among the people collecting tobacco. He then calls the False Faces. He turns on the door sill and starts singing *ganǫhwáiwih* [Onondaga] or *ganǫháo:wih* [Cayuga], and the maskers follow him into the longhouse crawling. [Simeon does not say that they circle the room during his first song.]

> When the maskers are all in, the leader goes to the fire and burns tobacco. He first sets some tobacco to one side to divide among the men when they have finished blowing ashes."

Invocation. The prayer of the leader of the False Faces at the longhouse, rendered by Simeon Gibson in Onondaga, is more elaborate.

o:nɛ waʔagayɛʔgwái:dɛʔ oyɛʔgwaʔu:we na:yeʔ sɔgwa:wi [12]
Now smoke has arisen   from sacred tobacco   which he gave us

sɔgwayaʔdísaʔi gayɛhíyadeʔ hana:ge: hawehí na:yeʔ
our creator   In the sky   he   he   that
                          dwells   intended

---

12. Some speakers say: *sǫgwayɛ́ʔntwɛ:ni*, "he planted for us."

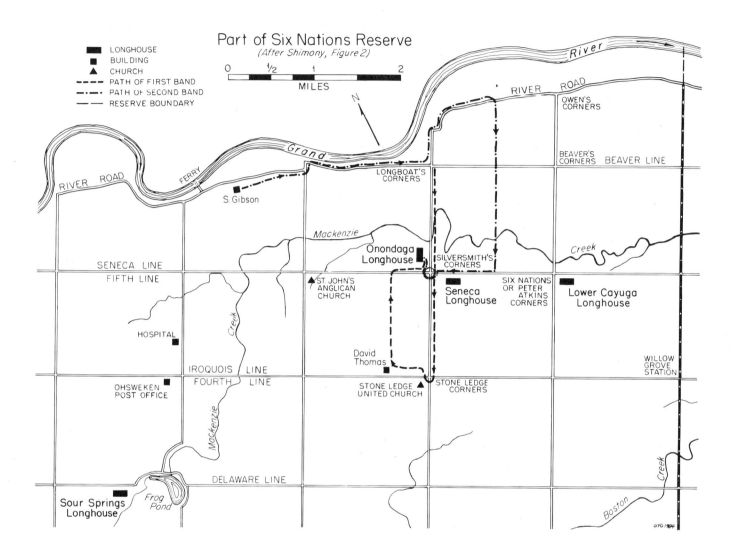

Figure 11-3. Part of Six Nations Reserve showing routes of the Traveling Rite to Onondaga Longhouse. Base map after Shimony 1961.

ɛyɔ:dwɛnónyna?tak ne? µ:gwe ɛyɔná:gä:t µ:hwɛdja?geh
we should employ mankind they will on earth dwell

o:nɛ díh ?i:s skwado:da:? ?i:s ?o:hni? sadu?igo:na[13]
Now then you our grandparents you also you great hunchback

wesayɛ?gwa?sɔ:wih
you tobacco inhale

13. Hadu?i', the name of the primordial doctor, as opposed to hadu?a, a hunchbacked man. Hɛnádu?a is the plural, but hɛnádu?i is used for the supernaturals.

Plate 11-14. Six Nations masks of the 1912 period. National Museum of Man. A: Small red mask from David Jack (Cayuga), 1914. Cat. No. III.I.10,03. F. W. Waugh, collector. B: Back of same reveals considerable age. 5 × 9.5 inches. C: Red mask, brass eyes, bifunelate mouth, prominent chin. Cat. No. III.I.124. D: Back of same shows seven-hole attachment, thin edges, much use. 6 × 10 inches. Collected by A. A. Goldenweiser.

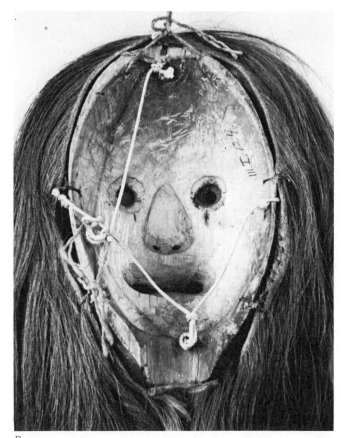

Plate 11-15. Six Nations masks of 1912 period, II. NMM. A: Red smiling mask with black hair. Collected by John Gibson, 1912. NMM, Cat. No. III.I.333. 6 × 10 inches. B: Massive red crooked-mouth mask. 7 by 11 inches. Pine. Nine-hole attachment, thick edges, used. NMM, Cat. No. III.I.185 (B2). From J. Gibson, 1911. C: Red smiling mask, brass eyes, bulbous nose, prominent chin, and cheeks. From J. Gibson, 1912. NMM, Cat. No. III.I.335. D: Back of same. Note five-hole attachment, deep, but little used. 6¾ × 10¼ × 3½ inches.

na:yeʔ ʔohneʔ neʔ gadjísaʔ oyɛʔgwaʔsɔ:wih
and also the Husk Face inhales the tobacco

na:yeʔ ʔó:hniʔ waʔaoyɛʔgwaʔsɔ́:wih ne:ʔ sastawɛ́:ʔshä:ʔ
and this also savors tobacco your turtle rattle

ʔo:hniʔ ne:ʔ sada:dítšäʔ o:nɛnóʔgagó:na haʔdegaɛhósädih[14]
and also your cane a giant hickory limbs lopped to its top

na:yeʔ diʔ tcaʔneyawɛ́haʔ ɛdwaduhɛ́hsɛ:n neʔ hegɛdjɔ́hgwagwé:gi
and this then shall happen we shall rejoice the entire crowd

dɛdowátgwaʔ neʔ deyuhɛsiʔdadíhas
we shall dance the alternating feet

na:yeʔ neʔ waʔgwaiwaʔné:gɛʔ ne skɛ:nu ta:ya:gwánage:kh
and this we ask a favor of good health we shall continue to live

neʔ ohɛ:du wahwɛdadeniyɔ́diye
in the future days to come

nɛʔ i:gá:yɛʔ odidjisgoni neʔ ɛthinóhaʔ ʔi:s ʔagwé:gi
and so it is ready the women have cooked mush our mothers you all

swayaʔdagwɛní:yuʔ nɛ:ʔ skwa:sodáshɔʔ
shall share it equally namely you our grandparents

na:yeʔ ʔóhniʔ dɛswakáhšiaʔ nɛ oyɛʔgwaʔú:we ne:ʔ etisó:daʔ
and also you shall divide the tobacco with our grandparents

hegaʔä:hgwɛs nitɛnétaʔ etiso:daʔ hadiwɛnó:dadye:s na:yeʔ
toward sunset they come from our grandparents their voices fumble whom

sagoʔihú:ᵐdaʔ neʔ sɔgwayaʔdísaʔi ɛhadi:ʔtyɛdénta:k tcaʔ-
he appointed the Creator they to moisten this

hoɛndjade[15]
earth

---

14. Simeon Gibson asserted that the maskers are supposed to carry a turtle rattle and a cane (or pole). In his view, the folded bark rattle is a makeup, but he conceded that possibly they had them in the olden days.

15. The Creator made four appointments: (1) our grandparents the thunders who

[The wind (*ogä:hao?*) also shares tobacco with the thunder.]

na:ye? ?ó:hni? deswakáhšia? ne:? oyɛ?gwa?ų:we nɛgɛ́
And this too   shall share   the tobacco   this one

ne? o:wä:de? na:ye? o:na? sagoiµ:ᵐda? ɛhanigɔ́hɛ:k
the wind   whom also he appointed   he shall look after

tcá? owä́:de? iya:djik thaga?oná?da? tca?dowana:ge¹⁶
   wind   to look   not to have too where we live
            out   heavy

[Translation]
Now the smoke has arisen from the sacred tobacco which was granted to us by the Creator who lives in the skyworld. He intended that we should employ it, we mankind who were about to inhabit the earth. Now, accordingly, you our grandfathers, namely you the great hunchback inhale (or savor) the tobacco. And this also partakes of the tobacco, your turtle rattle; and also your cane (staff), which is a giant hickory with its limbs lopped off to the top. And so it shall take place that we, the entire crowd in the longhouse shall rejoice by dancing the Alternating Feet. And particularly we ask the favor of good health that we shall survive in the days to come.

And so it is ready; our mothers have cooked mush for all of you. And so you, our grandfathers, shall share it equally. And also you shall divide the tobacco with our grandfathers who come from toward the sunset, our grandfathers of the rumbling voices, whom our Creator appointed to moisten the earth.

And another shall share the tobacco, namely the wind, whom he also appointed to control the atmosphere to make certain that it does not blow too hard on our settlement.

And these are all the words.

It is apparent that these tobacco invocations adhere to a formula, and the text that Gibson dictated includes the items that must be touched, however lightly or in full, depending on the speaker's style and the gravity of the occasion.

---

live in the West and bring rain; (2) the wind, charged with watching out that it is not too heavy and levels the settlement; and (3) Hadu?i, who also lives in the West where he promised to abide and look after disease. People offer tobacco when they want favors and enlist his help. Simeon mentioned and enumerated three men but omitted the fourth.

16. The wind is implored not to level the settlement.

THE DANCE FOR ALL THE PEOPLE TO ALTERNATELY SHUFFLE THEIR FEET. The officials will have appointed two singers to take their places astride the bench in the center of the longhouse to sing Deyoɛhsiʔdadíhas. As they take their places, the speaker announces the event to the maskers and the public. These announcements follow a formula, which Simeon Gibson recorded for both this event and for the Common Faces.

neʔ skwasó:daʔ
you grandparents

nigaiwagwaħaʔ ɛswadahǫsíyosdaʔ / ɛyetciyadɛ́notas neʔ i:s
a few words   you all pay   they will sing   your
               attention (listen)   for you   own

swaɛ:naʔ   deyoɛhsiʔdadíhas   ɛ:swadoháhshɛ:ʔ   gagwegíkhdiʔ
song   to alternately   you shall rejoice everyone must
           slide feet

dɛyetcidɛ́sdaʔ   čaʔniyų́ ganǫhsgų:´wa ethgodú:nyų etciyadesų́ʔa:h
they two shall   here   in the house   seated on   they your
stand you up   benches   grandchildren

[Translation]
You shall all pay attention to a few words, you our grandfathers, for they are going to sing for you your very own song, "to slide one foot ahead of the other," that you may rejoice. And they two[17] shall stand you up, everyone of their grandchildren who is seated on the benches inside of this house.

Before the maskers go into the longhouse the leader always appoints two senior members of the False Faces to clean off the benches. He warns them not to be rough, not to use their rattles [as weapons]. Once a Christian man refused to stand. He was not a longhouse member. A False Face hit him on the cheek with his rattle and cut him. He stood up.

Everyone must dance. Generally, people at Onondaga are willing to dance.

Members of the Society who wish to have ashes blown on them, toward the end of the cycle as they hear the cue song, go to the bench where the Faces will treat them. The particular song at the

---

17. Simeon explained the dual role of the maskers. "The two appointed hadúʔiʔ (maskers) will go around on the benches with their rattles to 'clean up the benches,' one going one way and the other going in the opposite direction, until no one remains seated. This is the time when the young ladies and the children 'shout' when they see the hadúʔiʔ coming. They have to jump up. Some persons are afraid [and become possessed]."

end of the cycle contains the words: *oda?gęho dagwęhadje?*,[18] "ashes fly every which way."

Several differences from the Seneca celebrations may be noted. There are no pails of medicine, the Thumbs-up Dance is omitted, and the doorkeeper concept is foreign. At Onondaga on Grand River, both maskers clean off the benches, and neither one guards the door. Shimony observed that a visiting Tonawanda Seneca assumed the doorkeeper role, and it was regarded as an innovation (Shimony 1961, 150).

HUSK FACES. The husk maskers, having acted as runners to warn the people that the masked company was approaching family dwellings and the longhouse, have a special song of their own at the end of the ritual. There should be at least two Husk Faces for each party or band, and sometimes there are as many as four. Billy Buck recorded their two songs (Fenton 1942, 26) and was aware that the Seneca have more Husk Face songs than those that are sung at Six Nations. The husk maskers dance at great speed around their staves and receive tobacco as they go out.

COMMENT

I shall now summarize the preceding accounts and comment on local variations in the spring and autumn purification ceremonies. The prominence of the two matrons, one from each moiety, at Coldspring, Cattaraugus, and Tonawanda, in initiating and managing the affairs of the society, at first blush is not borne out at Six Nations where, as Shimony noted, male dominance is the rule. But the women do have important roles at Onondaga Longhouse in oiling the masks and cooking, although their moiety affiliation receives less emphasis. The act of honoring the masks with sunflower oil, so important at Six Nations, is neglected among the Seneca, but the brewing of the medicine from manroot and sunflower seeds, so prominent at Allegany, compensates for neglect in not oiling the masks, although manroot is left out of the medicine at Cattaraugus and Tonawanda. The converging bands of maskers who purge the houses during the traveling rite are present everywhere. Collecting tobacco and food at the houses is an Allegany custom, whereas the Six Nations people bring flour and tobacco to the longhouse. Unmasked male conductors lead the bands of maskers at Allegany, Tonawanda, Cattaraugus, and Six Nations, although Morgan reported a "Mistress of the Band" in 1850 at Tonawanda. Parker did the same at Cattaraugus, whereas, in 1937, Jesse Cornplanter illustrated a matron offering tobacco for the maskers (Cornplanter 1938, 211) (Plate 11-16).

18. Billy Buck, a Seneca then living at Six Nations, recorded these songs for the Library of Congress (Fenton 1942b, Record 10 B).

Plate 11-16. Matron offering tobacco to the maskers. From the original drawing in the Library of the American Philosophical Society, Philadelphia.

Both Seneca and Six Nations Indians purify the springs. The belief that I encountered at Tonawanda in correlating colors with cardinal directions, red with the East and black with the West, may recall some earlier, more widespread cosmological concept, which is manifest in divided masks. Indeed, at Allegany black masks are deemed "poison" or are thought to be more powerful.

Two prominent features of the Seneca ritual celebrations are lacking at Six Nations: the Thumbs-up Dance of the two doorkeepers with the two matrons and then of paired men and women, selected by one of the two maskers from the crowd. This activity is the highlight of Seneca masked performances. The lack of the doorkeeper concept at Six Nations, as stressed by Shimony, detracts from any systematic association of mask types with particular roles. The status and role of doorkeeper masks was most highly developed at Cattaraugus in Newtown Longhouse. There is a certain emphasis on clowning at Six Nations—tales of Billy Buck kicking a clothesline (Jim Skye); the maskers cutting up during the tobacco invocation (Shimony); and visiting performers from Six Nations at Coldspring Longhouse. This may explain the behavior of "Ostrich" Bill and Charlie Fun.

The getup of the maskers varies little. They sometimes neglect to carry pine boughs. Six Nations maskers attach a thong from the turtle rattle to the waist. Special burlap costumes recall earlier suits of bearskin. One notes a variation in the prayers as to the species of the great tree at the center of the earth where Shagodyoweh pauses to rest and rub his rattle; likewise his cane is either a giant pine or a shagbark hickory uprooted and stripped of its limbs. The preoccupation with plague and high winds goes back at least a century. Finally, their is a certain ambivalence between mask and spirit, in which the mask takes on the qualities of the supernatural.

12. Family Feasts

Private Rites

Individual obligations to the tutelaries of the medicine societies run throughout the year and during the life of an individual who has been accepted by spiritual patrons of these societies. The person blessed with such a particular dream or who has been cured has a yearly obligation to fulfill his debt to the supernaturals by putting up a feast for them. This may occur anytime during the year, but the greatest incidence of such celebrations comes in the winter, particularly as the Great Ceremonial Mark of midwinter draws near. To let one's obligation slide until after that deadline is to forever have one's head stuck to the ceremonies, as the Iroquois phrase runs, and as we shall learn when the appearance of the maskers climaxes the Midwinter Festival.

FOR THE FACES ALONE

Private medicinal rites of the False Faces adhere to the same general pattern of sequence that governs the great public performances of purifying the houses. How much of the pattern is evoked and the complexity of the ritual depend on the number of orders to which the sponsor belongs and is called upon to have performed. The simpler ceremony is the so-called Common Faces, or the "Faces Alone," which requires only wooden masks, although Husk Faces may accompany them.

The reader may wonder how old this ceremony is, just how it appeared to an earlier observer, and what parts of the ritual program are evident in earlier accounts. A Quaker missionary account puts the ceremony back to 1800; the Seneca artist Ernest Smith, of Tonawanda, depicts from his mind's eye a traditional scene of the False Faces blowing ashes; two photographic essays contrast the ceremony at Allegany and Six Nations; and a content analysis of feasts that I attended, observed, and afterward discussed with informants should make it apparent that the ceremony adheres to a pattern of sequence, that tobacco invocations follow a formula, and that the behavior of the maskers is highly stylized and predictable. There is also room for individual variation in role fulfillment.

Halliday Jackson (1800)
The Seneca False Face medicine society is at least 200 years old. Halliday Jackson, one of the three young Friends who served as community workers on the Allegheny River in the 1790s, described a cure that he witnessed circa 1800 (Jackson 1830, 32–33):

> When a person has been a considerable time sick, in a lingering condition, and . . . [other means] . . . prove ineffectual to restore him to health, it is common for the friends of the diseased person

to collect, and dressing two or more men with masks and other accoutrements, as in times of public worship, they repair to the habitations of the sick, which they go round, rattling and rubbing the tortoise shell, and whooping in a frightful manner.

Although this is a known custom, and in time of health gives no alarm, yet on the debilitated Indian, whose fears are awakened by knowing what is to be endured, it has a considerable effect. The men enter the house, continuing the noise and acting every wild contortion and manoeuvre which their imaginations devise. Some times they pull the sick perrson [male or female] about the house, dirtying them with their black hands, rubbing their heads and bodies over with ashes, and handling the patient in so rough a manner, that a person unaquainted with their custom, might suppose they were going to kill him. After this wild treatment, and having thoroughly dirtied the house with ashes, they withdraw, and leave the nurse to clean after them.

Absurd as this practice appears, in many cases it is said to have had a beneficial effect, by restoring perspiration, working on the imagination, and rousing the indisposed person to a salutory exercise.

Their idea is that they drive away the evil spirit by this procedure.

Jackson's concluding remarks recall a statement frequently heard among the Seneca: "Perhaps all she/he needs is a little dance." The patient's mind is relieved at having fulfilled a ceremonial obligation, and getting the patient up and moving anticipates modern postoperative procedure.

Ernest Smith
In 1936, Ernest Smith, later a famous native Seneca artist, in one of his early works undertook to illustrate one of my first papers (Fenton 1937). His canvas represents a traditional view of a ceremony still current during his lifetime (Plate 12-1); (the painting is now in the Seneca Iroquois National Museum, Salamanca, NY).

The following extract, entitled "The Blowing Ashes Rite," (Fenton 1941, 428) reflects Smith's interpretation of his work:

The setting is the interior of a bark house, common among the Iroquois a few generations ago, and the time is presumably an evening of the Midwinter Festival. In response to a dream, the host has prepared a kettle of mush, or False Face pudding, and summoned the False Faces. The announcer, who is painted sitting on the bench, has returned thanks to all the spirit forces, explained the purpose of the feast, and invoked the Faces-of-the-forests with burning tobacco. They have entered. The singer straddles the bench to beat out the tempo for their dance, which they energetically

Plate 12-1. The Blowing Ashes Rite. Oil on canvas by Ernest Smith, Seneca artist of Tonawanda, 1936. Commissioned by the author. Seneca-Iroquois National Museum, Salamanca, N.Y.

commence, scattering ashes everywhere. They hasten to finish curing the patient, their host who stands before the fire, since they crave tobacco and hunger for the kettle of mush which he has set down for them. A tall, red-faced fellow vigorously rubs the patient's scalp before blowing the hot ashes into the seat of the pain. A dark one moans anxiously while rubbing hot ashes between his palms prior to pouncing on his victim's shoulder and pumping his arm. Across the fire, a red face stoops to scoop live coals, while another impatiently shakes a turtle rattle. They are naked above the waist, but wearing the masks is said to protect their bodies from cold and their hands from the burning embers.

Photographic Essay

Coverage of two private False Face rites was arranged with the willing co-operation of Iroquois colleagues who appreciated the value of pictures in conveying an understanding of the ceremony. In June of 1940, Chauncey Johnny John, at Coldspring, and I were deeply involved in the care and use of masks, the carver's art, the order of ritual, and the music. It was a natural progression from photographing the steps in carving a mask to covering the essential stages in the drama. Chauncey, as conductor of the ceremony, rounded up the models among his two grandsons and their peers and furnished masks, his own and his grandsons. Only the leader, his younger grandson, had a turtle rattle, and he received the tobacco when the maskers left.

1. Enter the Faces crawling (Plate 12-2A). The "buffalo" mask worn by the leader was made by Richard Kettle, of Cattaraugus, and sold to the Johnny Johns for five dollars (Plate 12-2A).

2. The tobacco invocation at the fire. The patient is seated. The second mask entering, and at the right is Chauncey's own mask that we reproduced. It frequently performed in the doorkeeper rite. The third, a human likeness smiling, is a beggar mask (Plate 12-2B).

3. "Arise and make medicine" (blowing ashes on the patient). A song here says: "They are back inside" (Plate 12-3A).

4. The conductor of the ritual rewards the False Face leader with tobacco as the maskers leave (Plate 12-3B).

Note that in these pictures no Husk Face stands by the door. Chauncey said that he need not be present with the Common Faces, unless specified. Moreover, there was no feast. Today the Seneca patient is passive; he stands or sits to receive the ashes; he is not led around, mauled, or carried.

A Renewal at Six Nations

The following winter, while recording Iroquois music for the Library of Congress, Simeon Gibson, who was assisting me, volunteered to put up a feast to renew his affiliation with the False Face Society. We were recording at the home of Councilor George Buck whose wife Lavinia Charles Buck, Simeon's mother's brother's daughter, agreed to host the feast and let the men do the work. Her husband assumed the roles of conductor, invoker, and singer. The three maskers were their son Hubert and two singers—Billy Buck, a Seneca of the Hawk Clan, and Russell Johnson.

By way of preparation, the sponsor (Gibson) had pounded corn and brought a pound of flour for the mush, cookies, and a pound of lard. He had also procured tobacco by borrowing it from a neighbor. (Not everyone at Six Nations grows tobacco in a summer garden [Plate 11-13] and hangs it to dry in winter.)

Because the sponsor no longer owned a mask, all equipment was furnished by the conductor (see earlier photograph of George Buck and his

Plate 12-2. A private False Face rite at Allegany. A: Enter the Faces crawling. B: The tobacco invocation at the fire.

mask collection, Plate 7-3 B, C, and of Simeon Gibson posed wearing one with Buck in the role of conductor [Plate 12-4 A].

The pattern of sequence that governs the ritual program of the False Face rite for an individual at Six Nations is illustrated in the following sequence of photographs:

1. Conductor makes mush; patient seated (Plate 12-4 B).
2. Outside, the hostess enters house; note rabbit hanging (Plate 12-5 A).

Plate 12-3. The cure with ashes and payment in tobacco. A: Maskers blow ashes on the patient. B: Conductor pays maskers tobacco.

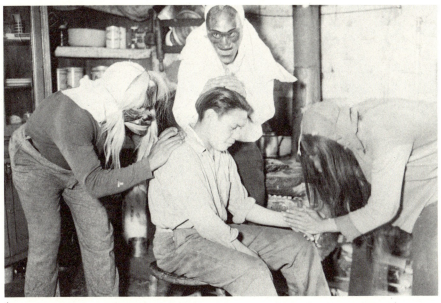
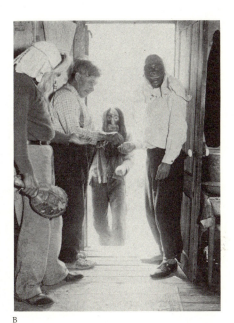

3. Outside, conductor oils masks, the maskers having dressed (Plate 12-5 B–C).
4. Maskers waiting signal to enter; crouch and enter (Plate 12-6 A–B).
5. Inside, conductor makes tobacco invocation; patient seated (Plate 12-7 A).
6. Conductor sings; maskers blow ashes on patient's head; other masker tackles ashes (Plate 12-7 B).
7. Masker carries patient pickaback around in dance (Plate 12-8 A).
8. Outside, maskers receive tobacco from conductor.
9. The feast; maskers return inside; conductor serves mush, sets down kettle; sit around telling stories (Plate 12-8 B).

Note that the three maskers donned masks that were not differentiated as to function or any prescription in the origin myth.

Two features unique in Six Nations False Face celebrations stand out clearly in this minifeast. The multiple roles of conductor as arranger, cook, invoker, and singer bespeak male dominance (Goldenweiser, Field Notes 1912; Shimony 1961, 148). Second, a masker picks up and carries the patient in a manner described by Sagard in 1623 in Huronia (Wrong 1939, 117–18). Whether the Seneca formerly lifted and carried patients before making them walk around in the dance is not apparent, although the patient does go around in the Doorkeeper Dance.

The Longhouse People: A Film

The False Face incident in Alan Worgon's film *The Longhouse People* (Worgon 1946) communicates better than words the essential pattern of a pri-

Plate 12-4. A private rite for Simeon Gibson at Six Nations, 1941. A: Conductor George Buck and Sponsor Simeon Gibson masked, the previous summer. B: Conductor makes the mush, sponsor seated.

Plate 12-5. Preliminaries outside. A: Hostess enters house (note rabbit hanging). B: Conductor oils faces of the maskers. C: Same.

12-4A

12-4B

12-5A

12-5B

12-5C

vate feast at Six Nations Reserve to relieve a particular dream. In this incident, a dying chief dreams of the False Faces, and he reveals his dream to his female relative who as sponsor calls in the headman of the False Faces. The headman acts as conductor, enlists a speaker to make the tobacco invocation as well as a singer. The late Deskaheh (Chief Alex General) performs the first role and the late George Buck the latter. The conductor enters, arranges the seating, stirs the embers in the woodstove, and exits to summon the maskers. The four maskers enter crawling, first rub-

Plate 12-6. A: Maskers await signal to enter. B: Maskers go inside.

Plate 12-7. Inside: the ceremony commences. A: Conductor invokes False Faces with tobacco. B: The maskers dance and blow ashes. While the conductor sings, two maskers blow ashes, while a third tackles ashes at the fire pit.

12-6A

12-6B

12-7A

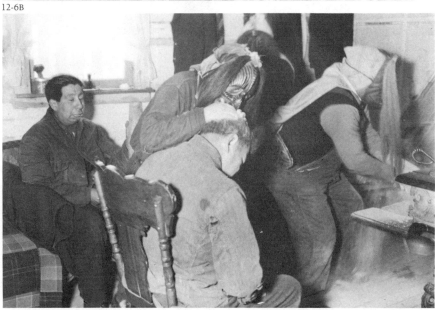

12-7B

bing their turtle rattles on the door, peering inside, feinting an entrance, then hesitating to look behind the open door, and finally approaching the fire. At this point the speaker takes up the tobacco pouch, which the conductor had handed to him, and commences the invocation, sprinkling a pinch of tobacco on the live embers at each "word" of the prayer: "Faces of the Forest," their promise to cure, their rattles, the provisions for the feast, and the final summons to rise and tackle the ashes. At each "word" the maskers scrape their rattles on the floor and utter their nasal cry. As the

Plate 12-8. A: Masker carries patient pick-a-back around in the dance. B: Maskers return inside unmasked for the feast.

crouching maskers listen to the invocation, the patron as sponsor oils the hair and face of each mask and reaches down to oil the carapace of the turtle rattle. The oiling of masks and rattles is the unique feature of the rite at Six Nations.

At the cure that ends the prayer, the singer beats the turtle rattle edgewise on a chair or bench, setting the tempo of the False Face song for ashing. The maskers dance in a most convincing and energetic manner, tackle ashes, and blow on the head and upper extremities of the patient. Perhaps as a concession to the severity of his illness, the maskers fail to get the patient out of bed, but they set him on a chair and carry him about. Nor did they carry him about pickaback. Nor do they treat his lower extremities.

Both the invocation and the songs are much abbreviated in the film, which is a pity, because Deskaheh was a master of this speech form, and George Buck was a virtuoso singer. Several of the songs come through, however.

The maskers end their treatment as the singer strikes twice. Each masker in turn receives a pinch of tobacco from the speaker and exits, again uttering his cry and shaking his rattle and rubbing it on the surfaces of the door. In contrast with their crawling entrance, the maskers depart standing erect. The conductor puts the room back in order. The speaker and singer depart with him.

I do not recall seeing the sponsor set down a kettle of mush for the maskers or the conductor carry it out.

Whatever the other merits of the film, this particular scene considerably amplifies the written word. In it the maskers are bigger than life, and their performance exceeds any description of their activities.

TWO COMPOUND PRIVATE FEASTS, INVOLVING COMMON FACES, HUSK FACES, AND THE DOORKEEPERS' DANCE (ALLEGANY SENECA)

From my observations of two compound private feasts and from interviews with sponsors and key participants, I have abstracted the ritual program or the pattern of sequence that one can expect the Allegany Seneca to follow. The two events are nearly identical, and the sequence of events is as follows:

   I. Preparations
       1. Preliminary cooking by the sponsors.
       2. Arrangements by the matrons: selection of conductor, speaker, invoker, singer, and maskers from appropriate moiety.
       3. Speaker returns thanks and announces program.

II. Hotigǫhsóska?a
4. Rite of Common Faces: enter crawling to stove.
5. Invocation with tobacco in fire.
6. Songs for applying ashes (maskers). Paid tobacco, exit.
7. Husk Faces at door (option), dance, and receive popcorn. Exit. (Intermission: matrons clean up. Maskers return inside unmasked.)

III. Doorkeepers' Dance: "Alternate Feet" (Deyęhsi?dadias)
8. Two doorkeepers enter, dance opposite patients, and blow ashes.
9. Thumbs-up Dance: two maskers opposite two matrons. Matrons organize unmasked men and women in pairs.
10. Two maskers dance opposite two matrons and blow ashes on them.
11. Round Dance: "Alternating Feet." Organized by two doorkeepers. One watches door; the other is the floor manager. This is Deyę:hsi?dadias proper, the name of rite.
12. Blowing ashes songs: on patients (sponsors).
13. Blow ashes on two matrons and exit. Receive tobacco.

IV. Aftermath
14. Conductor thanks participants.
15. Distribution of feast.
16. Crowd disperses carrying home soup in pails; also False Face pudding (mush).

The role of the doorkeeper (*hahoanǫsta:s* [Chafe 1963, 34]; *hade: hwoánǫs* [Sherman Redeye, personal communication, August 5, 1933]), which is prominent in the Seneca rite, is foretold in a Huron ceremony of 1623, described by Father Sagard (1939, 117). Although the Seneca version that has come down to us cannot be linked directly to the Huron observance, it should be remembered that large numbers of Huron captives came to live with the Seneca at midseventeenth century and presumably brought some of their customs with them. What is certain is that the doorkeeper role is not a recent innovation and may well be pre-Columbian.

With these structural considerations in mind, I shall describe the two ceremonial events. These observations represent my first opportunities to see the False Faces in action.

Henry Redeye Entertains the False Faces, August 11, 1933

The following is about Henry Redeye's entertaining the False Faces on August 11, 1933.

My Briefing. During the first summer of my fieldwork at Allegany, I worked more or less regularly with the family of Henry Redeye, speaker of the Coldspring Longhouse. Henry was the primary source, but his son

Sherman patiently explained what the old man was saying. And Sherman's wife Clara, niece of Jonas Snow, my host, interpreted. They were a good team. Clara suggested that the best way to make their answers to my queries about the False Faces explicit would be to sponsor a feast and let me watch the maskers in action. Clara, her mother, her mother's sister Alice Jones, and their brother Jonas Snow were all of the Hawk Clan into which I was being advanced for adoption. Henry (Bear Clan), Sherman (Snipe), and Henry's daughter's son (also Snipe) shared a joint obligation to the False Faces, and were, therefore, sponsors, patients, and hosts.

Sherman explained:

> If a man becomes ill, or wants to renew, he notifies the woman leader of the False Face company in his own moiety. She notifies the woman leader of the other side. [The two matrons at that time were Fannie Stevens (Heron), of Sherman's moiety, and Sadie Butler (Wolf), of the other moiety. The latter would bring her company to his house.] The rule is: The company of the other side is called in to cure anyone. They generally come in the evening. Both women take charge of the meeting.
>
> If the whole False Face ritual is to be performed, there are two parts:
>
> 1. Hodigǫhsóska?a ("The Faces Alone"). Someone who knows how to sing uses a turtle rattle, and all those members who have masks in both moieties enter crawling. Someone puts tobacco in the fire. Someone sings again, and the maskers dance and blow ashes on the head of the sick person. The maskers receive tobacco and depart.
>
> Sometimes the Gadjísa? [Husk Faces] appear with the wooden masks. They, too, are masked men wearing Husk Faces and carrying long sticks (staffs).
>
> 2. Deyɛ:hsi?dadias ["They Alternate Their Feet"], the so-called Doorkeepers' Dance. Two doorkeepers wearing powerful masks[1] enter and blow ashes on the sponsors. Then they go outside and watch [look in] while unmasked onlookers dance in the same manner. This is the Thumbs-up Dance. One of the headwomen would pick out a man or woman from her side [moiety], and the other headwoman would choose one of the opposite sex from her moiety to dance opposite. These paired couples are unmasked.
>
> Finally[2] the two masked doorkeepers return and dance opposite

---

1. The doorkeeper mask (hade:hwoánǫs, [Sherman Redeye]; hahoanǫ́sta:s, "he guards the door" [Chafe 1963, 34] worn in this ritual requires special care. To sell one courts sickness (Plate 7-3A). The mask of Henry Redeye is such a mask.
2. In this briefing, Sherman Redeye completely forgot the Round Dance from which this rite takes its name. This is a good example of how informant testimony must be combined with observation.

the two headwomen, each masker facing the matron of the other moiety. These men who perform this role receive tobacco sufficient to fill a little bag which is tied to the forehead of the mask.

On the day of the ceremony, August 11, 1933, while they were cooking, Clara Redeye and her mother's sister Alice Jones offered these further comments on preliminary plans. They confirmed that the Common False Faces who first enter from the outside are made up of men from both moieties. Alice, who had assumed the role of matron for her moiety, said she had appointed her husband Albert to sing for the Alternating Feet Dance (the second part). The two ladies did not forget the Round Dance. One said, "The doorkeepers [hade:hwoángs] will be watching from outside, and one will come over and organize the Round Dance, forcing the 'wallflowers' to enter. This dance is led by one of the two maskers." Alice had appointed her brother Jonas Snow to wear one Husk Face, which represented her moiety. It would be up to Sadie Butler, matron of the opposite moiety, to find someone to wear the Husk Face for the other side.

It is apparent that the selection of personnel to fill the required roles is the prerogative of the two headwomen.

These are my observations of the False Face ceremony at Henry Redeye's, in Quaker Bridge, on August 11, 1933.

Preliminary. Shortly after 8:30 P.M., men and women began to arrive on the road carrying tin pails for corn soup and bundles under their coats containing masks and rattles. Guests sat about on the porch conversing, the Redeye family inside, and Henry, the host, asleep on a couch. He had been feeling poorly.

Matrons. Alice Jones (Hawk Clan) came outside and handed her brother Jonas Snow a Husk Face wrapped up in a towel. Women then went inside, some of them taking children into an adjacent room where there was less chance of their being frightened by the maskers. Watchers sit anywhere (see floorplan of house, Figure 12-1). Men remained outside to get ready for their role as maskers. Alice Jones (Hawk) and Sadie Butler (Wolf) were in charge of the doings. There was much opening and closing of doors as one or the other of the headwomen went out to the men or returned inside.

Enter the Maskers. Suddenly, all was quiet. Sadie Butler opened the door to the porch and summoned the maskers. Levi Snow (Heron), wearing his red doorkeeper mask (Plate 5-2), followed by John Curry in a similar mask, entered the room crouching, peering about. They rubbed their rattles on the door and over the floor, while uttering the False Face cry. They were soon followed by the rest of the company—three wooden maskers. The backs of their heads were covered with towels, old sweaters, and rags. Jonas Snow (Hawk) and Arthur Johnny John (Beaver), of opposite moieties, came in last wearing Husk Faces. They leaned on four-foot staffs freshly cut. Weni Abrams (Beaver), in a Common Face, sat next

Figure 12-1. Floor plan of False Face ceremony for Henry Redeye at Allegany.

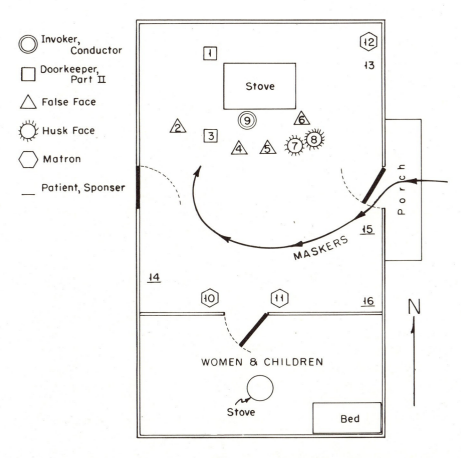

to the west door. The other maskers arranged themselves on the floor around the stove, at times groaning. All acted hungry and expectant.

Invocation. Albert Jones cast tobacco in the embers raked out of the kitchen stove, a pinch at a time, mentioning each kind of dance, the Husk Faces, and the Seneca names of the persons to be cured who were asking for health and good luck. (The structure of the invocation is contained in the text of the prayer offered in the longhouse.)

The accompanying floor plan shows the distribution of personnel, their roles, and clan affiliation. (See Figure 12-1). The participants are numbered and designated by roles with the following symbols: doorkeepers, []; Common False Face maskers, Δ; Husk Faces, 0; matrons, *; patient, sponsor,—. The actors in these roles were (1) Levi Snow (Heron), (2) Weni Abrams (Beaver), (3) John Curry (Bear), (4) Francis Abrams (Bear), (5) Ed Coury (Wolf), and (6) Avery Jimmerson (Bear). The two Husk Faces were (7) Jonas Snow (Hawk), and (8) Arthur Johnny John (Beaver). (9) Albert Jones (Snipe) served both as conductor and invoker. There were three matrons present, two of whom were performing that role: (10) Sadie Butler (Wolf), (11) Fannie Stevens (Heron) (not acting as such), and Alice Jones (Hawk), acting matron. Also in attendance was

(13) Carrie Armstrong (Bear). The three patients from a single family—grandfather, son, and grandson—received the ashes: (14) Henry Redeye (Bear) (15) Sherman Redeye (Snipe), and the latter's sister's son (16) (also Snipe). It would seem that the Bear Clan had turned out to honor their principal host.

Alice Jones (Hawk), acting matron, and Carrie Armstrong (Bear) went outside but quickly returned, for reasons I am unaware of.

Blowing Ashes. Meanwhile, Albert Jones sat astride a wooden bench in the southeast corner of the room. Grasping a turtle rattle in both hands, he commenced singing the songs of *hodigǫhsóskaʔa*. The wooden faces danced. Led by Levi Snow, the maskers dipped ashes out of the fire pit from a tray prepared by Sadie Butler and blew the ashes on the heads of the three patients, then on their shoulders near the back, and at the elbows. The Husk Faces followed with the same procedure but to their own tune. Here the singer laid aside the turtle rattle and took up a stick of firewood. While this was going on, the False Faces disappeared by the front door. At the end, the Husk Faces blew ashes on each other. The matron took the stick from her husband, the singer, and placed it behind the stove. (What was improvised for a sacred occasion was no longer needed and in all probability was burned the next day.)

Intermission. When all the maskers had gone out the front door, the Husk Faces last, the other matron, Sadie Butler, swept the floor and threw the ashes from the dustpan out the back (west) door.

Deyę:siʔdadías. The matron of Moiety 1 (Alice Jones) went out and returned with a turtle rattle for the singer (Albert). Henry Redeye, who had been sick that day, came in from the woodshed (west door) covered with ashes. Alice Jones made a second quick trip out the east door and then in again. The other matron, Sadie Butler, wrapped up a Husk Face that had been worn in the first part of the ceremony.

Two men, Myron Turkey and Jerry Jimmerson, arrived late, by the east door carrying pails. (They were not masked.) Emma Turkey (Hawk), Clara's mother, appeared about this time in the adjacent room where I was observing. All but two of the other participants in the first part of the ceremony entered singly or in couples, their masks bundled. They seated themselves around the room without any formal arrangement by phratry. The two exceptions were Weni Abrams (Beaver) and Levi Snow (Heron). The three sponsors and patients occupied the southwest corner.

Doorkeepers' Dance Opposite Patients. The two masked doorkeepers of opposite moieties (Levi and Weni) entered erect, not crawling this time, scraping their turtle rattles over the door and door frame, peering about. Now they danced the Thumbs-up Dance, confronting the three patients who were lined up on the west side of the room. Then they blew ashes on the heads of the patients. Levi did most of the blowing.

Thumbs-Up Dance (Unmasked). Men and women were paired in couples without references to moiety affiliation and sparred. I counted ten sets.

Some of the men and women obviously enjoyed themselves, with the more aggressive partners backing the persons of opposite sex to the wall. One woman started laughing, became embarrassed, and sat down. The doorkeepers were now outside, and one of them looked in at each dance, then closed the door, and withdrew his masked head. At the seventh set, neither doorkeeper looked in. Weni apparently forgot. At the ninth set, Levi looked in.

At the tenth song, Sadie Butler opened the door, and the two watchers or doorkeepers entered and danced opposite the two matrons of the two companies. This time moiety affiliation was observed with Matron 2 dancing opposite Doorkeeper 1 and Matron 1 dancing opposite Doorkeeper 2. When the song called for it, the two masked dancers scooped ashes in their hands from the fire pit and blew on the heads of the two matrons. (I neglected to note whether they treated the three patients again.)

The Round Dance (The Ceremony of the "Alternating and Bumping Feet"). Levi Snow now stood by the door with the turtle rattle in his hand to make certain that no one could leave. Weni, his opposite number, went about trying to induce watchers to join in the dance. He peered into the adjoining room and scared a little girl. During the second song the doorkeeper joined the dancers. Next, the two maskers circulated outside the ring of dancers, peering into the faces of observers. Levi looked me in the face and let out his questioning querulous moan; Levi is a funster who gets some fun out of everything he does. (Meanwhile the east door was open, and anyone could have escaped.) Levi stopped near the west door.

Women joined the dance during the sixth song. Now Weni, seeing the open door, hastened to prevent departures. Levi then danced. Next, the two doorkeepers faced each other and danced with the unmasked members.

At a particular song near the end, the two masked men again gathered ashes; all unmasked dancers sat down, as the maskers blew ashes on the heads of the three patients.

Last, the two masked men blew hot ashes from cupped bare hands on the heads of the two matrons. The two masked doorkeepers then left by the east door, and this ended the dance.

Aftermath. Sadie Butler once more swept up the ashes and threw them out the west door. Levi, no longer a masked doorkeeper, returned carrying a pail and his False Face wrapped under his arm.

The conductor (Albert) stood and returned thanks to the participants. During his speech, the boiler of corn soup made that morning was placed on the floor in front of the stove. At a signal from the matron, people shoved pails toward it. There was a platter of mush on the stove for the Common Faces. Beside it was a bowl of popcorn for the two Husk Faces.

Distribution of the Feast. One matron dished out mush into pail lids for all the masked dancers in the first part of the ceremony. Her opposite number ladled the soup into pails for the dancers and singers. Principal men and women had their pails filled first. Some food was set aside for members of the household, the sponsors, and the cooks.

False Face Feast
The family of Yendi Abrams (Beaver Clan) at Midwinter put up a feast for the False Faces (January 23, 1934).

Private feasts for medicine societies occur thick and fast during the first five days of the Midwinter Festival. I had gone back up to Coldspring for the "doings" at the Indian New Year and stayed with the family of Henry Redeye. The old man briefed me on the ceremonies we were going to attend, and then his son Sherman reviewed my observations afterward. Even though Sherman rarely attended, he could always fill me in on what I thought I had seen.

As Henry was to give the first tobacco invocation at Yendi's feast, we talked about the meeting during the afternoon before walking up to Coldspring about dark. During that morning at the longhouse, Henry was asked to attend, give the speech of thanksgiving to the spirit forces, and put the tobacco in the fire for the False Faces. He told me:

> There are two kinds of False Faces: the Common Faces that were here in the woods whom we call Hodigǫhsóskaʔah, "the Faces Only," and Shagodyowéhgo:wa:h whom the Creator met on the edge of the world and who is the chief or headman of this kind. He can eat people, and his dance is Deyę:hsiʔdadías [which is also called the "Doorkeepers' Dance"]. The great one is mentioned first in the tobacco-burning speech, and then the common kind who live in the forests receive tobacco second.

This explanatory note prefaced an abstract of the tobacco invocation that he greatly expanded in performance. The longer version was probably nearly identical to the prayer he later dictated for the spring and autumn purification of the houses. Omitting the text, only the main concepts will be quoted in the original Seneca.

Tobacco-throwing Prayer for the False Faces
[A pinch of tobacco is sprinkled on the fire for each item of which aid is asked.]

> Partake of this tobacco Shagodyowehgo:wa:h. [Mention of the Great False Face, literally, "The Great Defender," means that Deyę:hsiʔdadias, "Alternating Feet," the Doorkeepers' Dance will be performed. He is not mentioned if only the Common Forest False Faces, the Hodigǫhsoskaʔah, are to appear. Otherwise, Henry said the prayer is much the same.]
> And you also, of whom it is said "your faces are against the trees in the forest, namely 'Faces Alone,' Hodigǫhsóskaʔah."

(Here sprinkle a bit of tobacco.) All of you savor tobacco and bear in mind how this entire family whom you accepted [chose] derive your common membership [association].

(Here sprinkle tobacco in the fire.) So now then your turtle rattle receives tobacco. [Here the whole company of False Faces rubs rattles on the floor and say *họʔọʔọʔọ.*]

[Sprinkle tobacco.] And now then another thing inhales tobacco, namely the place where you rub your turtle rattle, the tree which is a giant elm.[3] [Again the maskers rub their rattles and talk.] [The reference to the great elm that stands in the center of the earth is an important concept in Iroquois thought.] Everytime Shagodyowehgo:wa:h traverses the world, he stops and rubs his rattle on the giant elm tree in the middle of the earth from which he derives and renews his strength. [Parker (1913, 128) specifies a great pine tree.]

[Again sprinkle tobacco. In fact, every time it is mentioned, or shortly thereafter.] So now at this time something partakes of the tobacco, namely your staff made of a giant pine tree its limbs lopped off to its top.

[Sprinkles tobacco.] Now then the sponsor is ready with what you prefer: mush that is laced with bear fat, and a kettle of corn soup is resting on the ground. [Clara Redeye commented, "Sometimes the speaker says, 'There are chunks of meat as big as your feet.' Here the maskers roll and try to put their feet in their mouths. Every man speaks differently when he puts tobacco in the fire."

Henry went on to comment on another speaker whose prayers are notably long.

He said the same thing twice and that is why he took so long.
[Sprinkle tobacco.] So now it is up to you to help that person, inasmuch as she has fulfilled everything.
So now arise and make medicine for her.
So it is said.

My mind was full of this briefing as the old Seneca speaker and I trudged through the snow that winter evening to the meeting at Yendi Abrams's home.

PART I
Ganonyonk. When everyone had gathered in the house, Henry Redeye stood where all could hear, removed his hat, and announced the purpose

---

3. Gaọgähgo:wa:h, "giant elm," is also a personal name in the Bear Clan, which at the time was held by Jerry Jimmerson. It is an exalted title of *hodiọt,* "longhouse officer," or faithkeeper rank.

of the meeting. He then launched into the familiar address of thanksgiving to the spirit forces on this earth and above it from the grasses and herbs to the sky world. He then enumerated the order of events that were to follow.

Headwoman of Opposite Moiety. Because Yendi's maternal family were Beavers, Fannie Stevens (Heron), headwoman of the False Faces in the other moiety, managed the masked dancers, enlisted the men who were participants, issued orders to the men who were dressing and masking behind the house, and finally told Willie Titus (Beaver) that he might commence the song. He sat in one corner and beat a turtle rattle on the edge of a wooden chair that he straddled, until someone provided him with a second chair on which to drum.

Enter the False Faces. The False Faces rubbed their rattles on the door and along the floor as they slid on their hips and hands toward the fire. Some of the same masks had appeared in another rite that morning, but now they were worn by different individuals, evidence that masks are loaned within the community. Although this was Hodigǫhsóskaʔah for the Common Faces of the Forest, with them were two masks that would later appear as doorkeepers; and a lone Husk Face entered last.

Invocation. The maskers grouped themselves about the stove, and Henry commenced the *hayęʔgontwas,* "tobacco speech." In the text that he had previously dictated in abstract, he failed to mention the Husk Face, but in the actual recitation of the prayer, which was far more elaborate and afforded ample room for his style of speaking, he named the Husk Face and mentioned his association with the False Faces and promised that the hostess had prepared popcorn for him. (Amos Johnny John acted in this role and later became Shagodyowéhgo:wa:h in the second part.)

Songs for Blowing Ashes. The singers (Atkins Coury had now joined Willie Titus) resumed the False Face songs that prompted the maskers to dip their bare hands in the hot embers and blow ashes on the patient's head, shoulders, and hands. The patient was one of Yendi's daughters. Then, one by one, the maskers blew ashes on the headwoman's head, received tobacco from her, and departed singly.

Husk Face Songs. Meanwhile, the Gajíhsaʔ stood by the door, except during the invocation when he crouched; he now danced to his own songs. The singer used a stick of wood to beat the rhythm. Usually Husk Faces circle their staffs but drop the sticks when called upon to blow ashes, as in this instance. The performer scooped hot ashes and blew them on the patient's head. The Husk Face has a special song and his own style of dancing, and he receives a special award, popcorn of which he is very fond. The matron handed the performer a bag of previously popped corn, and he departed, backing through the door.

INTERMISSION

People got up and stretched. Outside, False Faces were undressing as was the Husk Face. Meanwhile, two men were preparing for the role of doorkeeper. Inside, the matron swept ashes from the floor, tidied up about the stove, and cleared the floor for what was to follow. The guests, having nothing else to do, gossiped and joked in low key. Gradually, men who had served as False Faces returned at intervals carrying pails and their ritual equipment done up in bundles under their arms or in suitcases.

PART II

Deyę:hsiʔdadías. When all was in readiness, the singers commenced a third song called Deyę:hsiʔdadías, "They Alternately Bump Their Feet." Two men entered accoutered much the same as the previous maskers but wearing older and more powerful masks, one red, that of Levi Snow (Heron), and the other was black, that of Amos Johnny John (Wolf). (The red mask had appeared in the same role in the ceremony for Henry Redeye the previous summer. I was told that only the oldest masks are used for this ritual. But there is much confusion as to which masks are Common Faces and which ones represent the "Great False Face" [Shagodyoweh]. Masks with distended or bifunnelate lips of either color seem to qualify.) The two maskers blew ashes on the patient or hostess and departed.

Thumbs-Up Dance. On their second entrance, the two maskers, who themselves were of opposite moieties, danced opposite the two headwomen, each masker facing the matron of the opposite moiety. The maskers point their thumbs upward, while grasping their rattles in their right hands with the shell pointing downward, or dangling from a thumb by the loop that passes through the turtle's mouth or eye. A couple hops on one foot while bending the other knee and kicking the foot out in unison. At the same time a dancer spars toward his partner with the opposite hand (see Kurath's description (1964, 9, 100]). One bends his left knee, extends his right foot, and spars with the left hand, and vice versa.

Dance Organization. Third, the headwomen organize a dance, one matron picking out the men, and the other choosing the female partners. Selection proceeded counterclockwise around the room. Imitating the masked beings, the unmasked guests hold their thumbs erect and spar and kick in the same manner. The singer employs a turtle rattle. Each couple dances through a song or set. Alternately, one of the two doorkeepers looks in from outside once during each song. This dance elicits much amusement: A matron tried to back a senior man from the floor. A bashful youth may be roughed up, but this is done in good fun. One old lady, having succeeded in backing her male partner to the benches, whooped in triumph. Every onlooker must dance at least once, and at this meeting there were two rounds. I noted a tendency to choose partners of opposite moieties, for indeed the matrons are of opposite moieties. The element of female aggression is quite evident.

The action is supposed to represent what Shagodyowehgo:wa:h does when he dances. This pairing of couples is called *dęsädjogèwodę?*

Round Dance of Alternating Feet. After everyone had danced at least once, the two masked doorkeepers entered a third time and organized the watchers, including men who had already performed in Part I as Common Faces, in a round dance of two columns. The men formed the outside ring and the women the inside, each person stepping twice on each foot alternately and striking the heel against the floor, then raising his or her foot and setting it down ahead. Then this is repeated with the other foot. This bumping step gives the whole rite its specific name—*deyę:hsi²dadías*.

Sherman Redeye told me:

> In the Round Dance, one of the False Faces chooses the leader, that is, the first man selected from the wall. Then both masked men go about the room coercing the watchers to stand and enter the dance.
>
> One of the two masked men at a time must watch the door from the inside while the other superintends the dance. The doorkeeper must ensure that no one leaves or enters. This role lends itself to the popular Seneca name for the ceremony—"the Doorkeepers' Dance."

Blowing Ashes Songs. When the singers reach the song that signals that the three following songs are for blowing ashes—the "medicine songs"—each of the dancers sits down. Now the two False Faces, who were doorkeepers, blow ashes on the patient, who is their hostess and sponsor of the meeting. "Then they must blow ashes on the heads of the two matrons for which they receive a handful of tobacco." Sherman Redeye, who had played this role, continued:

> They pretend to take the tobacco first, but the matron points insistently at her head, and the masker gives up pointing to his mouth—a sign that he wants tobacco—and does his duty. Then the two maskers leave and, looking back, emit their cry for the last time, and then depart rubbing their rattles on the door. That is the end of it.

Thanks to the Participants. Now Henry Redeye spoke for the last time. He gave thanks to the headwomen who had organized and managed the ceremony, to the False Faces, and the people who came to watch and who had also joined the dance.

Feast. Both mush and corn soup were served to the participants. Pails of soup with mush on the inverted lids were stowed under chairs, pending a second ceremony.

A Second Order of False Faces Without Husk Faces

Willie Titus stood and announced a second kind of False Face ceremony similar to the first but without the Husk Face. This second performance was for Yendi's other children—two daughters and a son—of the Beaver Clan.

The second performance differed from the first in lacking the Husk Face. Also, the False Faces wandered about outside in the snow and rubbed their rattles up and down on the outside walls of the house while conversing mournfully, *họʔọʔọʔọʔọ, họʔọʔọʔọʔọ*. I was told that this was to drive all manner of disease and ill luck from the premises.

When the maskers finally entered the house, they were preceded by Henry Redeye singing *ganǫeo:wi:ʔ,* their marching song (Parker 1913, 128).

> This particular Dawn Song used to be sung by Shagodyowéhgo:wa:h, "the Great False Face," and it is his personal song addressed to the midpantheon, which stills the wind. Henry sang for the great one and for the lesser False Faces together.

That morning, Chauncey Johnny John had sung the same song when the maskers marched from Mary Armstrong's house to the longhouse.

PARTICIPATION OF MASKS IN THE MEDICINE COMPANY RITES

One rite of the Medicine Company, or the Society of the Mystic Animals (Parker 1909, 172–74), calls for the appearance of a wooden mask. Among the Seneca, the mask tends to be of a specialized type, but the masker, within my observation, behaves like other False Faces, dances in a round dance, co-opts dancers, and blows ashes on the patient. The ceremony also occurs at Six Nations where the masker impersonates the ancient shamans and juggles hot embers but no longer tosses hot rocks (Fenton 1942, 21). The ceremony is one order of ʔi:ʔdo:s or Hadí:ʔdo:s (Seneca); Hanahi:ʔdo:s (Onondaga).

At the turn of the century, Parker reported that the society possessed certain secret masks, which he illustrated (1909, fig. 25, p. 173), one of which has no eyeholes. He calls it a "conjuror's mask." This blind mask was worn by the leader of the society, and it was alleged to enable him to discover hidden objects, to juggle hot stones, and perform other magical feats. Parker asserted that the three masks that he collected and described were never used in the rites of the False Face Company (p. 174). These masks appear to be quite recent. Blind masks of apparent older vintage do appear, however, in collections. Their use seems to have been confined to Newtown on Cattaraugus.

At Coldspring, where there is no cultural memory of blind masks, certain black faces, such as the "buffalo" mask carved by Richard Kettle, of Newtown, and owned by the Johnny John family, perform in this rite and juggle hot ashes like the False Faces, although the songs refer to tossing hot rocks (Plate 12-9). I saw one black bifunnelate doorkeeper mask per-

Plate 12-9. "Buffalo" mask by Richard Kettle in Ido:s ceremony.

form in this role, and old John Jimmerson, a native of Cattaraugus, specified a white mask for ʔi:ʔdo:s.

Three Orders of ʔi:ʔdo:s

There are three orders of ʔi:ʔdo:s, and members celebrate only the orders that have assisted in their cure. Ordinary ʔi:ʔdo:s omits songs 34 to 50, in the version that Sherman Redeye sang, and these refer to the False Face. ʔi:ʔdo:s with Gagǫ́hsaʔ, the ceremony with the mask is called Gayǫwéoǫh, "Plunging the Sharp Point in Liquid," as mentioned in songs 32 and 33, or simply Ganónyahgwęʔ, the archaic term for a round dance. Here the masker enters and performs much as in Part II of the False Face ceremony. The longest ritual, which includes the others, is known as Hadi´hadi:yaʔs, "They Are Cutting through the Forests," which takes its name from the marching song of the visiting phratry who approach from a distance.

During the Round Dance, the mask enters on the cue, "the False Face is shouting," which is the fortieth song in the version that Sherman sang. He remains for about the next twenty songs. He dances around, peers at the watchers, isolates members of the society whom he forces to dance. He follows the dance, marshalls the dancers, and uses the same steps. My Seneca sources knew of no origin legend that explains the entrance of a masked conductor into the rites of the Medicine Company. At a later song that says "ashes he is scattering about," the masker goes to the fire, plunges his hands into the hot ashes, and blows them on the heads of the sponsors. During the last song the human conductor gives the masker some tobacco, and he goes out. In most respects the role is similar to that of the doorkeeper. And like the False Faces, he receives mush (Plate 12-9).

13. "Indian New Year"

Appearance of the Maskers at Midwinter

"OUR UNCLES," THE BIGHEADS

At dawn of the fifth day of the new moon, the first or second after the winter solstice that the elders have selected to start the new year, two matrons and two men meet in the longhouses of the Seneca. They should be of opposite moieties, and the men have been chosen in a dream. Each matron dresses her opposite number, her male "cousin," in a buffalo robe or old blanket and binds it with ropes of braided cornhusks from which the ears have been pulled; she puts a wreath of cornhusks about his hooded head and adds cornhusk anklets with trailers. Finally, they hand each of the men wooden corn pounders. A longhouse speaker charges them with a message and dispatches them about the settlement. They are to hail their nephews, announce the Feast of Dreams that marks the new year, and "run through all the fires." The Uncles symbolize the union of the trophies of the hunt and the fruit of the harvest—men and women's activities, respectively. The Bigheads should not be confused with the wooden False Faces or the Husk Faces, the two distinct but somewhat linked medicine societies that this book describes. This manner of announcing the Midwinter Festival is purely Seneca, for the Onondaga of Canada and those of New York do not observe quite the same custom. Their dream heralds go unmasked.

FALSE FACES ROUNDS

The False Faces commence to make their appearance toward dusk of the second or third day after the Big Heads have announced the Feast of Dreams and the officials have made the rounds of the houses singing the Dawn Song and stirring ashes. The particular day that the maskers appear varies, according to locality. Naming babies on the first day postpones by a day the renewal of dream obligations at Coldspring Longhouse; otherwise, the schedule resembles that at Newtown and Tonawanda. At Tonawanda, False Face beggars make the rounds on the evening of the second day, and False Face activity increases in intensity until the fourth night when the Husk Faces appear with the False Faces, a possible vestige of a once-longer Husk Face rite (Tooker 1970, 57). Such activity now occurs on the evening of the sixth day (Tooker 1970, 63). But a special celebration for the False Faces follows the weekend after Midwinter Festival concludes (Tooker 1970, 65). All masks are then assembled, and those not worn are carried and are bound together by men in a procession that includes the keeper of the False Faces. The Newtown and Coldspring Seneca False Face rites climax on the fifth and sixth nights, respectively, with the arrival of a great company of Husk Faces. At Newtown, the Husk Faces stage a mock hunt with bows and arrows, and the whole company returns on the eighth and final night, a feature no longer observed at Coldspring since a former longhouse leader, Hiram Jacobs, reasoned that in the first instance they said they were in a hurry to get on westward, and there was no point in bringing them back.

At Six Nations on Grand River, the Seneca Longhouse alone entertains the visiting Husk Faces modestly on the fourth night (S. Gibson, personal communication; Tooker 1970, 175). Formerly, the False Faces started to appear at nearby Onondaga Longhouse on the second day, were more active on the third, and wound up their rites on the fourth, when Husk Faces appeared with them. At Sour Springs, there is an unmasked dance for False Face Society members on the third day, and the maskers appear on this and the following day. Precise information on the Lower Cayuga Longhouse sequence is wanting.

At Old Onondaga, the False Faces and the Husk Faces arrive on the seventh day, and then on the fifteenth day, at night, False Face beggars and clowns perform in a riotous celebration that the entire community and guests attend in the longhouse. This occasion is well documented for nearly a century, from Beauchamp (1888) and DeCost Smith (1888) to Blau (1963), and I witnessed it in 1936 (see also Tooker 1970, 82). For the Seneca, however, historical accounts take the ceremony back to the eighteenth century.

EIGHTEENTH-CENTURY ACCOUNTS

In an account of the Midwinter Festival as celebrated by the Seneca on the Genesee River late in the eighteenth century by Mary Jemison (Seaver 1932, 164–67), on the second day, men wearing bearskin leggings and carrying turtle rattles, presumably False Faces, went around the settlement begging tobacco for an invocation. They are described as rubbing the walls of houses both inside and out. Midway into the festival, on the fourth or fifth day, Husk Faces made the rounds of the houses. Again they wore bearskin. They are described as besmearing themselves with dirt (offal) and bedaubing persons who refused to contribute alms (tobacco) in the baskets that they carried.

A generation later, Quaker missionaries observed and described the Midwinter Festival at Cornplanter's village on the Allegheny River. Halliday Jackson returned to Philadelphia in June of 1800 and wrote up his observations thirty years later from his diaries in the form of an ethnography; he then recalled the rounds of the False Faces on the second day (Jackson 1830, 24–25):

> After a day spent at this general rendezvous [wooden image], they divided into smaller companies, men and women apart, and

keep up the dance in each house of the town. These dancing companies are preceded by two men appointed for the purpose, who are dressed in the most frightful manner imaginable, being covered with bear skins, and a bag of ashes tied around their middle, behind them, with a hole to suffer the ashes to fly about as they move. Their faces are covered with a large painted mask, having a high mane on the crown, made of long coarse horse hair standing almost erect, and large eyes encircled with a flame coloured ring. The mouth is open, and shows their own teeth, with which they grin in a terrific manner, and their hands are blackened so as to leave the marks on every person they lay them on. They carry the shell of a mud tortoise, which has been dried for the purpose, with a stick thrust through it, which stretches the neck and a large head to their full extent, and inside the shell are a quantity of pebbles, with which they make a wonderful rattle.

These men go from house to house, and rub this shell on the sides and up and down the door posts. They also enter into the house, but say nothing, nor do any injury. As they travel about, if they meet with any person, male or female, in their way, they pursue them—those who turn and receive them in a friendly way, they shake hands with, but say nothing—but it is rather expected that many should run as if terrified; these are pursued, and if overtaken before they get into a house, are laid hold of, and blackened with their hands, but no other injury is offered, and, except a frightful yelling noise, nothing is spoken.

The design of these frightful representations is, to personify and imitate the bad spirit, and to remind the Indians of the necessity to amend their ways, and avoid all wrong things.

Several items in this account deserve comment. That there are just two of these maskers and that they function on the second day to precede parties of dancers making the rounds of the houses anticipate the role of the Bigheads at Coldspring in this century. The sack of ashes has disappeared, and the maskers no longer besmear those they encounter, either by shaking hands or roughing up persons who attempt to run away. One is reminded, however, that in recent years when the two parties of maskers converge and meet at Coldspring Longhouse after purging the settlement, their leaders shake hands. The rest of the account is straightforward False Face behavior.

Twelve years later, the Reverend Thaddeus Osgood, a missionary among the Seneca and the Iroquois in Ontario, gave an account of the Seneca Midwinter Festival to Timothy Dwight, which Dwight published in his "Travels" (1822, 4:213–14, in Tooker 1970, 131–32). He does not specify which of the seven days is devoted to False Face activity. Nor does he locate the scene. He simply says:

On one of the festival days they perform a peculiar religious ceremony, for the purpose of driving away evil spirits from their habitations. Three men clothe themselves in the skins of wild beasts, and cover their faces with masks of a hideous appearance, and their hands with the shell of the tortoise. In this garb they go from house to house, making a horrid noise, and in every house take the fuel from the fire, and scatter the embers and ashes about the floor with their hands.

At Squakie Hill (Mount Morris, New York) in 1816, the fourth and fifth day of the festival featured False Faces. There was begging for "an apple, a plug of tobacco, or a few pennies," and a case of hysteria and pawing in the ashes is described (Jedediah Horsford, in Doty 1876, cited by Tooker 1970, 132–34).

Such are the historical precedents out of which the behavior of the Society of Faces has evolved during the past 150 years.

THIS CENTURY AT COLDSPRING

In the decades before midcentury at Coldspring Longhouse, the False Face beggars commenced to make their rounds of the houses on the evening of the fourth day. They continued until the sixth night when the Husk Faces appeared at the longhouse. In closing the ceremony at the longhouse on the third day, the speaker announced that as soon as the Feather Dance had made the circuit of the houses the next day, the way was open for the beggars to visit private houses at dusk but not the longhouse. (One must remember that at Coldspring the fourth day of the festival is the third day of the new year.) Meanwhile, private feasts for the False Faces commenced in individual homes before making the rounds of the houses on the fifth and sixth days of the festival.

The beggar masks (*hatiyę ʔgwáne:s,* literally, "they beg for tobacco") include a great variety. Sherman Redeye asserted, "Any kind of False Face may be used during the Indian New Year when they go about the houses begging for tobacco." They are frequently comic masks representing, perhaps, a pig, and comic strip characters such as Mickey Mouse, Felix the Cat, and apes. Avery Jimmerson, later a renowned carver, in the early 1930s did a caricature of Charlie Chaplin that then belonged to Myron Turkey who dressed in a suit and wore a derby. In their rounds the beggars expect tobacco, and if not compensated, steal food from cupboards. Sherman Redeye once stole a pie.

The routine when the maskers arrive is to open the door for them. "If someone of the house sings for them, they will dance, but their hosts should be prepared with tobacco which they expect. And if you wish, they will stir ashes."

"One time Josephine Snow" (her mother's brother's wife and my hostess) "heard a noise, and thinking it Jones coming home drunk, came downstairs in her underwear and opened the door to the False Faces." Her traditional in-laws looked upon Mrs. Snow as ignorant of the old ways. She had attended Carlisle Indian School for a while, and when she returned, it was said that she did not know how to bake or cook.

The beggars usually carried a small tobacco basket, either a twined cornhusk tray, or a small splint basket.

During the winter of 1934, the beggars came to Henry Redeye's house, where I was staying, on the fifth night. They rubbed their rattles on the door, someone opened it, and they entered walking erect. Henry went and got some tobacco that he had put aside, so that he was ready when they entered. Holding the tobacco in his cupped open hands, Henry sat by the door where the leader would surely see it. The leader of the maskers accepted the tobacco and called off his mob who by this time were poking into cupboards for food. Other members of the company approached occupants of the house pointing to their masked mouths, to indicate that they wanted tobacco or something to eat. "If you give them nothing, they steal. If you give them tobacco, they will dance, providing you know how to sing." Sherman took the rattle from one of the maskers, and, beating on the edge of the wooden chair he was straddling, sang several of the *hodigohsóskaʔa* songs for them to dance. They bowed and left the house again, rubbing their rattles on the door, and emitted their mournful complaint—*hǫʔǫʔǫʔǫ*. They went off down the road to the next house toward Quaker Bridge.

AT TONAWANDA

It is always announced that on the second day, the way is open for the False Faces, or whoever would impersonate them, to go about the houses. The speaker cautions that whenever such a person approaches a house he must make a noise continually so that the people who live there will know that a False Face is coming. This notice is required so as not to frighten the children unduly or excite certain neurotic old women. (The reader is reminded of Peter Doctor's testimony regarding cases of hysteria and his own experience in this role when yet a novice.)

Chief Lyman Johnson boasted that Tonawanda then had the best False Face dancing among the Iroquois. And some of these False Face beggars were girls. He mentioned in particular the daughter of a chief whom he regarded as a particularly good dancer. "She wears overalls and other men's old clothes, puts on a False Face, and goes about begging and dancing. These girls look much like men" (Plates 13-1, 13-2).

Plate 13-1. Jesse and Yowehson Cornplanter are hosts to the False Face Beggars, Tonawanda, January, 1936. A: A single dancer amuses his hosts. B: The "Devil" as competition. C: A trio of dancers.

Plate 13-2. Tonawanda Beggars, January, 1936. A: Chief Edward Black sings for a dancer whom they watch intently. B: The Devil and Charlie Chaplin.

THE FOURTH DAY AT TONAWANDA, TWENTY YEARS LATER

Change is inevitable, even among the False Faces. On the evening of the fourth day in 1955, a party of False Faces came down the road in the gathering dusk toward the longhouse led by Harrison Ground who was singing *gaṇ̊eowi:ʔ*. Between house calls, they were joined by one volunteer. Emerging from a house, a few of the men took off their masks and gossiped in Seneca and English. Several of them recognized me and shook hands. In the next house, a woman was frying bread. The conductor offered tobacco and prayed that the custom of visiting the houses at this season would always continue. Several of the maskers whined words of their dance song, but no one offered to sing for them, and they went on to the next house. Yowésonh Cornplanter's house was no longer on the circuit, due to Jesse's illness.

In Jesse Cornplanter's view, the False Face ceremony was only a skeleton of what it used to be. Adverting to his boyhood at Newtown on Cattaraugus Reservation, Jesse declared:

> At Newtown they have no singers. On the fifth night at Newtown [the sixth at Coldspring, a difference that facilitates visiting back and forth], black-faced hunters with sacks over their heads used to come into the longhouse with a leader, just ahead of the Gajihsaʔ (Husk Face), and steal whatever articles of apparel they could lay hands on. The owners could recover their property by paying a bribe to the leader of the band who had the goods in a pool. The proceeds of their thievery went toward the soup next day. Any tradition of how this custom originated is forgotten.

THE FIFTH DAY AT COLDSPRING, 1934

On the fifth day at Coldspring, after the Drum Dance circuit of the houses, the medicine societies renew their rites in the longhouse as well as in private dwellings. Some of these rites actually go the circuit of houses. At the 1934 celebration, the rite of the Common Faces of the Forest (Hodigǫhsóskaʔah) was performed for a young woman of the Bear Clan in the house of the matron of that clan near the longhouse. The False Face matron of the opposite moiety conducted. She came into the longhouse and gathered up a group of False Face dancers, provided them with masks that she had borrowed about the community during the morning, and led the file of young men out of the longhouse in the direction of the private house where the ceremony was to take place. Chauncey Johnny John went along to sing and put tobacco in the fire.

Dressing Outside

The dancers dressed behind the house. The matron and singer went inside where the expectant family awaited the visitation of the maskers. Meanwhile, the matron made several flying trips to the rear of the house to make certain that all was in readiness. Presently, she notified the singer that he might begin.

Enter the Maskers

The singer commenced the songs of Hodigǫhsóska?ah, which is the curing dance. The company of maskers entered the house crawling. Several of the maskers were armed with turtle rattles that they rubbed on the doorposts and along the floor as they approached the stove. Others carried short sticks, for the matron had not rounded up enough turtle rattles, or they did not bring their own. In either case they had made substitutes. Most of the masks belonged to other persons.

Henry Redeye assured me afterward that moiety alignment is not important for Hodigǫhsóska?ah, but in the Doorkeeper Rite (Deyaęhsi?dadías), the participants must be of opposite moieties. Nevertheless, Sarah Armstrong, matron of the Bear Clan, had asked the False Face matron of the opposite moiety to organize and conduct the ceremony. However, the party she conscripted was mixed, being limited by the number of possibilities in her choice of men.

The maskers crawled up to the stove emitting their cries of *hǫ?ǫ?ǫ?ǫ?* and rubbing their rattles violently as they conversed in their nasal language.

Invocation

The matron conductor summoned the singer and handed him a dish of tobacco. (At one time a twined cornhusk basket was kept for this purpose.) The singer cast a pinch of tobacco into the fire and then periodically punctuated sections of the invocation with added pinches, item by item. As the tobacco is committed to the fire and the fumes pervade the room, the False Faces shake their rattles and groan energetically, particularly when the priest says: "savor this tobacco, you inhabitants of the forest"; and again, when their turtle rattles receive tobacco. When the priest describes the prepared mush as having pieces of meat in it, the False Faces become extremely enthusiastic. They peer at one another, frighten the children, amuse the old folks, and enjoy themselves tremendously. There is a natural amount of horseplay and good-natured humor in the execution of what is theoretically a very serious business. The patient, however, does not take it lightly.

Blowing Ashes

Having concluded the prayer, the priest or the matron draws out the ash pit of the stove. Then the False Faces drop their rattles and scoop up great handfuls of hot ashes, rubbing their hands to disperse any hot embers, and blow the hot ashes on the patient's head, shoulders, upper arms, hands, and knees.

I was told:

> It is thought that those maskers who really belong to the False Faces cannot burn their hands in the hot embers; but it is also believed that those actors who pretend to be members, assume the mask, and participate will burn themselves seriously.

After the ceremony, returning to the longhouse, I noticed that one of the participants was wrapping a handkerchief about a blister on one finger. This young man was from Tonawanda and had been hyperactive in the doctor role. He nevertheless insisted that he had not burned his hand.

The singer accompanied the blowing of ashes with the songs of Hodigǫhsóska?ah, and the maskers danced and blew ashes until the repertoire was finished. Before blowing ashes, each masker gave a short cry of *hǫ?ǫ?ǫ* to let the patient know that she was about to be treated.

Matron Pays Maskers

Having finished with the patient, the maskers turned to the matron who stood holding a basket containing the balance of the tobacco. Each masker in turn held up four fingers indicating that he wanted tobacco, but the matron did not comply until each masker blew ashes on her head and was paid off in order. She placed the tobacco in each masker's outstretched hand. The maskers then retired.

It is known in the community that certain individuals are especially apt at being False Faces, and they are always asked. In the 1930s, it was Amos Johnny John and Levi Snow, and they seemed to enjoy the role. But they did not joke about their serious or clowning behavior outside of actual participation. I have seen them perform all manner of antics as False Faces and then become quite sedate individuals on returning to the house for their mush.

The maskers departed from the house making the same racket as in entering. However, they walked, whereas they came in crawling.

To the Longhouse

The ceremony at the house concluded, the matron and singer departed, and the patient quickly donned her apparel and followed. The maskers repaired to the longhouse, followed by the matron and the patient. As the party approached the women's door, the singer commenced *ganǫeo:ei:?*. The procession of singer, matron, and patient entered the women's door. The maskers waited outside the building. Inside, the patient and matron sat on the south bench, and the singer took up his position straddling the center bench facing south. Once more he beat out the songs of Hodigǫhsóska?ah, and once more the False Faces entered crawling. The same rites were repeated in the longhouse.

Feast

At the end of the ritual in the longhouse, all of the men who had been False Faces took up their pails and returned to Sarah Armstrong's house for the mush that had been promised in the invocation. (I did not return with them.)

The preceding renewal of membership in the False Faces is typical of rites that begin in private and then are public in the longhouse, although in this example the ceremony did not complete the entire circuit of houses. This may be because it started in the last house on the circuit.

THE SIXTH DAY

On the sixth day of the Midwinter Festival at Coldspring, as it was celebrated during the 1930s, the participants in the Bowl Game (that commemorates the wager between the Creator and his twin) traveled a circuit of houses pausing to play against the householders, as was the time-honored custom. Returning to the longhouse from the last house on the circuit, the False Faces sometimes intercepted the party of gamers outside of the longhouse. Members of the society wearing masks played against the appointed ones, and the wagers were Indian tobacco. "They play right there in the snow wherever the False Faces meet them," asserted Levi Snow, but this does not always occur. Levi said that the game was played if the boys got together beforehand and decided to put on masks and intercept the players on the circuit. Ordinarily, the floor is not open for medicine society ceremonies until after the Bowl Game players have returned to the longhouse late in the morning. There is an element of impatience in this act of the False Faces, as if they were in a hurry to participate in the doings a bit ahead of schedule.

False Faces were frequently out in the settlement in the morning. If they met the gamers entering or leaving any of the houses on the circuit, the maskers forced a contest. This demand to participate on the part of the maskers operated also with other society dances that were making the rounds. These acts recall Halliday Jackson's statement, already quoted, that the maskers stopped persons or chased them outside of houses and that the house was a sanctuary.

The sixth day and night is certainly the frenetic day at Coldspring. All dream-related ceremonials must be fulfilled, lest someone who has neglected a ceremonial obligation has his or her head forever stuck to the ceremonies.

The 1939 Festival

During the 1939 festival, late in the afternoon of the sixth day, young men commenced a game of Snow Snake along Snow Street south of the longhouse. While the game was in progress, several rites of the False Face company were being performed in nearby private dwellings. There was a renewal at Yendi Abrams's house of the ceremony I observed in 1934. Another was about to begin at Amos Redeye's. On reaching the longhouse, I observed young men slipping out and crossing the snow to Amos's where they could be seen in the gathering dusk putting on their masks behind the house. Other people stayed at the longhouse, for no one could be sure, except the conductor, whether these rites would go public and come into the longhouse. Those of us who remained behind could observe from a distance through the longhouse windows the external preparations for the ritual and infer the rest.

A Husk Face Renewal

As in deer hunting, it is more rewarding to sit quietly where the game will pass than to beat the bush. We were presently rewarded by an anniversary Husk Face rite for Alice White of the Wolf Clan, which came from her house just north into the longhouse and returned there. There are records of her renewing this rite from 1934 to 1950, and I learned that she had this ceremony ever since she was a teenager and suffered an eye disorder. This dance was performed for her. She has repeated it ever since at the Indian New Year.

Eight or ten Husk Faces entered the longhouse through the women's door. Their heads were covered with rags of old clothes over which they had tied the faces. They all carried four-foot staffs. Amos Johnny John, also of the Wolf Clan, conducted the party, and his father, Chauncey, sang for them. The singer for the Husk Faces borrowed a pole from one of the maskers and rapped it smartly on the floor. The maskers danced in a lively manner around the poles, using them as pivots. On this occasion, the maskers took up ashes from the exposed fire pit, rubbed them between their hands in the manner of False Faces, and blew them on the sponsor's head, shoulders, arms, hands as she stood passively. Then each Husk Face blew on the head of the conductor. Unlike the False Faces, the Husk Face maskers were entirely mute. Each masker received tobacco from the conductor, and the party returned to Alice White's where they were paid in popcorn.

The entire ceremony was then repeated for Alice White's sister's son, as if the obligation had passed in the lineage. What distinguishes the Husk Faces from the wooden False Faces is the masks, the upright gait, the want of a nonsense speech, unique songs, dancing in circles, and the popcorn feast. The ritual pattern is otherwise identical.

Plate 13-3. Maskers go the circuit of houses at Coldspring Midwinter Festival, 1941. A: Returning from the circuit: masker, sponsor, invoker, and pig masker. B: Returning to the longhouse by the south door: masker, invoker, conductor.

Some False Face rites to renew dream obligations used to complete the full circuit of houses on the sixth day at Coldspring. The party might consist of sponsor, conductor, and several maskers, or just two maskers. At the festival of 1941, I photographed one such party as it returned to the longhouse, made up of conductor, invoker, and two maskers (Plate 13-3).

Plate 13-4. The Hula dancer (Dick Johnny John), who stole the show, and escort, Coldspring Midwinter, 1955. C. R. Roseberry photo.

HUSK FACE NIGHT AT COLDSPRING, 1955

A procession of at least five celebrations of the Bear Dance preceded the appearance of the False Face beggars. Tip Roseberry, who accompanied me, wrote afterward (*Times Union,* Albany, 13 February 1935, E-1, 3):

> At Coldspring we were in time for . . . the merry-andrew antics of the False Face Society. The False Faces are the clowns of the ceremonies, the comedy-relief as they say in show business. A group of them, wearing wooden masks, some comical, some hideous, burst in at intervals, cut capers, and do solo dances in return for cigarettes. [Plates 13-4.]

This year a Hula dancer, impersonated by Dick Johnny John, won the audience's acclaim.

During forty years of repeated visits to the Coldspring Longhouse, from 1934 to the early 1970s, the old men have complained to me about the decline of False Face activity. They say that people are failing to fulfill their ceremonies, yet at the times I have attended the sixth night of the Midwinter Festival, the False Face beggars and clowns have not lost their ingenuity. There is always some memorable performance. Edmund Wilson

(1960, 237ff.) reviewed the performance of 1958 in vivid language. My last visit before the removal of the longhouse to its new site near Steamburg was in 1965.

1968 OBSERVATIONS AT THE NEW LONGHOUSE

In 1968, I witnessed the ceremonies in the new longhouse and described the state of the art in the new setting (Fenton 1972c, 102–8) (Plate 13-5). The contrast between the old longhouse environs near the Allegheny River and the new modern facility replete with fluorescent lighting, suspended ceiling, and electrical wall outlets for hotplates had not only altered the setting but had changed the content of the ceremonies. Everything was now confined to the longhouse because the ceremonies no longer traveled the circuit of houses during five mornings. Such progressions as were celebrated simply went out one door of the longhouse and returned through the other. The heralds and conductors no longer knew their lines, and they mumbled their announcements. Constriction of space had telescoped content.

On the fifth morning as usual, the speaker announced that the door now stood open to admit all kinds of ceremonies revealed through dreams. He mentioned the False Faces. The Bear Dance continued to be the most popular of the dream dances.

> At dusk several performances of the False Faces disclosed substantial changes in that rite. In their new ranch-style houses people objected to the maskers' scraping rattles on the varnished doors, marring the woodwork, and tracking in mud. The two head women had thereupon quit because this objection meant that the circuit of houses at midwinter would no longer be observed, and they had abandoned spring and fall "housecleaning" throughout the settlement. The rites of the maskers now centered at the longhouse. [Fenton 1972c, 106]

"As the False Faces crawled and stooped toward the women's fire, I noted that their behavior lacked enthusiasm." Of two mature members of traditional families, only one "was properly raucous," and the other "danced while scooping hot ashes [and] moved the patient's head on its axis, and pumped her arms." Others failed to come up to expectations. One could scarcely hear the words of the tobacco invocation.

> One lady sponsor was wearing curlers, which embarrassed her, since under the old rules she would have left the ashes in her hair for three days. . . . Audience participation was quite limited: I saw no frightened children and no cases of hysterical possession; nor did anyone crawl toward the fire. When the doorkeepers cleared

Plate 13-5. The new Coldspring Longhouse near Steamburg, N.Y., Allegany Reservation, 1968.

> the benches, requiring everyone to join the dances, only the old people knew the steps. [Fenton 1972c, 106]

Evident though it might appear that the ceremonies were in decline, there is a certain built-in stability in Iroquois ceremonialism that keeps it going even in changed circumstances. This often comes out on the sixth night, which is the climax of the Midwinter Festival. Then visitors come regularly from the other Seneca reservations and bring their own singers and dancers.

Soon the benches were completely filled. Every Iroquois community where I had lived and made friends was represented. "It was interesting to meet the new generation because I have always been curious about the learning process in this society that afforded so few teaching situations." Johnson Jimmerson, now a speaker in the Newtown Longhouse, was there with his son. I recalled the father as a boy at Coldspring, how anxious he was to learn everything about the ceremonies, how he constantly practiced his songs, despite the ridicule of some elders. I was soon to be fascinated by

> the learning he had transmitted to his son, who proved the winner by acclaim in the False Face beggar dancing contest. Johnson had indeed, to use his words, "raised him right." The power of symbols and of certain stereotypes, much of it nonverbal, must be operative in this process. The masks are impressive enough when seen in museum collections, but they really come to life when worn by impersonators of the spirits that they represent. [Fenton 1972c, 107]

Indeed, the False Face clowns employ traditional dance steps but with variations of their own invention. The songs are from the repertory of Hodigǫhsóskaʔah: One song line says, "turn over," which is a challenge to a virtuoso performer to turn flips.

The False Faces, as everyone expected, led the program. Small boys slipped out to the cookhouse in twos and threes to return as masked beggars. The first beggar dressed in white overalls wore a Negro mask. Crossing the room to where I was seated, he thrust his stick at me and demanded that I sing for him to dance. Such a confrontation is a recognized contest between the generations, between singer and dancer. . . . Years ago someone had taught me a simple False Face song, and I recalled one other from my recordings. The beat was easy, and Clifford Crouse of my generation urged me to keep it going to tire the dancer. Accomplished singers try odd beats to throw the dancer off. Dancers prefer a fast tempo and short songs. The game is to stretch the beat, keeping the dancer at it until he tires and begs for his stick, at which the singer may speed up the beat again. This byplay appeals to the Iroquois sense of humor, in which an element of kindly torture persists. These contests are looked forward to and remembered long afterward. [Fenton 1972, 107–8]

There is always one memorable beggar. This year [1968] it was a visitor, Johnson Jimmerson's son, from Newtown Longhouse who impersonated Sumo, the Japanese wrestler. Wearing karati dress, he bounded barefoot into the women's end of the longhouse, combining karati postures with classic False Face antics. He wore a mask of lemon-colored wood with crooked mouth, but hairless. All of the youngsters in one voice mouthed, "Sumo!" Sumo stayed for a half hour, preempting the attention of the best singers whom the women sent the master of ceremonies to fetch, and he was still there at the men's stove at the second romp of the Husk Face Heralds. One of them rushed over toward the stove, cross checking with his stave, and they both kicked at each other in Karati style. This exchange produced much laughter. [Fenton, Inaugural Lecture 1969, 2–3]

These dance contests among the False Face beggars, with the exception of Old Onondaga, are confined to the three Seneca longhouses in western New York. There are no beggars at Six Nations, and no special night is set aside for them. Although the Husk Faces are prominent there, there is no special Gajíhsaʔ night. Indeed, the Husk Faces reach their climax form among the Seneca.

ONONDAGA ON SIX NATIONS RESERVE

Let us now observe the appearance of the Husk Faces with the False Faces at Six Nations to close out the Feast of Dreams. In Simeon Gibson's 1940 systematic account of the yearly cycle of ceremonies at Onondaga Longhouse, the speaker announced at the close of the third day that members of the Society of Faces should bring their masks to the longhouse and store them in the kitchen or at the nearest house. On the night before the burning of the white dog, the speaker announces that the Haduʔiʔ will enter. Thus, as among the Seneca, the False Faces and Husk Faces stop individual sponsoring and celebration of particular dreams on the fourth night. After that there will be no more reporting of dreams. The men go out to dress.

Enter the False Faces
The unmasked leader of the False Face Society enters first singing *ganǫhwai'wi* and circles the longhouse floor (in a clockwise direction) with the company of maskers crawling behind him. At the same time Gajíhsaʔ will be running around. Over the din of rattles the leader hollers: "*Swadaʔǫssíyusdaʔ yae:ʔ*" ("all of you listen [pay attention] for a while"), and they all quiet down. Then he announces: "The people have all kindly agreed, namely this crowd of your grandchildren, to promise you a present of mush."

Here the maskers make a great din of rattles and talk. When they quiet down, he resumes:

> Then something else is going to happen. You shall blow ashes on your grandchildren. All members of the society shall requicken [renew] their membership, as their individual fortune [luck] demands.
>
> There is something else that I request of you. Be careful when you blow ashes on them. Don't use too much strength. Don't get rough.

The officials then place two benches in the middle of the room, and members from both sides (phratries) who want ashes blown on them seat themselves on these benches, all mixed, regardless of phratry. They all sit. The leader of the Haduʔiʔ does not sing. The appointed singer sings alone accompanying himself with a turtle shell, or wooden replica, without a helper. After two introductory songs, the maskers stand and tackle the ashes. They blow on the heads of all members seated on the benches. These are mainly women and old men. When they have finished blowing ashes on the seated members, the False Faces then stand their patients up, and they are made to go around the benches in a round dance. But the maskers carry all of the men on their backs, dancing as they carry them. (This recalls the old Huron custom that is not observed among the Seneca.) The dancers make about two circuits, and then the singer stops and strikes the bench twice to signal the finish. The wooden maskers file out of the longhouse.

Husk Faces Remain
The speaker announces, "Anyone who desires to have ashes blown on him by the Husk Faces shall sit down here on the bench." People who are members of the Husk Face Society then come to the benches again. Meanwhile, the Husk Faces are waiting outside of the door. Frequently, a Husk Face masker will open the door and look in during the False Face rite, or he will enter and run through the house and out again. (They are not door tenders, and they take no bribes for passage in or out.)

The Husk Faces enter by themselves without a leader or conductor. There may be as many as six. They, too, have an appointed singer. He sings with a wooden turtle beater, and they come in. The Husk Faces also blow on the heads of patients, but they do not use ashes, as they sometimes do among the Seneca. There are no presents. The singer beats twice to mark the end, and the Husk maskers depart.

The maskers receive their feast at a later date when the traveling rite occurs in the spring.

PART FIVE

14. The Society of Husk Faces, or Bushy Heads

The Husk Faces are an agricultural people. According to Seneca lore, they dwell on the other side of the earth in a ravine where they till their fields amid high stumps. This belief is a relic of former Iroquois swidden horticulture. Coming from the east every New Year, they visit the Seneca longhouses during two nights of the Midwinter Festival. Preceded by runners, when they finally arrive, they announce themselves amid a great din of rubbing and beating the outsides of the building with staves. Their paired runners enter the building three times, and on the third pass break up the dances, mute the singers, and kidnap a headman to serve them as interpreter. They are themselves mute and require a speaker. As messengers of the Three Sisters—corn, beans, and squash—"our life supporters," they have great powers of prophecy.

The interpreter returns inside the longhouse and reports the message of the old woman, their leader, that they are hurrying westward to hoe their crops. They say that in fields about their houses they grow huge squashes, their corn produces giant ears, and string beans climb poles to touch the sky. They relate that some of their women have remained at home to tend to crying babies. During the Great Depression of the 1930s speakers used to comment on employment prospects on public works projects. Such messages at Coldspring and Newtown afford an opportunity for social commentary having moral force that supposedly comes from the Husk Face leader, who makes observations on Seneca communities visited, comments on behavioral lapses within the community, or by inference refers to some individual. This is an opportunity for the speaker to make a pointed joke. Sturtevant (1983, 41) confirms my observations that follow. These statements are accepted as an augury of fertility and hope. Regularly, the Husk Faces request the privilege of dancing with the people and specify two favorite dances—invariably the Fish Dance and Women's Dance (ʔen:skä:nye:ʔ). Early in this century, I was told, the party of visiting Husk maskers was composed entirely of men; but from the 1930s on, women participated dressed as males, and other men impersonated women and performed women's dance steps. Young Seneca women are very adept at men's dance steps. This reversal of sex roles causes much amusement.

The Husk Face Society is by no means as well integrated or as prominent as the False Face Society, although the two groups of maskers share certain functions. Unlike the False Faces, the Husk Faces are mutes, and they only puff as they run with great leaps. When two or four husk maskers suddenly appear racing between houses, they may be signaling the approach of the False Face Company. They loiter, policing the premises until the wooden maskers depart. Relatively few Iroquois belong to their society as such, but they set a kettle down for them to renew an old dream or celebrate a cure. Many more individuals put on the husk masks during the public longhouse rituals at midwinter, and other persons join them in the social dances, dancing at the end of the line. The Husk Faces have their own tobacco invocation, a particular medicine song, and they dance in circles about the staves that they carry. Like the wooden faces, the Husk Faces have the power to cure by blowing hot ashes on whomever sponsors a feast for them; but in Canada they sprinkle water on their patients. They like tobacco but prefer popcorn at Allegany, and they receive dumplings at Newtown and at Tonawanda, instead of mush. These features are treated topically later.

Origins

Old Seneca people placed the homeland of the Husk Faces off to the East. At Coldspring, Chauncey Johnny John said they came from somewhere east of the Hudson River, but John and Minnie Jacobs located their habitat nearer by—at the headwaters of the Allegheny River, in the mountainous region of Port Allegheny or Coudersport, Pennsylvania, "where you can jump across the stream." Arriving at Coldspring on the sixth night of the midwinter ceremonies, they go on from Coldspring to Lawtons (Newtown Longhouse on Cattaraugus Reservation), where they perform the following night. They used to return two days later to Coldspring (on the eighth night) to dance the Feather Dance on the eve of the Great Bowl Game. The Husk Faces come from the East but journey to the West, suggesting a circular world, or at least another side where the seasons are reversed.

Wherever home may be situated, the Husk Faces are said to inhabit "a place filled with stumps" (*ʔtgahǫʔtgänohǫ*), from "stump" (*ohǫ́ʔtgä:*) and "ravine" or "valley" (*deyo:dadáhgǫ*). According to Sherman Redeye, who lived at Newtown for several years:

> This ravine or valley filled with stumps where they come from is located off to the east. They come this way and go off northwest on their way to Newtown, where they perform the following night. They always repeat that they come from a stumpy ravine. They next go on to Tonawanda [north and east], and then they go on east to Syracuse [Onondaga Valley]. A different party may go west to Grand River in Canada. And when they are finished, I suppose, they go back east where they came from.

The original Husk Face people have a social structure denominated by four principals, whose names are revealed during their visitation. Each name represents a food source in augmented form. There is a chief and three women. At the 1939 Midwinter Festival, Chauncey Johnny John, their captive interpreter, named them as (1) "Big Potatoes" (Nanǫʔdowa:nɛʔs), their chief; (2) "Big Beans" (Osáidaʔwa:nɛʔs), a woman; (3) "Long Ears of White Corn" (Onɛ́hdesǫs), a woman; and, (4) "Dumplings" (Ganǫʔǫstaʔ), another woman. These were the renderings of John and Minnie Jacobs, although Sherman Redeye, a younger person, heard the fourth name as Ganoʔnustaʔ ("Cold").

Besides these symbols of plant fertility, human fecundity is symbolized by the female impersonators who sometimes carry representations of their babies. To hand one of these dolls to a man in the benches is a dead giveaway of suspected paternity. One young lady would not let the masker hold her baby. The Husk Faces are even thought to be cannibals. Small boys get restless during the long sixth night of the ceremonies at Coldspring; parents may caution them not to go outside, lest the Husk Faces kidnap and eat them.

The dramatic visitation of the Husk Faces to the longhouses of the Seneca Nation stops short of the longhouses of the Six Nations on the Grand River, although a night is set aside to honor them. What the Canadian Iroquois lack in ceremony is more than made up in mythology, whereas the Seneca have lost explanatory Husk Face tales (see Curtin and Hewitt 1918; Parker 1923).

A SENECA VARIANT

In connection with the 1939 ceremonies, Chauncey Johnny John came up with an account of Husk Face origins in an interview with Marjorie Lismer.

> There used to be a little Indian village from which a man went out hunting in the fall, and he went quite a ways and stayed in the woods alone. He had good luck and took lots of game. And he also had with him some dry roasted white corn, which hunters always carry. So he made a little grinder [mortar and pestle]. He got a little log about this high [?], and he put fire in it to make a hollow in one end, and then he obtained a stick as pounder. He ground the corn and made mush for himself. He put some maple sugar in it and some bear lard, and then he ate it. He drank hemlock tea. Then when he got done eating, he lay down for a rest, and soon he heard a noise outside. He sat up and watched out the door of his hemlock brush shanty.
>
> He then sat up by the fire [outside the door] and pretty soon he saw someone come in slowly and sit down on the opposite side of the fire. The hunter asked what he [the stranger] was here for, and this man told him that he wanted to be his friend forever. Asked where he was from, the visitor said he was from east of the rocky mountains beyond the Hudson River. (They are not there any longer because so many people have come to live there and they had to remove. It is not good for them to be around with people.) [Chauncey who had been over and beyond the Hudson River knew that *they* (Husk Faces) are no longer there.] The man said, "I know that you have some roasted corn." The hunter replied, "Yes, it is

for my lunch." And the visitor said, "I want some because I crave roasted corn." And he added that others of his people would come the following night.

The next night the visitor returned bringing twenty of his people. They said, "We want to show you how we dance when we are at home." So they put up the dance for him, and he saw what they do. Then they said: "Give us some corn, give us each one piece only all around." So the hunter passed the corn around. The visitor gave the hunter a little Husk Face to keep as long as he lived, and instructed him that when he returned home he was to show it to the people so that they can make just the same [replicas] out of cornhusks.

So the hunter did as instructed. He related all that he had seen in the woods. So the people of his village said, "We are willing to keep them [the masks] and call them "our grandfathers and our grandmothers." Thus the people are continuing to keep up what was told them about the dances. This is what the Husk Faces say when they come on the last night of the New Year's ceremony. They say that they are going somewhere else and that they will come back and have another dance on the way home. They say: "Good luck, goodbye, and God bless you."

THE ONONDAGA HUSK FACES

Between 1916 and 1928, J. N. B. Hewitt collected in Onondaga text from Chiefs Joshua and John Buck several variants of what appear to be a single myth genre involving the adventures of Onondaga hunters, their encounters with Husk Face beings, and the cultural gifts received—both luck at hunting and seeds of the cultivated plants. I subsequently translated these texts in 1941 with the assistance of Simeon Gibson.

"The Husk Face Legend," or How the Male Bushy Head Brings Seeds to the Hunter

This was later revised and translated by Hewitt. (Fenton 1941a, 417–18).

> [It is said] that in ancient times it thus happened that a man who was hunting in the forest saw there while on the hunt something [had a vision]. He was surprised to see there a deer standing at the bottom of the valley. He killed it. When he had completed dressing the carcass he looked as he turned around and saw standing there nearby a male Husk Face. He asked him, saying, "Where do you come from?" He replied: "From the place where the uprooted tree trunk is."
>
> Again the hunter asked, "Where then are you going?" He answered: "It is only you whom I am seeking. I am bearing corn, and

it is expressly for you that I am bringing it." The hunter then asked: "From what place do you bring it?" He replied: "On the far side of the bush [forest] one has planted it. Odendonníʔah (Sapling, or Sprout: the Master of Life) has planted it. He planted it for you human beings. It belongs to you people. I have come bringing it for you. You must mix it with what you are hunting, when you do eat."

He himself, Moving Winds (Gaendeh´sǫhk) sent me from there, and also Otcgǫwendéthhaʔ (the Tempest). [This association of the Faces with the wind gods ties the Husk Face spirits as messengers to the wooden mask spirits.] He [Wind] said, "You go deliver the corn. The hunter will carry it back to the people when he returns home! That is the reason I deliver it to you. You must take it home."

And Wind who is entirely face [no body] accompanied me. ["But one never sees him because he is invisible," commented Simeon Gibson.] Customarily, I go there [about the houses] whenever the Humpbacked Beings, the Honduʔi:ʔ, [False Faces] make their rounds.[1] I have my dwelling place where huckleberries grow. There in that place I pick up cornbread usually, when [once more] you human beings are again gathering berries. Ordinarily, I take the cornbread which is brought there [to the berry patches] as provisions. But you [people] never see me.

[Husk Face still speaking for the Wind:] Understand that I [deprecatively] have dwelt on the earth from the beginning with the Master of Life. I am free [wild] (to wander at will in the forests). [This seems to be the end of the message of the Wind God who is face only, speaking through the Husk Face.]

You must tell your people that you and they must prepare something with cornhusks which shall resemble the form of my body. And it shall be that when people wear this husk mask, that wearing the mask will enable me to aid them. Understand that it is I who will bring to you [people] all the seeds which you will plant— seed corn, seed beans, and squash seed. All the various kinds of

---

1. Again Gibson interpolated, "The Husk Face is messenger for the wind, who being entirely Face [without body], is the patron of the wooden masks representing the 'Faces Alone' who are wild and wander at large in the forests." [The Husk Face being, who is the narrator, therefore, in the ceremony becomes the messenger of the wooden faces, or the False Face Company. His association as messenger of wind explains why the Husk Face impersonators run so fast.]" The spirit of the Wind goes with the runner but one never sees him because he is invisible."

Gibson extended his remarks: He felt that "Face Alone," the tempest, the one who lives off to the North where the Huckleberries grow, is the one who comes unseen and takes the lunchbread that berry pickers carry there. "He comes here, but the people do not see him when the Husk Faces and the False Faces go around from house to house in fall and spring."

seeds will I deliver in full. I will bring them from the many planted fields of the Sapling (Odẹndǫni) [Master of Life]. So then don't let anyone complain of the amount of seeds which I shall bring [to maturity]. Understand also that it is Diyós?ahdih [Producer of All things], Mother of Sprout [Sapling], who brought them here for us to gather.[2]

This is what the Great Humpbacked One (Hadú?i?go:na) promised [to the Creator in return for his life], "I will aid you continually." Whereupon the Master of Life replied, "Then you shall continue to live."

Whenever and wherever you people shall set out groves [orchards] in many places, they shall bear fruit in the places where it is usual for fruits to grow where I come from.

Understand that customarily Face Alone [Hogǫhsó:gǫ:?] will aid you when once more you go hunting, since he [the Creator] placed him here, and he is free to roam here in these forests and to live where the game animals abound.[3]

Furthermore, whenever people think of me, appropriately they shall say, "Djohgwé?yani? Hajíhsa?" [Mr. Partridge (Ruffed Grouse) Bushy Head]. (This was the name of the Husk Face man, the speaker.)

So now you alone must carry home with you all the things which I have given to you.

That is the end of the story.

The Chief of the Husk Faces

While working with Chief Joshua Buck, Onondaga, at Brantford, Canada, in June 1916, Hewitt recorded a second text concerning a hunter's encounter with the leader of the Husk Faces. Hewitt subsequently reviewed the text in May of 1929, and again in June, 1931, with Chief John Buck, brother of Joshua who died in 1920. The title of this story is "Hadjíhsa? Thokstę́?ah (The Eldest Husk Face, the Chief One of the Husk Faces").

It is said to be a fact that they found a certain male person in the place where they were accustomed to make their annual hunts for game animals. They tell that a man was encamped there in the forest, where he hunted regularly for game animals. After some time elapsed, the story relates that he then killed a fawn, and at once

---

2. In the cosmology, the Creator's mother brought the seeds of cultivated plants from the skyworld in the hem of her skirt and under her nails when she fell through the hole in the floor of the skyworld.

3. The story of Face Alone cited here is taken from the episode of the Humpbacked One in the cosmology. He is the prototype of the Faces in the forest. The hunter thus has consumated a pact with the wind spirit. Moreover, both he and the Husk Faces, it appears, are custodians of the game animals.

grasped it so as to dress it. So when he had completed the task and had hung the several parts of the body in a tree, he moved off, saying, "Tomorrow I will come back for them." [Here we encounter the Iroquois hunting custom of quartering a deer and hanging it in a tree to be retrieved later.]

So when the next morning came, this man [hunter] returned there again. So now at that time he saw a person sitting [in the tree] above the place where he had hung the several pieces of meat. So then the hunter said, "What are you doing?" Then the stranger replied, "I am only watching for you to return. So now the affair has turned out right because we two in meeting have seen each other."

So now the hunter said, "Where did you come from?" He replied, "There in a valley in the forest is the place where I dwell. Surely it is a fact that you and your people are not aware that we travel about in the depths of the forest. Usually, it is we who can make a hunter successful in his hunting."

And it is a fact that at all times and even now we desire cornbread of the kind on which you people subsist. Therefore you shall inform your people when you return home. You must say, "I saw Djinagáihhäh (Mr. Whistler [an Onondaga Wolf Clan name]) who is Chief of the Husk Faces who travels about in the forests. He says that things [masks] which they will have patterned after them shall have the power to aid human beings dwelling on the earth. And they shall test [pattern] them by the mode and form of his body. He will give assistance to all persons who shall be born."

"It is he also who shall be at the head [lead] of all the Humpbacked Beings [Hondu?i?]. Customarily it shall be they [Husk Faces] who shall go in the lead when they [the maskers] go from place to place. [The Husk Faces shall precede the Society of Faces in their semiannual round of the settlements.] And as soon as the people are aware that the Humpbacked Man-beings are on the point of going from place to place, customarily a kettle of corn soup shall be prepared in whatever place they have been invited to come professionally. And, indeed Djinagáihhäh [Whistler] shall be in the lead, and next to him shall be the woman Gawęno?s (Voice in Water)."

"So thus it is that at all times they are just seven brothers and sisters; and indeed all these persons visit the planted fields of human beings, as does also their pet dog Dehhótha:?, "Echo" [The Barker], which they and the Little People own equally.

[The Little People, or pygmies (djigaähęhwa?) and their ritual, the Dark Dance, pertain also to hunting luck.]

"So then it shall be that whenever we have some business relating to the Great Darkness (Deyodahsǫndaigígo:nah) to transact, the two [humans and pygmies] shall have an equal share in it. And they [the Little People] will come a day's journey [coming from so far away that it takes overnight] to hear the songs [of Dark Dance]. Furthermore, they also have a hand (oʔnyaʔ) [a fetish, *otchinah-gę́ʔdaʔ*] which one must use when one gathers medicine.

"And thus it is that the care of all kinds of things that grow on the earth—the various kinds of medicines—devolves upon us, the Little People. We are the ones who have all the power which is necessary to make all of the medicinal plants grow peacefully and healthfully. So thus it is that we will help human beings, together with the full complement of our co-workers.

"Moreover, it shall be the custom for native tobacco to be provided when it is needed. "Whistler" and "Voice-in-Water" are at the head [lead] of the Husk Faces, and the Little People are at the head of the medicines. What is more, the ceremony of the great darkness shall be performed as a night feast regularly. And entirely native tobacco shall be used whenever we shall remember them! And this too, whenever the water drum shall sound the word shall go forth for even ten nights' distance, when the rite of the Little People [the Dark Dance] commences. [It is believed that the sound of the water drum travels and can be heard at a distance of ten sleeps where the Little People hear it and start immediately.]

So thus is that thing [end].

Chief John Buck, brother of Joshua, with whom Hewitt discussed the previous text in 1928, added the following notes on the costume of the Husk Faces and on their prerogatives and duties. (John Buck's remarks in Onondaga were translated for me by Simeon Gibson in 1941.)

Costume and Duties

From this account it appears that the Husk Faces probably wore, at one time, a faunskin mantle and garters of tanned hide below the knees. Deerskin is supposed to make the impersonator a swift runner when he precedes the main body of the False Face Company. The runner's duty is to discover who may be possessed with the False Face sickness.

Husk Face prerogatives are Indian tobacco and cornbread mixed with huckleberries. These things that humans have, the Husk Face craves. (This the usual contract theory of balanced desires and needs.)

Possibly the older cornhusk masks covered the entire head of the Husk Face impersonator, but within the memory of my interpreter Simeon Gibson, the husk masks have been face covers, and a cotton flour bag, or piece of cloth served as a headthrow. Buck's text follows:

> The particular way that the Husk Face is dressed.
> It would seem that the pelt of a newborn faun was the way he seemed to be dressed when the hunter first saw him at their initial meeting. Furthermore, because of the fact of the place they inhabit

in the hinterland, he [Husk Face spirit] always carries a cane [staff]. And he ties tanned deerhide about the calves of his legs; hence he is a fast runner.

He is always in a hurry, and he always calls here but briefly. Going ahead of the main body of maskers he clears the way to the places where someone may be possessed [of the False Face sickness].

That is what the Husk Face leader promised when the hunter met him. He added, "Also I [deprecatively] have the power to help the people. That is how I have promised. And [in return] Indian tobacco is what I prefer most [his particular prerogative] and also bread made from a certain maize, bread that has been mixed with huckleberries."

His head cover is made of cornhusk. Indeed his head is entirely covered with corn husk.

Hewitt's conversations with Chief John Buck in June of 1926, and two years later, inspired Chief Buck to relate two versions of his own. The first is a Cayuga legend, dictated in Onondaga, concerning a miniature Husk Face and its habitat in a rocky ravine, and its relation to the crops, fruits, and the deer. The text was redone for me by Simeon Gibson in January, 1941.

TEKAHSTǪYO:GĘH, MINIATURE HUSK FACE FROM THE ROCKY RAVINE

Hunters are camping where [they have been] for so long as they have been hunting. And it seems that one of them returned ahead of the others and stirred up the fire. He kindled the fire. As he was blowing the coals, he heard a noise and stood up. He thought it was the wind, which is the way that he perceived it. It seemed for a while that what he heard sounded like that. Again he stood up, he sensed that it was behind his back, and that time he turned around and saw him—way down low. The hunter spoke to him saying, "Who are you?" "I myself am a little Bushy Head [Husk Face]."

And at the time he spoke, he said to the hunter, "Will you please do it, give me cornbread [begging], that is lyed with the hulls off and mixed with huckleberries? And tomorrow at noon go there in the direction of the nearest hill yonder. There from the far side of yonder hill we all will drive the deer up the slope to the edge of the hill. And there it shall be fulfilled as you do what I have told you so that you may fell [with bow and arrow] a few in number. And therefore I will say, "I thank you, since we have been hungry for a long time, and you shall be lucky from now on into the future."

And then at that time the man, that is the hunter, spoke, saying, "Whereabouts do you come from?" Then the Husk Face spoke, "Amid rocks in a ravine is the name of the place where we all reside."

It was toward evening in the gathering dusk that he saw a diminutive Husk Face at the place where they were camping. When he awoke he went there to the place where the Husk Face had directed him it would be fulfilled. He went to the slope of the hill and stood there waiting a little while. Now the deer did come up over the crest and descend toward him. He did kill them, and so it was fulfilled just as the one called Ogahgwę́ʔodaʔ, "Black Eyes" [the small Husk Face] had promised.

There were three loaves of bread that the hunter gave to the Husk Face. And then he [Husk Face] said, "I thank you."

This is a tale that the Cayuga people used to relate.

The second myth of the Husk Face that Chief John Buck narrated was recorded by Hewitt at Brantford, Canada, in June, 1928, and revised the following year; it is a remarkable account of deer hunting. Again the title is in Cayuga, but the text is Onondaga, which Simeon Gibson redictated for me in January, 1941.

HADJÍHSAʔ OGAHGWIYOʔDAʔ (CAYUGA), THE BUSHY HEAD WITH BLACK CIRCLES AROUND HIS EYES

It seems that a man is getting ready to go away. Now he set out to go hunting. And at two sleeps' [overnights] distance, he camped temporarily overnight high on a hilltop. There at that place he completed putting on a roof [built a lean-to]. At that time he said, "Two days out ought to be sufficient. I shall rest to regain my strength and feel fresh." Having said it, he took a rest then and there.

And so three is the number of days that he saw dawn. It was a beautiful day. Right then he got ready and then he said, "Toward the sunrise I shall commence walking." Then he set out. So it was accomplished, it was toward the sunrise that he went.

At the time he was traversing a hill, climbing upgrade; about half way of the slope where he was at the moment, he noticed several things like wild game running toward him. They saw him standing there and veered off toward the midsky [South]. That surprised him. "My, that is unusual. That has never happened before to me. Perhaps something is wrong."

At that point he changed direction and went off to the South. He had not walked far when he said to himself: "Therefore I shall return to where I kindled my fire [camp]."

The account continues:

He just returned in time as night fell. When he got back safely to camp, then he sat down. Now he was thinking, "There surely must be something underhanded going on." Then he took a rest. He saw the dawn. He decided to go away, so he is saying, "This time to the South [midsky] I shall walk." He made ready now and started out, proceeding to the South. He had not gone far climbing a hill, when he was walking along thinking to himself how amazed he was at how scarce was the wild game. Just then he turned in a new direction, toward the sunset [West], where he made a beeline. He had not gone far in that direction when he said to himself, "I had better return toward the place where I made my fire [camp]." He arrived there and sat down. He was continually worried and thinking a great deal. Then he fell asleep, and there where he was lying now someone spoke, saying: "I shall go in that direction midway between where the sun sinks into the water and the midsky" [south; that is, to the southwest].

He himself saw another dawn [awoke] very early in the morning when he made ready to set out. Now he left his camp. Now for a fact he made a beeline there, when he saw a height of land with many wild game running along not far off. A particular great one of the deer species stood there with a great rack of antlers. He killed it. And then being not far from where his camp was he went back that way, he dragged it, he arrived just about dusk. Right then he commenced to clean it [dress it out]; he finished preparing it; he put a pole across; and there he hung the meat [venison]. At that time he stirred up the fire: Fresh embers remained all day long that he was away. While he was yet working at the fireplace and stooping there he heard a noise. He thought, "It must be the noise of a leaf rustling." Now when he raised up from stooping, he saw that the leaf hanging [on the tree] was quite still. He thought it might be the wind that had startled him, but there was nothing doing. Now once more he returned to what he was doing at the fireplace. Now once more he heard a noise. Now he faced around in a different direction towards it [the noise]. He was kneeling forward, turtlewise, with back arched; it looked almost human. At that time he [the hunter] spoke, "Where do you hail from?"

"Degahstǫniyó:gę, 'Between Two Rocks' [or] 'A Rocky Gorge,' is its name. That is the place where I [deprecative] [we] all reside."

Then the hunter said, "Truly that is it" [That is right, indeed]. "Now then," the person resumed, "I am going to tell you that our great leader of the Husk Faces ordered me to come. That which you have, namely cornbread, it is called, which has huckleberries mixed in it, is what we crave most. It has been a long time since we have had it to eat."

For a fact that is what happened: He gave him two loaves of

bread. Then at that time the Husk Face said, "Tomorrow, at halfway between sunrise and the midsky [noon] [when the sun is halfway to the zenith, about 9:30 A.M.], you should go in that direction. And then just once I am going to tell you that when you shall go home you shall tell your people that [it is] specifically for a lame back [caused by the Husk Face wanting a feast] [a kind of possession] that we can help people. If one appeals to us one must employ Indian tobacco, throwing it on the fire, and provide also two loaves of corn bread."

And now once more morning came (he saw the dawn), and he performed as instructed. He went in the direction of halfway between midsky and where the sun sinks into the water [to the Southwest]. And he had not traveled a very long time when surely wild game came running. It was fulfilled precisely as the Husk Face had said the previous day. And he killed several, as the Husk Face said, "You shall be lucky, but don't ever say, 'I am proud of myself [and can kill game any time],'[4] for it is we who control your luck, and people shall say, 'the black eyes' [ogahgwiyóʔdaʔ] who dwell in the rocky gorge [degastoyó:gęh],' whenever they speak of us."

Simeon Gibson commented: "When referring to the Husk Faces this place must be mentioned where they reside in a very narrow valley between two rocky ridges."

KINDS OF HUSK FACES

Having commented on the texts of his brother Chief Joshua Buck and having dictated the two previous myths in Onondaga, Chief John Buck distinguished three kinds of Husk Faces. These distinctions may reflect the then-current practice and are not entirely consonant with the myths. They are "(a) long-faced with projecting lower jaw; (b) round-faced; and (c) slant-faced. This one is said to be fleet of foot."

There are only three in all. It is their duty to take the lead when the Faces visit the houses, at the New Year fetes [Midwinter Festival]. Like the Faces [wooden masks], upon invitation of a sick person, they have the power and privilege to visit and blow ashes on the sick person to cure her of illness as the Faces do. Three large round loaves of cornbread must be provided. These give them great pleasure when they see them. The three [types of Husk Faces] go together. [Neither corn soup nor mush are mentioned, and Simeon Gibson did not know of their use at Six Nations.]

4. Simeon Gibson said that this means that "he should not be boastful, for it is the luck that they [the Husk Faces] gave him to get game."

I have quoted the preceding accounts of the origin of the Husk Faces at some length because such understandings have rapidly faded on the Six Nations Reserve during the present century. In 1912, Goldenweiser learned that in olden times they used to live in the East, and they went to the West. Between 1939 and 1943, when Simeon Gibson served as my interpreter, he was much interested in the stories of Chiefs Joshua and John Buck because very few of his contemporaries were aware of the origin legends of the Husk Faces. Having named several people who should know the background of their responsibilities in the Onondaga Longhouse, he turned to his wife's mother, Lucy Burning of Lower Cayuga, saying that her account was the first time that he had heard any of the old people speak of the Husk Face origins. Her version proved a direct transfer from the incident in the cosmology substituting Gajíhsaʔ for Honduʔi:ʔ in the confrontation for control of the earth. Certain elements found in the Buck versions, however, intrude: The Husk Faces have been here from creation; "I live to the *north* in a steep ravine where I tend my crops"; an offer to assist the people with their crops; volunteering to relieve sick persons by blowing; they are to be summoned by burning tobacco; agreement to stay to the North in their ravine; and to work together with the False Faces.

PERSONAL ENCOUNTERS

Although other contemporary sources seemed deficient in knowledge of Husk Face myths, several of them could quote sightings. Henry Redeye, speaker of the Coldspring Longhouse on the Allegany Seneca Reservation, related once such incident.

> The Husk Faces are said to live way out where no one ever goes in wooded ravines. [Henry said that he saw one himself one time when down in Wolf Run (a tributary of the Allegheny River) when he was hunting for ginseng roots (*djoädáwagǫ ʔokdéʔäʔ*) (*Panax quinquefolium*).]
>
> People used to see them way out in the hills. They are said to run, and they are capable of long jumps. [The one Henry saw was carrying a long cane or staff nearly as tall as himself.] They puff—blow out wind—which is their way of talking. He was built like a man, but his body was covered with fur except for his face, and the fur stood erect on top of his head, and in a ring about his face. [My interpreter added, "This is why they make the husk masks with a fringe of husks about the face to represent this halo of fur."]
>
> Others have sighted this same Gadjíhsaʔ at Wolf Run. He usually is sighted along Wolf Run ridge.
>
> Some people see them and then dream about their encounter;

> others do not dream about it. It is good luck to see one. If you dream about it afterward, you must put up a feast for the Husk Faces.

On second thought, Henry was not sure whether the Gadjihsaʔ he saw really had fur or was merely wearing a fur garment. "He was far off going away."

> The Husk Faces are supposed to eat popcorn, just as the False Faces prefer mush. False Faces, moreover, are no longer sighted; people only dream about them. Husk Faces have always been here since the beginning of things.
>
> Nor are the Husk Faces as powerful as the False Faces, nor as harmful. They also employ hot ashes in curing. But the Husk Faces cannot talk.
>
> Sometimes the Husk Faces are called in to a house alone without the wooden masks. At this time, they have a special tobacco-throwing speech. The man having charge of them, the conductor, is called hastéisthaʔ, the same as for the False Faces. They have a song and a dance peculiar to themselves. The singer beats out the tempo on a bench with a wooden stick, instead of the turtle rattle employed by the False Faces, for their dance.

THREE TONAWANDA VIEWS

Tonawanda, where Morgan worked a century before me, was still a center of traditional Seneca culture in the 1930s.

A Hunter's Adventures with the Husk Faces

Elijah David, "Twenty Pails," of the Hawk Clan then directed the activities of his moiety in the Tonawanda Longhouse. "Lige" was an herbalist as well as a ritualist, and he had worked for F. W. Waugh in 1912. Because I had Waugh's notes from the National Museum of Canada, I turned to "Lige" on a number of topics. He was also my clansman. He did not claim a personal encounter, but he knew an origin legend of the Husk Faces.

> The Husk Faces came from the woods. I heard this story the first time from Thomas Jones of the Wolf Clan. He was not my father's clansman, since my father was a Snipe. But he told me the story of the Husk Faces.
>
> Someone long ago went to the woods hunting. He hunted in the forests, but he could not find or kill any deer. Unsuccessful, he returned to his hunting camp. While he was there, someone came in. The hunter did not know him. That night this person said, "May

I stay for the night?" And the hunter answered, "Alright, you may stay here."

After supper that night, the hunter took out his tobacco pouch and offered some to his visitor so that they might smoke together. The hunter had one dog for hunting, and the visitor who had been appraising it, finally said, "I will tell you why you are unable to get any game, any deer, if you will give me that dog. I will give you good luck in hunting." "Alright," agreed the hunter.

Now this person who looked perfectly normal to the hunter said, "Tomorrow after the first meal, you go down to that big ravine in the forest and you will find me there. Then I will tell you how to hunt successfully." And the hunter said, "Alright."

Now the hunter went out that morning to the deep ditch, and he walked. And presently he saw another man walking and looking about as if he expected someone were coming. When this person saw the hunter, he said, "So now then you come down into the ravine." And the hunter replied, "Alright. Come along with me and you will see the other people" [the Husk Faces].

The hunter walked a little way and discerned men who appeared to be playing lacrosse. Seeing them, he tarried to watch the play. But the old Gadjihsaʔ said, "Come on, you have a dog to give to me." They went into the ravine where the hunter saw some female Gadjihsaʔ and another male.

The old Husk Face, who had met the hunter, killed the dog. Then he made soup out of it. He added dumplings to the soup. After that he said, "I will now give you good luck [a charm] for your hunting."

The Husk Face gave the hunter many pieces of skin with the hair intact, swatches from all of the animals. "When you go hunting, choose the kind of hair found on the animal you wish to kill." The hunter agreed, "Alright, I will accept them."

The hunter returned home. The next day he went hunting. He looked at the skin of the animal that he wanted to kill that day. When he went hunting he killed many of the species. There was lots of good meat that time.

Da: neʔho [That is it.]

Chief Barber Black

The Sachem of the Bear Clan at Tonawanda, was alone in placing the Husk Faces in the West, but he agreed with the others that they lived amid rocks. He said that they emerge from crevasses in the stone wall.

> Someone saw them go in there. The man followed and looked inside. It was full of Gadjihsaʔ. They were cooking soup with dump-

lings. That is why at Tonawanda we put up soup with dumplings in it for them.

They carry a stick and bump the ground when they walk. [They are earth shakers like the False Faces.] They have no language, unlike the False Faces, but they blow ashes on a person's head in curing. They are always in a hurry to finish, going out running in great leaps to the next house, where they repeat the action before going home, which they are always anxious to reach. They give as an excuse some necessity for getting home—to till crops which are immense, and this excuse becomes a prophecy for the next season on earth.

Chief Henan Scrogg

During the 1930s, Chief Henan Scrogg, Sachem of the Snipe Clan at Tonawanda, preached the Handsome Lake code on the circuit of longhouses. He was a frequent visitor at the home of Jesse Cornplanter, where these two savants used my questions as a foil for comparing notes on the rituals. They were at some pains to make me get things straight. During one such session in April of 1935, the subject was Gajíhsaʔ.

Scrogg said:

If you get up in the morning and your hair is all awry, then you look like the Gajíhsaʔ. That is why they [Husk Faces] bear the same term as the husk mats on which they pile sticks in all directions. The only difference is that the masks have holes for the eyes, nose, and mouth. The idea [of the coiled mask] came from the foot mats. [This explanation accounts for the coiled braided masks and the coiled braided doormats but not the twined Husk Faces.]

Unlike the False Faces, the Husk Faces have no language.

Like the False Faces, the Husk Faces blow hot ashes in curing.

They have their own special food: They crave dumplings [o:hǫ́:staʔ]. However, at Allegany they eat popcorn.

They run with the speed of the wind, taking great leaps.

On the occasions when they appear with the False Faces [spring and fall house cleaning and] during the Midwinter Festival, they precede the False Faces. Simultaneously, two Husk Face runners traverse the houses in opposite directions, coming in both doors, crossing in the middle of the house, and going out the opposite door. [This applies principally to the longhouse.] Where there is but one door, they enter, circle, and depart. Later the real False Faces appear. Then comes the main body of Husk Faces.

These systematic remarks and what follows represent a comparative Seneca view, reflecting the experience of Cornplanter's residence in three

Seneca communities and Scrogg's knowledge gained while preaching on the circuit. Scrogg was the principal source in this interview, with comment by Cornplanter. The opening statement of this chapter is based on this interview.

> The Husk Faces are a race of agriculturists. They dwell in the place of stumps (*gahǫtgánohǫ*) where they till their fields, for the Husk Faces are an industrious people. [The Seneca view does not mention rocky ravines.] Coming as they do at the Midwinter Festival, they have great powers of prophecy. They foretell bountiful crops. Giant string beans, which climb up poles to heaven, huge squashes, long-eared corn grow in their fields about their houses where some of their women have remained because they have so many babies. [The women are named for their crops.] Their prophecies of fertility are usually fulfilled during the coming year.

Scrogg then proceeded to enlighten me on the yearly visitation of the Husk Faces to the Seneca longhouses.

Apparently Chief Scrogg had not heard Elijah David's version of the origin of the Husk Faces, nor had Cornplanter. Scrogg rationalized that the Husk Faces were an offshoot of the life supporters (*djǫhéhgǫ*) because they dress in cornhusks, "they are forever telling of planting their fields and hoeing their crops, and they represent themselves as industrious agriculturists. In short, they are messengers of the Three Sisters."

> Since the Husk Faces are the messengers of the life supporters, they have to be careful what they say [their prophecies] when they come down here because it always comes true. When they say that they have left their women up there (where they live in the West), sure enough, we have babies here in the Tonawanda settlement.
>
> [Like Chief Black, Scrogg placed them in the West. Is this because they are thought to come from Newtown to Tonawanda?]
>
> There is always someone to receive them when they come to the longhouse. They usually ask for a certain man, usually a chief. He goes out and confers with one of their women. One year, when the Husk Faces arrived at the longhouse, they made the customary prophecy—that all was growing where they live; then they sent for the last speaker whom they called out. That time Charlie Hotbread was the Husk Face dressed as a woman. Brooks was the man he named. Hotbread, in the role of the old Husk Face woman, directed his speaker, the announcer, to tell the longhouse assembly for Brooks to come outside of the longhouse because his wife has come after him and wants to take him back after the dance to the place of the stumps in the country of the Husk Faces. (Hotbread intended this merely as a joke on Brooks.) Brooks came out of the longhouse after the dance and talked with his supposed Husk Face

wife, Charlie Hotbread. No one knows what was said in the conversation. Brooks returned to the longhouse and announced that his wife had come after him to take him back to her country. People in the longhouse were startled at this message. They remarked to one another: "Surely he will not live the year out." And surely he died. The Husk Faces must be careful not to make rash remarks, for what they say comes true.

SUMMARY

From the preceding myths and interviews, one may summarize the attributes of the Husk Faces in Iroquois thought. They inhabit a valley filled with stumps, or a rocky ravine, where huckleberries grow. They control game animals and hunting luck. Their concern is with fertility and growth, and they are donors of the seeds of cultivated crops. Indeed, they symbolize the introduction of horticulture to the Iroquois. As creatures of wind spirits, they are invisible save for their faces; they run and leap with celerity; they are always in a hurry; they carry canes or long peeled poles; and they are earth shakers. Suspected as being abductors and cannibals, they eat dogs and love dumplings and cornbread mixed with huckleberries. Some prefer popcorn. Like the False Faces, they crave tobacco; burning tobacco appeals to them, and they savor the smoke that seals a contract.

The Husk Faces have appeared to luckless hunters as visions and in dreams. Their instructions require a visitation to their country, adherence to specific hunting directions, and exchange of gifts: swatches of game animal fur as hunting charms and reciprocally feast foods and tobacco. In their various appearances, they reveal their personal names, their attributes, and afford glimpses of the social structure. Named are "Mr. Ruffed Grouse" (Bushy Head), "Mr. Whistler" (chief) paired with "Voice in Water" (female); "Black Circles around His Eyes"; a dwarf; and a linkage with the Little People. For the Seneca, their names revealed in visitations to the longhouses are augmentatives of the crops they grow and promise. One female is named "Dumplings." As supernaturals they have an affinity with the spirit world and with death. Hence, they must be careful in their prophecies.

Powers of Curing

By analogy with the wooden faces, the Husk Faces cure by blowing ashes, but they are not considered as powerful. Specifically, they cure backache, a kind of possession. They have no language, other than puffing, and they depend on interpreters. This deficiency is more than made up by speed and strength, both as runners for the False Faces and as police during masked ceremonies. The Seneca at Coldspring Longhouse recalled some rather memorable incidents of Husk Face power.

AS POLICE

Henry Redeye recalled two memorable incidents.

> The late Jonas Titus used to talk a lot in the crowd. One time at the New Year's dance we had a fight. They had just finished giving out white flour dumplings, and Jonas had a great pail of stuff which he had received as speaker. Melvin Jackson and Newman Redeye were fighting. Jonas had set his big old-fashioned dinner pail on the north stove [on the men's side]. Melvin grabbed it and swung it at Newman. The dumplings went on the floor. Somebody stopped the fight.

Here plainly was a job for the Gajíhsaʔ. Sherman and Clara Redeye commented:

> If the Gajíhsaʔ see anyone commence a fight in the longhouse, they go crazy and stop them. They hit the fighters with their sticks. Years ago someone nearly got killed when a Husk Face hit him with a stick. A Christian Indian from up Red House-way came drunk to the longhouse to poke fun and spoil the meeting. It was the sixth night of the Midwinter Festival when the Gajihsaʔ take charge. One of them went for the drunk, but Henry caught the stick in the crook of his arm, deflecting the blow and saving the man's life; for one gets great strength when he wears a Husk Face. The masker would have killed the man had he hit him.

The practice on these occasions did not always conform to native theory. At the 1939 celebration, I asked my neighbor Charlie Butler what they did about drunks in the longhouse. He told the following story to illustrate the fact that there used to be more fights than at present.

Years ago Charlie had a gang and they all went uptown (Salamanca) on the railroad (the now-abandoned Pennsy). And they got drunk. Returning, they landed in Crick's Run east of Coldspring community and across the Allegheny River. They had a few more drinks on the way to the landing where they found the river full of floating ice. How they ever got across in two trips is still a mystery to Charlie. The ice was thick; they jumped from cake to cake; and they were unsteady. When they came up the bank on the plain by the longhouse, they found it was Husk Face night so they all had another drink, and commencing outside, they danced the Fish Song, which was going on inside, from the common clear into the longhouse through the men's door.

The officers used to post huskies at the doors to pitch out drunks. Then a free-for-all would ensue because the relatives of the drunks would pitch into the doormen when they attempted to throw out the rowdies [such as Charlie and his friends]. And vice versa, the relatives of the doormen would pitch into the relatives of the rowdies until everyone was fighting in the middle of the room.

CHILDREN AND THE FACES

Children fear the Faces, both wooden and husk. The Husk Faces, however, have generated fewer cases of reported hysteria and possession. Some children were formerly told that the masks would hurt them, even bite them, and the practice of frightening children by threatening that the maskers will get them is generally deplored. Simeon Gibson's children were not members of either branch of maskers, and he kept no masks in the house in recent years. However his sister Jemima, a Cayuga matron of some prominence, took the children to visit a family near the Seneca Longhouse, at Six Nations:

The Senecas were having their annual round of the houses. One of the girls suddenly saw a Husk Face looking in through the window, and she almost fainted. My sister Jemima was with them in the house and she saw the Gajíhsaʔ, too. She told the girls not to be frightened because this was only a man wearing the Husk Face mask over his face, that the False Faces were coming not far off and not to be alarmed. And then the children quieted down, and the householders commenced to clear the floor for the coming of the Haduʔi:ʔ. [Although adults may express amusement at pictures of masks,] children are very much afraid of maskers, and they will hide anyplace they can get when they see them coming through the village. . . . The maskers do not chase frightened children when they catch them in the open because they know that the children are really afraid of them. . . . When children misbehave and want to go upstairs all of the time, contrary to a parent's wishes, some parents hang a mask at the head of the stairs to frighten the children into behaving. They warn the children that if they repeat their misbehavior, they will hang the mask up again. [Although these remarks of Gibson's apply mainly to the wooden masks, the discussion began with Husk Faces.]

Children who continually venture into the bush are warned that they might see Haduʔi:ʔ out there. This serves to keep them home. Old people used to warn us not to frighten the children too much with the mask, lest the children get sick. [Although Simeon knew of cases where parents put on a mask to frighten children, he thought this too much.] It might make the child sick. Children remember for a long time if they ever see a mask.

The old people used to tell us that some children are nervous. If you scare them too much, they might get sick. [This relates to cases of hysteria.]

Membership: The Society and Its Officers

KEEPERS AND CONDUCTORS

At the Coldspring Longhouse of the Seneca Nation in the 1930s, two women and two men of opposite moieties had charge of the Husk Faces and managed their appearance at the Midwinter Festival. One of the two ladies kept the community's collection of husk masks in a huge sack. For years their keeper was Hanna or Yendi Abrams of the Beaver Clan, and she was assisted by Alice White of the Wolf Clan, in later years Fannie Stevens (Heron) and Mrs. Amos Johnny John (Beaver) kept the mask. Anyone who needed a mask for a private feast knew where to borrow it. My host, Jonas Snow (Hawk), kept one there, and he also had several husk masks at home. The property lines between public and private ownership were vague. The two women keepers had charge of providing the costumes from bags of mission donations and dressing the maskers for the great performance. They are called *hǫwęnǫhsa:ní;* the two men are called *honǫ́ste:istǫ,* "the conductors." The latter were Amos Johnny John (Wolf) and Adam Clark (Snipe). Intermoiety cooperation was the ideal not always attained. I was advised that the two sets of functionaries were chosen each year. They were not in any way perennial officers, but they tended to repeat yearly.

The reversal of sex roles and dress at the Coldspring, Newtown, and Tonawanda longhouses of the Seneca is unique. At Six Nations, the Husk Face maskers are all men. Both sexes at Coldspring carry peeled poles. The male Husk Faces enter the longhouse on their knees in advance of their "women" who enter erect. My efforts to seek an explanation in 1939 came to naught: my informant, like so many of the Seneca, seemed both ignorant and unconcerned with symbolic behavior. He said, "That's the way they do!"

A PARTICIPANT'S VIEW

During the celebration of 1950, I inquired further into these matters with one of the participants, a young woman of college age, where I was staying. The participants that year spanned three generations, from a boy of eleven to his grandfather. My own son who was with me was co-opted by his Seneca friends and clansmen. That year there were three places where the maskers dressed: at Clayton White's, north of the longhouse, at Yendi Abrams's, and at her son's house across the road.

I inquired: "Who furnishes all the masks and costumes?" I was told that "there is an old woman who has charge of that from one year to the next. Yendi Abrams has most of the masks." My informant's father interposed, "Some, in fact most of them have their own [masks], and some are kept at Yendi's the year round for the ceremonies. Yendi is the keeper of the masks for the whole community—of both the wooden masks and the husk faces."

As to the purpose of the outlandish dress that people assume, I was told that "these people in overalls, old clothes, with pillows stuck inside of them, some to look like exaggerated pregnant women, others looking like men. That is the point. It is more of a disguise. Now, that is the main idea—to disguise yourself so that people will not know you."

My inquiries regarding reversal of sex roles were confirmed. More of this will come out in describing the performance.

15. Props to the Ceremony

Ritual Equipment

A cornhusk mask and a peeled, or unbarked, pole of five feet are the principal items of Husk Face equipment. Hoes, wooden paddles for stirring ashes, and cornbread paddles are sometimes seen, particularly at Six Nations (Shimony 1961, 149).

COSTUMES

The outlandish costumes that the maskers now affect are secondary to the masks themselves. The maskers no longer wear the traditional fawnskin nor the deerskin leggings and garters of mythology that are supposed to impart the speed of the wind to runners. These traditional accoutrements are recalled only by miniature groups of Husk Face dancers, toy replicas in cornhusks dressed in traditional garb and posed in antics known to ritual, which craft workers fashion at Six Nations Reserve for sale to museums, collectors, and tourists (Plate 15-1).

TYPES OF MASKS

Technically, Iroquois cornhusk masks are of two types: of coiled braids and twined. Specimens of the coiled variety predominate in museum collections, and twined masks are rare, comprising but three percent (two out of forty-nine) in the Museum of the American Indian collection, which holds the largest series of Iroquois masks that were field collected. I am indebted to my former student Marlene Martin for her study of this important series. One hardly ever encounters a twined mask worn in the ceremonies, and the art of twining cornhusks into tobacco trays, salt bottles, moccasins, and masks is all but obsolete. I did record the process of twining a cornhusk tray from Ella T. Jimmerson, one of the many descendants of the white woman of the Genesee, at Coldspring in 1933. She was then in her seventy-ninth year and was said to be the sole practitioner of the art (Plate 15-2). Besides Ella Jimmerson (also Mrs. Redeye), there was then at least one old lady at Cattaraugus still twining masks. Only the coiled variety was made at Six Nations and on other reserves in 1940.

A third kind of Bushy Head, or wooden Gajíhsaʔ, has a smooth wooden face, au naturel or painted a light color with red markings to delineate eyebrows, eye accents, nostrils, and mouth. Known specimens originated at Six Nations Reserve, on Grand River, Canada, in 1907–23 (National Museum of Man, Cat. No. III-I-225). One was commissioned by M. Barbeau at Wyandotte, Oklahoma, in 1911 and was made by Jackson Jamieson, a native of Ohsweken, Six Nations Reserve, Ontario, who was then living on the Seneca Reservation in Oklahoma (Plate 15-3). Two others, III-I-90

Plate 15-1. A: Cornhusk toy replicas of Husk Face and False Face dancers by Isabell Skye, Six Nations Reserve. Diorama in Schoharie Museum of the Iroquois Indian. Christina B. Johannsen photo. B: "Fuzzy Hair" (Husk Face) Society. Painting by Ernest Smith, Seneca artist of Tonawanda. Schoharie Museum of the Iroquois Indian. Christina B. Johannsen photo.

A

B

Plate 15-2. Ella T. Jimmerson, sole practitioner of the art of twining cornhusks, Allegany Reservation, 1933.

Plate 15-3. A wooden-face "Bushy Head" from Oklahoma. C. M. Barbeau, collector, 1911. NMM, Cat. No. III.I.225. Courtesy National Museum of Man, Ottawa.

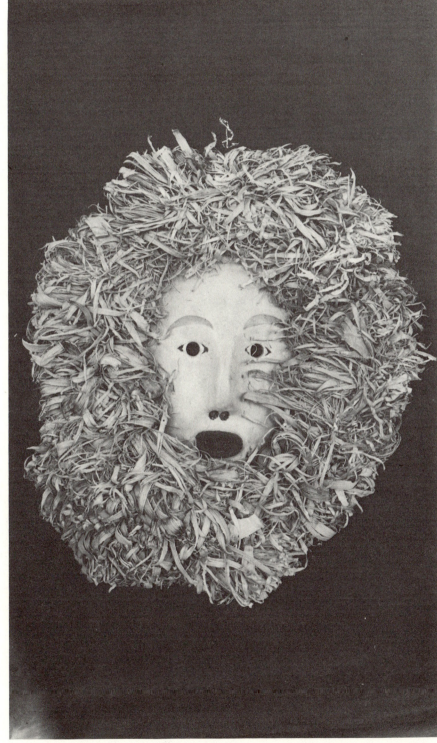

Plate 15-4. Coiled and braided Husk Faces from the Allegany Seneca. A: Top, a "grandmother." B: Bottom, a "grandfather." Fenton Collection, MAI-HF.

(58) and III-I-936, were collected at Six Nations. A fourth specimen, in the New York State Museum, was collected by M. R. Harrington from Albert Silversmith, an Onondaga at Six Nations Reserve (NYSM prefire, No. 4448; postfire, No. 37018; Plate 2-19B).

Working in cornhusks is a women's craft. Although women produce cornhusk masks, men predominantly wear them. As with wooden masks, they come in two sizes, full scale and miniature. They are also made to fit small boys. The miniatures are dream objects. They also appear at the Midwinter Festival, riding along on larger masks, or as faces on husk dolls that represent the babies of the Husk Face people. These are supposed to bring lots of babies to the Seneca people.

TECHNIQUE OF BRAIDING AND COILING

I shall rely on Martin's previously mentioned study for the technique of braiding and coiling. Three strands of husk, sometimes four, or even five are braided to form a rope. The technique then is to wind and sew the rope into a concentric circle leaving the center open. The wind starts at the center. It takes three of these circles—two for the eyes, and one for the mouth. The three pieces are sewn together to form the face. To a degree, sometimes exaggerated, the winding and sewing is done so that the openings are raised and the piece forms a cone. This is particularly true of the mouthpiece that is larger.

The rudimentary face is then framed with a braid that circles the whole with one or two courses. To this is added an outer and thicker braid into which bits of cornhusk are inserted to form a fringe that frames the entire face and imparts the bushy look.

The nose is formed by rolling a long, narrow piece of cornhusk around something firm, such as a corncob or folded cornhusk, as in making cornhusk dolls. The knobs for "tears" are made by rolling cornhusk into a wad and wrapping it with husk (Plates 15-4, 15-5A, B).

The artist has the option of adding decorations to this basic pattern of braided and coiled husk mask. One can add a spot of ceremonial red paint to each cheek or add the knobs as tears at the eyes. Such masks are said to represent women (Plate 15-5B). At Six Nations black-felt eyebrows and eye linings are favored (Plate 15-6). Even finer examples of Husk Faces are found in European museums (Plate 15-7).

TWINING

The technique of twining cornhusk has never been described in the literature. From my observations of and tutorials with Ella T. Jimmerson in 1933, the essential steps are as follows: In the fall after a husking party,

Plate 15-5. Twined and braided and coiled Husk faces from the Cattaraugus Seneca, 1910. A: Left, twined with fringe at eyes. Right, a senior citizen of the Husk Face Society. Note the puffy cheeks and red mouth. A. C. Parker, collector, NYSM, Cat. Nos. 36924, 36922. B: Left, a "grandfather" in the twined medium; right, a "grandmother," braided and coiled with "tears." NYSM. From Parker 1910, Plate 23, p. 82.

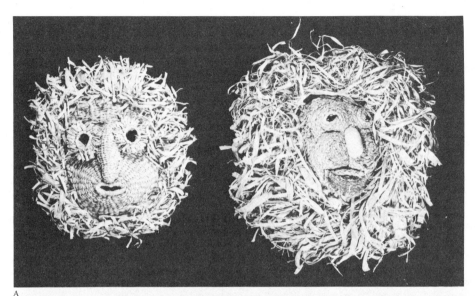

A

B

Plate 15-6. The Grand River baroque style at Six Nations favors eye liners, lolling tongues, and conical whistling mouths. A: Collected by J. N. B. Hewitt, 1916. USNM, Cat. No. 381404. B: Cayuga Husk Face in later baroque style. Collected by F. G. Speck, ca. 1940. MAI-HF, Cat. No. 18/4746.

Plate 15-7. *Even finer examples of Husk Faces are found in European museums. A braided and coiled example, ca. 1900. MME F/M, Cat. No. 10264. Photo courtesy Municipal Museum of Ethnology, Frankfurt am Main, Germany.*

old women and young girls eager to learn gather up the shucks from the longest and straightest ears and take them home. Only the inner husks from the white or squaw corn are used. These are then soaked to make them pliable.

First, the longest and smoothest leaves, having been well soaked, are drawn out with the fingers to feel out any defects. The inner leaves will be wide and silky. The butt ends and tops are trimmed to an even length with scissors. Then four leaves of similar texture are selected and torn to widths of an inch. The distal phalange of the thumb serves as the unit of measure. To produce strips of consistent width, the woman holds the leaf between opposing thumb tips and the second joints of the index fingers; a sudden outward thrust of the hands rips the leaf longitudinally along the grain (Figure 15-1A).

Weaving starts with a nucleus that consists of four evenly matched strips of cornhusk that are placed in a hollow overlapping square and then bent double. The ends are inserted through the adjacent member loop and interlocked to form a square nucleus or knot that is pulled up tight (Figure 15-1B, C, D). This same technique forms the nucleus of Pima and Papago basketry (Kissel 1916, 206–8). The ends of the four bent-double and interlocked strips of cornhusk now make eight warps, each of which in turn is split or divided in half to form sixteen radiating warps.

Forming the Nucleus
To form the nucleus, fold four strips of husk longitudinally along the midrib of the grain. Grasp one element midway between thumb and forefinger of the left hand; place a second strip at right angles to it (Figure 15-1B). Add a third element parallel to the first on top of the second with its tip toward the butt of the first. This third element passes over the second and at right angles to it, whereas the first was under it (Figure 15-1C). Now add a fourth element parallel and above the second, passing over the first and under the third (see schematic drawings of these steps (Figure 15-1D)). This is the nucleus of any plaited, over-one-under-one basket bottom.

By bending the end of each numbered element in turn over its transverse element, or elements, toward its other end (Figure 15-1E), in a counterclockwise direction and tucking the end of the last element through the loop made by the first, a square interlocking joint is made. When this knot is drawn tight and the ends are evened, the nucleus is complete (Figure 15-1F, G).

"Once the interlocking nucleus is dry," Ella Jimmerson assured me, "it will never come apart." Two elements, the ends of a single doubled element, protrude in four directions. These eight elements are spread fanwise, and each in turn is rent between thumb and forefinger of the opposing hands (Figure 15-1H). This makes sixteen warp elements that are spread to radiate in all directions. Now the twining can commence.

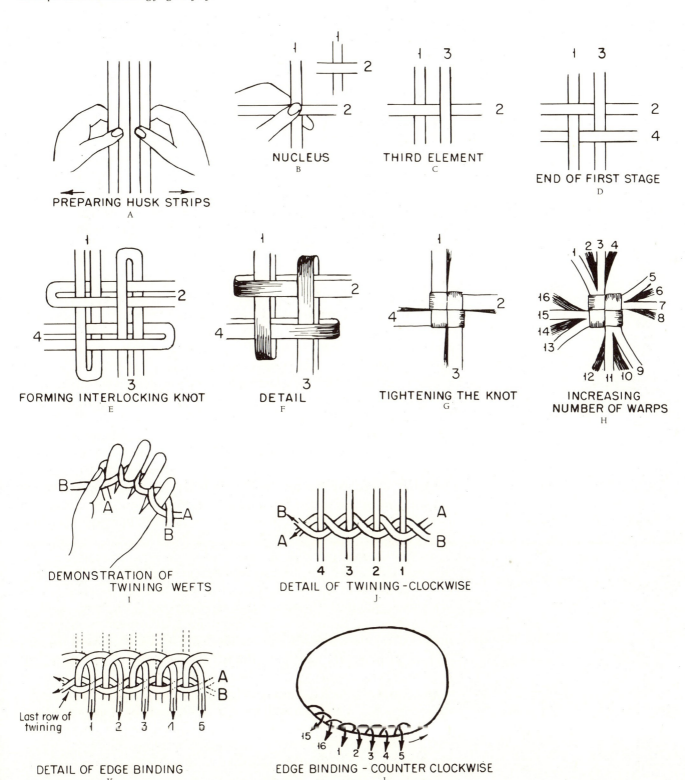

Figure 15-1. Details of twining cornhusk. A: Producing strips of consistent width. B–D: Forming the nucleus or knot. E–G: Steps in drawing the knot tight. H: Splitting the eight warp elements to make sixteen. I: Twining technique demonstrated using fingers of left hand. J: Detail of twining. K-L: Binding details.

Twining Technique

Ella demonstrated the twining technique using fingers of her left hand as warps and strips of cornhusk twisted between thumb and forefinger of her right hand as wefts. It is important to keep the husk damp while working it. She crossed the ends of two wefts, a and b, and pinched them between her left thumb and proximal knuckle. She then passed the end of the upper weft b inside her palm and between the interstices of her first two fingers, letting the end dangle down the back of her hand. The other element, a, was brought forward from the backside between the first and second fingers toward her binding the first element and then passing back between her second and third fingers. Element b was now brought toward her between her second and third fingers binding the preceding element that passed in the opposite direction. And she passed element b out between her third and fourth fingers. Each time a weft is brought between two warps it is twisted counterclockwise toward the weaver and pulled down hard, racking down its predecessor and binding it in place. It is apparent that in twining, two wefts are used simultaneously, and that each time they pass around opposite sides of a warp, they precede each other alternately, so that they are continually twisted one over the other toward the weaver as the work progresses (Figure 15-1I).[1]

Ella Jimmerson explained to me that the preceding demonstration was the method employed by her grandmother in teaching her. In turn, Ella had taught at least two other Seneca ladies who seem not to have put their lessons into practice. The fingers are used as warps to clarify what is an apparent puzzle to the beginner watching a proficient weaver twine wefts about husk warps so rapidly that the details are obscured by the motion of her fingers. Once the beginner mastered the detail of the weave, using her fingers as warps, Ella turned to the husk nucleus (Plate 15-2). She kept an extra nucleus (it lies on her left knee) in case the first was ruined in teaching.

Her weaving instructions, as I learned them, follow: "Hold the nucleus of warps in the left hand. Select two dampened wefts from the stock laid out parallel in your lap and cross them between two warps selected as the place of beginning." I observed that the long end of the lower weft (1) extends down and away from the basket bottom. (The inside is toward the worker.) The upper weft (2) is held down with the left thumb; it is twisted counterclockwise and passed to the right of the first warp element, out and away from the weaver. The first weft is then caught up, twisted counterclockwise with the right thumb and forefinger, drawn back toward the weaver to the right of the first warp, binding the previous weft in place. It is then passed out and away from the weaver, this time between

---

1. For plain twined weaving over single warps, see O. T. Mason, 1903, 190, Type E, and p. 232; also H. H. Roberts, 1929, 146. The latter study concerns San Carlos Apache basketry.

the second and third warp elements. It is dropped. "Now catch up the second weft, twist it, and pass it to the right of the second warp element bringing it toward the weaver, and then out to the right of the third warp element." Thus, the weaving proceeds in a clockwise direction providing the work is kept the same side up. This is quite important, Ella insisted, to insure that the knots are all on the inside of the work (Figure 15-1J).

Initial Circuit
This initial circuit of the warps is the most difficult because the beginnings of the wefts must be held down with the left thumb until a complete circuit is made and the ends are secured by the second spiral of wefts. Further, in making the first round, considerable care must be exercised in determining which warp elements are to be used in succession. Ella pointed out, as mentioned, that there are four warp elements extending from each loop of the nucleus, two upper and two lower. One must use up a unit of four elements before passing to the next four immediately adjacent on the right. It is well to select the upper left element as Warp 1 and the one beneath it as Warp 2, the next upper as 3, and the last lower as 4 (Figure 15-1H). (If one selects the first two upper elements as Warps 1 and 2, the transition from 2 to 3 will be too great and spoil the appearance of the weave.) This problem is solved at the end of the first round. By then the order of warps has been determined. The next obtrusive trouble is the weft joint.

Extending the Wefts
At the end of the first circuit, the wefts will be shorter, and as the basket grows, one or more joints become necessary in each circuit—the number growing as the work enlarges. This is because of the limited length of the husk strips available for wefts. Joints should be made on the inside of the basket or mask. Whenever a weft nears the end, or whenever the weft becomes too short to weave, the short-weft element is drawn toward the weaver between two warps, binding down the alternate weft element that has just passed in the opposite direction, and another weft element is selected from the supply in the worker's lap. Or it may be held temporarily in the teeth, and its butt end is twisted into the proximal end of the working weft. A deft twist and the natural cohesiveness of the wet cornhusk will tie them until the other weft element has passed over and bound it. Similarly, joints are made in the warp elements from time to time as the work grows in diameter beyond the initial radii.

The basket, bottle, or mask is shaped with the thumbs from the inside, and the shape and diameter may be constricted by drawing the warps up toward the weaver. However, in making a pail or jug bottom, one must keep the warps flat until the bottom diameter is attained. Then the warps are bent up sharply, and the sides may be fashioned.

Binding

Binding the rim calls for a reversal of tactics. When the desired dimensions have been achieved, there will be a number of loose ends of protruding warps. Beginning with the warp last passed by the twined wefts, Ella turned the basket over in her left hand, pinching down the wefts with the thumb of her left hand. She grasped the last warp in her right hand and passed it toward the inside of the basket behind the warp immediately adjacent in a counterclockwise direction and out between the second and third warps. The second warp was passed behind the third and out between the third and fourth warps in the direction from which the twining had proceeded. Each time, the warp is drawn down hard. Thus, she continued binding down the warps until the cycle was completed. The sixteenth warp was poked under the loop made by the first as it passed behind the second warp. The ends are all pulled taut and the work let stand for a week until thoroughly dry. Then all of the loose ends may be snipped off, and the basket is ready for use (Figure 15-1 L).

Ella Jimmerson assured me that these twined husk baskets and bottles last a family a lifetime.

For a tray or basket, the task of twining cornhusk is relatively uncomplicated, but twining a mask calls for greater skill and is more complex. The weaver starts with the nose, and creating the apertures for the nostrils, eyes, and mouth makes considerable demands on the skill of the artisan. A second or third nucleus may be required for the mouth and eyes. This means joining several sets of irregularly radiating warps with wefts. One mask at the Museum of the American Indian (22/4271) from Cattaraugus that Martin studied seems to have been mde in two basic sections: a mouthpiece and an eyepiece, which are joined. The warp ends form a stubble on the cheeks that the Seneca say makes it a "grandfather.

The twining technique admits of some interesting variations when weaving Husk Faces. A twined mask by Orphie Redeye, of Allegany, made about 1919 appears to have started from a single nucleus near the nose (Fenton Collection, MAI-HF, Cat. No. 20/2835). Smooth-faced, it represents a young woman. Eyebrows may be indicated by painting stubble ends left protruding over the eyes, and a round red spot may be painted on each cheek, indicating a person bound for the ceremonies at the longhouse (Plate 15-5).

The fringe on twined masks is attained by extending warps and not trimming them in binding the rim and by inserting added members of cornhusk in the binding. Some specimens are finished without fringe around the face and chin, only as hair at the top, whereas others have a complete halo with the fringe ends pointing in a clockwise circle.

PERTINENT VOCABULARY

This apparent diversion to describe what has become a lost art among the Iroquois may be concluded by listing some pertinent vocabulary.

Seneca
    Husk Face   Gajíhsaʔ (-jihs(a) :Kajihsaʔ [Chafe 1963, 1967 #851])
    Twined   ganǫshäʔ
    Salt bottle   ganǫhshäʔ djikheʔdaʔ
    Coiled   deganǫnyǫgádaseʔ
    Twining   waʔǫtwada:seʔ, "she goes around (with wefts)"
    Binding   eyǫntwada:seʔ, "to go around,"
                               ęsatwada:seʔ, "to round the bend, to circle a chair, to bind something"
    Miniature mask   Gagǫhsaʔ niwaʔa
                               gajihsaʔ niwaʔa
    Husk   ononyaʔ
Onondaga (Cayuga) of Six Nations
    "Black circles around eyes"   ogahgwiyoʔdaʔ, (JNBH Neg. No. 987-b-16)
    Husk   ono:yaʔ (S. Gibson)
    Husk Face (coiled)   (USNM #221, 153) µwäsiʔdagewaʔthaʔ gajíhsaʔ, "foot wiper,"
                               µdawdwęnahä:ʔgwęʔ gajíhsaʔ, "guardian Husk Face"

16. The Great Husk Face Drama

Appearances and Rituals of the Husk Faces

The Husk Faces make both private and public appearances. During the year, and especially at midwinter, they participate in private feasts held to treat some person who has had a particular dream involving them, or they respond to treat an uncured sickness on referral by a clairvoyant. For some patients, renewal of these cures is an annual event, which must not go past the Great Ceremonial Mark at midwinter. Their public appearances as heralds for the False Faces during the spring and autumn visitation of the houses has already been described. It remains to review the great drama when they appear en masse to climax the Midwinter Festival. My notes are most extensive on their yearly appearance at Coldspring Longhouse, which I witnessed several times; for Newtown on Cattaraugus, I rely on Sturtevant and others. While resident at Tonawanda for two and one-half years during the 1930s, I was present on at least one occasion. Information on Six Nations is from Simeon Gibson, Speck (1949), and Shimony (1961); and Onondaga, NY is after De Cost Smith (1888) and Blau (1966).

HUSK FACE NIGHT AT COLDSPRING

Husk Face night on the sixth day of the Midwinter Festival at Coldspring is a highly structured affair. The pattern of sequence that governs the program is always more or less the same. The details depend on the talents of the participants. Although Skinner (1925) preceded me and wrote a sketch of mask usages, I was the first to outline the daily program of the Midwinter Festival and isolate its major patterns (Fenton 1936).

In the gathering dusk of a winter's afternoon, the lads quit playing snow snake, and people converge on the longhouse to fulfill the ceremonial obligations of medicine societies and to enjoy an evening of social dances while waiting for the Husk Faces.

This is the last opportunity to put up one's ceremonies, "lest one's head be forever stuck to the ceremony" by failure to fulfill. It is an evening of frenzy as well as pleasure. It is also a homecoming, and visitors arrive from Newtown, the other reservation of the Seneca Nation, from Tonawanda, and from Six Nations. It is always a big affair at Coldspring. This is the last night that the False Faces go about the houses and come to the longhouse to compete in an impromptu dance contest. To keep things going in the proper way, the two headmen and two headwomen, one from each moiety, appoint a man from their respective moieties to serve as floor manager for the evening's events. These two arrange for singers, enlist lead dancers, place and remove benches as needed, and prompt the speakers.

The Ritual Pattern

Meanwhile, the two matrons in charge of the Husk Faces co-opt another man to enlist and take charge of the maskers.

Various medicine society rites go on simultaneously in opposite ends of the longhouse. There is always a sequence of Bear dances. Alice White, of the Wolf Clan, invariably put up a personal rite and received ashes from the Husk Faces who dance in circles about their peeled poles, blow, and depart.

Small boys dressed as False Face beggars enter in twos and threes to beg for tobacco, cigarettes, and to dance. They point a rattle at some older man who knows their songs. Their presence soon builds into a dance contest that usually features an outsider from Canada or Cattaraugus.

Three Traverses of Masked Runners. All of this goes on while waiting for the main event. Presently the speaker announces, "Watch out for the Husk Faces." This warning is to dancers, beggars, and anyone on the floor that the runners will presently burst into the longhouse from opposite ends, rush through the room knocking down anyone unfortunate to be in their path, and exit, banging doors.

There are two traverses of the Husk Face runners a half-hour apart, commencing about nine o'clock. Someone of the headmen shouts a warning: *haiʔ haiʔhaiʔ!* At each entrance the main party of the Husk Faces is drawing closer. The whole procedure is reminiscent of the "Woodsedge protocol" of runners announcing visiting embassies (Fenton 1978c, 319).

At their third traverse, the Husk Face runners break up the dance and quiet the singers. This means that the main party of maskers has arrived.

Meanwhile, announcements are going forward of the morrow's events: appointment of collectors of food, singers, and dance leaders. At this juncture the managers clear the longhouse floor.

Signal Arrival. A great din of rubbing staves down the clapboards of the building signals the arrival of the Husk Faces as a body. This is reminiscent of beating a house to drive away the soul of a tortured victim in the seventeenth century. (This custom has fallen away at the new longhouse erected in the Steamburg resettlement area since the U.S. Corps of Engineers built the Kinzua Dam and backed up the waters of the Allegheny River to inundate Coldspring in flood seasons. It is thought that the Husk Faces might damage the new building, just as the False Faces are discouraged from rubbing rattles on varnished doors of new houses.)

The Kidnapped Interpreter as Prophet. The two Husk Face runners as messengers return inside the longhouse to kidnap an old man to interpret their message. Often as a ruse to heighten tension, the first captive interpreter returns to say that they took the wrong person, and he names the right one. The interpreter mocks forgetfulness, feigns a desire to revisit some Husk Face lady, and makes several retreats for information. Ultimately, he names the Husk Face leaders.

Finally, the interpreter delivers the Husk Face prophecy. It invariably deals with bountiful crops on the far side of the earth, and it speaks to some issue of the moment.

Curing Songs on Request. An appointed singer, often the interpreter, is prepared to sing the three curing songs of the Husk Face males. Only men may assume this role. The singer strikes the floor and calls to them to enter. While the other Husk Faces wait without, the male Husk Faces treat any person who regularly relates to them as patient—it is the same people year after year.

Maskers. Then the interpreter leads in the main body. The male Husk Faces stoop to one knee; their women follow erect and sit on the singers' bench where the managers have moved it aside to await their requested dances.

Two Favorite Dance Songs. Toward the close of his hesitating discourse, the interpreter announces that the visiting Husk Faces request two dances: Old-time Women's Dance (for the women Husk Faces impersonated by men), and Fish Dance for the Husk Face men (who are impersonated mostly by women). The assembly may join. The ludicrous sight of men performing women's dance steps in heavy shoes contrasts with the skill and vigor of girls dressed as male Husk Faces dancing Fish Dance steps. (Later, both sexes are complimented for their respective performances.) The climax comes when the whole assembly joins in.

Feast and Departure. The Husk Faces depart presumably for Newtown on Cattaraugus or Tonawanda. For reasons stated later, they no longer return a second night for a grand social dance at the end of the midwinter ceremonies. Mush is available for the Husk Face doctors, and sometimes there is popcorn.

These are the bare bones of the ceremonial pattern. I shall now flesh out certain parts of it from observations extending from 1934 to 1968, stressing pattern over chronology and grouping observations of various years under topics as above. Clayton White's letters to M. H. Deardorff cover occasions when I was not present. Such informant testimony, including answers to queries generated by my own observations, carry the ritual pattern back before the twentieth century to the time of Handsome Lake at the close of the eighteenth century, although there are few historical records to substantiate such speculation. The ethnographic record for our own time is rich and merits extended treatment.

A Personal Rite in Public

From Skinner's 1925 account of Coldspring masking, before I regularly attended the midwinter ceremonies between 1934 and 1950, and presumeably up until her death a few years later, Alice White, of the Wolf Clan, discharged her obligation to the Husk Faces on the sixth night of the Midwinter Festival at Coldspring Longhouse. This minirite usually occurred in the evening, well before the big event. Its importance is that it became an expected part of the ritual program.

In 1934, Chauncey Johnny John, of the Turtle Clan, acted as both announcer and singer, while his son Amos, Alice's clansman, made the tobacco offering. During the prayer, the singer straddled a bench and on cue beat out the dance rhythm with a staff. Carrying shoulder-high poles, the maskers entered by the women's door, danced in circles around their staffs, tackled ashes, and blew them on their hostess, the patient. I did not observe whether they received tobacco or popcorn in payment of services before departing. Mush is sometimes provided.

I was present to observe Alice White's personal rite again in 1939. This time it was held in the late afternoon. On this occasion she conscripted Amos Johnny John, her clansman, to lead the maskers, a role later performed by his son Arthur, of the Beaver Clan. The then co-keeper of the Husk Faces, Sadie Butler, assured me that these are one-time appointments, and she added that women do not participate as maskers when the Husk Faces are curing, as in this rite, but women may participate later in the evening as dancers. Mrs. Butler went on to stress that the maskers, both husk and wooden, command and are accorded respect, saying that women should remove their hats whenever the maskers appear, and particularly when the women join the dance at the end of the line later in the evening. Otherwise, someone, even a masker, will take it off. Men are not exempt. This is the same mark of respect that one observes during the Old-time Women's Dance for the Three Sisters and the Great Feather Dance, which occur on the following day.

The timing of a personal Husk Face rite in public at the last possible moment of the Midwinter Festival occurs less frequently than similar rites for the Husk Faces held in private houses throughout the year. Such a ceremony can be held at any time of the year, but it tends to fall on the anniversary of the original cure. In 1939, a little boy was sick, and the parents consulted a famous visiting clairvoyant from Six Nations who was passing the winter at Coldspring and contributing to an intensification of orthodox observances. He told them to go through with the Husk Face ceremony.

A Husk Face Tug-of-War. The fulfillment and renewal of dreams through various rites commands greater attention at midwinter festivals on Six Nations Reserve than at Coldspring among the Seneca. The presence of Aldrich ("Ostrich") Bill at Coldspring during 1941 contributed two bits of orthodoxy to the ceremonies. On the evening of the sixth day, before the main body of Husk Faces reached the longhouse, six husk maskers entered the longhouse with "Ostrich" Bill to stage a tug-of-war by pulling against a horizontal pole in opposition, arms and feet braced, the back members of each team locking arms around the waist of the man ahead. The unmasked sponsor assumed the front position opposing three maskers with two other maskers behind him. There were two referees—the unmasked invoker of the tobacco prayer, and a sixth masker—standing on opposite sides at either end of the horizontal pole, the contestants between them. At a given signal the three maskers together pulled the sponsor and his two masked teammates across the line (Plate 16-1).

Had "Ostrich" Bill died within the following year, one can be certain that the people would have attributed his passing to the defeat of his side in the tug-of-war by the all-Husk Face team. Such was not the case. Recalling, however, the life-versus-death theme that pervades other encounters with the Husk Faces, one might have predicted such an interpretation. At the time of the contest, I heard no comment on the incident beyond the fact that the contest was a rarity at Coldspring. Perhaps I should have inquired.

Dance Contest of False Face Beggars
As the evening wears on and the crowd gathers, performances of the medicine societies give way to social dances. Meanwhile, the False Face beggars come and go, the young lads first and then the older men, and sometimes a few women who get themselves up for the lark. There is invariably one peak performance by a great dancer, frequently a visitor. People look forward to it and remember it long afterward. Although these demonstrations are variations on the theme of the wooden False Faces, these acts of clowning are associated with Husk Face night. Accordingly, I shall cite several memorable incidents that I witnessed.

"Hold My Cigar while I Dance." In 1934, a Cayuga man from Sour Springs (Upper Cayuga Longhouse) on Six Nations Reserve, then living with a Seneca woman at Coldspring, stole the show. My notes written at the time read:

> A pitch of excitement had been reached, when suddenly a man burst into the room in the role of a False Face beggar; but instead of the more orthodox ragged costume of his Coldspring counterparts and a recognizable beggar mask of wood, he wore a Halloween mask, he was smoking a cigar, he wore an old trench coat several sizes too small, and he sported a straw "boater" at a rakish angle. (False Face beggars are notably clowns, and whereas they symbolically derive their identity from mythical beings, their function is to provide amusement.) At first blush, it might appear that the visitor's behavior was a satire on the whole of pagan ritualism. In truth he had adapted modern dress to the current situation, and the comic element, the significant part of his act, was in character. Further, as a stranger living with the daughter of my host, this was his chance to validate himself with the community. Along with his tremendous sense of the ridiculous, he was somewhat sophisticated in a Western sense, at the same time that he was well versed in the traditional culture of his people. He sang most of the rituals, he was considered a fine dancer, and he preferred an Iroquoian language to English.

Plate 16-1. Husk Face tug-of-war for "Ostrich" Bill. A: The setup. B: The denouement. Photographs taken in 1941.

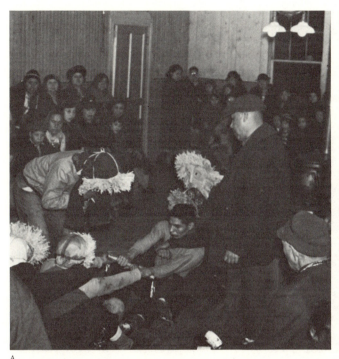

A B

The Trotting Dance was in progress and had reached the fourth or fifth song at his entrance. The file of dancers stretched down the west wall toward the women's end of the longhouse. At the other end the Bear Society quit dancing to watch the intruder, and one Bear dancer, appreciating the situation, dropped out to sing for him. In short, a False Face beggar had stolen the show. Uppermost in people's conversation was that crazy dancer from Upper Cayuga Longhouse, who the previous winter had appeared dressed as a woman who proceeded to lose her skirt while dancing. As the visitor commenced to dance, he turned to a neighbor saying, "Hold my cigar while I dance." Then he called upon the singer to heighten the tempo. His dancing, I was told, was a remarkable example of the true False Face dance style. His opening remark had doubled up the crowd in laughter. This was partly because normally False Faces do not speak.

Later Examples of Clowning. Three other short examples serve to illustrate that clowning is a regular feature of Husk Face night at Coldspring, and it probably continues to this day.

The sensation of the 1941 season was "Ostrich" Bill, also of the Six Nations Reserve, and then married to the daughter of a leading Seneca ritualist. Taking tradition at its word, namely that maskers are immune to frost and cold, even in the dead of winter, "Ostrich" startled the crowded

Plate 16-2. A naked False Face Dancer.
A: Entrance: "Ostrich" Bill. B: Dancing.

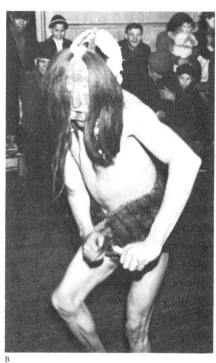

A   B

longhouse by appearing naked but for mask, moccasins, and breechclout devised from some old fur piece (Plate 16-2). Even the Coldspring people thought this a bit much.

With the return of Seneca veterans from the South Pacific, the rafia hula shirt reached Coldspring. To the False Face dancer's routine, Dick Johnny John added the bumps and grinds of nightclub performers.

The persistence of Iroquois culture and how traditional learning is transmitted is nowhere better illustrated than in the behavior of these masked clowns. After a lapse of many years, at the moon of midwinter 1968, I returned to see the ceremonies at the new Coldspring Longhouse where it had removed to Steamburg. On the sixth, or Husk Face, night, I spotted among the visitors from other reservations Johnson Jimerson (1918–84) whom I had known from my first residence on Snow Street as a young lad eager to learn. Since then, he had mastered everything of consequence concerning the cycle of longhouse ceremonies, including songs, formal speeches, and the order of ritual, becoming a speaker at Newtown Longhouse on Cattaraugus Reservation, where he had married. With him was an attractive lad, an older son. It was fascinating to witness the learning he had transmitted to the lad who presently outperformed all other False Face beggar dancers. His half-hour act was a satire on "Sumu" and the then-current karate cult. Barefoot, and dressed as a Japanese wrestler, his mask of lemon-colored wood featured the traditional crooked mouth of a False Face but was hairless. Johnson had indeed, to use his words, "raised him right," as he proudly told me in presenting the lad after the affair (Fenton 1969, 2; 1972c, 107; 1984, 15).

Content and Pattern

All of the preceding—both fulfillment of medicine society obligations and the clowning of beggars—is preliminary to the main event. The kinds of ritual activities go on from year to year, whereas their specific content changes. The pattern that governs these activities is the important thread that connects them all and gives them legitimacy. So when the speaker warns people to keep a path open for the expected Husk Face runners, this is a signal to persons who still have ceremonies to perform to get them over with, and the announcement marks a definite transition to the next phase of the ritual pattern. The total ceremony is building to a climax.

Runners. A general pattern emerges from my 1934 observations that were bolstered by comments of the Redeye family, and which can be taken as a baseline for later observations on special points. The Husk Face runners make two passes through the longhouse before their final entrance, and their course is always the same (Plate 16-3A). The announcer calls out again in the midst of a dance, "The Gajihsa? are coming."

Carrying long staves, a male Husk Face races in each door, passing each other on opposite sides of the singers' bench, and goes out by the other door slamming it shut. In 1934, the one coming from the south (women's door) ran around the singers' bench along the back of the longhouse and out the north (men's) door; his partner entered the men's door and ran down the east wall in front of the gallery.

The Course of the Husk Face Runners at Coldspring Longhouse, 1934 (Figure 16-1). Dancers stop as the Husk Face runners enter and resume after their departure. It is up to the audience and the dancers on the floor to watch out for them. Usually, someone watching shouts when he sees them coming. But people do get knocked down or shoved to the wall by the cross-checking Husk Faces.[1]

On their third entrance, the same two Husk Faces walk through the longhouse looking around to see who is there who may speak for them. Later, still, the same two enter, break up the dance, and kidnap some knowledgeable person to interpret for them.

I have already commented that the pattern of advance runners indicating the approach of a visiting people recalls Woodsedge protocol, which was widespread in the Eastern Woodlands during the seventeenth and eighteenth centuries. The act of running through the house recalls certain Seneca sky legends involving the sun looking in at the doorway of the

---

1. I was told that in the late 1920s the Husk Face runners bowled over Mrs. Alanson Skinner, wife of the anthropologist. She was standing near the women's door and apparently not paying attention to the warning shouts.

Plate 16-3. The Husk Faces arrive at the longhouse. A: First pass of the Husk Face runners. B: Leading in the crawling Husk Faces. Photographs taken in 1941.

A

B

Figure 16-1. The course of the Husk Face runners at Coldspring Longhouse during the Midwinter Festival, 1934.

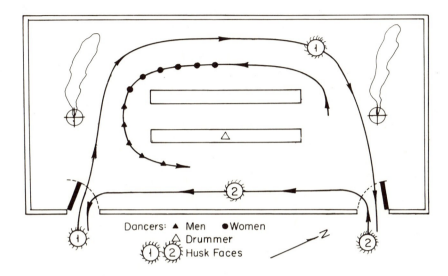

house inhabited by the Creator. Likewise, the parley that transpires between the Husk Faces and the man they choose to speak for them is not unlike the old Iroquois custom of visitors waiting outside a village at the edge of the brush until met by the resident chiefs and escorted to the principal fire, a protocol that is continued to this day in the Condolence Council for mourning and installing chiefs.

Later Observations of Husk Face Arrivals
Having established the general pattern in 1934, in later years my interest shifted to other things. In 1939, it was precise timing and participation. That year the three traverses of the Husk Face runners occurred at 9 P.M., 9:30, and 10:30. There was also a reversal of their route through the longhouse; the messenger came through the women's door east of the singers' bench, instead of west of it. On the second traverse, the courier coming down the west wall pushed an old woman who was leaving the floor after Garters' Dance onto the wall benches.

At the third entry of the masked runners in the 1950 doings, several young people attempted to continue a dance and resisted the Husk Face messengers who pushed them to the wall benches with their crossed staffs.

The New Year of 1965 was the last time the Husk Faces visited the Seneca Longhouse at Coldspring before the removal of the fire to Steamburg. Their two messengers made the customary three passes through the longhouse, knocking over a False Face beggar on the second pass. An amusing incident occurred on the third entry: They stopped the singers by taking the drum out of the hands of the first singer and seized the rattles of his assistants. When the leader persisted in singing, one of the

Husk Faces clapped a hand over his mouth, but the singer continued to emit sound each time the masker removed his hand, until finally the singer gave up. This caused much amusement.

The 1934 Prophecy as Pattern. The Pigeon Dance was in progress when the main body of Husk Faces arrived to rattle the longhouse and send in their messengers to arrest an interpreter. The two maskers walked in, holding their staffs horizontally, pushed the dancers from the floor, grabbed old John Jimmerson, and abducted him out the women's door. Presently he returned to the longhouse saying that the Husk Face men had taken the wrong man. "The Big Wet Woman (Enohwęhgo:wa) wanted to see me, but now she wants to see Ten Mornings [Wesley White]." Implied here is some sort of an affair between Seneca men and Husk Face women visitors, perhaps only a fantasy.

Wesley went out and returned momentarily saying that the Husk Faces were hurrying westward but that they would see all the doings on their way. Then he excused himself on the pretext that he had not seen "The Big Wet Woman" in a long time and that he would have to ask her again exactly what she told him to say.

(This mock forgetfulness on the part of interpreters is recurrent, and it serves to build suspense. It is a constant feature from year to year, but the speeches are not set and are never twice the same. The actors in this role are chosen for their artfulness and sense of humor.[2])

Wesley returned presently, having pretended to confer with his captors outside. He said, "They are working on their planted fields taking care of them. They are in a hurry because they are working, and there is lots of money where they come from, and it should be the same here where you people live, so that you shall have lots of money."[3]

Once more he forgot and conferred with the mythical woman outside the door. Going out a third time he said, "I am going to ask the people out there."

The ceremony was approaching a turning point. My informants of the Redeye household explained:

> Where the Husk Faces come from, the seasons are reversed from those on earth. They are just now planting, so they must hurry to their homes in the west and till their fields.
> A different speech [prediction] is made each year. Whatever message they bring, whatever is said at this time, is supposed to come true during the ensuing year. Next year we will have good crops."

Clearly, the Husk Faces are symbols of fertility, both as related to the earth and to women, although nothing is said of hunting luck. The pre-

2. Sherman and Clara Redeye, personal communication.
3. One should remember that this speech was made in 1934 at the bottom of the Great Depression, when work on the Erie and Pennsylvania railroads was slack, and most Seneca track workers were on relief projects.

occupation with insuring successful crops contrasts with declining Seneca farming. My informants continued:

> Sometimes they carry Husk Face babies, and should they mention babies, it would mean that many babies would come to the village during the following year.

Dance Requests
Wesley returned to announce the dances that the visitors requested. He said that Chauncey Johnny John would sing for them as they came in. Whereupon Chauncey called to the maskers and pounded the end of a staff on the floor to set the tempo for the Husk Face song. The male Husk Faces led the procession, stooping and crawling on one knee supported by their staffs. The women followed erect. Entering by the south, or women's door, they circled the room. It was announced that the men would perform their own dance, Fish Dance, first while their women sat on the singers' bench along the gallery waiting their turn at the Old-time Women's Dance, when they would stand up. Wesley had announced that Hanoje:nę?s would sing for them.

It is noteworthy that the "female" Husk Faces are actually men impersonating women, and this is the only time that Seneca men dance the Women's Dance. It affords them an excellent opportunity to ridicule their wives and mothers in a ceremonial setting. When they have started, the Seneca women are supposed to join them. Old-time Women's Shuffle Dance (ʔen:skä:nye:ʔ gainǫgáyonkha:ʔ) honors the Three Sisters—corn, beans, and squash— that Seneca women share with the supernaturals.

The Fish Dance follows. The Husk Face men, with their women (who are men) as partners, celebrate this favorite Iroquois social dance. It is also the favorite song of men's singing societies. It is customary for men to commence the dance, and when they are well started, Iroquois women usually enter in couples separating the male partners and making couples of alternate sex. Similarly the Husk Face men dance several songs alone before being joined by their women. Meanwhile, some Seneca men add themselves to the column, joining in couples. When it comes time for the women to enter the dance (and there is no set time for this), some of the Husk Face women (men) dance with Seneca men, and likewise some of the Seneca women join the Husk Face band up front. Thus, the people share this night with guests from the other side of the world. There is naturally considerable jesting and repartee between Seneca men and their mythical guests, although the Husk Faces are supposed to be mute. In the course of the dance, everyone comes to know who the Husk Face impersonators actually are, but for a time they go undetected.

As the drum strikes twice to end the Fish Dance, all of the gallery and the Husk Faces depart—the Seneca to their homes and the Husk Faces supposedly to their homes in the west.

The 1934 observations serve to set the pattern, a structure so to speak, for contrasting later observations. These I shall treat only as to their differences.

1939 Observations

By now thoroughly familiar with the ritual pattern and what to expect, I concentrated on the participants and noted variations. In 1939, two students from the previous summer's field seminar—Marjorie Lismer and Anne Schafer—attended and pooled their field notes. Because this ceremony is new to the literature I shall not spare the reader the details that seem important.

At their third entry, the Husk Face from the south door crossed the room to the men's side and grabbed Hanoje:nɛʔs and escorted him out the same way. In a few minutes, he returned to say that the Husk Faces really wanted Chauncey Johnny John who crossed the room and went out the women's door. These mock arrests, returns, and declarations that the maskers really want a different person are part of a pattern that recurs every year. How much of this is prearranged, I am uncertain, but it would appear that some of it is. On occasion though, there is an element of surprise, as in former times when the men who could play this role were more abundant.

Chauncey returned and, placing one foot on the hearth of the women's stove, learned on the now-cool stove with his left hand, while, after the manner of a story teller, he commented on flagging participation:

> They [the Husk Faces] have returned once more and are surprised not to find the people dancing. [The following day in an interview with Lismer, Chauncey changed the version of the Husk Face's message to what he should have said.] Thanks for everybody. They are glad to come and see the people in the Council House and the Indian doing his dances. They are going over to Cattaraugus tonight, and when they come back they will stop again tomorrow. They say further that if they don't stop it is because they may be going to another reservation, maybe Tonawanda.
>
> [He then named their leaders.] Their chief is "Big Potatoes," and he has three women—Big Beans, Long Corn, and Dumplings.

Following the usual lapse of memory, Chauncey went out to be prompted and came in again, this time to editorialize on the failure of farming at Coldspring.

> They say that they have fine crops and that we will also if we take care of them. The people here should plant, and we should take care of the crops that we do plant. [He added that some of their number had been left behind to look after their crops.] That is what they are doing now and why they are not all here. They also have

stock: cows, chickens, and pigs. They are wishing it to be here like what they got. And we had better work and take care of the crops so that we shall have the same.

After this editorial on domestication, Chauncey went out again. He returned to discuss women and abortion. He said, "Their women are strong because they let the babies come out when it is time. Let the child stay in the womb full term. They [the Husk Faces] do not force the child. If you did not do that we would have many people around here. Their women are healthy because they let the child come out when it is ready."

My notes state that Chauncey made four entrances. They indicate that he named the party on the first entry, but next day he told Lismer that he named them the last time. He probably named them the first time and then later reminded the audience of the names of their dance leaders.

On returning he said, "I have been asked to announce the names of the people in the dance."

> The first lady to lead the dance is "Long Ears of White Corn" (Oʔnísdesǫs). The second lady is "Large Purple Kidney Beans" (Osaídaʔwa:nɛʔs); the third is "String Beans" (Ganǫʔǫstaʔ). [Minnie Jacobs, an old lady once in charge of the Husk Faces, gave this name as meaning "dumplings"; Sherman Redeye said *ganoʔnystaʔ* ("cold").] Their leading man is named "Big Potatoes" (Nanǫʔdowa:nɛʔs). [Chauncey then went on to introduce the singer for the Old-time Women's Shuffle Dance.] Years ago over there on the far side of the Hudson River there was a good singer who used to sing for the ladies, and they want him to sing for them again, if he is still living. They want Dji:shäyɛʔ [Sherman Redeye] to sing Gainǫgayǫka:ʔ [traditional Women's Dance] for them. They want me to sing the Fish Dance.

Chauncey then turned and called the Husk Faces in by saying, *ka:ji ka:ji* ("come on, come on"), and at the same time banging a stick on the singers' bench. The men came in on their knees; their women were afoot.

The same names of Husk Face personalities persisted through the festivals of 1941, 1942, and again in 1950, and the same personnel performed key roles until Chauncey's death, after which Atkin Coury succeeded his mentor, and Hánoje:nɛʔs made the prophecies.

Photographs and Recordings

At the festival of 1941, I documented Husk Face behavior with the camera, and next day recorded the Husk Face songs.[4] At Coldspring, there are

---

4. A series of recordings for the Library of Congress at Six Nations Reserve on Grand River and at Coldspring on the Allegheny River were subsequently transcribed and published by Kurath (1964, 131). One of the Husk Face songs recorded by Joshua Billy Buck at Six Nations is available in Album VI, Folk Music

only three songs for the Husk Face men who crawl in on one knee. Their women who follow walking will await the Old-time Women's Shuffle Dance following the Husk Face Dance. Chauncey, in recording the songs told me, "I went to the door, struck my cane, and called them. I turned and they followed me around the room [Plate 16-3B]. I lead them around."

As in much other Seneca song recitative, the words of the three Husk Face songs resist analysis. The texts are (1) *hai hai* (repeatedly); *yoʔ hyoʔ hauʔ ga:ji:* (repeated six times), "come here"; (2) *ho ho ho hoʔhaogä:yęʔ* (repeated four times); and (3) *hyoʔ hyoʔhyoʔ hanoʔgä:yęʔ* (repeated).[5]

Children Warned

There are always children at Seneca ceremonies, and ordinarily they are let come and go with kindly tolerance, although during serious parts of the ritual they are urged to sit with their parents and listen. This they do with rapt attention, for that is how learning is transmitted. But on this occasion, when the longhouse is packed, and the temperature drops to near zero—"They say that when the Husk Faces come the temperature always drops"—the speaker appeals to the parents not to let their children run loose in the longhouse and indoors and outdoors during the ceremonies. One young lad who was often referred to as "that Alec" confirmed that as a youngster the old people used to tell him to be good while in the longhouse and not run outside lest the Husk Faces get him and eat him. My own son on one occasion was warned by his "brothers" of the Beaver clan as they were sitting in the longhouse: "Look out for the Husk Faces. If they point at you then you would have to go outside with them and they would eat you." Little children need no warning because they already fear the maskers and stick to parents or grandparents for security; but the older teenagers are careful not to let preteenagers follow them when they leave the longhouse to the rendezvous where the Husk Faces dress.

Costuming and Identity

In 1950, I taped an interview with a young lady who had been in among the maskers—both wooden and husk—with comments by her parents,

---

of the United States, Library of Congress, 1942, Record III-A, 4; and Fenton (1942, 25–26).

5. Although the words of the Husk Face songs resist analysis and their meanings are obscure, Chauncey ventured that *ganoʔgę:ʔ* refers to "a hoop of wood"; not to "snow on the ground," as others have suggested. It may therefore refer to the circular dance of the husk masker about a pole. A. Skinner (1925, 197) gives *ganiuhgwaieh*, as meaning "round about." This form is probably intended for *ganyoʔgwa:yęʔ*. Skinner was quoting A. C. Parker (1913, 129). Regularly, Iroquois words in song texts are accommodated to the song style; and they are frequently archaic words remembered only in the context of songs and are otherwise unintelligible to contemporary speakers.

my hosts on that occasion. "People can't really tell who the maskers are. They are both men and women, and they are both young and old people." She identified a boy of eleven, the youngest masker, and his grandfather, then approaching sixty. The latter's two sons were prominent participants—the former as a Husk Face runner, and the latter as the hula dancer in the beggar mask dancing contest. Chauncey Johnny John, patriarch of the extended family that included these males of four generations, told me he had no difficulty identifying them by their gaits and movements. The variety of costumes on these occasions is truly wonderful. They come out of grab bags and mission boxes and an endless supply of athletic equipment—a set of "tails," parts of baseball and lacrosse uniforms, and cast-off evening dresses. The resurgence of interest in Iroquois identity manifested itself in the 1950 procession when one of the men masquerading as a Seneca woman wore a traditional ceremonial costume right out of the plates of L. H. Morgan's *League* (1851).

Anonymity is further assured by the fact that Husk Faces are traditionally mutes, just as the False Faces speak a nonsense language of nasalized vowels. Pointing saves revealing identity by voice.

Interpreter Not Immune to Sanctions
By 1950, Atkins Coury had succeeded to the mantle of his late mentor, Chauncey Johnny John. Led out by one of the Husk Face messengers, he returned and spoke in the manner of his teacher. Outside, he had been instructed by the leading Husk Face matron. The man in this role was carrying out the orders of a true matron and keeper of the masks who was in charge of the ceremony. They wanted Hanoje:nę?s to come out and talk with them because he had left a family in the Husk Face country. (It was well known that Hanoje:nę?s had enjoyed some recent lapses from his last marriage to a longhouse headwoman, the daughter of the keeper of the Husk Faces; and that before that he had abandoned another family. His present wife's mother, as head of the Husk Faces, could thus visit a satirical sanction on her errant son-in-law in the context of the ritual. As speaker of the longhouse, the victim had no other course but to comply with instructions. My hostess assured me that Hanoje:nę?s's character was of no importance and did not detract from the things his status as longhouse speaker required him to say in the role of interpreter for the Husk Faces. The speeches that are made by the man abducted by the Husk Face messengers are the instructions of the headwoman of the Husk Faces, in this case the conductor of the ritual.) He told about his family in the Husk Face country and named them.

The next day I had a talk with Hanoje:nę?s about his role as interpreter for the Husk Faces.

> Indeed, the Husk Faces who enter first on one or both knees are Seneca young people who represent the Husk Face babies who are

yet crawling toward the people. [The unborn in Iroquois rhetoric are referred to as "they who are coming this way from beneath the ground."] The ones who follow them in are the "old folks"—their women escorted by their men. [He confirmed the reversal of sexes in their respective roles.]

Their message speaks of wonderful crops that are growing in the place that they come from. They say that there are lots of berries there, there is lots of work, that people plant a great deal. They urge the people of Coldspring to plant again—at least enough for their own use. They urge the people to work in the fields and keep good gardens, to can the produce.

The two dances that the Husk Faces invariably request are the Old-time Women's Shuffle Dance and Fish Dance for their men, and they name the singers. The Fish Dance is the climax form of all Iroquois social dances. On these occasions, women and girls as Husk Face men take the lead and dance the complicated men's steps. Men and boys as Husk Face women assume the more modest shuffle steps that women regularly employ in the Fish Dance until the dance reaches a pitch of excitement when—as in the Sunday social dances—young women break over into the men's dance steps. In 1950, I counted a column of fifty or sixty dancers led by the Husk Faces circling the room at midnight. Outside, the temperature had dropped as they say it invariably does when the Husk Faces visit the longhouse. The midcentury celebration was no exception.

Still Later Observations

Of five later records of Husk Face night at Coldspring Longhouse, three sets of observations are of other writers. In a remarkable piece of writing Wallace (1970, 54, 82) described the 1952 celebration. Three years later, I was present with C. R. "Tip" Roseberry, a reporter for the Albany *Times Union*.[6] In 1958, I shared observations with Edmund Wilson who devoted a chapter of *Apologies to the Iroquois* (1960, 198ff., 237–46) to an especially poignant account of Husk Face night, in which he noted the decline of satire and its replacement by preachment in the remarks of the speaker for the visiting maskers. It was an unforgettable experience for an ethnologist to interpret the culture of his adopted people to the foremost literary figure of our age and then to see how he constructed its image. I have already alluded to the climax year at the old longhouse in 1965, and I shall comment momentarily on stability and change at the new longhouse near Steamburg.

---

6. C. R. Roseberry, *Times-Union*, Albany, Sunday, February 13, 1955, Section E, 1, 5.

ORTHODOXY AND CHANGE

Elsewhere, I have described the first of two returns to the new Coldspring Longhouse near Steamburg (Fenton 1972c, 102–10). Husk Face night fell on February 7, 1968. It was a strange mixture of orthodoxy and innovation in an entirely modern building modeled after the old longhouse. Surprised at the quiet entry of the Husk Faces, I was told that they no longer announce their arrival by rubbing the outside of the building with their staves. This would mar the paint and the new woodwork! Moreover, the two young matrons who had succeeded to the responsibility of taking charge of the maskers had quit, and the longhouse officers had appointed two new ones because people objected to the False Faces and their Husk Face runners coming to the new houses at the Steamburg resettlement area, scratching the doors, and tracking in mud. This meant that the maskers no longer went from house to house in spring and fall and at midwinter. All masking activities are now confined to the longhouse. With one or two notable exceptions, the maskers lacked for enthusiasm. There is little new to report from observations made at a second visit to "New" Coldspring three years afterward.

Radical as these changes are in circumstances that can be explained by the second housing revolution of the Allegany Seneca, let me return to a change that occurred before my first fieldwork in 1933 (Fenton 1936, 1967), namely the abandonment of the dance honoring the Husk Faces on the eighth night of the Midwinter Festival on the eve of the Great Bowl Game. The stock explanation in 1934 was Hiram Jacobs's species of logic, that there was no point in recalling the husk maskers a second night when they professed to be in such a hurry to go elsewhere and to get home and tend to their crops and children.

THE SOCIAL DANCE HONORING THE HUSK FACES

The social dance that is held on the eighth night of the festival is in honor of the Husk Faces and is called *gajihsaʔ sadiyaʔdagwenini:yoʔ* because it belongs to them. At the close of the morning's activities on the eighth day of the 1934 festival, the speaker announced that people should return in the evening to honor the Husk Faces. This is the second night for the Husk Faces, according to the Redeye family, but they no longer return as they once did to dance because some years previously Hiram Jacob, the then-head of the longhouse, ruled that their return was inconsistent inasmuch as they said on the sixth night that they were going west after their first appearance. Therefore, they could not be present a second night also. He decided that henceforth they should not appear after the sixth night, but for want of another name the celebration on the eighth night continued to be a social dance held nominally in honor of the Husk Faces in absentia. Except for the failure of the maskers to reappear, the ritual order did not change.[7]

The same two men of opposite moieties whom the longhouse officers appointed to manage the affair for the Husk Faces on the sixth night continued to serve in 1934. By the time a performance of War Dance, sponsored by one of the longhouse leaders, had been celebrated, the room was full to overflowing.

The program honoring the Husk Faces consisted of three dances: (1) Great Feather Dance; (2) Old-time Women's Shuffle Dance (for the women and the Husk Faces, but danced by Seneca women); and (3) Fish Dance (for the Husk Face men, but danced by the youth of both sexes without costume).

These first three dances, according to Sherman Redeye, were always performed in honor of the Husk Faces at their second appearance. It was this way until Hiram Jacobs's decision. He died in 1932, and the headmen who succeeded him decided to eliminate the maskers on the second night and to continue to observe the dances as if they were present.

The second part of the evening is a social dance. It follows a customary pattern at Coldspring:

1. Trotting Dance (Ga?da:syo:t), "Standing Quiver"
2. Linking Arms Dance (Deyaodonę́hsotha?)
3. Sharpening-A-Stick Dance (Wa?ę́nothi:yo?)
4. Duck Dance (Twęt oeno?)
5. Naked Dance (Ka?nósta?ke:kha:?), or Shaking a Bush (kaskoę́ǫ́ta?toh)
6. Chicken Dance (Takä:?ę:? ?oęno?)
7. Raccoon Dance (jo?ä:ka? ?oęno?)

The program finished with a second Feather Dance, as always. The selection and order of social dances, however, is optional with the floor managers. They invariably begin with the Trotting, or Standing Quiver, Dance.

A Second Opinion

We come now to Albert Jones's explanation some sixteen years later. "The dance on the eighth night is indeed to honor the Husk Faces, but it is primarily held to entertain the people who put on the masks two nights previously, although no masks are worn on the second occasion at Cold-

---

7. The repetitive structure of the Midwinter Festival, which I first noted (1936, 13) and Tooker (1970, 39ff.) emphasized in her book, segments the ceremonies at Coldspring into a preliminary day to name babies, not part of the festival proper, five days of dream-fulfillment rites, which the Husk Faces climax, and three days devoted to the four sacred ceremonies. Sturtevant suggests that this general pattern, which more or less prevails in other Seneca longhouses, might require two nights of Husk Face visitations. They do appear twice at Cattaraugus.

spring." (I inferred from Albert's remarks that at Newtown Longhouse on Cattaraugus Reservation the Husk maskers do appear on a second night.)

The same mandatory program of dances obtained in 1950 with optional social dances. But Albert commented, "The people who wore the masks did not want to dance a second time." Certainly, there was far more enthusiasm when the people were masked than was manifest when they had to show their bare faces in public. Until 1950, I had relied on the previous explanation of Hiram Jacobs's logic, but by then it appeared that there was more to it. What persists is public masking, transvestism, preachment with sanctioned humor, and reversed sex roles in which the young people have always joined with enthusiasm. By 1950, the then-generation of bobby-soxers who went uptown to Salamanca High School would put on the cornhusk faces and be "Indian" once a year on the sixth night of the Midwinter Festival when during the rest of the year too-avid participation in Sunday night social dances embarrassed them. So, at the dance held in their honor as Husk Faces two nights later, they would bring their pails for mush but fewer of them took part. Furthermore, by the eighth night everyone was tired. In the entertainment of those who wore masks, the public recognizes their participation in the effort to entertain the supernaturals. Also, in effect, the dance celebrates persons coming out of seclusion, out of masking, their appearance in the public eye, and their return to the roles of daily life. And although the sexes are reversed in their roles as maskers, the participants once more resume their roles as normal members of Seneca society. These inferences drawn from Albert Jones's comments on the ceremony thirty years ago offer a better explanation of changes and continuity in the rite than the logic of Hiram Jacobs. We must assume, nevertheless, that husk maskers once returned a second night and probably unmasked during the intermission between their dances and the social dances that followed.

NEWTOWN ON CATTARAUGUS

The appearance of the Husk Faces at Newtown Longhouse on Cattaraugus was always regarded at Allegany as rather unique, and it contained a feature absent at Tonawanda. My knowledge of it derives from Jesse Cornplanter coupled with William C. Sturtevant's fieldwork with Solon Jones and his observations ca. 1958, for I never witnessed the ceremony myself.

On the fifth afternoon of the midwinter ceremony, and into the night, a band of black-faced "hunters" wearing sacks over their heads used to go around the settlement and into the longhouse ahead of the Husk Faces. They would steal whatever articles of apparel they could lay their hands on, which their leader put into a pool. The owners later could retrieve lost objects by paying the leader a bribe. The proceeds of their hunt went toward providing the soup in the longhouse kitchen next day. The tradition of the origin of this custom is long since forgotten. Years ago, the "hunters" came into the longhouse armed with miniature bows and arrows and proceeded to shoot at objects of their desire. Hits yielded forfeits. Coldspring sources regarded this behavior as rather bizarre, but they made the effort to get there if scheduling permitted. In Sturtevant's account, these hunters do not represent any supernatural beings; they are simply clowns (Sturtevant 1983, 40). The appearance of these "hunters" on the fifth night at Newtown recalls the origin myths in which lone hunters obtained hunting luck from Husk Face beings.

The black-faced hunters are followed into the longhouse by Husk Faces who request specific dances in their honor. The big dance for the Husk Faces to which they bring their prophecies falls on the eighth night at Newtown, instead of the sixth as at Coldspring, where the eighth night is a social dance for the participants. Otherwise, the Newtown and Coldspring performances are much the same and share common features.

The activities of the black-faced hunters at Newtown are consistent with the original purpose of the False Face beggars, which was to get tobacco in order to help put up the big feast. The beggars ordinarily carried a small basket into which householders could deposit a portion of tobacco toward the invocation to the white dog that climaxed the Dream Feast. John Jimmerson who grew up at Plank Road Longhouse, on Cattaraugus, recalled that the solicitation began on the third day, and Chauncey Warrior, who remembered when there were five longhouses on the Cattaraugus Reservation, said that each longhouse claimed that its procedure derived from the oldest great-grandfathers of the Seneca people.

TONAWANDA

Local diversity extends to Tonawanda. There, False Faces commence to make their rounds on the evening of the second day. Their activity intensifies on the following day when some Husk Faces appear with them and also independently (Tooker 1970, 55). On the fourth day, activity shifts from the houses to the longhouse, where the Husk Faces, having made the circuit of houses, perform what appears to be a vestige of the rites reported for Coldspring and Newtown longhouses (Tooker 1970, 57). The performance has evidently declined since the 1930s, judging by the previous testimony of Elijah David and Chief Henan Scrogg and my own observations. Tooker observed the complete cycle twenty years later. As at Coldspring, it is the sixth night at Tonawanda when the Husk Faces arrive in force to climax an evening of medicine society and social dances by disrupting the affair, capturing a speaker, and teaching him their prophecy (Tooker 1970, 61–63). A final dance is held for both the False Faces and the Husk Faces on the Sunday night following the festival (Fenton 1941, 162; Tooker 1970, 64–66).

THE TWO ONONDAGAS

The masked rituals of the Onondaga Longhouse in the valley south of Syracuse have been known since the late nineteenth century when they were monographed by Beauchamp (1888, 198–99; 1895, 209) and DeCost Smith (1888, 1889) in the early volumes of the *Journal of American Folklore*. Most recently, they have been studied and systematized by Blau (1966).

The Onondaga midwinter ceremonies are the most divergent of extant Iroquois rituals and preserve features of the Feast of Dreams described by Jesuit writers in the seventeenth century (Blau 1963, 1967; Tooker 1970, 79–82). The False Faces appear on several days and perform cures in response to dreams and for renewals, and they arrive en masse at the longhouse to entertain people including white visitors on the eighth night, reserving the fifteenth night for the more serious "Traveling Rite." On the other hand, the Husk Faces seem less developed than among the Seneca, and they do not perform the drama of fertility when they come in on the eighth night.

Another band of Onondaga settled on the Grand River some eighty miles west of Niagara after the Revolution, built a log longhouse at Middleport north of the river, and then shifted it over the river to its present location on MacKenzie Creek. A splinter group from this congregation formed the "Seneca Longhouse" nearby, late in the nineteenth century. Still farther east and down below is the Lower Cayuga Longhouse at Atkins' Corners, which is perhaps the most conservative congregation on the Six Nations Reserve. Up above and west toward Brantford at Sour Springs, the Upper Cayuga Longhouse, or "Sour Springs," has welcomed anthropologists from Speck to Shimony.

Husk Faces Less Developed

In his book on the midwinter rites, Speck (1949, 86–88, 93–95, 95–100) treats the masked rites in the longhouse, the "Traveling Rite" of the wooden and husk masks, and the cornhusk mask society in detail. Among the Cayuga, the Husk Faces are subsidiary to the "great ones," and I infer from a footnote describing the drama of fertility in which the Husk Faces appeared en masse at Seneca Longhouse in 1936 that its performance there is unique at Six Nations. (Speck 1949, 95–96).

Shimony's great study of conservatism (1961) covers all of the longhouse ceremonies at Six Nations and demonstrates how what Speck and I took to be tribal distinctions have blurred into congregational practices. She treats the False Faces at length, remarks on differences from my reporting of Seneca practices, links the Husk Faces with the False Faces in the "Traveling Rite," but she reports no drama of fertility (Shimony 1961, 148–53, 184).

No Beggars

My own fieldwork at Six Nations between 1939 and 1951 followed Speck and preceded Shimony by a decade. Before his tragic drowning in 1943, Simeon Gibson and I had commenced a complete catalog of the annual cycle of ceremonies at Onondaga Longhouse, which was not backed up completely by observations. Because I was already deeply into the subject of masking and these notes remain unpublished, I include them here rather than relying on Speck and Shimony whom they supplement.

> There are no beggars here at Six Nations, and no special night during the midwinter ceremonies is set aside for them, unlike Cattaraugus and Allegany among the Seneca. Contrary to the custom of the False Faces at Tonawanda, where the maskers go naked above the waist, they do not do this at Six Nations. [This is not true of Husk Face messengers at Seneca Longhouse, as we shall see momentarily.] The way we do is as follows: Individual members of the False Face Society go to the longhouse on the third and fourth days of the Midwinter Festival. There the community is divided according to phratries that sit opposite each other. Each side brings its masks to the longhouse and puts them in the kitchen [a separate building] against need. Any member of either phratry who feels the need to have ashes blown on his head reports to the speaker for his own side. That speaker announces to the "cousins" that an individual requests to be cured. The individual goes to the bench in the middle of the room and seats himself. The opposite side appoints a singer, and the singer sits beside the patient. The Gagǫhsaʔ will come in, sometimes only one masker, sometimes two; they go to the stove on their own side, get ashes, and blow on the patient's head, hands, limbs. There is no obligation for the patient to put up a feast [what Shimony's informants call "bare" or "dry pole"; no kettle is hung.] Nor does the patient have to pay in tobacco. Later the moiety of the individual will pay in kind for some member of the opposite phratry [or moiety].

No Special Night

As for the Husk Faces, no special night is set aside for them at Onondaga Longhouse during the Midwinter Festival. However, on the last night of Medicine Company dances (Day 4), the Husk Faces come into the longhouse ahead of the main body of wooden masks. "He [the Husk Face leader] runs around the room, jumps over benches, runs around again." [Onondaga Longhouse has but one door midway.] "He makes no noise, unlike Gagǫhsaʔ. Then he goes out. Sometimes as many as six Husk Faces perform as runners. A few minutes later the main body enters."

As previously indicated for Six Nations, the permanent leader of the False Faces, always a male, organizes the company of husk and wooden maskers. Some men impersonate Husk Face women. They have their own special dance at the end of the ritual.

> The leader of the society does not burn tobacco but makes a speech. He tells the society that the people of the longhouse are going to make them a present of mush. This is not delivered, however, until about two months afterward when the society makes its spring round of the settlement driving out disease.

SENECA LONGHOUSE

The Husk Faces have a special night during the Midwinter Festival at Seneca Longhouse when a special dance is held for them. Of all the ceremonies for the maskers in the several longhouses at Six Nations, this occasion most resembles Husk Face night among the Seneca of New York. One wonders whether the small band of Seneca who settled on the Grand River after 1784 brought the ceremony with them. There were several families of Seneca descent in the Onondaga Longhouse congregation, including Chief John Gibson and his brother, and the so-called "Seneca" Longhouse, which was founded by separatists, may perpetuate elements of Seneca ritualism besides its name. There, the fourth evening is devoted to all kinds of dances, and toward the end, the Husk Faces come in alone.

There is but one preliminary warning by Husk Face runners. They enter the men's door and go out the women's door. The main body does not announce its arrival by drumming on the building before entry.

Inside, an old man sits astride a bench and beats out the tempo with a wooden turtle rattle. The column of Husk maskers enters the longhouse, dances slowly around the bench, and as the leader reaches the singer, they are still coming in. Gibson recalled as many as 50 to 100 maskers; others report fewer. On this night, the Lower Cayuga and Onondaga combine with the "Seneca" to make up the company of Husk Faces. The leader of the column is someone who knows how to act in this role, and he is usually the eldest member.

The singer repeats but one song from start to finish: "*hu hu hä: yɛʔ*". He sings slowly, and the dance tempo is deliberate. Halfway in the song, the singer stops, and the speaker of the longhouse greets the maskers:

> We are very glad to see that the society has come. We are pleased, too, that you also rejoice that the New Year's dance has come. We will hope to see you again next year when we celebrate the Great Ceremonial Mark [Indian New Year]. Tonight we have prepared mush for you. That is your present.

[Then, Gibson continues:] The song and dance resumes. After two or three rounds, the maskers go out. When the maskers have undressed and put away their masks, the persons come back in. The pot of mush is set down in the middle of the room. The actors appoint one of their company to stir the mush.

I infer that the personnel is entirely male. Note that they do not perform Fish Dance and Women's Dance, unlike the Seneca of the other side.

Another View

Inasmuch as I did not witness the rite, I shall balance Simeon Gibson's account with that of Mrs. John L. Buck to Frank Speck, describing the ceremony of February 1, 1936. Speck quotes her in a footnote (1949, 95–96) and remarks on its absence from the program at Sour Springs Cayuga Longhouse. Because the account is published, I shall outline its features.

Abstract of Mrs. Buck

Mrs. Buck said in substance: A naked messenger Husk Face knocked at the longhouse door. He wore only breechcloth, moccasins, and husk helmet. He delivered a note naming Husk Face personages: a man (woman) named Corn Pounder and a second man (person) named Black Corn who were enroute. The messenger left without entering.

A speaker urged people to receive the guests, treat them well, and he read the note.

Then the two Husk Faces announced by the messenger came in. They were the man and woman already referred to. The male mask featured a long nose and no ruff; the female mask was large, heavily ruffed, with black fur eyebrows and moustache. [Are these reversed?] A spot of red paint was on each cheek.

The couple brought a message that this year's planting would yield bountiful crops. This they whispered to the speaker who spoke for them. They left by the same door.

Twenty members of the society then entered, representing both sexes of all ages. They danced around the singer, just as told by Gibson. At the end of the line came the naked messenger, then the named man, and third from the end the woman.

A woman from each moiety spoke; then two women from the Turtle Moiety and two from the Bear Moiety made speeches offering tobacco and cornbread that was promised for spring delivery when the society makes its rounds after the thaw.

Wooden maskers entered after the Husk Faces departed. The same speeches were made, and the same offerings were promised for spring delivery.

Mrs. Buck's last statement is not unlike the Onondaga version of Gibson.

Naked messengers do not feel the cold. One recalls the comment at Coldspring that the temperature always drops when the Husk Faces come.

A Seneca Manifestation
The Husk Faces seem to be a peculiarly Seneca manifestation. Among them, their rites reach a climax of intensity not found elsewhere. The presence of a prominent Husk Face rite only at Seneca Longhouse on Six Nations reaffirms this view. Among the Seneca, the Husk Faces are commemorated as donors of hunting luck and cultivated crops. They are symbols of fertility and harbingers of hope. Their activity dates at least from the late eighteenth century when Mary Jemison recalled parties of Husk Faces going from house to house on the fourth day of the Midwinter Festival among the Seneca on the Genesee River. Then the maskers dressed in bearskins, smeared themselves with dirt, bedaubed persons who refused to contribute tobacco to their baskets, and purged the settlement of sins (Seaver 1932, 166). Although rubbing walls of houses with turtle shell rattles—typical False Face behavior—is mentioned for a previous day, it is possible that the behavior of the husk and wooden faces is confused in this description by the recorder of Mrs. Jemison's narrative. Recall that Halliday Jackson attributed the handling and smearing of soot (and/or offal) to the False Faces at Allegany ca. 1800 (Jackson 1930, 24).

Personal Charms
As with the False Faces, miniature Husk Faces are given in response to particular dreams and are treasured during the life of the dreamer. This is a universal practice among Iroquois of the Five Nations. Nor does it belong only to the past. As recently as 1968, various sponsors put up feasts for the False Faces during the midwinter ceremonies at the new Coldspring Longhouse. A matron of my age group, whom I recall from my first residence on "Snow Street," now a grandmother, dressed fashionably and drove her relatively new Oldsmobile to the longhouse, bringing the fried meat and popcorn for the feast she was to sponsor. Standing midway of the women's end near the fire, she awaited the ministrations of the maskers. She held in one hand a miniature Husk Face with a tiny pole, a replica of the peeled staffs that the Husk Faces carry. "This is her guide," I was told, and when she came over to the men's side to prompt the speaker, I saw her wrap the objects carefully in a silk scarf and put it safely in her purse. This incident could be replicated in other longhouses throughout Iroquoia during the rites of dream fulfillment at midwinter.

HUSK FACE AND FALSE FACE ANALOGUES

It may serve to draw Iroquois masking together to contrast attributes and functions of the two principal kinds of masks:

Husk Faces	*False Faces*
Swift messengers of the wind	Earth stompers and tree shakers
Mutes	Nasal speech
Blow ashes	Blow ashes
Crawl on knees	Crawl on hip
Carry poles	Stripped trees as canes
Tobacco	Tobacco
Eat popcorn,[8] dumplings	Mush, corn soup
Subsistence and hunting luck	Disease control

8. The dietary preferences of Husk Faces versus False Faces are interesting because pod corn may be earlier than the varieties of flint and dent corn from which flour is ground for mush and hulled corn leached with ashes for corn soup. Fogelson has suggested in correspondence that the difference may indicate that Husk masks antedate wooden False Faces.

PART SIX

17. Prominence and Climax

Prominence of Masking and Related Concepts in Iroquois Life

Two features of Iroquois culture have captured the popular imagination—the False Faces and the famous League or Confederacy of the Five Nations. For the American public, it is the masks themselves and the idea that a representative government preceded our own in what Hewitt called the "Stone Age of North America." And this view is not far off the mark because, for the Iroquois themselves, the False Faces and their rituals and the Condoling Council, the great ceremony for mourning dead chiefs and installing their successors, constitute the two climax forms of their culture. The False Faces are preeminent among the medicine societies, rivaled only by the Little Water Medicine, which is far more restricted even in its celebration rites known collectively as I:ʔdo:s. The False Faces assert their priority by mythological reference to the cosmology and manifest it socially in two great public appearances to rid the settlements of disease. The spring and autumn visitation of the houses, known in Canada as the traveling rite, are a prominent and regular feature of the ceremonial calendar in all Iroquois longhouse communities. Attendance and sometimes participation are not limited to longhouse congregations. Even so-called Christians get involved as patients, if not as maskers. No one in an Iroquois community can be unaware of the False Faces. The associated Husk Faces provide the great spectacle at Midwinter that few longhouse adherents pass up and most other Iroquois attend at least once in a lifetime.

THE CLIMAX FEATURE OF THE MIDWINTER FESTIVAL

Husk Face night at the Seneca longhouses is the "Indian New Year" for many Iroquois. Actually, as we have seen, it is the culmination of several days of revealing and celebrating dreams. Celebration of the climax of the Dream Feast is shared with the False Face beggars, bands of masked boys who for two days have been circulating the settlement begging tobacco and cadging food in the houses that they visit. The boodle is supposed to go toward the feast at the longhouse, but the goodies are largely consumed by the hungry boys. Participation as beggars is, as we have seen, the first introduction for many lads to the role and responsibility of the False Faces. For, indeed, at any fireside they may be called upon to blow ashes. Their romp concludes on the second night at the longhouse in more begging for tobacco, impromptu dancing, and the dance contest that we have described. Surely, the False Face beggars are the least serious of the orders of maskers, and it is questionable whether they belong to the Society of Faces. But the activity affords a learning experience, an opportunity for clowning and comic relief, for satire, and what the Senecas call "heavy fun." In contrast with the more serious False Face "doctors," the beggars epitomize the more humorous aspects of False Face behavior as opposed to the more serious business of curing. The beggars and the doctor masks occupy the poles of an ambivalence with which the Iroquois regard the False Faces: They are at once amusing and threatening.

SECLUSION AND POWER

All of the maskers—both wooden False Faces and Husk Faces—stand in the relationship of "grandfathers" to the Iroquois people. Both the masks and their spirit patrons share this kinship term of respect with the thunders, medicinal herbs, the famous Little Water Medicine (once the War Bundle), and rattlesnakes. In common, they are powerful forces to be reckoned with.

The wooden False Faces share some of the inherent power of their supernatural donors. At Six Nations, the crooked-mouth and bent-nose portraits of Hadu?i? are constant reminders of the cosmology. Similarly, among the Seneca masks that are regarded as representing Shagodyowehgo:wa and are featured in the doorkeeper rite, they acquire the attributes of their patron. Certain masks come to be regarded as so powerful ("poison," in the vernacular) that they are, in a sense, "secluded" or at least restricted in their use. Such masks are not loaned out to boys for begging. One such mask that Alanson Skinner (1925, 200) collected at Coldspring from Lucy Gordon[1] was made at Horseshoe Bend on Allegheny early in the nineteenth century (MAI-HF Cat. No. 13/6609; Plate 17-1). Skinner described it as belonging to a class of "hidden masks," an idea that contributes to the notion that the False Faces are a secret society. They are not. Such masks are well known in the community and may be called upon in time of need. According to Skinner, this mask was believed to speak to its owner when danger threatened.

A LESS POWERFUL FORCE

The Husk Faces pose no such threat nor are they regarded as seriously. To be certain, the Husk Face runners as messengers for the False Faces and as advance men for the Husk Face troup run swiftly as the wind and knock down whomsoever gets in their way. Resisting them can be dangerous. As

---

1. Lucy Gordon, *gendaiyoa?* of the Snipe Clan, was ninety-four years old in 1925, when she sold the mask to Skinner. In 1934, when we reviewed Skinner's publication, Clara Redeye fondly remembered Lucy as her father's mother. It was from Lucy that Clara learned much of the lore that she imparted to me. Except for the prominent chin, the mask might be considered the type specimen for Allegany Reservation.

Plate 17-1. The "Hidden" mask of Lucy Gordon (Snipe Clan), Allegany Seneca. Collected by Alanson Skinner, 1925. MAI-HF, Cat. No. 13/6609 (see Plate 9-5).

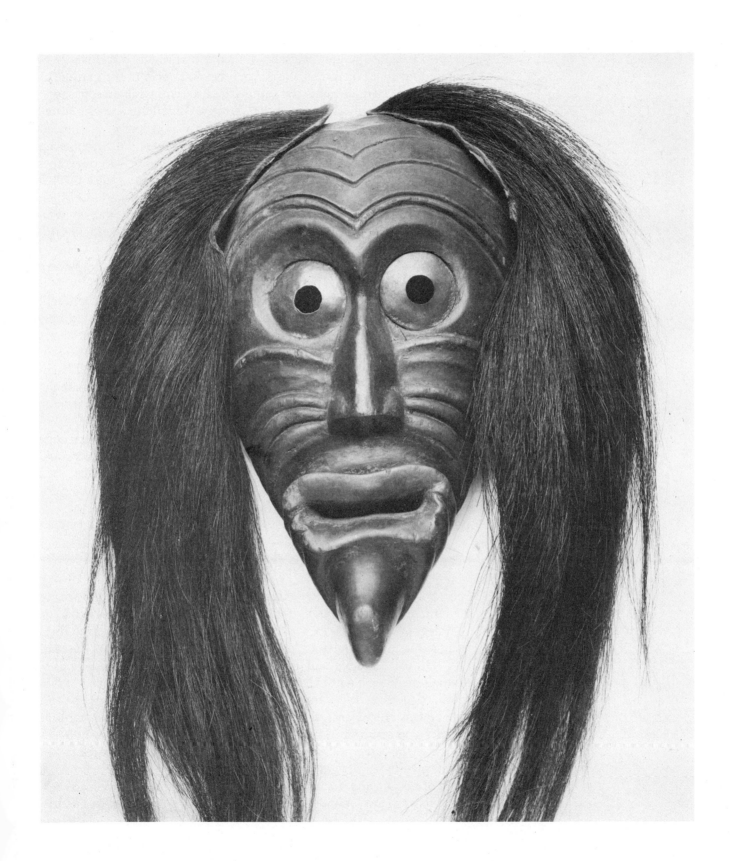

we have seen, at the great masked drama at midwinter, the Husk Faces represent a "race" of agriculturists from the other side of the earth. The high point of their advent is the capture of a speaker who is supposed to interpret their prophecy that he pretends the maskers have communicated to him. But the narrative is the speaker's own composition, which reflects the serious concerns of the community at the moment and their hopes for the coming year. His remarks are always laced with humor. Although he is expected to mention the prodigious crops that the visitors raise in their country where the seasons are reversed and to reveal the names of their leaders, which mirror their supposed prowess as farmers, these revelations and the prophecy are always more or less the same. Nevertheless, his role leaves considerable room for originality, the speech itself is an art form, and the speaker is selected as much for his wit as for his traditional knowledge. Accordingly, the prophecy varies with the times.

Today, the Iroquois are seldom farmers or even gardeners. One might infer from the heavy emphasis on crop production that swidden horticulture was the main business of the Husk Faces. Recalling the Husk Face origin myths as related by Joshua and John Buck to Hewitt early in this century, it would seem that the Husk Faces were once deemed keepers of the game and dispensers of hunting luck. For certain, at one time the Iroquois were more concerned with hunting success than small farming. One wonders whether the changed occupation of the Husk Faces represents a shift of Iroquois economic activity. There must have been a time when the Iroquois were primarily hunters and maize culture was brought to them from some center of higher culture to the South and West. In a way, the drama of Husk Face night symbolizes the introduction of cultivated crops to the Seneca by a visiting people of higher culture.

Masks as Material Manifestations of Dreams

Some forty years ago, I characterized the carved wooden False Faces as memorials to generations of nightmares. This statement aroused some comment from later scholars and friends of the Iroquois. I still think there is something to it. Given the preoccupation of the Iroquois with dreams during three centuries and the fact that one joins a medicine society through revealing a particular dream and hosting a ritual cure, persons do dream of the False Faces and often of a particular kind. However, the face may be generalized and nonspecific in the vision, and the dreamer asks the carver to make him a mask. The person may specify a type, or he may leave it to the carver's discretion. The person may even furnish the carver with a picture—a drawing or photograph. We know that there are local styles of carving and that the masks produced in a community by its carvers appear in the ceremonies and are seen by local residents. As Goldenweiser first suggested, these are the kinds of masks that people dream about. So the process is circular. There are also cases of persons commissioning a mask, dreaming about it later, and then joining the society through the appropriate feast. We have also seen that persons may inherit a mask, neglect the obligations due it, dream or become ill with one of the False Face symptoms, or even become possessed before participating actively in the society and its rituals. Once the link between the person and False Face spirit, or its surrogate, the mask, is established, the person has acquired a lifetime obligation that he dare not neglect and that he fulfills annually. Putting up one last feast for the False Faces may even be a deathbed request, as in the Worgon film, *The Longhouse People*.

Attitudes: The Paradox of Fear and Humor

Adults have been conditioned from childhood to respect the False Faces, and they learn to enjoy, and even be amused, by the antics of the maskers. The False Faces are at once awesome and funny. One does not let one's attitude get out of control in either direction. Most persons do not become possessed with classic False Face symptoms at one end of the range, nor does one ridicule the masks or the maskers at the opposite end. Somewhere in between, there is a nice balance of controlled behavior varying from respect to amusement. The False Faces evoke guarded smiles at fine performances but no belly laughs.

Children in the accounts of all observers are scared to death of the False Faces. Even the relatively harmless Husk Faces have been known to frighten the very young. Little children cry and run to their mothers, to a mother's sister, or to a grandmother for comfort and to hide their own frightened faces from sight of the maskers. I have seen this happen and have been told time and again by Iroquois women that individual children, now grown up, used to act in this manner. Individuals grow out of this initial fright as they grow older, and they are no longer threatened by parents that the maskers will get them if they do not behave. Initial fear at first sighting of the maskers is remembered long afterward.

The degree to which False Faces dominate the lives of traditional Iroquois is well illustrated in the testimony of a sophisticated woman of Shawnee and Cayuga parentage whom Margaret Mead met among the Omaha. Mead's informant had long since removed from her own tribesmen, but her childhood impression remained:

> I remember how scared I was of the False Faces; I didn't know what they were. They are to scare away disease. They used to come into the house and up the stairs and I used to hide away under the covers. They even crawled under the bed and they made that awful sound. When I was bad my mother used to say the False Faces would get me. Once, I must have been only 4 or 5, because I was

very little when I left Canada, but I remember it so well that when I think of it I can hear that cry now, and I was going along a road from my grandfather's; it was a straight road and I couldn't lose my way, but it was almost dark, and I had to pass through some timber, and I heard that cry and that rattle. I ran like a flash of lightning and I can hear it yet.[2]

Production and Collection of Masks

At the turn of the century, carvers were turning out False Faces, and women were fabricating Husk Faces for use in the local ceremonies on the several Iroquois reservations. Although Morgan did the first collecting in the midnineteenth century, it began in earnest during the closing decades of the century, notably in the activities of DeCost Smith and William Beauchamp at Onondaga, Harriet Maxwell Converse at Cattaraugus, and David Boyle at Six Nations Reserve. Evidently, there was an abundant supply of beggar or dancing masks already in use and available for sale, and a fair number of medicine masks were garnered for various museums. The Grider wash drawings in the Newberry Library convey the range and variation of local carving styles at the time. In reviewing these drawings recently, it was easy to detect features of carving treatment out of which the more pronounced local styles have since evolved. There are examples of the classic Newtown doorkeepers, both with straight lip and spoon-mouth lip treatment, and with and without spines above the nose. The great variety of "dancing" or beggar masks exhibit such features as peacock feathers and earrings. Most of these specimens went to the New York State Museum and were consumed in the fire of 1911. Grider's drawings are therefore important, although most of the label information from Converse must be treated critically.[3]

VICTORIAN COLLECTING ON THE RESERVATIONS

The intensification of collecting activity requires some explanation of trends operating in American culture and changes in Iroquois culture at the time. The close of the Victorian era saw the establishment of museums

---

2. Years ago Margaret Mead sent me this precious note culled from her Omaha field notes in an act of typical generosity to a younger anthropologist. Although published twice (Fenton 1937, 238; 1941a, 428–29), it is worth repeating here.
3. Chief Jacob Thomas, of Six Nations Reserve, a contemporary carver of note, also examined the Grider drawings with Mary Druke who tells me that he came to a similar conclusion about stylistic changes during his lifetime.

in America, increased respect for the amateur collector, and the rise of anthropology as a science, at first in the museum before it became an academic discipline in the university. Salvage ethnology was a concern of amateur and professional scientists alike, and the languages and cultures of Native Americans were the principal branches of study. Field trips to Native American communities to pursue these studies were largely supported at first by making a collection for a museum.

In the Iroquoian field, the descendants of the old Six Nations had been living on reservations since about 1800. Unable to hunt successfully as the land base shrank, they turned to small farming with domesticated animals. Residence patterns had changed. Subsistence was marginal. As agriculture declined toward the end of the century, they turned to working in the lumber woods and then on the railroads as laborers on seasonal wages. As we have seen, the traditional people who adhered to the Handsome Lake religion and were termed "pagans" by the Christian element clustered around longhouses on the reservations in western New York and Canada, keeping up the old ceremonies, including the rites of the medicine societies. Mortality in these communities, particularly among children, was high, and the intensification of the rites of these curing societies was one response to a threat that they perceived as coming from outside.

SURVIVAL

The histories of medicine societies parallel shifts in the economy and concern over public health and personal luck. In an earlier study, I demonstrated how the Eagle Dance Society evolved from a war society to a medicine society (Fenton 1953). The Society of Faces evolved in part as a response to the threat of periodic epidemics. Its concern has consistently been with public health. Smallpox and respiratory diseases swept the Iroquois settlements during the seventeenth and eighteenth centuries. The odd mask portrays facial pitting from smallpox (NYSM Cat. no. 36867; Plate 2-10B), which persisted until the present century. Cholera, typhoid, and various children's diseases—measles, mumps, diptheria, and scarlet fever—took their toll during the nineteenth and early twentieth centuries. And influenza hit the Iroquois reserves especially hard at the close of World War I. Tuberculosis came under control only recently, and pneumonia regularly greeted the spring thaw as late as 1935 before the discovery of antibiotics. For most of these diseases, the traditional herbal medicines were ineffective, and with all this sickness personal and public anxiety intensified. It was no time to neglect obligations to the medicine societies, especially the Society of Faces with its traditional concern for public health, namely the purging of windborne diseases. Although there is little solid evidence supporting this hypothesis, I think it accounts for the heightened activity of medicine societies and the perpetuation of their rites during this period. The dawn of an understanding of public sanitation and the spread of communicable diseases awaited the improvement of public education and the extension of medical services to the reservations.

CARVERS AND "PICKERS"

Among the traditional longhouse people, carvers worked part-time in the off-season from jobs as laborers and farmhands to satisfy two markets. Collectors coming from museums as well as dealers in Indian artifacts employed "pickers" as their contacts on the reserves. The family of Edward Cornplanter, Parker's informant on the code of Handsome Lake (1913), served Parker at the New York State Museum as well as Keppler and George Heye, of the Museum of the American Indian, in this capacity. Jesse Cornplanter grew up in this atmosphere, and his letters written as a boy artist document and illustrate this activity. Old masks were located and acquired from holders who wished to sell, and new ones were commissioned. Simeon and Hardy Gibson recalled serving M. R. Harrington and other ethnologists at Six Nations, where Joshua Buck was the agent for T. R. Roddy, a dealer of Black River Falls, Wisconsin. At Coldspring, on Allegany Reservation, Clarence White, Chauncey Johnny John, and Jonas Snow were my father's contacts in the twenties. Jonas Snow of the "Regular Gang" on the Erie Railroad section from Salamanca to Frewsburg (of whom it was said, "drunk or sober Jonas Snow could set and bank a curve with a piece of string and his own eyesight") carved masks in winter during slack periods of work for his longhouse neighbors and for collectors. I recall his scrawled postcards postmarked "Steamburg, NY," to my father saying, "I got a nice False Face. I just made it. Send me Five dollar." Or, "next time you come I know where we can get it, a good one." James Crow, of Cattaraugus, carried on a similar correspondence with Keppler and Heye. By 1930, picking old masks and carving new ones for collectors was a regular practice, and collecting was expected behavior of visiting ethnologists. I recall vividly the puzzlement of persons who showed me old masks and wondered why I simply wanted to photograph them. Indeed, I had no funds with which to purchase specimens, and I was more interested in learning the meaning and uses of False Faces already in museums.

FATE OF MASKS IN MUSEUMS

As the old masks left the reserves in numbers to be displayed in museum cases or curated in storage collections available to visiting scholars, one began to sense a gradual onset of regret that the finer pieces were no longer available for the ceremonies and concern that certain powerful masks might not be properly cared for by their new owners. One expedient adopted by museums was to get a knowledgeable Iroquois to visit the museum, burn tobacco, and "feed" the masks. Hardy Gibson regularly performed this service at the Royal Ontario Museum. Other individuals, some of whom had served as "pickers," performed this service at other museums. But this expedient did not satisfy the people back home. It is not easy to explain or convince descendants of former owners that museums as public trusts cannot easily divest themselves of collections once they are acquired and trustees have accepted the responsibility of preserving them. Accessioning is easy, but deaccessioning is very difficult, especially in state-supported museums. Hostility toward museum policy arose in part from guilt: Jesse Cornplanter who grew up in a family of pickers and himself collected for museums, in later life refused to understand why some of these objects could not be returned. There was the turtle rattle that Jonas Snow made in 1933 whose manufacture I have described and that was destined for the Yale Peabody Museum that Jesse said was just the proper size for singing Great Feather Dance. He never forgave my unreasonableness and kept returning to the subject in letters in later years. And there was a mask that he twice sold to Keppler and for which he twice received money that he still resented having gone to a museum.

NATIVE CONSCIOUSNESS

With the dawn of native consciousness during the 1970s, younger Iroquois, many of whom had been reared and educated in the cities, began to seek their roots. Few of these individuals had solid connections with longhouse communities. They began to read the ethnological literature on the Iroquois, a few apprenticed or were trained in museums that afforded access to collections, and they sought the traditional people. Too often they were bitten by the "genetic fallacy"—that being of Indian descent gives one especial insight into one's native culture, and they resented persons of other ethnic stock who had studied and written about their people. The next step was to chide traditionalists who had befriended and cooperated with ethnologists, pushing these equable individuals into a defensive posture. White persons would no longer be welcome at longhouse ceremonies. Teaching the Indian religion and even the language would be verboten. The third step was to draft and get the principals to sign white papers addressed to museums demanding that masks be removed from exhibition. This demand was later backed up by picketing a special exhibition at one museum that had preserved certain old masks in its collections for most of this century.

Some museums complied by taking False Faces off exhibit; other museums ignored the request. The Seneca Iroquois National Museum put the matter before its advisory committee of native Seneca. It was decided not to show masks still carrying bags of tobacco and presumably consecrated but to exhibit others that were not demonstrably sacred. Emboldened by partial success, the final step of the activists was to request repatriation.

Repatriation

The young men goaded the sachem chiefs in the communities that adhere to the traditional Grand Council of the Iroquois Confederacy that still meets at Onondaga. They drafted and got the council to adopt a policy statement. Directors of museums known to have Iroquois collections were presently greeted by a request dated March 18, 1981 (it was long delayed in the mail), signed by the legendary presiding officer of the confederacy, presently Leon Shenandoah (dateline Nedrow, New York, the post office serving the Onondaga Reservation), for the return of all manner and sizes of masks to the firekeepers of the Iroquois league. The letter and supporting memorandum stated that the masks are a part of the national patrimony and continuing spiritual beliefs. The communication proposed a regular method of receiving and distributing the masks from Onondaga to the several longhouses "after proper procedures and ceremonies have taken place."

The accompanying policy statement speaks to the medicine societies, to the status of masks, maintaining that they need not all be consecrated with tobacco to be powerful; it prohibits the sale of masks; it arrogates authority over masks to the Grand Council that assumes jurisdiction over local medicine societies; it forbids exhibition of masks; it restricts information about the medicine societies; it deplores all manner of reproduction; and finally, it holds that "there is no legal, moral or ethical way" that any non-Indian individual or institution can obtain or possess such a mask.

This proposal poses difficulties even for the Iroquois people. They face issues of jurisdiction and ambivalence. The authority of the Grand Council at Onondaga does not extend to all Iroquois communities in New York and in Canada. It does not represent the Seneca Nation of Indians, always the most populous body of the league, who withdrew from participation in 1848, formed a constitutional republic with elected councillors who have governed the Allegany and Cattaraugus reservations ever since. Late in the eighteenth century, the Loyalist Iroquois formed a parallel confederacy on the Grand River whose life chiefs duplicate those meeting today at Onondaga; they governed the Six Nations Reserve until 1924, when an elected council was imposed by the Canada Indian Act and the traditional system went underground and continued to meet at Onondaga Longhouse. Indeed, the traditions and rituals of the league have persisted in more vigorous form in Canada. Only the Tonawanda Band of Seneca, the Tuscarora, Onondaga itself, and most recently Akwesasneh (St. Regis) traditionalists adhere to the Grand Council at Onondaga. The writ of the Grand Council at Onondaga, therefore, runs thin; as a government it has no stature in U.S. law. Only on rare occasions do the two confederate fires meet, and then jurisdictional questions predominate. The Onondaga Grand Council in no way speaks for the whole.

LOCAL AUTONOMY

The medicine societies operate at the local level. Leaders holding traditional league titles may perform roles in the Society of Faces, and they do participate in policy decisions affecting the local ceremonies. But by and large such matters rest with the keepers of the faith (the *honondiont*) of each longhouse. In recent years, however, as the league in Canada has diminished in authority, its traditional chiefs have assumed new functions in its name (Shimony 1961).

Traditional politics are inevitably intertwined with the Handsome Lake religion. Following the annual autumn convention of longhouse leaders at Tonawanda, the so-called "Six Nations Meeting" at the central fire, preachers of the code who are selected from either side of the Niagara frontier travel the circuit of longhouses in New York and in Canada to deliver the "Good Message" of the prophet.

The push for repatriation of masks and related paraphernalia originated with a Handsome Lake preacher of Six Nations, himself a participant in films and traveling troups that have performed as False Faces. Likewise, an acknowledged master of the "Hai Hai" (condolence ritual) from Six Nations reserve is frequently borrowed to condole and install chiefs in the New York confederacy, and this ritual leader is also an accomplished carver who serves his own people, accepts commissions from museums, and sells masks to collectors. His indispensible knowledge of ritual grants him a certain immunity. Ambivalence among such persons must be considerable. Because of the high development of the arts at Six Nations, in which many of the traditionalists participate, there is virtually no local support for the policy and demand statement that emanated recently from Onondaga to confront museum trustees.

CONFLICTING VALUES

Two conflicting sets of values are at work—those of a native people who would hold their religion exclusively and persons of the larger society who act on behalf of museum goers in the name of the public benefit. Often, enough artifacts come into museum collections because sellers or donors from the larger society placed them in museum custody for the public benefit. The museum holds such objects as a special trust. Museum trustees accept and are charged with the responsibility of ensuring that the trust is maintained. Because museums are chartered for educational purposes and operate for the public benefit, few requests for repatriation of objects can be entertained. Native "activists" find this difficult to accept.

PART SEVEN

18. Comparisons and Implications for Ethnology

It now remains to place Iroquois masking in historical and ethnographic perspective. It may not be possible to determine the origin and direction of diffusion of masking in the Eastern Woodlands for want of comparable data on other ethnic entities within the area at the same period, but one can compare Iroquois masking with masking practices among their nearest neighbors at very nearly the same time. Our observations of the Iroquois False Faces and the Husk Faces pertain mainly to the twentieth century, backed up by similar descriptions from the midnineteenth century, which together afford a means of evaluating travelers' accounts from the previous century, reaching back to a baseline of 1687. Before that, relations from the neighboring Huron, linguistic congenors of the Iroquois, speak of masked shamanistic rites that may or may not contain the roots of later Iroquois practices. One who knows Iroquois False Face behavior at first hand sees in the accounts of Huron shamanism similar traits that undoubtedly belong to an earlier cultural stratum that are unreported for the Iroquois until after the Huron diaspora. Although these traits were conceivably present in Iroquoia, Iroquoianists from Beauchamp to the present writer have pointed to the Huron captives among the Seneca as agents for the introduction of False Faces to the Iroquois. The fact that many of these Huron captives were converts to Christianity and adhered to Christian observances, to the joy of the reporting Jesuit Fathers, does not mean necessarily that they had abandoned their own customs entirely, particularly the compulsion to fulfill dream obligations of some standing. Conversion had not saved their nation from destruction.

To extend such inferences through the media of prehistory by interpreting the widespread distribution of masquettes in stone, bone, and shell from New York to Arkansas as evidence of a still earlier stratum of masking customs once practiced throughout the area requires that one accept the fragmentary notices of masking among tidewater and southeastern peoples as clues to a more elaborate ceremonial cult that did not survive the impact of European culture.

Iroquois masking may or may not have such long cultural roots. But the rich tradition, to which I have devoted the previous chapters of this book, has evolved its own structural patterns during the period of its known existence. What one observes today, what one learns from its practitioners, and what one can deduce from myths and ritual texts perpetuate some core ideas and behavioral patterns that were shared by neighboring peoples, notably the Delaware. To our regret, Delaware masking has not survived with comparable vigor; we know it from Harrington and Speck's salvage of the now-extinct Big House Ceremony and from eighteenth-century missionary accounts.

Seventy-five years ago, when Harrington and later Speck first reached them, the descendants of the Delaware were living as a dispersed people in Oklahoma, Kansas, Wisconsin, and in western Ontario. These remnants had taken on the color of dominant neighboring native peoples making it difficult to separate Delaware customs from local ways. Harrington sought out Unami descendants in Oklahoma, and he visited Munceytown in Ontario (1913, 1921); somewhat later, Speck collaborated with a Munsee descendant from Oklahoma in a study of the Big House Ceremony (1931), then extended the study to other feasts and dances (1937), and afterward ran down the vestiges of these rites among Munsee–Mahican descendants living on the Six Nations Reserve (1945). Harrington already was quite familiar with Iroquois False Faces and their ways, and Speck was moving into Cayuga ceremonialism at the Sour Springs Longhouse where his neighboring Delaware informants attended (1949). An exchange of concepts and ritual customs between the two peoples had already occurred (Speck 1949, 1–2, 75). To separate the two traditions beyond identifying a few significant traits was no longer possible. What strikes one in reading their reports is that both men were superb field ethnologists and they both set Delaware masking apart from Iroquois practices.

Delaware-Munsee

There were both similarities and fundamental differences between Iroquois and Delaware masking usages. Although the ceremonial Big House, which Harrington found among the Oklahoma Unami, resembled Iroquois log and bark longhouses of the nineteenth century, the treatment of the interior was remarkably different. On the center post supporting the ridge pole were carved two human faces, having wrinkled brows and downturned mouths, one facing east, the other west, one greeting the dawn, and one the sunset. The six wall posts on each side carried similar carvings, and smaller faces adorned the door posts. The right side of each of the twelve faces was painted red, the left black (Harrington 1913, 219).[1] The same painting and symbolism applied to portable masks.

The symbolism of the center post recalls the Iroquois concept of the great tree that stands in the center of the earth and reaches to the sky, where the Great Defender pauses to rub his rattle and renew his strength. We have previously encountered the concept of the divided face and the east-west symbolism of red and black. The Delaware also regarded the

1. Raymond D. Fogelson, of the University of Chicago, on reading this chapter critically, added marginalia, some of which I have incorporated as footnotes. He calls attention to the Ojibwa Manitou-kan, which were human faces carved on top of planted stakes and painted, and these in turn may be related to the posts planted out of doors in the John White drawings of sixteenth-century Tidewater Algonquian ceremonies. One of the former adorns the dust jacket of Fogelson's *Contributions to Anthropology: Selected Papers of A. Irving Hallowell* (Hallowell 1976). Hallowell collected the specimen for the Museum of the American Indian. Fogelson suggests that the divided black-and-red symbolism may hint of some foreknowledge of brain lateralization.

faces as "grandfathers," the wrinkles on their foreheads being the symbols of their age (Speck 1931, 37). The Delaware, however, equated the color symbolism with gender—black resembling the warriors, red the women. These equate to death and life (Speck 1931, 37, after Harrington 1921, 83, 140–41). The faces carved on posts were regarded as portraits of man:it:owak (spirit forces) and were not worshipped as objects (Speck 1931, 36).

Although the Iroquois did not carve faces on house posts, they did carve them on living trees, and war posts sometimes featured human images; faces occasionally adorned gate posts on palisades, and there are the famous ball-headed war clubs inlaid with wampum, comprised of a human head and the shank of a leg.

LIVING SOLID FACE

It is in the concept of the "Living Solid Face" (Mεsinkhɔ:li:k:an) (Goddard 1978, 233), the mask being, that the Delaware and Iroquois masking traditions converge. "Solid Face," as guardian of all wild animals, controlled hunting luck, inhabited rocky mountains at the margin of the earth, and like Caribou Man among the Naskapi rode the back of a buck deer (Speck 1931, 39). As he traveled the earth he picked up and bagged snakes.[2] This character appeared on the fourth day of the Big House Ceremony, impersonated by a man wearing a bearskin shirt and leggings and a thick wooden mask painted one-half red and one-half black, carrying a staff and snapping-turtle shell rattle.

Unlike Iroquois specimens, the stick handle of the Delaware rattle was thrust clear through the shell. The Delaware mask, which Harrington collected, is more massive than Iroquois specimens: The face is round and smooth; the mouth is oval, reminiscent of Iroquois "whistlers," and there are modest radiating wrinkles above the brow. A headthrow and a bag of bearskin completed the ritual equipment (MAI-HF: Cat. Nos. 2/814, 2/878, 2/879; Harrington 1913, 229; 1921, 32). This character policed the camp, scared children into obedience lest they be taken and put in his bag of snakes, bestowed luck on hunters for the feast, and occasionally entered the Big House during the ceremony. While resident in Oklahoma, Solid Face had acquired the power of returning lost and stolen cattle and horses (Harrington 1913, 230). Lest one think that Solid Face represents a

2. The association of the masked shaman with rattlesnakes recalls the protective function of thunder and lightning. The "Thunder Boys" of Cherokee bear names that are cognate with the Iroquoian twins of creation, "Flint" and "Holder of the Heavens," at once evil and good, which enables Fogelson to make the speculative leap to red, indicating the "good brother"; black "the devious one." He also reminds me that the Cherokee "warrior masks" feature a coiled rattlesnake on the brow.

recent borrowing from the Iroquois, we are reminded of mideighteenth-century observations of the same character by Brainerd, Zeisberger, and Heckewelder, already cited. Brainerd suggests that a nativistic movement to restore the old religion was already afoot (Edwards 1822, 237–38).

At Munceytown, Ontario, among the descendants of a Delaware Band always closer to the Iroquois, Harrington's informant noted the absence of Solid Face and that none of the twelve mask holders was allowed in the Big House. Like the Iroquois, they formed a society of shamans who met in the spring, held a ceremony of their own, and expelled disease (Harrington 1913, 230; 1921: 152–53).

In general, medicine societies were not prevalent among the Delaware. The two that Harrington found were both among the Munsee—one of witches and the other maskers; the latter is reminiscent of the False Face Society of the Iroquois (Harrington 1913, 217). Both societies had stated meetings and rites. Like Iroquois False Faces, the Delaware Faces were representations of spirit forces, "dwellings of the spirits when worn by an impersonator" (Harrington 1921, 45). They were symbols and lacked latent power themselves. Their keepers burned tobacco, requesting hunting luck, help in retrieving lost objects and in cures.

IROQUOIS INFLUENCE ON DELAWARE MASKS

The few Delaware masks from the Six Nations Reserve that I have seen bear a marked resemblance to Iroquois masks in the Grand River style. If anything, they are more massive. There are at least three examples of masks and one face from a house post known to me, and they all date from the destruction of the Munsee-Mahican Big House on "Delaware Line" at midnineteenth century when most of the group converted to the Anglican faith.

A young Mohawk convert was the prime mover in the overthrow of the "Delaware idols." As a young man, Horatio Hale's informant and collaborator, Chief George H. M. Johnson, came into the Anglican movement through the Reverend Adam Eliott, who in 1840 had Johnson appointed interpreter for the English Church Mission on the reserve. On one occasion, in his zeal to bring the "Delaware idolators" into the fold, young Johnson seized an ax, made his way through the bush to Delaware Line, confronted the native congregation during their rites, and proceeded to smash the carved house posts, which he proclaimed "idols," and carried off one face as a trophy. It now reposes in the Royal Ontario Museum (Plate 18-1A; ROM Cat No. 922.I.25; Rogers 1959, A14). This massive face lacks the supraorbital wrinkles and downturned mouth of Unami house-post faces, its nose is massive, and the mouth oval. It was only his status as a principal Mohawk chief that enabled young Johnson to get away with this act of vandalism (Hale 1885, 133, 134–35).

An authenticated Delaware False Face was in the possession of Eliott Moses, himself a Delaware descendant living at Ohsweken on Six Nations Reserve in 1956, when I was privileged to photograph it and transcribe its documentation. It had belonged to the Delaware Longhouse (Big House) on the East Delaware Line highway before its congregation converted to the Anglican faith.

The mask is massive and measures at the back twelve and three-fourths inches by seven and one-half inches, and fourteen and one-half inches overall. It is much heavier than most Iroquois False Faces. There are seven ridges carved above the eyes, and the eyeholes are notably small. It appears to have been carved out of pinewood. Like older Iroquois masks, it features the five-hole attachment, and the original hair, which was tied on at these holes, was lacking when I examined and photographed it (see color plate).

> Pasted in the inside back an inscription read: Rev. Adam Eliott, the Missionary to Mohawk & other Indians tribes on the Grand River for over 40 years. One of the Chiefs was also a Medicine Man, who on his conversion to Christianity, gave this mask, which he had worn constantly, to Mrs. Eliott some time in 1860. Rev. and Mrs. Eliott lie buried in the church yard at Onondaga [north of the Grand River west of Middleport toward Brantford]. R. E. W. Mrs. Eliott gave the mask to Rev. G. W. Racey about 1876 and is now donated by Mrs. Racey to the Costume and Curio Department of Huron W. A. [Women's Auxilliary] October 1931.

OTHER "DELAWARE" MASKS

Speck (1945, Figure 2, p. 43) illustrated an unpainted mask with smiling mouth replete with dentures, prominent nose and chin, and wrinkles above painted eyebrows that was clearly carved in the Grand River style and resembles unpainted masks that I saw and photographed in the possession of Jake Henry and George Buck at Six Nations (Fenton 1941a; Zerries 1954, Plate 226). These masks clearly belong to the genre of Iroquois False Faces at Grand River.

Two Munsee-Delaware masks of the nineteenth century are illustrated in the Reverend Peter Jones's *History of the Ojebwa Indians* (1861, Figure 5, facing p. 83), and a third, having the Ojibwa term Pabookwaih, "The God That Crushes or Breaks Down Diseases," is shown on a following plate (6, facing p. 85). Delaware and Ojibwa, including Missisauga of the Credit, are Algonquian languages, a separate language family from Iroquoian that is spoken on the neighboring Six Nations Reserve. Peter Jones was a Missisauga by his mother, and he was born and missionized among the Six Nations Iroquois of Grand River, among the adjacent Delaware-Munsee,

Plate 18-1. A: House-post face from the Munsee-Mahican Big House on Delaware Line, Six Nations Reserve. Chiefswood Collection, ROM, Cat. No. 12631. B: Eastern Ojibwa Mask from Grand River. Teft Collection. Photo by M. R. Harrington. MAI-HF, Cat. No. X, Neg. No. 3251. The specimen went to AMNH, Cat. No. 50.1/1447.

A

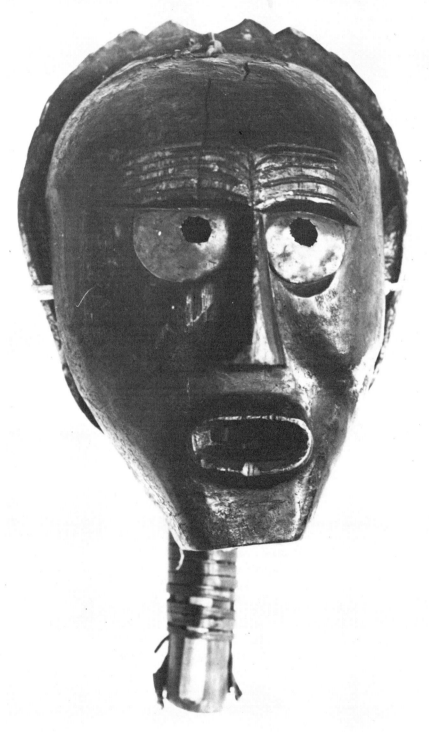

B

and among his own people whose dialect he spoke. Jones makes no explanation of these masks beyond the labels to the illustrations that attribute them to the Munsee.[3] The second mask of his first plate has a snapping-turtle rattle nested in its back, forming a bundle in the manner of keeping Iroquois False Faces. Both masks have hanging mouths, smooth faces, metal eye sconces, straight noses, and five or more wrinkles above the brow. These several masks belong to the decade of the 1840s and survived the breakup of the Big House on Boston Creek.

DELAWARE MINIATURES

The Delaware treasured miniature faces that they suspended on a string around the neck, kept in a bag, and later in a pocket, close to the person as health, or luck charms (Harrington 1921, 36; Speck 1931, 41, quoting Zeisberger). As among the Iroquois, these charms were given an annual feast and dance (Harrington 1913, 231). They were also reclothed. Such

---

3. Of the first mask Jones wrote: "*Me-Zeenk* is the name of this God," which he calls "a Muncey Idol," and he adds that it was "delivered up by Joe Nicholas on his Conversion to Christianity." The second mask on the same plate he labels: "A Muncey Devil Idol, . . . formerly belonging to the Logan family," which was "delivered up on the 26th of Jany. 1842." Harrington (1921, Plate III, op. p. 38) reprinted Jones's plate. The second of the two masks now reposes in the Indianer-Museum, Radebeul, East Germany, and is featured in color in Krusche (1975, opposite p. 176; Cat. No. 150; see also Feest 1980, Figure 177, p. 182.) This second mask is painted red, and in overall appearance it recalls certain older masks from the Seneca (MAI-HF, Fenton Collection, No. 20/2838; Plate 2-10A). In the same report, Harrington (1921, Figure 4) published a line drawing of a third mask from the Canadian Lenape (E. T. Tefft Collection, American Museum of Natural History, height 14 inches, Catalog No. 50.1/1447 [770]), which more nearly resembles the one here reproduced from Harrington's photograph (MAI-HF, Neg. No. 3251) and is reported by him in "Vestiges of the Material Culture of the Canadian Delawares" (1908, 408–18). The Tefft Collection went to the American Museum of Natural History with Harrington's usual ample fieldnotes. The catalog entry for 50.1/1447 (770) reads: "Mask/ PABOOKO WA IN/ Ojibwa./ With turtle rattle, very ancient." Harrington's notes say that he bought it from Peter Jones of the New Credit Reserve, Ontario, who said it was the original of the picture on page 85 of his father's book and that the son remembered when it was adorned by feathers, hair, and deer hoofs as illustrated in Peter Jones's book. Harrington was told that the mask and rattle were rarely used "but were bound together, and kept hung up in a special hut by the original Ojibwa medicine man who could prophesy from the way the mask hung" (Plate 18-1B). As noted, the Reverend Jones was a Missisauga-Ojibwa, but the mask apparently originated with the Munsey-Delaware.

miniatures go back to the trail of archaeological specimens that traces the Delaware migration westward.[4]

Although Harrington (1913, 235) minimized Iroquois resemblances, the parallels between the two masking complexes are striking and are of some standing historically. Both Harrington (1921, 36ff.) and Speck (1931, 93) noted this combined sharing: mask being inhabits rocky places; reveals his powers to humans; mask owners form a society; their chief function is to expel disease (Harrington 1921, 36); it controls wild animals of forest; is termed "grandfather"; patrols in early morning; frightens unruly children; begs tobacco; is paid not to scare; sees long distances despite small eye apertures; carries turtle-shell rattle and wooden staff; whinnies like a horse; indicates desires by pointing with rattle; kicks at persons; and carries a pouch or bag for tobacco in which he is said to keep snakes and offal lest someone try to rob him. He is the people's protector against disease (Speck 1931, 93).

These parallels notwithstanding, Speck (1937, 49–56), in pursuing Delaware ceremonies in Oklahoma, hesitated to link Iroquois and Delaware masking as one tradition. He noted, however, that of the Algonquians east of the Alleghanies and south of New England, only the Delaware shared in the mask tradition. As in the Iroquois traveling rite, since the eighteenth century, the Unami held a family feast in the fall after growing things had matured to seek hunting luck from the Master of Game. The latter may be a northern concept. Moreover, when neglected, the mask spirit was deemed capable of inflicting harm, and both the liability and the responsibility to hold a feast was inherited. Such a feast might be held to avert a "scare." Like many Iroquois ceremonies, the Delaware masked performance was held on the fifth day of the fall moon and was followed by an evening of social dances. The terminal feast was hominy.

Marking the transition from the harvest to the hunting phase of the annual cycle, the Delaware corn harvest ceremony, not unlike the symbolism of the Iroquois Husk Faces and False Faces, was heralded by two Husk maskers wearing suits of cornhusk and mounted on horseback. These mounted heralds carried excrement in a side pouch with which they smeared persons whom they encountered enroute unless these persons forfeited some trifling gift for the feast. Their behavior recalls the paired Husk Face messengers who precede the Iroquois False Faces in the Traveling Rite (Speck 1937, 79).

Speck (1937, 51–52) challenged someone to compare Delaware and Iroquois masking correspondences. It appears to me that we are dealing with a common cultural tradition that is quite old, although others have

---

4. The relationship of masquettes to the Delaware Doll Dance recalls the former use of dolls in the Seneca I:ʔdo:s at Cattaraugus, where Delaware were present, and the role of the Little People in the Dark Dance, still another medicine society; but these topics deserve separate treatment at another time.

argued that the Delaware Big House was post-Columbian and most probably derived from the Iroquois. Unquestionably, elements of Iroquois masking have reached the Delaware in historic times (Kinietz 1946; cf. Goddard 1978, 231–34).

Seneca-Cayuga of Oklahoma

When one considers that bands of the Delaware, Seneca-Cayuga, and Shawnee came to live as neighbors in northeastern Oklahoma midway in the nineteenth century, it is not surprising that they shared masking customs of both the Delaware and the Iroquois. Although the Seneca-Cayuga band abandoned its spring and fall purification rite about 1880, they are reported to have had twelve False Faces and six Husk Faces in their masked company (Sturtevant 1978, 542). Recall that twelve is precisely the number of house-post faces decorating the walls of the Delaware Big House. Besides, over the years, traditionalists from Six Nations Reserve have visited Oklahoma to missionize, and persons from Oklahoma have gone to Grand River in Canada to learn.

In 1950, enroute to the Southwest, I paused overnight at Quawpaw Agency and found an informant for an evening: himself one of the "Pot Hangers" (the local term for ceremonial officials). He described the maskers whom I did not see in action. Subsequently, Howard (1961, 1962, 1970) investigated the local ceremonialism and reported that the False Faces celebrated their renewal rite at Green Corn time until about 1954 when local whites ridiculed their public appearance and drove the society underground (Howard 1970, 11).

Shawnee

For the Shawnee "Shuck Faces" and False Faces, I am indebted to Erminie Wheeler-Voegelin who generously shared with me her ethnographic field notes from the 1930s. Speck (1950, 47–48) published an abstract of the same data. Taking off from Speck's Delaware study (1931, Figure 9, p. 40), Wheeler-Voegelin sought comparable information for the several Shawnee bands. She found variations in usage, which I am unable to evaluate, but certain generalities hold. The bearskin dress, staff, and turtle rattle were acceptable to Shawnee informants, although one remarked that the eyeholes were too close together in the Delaware solid face. She encountered the belief that wearing a mask intensifies eyesight (as in Seneca blind masks), which enabled a Shawnee masker to see a woman as if naked; so they blindfolded the masker. She found an exaggerated emphasis on "cleanness": It was taboo for the spouse of a pregnant wife or one who shared intercourse within four days to participate. Seneca, Delaware, and

Shawnee each had three "doctor" masks. One was divided. It is unclear whether all three wooden masks participated in the Traveling Rite. One Shawnee band, in removing from Kansas, had buried its wooden masks, and it was said that a tree grew on the spot. The Shawnee bands regarded the masks both as living properties and as grandparents.

One Absentee Shawnee[5] described a Seneca curing rite that he had witnessed. It involved an incident of putting out of the longhouse a woman who was believed to be unclean from having had intercourse the previous night. The blowing of ashes was then repeated. The taboos on pregnancy and intercourse during the four days preceding a ceremony is something that I failed to inquire about in my own fieldwork.

The Oklahoma Seneca purified their houses twice a year, in early May and before the Bread Dance in the fall. Three False Faces and three Husk Faces were selected. "Shuck Face" runners signaled the Traveling Rite, induced people to turn out, and frightened children who believed they were abductors. The Shuck Faces did not cure, but the usual False Face behavior was practiced. They were paid in tobacco. As mutes, the maskers replaced speech with gestures. As at Onondaga, the masks were kept in a rock cave, an appropriate residence for the spirit force.

Shawnee informants associated the origin of the False Faces and Husk Faces with the need to exorcise disease, specifically smallpox, and to prevent famine by exterminating worms in the corn plantings. One informant believed that the Shawnee had the maskers even in the Ohio days.

There is no mention of miniatures, but there was great stress on dolls, which had a dance of their own.

A False Face origin legend placed them in wild country to the west and related the vision of one lad who was put out to fast, had an encounter with a monster snake, which he frustrated by drawing faces on trees stripped of bark.

As in Iroquois myths, Shawnee Husk, or "Shuck," Faces dressed in deerskins, later in white trousers. As a quasi-curing society and as messengers for the wooden faces, their masks were braided and coiled, and some masks had brass eyes. A long nose fashioned from the pit of a cornstalk into which pins were stuck recalls the longnose mask of the Seneca. The maskers carried bells that simulated the noise of the great serpent. Swift runners like the deer, they made long leaps, and they rubbed dung on their hands to smear persons encountered. As mutes, they slammed their sticks to get attention and to receive tobacco. Their repertoire consisted of three songs that the singer accompanied by beating a board with a stick. Their reward was mush that they ate in the bush overnight. Performing the masking role transformed otherwise equable persons.

---

5. One of the three permanent, independent residence groups of the Shawnee formed in the late nineteenth century.

The dress and behavior of Shawnee maskers reads like a variation on Iroquois masking practices, which is not surprising because they were observing the neighboring Seneca-Cayuga and considering the long association of the Shawnee with the Iroquois, Cherokee, and Creek. If there are ethnohistorical sources that confirm my hunch of Iroquois and Shawnee sharing in the same mask complex as early as the eighteenth century, I am unaware of them.

Chippewa

North of the Lower Great Lakes, the Chippewa of Lower Michigan and southeastern Ontario, who are known as the Missisauga, displaced the Iroquois from the old Huron country. They are reported to have had a False Face ceremony possibly derived from the Iroquois (Skinner 1911, 117). Skinner inferred this from Peter Jones (1861, 138), whose Missisauga mother as a child witnessed a ceremony in which buckskin masks were worn in the manner of Sioux clowns. The eyes and mouth were bound with red flannel. This was at Owen Sound on Georgian Bay, Lake Huron. The Ojibwa used such masks to discipline children. Shamans of the Northern Saulteaux, however, had no knowledge of such masking customs (Skinner 1911, 160). The Ojibwa, moreover, knew Bokwewa, a humpbacked folk character whose deformity was mimicked by the False Faces (Schoolcraft 1839, 1:175). Skinner notwithstanding, it seems highly unlikely that the Missisauga or Chippewa had a full-fledged Society of Faces.

Oneida of Wisconsin

Although substantial numbers of the Oneida were converted to Christianity by the Reverend Samuel Kirkland (1741–1808), traditionalists among them carried at least one False Face to Green Bay, Wisconsin, early in the nineteenth century. Green Bay has been a predominantly Christian community, and the Oneida Society of Faces was never as well developed as among the Seneca and Six Nations of Grand River, and it is now extinct. (Campisi 1974, 211; Ritzenthaler 1950, 38; 1969, 30). However, the Oneida on the Thames River, near London, Ontario, as we have seen, have maintained the False Face Society, reinforced by frequent contact with the Six Nations to the east (Campisi 1978, 488).

Wabanaki

Of the Wabanaki Algonquian peoples of New England and the maritimes of Canada, northeast of the Iroquois, the Penobscot, of Maine, are reported to have performed a gaming ceremony featuring a Trading or Clown Dance, which played two or three times a week during the winter months (Speck 1940, 297–99). The clown wore a mask of skin and antlers of a deer that seems unrelated to the False Faces of the Iroquois, although the masker affected women's clothing and stuffed out his back with a hump. This whole drama, which involved exchange of goods, apparently has other roots, possibly in Europe.

Eskimo

The Penobscot Trading Dance may be related to Eskimo masking as reported for Labrador (Speck 1935), southern Baffin Land (Boas 1888: 605–6; 1901, 39–42), and elsewhere in the Arctic littoral (Birket-Smith 1929). Performances in Alaska occurred during trading occasions; in Baffin Land masks appear during rites of conjuring in fall and winter. Eastern Eskimo masks are representational; they are usually of skin but sometimes are distorted wooden human faces. The seal- or dogskin masks of Labrador contrast with the complicated wooden masks of the west. Even more so than Iroquois beggar maskers, the Eskimo masker is self-appointed, he carries a staff, and he visits houses to entertain with lewd and comic antics. Eskimo masked clowns, like the Cherokee "Booger Men," sometimes sport an exaggerated phallus that is raised and lowered by an invisible string to the delight or feigned anguish of the audience. Acrobatic feats of physical prowess are an Eskimo specialty. Dancers have been known to climax their act by exposing the buttocks in a climactic gesture of chagrin or contempt for the audience. There is nothing in Iroquoia quite like the Central Eskimo custom during the fall festival when two shamans wearing sealskin masks pair off men and women to mate out of marriage bonds for several days, unless it is the pairing by a masked conductor of men and women during the Thumbs-up Dance of the Seneca that has definite sexual implications.

Richling (1983) has interpreted Labrador *nalujuk* (masking) as the transformation of an aboriginal ritual complex in a postcontact setting. In his account, the Labrador Eskimo maskers share some remarkable similarities to Seneca masking: their concern with the behavior of children, children following maskers and being chased by them, clubbing persons overtaken with a stick, the belief that the mask spirit abducts children in a bag, and control of game animals. It would appear that the complex is older than Speck thought. The theme of renewal is predominant, and the tension between Inuit and Moravian customs and innovations is embodied in the current masking practices.

The Southeast

Turning to the southeastern Woodlands, we are no longer under the compulsion to seek the roots of Iroquois culture in that quarter because Iroquois culture is now thought to have evolved in its historic locale. This interpretation of Iroquois culture history does not rule out, however, the genetic connection between Iroquois in the North and Cherokee and Tuscarora in the Southeast at an earlier horizon. Remote as this connection must be, establishing a genetic relationship for masking in the two areas is not helped by the unsubstantial character of the ethnological literature on masking in the Southeast as compared with the more ample information on Delaware and Iroquois masking. It affords small basis for comparison. But masking was once prevalent and widespread in the Southeast during prehistoric and early historic times, judging by the distribution of conch-shell face images that covered a wide area from Arkansas to Ontario with the center in Tennessee. Illustrations of such masks in published archaeological reports (Lilly 1937, 228; Webb 1938, 373) bear a striking resemblance to Hagónde:s, "Longnose," the Seneca trickster, and to Husk Faces featuring conventionalized "tears." Both shell and copper masks of a "long-nosed god" are reported from Mississippian sites (Hudson 1976, 90, Figure 33), and archaeologists have compared elements of the "Southeastern Ceremonial Complex" with the art of Mesoamerica: Yucatecuhtli, the god of Aztec traders (Pochteca) who were also healers, is featured in sculptures (Griffin 1967, 190; Howard 1968, 10, 64; Hudson 1976, 89–90). These traders may have reached southeastern peoples via the coast of the Gulf of Mexico.[6]

From prehistoric into protohistoric times, the southeastern peoples were accomplished wood-carvers and sculpted both animal and human masks. The Spiro Mound in Oklahoma yielded a human mask replete with spool-ringed ears, shell-inlaid eyes and mouth, and a rack of deer antlers of wood (see Hudson 1976, 381), which recalls the antler symbolism of League Iroquois chieftainship. And from Key Marco in Florida come both human and animal masks, both finely carved and painted, of which a deerhead is one of the greatest works of pre-Columbian art (Hudson 1976, 382; University Museum, University of Pennsylvania

---

6. My editor, Robert Chadwick, himself a Mesoamericanist, comments, "I am not aware that the Pochteca were also healers. Yucatecuhtli is probably an aspect of Quetzalcoatl. That deity, in his avatar as the Wind God, has a long nose in the Mixtec codices" (Robert Chadwick, personal communication, 1985).

Negative No. 13256-7). Some masks of red cedar, both miniature and full-size, were hollowed out at the back to fit the human face, and bored at the rims for string attachments. The presence of paired animal and human masks painted in identical colors has suggested that dancers might shift from wearing one mask to the other as on the Northwest Coast to symbolize transformation (Hudson 1976, 384). Nor is this interpretation far-fetched.

From De Soto onward Spanish observers remarked on the examples of woodcarving in southeastern towns, and some of this high art survived among the Calusa of southwestern Florida. There masks were kept in temples erected atop mounds. In one ceremony, a masked procession came down from the mound and passed through a corridor in view of the public while women sang. Animal masks appeared during an autumn ceremony (Goggin and Sturtevant 1964, 199).

To the north, up the Atlantic coast, at this period, Carolina Algonquians carved and painted faces on posts. Between them and the Delaware, the intervening Nanticoke and neighboring Algonquian left no examples of such art. In a famous watercolor drawing, the English artist John White in 1585, at Secotan, sketched a ceremonial dance about an enclosure of seven to eight "posts carved on the topps lyke men's faces," all facing inward. They also had idols set up in temples (Feest 1978, 274; Hulton and Quinn 1964). There is no mention of portable face masks.

A century later, the Neusiok (Sturtevant 1964, 97), adjacent to the Tuscarora on the Neuse River, had erected two images in a dome-shaped shrine. One was set to the East and painted one-half red, half white; facing it on the West, the other was half red, half black, an "ugly face." Before the first image was stuck a long staff topped by a "crown", and striped in rings of red and white. The Swiss Graffenreid, ca. 1711, equated the second image with the "devil" (Todd 1920, 277–78). From this account, one may infer color symbolism marking opposite cardinal directions, sunrise and sunset, red and black, and probably life and death. Whether Graffenried was right in inferring good and evil spirits must remain uncertain. The Neusiok are extinct; the later Tuscarora had no such cultural memory.

Lawson, who accompanied Graffenreid until the natives killed him, failed to gain admittance to the house where the idols were kept secluded, as only the chief and conjuror with some old men were allowed access to the mysteries (Lawson 1967, 219). But in 1701, Lawson attended and described a masked dance among the Siouan-speaking Waxhaw, near Catawba. The dancers entered, wearing gourd masks and feathers, and carrying clubs, which he described as "falchions"; they engaged in mock combat, "cut two or three high Capers and left" (Lawson 1967, 44). At the conclusion of the dance, the young men made sport with the local girls. Such gourd masks were characteristic of the Southeast, and they prevail among the Cherokee today, although earlier specimens would have perished quickly and would not turn up in archaeological sites.

The eighteenth-century Creek decorated the posts supporting the arbors of square grounds with elaborately painted sculptures, which William Bartram described as caricatures of men, animals, and birds, often with human heads. Speckled serpents ascended pillars supporting the council house porch (Bartram 1928, 361).

Cherokee

Until recently, the Eastern Cherokee of Qualla Reservation in western North Carolina knew a dozen varieties of wooden and gourd masks in their famous "Booger Dance." One might think that any connection with prehistoric masking has been lost, but Fogelson has recently demonstrated the contrary. Speck held that this performance satirizes early Europeans who first invaded the Cherokee country; De Soto came in the sixteenth century, but the English traders were persistent visitors in the eighteenth century. Fogelson contends that the Booger Dance may be construed as descended from an earlier masking complex, which is suggested by the evidence of prehistory. Although I found that it shares few traits with Iroquois masked ceremonies and was disappointed in demonstrating that the two masked complexes derive from a proto-Iroquoian source, Fogelson has produced some positive evidence that holds out hope of establishing a common source for Iroquois and Cherokee masking (Fogelson, personal communication, April, 1983).

Speck (1950, 56) isolated the essentials of the Booger Dance, and he and Broom (1951, 24–39) described the ceremony in which the maskers appear. Essentially, the dance is a dramatic performance lacking religious function, but it does serve as an antidote to disease and misfortune, a purpose it shares with the Iroquois False Faces. The Booger masks satirize whites, Negroes, and other Indians; but they do not impersonate supernaturals. The maskers carry no rattles. There is no tobacco invocation. A variety of masks relate to hunting rites and serve as decoys. There is no color symbolism.

In a program of all-night dancing, the Bear Dance circles counterclockwise and is accompanied by a water drum and gourd rattle. Unlike the Iroquois, this is not connected with a medicine society. Midway, masked strangers from afar arrive outside, interrupt the proceedings, and stop the dance. Like the Iroquois Husk Faces, the visitors speak another language and require an interpreter, who announces their names, which are invariably obscene. Women and children register visible anxiety because the masked strangers cavort in the dances, jostle, and fondle the women, chase some into corners exposing gourd phalli, but they say nothing. Speck (1950, 24) interpreted this outlandish behavior as a reminder of the baleful character of European visitors from DeSoto onward. He further identified the concern of masked rituals with prevention, reduction, and curing of disease as a common property of Iroquoian speakers—both northern and southern—going back before their separation (Speck 1950, 28). Moreover, the rite normally took place in late fall or winter.

MY INVESTIGATION

It was to investigate parallels between Iroquois False Faces and Cherokee maskers that sent me to Qualla Reservation in 1946. I sought out Will West Long at Big Cove and found him and his son Alan carving masks. I found very little correspondence between Cherokee and Iroquois masking. Will West told me there were a dozen types of masks and named eleven of them. He and his son posed for photographs illustrating stages in mask carving. We discussed the Booger Dance, which I inferred was nearing extinction. In contrast with the Iroquois False Faces and the structured rituals of the Society of Faces, the individualism of the Cherokee rite was striking. Will West stressed sacred formulas, which were the property of particular medicine men who whispered the prayers, went to water night and morning, and divined over beads. Will West allowed that a mask might be used to scare a sick person out of an illness, and he thought that once there had been a feast.

My questions based on False Face traits evoked a memory of a visit by Harrington who sought the comparisons by a more dramatic means. Harrington put on an Iroquois False Face and entered the house crouching and whining in the manner of Iroquois maskers. Will West admitted that he was frightened: He supposed that it was a medicine-man mask, but the wearer behaved differently. It sought the fire, tackled the ashes, scattering them, and blew. This act in itself was alarming because Cherokee maskers do not go to the fire; they do not take up and scatter ashes and blow on the patient. Will recognized the transfer of heat, as from charcoal to a child's stomach, as Cherokee practice. There was also some association of masks with toothache, but the main stress was on fear.

IROQUOIS PARALLELS

As for Iroquois parallels with the Booger Dance, the two cultures share the common traits of maskers speaking in foreign tongues, whispering, doing caricatures, masquerading as hunters, carrying bows, having a gross distortion of the figure to represent pregnancy, handling offal, and the use of augmented names. The Boogers favor names having anal, sexual, or alien reference; the Husk Faces affect symbols of fertility. In either case, the maskers evoke anxiety. Both cults represent invaders or visitors from afar who enter, disrupt social dances, and request dances of their own choice.

Contests of solo dancing are more a feature of the Iroquois Midwinter Festival when False Face beggars may call upon a particular singer to accompany them. In Iroquoia, the Bear Dance is a distinct medicine society rite; in both cultures the conductor (driver) lights and passes a pipe among the participants. Ultimately, in the Booger Dance, the intruding foreigners wearing masks depart, hastening on to some other mission. Cherokee scholars have projected this satire on the whites. For the Iroquois, the visiting Husk Faces commemorate some prehistoric gift of maize, and they relieve anxiety over the next growing season. The Booger Dance may be prescribed as a cure "to scare away sickness." The same is true of the Husk Faces (Fenton 1946–47, 5; 1978b, 241–42; Speck and Broom 1951, 38).

Cherokee and Iroquois masking occupy a special place in the ethnology of Eastern North America. They both have survived into modern times, and each has evolved in its own peculiar way. Although their respective present forms might suggest that they are both post-Columbian developments, there is too much depth to masking, it is too widespread, and the evidence of prehistory argues that masking was present in pre-Columbian times. Indeed, it was present and noted in some quarters at discovery.

19. Alternate Interpretations of Eastern Masking

Three Levels

Cherokee and Iroquois masking may be viewed at three levels of historical interpretation: since the eighteenth century as a response to European agression, at a more remote level of proto-Iroquoian culture, and in relation to masking in the Eastern Woodlands generally. Beyond that are the far horizons of masking in the Americas and in Eurasia that lie beyond the purview of this study.

At the first level—since the eighteenth century—we know that rituals may persist in form but acquire changed purposes, as I demonstrated in a study of the Iroquois Eagle Dance, another medicine society (Fenton 1953). It is equally possible that the Cherokee Booger Dance, until recently a satire on Europeans, blacks, and other Indians may have evolved and changed its purpose from some earlier form of masking association with hunting, fertility, and conceivably dramatizing trading relations with earlier peoples.

At the second level—during protohistoric times—masking north and south may represent "an old common property" of Iroquoians, as Speck proposed (1950, 28) (his argument is summarized later), before the northern and southern divisions drifted apart. This argument rests on the proposition that in both places masked dances function to prevent, reduce, and cure sickness and bad luck. It is equally logical to suggest that the purging and curing functions of the maskers arose in response to the devastating epidemics of European diseases that depopulated native America in advance of the frontier. Indeed, the Iroquois False Faces at midnineteenth century were responding to smallpox, cholera, and influenza, as they may have been much earlier.

At the third level—masking in the Eastern Woodlands, as we know it—has an interrupted distribution. Several hypotheses have been advanced to explain the sporadic and variable incidence. Speck separated a northern area of portable face masking from a mid-Atlantic area of faces carved on planted posts (Speck 1945b, 73–76; 1950, 53–55). Krusche, whose ideas I shall treat momentarily, proposed a revision of the ethnohistorical and archaeological data with the thesis that wooden masks of the Eastern Woodlands evolved out of faces carved on trees and posts (1975, 171). Both views deserve examination.

Formerly, when ethnologists were concerned with the age-area hypothesis and the alleged southern origins of Iroquois culture, I had conjectured as to whether Iroquois masking was a diagnostic trait supporting the southern hypothesis "or whether it related to northern shamanism and the use of masks across the Arctic littoral, or whether the complex was original with the Iroquois themselves from whom it spread to the neighboring Delaware" (Fenton 1941a, 405). Speck took up this challenge and advanced his own view derived from fieldwork and mature consideration of the problem.

THE SPECK HYPOTHESIS

Speck's argument ran the following course: (1) No group dwells in isolation. In this regard, the Iroquois had been large-scale donors as well as takers, notably in their contributions to northern Algonquians. (2) He made a fourfold tabulation of eastern tribes using masks: northern Iroquoians; Algonquians of the Atlantic slope—Lenape subdivisions, the Mahican of the Hudson Valley, and the groups that had drifted west, including the Shawnee; Iroquoians of the near Southeast—the Cherokee; and Siouan tribes of the Southeast—Catawba and Tutelo. (3) He noted that the distribution of face masks over the area was uneven and was interrupted by tidewater groups and those from whom there are no data. He concluded that my conjecture should remain unanswered. (4) He inferred that the Huron and Iroquois were the agents for diffusing face masks to the Delaware, Munsee, and Mahican. The Cherokee were, in his view, disseminators in the Southeast. (5) Stationary wooden-face images of spiritual beings erected in open places and in buildings predominated to the exclusion of portable face masks on the mid-Atlantic slope from Pamlico Sound through Tidewater Virginia. (6) The Delaware had both stationary and portable masks. Presumably, these two classes of images represented different classes of spiritual beings and functioned differently.

Having taken the preceding steps, Speck intuited three other things: (1) At an early time Algonquian peoples from the Hudson to Carolina Sound held rituals connected with these carved posts; (2) early Iroquoians celebrated other rites employing face masks; (3) meanwhile the Delaware and Munsee, under the influence of neighboring Iroquois, began employing masks in addition to stationary icons and developed the functions of both (Speck 1945b, 73–76).

In his final paper on masking, Speck very nearly solved his own problem. He assumed that fixed images preceded removable face masks, citing the proposition "that permanent fixtures in architecture are temporally anterior to mobile ones" (1950, 43). Having previously reasoned that the Delaware Munsee, in addition to stationary images, had adopted the use of masks from the neighboring Iroquois, he remarked how they returned to hang portable face masks on house posts (1945b, 76). What he failed to notice and include in his argument is the fact that the Iroquois first carved faces on trees and that this former practice continues to be the native theory of mask origins, even if it is no longer practiced. Oddly enough, I noticed this on reading Speck's final paper and wrote a marginal note, not realizing that later it would become the linchpin of Krusche's thesis (1975).

Speck's argument has several flaws. Although there is good reason for saying that the Iroquois influenced Delaware masking customs and were the agents of diffusion to the Shawnee, there is no evidence that the Cherokee performed a similar role in the Southeast.

He is right about some other things. Of his eight final conclusions (1950, 53–55): (1) Eastern masking behavior, ranging from Labrador to Florida, is too diverse to be regarded as a basic common property of the various ethnic entities. (2) Distribution is spotty, and reportings are at different levels of time. (3) The characteristic traits of eastern mask typology are found wherever masks are made. (4) He held it reasonable to focus attention on two territorial types of masking. (Actually, only on these are comparable data available.) The highly religious complexes of the Iroquois and Delaware, which are aimed at expelling disease, suggested a common source. East and West color symbolism, particularly among the Delaware groups, coordinated with specialized social functions (of the dual divisions of society). The parallel forms of clowning among the Labrador Eskimo and the distant Cherokee remain inexplicable. Speck regarded Cherokee masked drama as a weakly developed variant of Delaware-Iroquois prophylaxis. (5) He considered other instances of masking too marginal for consideration. (6) He held that one need not look to Europe for sources of the songs, dances, or drama that the Delaware, Iroquois, and Cherokee perpetuated into historic times. He regarded the use of masks to frighten children into obedience as marginal to, and unrelated to, the major trends of eastern masking. (7) Speck observed that the history of masking elsewhere generally has been that religious symbolism fades as dramatic behavior takes over, as in the case of the Cherokee and Labrador Eskimo. (8) He reiterated the conclusion that stationary face images and portable masks have separate histories, the former center among the Delaware, the latter among the Iroquois.

Krusche's Revision

For twenty-five years, no one took a serious look at the historical development of masking in the Eastern Woodlands of North America, until Krusche (1975), who before that had never visited the United States, reexamined the literature available in libraries of central Europe. Not since Friederici (1906) wrote on scalping has a German scholar demonstrated such rigor in the use of sources or comparable familiarity with the American literature. Virtually nothing of importance has been overlooked. An English translation by Annemarie Shimony is most welcome (1986).

Starting with Iroquois False Face practices still current and known since the seventeenth century, Krusche remarks that Iroquois masks have been taken as typical of Eastern Woodland art and collections of False Faces are found in major museums. He then acknowledges the major primary and secondary sources and sketches the distribution of masking throughout the area. The disappearance of masking customs among Siouan, Algonquian, and some Iroquoian peoples has left the Iroquois, the Cherokee, and the Delaware (as of 1910) the exemplars of a tradition that was once more widespread. The predominance of Iroquois masking customs both in practice and in the literature and the overwhelming frequency of Iroquois masks in collections have all but obscured the handful of Delaware masks that Harrington collected.

AN IN SITU DEVELOPMENT

These considerations and the previously accepted assumption that the Iroquois were a southeastern people made the Iroquois the logical center of the masking complex. When archaeologists overset the southern hypothesis and substituted the in situ explanation of the origin of Iroquois culture (MacNeish 1952), the way was open for Krusche to reexamine the question of the origin of masking customs and to expose previous explanations to critical examination. Speck (1950) and I are the principal victims. There has been considerable advance in all branches of Iroquois studies since the founding of the Conference on Iroquois Research in 1945. Krusche cites some of this research. It is now evident that the separation of the Iroquoian family into northern and southern branches occurred several millennia ago (Lounsbury 1961). And of a similar order was the separation of Algonquian into eastern and central branches (Siebert 1967). Moreover, maize culture was just as intensive among Algonquian peoples of the Middle Atlantic coast and the Ohio Valley as among the Iroquois (Trigger 1963).

These revisions led Krusche to indicate the need for a new explanation of the masking complex. He finds recent ethnographic materials of little help in demonstrating connections with widespread prehistoric archaeological evidence. For him the central question is one that I raised earlier, namely whether the masking complex belongs to the hunter culture of the sub-Arctic or derives from the maize culture of the Southeast. I found no way of solving this riddle (1941a, 405). He credits me with stressing the importance of game animal spirits and of certain northern shamanistic practices in False Face rites. Chafe (1964, 281, 284) then analyzed ritual terms and demonstrated that shamanistic rites of Iroquois religion are older than the cycle of festivals that Speck and I thought had an agricultural orientation. Kurath (1961, 182, 187) anticipated this in analyzing Iroquois songs that I had recorded, finding that the False Face and Great Feather Dance songs and other music of the Midwinter Festival rites adhere to a narrow melodic line that is distinctly northern in style. With these, she lumped certain Cherokee songs.

Although one cannot posit an in situ development to masking, Speck's two-center approach—one in Iroquoia, the other in Cherokee—is not much better. Instead of my earlier characterization of Iroquois economy as comprised of northern hunting overlaid by southern agriculture, Krusche (1975, 145) accommodates the two aspects of the economy to summer and winter activities that fit the alternation of the seasons. In his view, the False Faces belong to the winter hunt, the Husk Faces to summer growth. But the trouble with this interpretation is that the Husk Faces do not appear at the Green Corn Festival,[1] that their original concern was dispensing hunting luck, that they invariably appear in spring and autumn as messengers for the wooden maskers in the Traveling Rite, and that their big act comes at midwinter when they predict the next season's agricultural productivity. Their profession of horticultural concerns is not borne out by the myths, as we have seen. Indeed, the Husk Faces, too, have a shamanistic aspect.

If culture-historical methods and interpretation yield unsatisfactory results, ethnohistory fails also for want of definitive early sources. Krusche questions Beauchamp's hypothesis that the Seneca acquired masked ceremonies from Huron captives at midseventeenth century, inasmuch as many of the Huron captives were Christian converts who later welcomed Jesuit missionaries among them. But there were also traditionalists among them who resisted conversion, which had been the downfall of Huronia (Trigger 1976). The real problem is one of methodology—whether it is legitimate to infer from accounts of Huron masked ceremonies during the early seventeenth century that the Five Nations Iroquois south of the lakes could have had similar customs that were not described until much later. Indeed, at least one Jesuit writer admits the error that the Iroquois had no masks. Krusche maintains that such diffusion from Huronia to Iroquoia might just as well have taken place in precontact times.

DELAWARE AND IROQUOIS SHARED TRADITION

The silence of early writers on the Eastern Algonquians, in Krusche's opinion, is of greater significance than the failure of observers in Iroquoia to be specific about masks. The sources are short and of bad quality. Even the Delaware accounts date only from the mideighteenth century, and the want of records for the Nanticoke led to the assumption that the Iroquois were the originators. There is, however, a specific record by a competent observer that, in 1654, the Delaware were using masquettes as amulets in a way entirely consistent with later Delaware and Iroquois usage, and Krusche notes that these masquettes were fairly accurate copies of larger masks reported later (Lindeström, in Krusche 1975, 150).

Similar stone masquettes occur archaeologically in Huronia, Iroquoia, and wherever the Delaware migrated. Indeed the face motif goes back to the Chance Horizon and is older than true Iroquois culture. It exhibits a

---

1. If the Green Corn Festival is of late diffusion to the Iroquois, or a later development, as some evidence would indicate, this may explain the want of appearance by the Husk Faces whom the earlier myths associate with hunting luck.

continuity of style during several hundred years. Thus, Krusche concludes that the Iroquois had masks in prehistoric times. But to be significant, the same must hold for the Algonquian tribes of the mid-Atlantic coast. Such stone faces, both small and large, do occur in the habitat of the Delaware and Shawnee and resemble the wooden Mising faces (Krusche 1975, 152–3). These things and the fact that eastern Delaware sites were abandoned soon after contact lead to the conclusion that the mask rites of the Delaware cannot be copies of Iroquois ceremonies: The mask traditions of the Iroquois and the Delaware appear to be independent developments from a common heritage.

Krusche derives *two theses* from his investigation: (a) an in situ development of the masking complex in the Eastern Woodlands; and (b) both the Iroquois and the Delaware shared in this development. But he recognizes that this attribution to a local development does not explain how a mask originated.

In their preoccupation with masks, scholars have paid too little attention to how maskers dressed, how they manipulated faces, and where they were put when not worn. He notes that the animal masks from Spiro and Key Marco have no eyeholes, were not hollowed out, and could not be worn. But Sturtevant and Goggin (1964, 198) indicate that the ancestors of the Calusa did indeed have hollowed masks with eyeholes that were worn, although the former carvings were carried in processions, put on poles like trophy heads or scalps, or hung on stakes or posts as Krusche suggests (1975, 154). Hanging masks on posts has both a prehistoric and an historic dimension, as witness the Munsee-Mahican in Canada hanging faces on house posts, as if in substitution of faces already carved on the posts of the Big House in Oklahoma.

In Krusche's view, Speck's distinction between faces on house posts as icons and portable masks is bogus, the difference between "static" and "moving" images is not supported by the sources, and the hypothesis of an Iroquois tradition of movable masks and an Algonquian tradition of post icons does not hold. Actually, we are confronted with different aspects of an old and widespread cult tradition (Krusche 1975, 156).

THE HOUSE POST SET IN MOTION

On reexamining Speck's information on the relationship of the Delaware mask being to the post faces, which Speck held was of different conceptual orders, Krusche suspects that the distinction is recent. He notes that the two are painted identically—half red, half black. They both rate the honorific kinship term "grandfather," which is generally accorded to powerful supernaturals; they both are clothed or reclothed in bearskins. He also notes that the terms *Mising*, "Solid Face," and *Misinghalikun*, "Living Solid Face" bespeak a generic relationship, one stationary and the other dynamic, and that the number of twelve houseposts and their arrangement into dual divisions corresponds to the number of masks later introduced into the Big House. To Krusche, the masked spirit clad in bearskin, who is master of the game, appeared to the Delaware as the house post set in motion. (1975, 157–58).

Further evidence of the generic connection between face posts and face masks and between Delaware and Iroquois carving is the fact that the Iroquois formerly carved faces that became masks on a living tree, which Krusche maintains is not essentially different from carving a face on a planted post. And he holds that wooden face masks developed from the stake icon. But the living tree contrasts with the lifeless post (1975, 160–61, Figures 3, 4). (Although not mentioned, I am reminded of the line in the tobacco invocation to the False Faces that speaks of "Faces against the trees.") In both cultures, one finds the concept of the world tree that stands in the center of the earth, where the Iroquois False Face prototype pauses to rub his rattle and from which he derives his strength and the center post of the Delaware Big House. There is, moreover, a natural progression in the carving of a mask, which I had reported (1937, 233; 1941a, 423–24, Figures 21–22), before the back is hollowed and the eyes and mouth apertures are opened, when the block face resembles Delaware post icons, and before the refinements of wrinkles are added. As in old Iroquois masks, the smoother faces could be taken for Delaware solid faces. If the eyes are never opened, as in certain secluded Seneca blind masks, and a chin hold is left for adjusting the mask to one's face temporarily, there is the possibility of recapturing an earlier method of holding masks to actors' faces before holes were bored in the rim to accommodate head ties. Krusche illustrates this transition (1974, Figures 5–9) and documents his comparisons (1975, 162–63). This is a fascinating suggestion that, unfortunately, can no longer be tested in the field. Nor can ethnologists, as I have previously indicated, recapture the ritual of carving a mask on a living tree, which in Krusche's thesis recapitulates the evolution from tree, or post face, to portable mask (1975, 165).

EVOLUTION OF MASKS FROM TREE AND POST FACES

In defending his thesis that wooden masks of the Woodland Indians evolved from tree and post faces, Krusche confronts Speck's hypothesis of separate origins, and in due regard for Speck's eminence in the field, he reviews the ethnohistorical scraps that demonstrate that the Iroquois did indeed participate in the post face tradition. Much of this material we have already cited. Such post faces as there were among the Iroquois had disappeared before the dawn of modern ethnography, and so it is not strange that Iroquoianists have not inquired about them (Krusche 1975, 169).

The anomaly of having to explain the evolution of Eastern Woodland masking customs that were widespread in prehistoric times in terms of the Iroquois and Delaware data proves an embarrassment to the scholar that can only be explained by their survival into the present century. Disappearance of these customs elsewhere poses no difficulty; survival is far more sensational and due, in these two cases, to integration into reformed religions that are the outgrowth of nativistic movements. The Delaware movement had begun by the mideighteenth century, as Brainerd noted in 1745, and the masking complex was installed in the Big House. The Iroquois case started with Handsome Lake's revelation at the close of the eighteenth century, and masking has been perpetuated by the adherents to his code to this day. Masking among the Eastern Cherokee that has survived in the coves of the Great Smoky Mountains is attributed to their long isolation from contact (Krusche 1975, 170ff.).

In Kansas, the Living Solid Face became the target of frontier prejudice that equated him with the devil, and the Delaware leaders in self-protection reinterpreted his role in the Big House. And, in Canada, many of the old masks were destroyed by Christian zealots. Likewise, among the Seneca when the medicine societies were temporarily suppressed by the followers of the prophet, the False Faces went underground with their con-fraternities, and, according to Parker (1909, 163), maintained that the order in council was not valid because the order to dissolve and disband was not accompanied by a proper tobacco invocation. Indeed, this episode and the pressures later from the Christian party on the reservations contributed to the element of secrecy, although ceremonies were performed in the longhouse districts more or less publicly. As Wallace (1970, 336) has pointed out: "What was revolutionary in the prophet's day is now . . . the extreme of traditionalism." Thus the Society of Faces has emerged, almost 200 years later, as the hallmark of Iroquois religious expression (Krusche 1975, 174).

Krusche makes another point that I have made earlier, namely that the masked societies that originally had to do with hunting luck lost some of their purpose as the land base shrank, game declined, and reservation life set in. Except for the early association of animals with disease, their present preoccupation with sickness, healing, and psychic disorders seems recent (Krusche 1975, 175).

The convergence of like-minded, conservative ethnic entities on the Six Nations Reserve in Canada contributed to the maintenance of masked ceremonies and mutual interchange of customs. We have alluded to the Munsee of Boston Creek seeking sanctuary in Sour Springs Cayuga Longhouse after the defection of members to the Anglican faith. Krusche (1975, 176) wonders whether the Tutelo who found refuge among the Cayuga at mideighteenth century and followed them to Grand River brought masked ceremonies with them. By the close of the nineteenth century, Tutelo rites had become integrated into Cayuga Longhouse ceremonies, and the last speakers of Tutelo were culturally Cayuga, as witness Boyle's (1898, Plate VIII B) photograph of John Key posed with his artifacts, which include a typical Grand River wry-mouth mask and turtle rattle.

DELAWARE MASKING SIMPLER

I have always been struck by the relatively uncomplicated nature of Delaware masks and masked ceremonies as opposed to the relative complexity of Iroquois masks and the more elaborate masked rituals. I have commented on the evolution of carving styles and noted that the earliest known Iroquois False Faces are rather smooth-faced and lack the distortions and wrinkles of later carvings. Krusche (1975, 179–80) reaffirms this. The color symbolism of divided Delaware masks and the cardinal orientation of red and black is clear-cut, and masks of a single color (red or white) are associated with the moieties. The red or black polarity of most Iroquois masks, identified with east and west and morning and afternoon by learned Tonawanda informants of the 1930s, is not shared by all Iroquois groups, and the relative power of black versus red masks remains a moot issue with my informants. The divided mask at Six Nations Reserve is an Iroquois anomaly and is quite probably of Delaware derivation.

Ethnologists are certainly aware of the importance of the moiety principle in Iroquois social organization and how the moieties function in ceremonial contexts. Designation of the moieties as "red" and "black" has been known since 1666 (Fenton 1978c, 299) (O'Callaghan 1855, 9:47–50), but during the intervening centuries this clear-cut symbolism has fallen away. Krusche's suggestion (1975, 181), which is supported by Shimony's information (1961, 151), that the red and black masks were formerly keyed to respective moieties is an intriguing possibility that can only be inferred at this late date.

I find no evidence, however, that masks were ever clan property.

Although the Delaware and Iroquois share certain traits of masking, it would appear that the Delaware kept the mask tradition of the Eastern Woodlands in a relatively archaic form (Krusche 1975, 182). This being so, the Iroquois can no longer be considered as donors of masked rites to the Delaware. Rather, as in other matters, just as the Iroquois have adopted whole peoples, they accepted and reinterpreted customs of neighboring peoples and then elaborated them.

In devoting considerable space to the elaboration of Krusche's arguments and commenting on his conclusions, I am mindful that his contribution may be missed by students of Iroquois masking, and my review of it here may be useful. He has gone beyond the usual cultural-historical method, and I find his perceptions most challenging and his findings admirable.

Fogelson's Ideas on Common Folk Beliefs

In a wide-ranging essay on stone-covered anthropomorphic beings that populate Iroquoian mythology, both south and north, and find their counterparts in the folklore of neighboring Algonquians, east and west and north to the sub-Arctic, Fogelson (1980) has isolated traits of these supernaturals that link Cherokee and northern Iroquois culture through commonly shared beliefs that up to now we have not considered and that are not clearly evident in the masking complex.

STONE GIANTS

The relevant attributes of these beings are stone- or flint-covered bodies, gigantic stature, cannibalism, and a heart of quartz or ice crystal. Secondary features comprise transformation to human form, a spear-shaped finger for extracting livers of victims, a detached finger that magically points to human game, and a magical cane or staff that also serves as a weapon, as a sensing device in tracking, and can be projected and transformed into bridges and other works. Such stone beings inhabit the north or dwell in caves or mountains. They profess and are believed to have preceded humans on earth and require special treatment to nullify their powers lest they destroy humans and the sources of sustenance left on earth by the Creator for human use and enjoyment.

Not all of these attributes are shared by the supernaturals whom the False Faces represent. But the obvious shared features include stature, cannibal tendencies, transformation, the cane or staff, affinities for the margins of the earth, caves, and mountains, and awesome power that can be converted to human benefit with native tobacco, prayer, song, and imitation. Indeed, the Iroquois know the cane as a sensing device in tracking, which when pointed causes paralysis of the victim, a theme that is celebrated in "The Oneida Tracker's Boasting Song" (Fenton 1942b, Record IB3, Program Notes, 19–20). Other attributes occur in other contexts.

CHEROKEE AND SENECA CONNECTIONS

At this level of investigation, Cherokee and Iroquois connections assume reality. Although Fogelson's research stems from the Cherokee "Stone Man," he finds a northern Iroquois affinity in the Seneca Genonskwaʔ, the so-called "Stone Giants" whose activities Parker (1923, 394–400) collected in several versions and merged into a single narrative. In this account, Genonskwaʔ (literally "It Eats Leather [or] Human Flesh") was the progenitor of the Society of Faces.

In Seneca folk literature, Stone Giants manifest important parallel attributes to the Cherokee Stone Man: detached finger as game finder, acute hearing (poor eyesight), powerful spittle, can wade under water, and northern origin. At the behest of Skyholder, Thunder ambushes an invading army of Stone Giants, traps them in a narrow defile, and crushes them with boulders hurled down by West Wind.

Stone Coats were nocturnal and holed up in caves during daylight. In one incident, they were infiltrated by Skyholder who transformed into one of them and who by magical feats became their leader. During an attack on Onondaga, he bade the others hide in caves, while he caused an earthquake to collapse the caves and bury them alive forever (Parker 1923, 394–96). One lone survivor escaped to a cave in the Allegheny Mountains where a lone hunter seeking shelter from a hail storm (flint or ice) took refuge.

The last of his kind, Gęnonskwaʔ, in a culturally charged conversation, spared the hunter, informed him that the spirits of the dead kindred Gęnonskwaʔ survived in living trees, and charged him to go forth and carve faces on the living basswood, the great healing tree, to carry home the load of carvings, and to form a society that would preserve his teaching (Parker 1923, 396–400). The new learning would cover the use of herbs in healing and the control of windborne diseases by blowing ashes.

The proscriptions on secrecy have been treated earlier as has the ritual of mask making (Parker 1923, 401–2).

RELATED MONSTERS

Fogelson's analysis demonstrates a connection between the southeastern Stone Clad, with his heart of quartz crystal, the Iroquois Stone Coat, and the northern Windigo, with his heart of ice. He holds that these anthropophagous monsters pertain to the realm of nature. In the Iroquois case, by the intermediary of sacred tobacco and a contractual agreement with a good hunter to sponsor ceremonies in their behalf, their evil power is transformed to positive culture. Monsters occupy a polar position to human values and become humanized. The legacy of Gęnonskwaʔ transformed is the Society of Faces. In the Onondaga version of the cosmology, it is Haduʔiːʔ who is bested by Skyholder, and for most Seneca it is Shagodyowéhgo:wa:h and the less dangerous Faces of the Forest. These are the folk characters that are commemorated in the great drama that this book describes.

BOOGERS AND HUSK FACES

Inspired by the Stonecoat, in yet another paper, Fogelson and Bell (1983) have reexamined the "Cherokee booger mask tradition" at a deep level of analysis and have found parallels and established a connection with northern Iroquois masking traditions that I failed to discover in the field but hinted at in the previous discussion of Speck and Broom's interpretation. The parallel is particularly evident between the Cherokee buffoons and the northern Husk Faces.

The essential points in their analysis and findings are the following:

1. A redefinition of the event that occurs in late autumn after the first killing frost parallels the northern Iroquois masking rites when the Husk Faces and False Faces revisit the settlement in the traveling rite, and especially at midwinter when the Husk Faces arrive from the other world at the longhouse and request the privilege of dancing with the people in friendship.

2. "Booger" may be a misnomer for "beggar," which immediately recalls the Iroquois beggar mask performances at midwinter. (Fogelson now considers this equation very hypothetical.)

3. The close association of both groups of maskers with disease is probably older than the European invasion.

4. A reexamination at a deeper level of similarities and differences in Cherokee and Iroquois masking reveals that the former tradition is weaker and not hedged in by taboos and requirements that are incumbent on Iroquois mask holders. As I noted previously, the Cherokee lack the elements of possession, transformation, and the handling of live embers and ashes. As a restricted, if not secret, society, the Iroquois False Faces resemble dancing societies on the Plains, notably the Dakota Heyoka and the Pawnee Iruska and the closer Ojibwa Windigokan. Ritual buffoonery has even wider implications as far away as the Pueblos.

5. Profound surface differences between Iroquois and Cherokee masking obscure basic similarities: begging, relation to disease, communicating in whispers and in a nonsense language, advent of visitors from afar who bear weapons of the hunt, visage and stooped gait, and the use of canes or staffs as old people.

6. Invoking Lévi-Strauss's theory that poses a dialectic of culture versus nature, the Iroquois fulfill the opposition nicely, the Cherokee less so. In the analogy, in which the Iroquois wooden faces are to the Husk Faces, much as the Cherokee wooden faces are to gourd masks, we are reminded that Iroquois False Faces personify nature; ideally they are carved from living basswood trees; they are denizens of the forest; and they bear a symbolic association with game animals and diseases that are windborne. Similarly, animals are the tutelaries of other Iroquois medicine societies: Bear, Buffalo, Otter, and Eagle. At the same time, Iroquois Husk Faces and Cherokee gourd masks personify man's involvement with cultivated plants, namely his subsistence culture.

A further dialectic is resolved by a ritual contract: In the exchange between tutelaries and man, for access to wild game, for relief from disease, and for safe passage through the woods, man offers the cultural gifts of tobacco, mush, sunflower oil, sponsors a ritual, and puts up a feast.

7. The Haduʔiʔ are male, False Faces are carved by men, they are worn by men, and they impersonate older men (grandfathers). In an age differential, small boys impersonate older men, and the society in its rounds is led by men.

8. Iroquois Husk Faces occupy the cultural pole of the dialectic. Women fabricate them; weaving is a cultural act, and magic is a cultural product. Again, there is an age differential between maskers and the spirits they impersonate. Husk Faces are less formalized, less powerful, less dangerous, less sacred. There is a reversal of sex roles in their appearance at midwinter, but most of the roles are played by men. Their keepers, however, are women. They are messengers for the False Faces; they imitate them in curing; they are old but spritely; and their performances are profane and sometimes obscene. They are otherworldly and are associated with the planting and cultivating of prodigious food crops. (Their former association with game control has been forgotten.) Fertility is of their essence. They are generators and donors of culture.

9. The analogy can be stated in terms of shared traits: both the Cherokee wooden Booger masks and Iroquois wooden False Faces are concerned with disease, they share the attributes of wildness and masculinity, their locale is the forest, and they have similar origins. Cherokee gourd masks and Iroquois Husk Faces are fabricated from domestic plant residue, and they barge in and interrupt social dances. But between the Booger masks and the Husk Faces there are contrasts: The former are less organized, they are overtly sexual, whereas the latter are hierarchical, and the scatalogical element of the Boogers has been lost among the Husk Faces.

The weakness of the foregoing analogy is that the functions of Cherokee wooden and gourd masks have merged, whereas the Iroquois differentiation of wooden and husk masks is clear-cut.

10. The two peoples share a common cosmology. A further parallel lies in the Cherokee tradition of a visit to another world—a place of great plant fertility in winter—where seasons are reversed.

In sum, the authors view the Cherokee Booger Dance as being genetically related to northern Iroquois masked dancing.

OTHER SOUTHEASTERN PARALLELS

The balance of this stimulating paper seeks parallels in other cultures of the Southeast. In the Creek Old Man's Dance, the young impersonate the elders; they wear gourd masks; their performance features buffoonery; and a pantomimic hunt (reminiscent of the Cattaraugus Seneca) manifests concern with animals and hunting. Similarly, among the Choctaw, the performance with gourd masks preceded departure on the fall hunt. Unfortunately, masking in the Southeast is not viable nor available for ethnological study, as in the northern Iroquois case. Its main theme, however, was impersonation of the elders by young people in which the old men gain strength and power from the young—a theme not unknown in Iroquois mythology. Whereas Iroquois masking borders on the sacred, a profane attitude pervades southeastern masked dancing: Carnival, or burlesque, is its life's blood. Through it, overt sexuality is expressed.

The authors conclude with the following suggestion:

> that the Cherokee Booger Dance is one such performance in which young men masked as old men symbolically journey from a distant land, intrude upon, frighten, and entertain the audience of kinsmen and potential affines, achieve social solidarity by dancing with the women of the local group, and then abruptly take their leave [Fogelson and Bell 1983, 62.]

Almost the same statement could be made of the Seneca Husk Faces, who, as we have seen, are a constant reminder of the southeastern origins of Iroquois horticulture. It would seem that their presence represents an overlay on an older hunting economy. They are concerned with summer activities, and they return at midwinter to encourage the people to hope for a warmer season.

PART EIGHT

20. Postlude
The Startling Parallel of Carnival in Europe

Preconceptions

European observers coming to New France during the seventeenth century constantly compare face painting and masked shamanism of the native Indians to the more familiar antics of the jugglers and clowns who ran riot on Shrove Tuesday in provincial France. Indeed, Father Gabriel Sagard, a Recollect priest, and the Jesuit writers who followed him saw in these New World customs an example of unredeemed paganism that they deplored as persisting at home despite the Counter-Reformation. Inevitably, they saw these shocking customs in terms of what they already knew, and they invariably described the frenzy of Huron and Iroquois midwinter dream fulfillments by resort to the concepts and vocabulary of their own culture.

Sagard's *Long Journey to the Hurons* and the *Jesuit Relations* are the bread and butter of Iroquois ethnohistory, but I previously read them through the screen of ethnological fieldwork among the Iroquois and discounted as irrelevant references to the Feast of Fools, or Carnival, as misreading the situation. The late Marius Barbeau, the distinguished Canadian savant, used to insist that Huron and Iroquois masking derived directly from folk customs transplanted to the New World by the habitants of New France. At the time, I paid little attention to Barbeau's views and dismissed them as an abberation of an otherwise accomplished folklorist and ethnologist, until I visited the museums of Switzerland in 1962. I then experienced a culture shock of my own on seeing the remarkable parallels between the masks of the Swiss folk and Iroquois False Faces. I was unprepared to cope with this dilemma—other than by resort to familiar ethnological theory on diffusion versus independent invention—until I read a noteworthy paper by an American scholar of the theater who has made a special study of Carnival as it survives today among folk peoples in Central Europe and has used this background to analyze the *Jesuit Relations*. I shall recount my own museum visitations and then discuss Martin W. Walsh's paper.

SWISS MASKS

In the summer of 1962, I made an extended search of European museums for ethnological specimens that were possibly carried home from the natives of northeastern North America to repose first in Cabinets of Antiquities and then museums. I was looking particularly for early examples of Iroquois masks. Arriving in Zurich, I was greeted by a grand display in the windows of a principal department store featuring the "Customs and Usages of the Swiss People." Here were brilliantly lacquered masks with bent noses and distorted mouths that, save for an element of decorative style, could have been straight out of Iroquoia. This discovery sent me to the nearby Rietberg museum that holds an extensive collection of Swiss masks. Inasmuch as the Swiss maskers, I was told, like the Iroquois False Faces, are most active in winter, there was no opportunity to witness them in action.

From readily available literature on the subject, one learns that the Swiss maskers who are garbed in animal skins represent old people and that they frighten women and children who hide from them. Among the mountain folk they come at midwinter begging, they steal food, they carry cowbells instead of turtle rattles, they commit excesses, engage in reverse behavior, and there are other striking correspondences to False Face behavior (Christinger and Borgeaud 1963, 1–24; Hansmann 1959).

WALSH'S STUDY

All of this seemed beyond my ken until I read Walsh's "The Condemnation of Carnival in the *Jesuit Relations*" (1982) and heard him discuss the subject at the Conference on Iroquois Research. Walsh cites and analyses passages in which the missionaries from 1632 onward describe face painting and masking among the Montagnais, Huron, and Iroquois of the Five Nations, likening what they saw to the old French Carnival. Brilliant hues of face pigments evoked "brightly colored and highly lacquered masks," which are still characteristic of European carnivals (Le Jeune in JR 5, 22–23; Walsh 1982, 13). Walsh is the first European folklorist familiar with Carnival to look at the *Relations,* and he finds Carnival to be a constant throughout the seventeenth century for comparison with the frenetic shamanistic rites of Huron–Iroquois medicine societies performing at the Midwinter Festival. Indeed, as he points out, the Jesuit Fathers constantly engaged in a species of social criticism aimed at their audience in France that they couched in metaphors already familiar to their readers, at the same time deploring the survival of pagan customs in civilized France. In a passage that I have previously cited as ethnological evidence of Huron masking, Father Brébeuf, who knew French folk performance, fully articulated the Carnival analogy (JR 10:201–3).

In commenting on this passage in Brébeuf's relation, Walsh reminds us that the improvised bag mask and the padded belly of the man-woman are depicted for us in Bruegel's famous painting *The Battle of Carnival and Lent.* To the French Jesuit missionary, the cures and renewals of Huron medicine societies celebrated during Ononharoia ("The Reversed or Addled Mind"), which is the linguistic and cultural ancestor of the Iroquois Midwinter Festival, presented a clear analogy to the antics of Carnival fraternities, to the *sociétés joyeuses* that were certain confraternities of fools that recently had been suppressed in France who in turn were descended from the medieval *Festa stultorum.*

Again Brébeuf provides a case study of how one Huron male attempted to achieve the rank of principal shaman (JR 10:200–1). The man went about naked at midwinter night and day and accompanied his singing with a turtle rattle in the manner of later Iroquois maskers. But Brébeuf equated the turtle rattle "with the parodic scepter of the Court Fool," thus identifying the actor for French readers of the period. The same individual was later treated and admitted to membership by a society of medicine men who recognized the symptoms when the man fell over backward, in a kind of hysterical seizure, and vomited. Brébeuf likened the society of shamans to a brotherhood of fools and their behavior to the orgies of the Bacchantes of ancient times (JR 10:206–9).

"Already in Brébeuf," Walsh writes, "we can see a full vocabulary drawn from popular and carnivalesque performance applied perjoratively to native ceremonies."

A decade earlier, having preceded the Jesuits to Huronia, Sagard witnessed a bearskin-clad doorkeeper in one ceremony that suggests to the ethnologist the garb of eighteenth century Delaware and Iroquois maskers, but he equated the role with that of the French *boufon*. Again, cornhusk figures that the Huron set up on lodges during an epidemic in 1639 reminded Father Le Mercier of "orchard scarecrows," and wooden maskers struck him as "altogether ridiculous" (JR 13:231, 263).

Yet another Jesuit writer likened the turtle rattle to a French children's toy, called the Ononharoia a "general mania," and wondered should he compare it "to the most extravagant of our maskers . . . or to the bacchantes of the ancients, or . . . to the furies of Hell" (Jerome Lalement, in the Relation of 1639, JR 17:157, 176–77). Although we can understand the good father's annoyance at having the solemnity of Christmas Eve disrupted, he does document the role of the crier or herald who announces the ceremonies and urges all to participate. When he adds that "he is judged most valiant who best acts the maniac," he underscores the fact that in Huron and in Iroquois society prestige attaches to role playing and to fulfilling one's ceremonial obligations (JR 20:28–31).

When at midcentury, the Jesuit missionaries reached Onondaga, the central fire of the Five Nations Iroquois Longhouse, they found the equivalent of the Huron Ononharoia flourishing. One wishes that they had been more matter of fact in describing its proceedings, rather than likening it to the "Feast of Fools, or to the Carnival of the wicked Christians" and that they had refrained from resorting to classical analogies—to Satyrs, Megaras, and Amazons (JR 42:154–55, 160–61). Their *Relation* leaves us wondering: Were there maskers at Onondaga at this time?

Having collated Jesuit observations both in Huronia and in Iroquoia during forty years of the century, Walsh finds that the "number and depth of correspondences between the Midwinter Ceremony and the old European Carnival" cluster around nine subjects.

CARNIVAL PARALLELS WITH HURON-IROQUOIS RITES

Following are some Carnival parallels with Huron-Iroquois rites.

1. *Calendric position.* Both the Ononharoia, with its associated shamanistic rituals, and Carnival occurred in late winter or early March. Carnival fell on the Sunday, Monday, and Tuesday before Ash Wednesday, as it still does. Setting the date for the Midwinter Festival by observing the Pleiades and the new moon, as among the modern Seneca, lacks early historical documentation.

2. *Origin myth.* The beginnings of the Huron festival were associated with a cannibalistic giant, possibly a "Stone Giant." An all-devouring giant, or giants, dominates Carnival.

3. *Social structure.* Youth, as among False Face Beggars today, comprised the main participants in public frenzy and ensured maintenance of the festival. Healing was left to experienced shamans. Medicine societies equated with Fool confraternities. Both systems featured village criers. Although the Jesuits found nothing in Huronia comparable to the "burying of Carnival," today the climactic visitation of the Husk Faces performs this function.

4. *Masquerading.* "Hunchbacks, 'Bessies,' creatures reminiscent of the European Straw-bear and the witchlike Perchten (Dablon's Satyrs and Megeras) are common in the *Ononharoia.*" Grotesques, ogres, idiots, and forest spirits people both traditions. Even the material culture similarities are striking: cornhusks (straw), antlers (cow and goat horns), skin garb, bright paint, grotesque wooden masks, blackening with ash or soot, or even smearing with excrement.

5. *Monde reverse.* Ononharoia is a *renversement de tête,* a turning over of the mind, which permits and demands reversal of sex roles and outlandish appearance. The common Carnival "topos" is suggested.

6. *Gluttony.* The famous "eat-all" feasts did not rival the drunken frolic that was Carnival.

7. *Sexual license.* The unspecified obscenities of the Huron Midwinter Festival, the all-night mating of young girls and men in a particular Huron ceremony, did not draw from Walsh a Carnival parallel.

8. *Frenzy.* Hysterical possession was the predominant characteristic of Ononharoia, a wild racing between and through lodges, a *folie publique* (JR 30:100), howling, beating on houses, and shaking rattles. Walsh notes that keen competition at various stunts—climbing, walking on all fours, and tricks—termed *lazzi* in the theater, had close parallels in the great press and din of bells and drums in the old French Carnival. "Disorders," whether violent or self-befouling, are similar in both traditions. Handling live embers and ash, juggling hot rocks, and feinting with knives and clubs "have parallels in the bonfire faulting, twirling of *brandons* and sword dances of French Carnival." Firewalking, rolling in hot ashes, and having ashes rubbed into body orifices evokes the straw-padded Pailhasses of

Languedoc who wash themselves and their victims in liquid mud. Fear and amusement, cure and mischief intergrade. Throwing and spraying water on persons met (JR 42:157), as in the modern Bear Dance (JR 20:30; 42:163), find a common feature in old French Carnival in "aspersion with *andouille,* or chitterling broth."

9. *Catharsis.* The compulsions to renew old dream obligations and to fulfill new dreams via the ritual of dream guessing that were so essential to the catharsis of Ononharoia are the driving forces that maintain the Midwinter Festival today. Walsh finds they correspond "to that host of forbidden desires brought out during the shameless period of Carnival."

Despite their prejudices and their attitude of cultural superiority, Walsh concludes that the Jesuits recognized that the "deep structure" of the *Ononharoia* and Carnival were identical.

Although I have leaned very heavily on his paper, and paraphrased much of its body in rewriting sections that seemed germane to the present inquiry, I cannot cover all of his points. One minor point, however, is of interest. It appears that Barbeau was wrong in insisting that Huron–Iroquois masking was borrowed from the settlers of New France. Walsh finds only scanty records of Carnival in Quebec in the seventeenth century. Although it did exist, the cited dates from the *Relations* are after the destruction of Huronia in 1648 and well after Brébeuf's observations of Ononharoia. The intensity of the Huron festival far exceeds the minor celebrations of Carnival in Quebec after the midcentury. The Jesuits were not above incorporating native dream images in their morality plays.

CONVERGENCE

This brings us back to square one, where American ethnology began: diffusion versus independent invention or parallelism, which, on investigation, usually turns out to be convergence. Alexander Goldenweiser articulated the concept of convergence as it applies to cultural phenomena, early in this century, in a brilliant article entitled "The Principle of Limited Possibilities in the Development of Culture" (Goldenweiser 1933, 35–55). Unless they go back to some deep infrastructure or universal culture pattern that is rooted in the human psyche, I do not think for a moment that Iroquois masking and the masqueraders of Carnival are generically related, despite the parallels cited. Ritzenthaler, to whom I loaned the two monographs on Swiss masking, regarded it as a somewhat astonishing case of parallelism but not diffusion (Ritzenthaler, personal communication, December 19, 1968). Iroquois masking, as I trust this book has demonstrated, conforms to a ritual pattern that is perpetuated by the felt need to honor obligations revealed through dreams and to renew previous cures by particular medicine societies, of which the False Faces are one. Carnival strikes the counterpoint between ancient paganism and Christian piety on the eve of the Lenten season between release from repression of human desires and sanctions imposed by penances. Among the Iroquois, the dyad is between revelation and fulfillment of dreams, which are regarded as the window of the soul. In contrast, the opposition between Carnival and Christian sanctions is pronounced.

Masking the World over

Masking has a worldwide distribution. It is found on every continent, at the margins of the Arctic, and in the Southwest Pacific. Although seemingly infinite, the patterned ways in which the human physiognomy may be stylized in plastic art are limited. There are bound to be convergences in mask types. Distortion of the mouth and nose, twisted to one side as in paralytic strokes, can occur anywhere, and are strikingly so in masks from the Inuit, of Greenland. Masks representing the muses of comedy and tragedy in the tradition of classical Greek drama are replicated in two Iroquois mask mouth types—smiling and hanging. The pursed mouth of the "whistler" is probably universal. As portraits of "grandfather" spirits, the False Faces are frequently wrinkled; Swiss folk masks representing old people mark the generation gap in similar ways. Scholars familiar with the masks of New Guinea and Africa will find other parallels.

21. Conclusions

The Society of Faces is a viable concern among traditionalist descendants of the native Iroquois of New York and Ontario. Largely undocumented before 1940, the present work puts on record its paraphernalia, origin myths, beliefs, ceremonies, and cures, first for the native people themselves, second to enhance programs of interpretation and education in museums, and third to enlighten collectors of masks. Because the masks have a considerable popular appeal to a wide variety of publics, I have striven to fulfill the need for a definitive monograph, which I trust will serve as a reference work for curators in museums having substantial collections of masks and will stand as a definitive contribution to the ethnology of the Eastern Woodlands and to the history of religions.

The problems imposed by the task and the methods employed, both in fieldwork and museum studies, stem from my early training under students of Franz Boas and reflect the state of the art in anthropology when I took to the field in 1933. I have striven to make the historical dimension more explicit, both the comparative ethnographical coverage of masking in the Eastern Woodlands, a dimension inspired by Clark Wissler and Leslie Spier, and my own contribution to the approach now widely understood by the term *ethnohistory,* which employs the perspective of the native culture for interpreting the past.

Although I have not succeeded in tracing Iroquois masked shamanism beyond the midseventeenth century by direct historical methods, I have invoked other inferential approaches employed by anthropologists to deepen and widen the perspective.

Structural considerations alone place the False Faces near the top of the hierarchy of Iroquois medicine societies. The Husk Faces are linked with the wooden faces in a coordinate capacity. Having defined the orders of membership and described the form and content of the masked rituals, one gains some appreciation of the importance of the False Faces and the Husk Faces in Iroquois life. In fulfilling obligations to mask spirits by putting up feasts for them and celebrating their rituals, the Iroquois guarantee the maintenance of the Society of Faces, ensure its future, and proclaim a distinguished past. The importance of the False Faces and Husk Faces in traditional Iroquois life derives from these continuing activities.

The true meaning of the wooden faces should now be clear. We now know how the Iroquois regard the masks and the mask spirits in general. The native classification of masks, however, remains poorly understood and awaits further research. Whether cognitive approaches of ethnoscience will clarify our understanding remains to be demonstrated. Sources of such knowledge are fading fast. My approach to this problem has succeeded only partially in illuminating this topic. Tradition projected in dreams and visions affords a species of native theory on kinds of masks, but mask type depends more on the pragmatic needs of the ceremonies. Role behavior of actors in the ceremonies is more important than mask morphology. Dramatic behavior of the maskers is compelling.

One may, nevertheless, essay a classification of masks based on morphological features and come up with a system that helps the layman, the collector, and the curator arrange the masks in some order. Such a classificatory system may have small meaning to the Iroquois themselves. In seizing on the most variable feature—the mouth shape—which Iroquois sources first pointed out to me, I achieved a classification that the Iroquois themselves substantiated in part. This semiemic approach produced results that at least one other scholar confirmed in a later study (Mathews 1978).

The Husk Faces, who at first blush appear as a group of agriculturists, as donors of cultivated plants, on deeper investigation turn out to have an original preoccupation as donors of hunting magic. The masks that represent these spirits comprise three techniques of fabrication in two media—braided and coiled husk, twined husk, and wood fringed with husk. The Husk Face Society, its origins, ritual equipment, and the appearances of the husk maskers have received systematic treatment for the first time in the Iroquois literature in this volume.

Miniature masks, or masquettes, that boys learn to carve and adults treasure as talismans in response to dreams and as memorabilia of cures are the products of the dream-guessing rite at midwinter, now virtually extinct among the Seneca, but still observed at Onondaga and at Six Nations. Owning a masquette entails both a personal obligation to renew a ceremony and a social relationship with the dream guesser and donor of the masquette that is sanctioned by ritual and celebrated during the lifetime of either partner. Of all Iroquois mask forms, masquettes afford the clearest evidence of having evolved from examples known to prehistory. Neither the larger wooden or husk masks have such clearly established roots in protohistoric or prehistoric horizons.

The search for a time perspective on Iroquois masking, forecast previously, brought into focus some methods outlined by Sapir (1916), to which I have added the direct historic approach of ethnohistory. Archaeology has produced mixed results: failure to find demonstrable artifacts of wooden masks or fragments of snapping-turtle carapaces showing the telltale edges worn from use by maskers and singers. This negative evidence belies descriptions of masked shamans in action during the early seventeenth century in Huronia and turtle shell rattles illustrated and described in contemporary sources, predating their modern counterparts. There are no such illustrations of masks. To be certain, informant testimony by my Seneca sources holds that folded bark rattles preceded snapping-turtle rattles, an assertion of tradition that cannot be verified archaeologically. Of one thing we may be certain, however: Early preoccupation with dreams and dream fulfillment, attested to by seventeenth-century missionary observers, began early and created the social and religious contexts for the medicine societies, which this book describes, and afforded an environment in which the masking complex could flourish. Indeed, the face motif occurs in several media, of which pottery, bone, and stone objects have survived as archaeological specimens. Although the modeled faces with hands to mouth on pottery pipes may not represent maskers blowing ashes, there is one solid bit of evidence that the Seneca knew masks before the Huron diaspora, namely an antler figurine of a person adjusting a mask to the face by the chin. The evidence of mask parts found in Seneca graves remains shaky. The evolutionary sequence of miniature masks from archaeological objects to their modern counterparts is reasonably established. The Iroquois mask complex is old and need not rest on an historic Huron connection.

Huron and Iroquois masked shamanism are cut from the same cloth. Whether one is derived from the other is irrelevant because both were in continuous contact during the first half-century of European contact. Huron masked shamanism enjoyed a better press early on. Ethnohistory has failed to resolve this enigma.

It should be evident to anyone who examines older Iroquois masks that two carving styles are represented by earlier specimens. Smooth, plain likenesses predominate in older collections, although the heavily lined and protruding tongue of the Morgan mask collected in 1849 foretells a distinctly Grand River style of carving. I previously ascribed an evolution from smooth likenesses to grotesque caricatures to the acquisition of steel carving tools. But it is clear that prehistoric artisans fashioned spectacular wood carvings using tools available in the then-contemporary inventory. The sequence from plain to grotesque occurs in miniature masks that reach solidly into prehistory and have a wide distribution in the woodlands. Whether larger masks evolved in parallel fashion or synchronically we cannot say for want of a continuous chain of artifacts. Whether periodic epidemics brought a reevaluation of mask tutelaries and influenced carving style toward portraying exaggerated disease symptoms, as Hamell suggests, remains an unconfirmed hypothesis.

Linguistic evidence of the face concept occurs among extant Iroquoian languages and finds expression in several contexts. The earlier vocabularies do not include a term for "mask" as such, but because it is coterminous with "face" this lack may not be significant. Examples cited for Bruyas's roots, however, relate to the masking complex.

Onondaga and Seneca are the focuses of the masking complex. The Haduʔiʔ tradition migrated from Onondaga to Grand River. Shagodyoweh of the Seneca spawned the greater intensity and proliferation of masking. The greater number of False Faces now in museum collections derive from Seneca sources.

Both the Iroquois and the neighboring Delaware had portable masks, painted red and black, often divided, carried turtle rattles, and dressed in bearskin suits, but only the Delaware carved faces on house posts of their ceremonial centers. The Iroquois, however, carved masks on trees, on posts that they danced around, and on gate posts. The affinity of faces (masks) to trees is compelling. The figure of the great tree at the center of the earth where the masker pauses to renew his strength, and the theme "faces against the trees" for the forest spirits strengthen the association.

The ethnological literature on the False Faces parallels the history of anthropology in America. It began with Morgan, stagnated for fifty years while collecting progressed, and then expanded exponentially after Parker demonstrated that the Seneca as well as the Plains tribes had societies. Theoretical aspects of masking have come to the fore just recently.

No extant Iroquois mask is of any great antiquity. None of which I am aware predates the end of the eighteenth century. Since then, False Faces have evolved with the times, particularly the class of Seneca beggar masks, which mirror folk characters of the larger society.

The fanciful names that Converse labeled her mask collections had best be laid to rest.

This book represents the first comprehensive description of the Society of Faces in all its aspects. The two types of origin legends forecast two classes of beings and two fundamental classes of wooden masks—representatives of the primal masker in the cosmology and the "Faces of the Forest." Each class has its own ceremony. Three orders of medicine societies—False Faces, Husk Faces, and the Medicine Company (I:ʔdo:s)—employ masks. Each has its own ritual, and patients participate at one or all levels. Hysterical possession during sightings or encounters, dreams calling for tokens, and certain "red" diseases demand relief by maskers who cure by blowing hot ashes. These are the avenues of entry to the society that the case histories of patients confirm. The requirements for care and propitiation of mask and rattle recall the bundle concept so prominent and widespread among prairie and plains peoples. There is a tobacco prayer to sanction every contingency involving mask and rattle from the time the carver takes the block from the tree, dedicates the finished mask to service, compensates it for cures, propitiates it when it falls or "sweats," loans it, recovers it, or dispatches it to a museum.

Nowhere else are the props to the ceremony described and their manufacture recorded, except for the "singing tools," by Conklin and Sturtevant (1953). Turtle rattles, bark rattles, masquettes, costume, staff, and emblem pole are items of the inventory mentioned in the literature and often exhibited in museums.

The traditional ritual of carving a mask on a basswood tree was already passée in Parker's time and is now only performed for ethnologists. But we have followed the careers of some ten carvers and observed them at work, producing, I believe, a clear picture of their art, its uniformities, individual variations, and local styles.

The purification of the houses, or the so-called "Traveling Rite," first mentioned by Morgan (1851) and fully documented for Six Nations by Shimony a century later, has been described here for Coldspring on Allegany Reservation at length, observed repeatedly, and photographed. Two paradigms emerge: the Coldspring Seneca paradigm features administration of a medicine to the public and the Thumbs-up Dance; and at Six Nations we have matrons oiling the masks before their departure. These public spectacles belie the claim that the False Faces are a secret society; on the contrary, everyone knows who the matrons are, what they do, and who are the conductors. At Six Nations, a man has charge of the maskers, and his office is considered permanent. The names of male leaders since 1880 are well known. People speak familiarly of the individuals who impersonate the mask spirits and recall their antics. Rather than being a secret society, participation is restricted to those invited when sponsors put up a private feast. The same ritual pattern prevails at these private rites as in the more public traveling rite.

The appearance of the maskers at the Midwinter Festival compounds public and private rites and includes, in addition, the antics of a class of beggar maskers who function as clowns, make rounds of the houses begging, cadging tobacco and food during one night, and who perform a gala show a second night at the Seneca longhouses. Six Nations lacks them. The Onondaga of New York devote a special night to similar performances, all in the longhouse. Generally, beggars are small boys, young men, and women and should not be confused with the False Faces proper.

Together, the False Faces and the Husk Faces constitute one of the climax forms in Iroquois culture. The traveling rite occurs twice a year on the calendar of traditional Iroquois communities. Husk Face night at the Seneca longhouses, which for many of the faithful is the Indian New Year, draws visitors from communities that lack this celebration to Coldspring, Newtown, and Tonawanda to witness the spectacle. All forms of masks and mask spirits stand as "grandfathers" to the people, a term reserved for powerful medicines from rattlesnakes to thunders.

Certain masks alone are thought to have inherent power that they share with the supernaturals; they require special treatment and are referred to as "secluded," "hidden," or plain "poison." Husk Faces are taken less seriously.

One maintains a guarded attitude toward the supernaturals and the masks that represent them. Ambivalence, fear, amusement, and respect require constant adjustment. Balance and restraint are the ideal. That maskers frighten children is remarked by everyone and long remembered by persons from their childhood.

Diseases and plagues were regarded as windborne. The Society of Faces evolved as a medicine society in response to the threat of periodic epidemics of introduced diseases for which the Iroquois had no immunity. It was thought that the traveling rite, by going through houses and visiting springs, could quiet the wind and purge sickness from the community.

Collecting activities at the turn of the century stimulated mask production as the available supply diminished and was siphoned off to museums. Selling ethnographic objects to "pickers" who acted as agents for collectors and museums provided supplementary income to people living a marginal existence. Carving masks became a part-time activity like basket making in the off season when work for wages slackened. The accepted way for an ethnologist to finance a field trip was to make a collection for a museum. Lacking such commissions, ethnologists bent on salvage ethnology collected and then sold documented objects to museums to recover field expenses.

Once these objects were accessioned by a publicly chartered museum, they became part of a public trust for which museum trustees are accountable. Ultimately, the concept of a public trust came into conflict with a growing sense of corporate or tribal loss of cultural treasures that has in recent years inspired nativists to demand repatriation of "sacred" objects. There is really no solution to this problem other than loaning collections temporarily or long term to Native American museums that have been recently established and are chartered as educational institutions.

Finally, turning to comparisons and implications of Woodland masking for ethnology, Delaware and Iroquois masking correspondences comprise a common cultural tradition that is quite old. Not surprisingly, the Cayuga-Seneca carried their masking customs to Oklahoma and shared them with the Delaware and Shawnee. The latter appear to have participated in the Delaware tradition. However, accounts of Shawnee masking read like Iroquois masking practices. The two groups were in contact at various times as neighbors and as enemies. By contrast, Chippewa masking seems of small consequence, and Eskimo and Iroquois parallels lack sufficient precision to claim relationship.

The southeastern masking complex reaches to a remote past, although the evidence is fragmentary and lacks the cohesion of the Delaware–Iroquois complex. Both portable masks and faces carved on posts are reported.

The Eastern Cherokee afford the only example of a southeastern people with whom a comparison of Delaware–Iroquois masking is possible. Fogelson contends that the Booger Dance is descended from an earlier masking complex; and although I found few traits shared with Iroquois masking, Fogelson, by deeper analysis, has discerned evidence of a common source for traits found in the Booger Dance and shared with the Husk Faces of the Iroquois. Each masking complex, in this view, has evolved separately from some pre-Columbian source.

Speck's hypothesis of a northern complex of portable masks separate from a mid-Atlantic area of faces carved on posts collapses before Krusche's revisionary thesis that Eastern Woodland masks evolved out of faces carved on trees and posts (Krusche 1975, 171). In his favor, Speck saw Iroquois influence on Delaware and Shawnee masking, but the Cherokee seem not to have performed that role in the Southeast. Moreover, he held that eastern masking from Labrador to Florida was too diverse to be one complex, that spotty distribution and different time levels vitiated comparison, and that similar mask typology is found wherever masks are made. His other points are not easily dismissed.

Because of its importance, Krusche's thesis has been reviewed critically and at length for readers not familiar with German scholarship. Krusche's contribution exceeds the limits of the culture-historical method: His perceptions are challenging, and his findings are admirable.

Fogelson's analysis has gone beyond masking to encompass folk beliefs common to the Cherokee and Iroquois, which enables him to demonstrate a genuine connection between the two masking complexes. Again, the reader is referred to my commentary. By applying Lévi-Strauss's theory of the dialectic between nature and culture, he has produced startling results: In this dialectic the False Faces represent nature, the Husk Faces, culture. By contrasting the traits in this dyad, Fogelson and Walker juxtapose the Cherokee Booger Dance and the annual appearance of the northern Husk Faces in a series of paired correspondences.

The even more startling parallel between Carnival in Europe and Iroquois masking has been long suspected but only recently demonstrated for us by Walsh, a scholar of the theater, who comes to the problem from a study of folk masking in Europe. Walsh finds a series of correspondences between the Huron–Iroquois midwinter ceremony, as observed by Jesuit missionaries in the seventeenth century, and European Carnival. The case for parallel development on the two continents is most convincing. The two phenomena are clearly not related. The reader need but look at the sources cited by Walsh and by me in reviewing his findings.

We are as yet some distance from reaching a general theory of masking. Such a theory must probe the nature of the human psyche that leads persons everywhere to transform themselves by masking, to impersonate spirits, and to exceed the limits of conventional behavior. We need to know what state of altered consciousness occurs when a person dons a mask, and what supernatural attributes and powers does he or she acquire that are imputed to the mask itself. The search for such a transformational model, which we have seen in the behavior and beliefs regarding the False Faces, has begun (Crumrine and Halpin 1983).

Iroquois Mask

This Iroquois False Face mask replicates those used in dance ceremonies to heal or prevent disaster. Broken Nose is a healing mask, and came about as a result of a conflict between the Creator and a Being who claimed to have created Mother Earth. The being was challenged to a contest of power and was able to move a mountain slightly as his show of strength. The Creator then caused the mountain to roar, and startled the Being who smashed his face on the mountain as a result. Created by Onondaga artisan Hoʔnhyagéhdeʔ (Stick-on-the-Shoulder), this mask has not undergone the blessing necessary to give it healing power. Crafted of pine, copper and horsehair.

12" (30 cm) long plus hair

Stick-on-the-Shoulder

I haven't heard of the artist you mention, and don't know the name. But I can make a guess that, as is usual, the name consists of a verb with an incorporated noun (there's no construction consisting of two noun roots). My guess is that the verb may be -gehd- *carry on one's back, carry around one's body* (there's a famous chief named Ax Carrier, whose name is **hoʔsgwehsagéhdeʔ** and who is pictured carrying an ax on his shoulder), with the incorporated noun -ʔnhy- perhaps, or -aʔęn-, so **hoʔnhyagéhdeʔ** or **hoʔęnagéhdeʔ**. But, of course, I'm only guessing. If it's a female, substitute g for initial h I suppose.

Hanni Woodbury

April 1, 2010

Bibliography

Abrams, G. 1967. Moving of the fire: A case of Iroquois ritual innovation. In *Iroquois culture, history, and Prehistory: Proceedings of the 1965 conference on Iroquois research*, ed. Elisabeth Tooker, 23–29. Albany: New York State Museum and Science Service.

American state papers—Indian affairs. Walter Lowrie et al., eds. 2 vols. Washington, D.C., 1832–34. (Contains the journal of Col. Thomas Proctor, 1791–92).

Barbeau, C. M. 1912. On Huron work, 1911. In *Summary Report, Geological Survey, Canada, Anthropological Division, for the calendar years 1910 and 1911*, 7–12. Ottawa.

———. 1913. On Iroquoian fieldwork, 1912. In *Summary report, Geological Survey, Canada, Anthropological Division, for the calendar year 1912*, 454–60. Ottawa.

———. 1915. *Huron and Wyandot mythology.* Memoir 80, Canada Geological Survey, Anthropological Series, No. 11. Ottawa.

Bartram, J. 1751. *Observations on the inhabitants, climate, soil, rivers, productions, animals, and other matters worthy of notice, made by Mr. John Bartram, in his travels from Pensilvania [sic] to Onondago, Oswego, and the Lake Ontario, in Canada.* London: Printed for J. Whiston and B. White.

Bartram, W. 1928. *The travels of William Bartram*, [Philadelphia, 1791]. Ed. M. Van Doren. New York: Dover Publications.

Beauchamp. W. M. 1888. Onondaga customs. *Journal of American Folk-Lore* 1(3): 195–203.

———. 1892. *The Iroquois Trail, or foot-prints of the Six Nations, in customs, traditions, and history, in which are included David Cusick's sketches of ancient history of the Six Nations.* Fayetteville, N.Y.: H. C. Beauchamp.

———. 1895. Onondaga notes. *Journal of American Folk-Lore* 8(30): 209–16.

———. 1905. Aboriginal use of wood in New York. *New-York State Museum Bulletin* 89:87–292. Albany.

Biggar, H. P., ed. 1924. *The voyages of Jacques Cartier: Published from the originals with translations, notes and appendices.* Publications of the Public Archives of Canada 11. Ottawa.

Birket-Smith, K. 1920. Some ancient artifacts from the eastern United States. *Journal de la Société des Americanistes de Paris*, n.s., 12:141–69.

———. 1929. The Caribou Eskimos. *Report of the Fifth Thule Expedition, 1921–24* 5, pt. 2:201–202, 288. Copenhagen.

———. Blau, H. 1963. Dream guessing: A comparative analysis. *Ethnohistory* 10:233–49.

———. 1966. Function and the False Faces: A classification of Onondaga masked rituals and themes. *Journal of American Folklore* 79 (314): 564–80.

———. 1967. Onondaga False Face rituals. *New York Folklore Quarterly* 23(4):253–64.

Boas, F. 1888. The Central Eskimo. In *6th Annual Report of the Bureau of American Ethnology for the Years 1884–1885*, 299–669. Washington, D.C.: Smithsonian Institution.

———. 1901. Eskimo of Baffin Land and Hudson Bay. *American Museum of Natural History Bulletin* 15:139–42. New York.

Boyle, D. 1898. The pagan Iroquois. In *Annual Archaeological Report for 1898 . . . , Appendix to the Report of the Minister of Education, Ontario*, 34–211. Toronto.

———. Iroquois medicine man's mask. In *Annual Archaeological Report for 1899 . . . , Appendix to the Report of the Minister of Education, Ontario*, 27–30. Toronto.

———. 1905. Husk False Faces. In *Annual Archaeological Report 1904 . . . , Appendix to the Report of the Minister of Education, Ontario*, 58–59. Toronto.

Brasser, T. J. C. 1967. Blanken zijn geen echte mensen. Verre naasten nader bij Rijksmuseum voor volkenkunde, Te Leiden. *Eerste Jaargang NR* 2 (April):1–8.

Bruyas, J., S. J. 1863. *Radices verborum Iroquaeorum* [Radical words of the Mohawk language, with their derivatives]. [J. G.] Shea's Library of American Linguistics 10. New York: Cramoisy Press.

Campisi, J. 1974. Ethnic identity and boundary maintenance in three Oneida communities. Ph.D. diss., State University of New York at Albany.

———. 1978. Oneida. In *Handbook of North American Indians*, Vol. 15, *Northeast*, ed. B. G. Trigger, 481–90. Washington, D.C.: Smithsonian Institution.

Chafe, W. L. 1963. *Handbook of the Seneca Language.* New York State Museum and Science Service Bulletin 388. Albany.

———. 1964. Linguistic evidence for the relative age of Iroquois religious practices. *Southwestern Journal of Anthropology* 20(3):278–85.

———. 1967. *Seneca morphology and dictionary.* Smithsonian Contributions to Anthropology 4. Washington, D.C.: Smithsonian Institution.

Champlain, S. de. 1922–36. *The works of Samuel de Champlain.* Ed. H. P. Biggar. 6 vols. Toronto: Champlain Society.

Charlevoix, P. F. X. de. 1761. *Journal of a voyage to America.* 2 vols. London.

Christinger, R., and W. Borgeaud. 1963. *Mythologie de la Suisse ancienne.* Musée de Institut d'Ethnographie de Genève. Geneva.

Librairie de l'Université Georg.

Clark, J. V. H. 1849. *Onondaga; or reminiscences of earlier and later times* . . . . 2 vols. Syracuse, N.Y.: Stoddard and Babcock.

Congdon, C. E. 1967. *Allegany Oxbow: A history of Allegany State Park and the Allegany Reserve of the Seneca Nation*. Little Valley, N.Y.: Straight Publishing Co.

Conklin, H. C., and W. Sturtevant. 1953. Seneca Indian singing tools at Coldspring Longhouse: Musical instruments of the modern Iroquois. *American Philosophical Society Proceedings* 97:262–90.

Converse, H. M. 1899. Iroquois masks. *Buffalo Express*, October 18. Buffalo, N.Y.

———. 1908. *Myths and legends of the New York State Iroquois*. Ed. A. C. Parker. New York State Museum Bulletin 125. Albany.

———. 1930. The Seneca New-Year Ceremony and other customs. *Indian Notes* 7:68–89. New York: Museum of the American Indian—Heye Foundation.

Conover, G. S., ed. 1887. *Journals of the military expedition of Major General John Sullivan against the Six Nations of New York in 1779* . . . . Auburn, N.Y.: Knapp, Peck and Thomson.

Cook, F. 1887. See New York (State) Secretary of State.

Cornplanter, J. J. 1900–37. Cornplanter Papers, in Fenton Collection, American Philosophical Society Library.

———. 1903. *Iroquois Indian Games and Dances, drawn by Jesse Cornplanter, Seneca Indian Boy*. Published privately

———. 1938. *Legends of the longhouse*. Philadelphia: J. B. Lippincott.

———. 1978. Original drawings, NYSL. In *Handbook of North American Indians*, Vol. 15, *Northeast*, ed. B. G. Trigger. Washington, D.C.: Smithsonian Institution.

Cresswell, N. 1924. *The journal of Nicholas Cresswell, 1774–1775*. Ed. S. Thornely. New York: Lincoln MacVeagh, Dial Press.

Crowell, S. 1877. *The dog sacrifice of the Senecas*. Reprinted from the *Cincinnati Miscellany*, February, 1845, 137–40 in W. W. Beach, ed. *The Indian miscellany* . . . . Albany, N.Y.: J. Munsell.

Crumrine, N. R., and M. Halpin, eds. 1983. *The power of symbols: Masks and masquerade in the Americas*. Vancouver: University of British Columbia Press.

Curtin, J., and J. N. B. Hewitt. 1918. Seneca fiction, legends, and myths. Ed. J. N. B. Hewitt. In *32nd Annual Report, Bureau of American Ethnology*, 37–813. Washington, D.C.: Smithsonian Institution.

Deardorff, M. H. 1951. The religion of Handsome Lake: Its origin and development. In *Symposium on local diversity in Iroquois culture*, ed. W. N. Fenton, 77–107. Bureau of American Ethnology Bulletin 149. Washington, D.C.: Smithsonian Institution.

———, and G. S. Snyderman. 1956. A nineteenth century journal of a visit to the Indians of New York. *Proceedings of the American Philosophical Society* 100:582–612.

Edwards, J. 1822. *Memoirs of the Rev. David Brainerd, missionary to the Indians on the borders of New-York, New-Jersey, and Pennsylvania: Chiefly taken from his own diary*. Ed. S. E. Dwight. New Haven, Conn.

Eliade, M. 1972. *Shamanism: Archaic techniques of ecstasy*. Princeton, N.J.: Bollingen Foundation. First published 1964.

Feest, C. F. 1978. North Carolina Algonquians. In *Handbook of North American Indians*, Vol. 15, *Northeast*, ed. B. G. Trigger, 271–81. Washington, D.C.: Smithsonian Institution.

———. 1980. *Native arts of North America*. London: Thames and Hudson.

Fenstermaker, G. B. 1959. Reminiscences of Susquehannock archaeology. In *Susquehannock Miscellany*, ed. J. Witthoft and W. F. Kinsey III, 148–54. Harrisburg: Pennsylvania Historical and Museum Commission.

Fenton, W. N. 1933–73. Field notes of Seneca and Iroquois research. Fenton Papers, American Philosophical Society Library, Philadelphia.

———. 1936. An outline of Seneca ceremonies at Coldspring Longhouse. In *Yale University Publications in Anthropology* 9:1–23. New Haven, Conn.: Yale University Press.

———. 1937. The Seneca Society of Faces. *Scientific Monthly* 44 (March): 215–38.

———. 1941a. Masked medicine societies of the Iroquois. In *Annual Report of the Smithsonian Institution for 1940*, 397–430. Washington, D.C.

———. 1941b. Tonawanda Longhouse ceremonies: Ninety years after Lewis Henry Morgan. *Bureau of American Ethnology Bulletin* 128: 140–66. Washington, D.C.: Smithsonian Institution.

———. 1941c. Museum and field studies of Iroquois masks and ritualism. In *Explorations and Field-Work of the Smithsonian Institution in 1940*, 95–100. Washington, D.C.

———. 1942a. Review: Comments on certain Iroquois Masks. Joseph Keppler. *American Anthropologist* 44:118–19.

———. 1942b. *Songs from the Iroquois*

longhouse: Program notes for an album of American Indian music from the Eastern Woodlands. Smithsonian Institution Publication No. 3691. Washington, D.C.

———. 1944. Simeon Gibson: Iroquois informant, 1889–1943. *American Anthropologist* 46(2): 231–34.

———. 1950. The roll call of the Iroquois chief: A study of a mnemonic cane from the Six Nations Reserve. *Smithsonian Miscellaneous Collections* 111(5):1–73. Washington, D.C.

———. 1953. *The Iroquois Eagle Dance: An offshoot of the Calumet Dance; with an analysis of the Iroquois Eagle Dance and songs by Gertrude P. Kurath.* Bureau of American Ethnology Bulletin 156. Washington, D.C.: Smithsonian Institution.

———. 1956. Some questions of classification, typology, and style raised by Iroquois masks. *Transactions of the New York Academy of Science,* 2d ser., 18:347–57.

———. 1962. This island, the world on the turtle's back. *Journal of American Folklore* 76(298):283–300.

———. 1967. From longhouse to ranch-type house: The second housing revolution of the Seneca Nation. In *Iroquois culture, history, and prehistory: Proceedings of the 1965 conference on Iroquois research,* ed. E. Tooker, 7–22. Albany, N.Y.: New York State Museum and Science Service.

———. 1969. Anthropology and the university: an inaugural lecture. State University of New York at Albany, May 8, 1968. Albany: SUNYA, Department of Sociology and Anthropology.

———. 1971. Converse, Harriet Maxwell (1836–1903). In *Notable American women, 1607–1950: A biographical dictionary,* ed. E. T. James. 3 vols. 1:375–77. Cambridge, Mass.: Harvard University Press.

———. 1972a. Howard Sky, 1900–1971: Cayuga faith-keeper, gentleman, and interpreter of Iroquois culture. *American Anthropologist* 74(3):758–62.

———. 1972b. Iroquois masks: A living tradition in the Northeast. In *American Indian art, form and tradition: an exhibition organized by the Walker Art Center, the Indian Art Association, and the Minneapolis Institute of Arts, 22 October–31 December, 1972,* 42–47. Minneapolis.

———. 1972c. Return to the longhouse. In *Crossing Cultural Boundaries . . . ,* ed. T. Kimball and J. B. Watson, 102–18. San Francisco: Chandler Publishing Co.

———. 1978a. "Aboriginally yours," Jesse J. Cornplanter, . . . Seneca, 1899–1957. In *American Indian Intellectuals: 1976 Proceedings of the American Ethnological Society,* ed. M. Liberty, 177–95. St. Paul, Minn.: West Publishing Co.

———. 1978b. Cherokee and Iroquois connections revisited. *Journal of Cherokee Studies* 3(4):239–49.

———. 1978c. Northern Iroquoian culture patterns. In *Handbook of North American Indians,* Vol. 15, *Northeast,* ed. B. G. Trigger, 296–321. Washington, D.C.: Smithsonian Institution.

———. 1979. The "great good medicine." *New York State Journal of Medicine* 79(10):1603–1609.

———. 1980a. Frederick Starr, Jesse Cornplanter, and the Cornplanter Medal for Iroquois research. *New York History* 61(2):187–99.

——— [with H. Redeye]. 1980b. Tobacco invocation: Seneca. Ed. W. Chafe. In *Native American Texts,* ed. M. Mithun and H. Woodbury, 3–8. International Journal of American Linguistics, Native American Texts Series, Monograph No. 4. Chicago: University of Chicago Press.

———. 1984. Johnson Jimmerson (1918–1984). *Ohiyonoh: Allegany Reservation Newsletter,* November 16, 1984, 14–15. Salamanca, N.Y.

———, and E. L. Moore, trans. and eds. 1974–76. *Customs of the American Indians, compared with the customs of primitive times, by Father Joseph-François Lafitau.* 2 vols. Toronto: Champlain Society.

Fogelson, R. D. 1980. Windigo goes south: Stone Clad among the Cherokees. In *Manlike monsters on trial: Early recordings and modern evidence,* ed. M. M. Halpin and M. M. Ames, 132–41. Vancouver and London: University of British Columbia Press.

———, and A. R. Bell. 1983. Cherokee Booger Mask tradition. In *The power of symbols,* ed. N. R. Crumrine and M. Halpin, 49–69. Vancouver: University of British Columbia Press.

Friederici, Georg. 1906. *Skalpieren und Ähnliche Kriegsgebräuche in Amerika.* Braunschweig: Frederick Vieweg und Sohn.

Furst, P. T., and J. L. Furst. 1982. *North American Indian art.* New York: Rizzoli.

Gilbert, B. See W. Walton, ed.

Goddard, I. 1978. Delaware. In *Handbook of North American Indians,* Vol. 15, *Northeast,* ed. B. G. Trigger, 215–39. Washington, D.C.: Smithsonian Institution.

Goggin, J., and W. C. Sturtevant. 1964. The Calusa: A stratified non-agricultural society. . . . In *Explorations in cultural anthropology in honor of George Peter Murdock,* ed. W. C. Goodenough, 179–219. New York: McGraw-Hill.

Goldenweiser, A. A. 1912. On Iroquois work, 1911. In *Summary Report, Geological Survey, Canada, Anthropological Division, for the cal-*

endar years 1910 and 1911, 12–13. Ottawa.

———. 1913. On Iroquois work, 1912. In *Summary Report, Geological Survey, Canada, Anthropological Division, for the calendar year 1912*, 464–75. Ottawa.

———. 1914. On Iroquois work, 1913–1914. In *Summary Report, Geological Survey, Canada, Anthropological Division, for the calendar year 1913*, 365–72. Ottawa.

———. 1922. *Early civilization*. New York: Alfred A. Knopf.

———. 1933. *History, psychology, and culture*. New York: Alfred A. Knopf.

———. 1937. *Anthropology*. New York: Crofts.

———. N.d. Field notebooks of Iroquois research, National Museum of Man, Ottawa. Xerox copies in the American Philosophical Society Library, Philadelphia.

Graffenried, C. von. 1920. *Christoph von Graffenried's account of the founding of New Bern*. Ed. V. H. Todd. Publications of the North Carolina Historical Commission. Raleigh.

Grider, Rufus. 1897. Original drawings of Iroquois masks. Portfolios. Newberry Library, Chicago.

Griffin, J. B. 1967. Eastern North American archaeology: A summary. *Science* 156:175–91.

Hale, H. E. 1885. Chief George H. M. Johnson, Onwanonsyshon: His life and work among the Six Nations. *Magazine of American History* 8 (February): 130–42.

Hallowell, A. I. 1976. Anthropology in Philadelphia (1967). In *Contributions to anthropology*, ed. R. Fogelson et al. Chicago: University of Chicago Press.

Hansmann, C. 1959. *Masken Schemen Larven: Volksmasken der Alpenländer*. Munich: Verlag F. Bruckmann.

Harrington, M. R. 1908. Vestiges of the material culture of the Canadian Delawares. *American Anthropologist*, n.s., 10(3):408–18.

———. 1909. Some unusual Iroquois specimens. *American Anthropologist*, n.s., 11(1):85–91.

———. 1913. A preliminary sketch of Lenape culture. *American Anthropologist*, n.s., 15(2):208–35.

———. 1921. Religion and ceremonies of the Lenape. *Indian Notes and Monographs*, 2d ser., 19. New York: Museum of the American Indian—Heye Foundation.

———. 1922. A midcolonial site in Erie County. In *The archaeological history of New York*, ed. A. C. Parker, 2 pts., 207–37. New York State Museum Bulletin, 235–38, 1922. Albany.

———. 1925. Alanson Skinner (1886–1925). *Indian Notes and Monographs*, 2d ser., 4:247–57. New York: Museum of the American Indian—Heye Foundation.

Heckewelder, J. 1819 (1881). *An account of the history, manners and customs of the Indian nations, who once inhabited Pennsylvania and the neighbouring states*. New and rev. ed., intro. and notes by W. C. Reichel. Philadelphia: Historical Society of Pennsylvania.

Hendry, J. 1964. Iroquois masks and maskmaking at Onondaga. Anthropological paper no. 74. *Bureau of American Ethnology Bulletin* 191: 349–409. Washington, D.C.: Smithsonian Institution.

Hewitt, J. N. B. 1888–1936. *Iroquoian texts*. National Anthropological Archives. Washington, D.C.: Smithsonian Institution.

———. 1916. Ethnology of the Iroquois. *Smithsonian Miscellaneous Collections* 66 (17):121–29. Washington, D.C.

———. 1921. Iroquoian cosmology, part 1. In *21st Annual Report of the Bureau of American Ethnology*, 127–339. Washington, D.C.: Smithsonian Institution.

———. 1928. Iroquoian cosmology, second part, with introduction and notes. In *43d Annual Report of the Bureau of American Ethnology*, 449–810. Washington, D.C.: Smithsonian Institution.

———. 1929. The culture of the Indians of eastern Canada. In *Explorations and field-work of the Smithsonian Institution in 1928*, 179–82. Washington, D.C.: Smithsonian Institution.

Howard, J. H. 1961. Cultural persistence and cultural change as reflected in Oklahoma-Seneca ceremonialism. *Plains Anthropologist* 6(11):21–30.

———. 1963. Environment and culture: The case of the Oklahoma Seneca-Cayuga. *North Dakota Quarterly* 29(3):66–71; (4):113–22. Reprinted with revisions in *Newsletter of the Oklahoma Anthropological Society* 19(7):5–17; pt. 2 of the above, 1970.

———. 1968. The southeastern ceremonial complex and its interpretation. *Missouri Archaeological Society Memoir* 6:1–viii, 1–169. Columbia.

———. 1970. Environment and culture: The case of the Oklahoma Seneca-Cayuga. *Newsletter of the Oklahoma Anthropological Society* 18(6):5–13; (7):5–21.

Hudson, C. 1976. *The southeastern Indians*. Knoxville: University of Tennessee Press.

Hulton, P. H., and D. B. Quinn. 1964. *The American drawings of John White, 1577–1690*. 2 vols. London: Trustees of the British Museum; Chapel Hill: University of North Carolina Press.

Isaacs, H. L., and B. Lex. 1980. Handling fire: Treatment of illness by the Iroquois False-Face Medicine Society. In *Studies in Iroquois culture*, ed. Nancy Bonvillain, 5–13. Occasional Publications in Northeastern Anthropology, no. 6. Rindge, N.H.

Jackson, H. 1830. *Sketch of the manners of the Seneca Indians, in 1800.* Philadelphia: Marcus T. C. Gould; New York: Isaac T. C. Hopper.

Jameson, J. 1909. *Narratives of New Netherland.* New York: Charles Scribner's Sons. (Contains *Narrative of a Journey into the Mohawk and Oneida country, 1634–35,* 135–57).

Jesuit Relations [*JR*]. See R. G. Thwaites, 1896–1901.

Jones, Rev. P. 1861. *History of the Ojebway Indians; with especial reference to their conversion to Christianity.* London: A. W. Bennett.

Keppler, J. 1941. Comments on certain Iroquois masks. *Contributions from the Museum of the American Indian—Heye Foundation* 12(4):1–40.

Killan, G. 1983. *David Boyle: From artisan to archaeologist.* Toronto: University of Toronto Press.

Kinietz, W. V. 1946. Delaware culture chronology. *Indiana Historical Society Prehistory Research Series* 3(1):1–143. Indianapolis.

Kinsey, W. F., III. 1977. *Lower Susquehanna Valley prehistoric Indians.* Ephrata, Pa.: Science Press.

Kissel, M. L. 1916. Basketry of the Pima and Papago. *Anthropological Papers of the American Museum of Natural History* 17:115–264. New York.

Kroeber, A. L., and C. Holt. 1920. Masks and moieties as a culture complex. *Journal of the Royal Anthropological Institute of Great Britain and Ireland,* n.s., 50:452–60.

Krusche, R. 1975. Zur Genese des Maskenwesens im Östlichen Waldland Nordamerikas. In *Sonderdruck aus Jahrbuch des Museums für Völkerkunde zu Leipzig,* 137–90. Berlin: Akademie-Verlag.

———. 1986. The origin of the mask concept in the Eastern Woodlands of North America. Trans. Anne Marie Shimony and W. C. Sturtevant. *Man in the Northeast,* no. 31 (Spring): 1–47. Albany: State University of New York at Albany.

Kurath, G. P. 1951. Local diversity in Iroquois music and dance. *Bureau of American Ethnology Bulletin* 149(6):109–37.

———. 1961. Effects of environment on Cherokee-Iroquois ceremonialism, music, and dance. In *Symposium on Cherokee and Iroquois culture,* ed. W. N. Fenton and J. Gulick, 173–95. Bureau of American Ethnology Bulletin 180. Washington, D.C.: Smithsonian Institution.

Kutscher, G. 1953. *Exotische masken.* Stuttgart.

Lafitau, J.-F. 1724. *Moeurs des sauvages amériquains, comparées aux moeurs des premiers temps.* 2 vols. Paris: Saugrain l'aîné.

———. 1974, 1976. *Customs of the American Indians.* Trans. and ed. W. N. Fenton and E. L. Moore, 2 vols. Toronto: Champlain Society.

Lawson, J. 1967. *A new voyage to Carolina.* Ed. Talmadge Lefler. Chapel Hill: University of North Carolina Press.

Leechman, D. 1934. Dental caries in prehistoric skulls from Canada. *Dominion Dental Journal* 46(2):351–58.

Lilly, E. 1937. *Prehistoric Antiquities of Indiana.* Indianapolis: Indiana Historical Society.

Linton, R. 1936. *The study of man.* New York: D. Appleton-Century.

McElwain, T. 1980. Methods in mask morphology: Iroquoian False Faces in the Ethnographical Museum, Stockholm. *Temenos: Studies in Comparative Religion* 16:68–83. Helsinki.

Macgowan, K., and H. Rosse. 1923. *Masks and demons.* New York: Harcourt, Brace.

MacNeish, R. S. 1952. Iroquois pottery types: A technique for the study of Iroquois prehistory. *National Museum of Canada Bulletin* 124. Ottawa.

Mason, O. T. 1903. Aboriginal American basketry: Studies in a textile art without machinery. In *United States National Museum, Annual Report for 1902,* 171–548. Washington, D.C.

Mathews, Z. P. 1978. *The relation of Seneca false face masks to Seneca and Ontario archaeology.* New York: Garland.

Megapolensis, J. 1644. A short account of the Mohawk. In *Narratives of New Netherland, 1609–1664,* ed. J. F. Jameson, 163–80. New York: Charles Scribner's Sons, 1909.

Michelson, G. 1973. *A thousand words of Mohawk.* National Museum of Man, Mercury Series, Ethnology No. 5. Ottawa.

———. 1974. Upstreaming Bruyas. In *Papers in linguistics from the 1972 conference on Iroquois research,* ed. M. K. Foster, 36–46. National Museum of Man, Mercury Series, Ethnology No. 10. Ottawa.

Mithun, M. 1977. *Iontenwennaweienstahkhwaʔ: Mohawk spelling dictionary.* New York State Museum Bulletin 429. Albany.

Morgan, L. H. 1851. *League of the Ho-de-no-sau-nee, or Iroquois.* Rochester: Sage.

———. 1852. Report on the fabrics, inventions, implements and utensils of the Iroquois, made to the Regents of the University, January 22, 1851. Assembly Document No. 122. *New York State Cabinet of Antiquities' Annual Report* 5:66–117. Albany.

———. Cited in W. H. Dall. 1884 [1885]. On Masks, labrets, and certain aboriginal customs with an inquiry into the bearing of their geographical distribution. In *Third*

Annual Report of the Bureau of American Ethnology, 1881–82, 57–202. Washington, D.C.

———. 1901. *League of the Ho-de-no-sau-nee, or Iroquois.* Ed. H. M. Lloyd. 2 vols. New York: Dodd, Mead.

O'Callaghan, E. B., ed. 1855. *Documents relative to the colonial history of the state of New-York.* Vol. 9. Albany. [Also NYCD.]

Orr, R. B. 1922. The masks or false faces of our Ontario Indians. In *33d Annual Archaeological Report, 1921–22,* 32–37. (Appendix to the report of the Minister of Education of Ontario, Toronto.)

Parker, A. C. 1906. Report of the Archaeology Section. In *Annual Report of the Director of the New York State Museum for 1906,* 73–80. Albany.

———. 1908. Report of the Archaeology Section. In *Annual Report of the Director of the New York State Museum,* 85–110. Albany.

———. 1909. Secret medicine societies of the Seneca. *American Anthropologist,* n.s., 11(2):161–85. Reprinted in Parker 1913:113–30.

———. 1910a. Iroquois uses of maize and other food plants. *New York State Museum Bulletin* 144. Albany.

———. 1910b. Ethnology. In *Sixth Report of the Director of the Science Division of the New York State Museum,* 61–62. Bulletin 140. Albany.

———. 1913. The code of Handsome Lake, the Seneca prophet. *New York State Museum Bulletin* 163. Albany.

———. 1922. The archaeological history of New York. *New York State Museum Bulletin,* 235–38. Albany.

———. 1923. *Seneca myths and folk tales.* Buffalo Historical Society Publications 27.

Pasztory, E. 1975. Shamanism and art. Paper presented at Skidmore College symposium: Shamanism and the Arts of Asia and the Americas, January 18, 1975.

Potts, W. J. 1889. Du Simitiere, artist, antiquary, and naturalist, projector of the first American museum, with some extracts from his notebook. *Pennsylvania Magazine of History and Biography* 13(3):341–75.

Proctor, [Col.] T. [1791]. 1832. Narrative of Colonel Thomas Proctor to the Hon. Secretary of War. In *American State Papers—Indian Affairs,* ed. W. Lowrie, and M. St. C. Clarke, 149–65. Washington, D.C.: Gales and Seaton.

Richling, B. 1983. Labrador Nalujuk: The transformation of an aboriginal ritual complex in a post-contact setting. In *The power of symbols: Masks and masquerade in the Americas,* ed. N. R. Crumrine and M. Halpin, 21–19. Vancouver: University of British Columbia Press.

Ritchie, W. A. 1954. Dutch Hollow, an early historic Seneca site in Livingston County, N.Y. *Researches and Transactions of the New York State Archaeological Association* 13(1). Rochester.

———. 1965. *The archaeology of New York State.* Garden City, N.Y.: Natural History Press. Rev. ed., 1969.

Ritzenthaler, R. E. 1950. The Oneida Indians of Wisconsin. *Bulletin of the Public Museum of the City of Milwaukee* 19(1):1–52. Milwaukee.

———. 1969. Iroquois false-face masks. In *Milwaukee Public Museum Publications in Primitive Art* 3, 1–71. Milwaukee.

Roberts, H. H. 1929. San Carlos Apache Basketry. *Anthropological Papers, American Museum of Natural History* 31(2). New York.

Rogers, E. S. 1959. Masks: The many faces of man: An exhibition presented by the Division of Art and Archaeology of the Royal Ontario Museum, Toronto.

———. 1966. *What? How? Why? Where? When? Who? The False Face Society of the Iroquois.* Toronto: Royal Ontario Museum/University of Toronto.

Sagard, G. 1939. *The long journey to the country of the Hurons.* Ed. G. M. Wrong. Toronto: Champlain Society.

Sapir, E. 1916. *Time perspective in aboriginal American culture: A study in method.* Anthropological Series 13. Memoirs of the Canadian Geological Survey 90. Ottawa.

Schaeffer, C. E. 1941. A stone pipe bowl from northern Pennsylvania. *Pennsylvania Archaeologist* 11(3):53–56.

Schmidt, Leopold, ed. 1955. *Masken in Mitteleuropa.* Sonerschriften des Vereines für Völkskunde in Wien 1. Wienna: Verein für Völkskunde.

Schoolcraft, H. R. 1839. *Algic researches.* 2 vols. New York: Harper and Brothers.

Seaver, J. E., M.D. 1932. *A narrative of the life of Mary Jemison: The white woman of the Genesee.* New York: American Scenic and Preservation Society.

Sellers, C. C. 1980. *Mr. Peale's museum: Charles Wilson Peale and the first popular museum of natural science and art.* New York: W. W. Norton.

Shimony, A. A. 1961. *Conservatism among the Iroquois at the Six Nations Reserve.* Yale University Publications in Anthropology 65. New Haven, Conn.: Yale University Press.

Siebert, F. T., Jr. 1967. The original home of the proto-Algonquian people. In *Contributions to Anthropology: Linguistics I (Algonquian).* Anthropological Series 78. Ottawa: National Museum of Canada.

Skinner, A. 1911. Notes on the Eastern Cree and Northern Saulteaux. *American Museum of Natural History Anthropological Papers* 9(1):1–177. New York.

———. 1925. Some Seneca masks and their uses. *Indian Notes and Monographs* 2(3):191–207. New York: Museum of the American Indian—Heye Foundation.

Smith, DeCost. 1888. Witchcraft and demonism of the modern Iroquois. *Journal of American Folk-Lore* 1(3): 184–94.

———. 1889. Additional notes on Iroquois witchcraft and Hondo-i. *Journal of American Folk-Lore* 2(7): 277–81.

———. 1943. *Indian experiences.* Caldwell, Idaho: Caxton Printers.

Snyderman, G. S. 1957. Halliday Jackson's journal on a visit paid to the Indians of New York, 1806. *Proceedings of the American Philosophical Society* 101:565–99.

Speck, F. G. 1931. *A study of the Delaware Indian big house ceremony.* Publications of the Pennsylvania Historical Commission 2. Harrisburg.

———. 1935. Labrador Eskimo mask and clown. *General Magazine and Historical Chronicle* 37(2):159–73. Philadelphia.

———. 1937. Oklahoma Delaware ceremonies, feasts, and dances. *Memoirs of the American Philosophical Society* 7:1–161. Philadelphia.

———. 1940. *Penobscot man.* Philadelphia: University of Pennsylvania Press.

———. 1942. Review of Fenton, Masked medicine societies of the Iroquois. *American Anthropologist* 44(4):696–697.

———. 1945a. *The celestial bear comes down to earth.* Reading Public Museum and Art Gallery, Scientific Publications 7. Reading, Pa.

———. 1945b. *The Iroquois: A study in cultural evolution.* Cranbrook Institute of Science Bulletin 23. Bloomfield Hills, Mich.

———. 1949. *Midwinter rites of the Cayuga Long House.* Philadelphia: University of Pennsylvania Press.

———. 1950. Concerning iconology and the masking complex in eastern North America. *University of Pennsylvania Museum Bulletin* 15: 7–57. Philadelphia.

———, and L. Broom. 1951. *Cherokee dance and drama.* Berkeley and Los Angeles: University of California Press. New ed., Norman: University of Oklahoma Press, 1983.

Spittal, W. G. 1961. Iroquois False Faces. Caledonia, Ontario. Xerox.

Sturtevant, W. C. 1961. Comment on Gertrude P. Kurath's Effects of environment on Cherokee-Iroquois ceremonialism, music, and dance. In *Symposium on Cherokee and Iroquois culture,* ed. W. N. Fenton and J. Gulick, 197–204. Bureau of American Ethnology Bulletin 180. Washington, D.C.: Smithsonian Institution.

———. 1964. John White's contributions to ethnology. In *The American drawings of John White, 1577–1590,* ed. P. Hulton and D. B. Quinn. 2 vols. 1:85–99. London: Trustees of the British Museum; Chapel Hill: University of North Carolina Press.

———. 1978. Oklahoma Seneca-Cayuga. In *Handbook of North American Indians,* Vol. 15, *Northeast,* ed. B. G. Trigger, 537–43. Washington, D.C.: Smithsonian Institution.

———. 1983. Seneca masks. In *The power of symbols: Masks and masquerade in the Americas,* ed. N. R. Crumrine and M. Halpin, 39–47. Vancouver: University of British Columbia Press.

Thwaites, R. G., ed. 1896–1901. *The Jesuit relations and allied documents.* 73 vols. Cleveland: Burrows Brothers. Reprinted, New York: Pageant, 1959.

Todd, V. H. 1920. See C. Graffenried.

Tooker, E. 1964. *An ethnography of the Huron Indians, 1615–1649.* Bureau of American Ethnology Bulletin 190. Washington, D.C.: Smithsonian Institution.

———. 1968. Masking and matrilineality in North America. *American Anthropologist* 70(6):1170–76.

———. 1970. *The Iroquois ceremonial of midwinter.* Syracuse, N.Y.: Syracuse University Press.

———. 1978. Iroquois since 1820. In *Handbook of North American Indians,* Vol. 15, *Northeast,* ed. B. G. Trigger, 449–65. Washington, D.C.: Smithsonian Institution.

Trigger, B. G. 1963. Settlement as an aspect of Iroquoian adaptation at the time of contact. *American Anthropologist* 65:86–101.

———. 1976. *The children of Ataentsic: A history of the Huron people to 1660.* 2 vols. Montreal and London: McGill-Queens University Press.

Tuck, J. A. 1971. *Onondaga Iroquois prehistory.* Syracuse, N.Y.: Syracuse University Press.

———. 1978. Northern Iroquoian prehistory. In *Handbook of North American Indians,* Vol. 15, *Northeast,* ed. B. G. Trigger, 322–33. Washington, D.C.: Smithsonian Institution.

Wallace, A. F. C. 1952. Halliday Jackson's Journal to the Seneca Indians, 1798–1800. *Pennsylvania History* 19(2):1–55.

———. 1958. Dreams as wishes of the soul: A type of psychiatric theory among the seventeenth century Iroquois. *American Anthropologist* 60(2):234–48.

———. 1970. *The death and rebirth of the Seneca.* New York: Alfred A. Knopf.

Walsh, M. W. 1982. The condemnation of carnival in the Jesuit relations. *Michigan Academician: Papers of the Michigan Academy of Science, Arts, and Letters* 25(1):13–26.

Walton, W., ed. 1904. *Narratives and captivities: The captivity and sufferings of Benjamin Gilbert and his family, 1780–83.* Reprinted from the original edition of 1784, with introduction and notes by Frank W. Severance. Cleveland: Burrows Brothers.

Waugh, F. W. 1913. On work in material culture of the Iroquois, 1912. In *Summary Report, Geological Survey, Canada, for the calendar year 1912,* 476–80. Ottawa.

———. 1916. *Iroquois foods and food preparation.* Anthropological Series 12. Memoirs of the Canadian Geological Survey 86. Ottawa.

———. N.d. Field notebooks on Iroquois research. National Museum of Man, Ottawa.

Webb, W. S. 1938. *An archaeological survey of the Norris Basin in eastern Tennessee.* Bureau of American Ethnology Bulletin 118. Washington, D.C.: Smithsonian Institution.

Wilson, E. 1960. *Apologies to the Iroquois.* New York: Farrar, Straus and Cudahy.

Wintemberg, W. J. 1931. Distinguishing characteristics of Algonkian and Iroquoian cultures. In *National Museum of Canada Annual Report, 1929.* Ottawa.

———. 1936. *Roebuck prehistoric village site, Grenville County, Ontario.* Anthropological Series 19, National Museum of Canada Bulletin 83. Ottawa.

Wissler, C. 1928. The lore of the demon mask. *Natural History* 28(4):339–52.

Worgon, A. 1946. *The Longhouse people.* Ottawa: Canadian Film Board.

Zeisberger, D. 1910. History of the Northern American Indians. Ed. A. B. Hulbert and W. N. Schwarze. *Ohio State Archaeological and Historical Quarterly,* 19–189. Columbus.

Zerries, O. 1948. *Religiose Kunst bei Naturvölkern.* Wiesbaden. (For a special exhibit marking the 50th anniversary of the Frobenius Institut.)

———. 1954. Wild- und Buschgeister in Südamerika. In *Studien zur Kulturkunde* 11. Wiesbaden.

———. 1961. Nordamerika. In *JRO-Völkerkunde,* 167–84. Munich: JRO-Verlag.

Index

Abeel, Henry (son of Cornplanter): 84
Abrams, Hannah (Yendi, matron at Coldspring): 356
Akwesasneh ("Where the Partridge Drums"): 5; *see also* St. Regis Reservation
Albany, N.Y.: 5
Allegany Reservation: 4; *see also* Seneca Nation of Indians
Allegheny River: 4
American Museum of Natural History: 5, 10
Anthropology: 89–90, 453; scholarly trends in, 89–90; rise of, and amateur collectors, 453
Antlers, Iroquois and Spiro Mound: 473
Art form, masks as: 71
Ashing: 298 n.
Auburn, N.Y.: 6

Barbeau, C. Marius: 493, 495, 499
Bark rattle: 123, 197, 201, 335 n., 502; *see also* Cherokee
Barrett, S. A.: 6
Bartram, John (masker at Onondaga, 1743): 78
Basswood (*Tilia americana*): 127
Batavia, N.Y.: 4
Bearfoot Band (Onondaga): 4
Bear Society rite: 48, Onondaga, seventeenth century, 77; *see also* Midwinter Festival
Beating on bark, in exorcism: 74; *see also* Huron; Husk Faces, appearances at midwinter ceremony
Beauchamp, Rev. William M. (1830–1925): 10, 75, 90, 91, 461; Huron hypothesis of, 75, 461; on Converse nomenclature, 91
Beschefer, Thierry, S.J., and first report of Iroquois mask, 1687: 77; *see also* Denonville expedition
Bigheads, Our Uncles: 63; *see also* Midwinter Festival
Bill, Aldrich ("Ostrich"), of Six Nations: 421
Black, Chief Barber (Tonawanda): 397
Blind masks: 361
Boas, Franz (1858–1942): 19, 92, 501; *see also* Sapir, Edward; Spier, Leslie; Wissler, Clark
Bogaert, Van den: 83
Bows and arrows: 118
Box turtle: 39 n.; rattle, 69; distribution of, 69 n.

Boyle, David (1842–1911), 7; on rite of mask transfer, 174
Boys, carving learned by: 60; *see also* masquettes
Brainerd, David (1718–47): 80
Brant, Joseph (Thayendanegea, 1742–1807): followers of, to Grand River, 1784, 85; alleged mask of, 91 n.
Brantford, Canada: 3, 4
Brébeuf, Jean de, S.J.: 73, on carnival in Huronia, 496
Brodhead, Col. Daniel (Allegheny campaign leader, 1779): 84
Bruegel, Pieter, *The Battle of Carnival and Lent* by: 496
Bruyas, J., S.J., on "face": 75&n., 76
Buck, Abraham (Onondaga, Six Nations: chief of False Faces, 1898): 141
Buck, Billy (Seneca), recordings by, for Library of Congress: 338 n.
Buck, Chief John: on divided mask, 36; on origins, 104–105; on Husk Face origins, costumes, 390–93
Buck, George: 343; collection of, 179–80; *see also* photographic ethnology
Buck, Joshua: on divided mask, 36; on origins, 104; on Husk Face origin, 386, 388
Buck, Mrs. John L., on Husk Face appearance at Six Nations: 442
Buffalo, N.Y.: 3, 4
Buffalo (Buffaloe) Creek: 4, 5; Reservation, 35; *see also* hanging-mouth mask
Buffalo Museum of Science, masks in: 240
Bureau of American Ethnology: 12
Burning, Lucy: 395

Calusa (Florida tribe), masks of: 474
Canada: 3, 456
Cannibal clown, Algonquian: 36 n; *see also* Longnose
Carnival, European, parallels: 495ff.
Cattaraugus Reservation: 4, 237; *see also* Seneca Nation of Indians
Caughnawaga, P. Q.: 5
Chadwick, Robert: 473 n.
Chafe, Wallace L., on Seneca language: 277
Chance Horizon, face motif of: 482
Chandler, Milford, collection of: 7; *see also* Cranbrook Institute of Science
Charles, Chief Abraham (Cayuga): 153; *see also* possession
Chemung, N.Y.: masks found by soldiers in, 1779, 81; carved posts reported in, 84

Cherokee: and Iroquois parallels, 158 n., 197, 473, 476–78, 487ff.; Booger Dance and Husk Faces of, 475, 488; *see also* Fogelson, Ray D.
Chiefswood Collection: 7
Children, discipline of: 38 n., 167; *see also* Longnose; maskers
Chippewa masking: 471
Cholera: 8, 322–23
Clairvoyance: 153, 157
Clark, Gen. John S.: 141
Classification of masks: morphological v. native, 28, 501, 503; by mouth shape, 30; reduced to seven types, 48; confirmed by Mathews, 52; *see also* Sturtevant, W. C.
Clinton, Gov. George, mask donated to Du Simitiere Museum by: 82
Clute, Alex (Handsome Lake preacher): 5
Coldspring: 4
Collecting, ethnological: 454
Collections: 12
Condolence Council: 70
Congdon, Charles E. (Salamanca, N.Y.): 133 n., 216 n.
Conklin, Harold: 48
Conservatism: 159; *see also* Shimony, Annemarie
Contract, between masker and creator, man and supernaturals: 113
Convergence, and limited possibilities of mask types: 499; *see also* Goldenweiser, A. A.
Converse, Harriet Maxwell: mask titles of, 10, 17ff.; collections of, 17, 237
Cornhusk craft: 408
Corning, N.Y.: 84
Corn-meal mush: 122
Cornplanter (Seneca chief, ca. 1732–1836): 7; village of, 84; *see also* Abeel, Henry; OBail, John
Cornplanter, Edward (Parker's informant, father of Jesse): on blind masks in I:?do:s Society, 48, 237; as "picker," 454
Cornplanter, Jesse: on origin of horned mask, 39; revisits Newtown, 31 n., 237–38; drawings of, 48; carves classic doorkeeper masks, 134–35; interprets prayer, 287; on symbolism, 287; *see also* traveling rite
Coury, Atkins ("Ed," Husk Face interpreter): 433
Creek Indians, carved arbor posts of: 475
Cresswell, N., and Delaware masker: 80
Crooked Nose episode: 97
Crow, James: premier carver at Newton,

Crow, James (*continued*)
31n., 237; *see also* Heye, George C.; Keppler, Joseph
Culture: change and stability of, 90, 379; maintenance of, 159; memory of, 395; persistence of, 424; climax of, 505; *see also* Midwinter Festival
Cusick, David, on traveling rite, 1825: 86

Danford, Chief John (Oneida), joins False Face society: 145ff.
Dark Dance: 468n.; *see also* Little People
David, Elijah (Twenty Kettles, Tonawanda): 276; and tobacco invocation to False Faces, 285–86; and Husk Face origin, 396
Deardorff, Merle H.: 312
Death: 70
Delaware: Munsee, among Cayuga of Six Nations, 36; divided mask of, 36, 80; skin-beating dance of, 48; costume of, 82; house posts of, 82; masking extinct among, 461; and Iroquois parallels, 462; and Living Solid Face, 463; turtle rattle of, 463; influence of, 464, 465, 468; medicine societies of, 464; Doll Dance of, 468n.; and Iroquois shared tradition, 483; and nativistic religions, 485; masking of, 486; *see also* Krusche, R.
Denonville expedition, 1687, and first report of Seneca mask: 77; *see also* Beschefer, Thierry, S. J.
Denver Art Museum: 7
Dependencies, and mask care: 169
Derangement, as heritage of Dream Feast: 151
Dew Eagle: 39
Disease and high winds: 315
Divided body: 106, 108
Divided mask: first mention of, 1745, 80; *see also* Brainerd, David
Divided mask, dream of: 167
Doctor, Peter W. (lay preacher at Tonawanda): 148ff.
Doorkeeper role: roots in Huronia, 37, 350; Hadu?i? and Shagodyoweh, 129; dance, 139; *see also* maskers
Douglas, Eric: 7
Dreams: 14, 27, 159–67; styles of, 27; objects in, 60; miniature, 161; without guardian, 167; guessing, 63, 159; after encounter, 115; entrance and release

from Society of Faces, 142; and dream song, 273; of masks, 451; *see also* Midwinter Festival
Druke, Mary A. 450n.; *see also* Grider, R. A., drawings by
"Dry pole": 138
Du Simitiere Museum, Philadelphia: 82

East-west symbolism: 134, 287, 474, 480; *see also* Graffenreid; Lawson, John
Eliott, Rev. Adam (missionary at Six Nations): 464
Elm, giant (World Tree): 123
Emblem pole: 204
Epic myths: 101
Eskimo masking: 472
Ethnohistory: historic approach, 22; and failure of early sources, 482; *see also* Krusche, R.
Ethnological literature: 86; 504
Evolution of masking style: 71
Excrement, handling of: by Delaware of Oklahoma, 468; by Shawnee, 470

Facelessness: 70
Face motif: in other media, 66; in Chance Horizon, 70
Faces: 106, 108, 115; carved on posts, 83, 84; carved on trees, 209
Facial paralysis: 158; *see also* False Face Society, and False Face sickness
False Face Society: 13, 23, 24; and fire and ashes, 27; speech of, 27; food habits of, 27, 124; power of, 27; criteria of, 65; mask and bundle in, 65, 168–72, 178, 180, 486; protohistoric evidence for, 66–67; "grandfathers," 94; origins and kinds of, 95ff.; versus cannibal spirits, 115; preference of, for rocky places, 126; versus stone giants, 122; affinity of, for trees, 127, 128; and lightning and thunder, 128, 503; two main classes of, 129; membership in, 140; participation in, 140, 505; Common Faces of Forest, 141; and dreams, or sickness, 142; conductor and singers in, 143; and False Face sickness, 143–85; officers in, 151; matrons in, 153ff.; paraphernalia of, 191; evolution and survival of, 453; and plagues and windborne diseases, 453; rank of, among medicine societies, 501; *see also* maskers; masks; rituals

Fenton, John William: 160
Fenton, John William, II: 432
Field method: 15, 350
Field Museum of Natural History, Chicago: 6
Fish Dance: 434
Five Nations, first observers of: 75
Fogelson, Ray D.: on facial distortion, 31n., 72n.; on tobacco invocation and Cherokee formulas, 165n.; on covering bundle, 180n.; on Cherokee-Iroquois parallels, 337–38, 473, 487; on relative age of False and Husk faces, 551n.; on Ojibwa manitoukan, 462n., 463n.
Four, as magic number: 114
Four sacred rites: 85
Frankfurt-am-Main, West Germany: 5
Friederici, Georg: 480

General, Chief Alex (Deskaheh): 7
Genesinguhta (Cornplanter's upper village): 84
Giant Raven: 39
Gibson, Chief John Arthur (ca. 1850–1912): 100
Gibson, G., prayer of, to False Faces: 162–63
Gibson, John Hardy: 455
Gibson, Simeon (1889–1943): 11, 335n., 395, 454
Gillette, Charles E.: 49n.
Goldenweiser, A. A.: observes carving, 211ff.; on convergence, 499
Good Hunter: 126–27
Gordon, Lucy (grandmother of Clara Redeye), mask of: 448&n.
Gordon, Mandy (storyteller): 122
Graffenreid (Swiss): 474
Grand River, Ontario: 35; *see also* Six Nations Reserve
Grand River style: 30, 85, 237; *see also* Morgan, Lewis Henry
Great Humpbacked One (Hadu?i?gó:na, Onondaga): 27, 106, 129
Green Bay, Wis.: 5
Grider, R. A.: drawings by, 237; *see also* Newberry Library
Ground, Harrison (Tonawanda carver): 259–60
Guardian mask: 166

Hunchback (Hadu?i? or Hondo:wi?, mask prototype, Onondaga): 27, 129; and

wind, 107–108; in belt of Orion, 113–14; etymology of, 332 n.; in cosmology, 448
Hale, Horatio (1817–96): 464
Hamell, George R., on mask history: 67
Hamilton, Ontario: 3
Handsome Lake (Seneca prophet): 3, 84, 91, 457
Harrington, M. R.: 11, 237, 243
Harris, Tom (carver): 7, 249ff.
Heckewelder, John (Moravian missionary), on Delaware masker: 80
Henry, Jake (carver): 261
Hewitt, J. N. B., fieldwork of, at Six Nations: 103, 386
Heye, George G.: 11, 237
Hill, Cephas (Tonawanda Seneca): 260
Historic approach, 65, 502
Holt, John (trader at Quaker Bridge): 160
Howel (curved adze): 216 n.; see also Congdon, Charles E.
Hunter, good (theme): 114–18
Huron Dream Feast: 497
Huron hypothesis: 75; see also Beauchamp, Rev. William M.
Huron shamans: 68, 72
Huron town (Seneca): 78
Husk Faces, or "Bushy Heads": 54; etymology of, 54–55, 398, 400; techniques of creating, 54ff., 285, 407ff.; types and vocabulary of, 58, 403, 406, 417; Speck's five types of, 59; rites of, 138; and runners, 272, 329; and Alice White's renewal, 276, 420–21; at Six Nations, 382; among Seneca, 383; as messengers of "Three Sisters," 383, 399; powers of prophecy of, 383; compared to False Faces, 383; and interpreter's role, 383ff., 420; crops of, 384; origins and homeland of, 384, 396, 398; as symbols of fertility and fecundity, 385; hunting of, 386ff., 394; in Onondaga of Six Nations legends, 386ff.; and Little People, 389–92, 394, 395, 399–401; food of, 394; keepers of, 403; reversal of sex roles in, 403; ritual equipment and costume of, 406; appearances of, at Midwinter Festival, 418ff.; recordings of, 431 n.; texts of, 432 n.; rites of, at Six Nations, 439: rites of, among Onondaga, 440; at Seneca longhouse, 441–43; miniatures, as charms, 443; and False Face analogues, 444; power of, compared to that of False Faces, 448–49; danger of resisting, 449; as guardians of game, 450

"Indian New Year:" 366, 447; see also Midwinter Festival
In situ hypothesis: 13
International Congress of Anthropology and Ethnology: 7
Invocation ("throwing tobacco"): 119, 162–63, 276ff., 285–86; on joining society, 165–66; for dedication of mask, 177–78; for making, owning, lending mask, 181ff.; Clayton White's rendering of, 317–18; for a person (Six Nations), 329; at Onondaga Longhouse (Six Nations), as climax of traveling rite, 331ff.; by Henry Redeye at Abrams family feast, 356–57
Ipomoea pandurata Meyer (manroot), Ohio River distribution of: 269
Iroquoia (upstate New York): 3
Iroquoian cosmology: 68
Iroquois Confederacy, or League: 447; policy statement of, on masks, 456, 457; legal status of, 457; see also Five Nations
Iroquois shamanism: 13

Jackson, Halliday (Quaker missionary): on maskers on Allegheny River (1800): 343–44
Jacob, Hiram (longhouse officer): 435; see also Husk Faces, appearances of
Jamieson, John (Cayuga), conductor of maskers: 101; see also traveling rite
Jemison, Mary (white captive): 80
Jimmerson, Avery (1914–86): drawings of, 159; as carver, 257
Jimmerson, Ella Tandy, husk twining technique of: 407ff.
Jimmerson, Howard (Seneca), on False Face encounter: 65
Jimmerson, Jerry (Giant Elm): 360 n.
Jimmerson, John (Seneca, father of Avery), on four classes of masks: 133, 438
Jimmerson, Johnson (1918–84, Seneca): 424
John, Andrew (Seneca): 7
Johnny John, Chauncey, 7, 99 n., 172, 297; on bark rattles, 201ff.; photos of False Face rite by, 346; on origin of False Faces, 385; as Husk Face interpreter, 430ff; as mask maker, 215ff.
Johnson, Chief George H. M. (Mohawk of Chiefswood), Delaware idols destroyed by: 464; see also Hale, Horatio
Johnson, Chief Lyman (Tonawanda), on east-west symbolism: 134
Johnson, Evelyn H. C. (Mohawk): 7
Jones, Albert (Seneca): 256–57, 298, 436–37
Jones, Helia (Seneca), on False Face prototype and Stone Giant: 122
Jones, Rev. Peter (Ojibwa historian): 465, 467 n.

Kanadasego (Geneva, N.Y.): 82
Keppler, Joseph: 11, 90 n., 237
Kinship: 318, 448, 505
Kirkland, Rev. Samuel (1741–1808; missionary to Oneida): 471
Krusche, R.: contradicts Speck, 83; on roots of Delaware and Iroquois masking, 89; on evolution of, 478ff.
Kurath, Gertrude P.: choreography by, 289, 291–93; on round dances, 294–95

Lafitau, J.-F., S.J., on masks at Caughnawaga: 76
Lake Ontario: 75
Laurentian Mohawk: 5
Lawson, John, on Waxhaw masked dance: 474
Lévi-Strauss, C., on nature v. culture: 507
Leningrad: 5
Library of Congress, recorded music in: 293 n.
Lismer, Marjorie: 385
Little People: 95; see also Dark Dance
Little Water Society: 39, 447
Longhouse adherents: 23
Longhouse People, The (film): 348–49; see also Worgon, Alan
Longnose: sightings of, 168; and long-nosed god of the Southeast, 474
Lower Cayuga Longhouse: 5

MacKenzie Creek: 5
Magic staff, or cane: 283 [8]; see also Cherokee
Manroot: 269; see also False Face Society
Maple tree: 256–57; see also invocation; Jones, Albert
Martin, Marlene, on Husk masks: 406
Mask carvers: observations and patterns

Mask carvers (*continued*)
of, 209–11; Godenweiser (Gus Yellow), 211ff.; tools of, 211–12, 215–16; C. Johnny John, 215ff.; Allegany from Cattaraugus, 237; at Grand River, 249; Tom Harris, 249ff.; Jonas Snow, 255ff.; Avery Jimmerson, 257; Harrison Ground, 259–60; Jake Henry, 261; Elon Webster, 261; and "pickers," 452; Jake Thomas, 452n.; evolution of styles of, 503

Maskers: as actors, 28, 29, 371; and medicine, 73–74; frighten children, 86, 167, 402, 451; blind, 136; three orders of, 138; and blowing-ashes rite, 139; costume of, 204, 322; staff and cane of, 204; at Six Nations, 348; in Medicine Company rite, 361, 362; in Iroquois life, 447; in Eastern Woodlands, 478; distribution of, worldwide, 500; ambivalence toward, 505; lack of general theory on, 507

Masks (wooden False Faces): type specimen of, 8, 91; and tobacco bags, 8; hair attachment of, 8; studied, 18; eye reflectors on, 18n.; pictures and styles of, 19; styles of, and dreams, 27; native terms for, 27; true meaning of, 27; as projections to mask spirits, 28; types of, 28, 29, 31ff.; general features of, 30; classification of, based on specimens, 30ff.; informants on, 32; early beggar, 35, 131; pig, 48; blind, 48; and trees, 85; Seneca production and use of, 91; color and power of, 103; symbolism of, and cardinal directions, 108–109; Onondaga color-coordinated, 111–12; restricted, 131ff.; ambiguity in function of, 135; and mask of C. Johnny John, 172–77; and carving-tree rite, 175, 206, 209; and emblem pole (matron's staff), 204–205; classic doorkeeper, 237; prototypes of, 244; author's collection of, 248; and matron's role, 352ff., 371, 378; dreams of, 450; attitudes toward, 451; childhood memory of, 451; production and collection of, 452–53; evolution of, 484; age of, 503; *see also* maskers; rituals; Mathews, Zena Pearlstone; Morgan, Lewis Henry

Masquettes (miniature masks): 60, 66, 204; in antiquity, 69; as class, 136–37; as protectors of house, 138; as dream guardians, 161; and classes of membership, 164; evolution of, from prehistory, 502; *see also* dreams, guessing

Master of game: 106
Material culture studies: 17
Maternity concept: 60, 133–34, 181, 241
Mathews, Zena Pearlstone: 12, 52–53
Medicine societies, 23, 39, 91, 114, 140, 447, 458
Midwinter Festival ("Indian New Year"): 366, 367; eighteenth-century accounts of, 367–69; of this century, 369, 421ff.; observations of, 370, 427, 428; at Tonawanda, 370; and bowl game, 372; contests at, 373, 379, 380, 422ff.; at new Coldspring Longhouse (1968), 378; participation in, 378; Husk Face night pattern at, 425; sex-role reversals at, 429; Husk Face visitors at, 431, 435ff.; photographs and recordings of, 431; and children, 432; costume and identity at, 432–33; interpreter at, 433; and instructions of matron, 433; Fish Dance at, 434; orthodoxy and change at, 435; structure of, 436n.; at Newtown Longhouse, 437; at Tonawanda, 438; at Onondaga, 439; Seneca, 440, 505; climax of, 447; *see also* Husk Faces; maskers; False Face rituals

Mifflin, General Thomas: 82
Milwaukee Public Museum: 6
Mississauga of the Credit: 465
Mohawk: shamans, 68n.; face motif of, 75; masks of, at Caughnawaga, 76
Moieties, color coding of: 108
Montreal: 3
Morgan, Lewis Henry (1818–81): 9, 85; collection of, 237
Moses, Eliott (Delaware of Six Nations), mask of: 465
Munceytown, Ontario: 464
Munsee-Mahican, descendants of, at Six Nations: 462; *see also* Delaware
Museum für Völkerkunde, Berlin: 9
Museum of the American Indian—Heye Foundation: 5, 10
Museum of Natural History, Denver: 7
Museums: studies of, 17; attitude of natives toward, 454–55; Seneca masks in collections of, 503; and public trusts, 506
Mush, maskers' food: 27

Nationalmuseet, Copenhagen: 8
National Museum of Ethnology, Stockholm: 11
Native consciousness: dawn of, 455; and nativist movements, 485
Native texts, importance of, for research: 19
Native theory v. practice: 15, 131
Newberry Library, Chicago, Grider drawings in: 237
Newtown, Cattaraugus: 4, 35; tradition of, 237; *see also* Cornplanter
Nedrow, N.Y.: 30
Neusiok of Neuse River, N.C., images in shrine: 474
New York State: 3; Cabinet of Antiquities: 8; State Capitol, fire in (1911), 237; Museum, 90, 170
Niagara Falls: 3
Nieder-Walluf, West Germany: 5
Nonbeliever (matron of False Faces): 159–60
Norris, Major James (Sullivan's army, 1779): 84
Northern shamanism: 65

Obail, John: 7; *see also* Cornplanter
Oneida: nation, 3; of Green Bay, Wisconsin, 5, 471; on Thames River, 5
Onondaga: nation, 3, 439; Reservation, New York, 3; Valley, 35; twice invaded and burned, 111n.
Onondaga Historical Association, Syracuse, N.Y.: 10
Onondaga Longhouse (Canada): 5
Onondaga masks: brought to Grand River, 112
Onondaga Midwinter Festival: in seventeenth century, 76; and shaman and turtle rattle, 77; False Face at (1743), 78
Ontario, Lake: 75
Origin legends (False Faces): epic and human adventures in, 95ff.; Six Nations versions of, 100ff.; *see also* Buck, Chief John; Buck, Joshua; Hewitt, J. N. B.
Owen Sound, Georgian Bay, Lake Huron: 471

Painted Post, N.Y.: 84
Pan-American Exposition, Buffalo, N.Y.: 7
Parker, Arthur C.: 10; fieldwork of, at Cattaraugus, 48; influenced by research on age-grade societies, 86; on Stone Giants, 99; as collector, 237
Participation in Society of Faces: 140, 156ff., 159, 316
Patterns: of sequence, 23; consistent, 318;

ideal v. practice, 319; in compound feasts (Allegany), 349–50; of Husk Face night, 418ff.; in prophecies, 428; structural, 461
Peabody Museum, Harvard: 7
Peale's Museum, Philadelphia: 82 n.
Penobscot of Maine: 472
Photographic ethnology: 16, 191ff., 216ff., 249ff., 301ff., 343ff.
"Pickers" (collectors): 454
Possession: by bear, 150; by buffalo, 150; by participation, 152; by ridicule, 152–53; by imitation, 154; and singing songs, 153; and maskers, 154; and trickster, 154; white observer of, 155; at visitation of maskers, 155
Power: 98, 122, 315
Putnam, F. W. (1839–1915): 7

Quaker journals: 84 n.

Rassloff, Count W.: 8
Rattlesnakes, associated with maskers: 463 n.; see also Fogelson, Ray D.
Raven, Giant: 39
Recordings: of Iroquois music, Library of Congress: 431&n.
Redeye, Clara (Seneca interpreter): on Longnose, 38 n.; 282 n.; on invocation, 284–85
Redeye, Henry (Seneca preacher, 1864–1946): on mask types, 28; on Shagodyoweh, 97; on origin of False Faces, 115ff.; on mask care, 172; invocation of, 276ff.; entertains False Faces, 350ff.; encounters Husk Face, 395
Redeye, Sherman (son of Henry), miniature mask of: 148
Repatriation, of masks, Iroquois: 45–57
Rietberg Museum, Zurich, mask collection of: 494
Ritchie, William A.: 49 n., 68
Ritual pattern: 16; components of, 267ff.; map of, 309
Rituals: form and content of, 23; and dream guessing, 164; traveling (purification) rite, 267ff.; medicine of, 269, 288; house-to-house, 270; conductor's role in, 272–75; of Faces alone, 289; and dance songs, 289–90; and mush, or False Face pudding, 290–92, 290 n.; and Husk Faces and False Faces, 292; and Doorkeeper's Dance, 292; and thumbs up, 293; song texts of, 293, 295, 297; and ashing, 298; and feast-distribution pattern, 299; purging sickness (house to house), 301ff.; decline of, at Coldspring, 320; see also photographic ethnology
Rituals (family feasts): in midwinter, 340; renewal at Six Nations, 343–44; at Coldspring, 356ff.; structure and pattern, 357ff.; False Faces without Husk Faces, 360–61; see also photographic ethnology
Rituals, Six Nations: 324ff.; men dominate in, 324, 378; women's role in, 143, 325–26; and traveling rite, 330ff.; and "advancing feet," or round, dance, 337; differences in, from Seneca rituals, 338; on diversity, 338–39; male unmasked conductor of, 378
Rituals, Tonawanda: observations of, 320; house purification, 321; and dawn, or marching-song, texts, 323; ritual components of, 323–24; see also Cornplanter, Jesse; Scrogg, Chief Henan
Rochester, N.Y.: 3
Rochester Museum and Science Center: 5
Roddy, T. R.: 6, 454
Royal Ontario Museum, Toronto: 7, 10
Roseberry, C. R. ("Tip"): 374, 433
Running water (purification): 273 n.; see also Cherokee

"Sacred" objects: 506; see also repatriation, Iroquois, of masks
Sagard, Father Gabriel: 495
Saint Lawrence River: 5
Saint Regis Reservation: 5
Salamanca, N.Y.: 4
Sanborn, Rev. J. W.: 7
Sapir, Edward (1884–1939): 19
Sapling (Creator): 107
Scrogg, Chief Henan: 321, 323, 395
Secrecy: 140
Seneca: 27; Nation, 3, 4; Nation of Indians, 4; Longhouse (Canada), 5; language of, 55 n.; New Year, 63; reservations, 85; at Sandusky, 85; Arts Project of, 259; of Oklahoma, 470; masks of, in collections, 504
Seneca Iroquois National Museum, Salamanca, N.Y.: 455
Seneca Nation of Indians: 4; see also Seneca
Shamokin, Pa. (former home of Delaware): 80
Shawnee, masking parallels: 469ff.
Shenandoah, Leon (Thadodaho), presiding officer of Grand Council: 456
Shikellamy (Bartram's guide, 1743): 79
Shimony, Annemarie: 159, 439, 480
"Shooting spells," Onondaga, seventeenth century: 77
Six Nations: 3; Reserve, on Grand River, 5–7; tribal distinctions among, 439
Skaneateles, N.Y.: 9
Skinner, Alanson: 11, 448
Skinner, Dorothy: 12
Smith, DeCost: 9, 259
Smith, Ernest (Seneca artist): 17, 151–52, 341–42
Smithsonian Institution: 7
Snapping turtle (*Chelydra serpentina*) rattle: 65, 67, 68, 97, 123, 191
Snow, Amos (father of Jonas): 248
Snow, Bemis (son of Jonas): 138
Snow, John (Seneca of Six Nations): 181
Snow, Jonas: 15, 123, 191, 200, 454
Snow Snake on Snow Street, Coldspring: 372
Sour Springs (Upper Cayuga): 5
Southeastern migration hypothesis: 22
Southeastern parallels: 490–91
Speck, Frank G.: 12, 48, 469, 479ff.
Spier, Leslie: 19, 501
Spiro Mound, Oklahoma, masks at: 474
Spittal, William Guy: 170–71
Stone coasts (giants): 95, 97, in origin of False Faces, 100; as cannibals, 122; description of, 127; and crystals, 487, 488
Sturtevant, W. C.: on classification, 53–54; on "Niagara Falls" style, 63; on False Faces, 161 n.; observes carver, 209 n.; on pattern, 436 n.
Stuttgart, West Germany: 5
Sullivan-Clinton expedition (1779), masks collected on: 81
Sunflower medicine: 270
Symbolic dyads: 104; east-west (Tonawanda), 134; center post and world tree, 462
Syracuse, N.Y.: 3
Steamburg, N.Y.: 4

Thanksgiving Speech, False Face: 276
Thunder, contest of, with Creator: 98
Tobacco (native, *Nicotiana rustica* L.): 27; invocations, 74ff.; in cosmology, 103
Tonawanda Reservation: 4, 8, 35; informants at, 320
Tradition: in visions and carving, 28; and direct history, 48; and Onondaga masks

Tradition (*continued*)
   at Six Nations, 108–109; *see also* Beauchamp, Rev. William M.
Traveling rite: 48, 65, 138ff.
Tree, medicinal power of, 175–76
Turkey, Emma (Hawk clan matron): 38 n.
Turkey, Myron, as Longnose: 168
Turtle rattle: Onondaga, seventeenth century, 77; manufacture of, 191, 192ff.; in Great Feather Dance, 195; four Allegany makers of, 196; at Six Nations, 196; wooden replica of, for Great Feather Dance, 197
"Tuscarora Faces": 63–64

U.S. National Museum of Natural History, Washington, D.C., 7
University Museum, Philadelphia: 7

Values: native v. trustees': 457

Wabanaki clown dance: 472
Wallace, A. F. C., on Iroquois dreams: 159
Walsh, Martin W.: on carnival in *Jesuit Relations*: 495ff.
Warrior, Chauncey: 438
Waxhaw masked dance: 474
Weapons, in dating tale: 118
Webster, Elon: 261
Weiser, Conrad: on False Faces at Onondaga (1743): 78
West, Will (Cherokee source): 476
Wheeler-Voegelin, Erminie, on Shawnee masking: 469ff.
Whistling God: 35
White, Alice (mother of Clayton): on tobacco invocation, 315; on Husk Face rite, 420–21
White, Clarence (carver at Coldspring): 454
White, Clayton: on False Face visits, 312, 313ff.
White, John (English artist), drawings of (1585): 474
Williams, Mrs. Peter (Six Nations matron), on origin of False Faces: 102
Wilson, Edmund: 374, 434
Wissler, Clark: 19, 501
Women, role of, at Six Nations: 328; *see also* rituals, Six Nations
Wooden Faces Society: 139; *see also* False Faces
Woodworking, burning, boring: 176
Worgon, Alan, film of, on Six Nations: 345
WPA Indian Arts Project: 6, 17
World tree (giant elm or pine): 85, 114, 484
Wry-faced, or split-faced, being: 104; *see also* Buck, Joshua

Yellow, Gus (carver): 211ff.

Zeisberger, David (Moravian missionary to Delaware), on masker: 79
Zurich, Switzerland: 5